W9-COO-277

Operations Management

McGRAW-HILL SERIES IN INDUSTRIAL ENGINEERING AND MANAGEMENT SCIENCE

Consulting Editor
James L. Riggs, *Department of Industrial Engineering, Oregon State University*

Operations Management

Kostas N. Dervitsiotis

GRADUATE SCHOOL OF INDUSTRIAL STUDIES
THESSALONIKI, GREECE

FORMERLY WITH
SCHOOL OF BUSINESS ADMINISTRATION
PORTLAND STATE UNIVERSITY

McGraw-Hill Book Company

NEW YORK □ ST. LOUIS □ SAN FRANCISCO □ AUCKLAND □ BOGOTÁ □ HAMBURG □ JOHANNESBURG
LONDON □ MADRID □ MEXICO □ MONTREAL □ NEW DELHI □ PANAMA □ PARIS □ SÃO PAULO
SINGAPORE □ SYDNEY □ TOKYO □ TORONTO

This book was set in Times Roman.
The editors were Julienne V. Brown and Susan Hazlett;
the designer was Anne Canevari Green;
the production supervisor was Leroy A. Young.
The drawings were done by Santype International Limited.
R. R. Donnelley & Sons Company was printer and binder.

Library of Congress Cataloging in Publication Data

Dervitsiotis, Kostas N
    Operations management.

    (McGraw-Hill series in industrial engineering
and management science)
    Includes index.
    1. Production management. I. Title.
TS155.D475   658.5   80-11641
ISBN 0-07-016537-8

OPERATIONS MANAGEMENT

1234567890 DODO 89876543210

TO MY PARENTS, NICHOLAS AND ANNA

ΓΙΑ ΤΑ ΘΕΜΕΛΙΑ

Contents

PART THREE
Operations Planning and Control

Preface

From its emergence as a recognizable field of study to this date, production or operations management has been subject to dynamic change. In its brief history we have seen its boundaries expand, its outlook mature, and its methods increase in power and sophistication. This is the cumulative result of successful efforts by both practitioners and scholars challenged by technological, social, and economic developments that affect the means and methods for satisfying human needs for products and services.

More recently, managers of both private and public organizations have been challenged to respond to problems related to sagging productivity rates, inflation, energy, pollution, and other issues created by the complexities of modern societies. This book has been written to present several of the standard topics of operations management in a framework that accounts for the above concerns. This stems from a strong belief that operations managers can contribute significantly toward a solution of such problems.

The content of the text and the level of presentation aim at providing a balanced response to several of the conflicting demands facing every instructor of the subject. The material included can be used for an introduction to operations management at the undergraduate or graduate level for students in business administration, economics, engineering, or related programs.

Depending on the instructor's interests and time available, the book can be used for a course of one or two academic quarters. For those preferring a rather descriptive problem-oriented treatment of the subject, the chapters have been arranged so that basic material is presented in the early sections, reinforced with numerous diagrams and comparative summaries. The more quantitative material on various decision-making techniques is usually presented toward the end of each unit. It is assumed that the reader has been exposed to an elementary course in statistics and management science. However, for those wishing a refresher on needed concepts and methods, not discussed in the body of the text, supplementary chapters have been included for easy review.

The sections on issues relating to energy, recycling, pollution, and legal considerations about safety (OSHA), product liability, and environmental impact statements (EIS) can be covered in lectures, assigned for reading, or used as a basis for class projects on specific problems. They have been included to add more realism and relevance to the more traditional topics, but the extent of their use will vary with the course and time available.

The material in this book is organized into three parts that offer a logical development and allow the most effective coverage of both standard and special topics.

Part One provides an overview of operations management, discusses basic concepts, and gives definitions of terms and decision types that are referred to repeatedly throughout the text. Included here is a discussion of systems and models as primary tools for problem solving. In examining decision-making methods we focus not only on rational types but on organizational and political approaches as well. This part closes with an analysis of environmental conditions, both inside and outside an organization, as a key requirement for identifying opportunities and constraints in pursuing objectives and minimizing friction with other parts of the organization.

Part Two looks at long-term decisions which commit large amounts of resources for long periods of time with a limited degree of reversibility. Decisions about the design of products or services and processes, the location and layout of facilities, and the capacity of a firm establish a broad framework for its operation. These are also the most critical decisions with respect to environmental impacts. For this reason, we have included here fairly extensive sections on pollution (air, water, noise, and solid waste), energy, and recycling. Environmental impact analysis is discussed as a comprehensive approach for evaluating the effects of strategic decisions, i.e., new technologies, plant location, and other large projects on social, economic, and natural processes.

In Part Three we turn to medium- and short-term decisions, i.e., the month-to-month or even day-to-day decisions for achieving the best utilization of available productive capacity. Included here are topics on demand forecasting, aggregate planning, inventories, scheduling, quality control, and maintenance. Our approach in these chapters is to describe first the relevant decision system in terms of information inputs and outputs, control variables, and performance criteria. Then we proceed to examine methods by which representative problems are solved and illustrate them with detailed numerical examples. Part Three ends with a final chapter which reviews and synthesizes key aspects of the various decision areas of operations management and attempts to extrapolate likely future developments from current trends.

The following features of this text should make it especially effective for preparing students and aspiring practitioners in the fundamentals of operations management and its projected development.

1. The emphasis of the text on social, economic, legal, and environmental issues can increase the student's awareness of how specific operations decisions are affected by these issues to arrive at more realistic policies. In addition, the detailed analysis of the internal environment provides an understanding of how other parts of the organization are affected and are likely to react to proposed changes.

2. The inclusion of organizational and political decision-making approaches can help increase the awareness of operations managers to certain factors so they are more

able to bridge the frustrating gap between rational solutions and their effective implementation. In today's complex organizations, these considerations must be dealt with explicitly, especially with regard to strategic level decisions.

3. A balanced treatment of both manufacturing and service sectors in the presentation, examples, and review questions and problems is designed to strengthen the student's confidence about the range of applications.

4. Extensive use of diagrams, flowcharts, and detailed examples are provided to clarify difficult concepts and techniques.

5. Inclusion of material on recent developments on material requirements planning (MRP), safety considerations (OSHA), and product liability enable the student to keep abreast of the contemporary scene.

6. Inclusion of chapter summaries for quick review of important points in descriptive form and a final chapter with a synthesis of all decisions areas helps the student concentrate more easily on important problems, their information requirements, decisions variables, and solution methods.

7. Numerous review questions and problem sets at the end of each chapter provide ample opportunity to reinforce understanding of important concepts and develop needed skills for solving problems at various levels of complexity.

This text reflects the cumulative influence of inspiring teachers, path-breaking writers in operations management and related areas, and the many students who have made teaching this subject over the last ten years exciting. For the completion of this project, a special word of thanks belongs to Professor James L. Riggs, Oregon State University, for encouraging me to undertake this project and for his unfailing help as an editor of the series; Professors William F. Boore, Portland State University, and Arthur F. Gould, Lehigh University, for their careful review of the manuscript that helped make it more balanced, more down-to-earth, and more readable; Professors Richard R. Robinson, Portland State University, and Michael S. Inoue, Oregon State University, for many discussions that helped sharpen my thinking about people, systems, and their management; the School of Business Administration at Portland State University for providing over the years a stimulating academic atmosphere and time to think, to learn, and to write.

Finally, no words can express my gratitude and appreciation to Nancy S. Ritchey whose help with every aspect in the preparation, multiple revisions, and editing of the manuscript created order in what often seemed to be an unmanageable project.

Kostas N. Dervitsiotis

To the Student

You are about to embark on a learning experience exploring a subject that is dynamic in nature and diverse in applications, *operations management*. It is the study of a field where knowledge from the social sciences (economics, psychology, sociology), engineering, and mathematics comes together to create and operate productive systems for the satisfaction of human needs in products and services.

Other subjects that you may have studied so far had a focus or language that enabled you to make an easy adjustment. Operations management seems to require a greater effort than most. You will be asked to examine, analyze, and solve problems that do not always have one best solution. Some of the more technical topics may require more than one reading with pencil and paper. Do not become frustrated if some concepts or methods do not become clear the first time around.

The first and last chapters have been designed to give you an overview of the whole area before you become too involved in the more detailed parts. Refer to them often and make sure you do not lose sight of the forest by standing too close to the trees.

Most chapters have been written to be as self-contained as possible, for those desiring familiarity with a specific topic. For those exposed to the entire text, your efforts will be rewarded with an understanding of what it takes to design, plan, and control productive systems and the importance of being aware of the demands and restrictions placed on them by social, legal, economic, and technological considerations.

In a world confounded with problems for better utilization of our limited resources, a cleaner environment, a more satisfied worker, and many others, your decision-making ability as a manager, an administrator, or a technical specialist represents a most valuable resource. If this book can contribute, even modestly, to the development of this ability, it will have succeeded.

Your comments or suggestions to the author for the improvement of this text will be welcome and appreciated.

Kostas N. Dervitsiotis

Operations Management

Part One

INTRODUCTION

Part One provides an overview of operations management and sets the conceptual framework for the text. Chapter 1 describes the evolution of operations management marked by changes in focus and methodology. It also provides definitions of key concepts, highlights major problem types, and establishes the criteria for evaluating performance.

Chapter 2 presents the basic conceptual tools of "systems" and "models", discusses the model-building process, and presents three approaches for decision making (rational, organizational and political). Operations management uses these singly or in combination depending on problem complexity and the number of participants. Chapter 3 examines the internal and external environment for an operations system based on the manager's degree of control. The first, partially controlled, includes other parts of the organization and how they interact with operations management problems. It emphasizes the need to focus on organizational rather than functional objectives and examines some of the problems caused by "local" criteria for evaluating performance. The external environment is defined by the factors that affect performance, but cannot be controlled (economy, politics, technology, nature, etc.). This is viewed as the source of opportunities and constraints in reaching organizational objectives.

Included in Part One are also Supplementary Chapters A and B, in decision analysis and economic analysis, designed to provide review material for important decision-making tools.

Chapter 1

AN OVERVIEW OF OPERATIONS MANAGEMENT

1-1   INTRODUCTION

In today's complex society we are closely associated with numerous production systems. In some systems we may be a part of the production process, but we consume the diverse products and services of many others.

The word "production" is used here to describe any organized activity intended to provide services or to increase the value or usefulness of material things. These activities serve to satisfy human needs, from basics, such as food and clothing, to luxuries, such as a 15-day cruise in the Caribbean. The nature of a production process is thus associated with the type of conversion responsible for the value added to the final product, e.g., lumber transformed into a dining room table or people transported from one location to another.

Until recently, the study of production systems focused mainly on manufacturing activities, and it has been common to analyze the operation of a factory from the time of arrival of raw materials to the delivery of the finished product. The development of methods for planning and controlling the numerous activities required for making a complex product gradually led to a body of knowledge that changed the nature of production management from an art to a mixture of art and a considerable amount of science.

It has become increasingly clear that the concepts and techniques appropriate for the management of production activities in a factory can be effectively applied to service organizations, e.g., a school, a hospital, or a commercial bank, as well as many government agencies. To the layperson these appear to be drastically different systems with unique problems and different technologies. In the eyes of the experienced analyst, however, the problems encountered in all of them have many similarities. The analyst recognizes inventories not only in piles of raw materials or cases of finished goods but also in a bank's excessive cash reserves or a hospital's idle beds. The great diversity of activities to which the methodology can be applied has led many writers in the field to refer to it as *operations* (rather than *production*) *management*. We shall use these terms as synonyms.

For present or future managers the importance of studying operations management is great whether they will work in the private or public sector of the economy. From an economic point of view, the production phase in most organizations absorbs the largest expenditures for plant and equipment as well as raw materials and labor to satisfy the economy's needs in products and services.

From a social viewpoint, the various operations systems employ the largest percentage of the nation's labor force. As a result they play a dominant role in shaping the social interaction between employees, and they offer opportunities to satisfy social needs for power, status, and community involvement.

From an ecological point of view, it is clear that production systems profoundly affect the ecological balance both by depleting natural resources to secure production inputs and by generating wastes, thus polluting the land, water, and air of the natural environment.

Finally, from a more personal point of view, understanding how various operations systems operate, especially on the basis of sound analysis, makes it possible to form a better opinion of their effect on the economy and other societal problems.

1-2 HISTORICAL BACKGROUND

The study of the historical development of production systems is intimately related to the study of human beings. From the beginning of our existence on this planet, production has been our main preoccupation. In the early stages productive activity was aimed at finding the means for satisfying the most basic needs (food, clothing, and shelter). Since then, through productive activities, people have striven to enjoy the "good life" made possible by modern technologies and desirable by the value system of their culture.

Phase 1: The Age of Empiricism

The evolution of production systems beyond the form of self-sufficient households or artisan shops in the Middle Ages had to await the development of the intellectual foundation of the Renaissance (fourteenth to sixteenth centuries). In this period we discern the beginnings of contemporary science and a willingness to experiment as an approach to understanding natural laws.

The impact of the *industrial revolution* in the eighteenth century was felt in terms of new technologies (the hardware aspect)—and in new forms of organization and management of the production process (the software aspects). In the period that followed the distinctive trend was the replacement of people as a source of muscular power by an increasing number of machines. Continuous improvements in machines, combined with the principles of parts standardization and interchangeability,[1] gradually led to mass-production systems, and, in the early twentieth century, to the introduction of the first moving assembly line for automobiles.

While the types of basic problems encountered in production management were perceived early in the industrial revolution, the emphasis on technological developments and the trend toward increased work specialization acted as obstacles to the formulation of an integrated approach for their systematic study. Despite some sporadic efforts to describe and analyze production processes, such as those of Adam Smith (1785), the famous Scottish economist, and later of Charles Babbage (1832), for the next 50 years we observe a lack of the conceptual framework and terminology that give a discipline a scientific form and unity. Decision making until the end of the nineteenth century relied on the cumulative experience of managers and the mentality of the times.

Phase 2: The Age of Analysis

In 1895, the work of Frederick W. Taylor initiated a new era in the manner of viewing production systems. Influenced greatly by the outlook of his time, Taylor developed a management philosophy based on analyzing and measuring work

---

[1] It is worth noting that the ideas of standardization and interchangeability of parts were invented independently about the same time by Eli Whitney (1798) in the United States and by Leblanc (1788) in France.

according to the scientific method.[1] Despite the intense reactions from many sides that followed the application of Taylor's *scientific management*, his contributions helped advance production-system analysis to the status of a new discipline.

Taylor's work was continued in new directions by Lillian and Frank Gilbreth, Henry Gantt, H. Emerson, and others. Their objective was to study work methods in terms of their component parts in the light of human abilities and limitations.

Many psychologists and sociologists considered Taylor's view of man as a machine as an insult to human dignity. Their aim was an attempt to differentiate man's role from that of the machine when examined as an element of a production process. In a series of experiments known as the *Hawthorne studies*, F. J. Roethlisberger (1924) concluded that psychological factors affect a worker's performance significantly and are more complex than explained in Taylor's theories. Similar conclusions were reached by comparable experiments performed at the Mayo Clinic (1935). As a result, the role of people as elements of a production process was defined in more humane terms without diminishing the importance of Taylor's contributions.

Phase 3: The Age of Synthesis and Systems

The next significant development in the study of production systems came during World War II. The urgent need to make the best use of available resources led to the creation of special teams in Great Britain with scientists of diverse training and background. These teams, including biologists, mathematicians, economists, and others, were assigned problems relating to war operations.[2] The success of their efforts contributed a great deal to the victory of the Allies. As a result a new discipline was born, and the so-called *operations research* (OR) teams were continued after the war in defense projects and later in industry.

The essence of the new approach consisted of looking at complex problems in a way that accounted for the most significant variables and their interactions. Taylor's approach emphasized analysis. Accordingly a large problem was decomposed into simple ones, which were solved independently, and the optimum results for each part were then combined. Throughout the analysis, there was no serious attempt to capture the interactions between variables in the component problems. The OR approach looked at a system as a whole. In developing a solution the emphasis was not only on problem analysis but also on a well-integrated synthesis aimed at producing the best possible (or *optimum*) solution.

Coupled with the power of computers, OR (also known as management science) developed an impressive variety of techniques helpful in solving several production problems. Today, management science offers a *systems approach* for solving problems of resource allocation, inventory control, operations scheduling, maintenance, and others. The use of computers and mathematical models initiated a new era known as the *second industrial revolution*. Its main characteristic is the gradual substitution of machines for people as a source of control (see Fig. 1-1).

---

[1] F. W. Taylor, *Principles of Scientific Management*, Harper, New York, 1911.

[2] Their studies included radar effectiveness, submarine bombings, optimum size of convoys, and others.

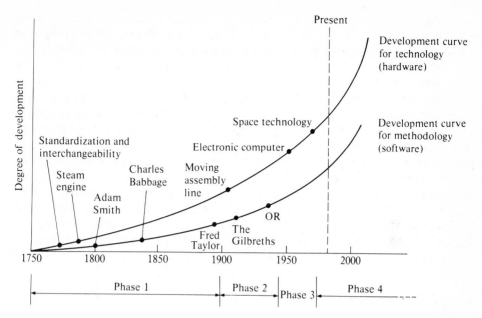

Fig. 1-1 Chronological development of production technology (hardware) and production methodology (software).

The initial applications of management science in production were in the category of *tactical decisions*. These concern problems of limited scope, involving limited resources, and having a limited impact on the effectiveness of the whole organization, e.g., inventory and scheduling decisions. *Strategic decisions* relate to problems of greater scope, affecting more parts of the organization, requiring the commitment of large amounts of resources, and having a long-term impact on the organization. Such problems may involve new products, new markets, new plant locations, or integrated investment strategies. By their nature strategic decisions are more difficult to define and solve.

During the last 15 to 20 years we have witnessed a shift in emphasis from rather *well-structured* problems at the tactical level to the *ill-structured* ones at the strategic level. This enables management to view more objectively certain problems which until recently were solved subjectively. The availability of computers makes it possible to integrate managerial experience through common sense rules with the more quantitative aspects in the form of *heuristic* procedures or models.

Phase 4: The Age of Earthmanship-Oriented[1] Production System

Until the late sixties production systems were viewed as operating in an environment with unlimited resources for needed production inputs and an infinite capac-

---

[1] The term is from G. Tyler Miller, *Living in the Environment: Concepts, Problems and Alternatives*, Wadsworth, Belmont, Calif., 1975.

ity to absorb polluting wastes from human productive activities. The ensuing dangers from pollution of our landscape, air, and water, coupled with the threat of rapid depletion of natural resources, have increased our awareness of the finite limits of the planet Earth.

The undesirable environmental impacts of operations systems have resulted in new pressures for resource conservation and a cleaner environment. One important result of public concern for such issues has been to pass new laws regulating the pollution characteristics of industry. If resource depletion continues at present rates so that our dependence on certain materials becomes too critical, it is not hard to visualize laws being passed to regulate the use of such resources, too, particularly energy.

Present and future managers must develop a sensitivity for the environmental impacts of productive activities. Adjustments for making this shift more effectively will become part of the next stage, or phase 4, in the evolution of operations management. The importance of this adjustment is examined more closely later in this chapter and in other relevant chapters that follow.

1-3 SOME BASIC CONCEPTS

Before proceeding with our discussion of production-management methods, it is necessary to define some of the key terms and concepts that will be used repeatedly throughout the book.

Management Process

The term *management process* refers to the *set of activities undertaken in order to determine* (1) *the value system and objectives*, (2) *the organizational structure*, (3) *the design*, (4) *the planning*, and (5) *the control of operations of an organization* in the private or public sector of the economy. In the sense that the behavior of organizations, like that of human beings, is not random but motivated by the desire to satisfy certain needs, it is useful to define the concepts of basic purpose, objectives, and targets for an organization more sharply.

Basic Purpose

We view the *basic purpose or mission of an organization* as *the reason for its creation or existence*, independently of the means or methods employed for its achievement. For example, the basic purpose of a private firm is the satisfaction of the needs of all those that have an interest in it. Thus, the firm attempts to satisfy:

1. Its owners, through an adequate return on their investment or other direct or indirect benefits (influence, power, etc.)
2. Its customers, through the sale of products or services that meet quality requirements at a competitive cost
3. Its employees, through adequate compensation in salaries or wages and through a working environment that provides job satisfaction

4. Society or the public, through active involvement in projects for community improvements and assistance in resolving societal problems

Objectives

In order for an organization to fulfill its basic purpose, it is necessary to determine its *objectives*, i.e., the *desirable states in which it seeks to find itself.*

For a private firm some of the (stated or concealed) objectives might be (1) a satisfactory rate of return on invested capital, (2) a reputation for high-quality products, (3) a certain position concerning its share of the market, (4) a high degree of employee motivation or loyalty, etc.

For a community hospital some of the objectives might be (1) a high level of general patient services, (2) a satisfactory utilization rate of expensive facilities such as operating rooms, x-ray laboratories, etc., (3) a low absenteeism rate for its employees, and so on.

At the level of defining objectives for an organization we are confronted for the first time with the conflict between them. Each objective makes important demands on the limited resources available. Advancement toward satisfying one objective is generally obtained at the expense of others. Thus, *as an organization begins to concentrate too much effort on excelling with regard to one objective, its overall performance may suffer as a result of inferior achievement of other objectives.* The firm that attempts to maximize its profits may resort to rather dangerous compromises with regard to the quality of its products or the satisfaction of its employees. This phenomenon, known as *suboptimization,* is pervasive in all decision-making behavior. Suboptimization is present at the level of personal decisions, organization decisions, or even national priorities.

So far the most common approach is to identify a dominant objective, say service quality, and attempt to achieve it to the maximum degree allowed by certain restrictions. The latter are imposed by acceptable levels of achievement for the remaining objectives such as return on investment, employee morale, and so on. As conditions change, management may alter its priorities to adjust to new pressures or exploit new opportunities.

Targets

Once a set of objectives for an organization has been adopted, target setting involves determining the specific degree of achievement for each objective in a given planning period. Some writers prefer the term *goals* instead of targets, but they mean the same.

For a firm seeking a dominant position in the market, the target for the next year might be an increase of 5 percent in its market share. For a community hospital seeking a lower absenteeism record, its target might be a reduction in absenteeism of 15 percent for the following 2 years.

An objective represents a desirable direction in which we want to move, while a target represents how far in that direction we wish to advance in a given time. Specifying targets for successive years with regard to the organization's objectives is equivalent to the formulation of a long-term strategy or a path for growth and development. It is helpful to display objectives and targets in a form resembling an organization chart. This representation allows management to recognize a hierarchy in the objectives that motivate the organization's behavior and to indicate the most significant interactions between them.

Production Process

Some of the most important objectives of an organization are achieved by offering the public material goods or services for a price or (in the case of government agencies) through taxation. A *production process* is the *set of all activities that are required to transform a set of inputs (human resources, raw materials, energy, etc.) into more valuable outputs such as finished products and/or services.*

The issuance of a passport, the hospital treatment of a patient, the manufacture of an appliance, or the repair of a car are all representative examples of a production process. In all these cases we can describe the appropriate transformation through an input-output diagram like Fig. 1-2.

Production or Operations System

By itself, a production process as shown in Fig. 1-2 is undirected and unable to function effectively. To make such a process viable in the long run, it is necessary to couple it to another type of process that will provide guidance, evaluate its performance, and adapt it to an ever-changing environment. For this purpose we need a management process. *Coupling a conversion process with an operations-management process yields a production system. This is an entity with a basic purpose, objectives, targets, and the ability to evaluate its performance and adjust to the varying demands placed on it by a dynamic environment.*

A more detailed analysis of systems in general and production systems in particular is given in the chapters that follow. Control is made possible through a *feedback loop*, which measures the system's output, compares it with existing plans or standards, and proceeds to make corrections to bring performance within desired limits. The elements of a production system are shown in Fig. 1-3.

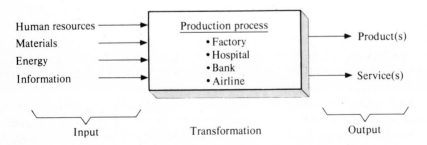

Fig. 1-2   An input-output representation of a production or operations process.

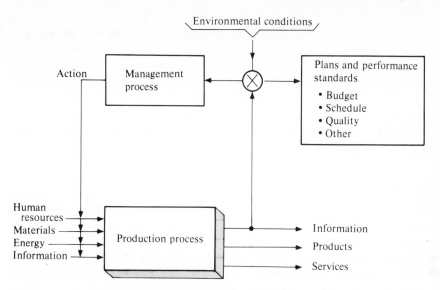

Fig. 1-3 An input-output representation of a production system.

1-4   TYPES OF PRODUCTION OR OPERATIONS SYSTEMS

The huge variety of existing production systems can be studied more easily if an attempt is made at grouping them into meaningful categories. Such groupings can help in selecting appropriate methods for their analysis, design, planning, and control. Here we have chosen to classify production systems in terms of their main objective and the form of their output. Another classification scheme, discussed in Chap. 7, is based on the type of the conversion process used.

Profit-Oriented versus Non-Profit-Oriented Production Systems

In a free, or mixed, economy the major objective of many production systems is to earn profits. From the sale of their products or services such systems seek to maximize profit or the return on invested capital. Other objectives such as output quality, employee satisfaction, etc., assume the role of *operating restrictions*. The aggregate of all such systems makes up the private sector of the economy, and their behavior is governed mainly by the interaction of the supply and demand mechanisms of the marketplace, which can take the form of free competition, oligopoly, or monopoly. Since profit is the difference between revenues and costs, it is often more fruitful to analyze production decisions for profit-oriented systems with the objective of minimizing costs.

As societies become more complex, there is a need for some production systems that operate without a profit motive. Such systems exist to satisfy human needs primarily through services, i.e., defense, police protection, education, medical care, welfare, transportation, and, of course, government at the federal, state, and local level. The aggregate of all such systems constitutes the public sector of the economy. For non-profit-oriented systems we seek to maximize some measure of effectiveness in providing needed services subject to restrictions concerning their budget, existing laws, etc.

Somewhere between the above categories we have a third type of quasi-public systems operating under strong government regulation. In this group we include public utilities for water, electricity, communications, and others. They are generally evaluated in terms of both economic and effectiveness criteria.

Product versus Service Systems

An operations system may have as its output products, services, or both. The distinction becomes important when we must choose the appropriate methods for the system's design, planning, and control.

The physical product of a process may be intended for direct consumption or use, such as foodstuffs, clothing, or private cars. In economics these are called *consumer goods*. Their design and production must take into account not only functional needs but aesthetic ones as well (color, style, and so on). Since consumer tastes display a great deal of unpredictability, the demand for many consumer goods may be rather volatile.

Certain products, on the other hand, are used as elements of another production process. They may be machines, like lathes or drill presses, materials-handling equipment, or others. In economics these are called *producer's goods*. Since they are intended for use in a productive capacity, we are more concerned with their functional characteristics (output rate, safety, reliability, etc.) than their aesthetic qualities. Furthermore, their longer life, planned use, and generally high cost result in more stable demand patterns.

In addition to products, people require a wide variety of services ranging from police protection to education and entertainment. Physical products often lend themselves to a considerable amount of standardization that permits mass production. This is not usually the case with service systems, for which there is a more

TABLE 1-1 Production systems classified by form of output†

Product-oriented		Service-oriented	
Consumer goods	Producer goods	Standardized	Customized
Manufacture of: Foodstuffs Clothing Appliances Furniture	Manufacture of: Machine tools Materials-handling equipment Earth-moving equipment Office machines	Insurance Wholesale stores	Medical care Legal services Accounting services

† Only a few examples are given for each group.

pronounced need for personalized care. Treating a patient, catering to a restaurant customer, defending an alleged criminal, or repairing a car all require special attention to the needs of the particular person receiving the service (see Table 1-1).

Despite their distinctive differences, it is highly rewarding to see that both categories have considerable similarities in the problems that arise and the way they are resolved.

1-5 OPERATIONS MANAGEMENT

The Role of Operations Management

The success of an organization rests on the satisfactory performance of at least three basic functions, marketing, finance, and production. The *marketing function* is mainly responsible for generating the demand for the organization's products or services. The *production function* carries the responsibility of creating the products and/or services to satisfy the expected demand for them. The *finance function* is responsible for generating the short- and long-term capital requirements to support the system's operation.

These basic functions present in all organizations interact very strongly, sometimes fiercely. The most significant interactions are discussed in Chap. 3. To avoid letting each function attempt to achieve its own limited objectives at the expense of the overall objectives, their activities must be coordinated and controlled by *top management*, which formulates a strategy and develops policies aimed at the success of the entire organization (see Fig. 1-4).

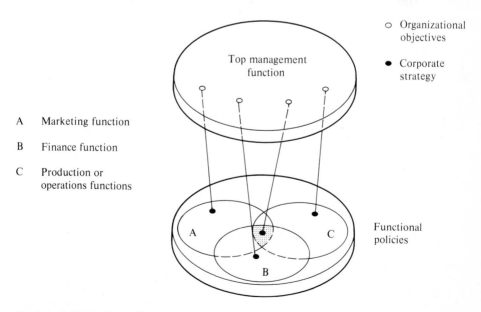

A   Marketing function

B   Finance function

C   Production or
     operations functions

○ Organizational
   objectives

● Corporate
   strategy

Functional
policies

Fig. 1-4 Basic functions within an organization.

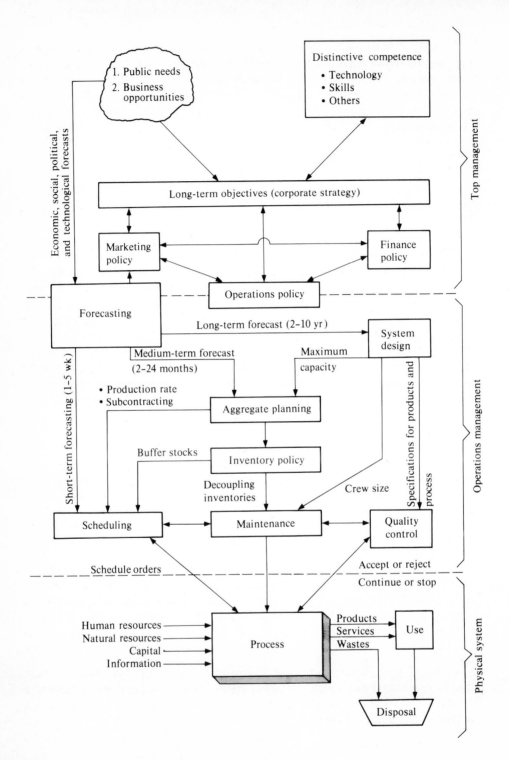

Fig. 1-5 Specific functions of operations management.

14

It is the role of operations management to manage the production or operations function of an organization. This must be done so that it satisfies performance criteria unique to the production function itself while remaining well integrated with marketing and finance and consistent with the overall objectives for the organization. The interrelationships of policies for operation, finance, and marketing with corporate strategy at the top level and specific operations-management functions at lower levels are shown in Fig. 1-5. These functions are described briefly in the next section to set the stage for more detailed discussion later.

Specific Functions of Operations Management

Translation of an organization's value system into operational objectives   One of the most important and difficult functions of operations management is to examine the more general objectives of the organization derived from its value system and give them operational meaning, i.e., relating the organization's broad objectives to the operational characteristics of the production process. For example, an objective relating to excellence in product quality must be expressed in such terms as percentage defectives allowed in the process output, product reliability, forms of warranties offered, and so on. Similarly, the objective of providing good service must be translated in quantitative measures for service time and waiting time, maximum allowed shortages, or number of complaints from dissatisfied customers, and so on.

Organizational structure and utilization of human resources   Despite the rapid technological advances of our age, human resources represent an organization's most valuable asset. For operations management this means that a great deal of thought must be given to the most desirable form of organizational structure and deployment of people in the production process. More specifically, it is necessary to consider the following:

1. Specification of *job descriptions* that allow the most effective matching of people to jobs and their proper utilization
2. Determination of clear lines of *authority* and assignment of *responsibility* appropriate to a given organizational structure
3. Determination of a smooth and efficient *communication network* that provides timely information to satisfy decision requirements
4. Determination and complete descriptions of effective *decision mechanisms* for resolving the variety of problems encountered in managing a production process

Recent studies have pointed out the importance of organizational structure (flexibility, management layers, supervision styles) in the survival and success of a business.[1] The most appropriate structure for a firm appears to depend heavily on the type of technology it uses.

---

[1] Tom Burns and G. M. Stalker, *The Management of Innovation*, Tavistock, London, 1961.

Design of the production system   The overall effectiveness of a production system depends not only on the quality and utilization of its human resources but on the characteristics of the physical resources (facilities, equipment, etc.) it uses and of the products and/or services offered.

The design of a production system involves a number of critical long-term decisions that establish the technical performance and operational characteristics of the organization. In particular, it covers the following areas:

1. *Product design,* or the development of general and engineering specifications for the output(s) of the process(es) in products or services (see Chap. 4)
2. *Capacity determination,* or the determination of the desired maximum output rate or resources needed to meet expected demand in the planning period (see Chaps. 5 and 6)
3. *Process design,* or the development of specifications for the technologies used in the various stages of the production process and for the equipment needed in each stage (see Chap. 7)
4. *Work design and measurement,* or the determination of job content, work methods, and time standards (see Chap. 8)
5. *Facilities layout,* or the selection of the best configuration of facilities, machines, and product flows (see Chap. 9)
6. *Facilities location,* or the determination of the specific site of the production system (see Chap. 10)
7. *Management information system,* or the determination of information requirements for the variety of decisions made in operations management

Even though these problems have a high percentage of technical content, thus requiring engineering expertise, their successful resolution depends on the satisfactory collaboration with nontechnical management personnel familiar with the objectives of the system, budget constraints, market characteristics, and other nontechnical details.

Operations planning   Specification of the desired organizational structure, the necessary human resources, and the configuration of the physical facilities sets an upper limit on the capacity available for the near future. Within such a framework *operations planning seeks to determine the best utilization of existing resources (labor force, inventories, facilities, etc.) that will satisfy expected demand.*

With capacity assumed relatively fixed, a common planning horizon is 1 year. For products displaying seasonal fluctuations there is thus an opportunity to consider a complete annual cycle and develop appropriate strategies for absorbing demand fluctuations at minimum cost. Such strategies include the use of inventories or backordering, changing the production rate through overtime and undertime or through hiring and firing, and subcontracting. Planning production activity in broad terms for a period up to 1 year is called *aggregate planning* (Chap. 12).

For shorter periods, say up to 1 month, the planning activity is constrained by the previously developed aggregate plans and is more detailed. Here we proceed to assign actual orders to specific resource centers and sequence them to meet specific criteria. This type of planning is known as *operations scheduling* (Chap. 15).

As the planning horizon becomes longer and longer, exceeding 1 or 2 years, the distinction between planning and design becomes rather fuzzy because now there is an opportunity to change the capacity available. In short, in order to know how to design a system we must know how its capacity will be used; this involves planning. This is true whether we consider the construction of a hospital or a factory.

Operations control In order to operate a production system satisfactorily relying on plans or schedules prepared in advance, it is necessary to have control. *A control system seeks to secure conformance to a plan or to identify reasons for adjusting such a plan.* More specifically, a control system is responsible for the following:

1. Sensing significant deviations of actual from planned performance
2. Initiating corrective action to remove such deviations
3. Proposing desirable adjustments to the plan or even to the production system itself if warranted by changes in the environment
4. Evaluating the degree to which broad organizational objectives are served by accepted operations-management objectives and revising the latter if necessary

The management of operations requires appropriate policies for inventory control (Chaps. 13 and 14), quality and cost control (Chap. 16), and maintenance of the physical and human resources (Chap. 17).

Performance Criteria for Operations Management

Since it is responsible for generating the goods and/or services to satisfy anticipated demand, the production function and its management can be evaluated on the basis of both physical and economic performance. Criteria of *physical performance* relate to how well inputs are converted into outputs that satisfy consumers. Those related to *economic performance* measure how effectively production contributes to the achievement of the overall objectives of the organization.

Demand can be described in terms of quantities wanted, their timing, the desired quality of the output, and where it is wanted or its location. Table 1-2 lists

TABLE 1-2 Physical performance criteria for demand satisfaction

Dimensions of demand	Performance criteria	Some determining factors
Quantity (how much?)	Output rate	Labor-force efficiency
	Inventory levels	Equipment efficiency
Timing (when?)	Inventory service levels	Supplier's reliability
	Production schedules	Manufacturing lead time
Quality (what?)	Percent defective	Product design
	Reliability	Process technology
	No. of complaints	Quality-control effort
Location (where?)		Transportation system
		Warehouse location

some of the most common performance criteria used for evaluating the production system's effectiveness in satisfying demand. All dimensions, especially quality and location considerations, are taken into account in the phase of system design. Quantity and timing, however, are regularly analyzed during planning and scheduling.

The physical performance of a production system must next be translated into economic terms in order to assess its contribution to the overall objectives of the organization. Let us assume that for a private firm the dominant objective is to maximize profits within certain restrictions on quality, service levels, etc. Since profit is the difference between revenues and costs, for a given level of demand and pricing policy the revenues are determined. The production system's performance is related to the production costs incurred to satisfy that demand. The smaller these costs the greater the profits. Therefore, in rough terms, operations management contributes to the achievement of the firm's objective by minimizing the costs of the production function without sacrificing other objectives such as product or service quality or employee safety.

The evaluation task would be relatively simple if all production costs could be accurately measured by the firm's accounting system. Unfortunately, this is not the case. Certain production costs, e.g., those related to materials, labor, and overhead (power, supervision, etc.), are *explicit* and can be adequately measured or approximated by standard accounting techniques. Others, however, are intangible and difficult to assess satisfactorily.

In the category of *intangible or implicit production costs* we include: (1) the costs resulting from dissatisfied customers, which may be due to products of poor quality

Inputs	Performance criteria		
	Physical	Economic	
		Measurable	Intangible
Labor Materials Energy Other	Labor efficiency Materials utilization (scrap, etc.) Energy utilization Other	Labor cost Materials cost Energy cost	Poor selection of • Suppliers • Parts and/ or materials
Production process	Equipment utilization Output rate Inventory levels	Production overhead • Rents • Salaries • Insurance • Utilities • Etc.	Improperly trained workers Unused capacity Machine breakdowns Shortages
Products Services Outputs	Quantity Timing Quality Location		Loss of goodwill from dissatisfied customers • Poor quality • Late deliveries • Poor service

Fig. 1-6   Physical and economic performance criteria for evaluating operations management.

or to poor service, attributed to lack of parts, late deliveries, etc.; (2) intangible costs due to poor utilization of productive resources (improperly trained operators, machine breakdowns, unused capacity because of poor scheduling and so on); and (3) opportunity costs, resulting from failure to make the best decisions in the selection of suppliers of parts or materials, the choice of equipment, the selection of a warehouse or plant location, and others.

The evaluation of operations management on the basis of physical and economic criteria with reference to the inputs, the process, and the output of the production system is shown in Fig. 1-6. Supplementary Chap. B covers the basic concepts and methods employed in the economic analysis of typical decisions related to the production function.

1-6 OPERATIONS MANAGEMENT AND ENVIRONMENTAL IMPACTS

The input-process-output representation of a production system has been a useful framework for studying many of the decisions related to operations management. Nevertheless, the increasingly serious problems of environmental pollution and depletion of natural resources suggest that this and other views of such systems have been deficient in some important respects.

A more realistic framework for productive activities must account for two additional considerations: (1) it is essential to acknowledge, early in the design phase, that along with the products and services for which there is a demand the system also produces wastes that may bring about dangerous environmental disruption; (2) the natural resources (in the form of matter and energy) used as inputs to the production system are drawn from an environment that has finite limits on what it can provide.

The dangers attributed to rapid resource depletion and to environmental pollution have resulted in drastic changes in the attitudes of the public toward wasteful or polluting systems. Operations management is still confronted with the traditional problems of design, planning, and control, but these problems must now be solved in a new context. The new reality assigns high priority to the need for managing private operations systems with a strong concern not only for profitability but also for the integrity of an environment threatened by pollution and resource depletion.

Depletion of Natural Resources

Until a few years ago most planning effort did not take into account the extent of a natural-resource base. The variety of inputs to production activities were assumed to be derived from almost inexhaustible reserves of energy, raw materials, and other resources. The energy crises that shook the Western world in 1973 and 1979 and food shortages in various countries have served as stern warnings that the limits of resources available on our planet are indeed finite and may be reached much sooner than anticipated.

Causes of resource depletion   There is considerable agreement among experts that the most serious contributing factors to the rapid and sometimes unwise depletion of natural resources are three:

1. The population explosion
2. The increase in our standard of living or affluence
3. Technological advances

Let D = natural-resource depletion
   P = population size
   C = consumption of products and services per capita

Then
$$D = P \cdot C \tag{1-1}$$
or

$$\begin{bmatrix} \text{Natural-} \\ \text{resource} \\ \text{depletion} \end{bmatrix} = \begin{bmatrix} \text{population} \\ \text{size} \end{bmatrix} \begin{bmatrix} \text{consumption} \\ \text{per} \\ \text{capita} \end{bmatrix}$$

The important point to keep in mind about this relationship is that the combined effect of the factors that cause resource depletion is *multiplicative* rather than additive. This means that even though each factor may increase slowly, when they are combined and multiplied, they result in rapidly increasing total effects. Thus, when the population of the United States increased fourfold between 1880 and 1966 and consumption per capita for the same period increased threefold, the total energy consumption increased twelvefold.[1]

Population changes are tracked through a periodic census, but consumption per capita as a measure of affluence is more difficult to estimate. Economists generally rely on the conventional but controversial gross national product (GNP), which consists of expenditures by consumers and government for goods and services plus investments. The GNP is criticized for including costs that it should not, e.g., costs of prosecuting criminals or cleaning pollution, and for not including other costs that should be taken into account and subtracted, e.g., those related to environmental or city deterioration.

Alternative approaches for assessing affluence may be directed at measuring the *capital stock* (goods, machinery, etc.) in existence. Certain *flows*, such as the annual production and consumption of steel, water, or energy, may be more appropriate as indicators of a country's standard of living. In the opinion of many experts, energy consumption per capita is one of the most accurate and reliable yardsticks for measuring affluence.[2] The impressive increases in the affluence of most countries are a matter of record, regardless of the method of measurement.

Technology is the critical factor needed to explain the relationship between consumption per capita and affluence. It is the type of technology used that determines the input requirements in natural resources that will be transformed into final products and services for consumption.

---

[1] P. Ehrlich, A. E. Ehrlich, and J. P. Holdren, *Human Ecology*, Freeman, San Francisco, 1973, p. 207.

[2] Ibid.

The stimulus for technological advances can be traced to economic pressures. The need for less expensive production methods, for new products and services, and for exploiting less accessible sources of raw materials or energy is constantly motivating technological improvements or breakthroughs.

Environmental Pollution

Equally alarming and perhaps more apparent than the problem of resource depletion is that of environmental pollution. Public concern for pollution started after World War II and is an important contemporary issue. A production process may alter the natural environment by wastes that pollute the ground, the water, and the air, singly or in combination. Noise, thermal, and radiation pollution adversely affect various forms of plant and animal life.

Causes of pollution Impurities in the water or the air have existed for many centuries. The real concern about them emerged when the degree of such impurities disrupted the environment to the point of making it unfit for plant and animal life, including human beings. The present level of environmental pollution is attributed to the following factors:

1. The population explosion and its concentration patterns
2. The unprecedented affluence of industrialized countries
3. The development of new technologies, some of them faulty
4. The inability of our economic system to evaluate the impact of ecological disruptions adequately

The first three factors are the same that have also contributed to the rapid depletion of natural resources, and the two problems are intimately related.

Let E = environmental impact
P = population size
C = consumption per capita (in goods and services)
I = environmental impact per unit of goods consumed
I_p = environmental impact *from production* per unit of goods consumed (water, air, thermal, noise pollution)
I_c = environmental impact *from consumption* per unit of goods (solid waste plus other forms of pollution)

Then
$$E = P \cdot C \cdot I = P \cdot C \cdot (I_p + I_c) \tag{1-2}$$

or

$$
\begin{bmatrix} \text{Environmental} \\ \text{pollution} \end{bmatrix} = \begin{bmatrix} \text{population} \\ \text{size} \end{bmatrix} \begin{bmatrix} \text{consumption} \\ \text{per} \\ \text{capita} \end{bmatrix} \left(\begin{bmatrix} \text{industrial} \\ \text{pollution per} \\ \text{unit production} \end{bmatrix} + \begin{bmatrix} \text{consumer} \\ \text{pollution} \\ \text{per unit} \\ \text{consumption} \end{bmatrix} \right)
$$

It is important to note again that the combined effect of these factors is *multiplicative*. This means that even small increases in any one contributing factor are amplified in proportion to the rate of increase and magnitude of the remaining factors.

The population explosion has resulted in greater and greater pollution simply because more people generate more wastes. Furthermore, as these people tend to cluster in highly populated areas, the generated wastes exceed the capacity of the local environment to assimilate them.

The unparalleled increase in the standard of living of many countries intensifies the pollution problem because of increased consumption per capita of goods and services. This creates opportunities for more and bigger production systems to absorb the increased demand. With most products being disposable, even those having a longer life such as cars, solid waste is polluting the ground after consumption, while industry pollutes the water and the air in the process of producing.

Some industrial technological advances have aggravated the pollution problem even more. The changes in the material makeup of many products and their containers or packaging make disposal more difficult. Examples are nonbiodegradable compounds, indestructible containers, harmful pesticides and industrial wastes. These often represent a menace to our countryside and a threat to our health.

Sometimes the ecological aftereffects of technological advances can be estimated in advance. In the soap industry, switching from a fat base to a nondegradable detergent base resulted in suds from contaminated reservoirs returning to households through the kitchen faucet. In other instances, the best-intentioned efforts have unpredictable consequences. The development of detergents, pesticides, even complex projects such as the Aswan dam in Egypt,[1] were intended to help mankind. They have all somehow backfired, resulting in serious ecological disruptions whose overall impact will take years to assess.

Some effects of pollution   Many of the effects of pollution can be determined in a direct way through our sensory organs. The ugliness of garbage piles or junked cars in the countryside, the offensive odors of a polluted stream or lake, and the burning sensation in our eyes from smog are hard to ignore. However, other effects of pollution, especially on the health of human beings and other forms of plant and animal life, have been observed but are more difficult to assess.

Potential Contributions of Operations Management

An effective attack against the problems of unwise resource depletion and environmental pollution is a complex problem requiring far-reaching decisions at the federal, state, and local levels. For certain parts of the world international cooperation appears also necessary due to the complex web of interlocking economic, trade, and other relationships.[2] The effectiveness of such policies depends on sound decisions with regard to all interacting factors, i.e., population, consumption per capita, and technology.

---

[1] Marshall I. Goldman, *Ecology and Economics: Controlling Pollution in the 70's*, Prentice-Hall, Englewood Cliffs, N.J., 1972, p. 11.

[2] Countries in the Mediterranean have in recent conferences agreed to certain common policies to combat pollution.

Operations management can play a significant role in such an effort. Production systems represent the basic transformation mechanisms of natural resources into products and services with attendant waste and/or by-products. Through correct decisions in product design, process design, and plant location operations management can exercise considerable control. On the input side, resource depletion can be controlled through appropriate selection of raw materials, sound product design, and efficient technologies that do not result in wasted energy or excessive scrap losses. On the output side, pollution can be partially controlled through improved product and packaging design, tighter quality standards, incorporation of antipollution devices, and the selection of cleaner technologies with regard to water, air, noise, and thermal pollution. These approaches will be discussed in more detail in the chapters on product and process design and facility location.

If prevention of pollution or its significant reduction before it occurs is technologically impossible or infeasible, the next defense line is in its abatement through recycling and treatment. Through *recycling* operations management attempts to help in the recovery of the usable portion of a product or its container after consumption. It has been applied with various degrees of success by several industries (steel, aluminum, paper, etc.). *Treatment* is employed for the wastes of a process or from consumption of products that are not recyclable. Wastes flowing into water streams may be treated mechanically, chemically, or biologically. Effluents that may pollute the air, such as smoke from a stack, can be filtered, scrubbed, or precipitated. Noise can be treated by suppressing its intensity at the source or through insulation of the affected space.

A Revised View of Operations Systems

If operations management is to be effective in the future, it must rely for its decisions on a framework that will assist in achieving a proper balance between profitability and concern for the environment. In terms of the preceding discussion on the importance of resource depletion and pollution, such a framework must allow for an evaluation, even in general terms, of the environmental impacts produced. Figure 1-7 maintains in focus the relevant aspects that must be taken into account if such a balance is to be achieved. This revised input-process-output representation brings out the following points explicitly:

1. The natural environment is finite, i.e., limited in its capacity to provide needed inputs (such as raw materials and energy) and absorb polluting wastes.
2. Operations management can reduce the amounts of polluting wastes discharged in the environment through preventive measures (improved product and process design) and through recycling and treatment.
3. Operations management can assist in the improved utilization of natural resources through improvements in product design, selection of more efficient processes, and recycling.

In addition, it is also important to consider significant interactions of operations management with other parts of the environment such as the economy and the value system of our culture.

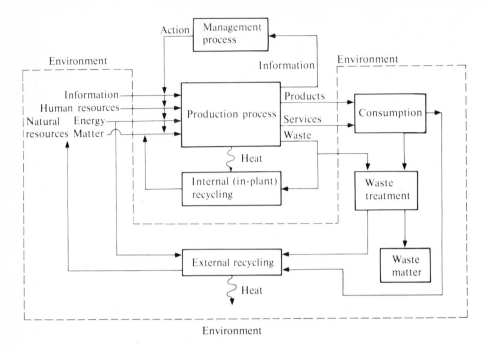

Fig. 1-7   A revised view of operations systems.

As one may conclude from this survey, operations management is a dynamic subject that has displayed significant progress and growth in the last few decades. Today's managers can approach many of their problems with a rich background of concepts and techniques. However, the complexity and evolution of production systems combined with external uncertainties defy clear-cut solutions that will remain valid for long periods. Furthermore, the pressing need for solving such problems in a new environmental context poses important new challenges.

In the chapters that follow, the reader will study how operations management can contribute to satisfying human needs for diverse products and services while preserving a quality of life that at times is threatened by unwise assaults on our natural environment.

1-7   SUMMARY

This introductory chapter previews the entire book. It emphasizes that the study of operations management is important for economic, social, and ecological reasons. In tracing the historical development of the field we describe the successive phases of its evolution from Frederick Taylor to today's era of the systems approach and our concern for the environment.

To set the stage for later discussions, we define early basic concepts about the management process and the production process (or operations process) and how the two are coupled to form adaptive productive systems. Following a classification of such systems, we examine the physical and economic criteria employed to evaluate their contribution in achieving organizational objectives. The latter are set by top management and translated into action through coordinated policies and plans for functional areas such as marketing, finance, and operations.

After discussing the interrelationships between functional policies and top management, we focus on the specific functions performed by operations management. Their importance or particular content may vary between sectors, e.g., manufacturing and services, or even within systems of the same kind. However, they must be performed in a well-integrated fashion to ensure smoothness and economy of operation.

Our primary interest in this text centers on the specific functions pertaining to systems design, operations planning, and control. These parallel more general managerial functions but have as their focus the long-term decisions for creating the physical facilities with desired productive capacity and short-term decisions for their effective utilization to attain organizational objectives. More specifically, long-term decisions relate to the design of output(s) and conversion processes, the layout and location of facilities, and the determination of capacity needed to meet expected demand. Short-term decisions involve the allocation of available productive resources (aggregate planning), setting inventory levels, and scheduling work loads. These represent short-term plans for action. However, actual operations are often disturbed by unforeseen events as trivial as equipment breakdowns or as serious as labor strikes. To accommodate such events plus random fluctuations in demand, operations management relies on short-term decisions for control. Inventory control, quality control, and maintenance are used to minimize the deviation from plans.

In recent years we have seen increased air, water, and land pollution combined with higher prices and/or shortages of critical materials and energy. These have made industrialized societies aware of the danger of assuming no limit for supplies of natural resources or the environment's capacity to absorb wastes. The need to revise our view of operations systems is a conclusion drawn from our general discussion of the factors that have caused these developments. These factors are examined in detail in later chapters as they interact with specific operations-management decisions.

REVIEW QUESTIONS

1. Give some of the reasons why the study of operations management is important for future managers.
2. Describe the key characteristics of, and main contributors to, each phase in the historical development of operations management.
3. Which are the major contributions to operations management of Frederick Taylor?
4. Define (*a*) management process, (*b*) production process, and (*c*) production system.
5. State the difference(s) in the meaning of the terms *basic purpose*, *objectives*, and *targets* as used in this text.
6. Discuss the criteria for classifying operations systems and give an example for the types in each category.

7. Discuss the roles of the basic functional areas within an organization and their relationship to top management.
8. Describe the specific functions performed by operations management.
9. What types of performance criteria are employed in operations management? Give some examples with respect to the operations area in (*a*) a manufacturing firm, (*b*) a commercial airline, and (*c*) a hospital.
10. Discuss the causes of environmental problems associated with (*a*) natural resource depletion and (*b*) pollution.
11. What is the difference between a *multiplicative* and an *additive* relationship of the causes responsible for environmental pollution such as solid waste?
12. In what ways can operations management assist in reducing adverse environmental effects associated with productive activities?
13. What are the major differences between the traditional and revised viewpoints of an operations system?

SELECTED REFERENCES

1. Bowman, Edward H., and Robert B. Fetter: *Analysis for Production and Operations Management*, 3d ed., Irwin, Homewood, Ill., 1967.
2. Buffa, Elwood S.: *Modern Production Management*, 3d ed., Wiley, New York, 1969.
3. Buffa, Elwood S.: *Basic Production Management*, Wiley, New York, 1971.
4. Chase, Richard B., and Nicholas J. Aquilano: *Production and Operations Management*, Irwin, Homewood, Ill., 1973.
5. Ehrlich, Paul, et al.: *Human Ecology*, Freeman, San Francisco, 1973.
6. Elmaghraby, Salah E.: *The Design of Production Systems*, Reinhold, New York, 1966.
7. Gavett, J. William: *Production and Operations Management*, Harcourt, New York, 1968.
8. Greene, James H.: *Operations Planning and Control*, Irwin, Homewood, Ill., 1967.
9. Miller, T. G. Jr.: *Living in the Environment: Concepts, Problems and Alternatives*, Wadsworth, Belmont, Calif., 1975.
10. Riggs, James L.: *Production Systems: Planning, Analysis and Control*, Wiley, New York, 1970.
11. Starr, Martin K.: *Production Management: Systems and Synthesis*, 2d ed., Prentice-Hall, Englewood Cliffs, N.J., 1972.

Chapter 2

SYSTEMS, MODELS, AND DECISION-MAKING APPROACHES

27

Organizational Approach to Decision Making
Political Approach to Decision Making

2-9   SUMMARY

2-1 INTRODUCTION

Those responsible for managing an operations system are under steady pressure to make difficult decisions about complex activities involving valuable human resources, raw materials, technology, information, etc. Despite their diversity, the multitude of decisions that must be made all have as their aim the coordination and smooth operation of several components to achieve the organization's objectives.

Confronted with so much complexity, management has the major task of formulating a general framework and employing a methodology that simplifies the structure of required decisions. The concepts of a *system* and a *model* play an important role in improving the decision-making process. Even though in everyday usage these terms may be vague or confusing, properly defined they become the pillars of the most powerful approach available for the analysis of operations problems.

2-2 THE CONCEPT OF A SYSTEM

Even though *system* has been defined in a variety of ways, for our purposes its meaning is best explained as follows:

Definition

A *system* refers to an organized set of component parts that are functionally interrelated in order to achieve some common predetermined objective(s).

For many work situations a human being as a "production machine" is one of nature's most advanced systems. A Boeing 747 airplane flying with an automatic pilot represents a mechanical system. The same aircraft during takeoff or landing under the pilot's control represents a good example of a *man-machine*[1] *system*.

The term "system" can be correctly applied to describe a hospital, a post office,

---

[1] The term "man-machine" is generic and is intended to cover both men and women in strong interaction with a machine, e.g., driving a car, using a computer or a typewriter, or operating a machine in a production line.

a factory, or a service garage. All these examples show the presence of component parts whose coordinated activities serve some predetermined objective(s).

Basic System Characteristics

To enrich the meaning of a system as defined previously, it is desirable to describe its basic characteristics. Churchman (Ref. 7, p. 29)[1] identifies five important attributes of a system: its objectives, its environment, its resources, its components, and its management. These attributes are explained in detail below and related more closely to production or operations systems.

System objectives and measures of performance In Chap. 1 a system objective was defined as *a desirable change in its characteristics*. It is therefore possible for a system to have several concurrent objectives. With regard to complex systems such as a business firm or a university, it is very important to attempt to identify the real objectives pursued, which may differ from those stated in public. For example, a car-rental company may adopt as its objective maximum customer service with a reasonable return on investment. At the same time, however, this company may be seeking to expand its market share, with limited profits being only a temporary goal.

To the experienced systems analyst, the real objectives are revealed when management knowingly sacrifices one objective, say profit, to satisfy others, such as market dominance. The same might be true of a senator's activities when the stated objective of serving his constituency takes a back seat to an intensive schedule of public appearances designed to enhance his chances for a higher office.

It can be seen that any worthwhile analysis must penetrate beyond socially approved stated objectives. This requires a careful selection of the measure(s) of performance used to evaluate the system. Volume of mail handled by a post office branch may thus be inadequate as a measure of performance unless it is related to the cost of operation, the number of wrong deliveries, the value of damaged items, or other characteristics.

System environment Deciding what is a part of the system and what is not is often a crucial question, and the answer can play an important role in how well a management problem is solved. *The environment of a system consists of all significant factors that affect the system's performance but cannot be controlled.*

Defining system boundaries is difficult because for most operations systems they do not take the form of walls, as in an office building, or geographical barriers, like a river. We often deal with component parts that are members of other systems as well.

A system's environment is usually analyzed in two ways. The first refers to the demand, or load, the environment places on the system, and the second involves the set of constraints imposed on the system's behavior. The *demand aspect* of

---

[1] Numbered references appear at the end of each chapter.

the environment can be further analyzed in terms of quantity, timing, quality, and location. The *constraints aspect* refers to legal, social, economic, and technological limitations. In recent years, as a result of rapid resource depletion and excessive pollution, management has come to reckon with societal and political pressures that set ecological constraints. These will play an increasingly important role in selecting optimum operating patterns. Periodically, it is also desirable to consider new *opportunities* and *threats* to the system's success or survival. A more detailed examination of the environment for an operations system is the subject of Chap. 3.

System resources   In contrast to the environment defined by uncontrollable factors, *a system's resources represent the variety of means under control that management can use to achieve its objectives.* Included here are the human resources and know-how, available capital and technology, raw materials, finished goods, and others.

It is customary for a business to specify its resources at a given time with a balance sheet. Similarly, how resources were used for a given period is described by an income statement. Useful as these accounting devices may be, they nevertheless are limited in the information they provide for analysis. Grouping similar resources in a balance sheet may conceal some important characteristics, i.e., the flexibility of equipment, the capabilities of personnel, and so on. Similarly omitted from an income statement is information about experience gained, lost opportunities, the potential for significant improvements through better motivation, training, new products or processes, and the like.

A realistic inventory of resources for systems analysis must go beyond the documents prepared on a routine basis, so that it can focus more closely on both tangible and intangible strengths and limitations.

System components and their outputs   Even though one is tempted to use an organization chart to identify a system's components in the divisions and departments that constitute its formal structure, we must strive to go beyond such a static description. *A system's components are the parts of an organization performing activities that contribute to achieving its objectives.* Some of these components contributed directly and perform "line" activities. Others contribute indirectly and perform "staff," or "maintenance," activities.

In a hospital line activities refer to the types of services offered, e.g., emergency aid and general or specialized surgery. The same would be true of a law firm (corporate tax, divorce cases, property transfers, etc.). For a manufacturer line activities refer to the products made.

By relating performance to those activities which determine a system's effectiveness we can concentrate on the load-bearing components deserving the most thorough analysis and design efforts.

System management   The preceding parts of the system require coordination and direction that must be provided by another system entity known as management. This is the *brain of the system responsible for setting values, defining objectives, and planning and control of the activities undertaken.* In advanced systems, management

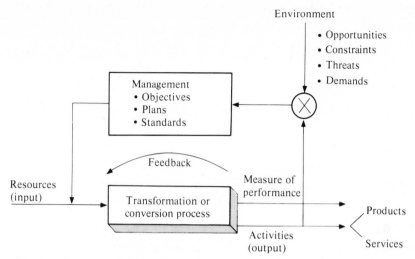

Fig. 2-1   Input-output representation of a system.

behavior follows certain principles of cybernetics, or steersmanship, to provide the system with stability, dynamic balance, and effectiveness in pursuing objectives.

System Representation

Our understanding of the concept of a system and its basic characteristics can be enhanced by representing it by an input-output diagram, as shown in Fig. 2-1, where the system objective(s) can be represented by the appropriate measure(s) of performance. The resources represent the inputs to the system, which are converted, in one or more transformations, into those activities (products, services, etc.) which contribute to achieving the selected objective(s). Information about activities, actual performance, and environmental conditions is fed back to management responsible for planning and control. Depending on observed deviations from plans and environmental changes, management undertakes corrective action with regard to resources under its control. Such actions aim at reducing the deviations from plans or at readjusting objectives to make them more realistic under prevailing conditions.

System Hierarchies

The reader may have by now realized that the notion of a system is a relative one. How we draw the system boundaries and define the environment depends greatly on the scope and purpose of the analysis and the degree of authority vested in the person(s) requesting the study.

A very important consideration when undertaking a system analysis is that *any system is part of, or embedded in, another larger system.* A container-manufacturing plant may be owned by a food-processing company, which is part of the food industry. The latter is part of the national economy, which is a component of the global economy, and so on. The result of this phenomenon is a hierarchy of systems. *Each level in the hierarchy of interest has, in general, a different value system from the others.* Therefore, what is the best course of action for management at one level, say a product design for the container manufacturer, may not be appropriate for the food industry because of marketing considerations. Furthermore, it may be quite bad for the economy in terms of the solid-waste pollution it creates.

Since we cannot solve specific problems with reference at all times to the highest-level value system, a good practical rule is to perform the analysis by defining the system boundaries one or two levels above that of the person requesting the study. Insofar as there is a need to consider the impact of our decisions on the environment at large, either in terms of resource utilization or pollution, the higher-level objectives can take the form of operational constraints. Thus, for the auto industry the need to protect the environment against air pollution takes the form of design requirements to limit exhaust fumes.

2-3   SYSTEM CLASSIFICATION

In studying economic, social, biological, and other processes we encounter an enormous variety of systems. Our understanding and description of them is assisted greatly by classifying systems in groups with common properties.

Natural versus Artificial Systems

When component parts and their functions are connected to form an integrated organic whole, we have a natural, or organic, system. Human beings, other animals, the plant and animal life in a lake or a forest are just a few examples of natural, or biological, systems. A school, a business, a hospital, and a commercial airplane in flight, on the other hand, are all artificial systems even though some of their components, the people, are natural systems.

Open versus Closed Systems

A system is considered open when it both has an affect upon and is affected by its environment. This interaction is possible through the exchange of energy, matter, and information between the system and its environment.

Natural systems are open, and the same is true for most social and economic systems of which private and public organizations are good examples. Closed systems are rather rare, except for some primitive tribes in the Philippine Islands and some colonies of bacteria in controlled laboratory experiments.

As we expand the boundaries of an operations system to account for the aggregate effects related to resource depletion and environmental pollution, the concept of a closed system assumes a special significance. Here we realize that an economic system is embedded in a complex ecological system from which it draws scarce natural resources (matter and energy) and to which it discharges its wastes. Unless the flow of resources through the system can be maintained at levels that do not exceed certain threshold limits, the rapid use of resources and excessive pollution can bring the collapse of the ecological system of which the economy is only a subsystem. In this sense, the concept of the earth as a closed system (except for the energy received from the sun) has helped focus attention on the importance of ranking national and global priorities in a manner consistent with our long-term well-being and survival.

Stable versus Unstable Systems

The state or condition of a system can be described by the values or descriptions assigned to its most significant characteristics. They may change with time, but the size and rate of variation play an important role in how effectively a system advances toward its objectives.

A system is considered stable when the variations in the values of its basic characteristics remain within predetermined limits. In a production system certain measures of quality or performance, e.g., defects per unit, personnel absenteeism, or toxic content of wastes, may vary within limits without serious consequences; however, if absenteeism becomes excessive due to an epidemic or the number of defects in the output increases greatly because of a faulty process, the system may no longer function properly.

When important system variables exceed certain limits or thresholds, we say the system is unstable. If corrective action cannot bring such variables under control, the viability of the system becomes questionable.

Adaptive versus Rigid Systems

When a system loses its stability due to some extreme overload or other reason, the resulting imbalance may lead to important changes in its characteristics or even to its destruction. This can be prevented only through action designed to restore its stability, redefine its goals, or change its environment.

A system is said to be adaptive when it can restore its disturbed stability on its own or modify its objectives. The effects of environmental or internal causes of imbalance initiate automatically self-corrective mechanisms designed to bring the system to the same or a new stable condition. Human beings are perfect examples of adaptive systems. The same holds for all natural and some social and economic systems.

The same property is present to a lesser extent in artificial systems, such as governments, oil refineries, ocean liners, and airplanes. How well such systems adapt to disturbances depends on their structure and "nervous system," i.e., the coordination and integration of their components as determined by their information systems.

2-4 THE CONCEPT OF A MODEL

A great deal of managerial and personal decision making is based on experience and develops like an art. One of the most important developments in the evolution of managerial thought has been to help the decision-making process by using models, a phenomenon that has gained momentum in this century. In a sense almost everyone makes decisions based on a mental image, or model, of a situation which focuses on the key variables and how they may be related. The value of modeling in management is in making such models explicit so that we can check the assumptions behind them and their ability to help us make better decisions.

Definition

A *model* is a representation or abstraction of the significant parts of a real system and their interactions.

Some models, like the map of a city, the wooden replica of a ship, or the drawings for a building, have been used for centuries. More sophisticated models, however, like those used to study an inventory system or the structure of the economy, are of more recent origin.

In any event, the development of a model can be undertaken with one or more purposes in mind. The most important ones, however, include the following:

1. To *describe* some part of reality, i.e., the system under study
2. To *understand* the structure and function of the system
3. To *predict* the behavior of the system as a whole or that of its parts under various conditions
4. To *prescribe* or control the behavior of the system for achieving its objectives most effectively

The decision-making process for management is made easier by using a model in two ways: (1) by representing only the relevant parts of reality and how they interact we simplify the system by reducing its immense complexity and (2) the ability to generalize from the model makes it easier to study the same system under different conditions or to understand other similar systems.

2-5 MODEL CLASSIFICATION

As a system consists of component parts described by their key characteristics and significant interactions, a model is similarly made up of enough elements to provide an adequate system representation. The specific form of a model depends on its type and intended application. A widely used classification scheme is based on the model's ability to generalize. In such a scheme we have three categories, covering iconic, analog, and mathematical models.

Iconic Models

When the representation of a system maintains certain physical similarities to the real object or situation, the model employed is called *iconic*. The simplification of actual characteristics and component interactions is achieved by scaling physical dimensions up or down, depending on the application.

Examples of iconic models involving scaling relevant physical characteristics down include a wind-tunnel airplane model, a three-dimensional plant layout, a model of a final product, e.g., an automobile or a crane. Iconic models representing the chemical structure of DNA or the construction of a small integrated circuit are scaled-up versions of the relevant physical variables of the real thing.

Analog Models

Sometimes our understanding and analysis of a real system can be enhanced by representing one kind of variable, say inventory levels, by another kind of variable, say, water level in a tank or electric charge in a capacitor. In such cases we have an *analog* model. The study of a real system, like a factory or city traffic, can be assisted by deducing the form of interactions and the effects of certain changes in the variables of interest from the information provided by the behavior of an equivalent hydraulic- or electrical-network analog model.

Analog models can be static or dynamic. A work-flow diagram, a city map, or a logarithmic slide rule are examples of static analog representations. More valuable, however, are the analog models used to study dynamic phenomena.

Analog representations are more flexible than iconic ones and allow the analyst to generalize more easily from the model to the real situation being investigated. An interesting application of such a model was a grid made from ropes of different thicknesses to study city traffic patterns. The grid from ropes represented the actual traffic network of roads and streets. Nests of ants were placed in positions representing residential areas, whereas employment and shopping areas in the city were represented by open containers with honey. The stable pattern of traffic for ants that developed for several urban configurations provided many useful insights into city traffic patterns.

Symbolic, or Mathematical, Models

In a mathematical model the key activities of the real system are represented by symbols, or mathematical variables; the fixed aspects, or parameters, by constants or numbers; and the significant relationships by equations, inequalities, or other logical relationships.

A symbolic model allows the greatest degree of generalization possible and can be quite versatile and accurate. In physics and chemistry such models have been used with great success for many decades. However, their application in the social sciences has proceeded more slowly due to the immense complexity of the processes studied. An encouraging stimulus to the use of mathematical models for studying socioeconomic systems has been the increasing storage and computational capability of modern computers, combined with lower cost for their use and greater availability.

The use of mathematical models for the study of production-oriented problems has been more extensive and successful than for any other functional area within a business (marketing, finance, etc.). Their application generally involves considerable cost, specialized personnel, and the availability of adequate data. Consequently the development and use of such a model is not only a technical problem but an economic one, based on a benefit-cost analysis.

A mathematical model is *static* if it suggests what will happen for certain decisions in only one planning period. An example would be the desired allocation of existing resources to different activities for the next year. The model is considered *dynamic* when it provides solutions for successive periods as new information becomes available. An inventory policy providing decision rules for each month as actual demand becomes known is an example.

Sometimes it is reasonable to assume that all variables in the model behave in a completely predictable manner. Such models are *deterministic* because they do not allow for any uncertainty in the variables and their assumed relationships. This simplification of reality may be justifiable because of limits on the time, funds, and knowledge available for a study. On other occasions it is warranted by the long experience available for a particular activity, say preventive-maintenance times for preparing a production schedule. When it is important to account explicitly for the uncertainty in the behavior of one or more variables in the model, we have a *probabilistic* (for one time period) or *stochastic* (for successive periods) model. This may be desirable when we deal with such uncontrollable factors as the monthly demand for a jet-engine spare part, daily arrivals for emergency aid in a hospital, etc.

With regard to the purpose of a model, we recognize two important categories. When all we expect of a model is to describe a system's behavior, say the average time to make a reservation by telephone with an airline or the process-failure rate for a given maintenance policy, the model is called *descriptive*. If beyond such descriptions we require the model to suggest how best to manage the system under study, the result is a *prescriptive*, or *normative*, model. Such a model can be used to determine which of several possible products to make, how much productive capacity to provide for a future period, how much and when to order when replenishing inventory, and so on. In building a normative model, in addition to the relationships needed to specify how the component parts interact or how their activities are limited we require a quantitative statement of the measure of performance by which the system is evaluated. This is known as the *objective function*.

A model becomes more complex when we must account for the uncertainty about key variables. This complexity is multiplied further when system performance is evaluated by several criteria and the model must therefore have several objective functions. In the end, it is necessary to settle for the degree of complexity in the model that allows accurate enough representation with ease in acceptance and implementation by management.

Sometimes the mathematical model of a system is too complex to be solved by known methods, and direct experimentation with the system itself is too dangerous or expensive. It may then be possible to use a *simulation model* which allows management to evaluate different policies by using such a model to imitate the real

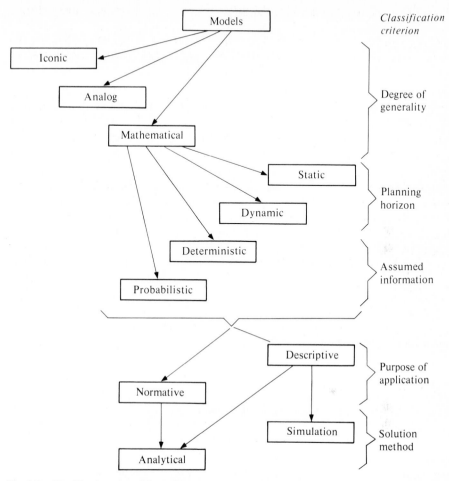

Fig. 2-2 **Classification of models used in operations management.**

system's behavior with the aid of a computer. Simulation is discussed in Supplementary Chapter D. The variety of model categories is summarized in Fig. 2-2.

In the analysis of operations systems we can use any one of the types of models discussed. Some have direct applications for production problems, whereas others are more general. It is quite remarkable that the basic forms for such models are few and have been developed extensively in the area of operations research. These forms cover problems of resource allocation, inventory control, waiting lines, scheduling, sequencing, replacement, and maintenance of equipment. Combined with a variety of statistical models for forecasting demand, quality control, and others, these basic forms represent a powerful decision technology of the modern manager. When supported by the manager's experience and intuition, these models can enhance the decision-making process for the achievement of stated objectives.

2-6   THE STRUCTURE OF A MODEL

As we have indicated, the structure of a mathematical model can be subdivided into two parts, one referring to the objective(s) being pursued by the management of the system and one describing how system components interact and how their activities are restricted by internal or external factors. In the discussion that follows these concepts will be illustrated with an example.

▶ EXAMPLE 2-1: A STATEMENT OF AN INVENTORY PROBLEM
Suppose that the management of the maintenance shop for a city's mass-transit bus system wishes to study its inventory problem for spare parts. For the hundreds of parts kept in stock it is desired to have a policy of inventory replenishment that will result in best performance. After a preliminary analysis management comes to the following conclusions:

1. The measure of performance for the inventory system is related to the variable or incremental costs required to support the stock room, i.e., holding, shortage, and ordering costs.
2. The controllable variables in operating the system are the size and timing of the orders for parts.
3. The uncontrollable variables consist of the demand for parts needed for repair work and the lead time of suppliers in meeting the orders.
4. The level of service provided, i.e., allowed stockouts, the prices for parts,
▶   and the unit costs for operating the inventory system, is assumed to be fixed.

The development of a model that would help manage the maintenance shop more effectively can be understood using the following conceptual framework.

Objective Function for Measure of Performance

The *objective function* of a model is usually a quantitative statement of the criterion for evaluating system performance. This measure of performance or effectiveness is a function of the system activities (controllable variables) and important environmental factors (uncontrollable variables). Thus, we have

$$\begin{bmatrix} \text{Measure of} \\ \text{system effectiveness} \end{bmatrix} = f(\text{controllable variables, uncontrollable variables})$$

or
$$E = f(X_j, Y_k) \tag{2-1}$$

where E = measure of effectiveness for system performance, e.g., profit for business or operating cost for public agency

X_j = levels for system activities viewed as controllable variables ($j = 1, 2, \ldots, n$), e.g., work-force size, production rate, order quantities

Y_k = effects of environmental uncontrollable conditions ($k = 1, 2, \ldots, 9$), e.g., demand for a product or service or amount of rainfall in reservoir

Management seeks to make decisions about the controllable variables in a way that will yield optimum system performance. If effectiveness is measured by something desirable, such as profit for a business or reliability for an airplane jet engine, E is to be maximized. On the other hand, if the measure of performance refers to something undesirable, like operating cost, amount of polluting waste, probability of failure, or extent of possible damage by fire, flooding, or other calamity, E is to be minimized.

For the spare-parts-inventory example we have

E = variable costs related to inventory
X_1 = order quantity for replenishment
X_2 = timing of order
Y_1 = demand for part in given period
Y_2 = delivery time from part supplier

Since demand and delivery time are uncertain, we must describe them in terms of their statistical distributions, that is, $f_1(Y_1)$ and $f_2(Y_2)$, so that we know their average values and the expected variability.

For a desired service level inventory cost is something to be minimized. Thus, the objective function will be of the form

$$\text{Minimize } E = f(X_1, X_2; Y_1, Y_2)$$

For many real problems a complicating factor is the existence of several objectives pursued simultaneously. If they can be stated in quantitative terms, we can attempt to synthesize them in a more general form of an objective function or we can treat one of them as the dominant objective and consider the others as constraints. Mathematical and other techniques for solving multiobjective models, which are beyond the scope of this work, are given in Refs. 9 and 16.

Functional Interrelationships and System Constraints

The second part of a model consists of a set of mathematical relationships that describe operating conditions. Some of them describe how the parts of a system interact given an assumed structure and technology. For example, the production of a piece of furniture requires certain quantities of materials and parts (wood, plywood, veneer, nuts, bolts, etc.) to be processed by certain skilled operators on various types of equipment. The variety and amounts of resources needed are determined by the product design of the items made and the technology used.

In addition to relationships dictated by product design and technology, it is important to include any restrictions imposed by the environment. The size of the market, pollution regulations, union contracts, safety laws, and many other considerations may limit considerably the type and range of activities that contribute to the system objective(s).

All constraints must be formulated in a mathematical or logical form of one of the following types:

In symbols	Description
$g_1(X_j, Y_k) \le b_1$	Total use of equipment A in hours must be less than or equal to the total time available on equipment A
$g_2(X_j, Y_k) \le b_2$	Total use of raw material B in tons must be less than or equal to the total quantity available of that material
. . . .	. . . .
$g_m(X_j, Y_k) \ge b_m$	Total labor hours used must be greater than or equal to the minimum amount provided by union contract

where b_i = constants for system and environmental parameters $(i = 1, 2, \ldots, m)$
$$g_1(X_j, Y_k), g_2(X_j, Y_k), \ldots, g_m(X_j, Y_k)$$
= functions, i.e., relationships between system variables

In the inventory problem for the maintenance shop of city buses, we may have constraints imposed by a fixed budget, by limited storage space, by internal administration policies, supplier policies, etc.

Our objectives in developing a model include the following:

The determination of decision rules for managerial action   Such rules enable managers to assign values to the controllable variables X_j, that is, for the levels of system activities, in view of expected values and variation for the uncontrollable variables Y_k that define anticipated environmental conditions. Decision rules may take the following form:

$$X_1 = r_1(Y_1, Y_2, \ldots, Y_q)$$
$$X_2 = r_2(Y_1, Y_2, \ldots, Y_q)$$ Decision rules for optimum
. . . . system performance
$$X_n = r_n(Y_1, Y_2, \ldots, Y_q)$$

where $X_j = r_j(Y_1, Y_2, \ldots, Y_q)$ $j = 1, 2, \ldots, n$

is a decision rule that tells management what value to assign to the controllable variable X_j when the uncontrollable factors are expected to take values $Y_1, Y_2, \ldots, Y_q$. The functions $r_1(\ldots), r_2(\ldots), \ldots, r_n(\ldots)$ may be described by linear or nonlinear relationships; $X = r(Y)$ is a different but equivalent way of saying $X = f(Y)$.

For the spare-parts-inventory problem the *decision rules* would be as follows:

Descriptive		Symbolic†
$\begin{bmatrix} \text{Order} \\ \text{quantity} \end{bmatrix}$	$= r_1(\text{demand for part, delivery time})$	$X_1 = r_1(Y_1, Y_2)$
$\begin{bmatrix} \text{Order} \\ \text{timing} \end{bmatrix}$	$= r_2(\text{demand for part, delivery time})$	$X_2 = r_2(Y_1, Y_2)$

† r means "a function of."

The solution of a problem using a model, i.e., the derivation of decision rules, can be accomplished either by mathematical analysis or by simulation. Simulation is preferred when the mathematical relationships are too complex to be solved with available analytical methods.

A sensitivity analysis for the derived solution   Several aspects of a real situation can be assumed to be fixed; i.e., they are treated as problem parameters. A sensitivity analysis attempts to evaluate the direction and magnitude of changes in system performance that would result if one or more of the parameter values change. Such changes may apply to the amounts of resources available, the production technology used, the price of raw materials, the wages for labor, and others.

In short, *through sensitivity analysis we try to assess the impact on performance of changes in the environmental conditions and the system characteristics.* The entire modeling process is a series of simplifications, approximations, and imperfect estimates. It is therefore desirable to have an idea of how errors in the assumptions and estimates made as well as future changes in operating conditions are likely to affect system performance.

In the example with the maintenance shop, through sensitivity analysis we would try to determine the effect on inventory cost of changes in the distribution of demand, in holding and ordering unit costs, in prices of parts, etc. A change in one or more of these parameter values or in the assumed relationships would result in different values for the controllable variables, with subsequent effects on inventory costs. In some models, such as those used to study inventory systems, the measure of performance may not be seriously affected by changes in some parameter values. Other models, however, offer solutions that are highly sensitive to such changes.

2-7   THE ART AND SCIENCE OF MODEL BUILDING

Model building usually follows a procedure of successive approximations. The purpose here is to construct a representation of the real system with two important attributes. The first would allow the model to improve our understanding of the system's key features and enable us to predict its behavior and perhaps control it. The second would make it possible to accomplish this at a reasonable cost and in time to assist the decision-making process.

If we wished the model to represent all aspects of the real system, it would have to be as complex and difficult to understand as the real thing. It is possible, in many cases, with enough simplification to build a model that can help us understand and predict the system's behavior with sufficient accuracy. This is due to a *fundamental property* of systems. *Whereas for prediction with very high accuracy we need to include in the model an extremely large number of variables, it is possible to have predictions with satisfactory accuracy by incorporating only a small number of key variables.* Consequently, the art in building good models depends on the careful selection of a few critical variables and the correct assumptions of how they are related.

In many respects the model-building process for management problems resembles the scientific method employed in the physical sciences. It begins with careful observation of the system's behavior and the evaluation of available relevant data. The analyst in the first phase attempts to arrive at an adequate system description that includes its objective(s), activities, resources, environment, and management. At this point, it is helpful to make several (sometimes excessive) simplifications. Iconic and analog models may provide considerable information about the system's structure and operation.

Subsequently, the analyst searches for correlations and analogies with better-known systems in order to enrich the initial somewhat crude representation of important system parts and properties. Even at this early stage, the benefits to management from a better understanding of the situation studied can be quite remarkable.

From the early approximations and a tentative rough representation, the analysis can proceed to develop a simplified mathematical model. Included in the latter are key relationships that govern the system's operation. Examples of such relationships include the flows of materials, products, and information; restrictions on available resources; market considerations; and others. If the objectives of the system have been determined, they can also be included in the model as an objective function.

After sufficient mathematical analysis or experimentation with the model, we can test the consequences of assumed relationships. Similarly, trial predictions can be attempted and the results compared with actual system behavior. As a result, a number of adjustments are made, and the model is further enriched by adding more variables and/or relationships. This process is repeated in a cyclic fashion until successive approximations lead to a model form that can be helpful in managerial decision making. It should be remembered at all times that *a key purpose of the model is to offer insights in addition to numerical solutions.* The cyclic model-building process with its major phases is shown in Fig. 2-3.

Evaluation of a model in the form used by management can be made with several criteria, but the two most important qualities of a model are the *accuracy* with which it represents the real system and its *ease of implementation.* The latter includes user acceptance, model adaptability, and the cost of producing solutions to the class of problems for which the model was constructed.

According to Morris,[1] it is also desirable for a model to display the following properties:

Relatedness to other well-developed and tested models

Transparency with regard to the interpretation of its results and their validity

Robustness with regard to its usefulness under assumption variations

Fertility with regard to the variety and quality of the model-derived conclusions

Ease of enrichment for adaptability to varied and more complex applications

[1] William T. Morris, *Management Science: A Bayesian Introduction*, Prentice-Hall, Englewood Cliffs, N.J., 1968.

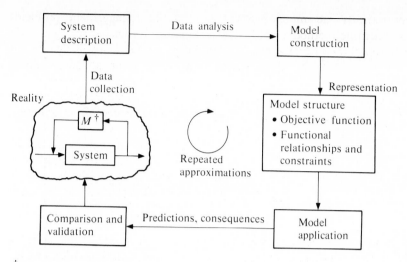

Fig. 2-3 **Steps in the model-building process.**

In conclusion, the development of a model requires not only specialized knowledge but a creative talent, an ability to focus on the significant variables, and skill in synthesizing the correct interrelationships of system components.

2-8 DECISION-MAKING APPROACHES

General

A manager's major responsibility is to make decisions and put them into effect. A decision in this context refers to the selection of an alternative solution in response to a perceived problem. Decision-making approaches in management vary in the way an alternative is chosen. The three major methods or models are (1) the rational, (2) the organizational, and (3) the political (Ref. 3), discussed in some detail below. Sometimes one is more appropriate than the other; often, however, they can fruitfully be used together.

Even though most textbooks in operations management discuss and recommend rational models for decision making, the limited success these models have enjoyed in practice suggests the need for including organizational and political considerations. The latter are especially important in assuring successful implementation without which the selection of an "optimum" solution is more of an academic exercise.

The Essence of a Problem

For a problem to exist or for a condition to be perceived as a problem it is necessary to feel pressure to take action for a change. For management the change relates to whatever activities are managed. With individuals such a change may refer to one or more aspects of their life. This feeling of pressure implies a dissatisfaction either with the status quo, or *state A*, or with projected developments from state A if nothing is done. Therefore, there is a desire to change things in a given direction and perhaps by a certain amount, in order to find the system managed in a preferred future condition, or *state B*. Such a change may often be needed within a given time frame.

The second aspect of a problem situation that influences how a decision will be reached is the *number of participants* or decision makers. A participant may be defined as an individual or an organized group that has the power to influence the outcome of the decision (Ref. 16). Even though, for simplicity, we often assume that a decision is made by only one person, further examination may reveal that this is an unjustified assumption. The effect of two or more decision makers varies with their power and the information they have.

A third aspect of a problem is the *environment* in which it occurs, determined by the economic, social, technological, and other characteristics as well as their dynamic nature.

The complexity of the problem increases rapidly with the size of the system affected (one or several facilities versus a work station), with the number of decision makers, and with the uncertainty of the available information.

Problem Diagnosis

In an existing system, a problem arises when one or more of its components fail to function as expected, e.g., through excessive downtime or absenteeism, or when there are drastic changes in the environment, like technological developments, shortages in production inputs (materials, energy, or other), or new restrictive laws about safety or pollution.

Quite often while studying the symptoms of what is thought to be a problem, management discovers hidden causes in other parts of the organization. For example, the excessive congestion in a factory warehouse originally attributed to limited space or inadequate materials-handling capacity may be traced to poor scheduling in the factory. At times, problems are diagnosed not from disturbing symptoms but from projected inadequacies in carrying out a plan for future activities, such as capacity expansions due to an increase in demand. Higher prices combined with limited supplies of oil have recently created such problems.

The timely diagnosis of a problem depends to a large extent on the information system being used, in terms of completeness, reliability, and frequency of status reports submitted to management. This process is also affected by the experience and ability of the managers themselves, both in the choice of information used and in how it is interpreted and acted upon.

Three Views of a Decision Problem

When an operations-management problem is localized and can be decided by a single person, say the layout of a particular work station on a production line, the

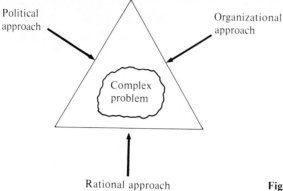

Fig. 2-4　**Three views of a decision problem.**

approach involves a limited analysis or routine procedure developed from past experience. In situations that involve several departments or organizations, many participants, and a commitment of large amounts of resources, it is possible to view a problem in one of three ways shown in Fig. 2-4, explained in detail in the following sections. Each approach rests on different assumptions, yields different results, and offers different insights. The conceptual framework allowing a complex problem to be viewed in rational, organizational, and political terms is discussed at length in G. T. Allison's *Essence of Decision* (Ref. 3).

Rational Approach to Decision Making

The use of a rational approach to solve a problem rests on a number of important assumptions:[1]

1. There is only one decision maker with a well-understood and consistent method for expressing preferences. If the decision involves several people, we assume that they act as one.
2. The objective is to select the alternative that maximizes the degree to which the decision maker satisfies a known objective or criterion (maximize profits, minimize costs, etc.)
3. The decision maker has complete information about available alternatives, their outcomes, and their values.

　The procedure employed to reach a decision using the rational method consists of the following phases: (1) define the problem, (2) analyze the problem, (3) develop alternatives, (4) evaluate alternatives, and (5) implement the best proposal. The process allows the decision maker to return to previous phases, as necessary, in order to redefine key issue(s) and redirect or improve the search and evaluation of the alternatives.[2]

---

[1] The ideal example of a rational decision maker is that assumed in classical economics, whether the decision involves the consumption or production of various goods.

[2] The discussion in this section has been influenced by the ideas for a design approach presented in E. Krick, *Methods Engineering*, Wiley, New York, 1961.

TABLE 2-1   Specification of states A and B in problem definition

System description		State A present value (1980)	State B future value (1982)
Characteristic	Symbol		
Annual sales	x_1	$12 million	$15 million
Percent defective	x_2	4%	2%
Market share	x_3	10%	15%
. . . .	. . . . .	. . . .	. . . .
Absenteeism	x_n	7%	4%

Phase 1: problem definition   Attempting to define a problem requires collecting data available in the form of facts, opinions, beliefs, etc., and screening them to sort out what is relevant and useful to the case at hand. The important outputs of the problem-definition phase include a complete specification of states A and B, based on what are considered to be the most significant system characteristics, the criterion by which various alternatives will be evaluated, and the time frame in which a solution must be found.

Suppose that in the next 2 years the management of an electronics firm wishes to improve the quality of a new product that has met intense competition. A specification of states A and B may be given in the form shown in Table 2-1, which includes additional desired changes.

To bring about the desired improvement in product quality, management has identified the following alternatives:

a_1 = increase number of inspectors
a_2 = provide additional training of machine operators
a_3 = use higher-quality materials
a_4 = change to new equipment
a_5 = redesign product

We shall assume for simplicity that management expects future environmental conditions to be the same as those in the present. This allows the estimation of the consequences for each alternative to be made under conditions of certainty. Otherwise, state B must be described using averages (or expected values) from the probable values of the system characteristics included in the problem definition. Decision-making methods under conditions of uncertainty are examined in Supplementary Chapter A.

Since the alternatives considered require different amounts of resources (capital, labor, other) or organizational readjustments, it is important to identify the criterion or criteria by which they will be evaluated. In most cases, we must deal with multiple criteria such as economic, psychological, social, environmental, or other.

However, for private firms with a profit objective, the evaluation is usually based on economic criteria, e.g., present value, rate of return on investment, or other. Rational models based on economic criteria are used extensively for many

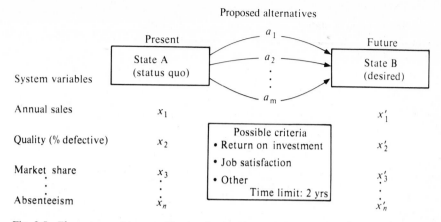

Fig. 2-5   Elements requiring specification in the phase of problem definition under conditions of certainty.

types of problems and are discussed in Supplementary Chapter B. Methods for handling problems with multiple criteria are quite complex. Two of them are described in Chaps. 4 and 10 on product design and facilities location. The problem definition as suggested above is shown in Fig. 2-5. The reader is reminded that this applies only to conditions of certainty about the future.

Successful problem definition depends on a correct interpretation of the system's structure and function, its goals, and its environment. In the early stages of problem definition it is important to avoid too narrow a formulation in terms of the scope of activities covered.

Phase 2: problem analysis   After specifying the problem based on a description of states A and B, the criterion for evaluating alternatives, and the time limit for developing a solution, we begin the analysis by specifying the key components of the system in which the problem occurs, their basic properties, and the most significant interactions. These tasks demand the collection, analysis, and evaluation of considerable amounts of data. The result of the analysis phase is an improved understanding of the system structure, its operation, and the important interactions with the system's environment.

It is in the analysis phase that we find the use of iconic, analog, or quantitative models helpful in identifying critical variables and interactions and dynamic characteristics of the system's behavior. The proper interpretation of current conditions leads us to the specification of external or internal restrictions that may limit the number of alternatives considered. Figure 2-6 shows how genuine, as well as nonexisting (or fictitious), restrictions limit the range of options that may be perceived in going from state A to state B.

External constraints are usually beyond control, at least in the short run, and represent rather rigid limitations to what a firm can do in response to a given problem. They refer to technology, the state of the economy (labor markets, interest rates, etc.), environmental regulation, social norms, and other sources. *Internal*

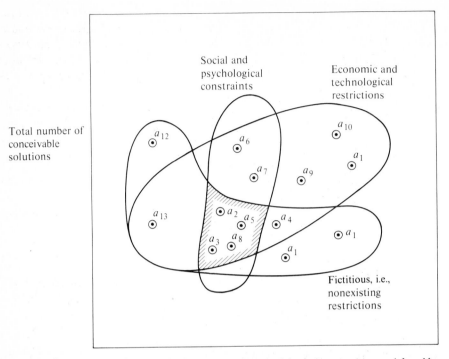

Fig. 2-6   The effect of real and assumed restrictions on potential solutions to a managerial problem.

constraints stem from limits in productive capacity, financial strength, managerial or technical expertise within the firm, and so on. As such they can be influenced to some extent.

With reference to Fig. 2-6, alternatives a_9, a_{10}, and a_{11} are feasible but undesirable for psychological reasons. Alternative a_4 is feasible but is assumed unacceptable for nonexisting social reasons. In the end, the solutions that will be examined are those which satisfy all perceived restrictions whether they are genuine or assumed. In our example, this feasible set would include a_2, a_3, a_5, and a_8.

Phase 3: generation of alternatives   In the phase of generating alternatives we seek to formulate options or courses of actions a_1, a_2, ..., a_m that will enable us to go from state A to state B. Success in this phase depends on a good formulation of the problem and is limited only by the imagination of those studying the problem.

Generating alternatives is the creative step in the problem-solving process and must be free-flowing and spontaneous. It is important for this reason to ignore temporarily the effect of restrictions and to encourage suggestions from people that are not so familiar with the status quo that they take much of it for granted. In operations-research teams the potential of new ideas for solving complex problems is encouraged by the use of interdisciplinary teams, including not only engineers and economists but also psychologists, biologists, and others. Figure 2-7a states that the generation of alternatives is a *branching-out process* uninhibited by the fear of perceived restrictions. The range and quality of proposed alternatives depends on

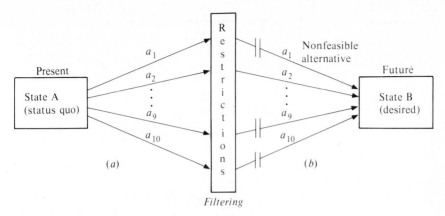

Fig. 2-7 *(a)* **Generation and** *(b)* **evaluation of alternatives.**

the creativity of the participants and the time and funds available to encourage the search for new ideas.

Phase 4: evaluation of alternatives With as many alternatives formulated as allowed by the time, funds, and skills available, the evaluation phase begins by filtering alternatives through perceived restrictions and then ranking the feasible, i.e., acceptable, solutions according to the criterion selected in phase 1. Whereas the generation of alternatives is a branching-out process, their evaluation is a tree-pruning, converging, and *elimination process*. This is shown in Fig. 2-7*b*, in which alternative a_1 is eliminated because it violates budget limitations, a_4 is eliminated because it causes poor relations with the community, and so on.

A perplexing feature in a problem exists when we have to deal with *multiple criteria* simultaneously. A common approach in this case is to select one criterion as the dominant one and treat the others as constraints. For example, if in designing a new product we seek to maximize return on investment, safety, reliability, and customer service, we may select return on investment as the dominant criterion and design the product so that we meet acceptable levels of safety, reliability, and customer service. More sophisticated methods attempt to assign relative weights to each criterion and then proceed to derive an overall measure of effectiveness.

Whatever the evaluation procedure, the end result is the selection of the "best" alternative which is then recommended for implementation. Up to this point we have covered the phases of the "pure" rational approach whose effectiveness may be in doubt unless it is accompanied by the next phase.

Phase 5: preparation for implementation The whole problem-solving process is undertaken in vain unless those recommending a specific "optimum" alternative take advantage of every opportunity available to enhance its implementation. This endeavor must start as early as possible, i.e., in the problem-definition phase. How recommendations are made must first convince those responsible for the approval of the proposed change(s). This requires incorporating their criteria of evaluating proposals in the selection process.

Next, assuming that approval has been secured at the top level, it is essential to have the understanding and cooperation of key personnel who will play a crucial role in implementing the proposed solution during its installation, use, and maintenance. If the process of generating alternatives has not considered the ideas, sensitivities, and priorities of such people, it is unlikely that their support will be especially strong. It is therefore essential that they be part of the whole process as early and as much as possible. Finally, provisions must be made to let people affected by the proposed changes know of the advantages to be gained by moving to state B and if possible contribute ideas how this can be accomplished.

The literature abounds with examples of sound proposals that failed because people felt threatened by the perceived changes. Supervisors, operators, inventory clerks, and others at the lower levels of an organization have often ignored or sabotaged efforts to modify new procedures for fear they would lose control of their jobs and opportunities for growth, higher pay, and advancement.

The entire decision-making process as suggested by the rational model is summarized in Fig. 2-8.

Summary of the rational decision-making approach   The key features of a rational approach to making decisions include (1) a single decision maker, (2) a set of alternatives from which that person must choose, (3) the consequences or subjective values of the different outcomes of each alternative, and (4) a selection criterion in the form of a payoff, return, or utility function to be maximized by that person's

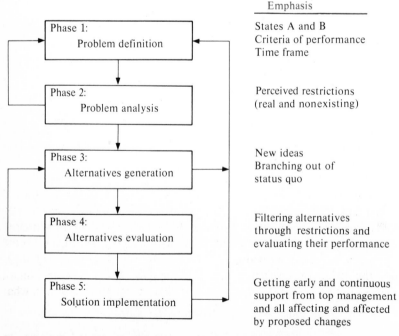

Fig. 2-8   A flowchart for the phases in the rational decision-making approach.

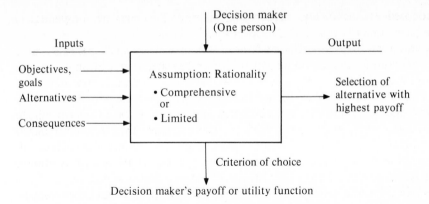

Fig. 2-9   **Key features of the rational decision-making approach. Adapted from Graham T. Allison,** *Essence of Decision: Explaining the Cuban Missile Crisis,* **p. 256. Copyright ©
1971 by Graham T. Allison, reprinted by permission of Little, Brown & Co.**

decisions. An important assumption in this approach is the *rationality* of the decision maker, i.e., the ability to make consistent preferences among the alternatives considered. The above elements are shown in Fig. 2-9.

These features characterize the majority of models developed to assist managers, especially in the field of management science or operations research. In real life, the rational approach may work satisfactorily for problems of limited scope and in situations controlled considerably by one person or a group acting as an individual. However, quite often the powerful mathematical or computer management models (the best examples of the rational approach to decision making) meet with limited success in the implementation phase, especially when the scope of the problem encompasses important organizational and political factors that cannot be accounted for in the rational models.

Organizational Approach to Decision Making

In large organizations, such as government agencies, large hospitals, or multiplant manufacturing firms, it has been found instructive to explain the response to a problem more as a result of standard patterns of behavior, i.e., coordinated predetermined outputs or reactions of their component units, than as conscious choices among well-defined alternatives.

The complexity of tasks performed by large organizations to achieve their goals can be handled only with proper coordination of their component parts and the large number of people who run them. Such coordination is normally achieved by the use of routine decision rules known as *standard operating procedures* activated to handle a new order, a customer complaint, a maintenance inspection, and so on.

According to Simon,[1] both individuals and organizations display considerable deviation from the behavior implied by rational models. The limits on human capacity to process information relevant to the problem under study result in what

[1] Herbert Simon, *Administrative Behavior*, 3d ed., Harper & Row, New York, 1976.

Simon calls *bounded rationality* in decision making. This view is supported by several arguments. (1) Large problems are usually factored or split up into several organizational units or individuals, and the solutions to the subproblems are then combined. (2) Rather than looking for the optimum alternative from a set, the search stops when coming across a solution that is good enough. Hence, organizational decision making works on the principle of *satisficing* rather than optimizing. (3) The generation of alternatives is sequential, and since the search stops with the first one that is satisfactory, the process is rather limited in scope. The search procedure therefore becomes critical for finding good alternatives. (4) Whereas in rational models environmental uncertainty is treated explicitly, in organizational decision making it is avoided by relying on procedures that allow short-run feedback. Like house thermostats, which make speedy adjustments instead of predicting tomorrow's temperature, such procedures try to avoid dealing with an uncertain future. (5) Organizations, like concert pianists, develop a repertoire of action programs that describe their behavior in response to recurring problems. Since organizational learning is rather slow, such repertoires change at a slow pace except in situations of crises or major disaster.

The organizational approach to decision making attempts to explain a choice made in response to a particular problem on the basis of the goals and the expectations of the organization. Since in a large organization individual departments or divisions may have considerable independence, their operational goals may be in conflict, even though they are "rational" at the local level. Each unit has parochial perceptions of the problem and parochial priorities. Marketing seeks to maximize sales, production attempts to minimize unit production costs, etc. The overall company policy attempts to coordinate the standard routines of the component parts. Existing conflicts are resolved by attending to conflicting goals sequentially. Problem solving takes place by attacking the most pressing problems first, rather than taking a global view of the organization's activities, and by avoiding environmental uncertainty relying on routine procedures, industry tradition, and short-run feedback loops. The outputs of the various subunits of an organization or agencies for the government are brought together and coordinated by top managers or administrators to compose an organizational response to the problem that provided the initial stimulus.

The key features of the organizational approach to decision making are summarized in Fig. 2-10.

Political Approach to Decision Making

Power within large organizations becomes quite diffused among those in charge of subunits asked to respond to a problem. Similarly, a specific issue may involve several firms and/or government agencies. The decision-making result in such cases can be viewed neither as a deliberate choice among alternatives (rational model) nor as a coordinated output of the organizations involved (organizational model). In this situation, the solution to a problem can be best understood as a result of political bargaining between the participants involved with power to influence the outcome.

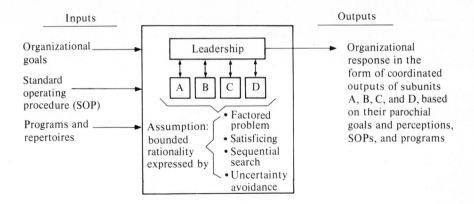

Fig. 2-10 Key features of the organizational approach to decision-making. Adapted from Graham T. Allison, *Essence of Decision: Explaining the Cuban Missile Crisis,* **p. 256. Copyright © 1971 by Graham T. Allison, reprinted by permission of Little, Brown & Co.**

In the political model the distinct features are: (1) the many decision makers and their characteristics, (2) the manner in which they become involved in responding to a particular problem or issue, (3) the process by which they arrive at a "solution," and (4) the characteristics of that solution. Examples in which the political approach to decision making may provide valuable insights include the decision to install a new plant in a foreign country, the decision to install a new safety feature in a product, such as airbags in automobiles, the decision to comply and at what rate with antipollution laws, or the decision to implement a new energy policy by the government.

Many decision makers and their characteristics   Complex problems or issues that affect many parts of an organization, several agencies of the government, or one or more groups of a community require the involvement of several decision makers. All decision makers or participants approach the problem with their own value systems, which influence their goals and priorities. Their position also affects the information available to them and their perception of the important aspects of the problem. In general, perceptions and priorities are parochial, reflecting each decision maker's stakes and stands on the issue.

Since participants in a complex decision are also involved in solving other problems, they operate under the pressure of deadlines; this limits the amount of information they can acquire. As a result, different individuals come to see different angles of the same problem.

The importance of a participant in shaping the final solution depends on his power. This is determined by the bargaining advantages inherent in his position and by his personal skill in using them. The power of an individual derives from his authority and responsibility, his control of resources needed to implement a solution, his information about the problem and other participants, and his ability to persuade others to act as he wishes using their bargaining advantages. A participant's power varies, in general, from one issue to another. Therefore, to maintain his long-term effectiveness a decision maker must select how to use his power so that he maximizes the probability for success.

Engagement of participants in action channels   As indicated previously, the participants who count in a given situation are those with the power to influence the outcome of the decision. To a great extent a person's involvement or not in the solution of a problem depends on the person's position and responsibility at the time the problem arises. For many complex problems the structure of an organization, of government at all levels, and even of international bodies provides well-defined procedures of taking action in response to specific issues. These are called *action channels*, which automatically engage those individuals holding positions in specified offices of authority.

A proposal to introduce an additional new product or service would activate an action channel engaging those in charge of research and development (R & D), marketing, production, and finance. A proposal for a new national energy policy would first activate an action channel within the administration, a second action channel for passing it through Congress into law and a third action channel for its successful implementation based on domestic and international mechanisms. Action channels thus specify who the participants will be and how they will be brought into the picture in terms of timing, bargaining advantages, and limitations.

Process for arriving at a response to a problem   Once a problem has been introduced to a particular action channel, specifying the participants that "have the action," the process of political bargaining begins. This is a complex activity aimed at building a consensus among participants with varied goals often in conflict, with diverse viewpoints due to different information available, and with different power as a result of their position and personal skills. In a sense, political decision making is a game, and each player is involved in several such games on different issues with pressing deadlines and conflicting interests.

Rather than dealing with *the* problem, each participant has a narrower view of the specific issue and broader concerns as a spokesman of an organization or a subunit with long-term interests in this and many other problems. This forces him to argue much more confidently than a detached analyst, because of the need to persuade others and enhance the status of his area of control.

Allison (Ref. 3) argues that political decision making is typically characterized by (1) *misperception* due to limited information, (2) *misexpectation* due to ignorance of the problem of other players, (3) *miscommunication* due to time pressure and a noisy environment in which others assume they have been understood, (4) *reticence*, i.e., reluctant silence or intended soft-spokenness, due to engagement in many other problems and the wish to have others interpret an outcome as they desire.

Nevertheless, the process of political bargaining follows certain rules which define the game. These rules may be written in the form of corporate charter provisions, laws, regulations, or long-standing policies. However, some of the rules of bargaining are unwritten and derive from tradition, convention, and culture. The rules specify (1) the structure (positions and paths) of the appropriate action channel, (2) the range of acceptable decisions, and (3) the propriety of various behaviors for bargaining, persuasion, coalition, threats, bluffs, and other actions.

Characteristics of the political response to a problem The final action taken in response to a complex problem is a result of political bargaining. As such, it represents a compromise of the proposals of the different participants. It is achieved by reducing the conflicts in the goals, perceptions and priorities of the players, so that there will be a consensus on the action needed. The final outcome reflects the personalities of the players and tends to protect the vested interests of the organizations they represent. In this regard, it may bear a limited resemblance to what might have been an optimum response since its main virtue is that it is acceptable to all or the majority of the participants. The key features of the political approach to decision making are represented in Fig. 2-11.

Comparison of decision-making approaches

The need to function effectively as an operations manager requires an awareness and development of skills in all three approaches to decision making. The rational approach requires the decision-making power to be concentrated in one individual with a well-defined objective who can select among several alternatives the one that advances him most satisfactorily towards his objective. This requires considerable creative and analytical ability in formulating a problem, developing alternatives, evaluating them, and selecting the best for implementation. The above holds for relatively well-structured problems. If there are several decision makers, we assume that they can agree on the objective(s) pursued and the reasonableness of the proposed alternatives.

Life in large organizations is considerably more complicated in regard to decision making. Here the effective manager realizes that such complexity has brought about standard behavior patterns by different units to specific problems. As a

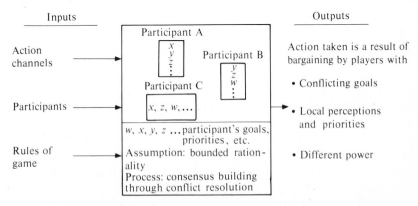

Fig. 2-11   Key features of the political approach to decision-making. Adapted from Graham T. Allison, *Essence of Decision: Explaining the Cuban Missile Crisis,* **p. 256. Copyright ©️ 1971 by Graham T. Allison, reprinted by permission of Little, Brown & Co.**

result, when a complex problem arises, it is split up and assigned to affected units; these develop partial solutions that are then combined or coordinated to form an overall response to the initial total problem. Decision making thus produces small incremental changes. The slow organizational learning yields solutions designed to avoid uncertainty rather than address large strategic problems in their entirety. The parochial priorities and perception of individuals representing different units are partially coordinated by the top leadership.

The relative independence of participants engaged in the action channel activated by a specific problem brings out the significance of considering the political dimensions of decision making. This is appropriate for large organizations with diffused power or for issues involving several organizations. Decision making is thus reduced to a bargaining process aimed at reconciling conflicting goals, priorities, and perceptions of participants to produce a response acceptable to all or most.

Each decision-making approach reveals different aspects of a complex problem and assigns different weights to different considerations. It is through the understanding and insights provided by "walking around" the problem looking at it through the lenses of the rational, organizational, and political modes that we can arrive at the most satisfactory solution. The need for successful implementation requires that decision making focus not only on the formulation and evaluation of alternatives but on those elements which enhance implementation by encouraging acceptance.

As operations managers become responsible for decisions that interact significantly with the environment, the need for understanding the organizational and political approaches to decision making, as well as rational models, cannot be overemphasized.

2-9   SUMMARY

A manager's most challenging role is to make decisions about resources under his control as a means of achieving organizational and personal objectives. To reduce the complexity of problems confronting him, it has been fruitful to make use of the two powerful concepts of a system and a model. The first makes it easier to address the relevant part of the real world in which he operates. The second helps him simplify that part to manageable proportions by abstracting from it the most significant of its characteristics. Systems and models can be classified in a number of ways to describe specific circumstances.

The model-building process, a mixture of art and science, enables one to arrive at a statement of a problem and its solution with various degrees of generality. The purpose may be to understand, to describe, mainly to predict, and sometimes to control the system in which the problem occurs. Supported by computer developments, the modeling of many common types of managerial problems has advanced admirably since World War II and has matured to full-fledged professional fields known variously as operations research, management science, or system analysis.

The majority of available mathematical models are good examples of the rational approach to decision making. Here a decision maker has to select one of several alternatives that has the most favorable consequences to advance him toward his objectives. Rational models have been developed extensively to handle primarily well-structured problems under conditions of certain or uncertain information. However, in situations with many participants, in which power is quite diffused, goals and problem perceptions are parochial, and rationality as an assumption is quite unrealistic, the above OR type of models can be of limited use. Decision making in such contexts can be better understood as an organizational process of coordinating the responses of different departments that have been assigned part of the total problem.

For complex problems in which the influence of leadership is limited, the decision-making process can also be understood as a political game in which the various participants have conflicting objectives. What follows is a bargaining process in which there is an attempt to reach consensus on a response that reflects the goals and power of those participants who can influence the outcome.

As we move from well-structured problems to be solved by one criterion of choice to more complex situations with ill-defined issues, many participants and multiple objectives, the organizational and political approaches assume greater significance in explaining the behavior of complex organizations. Their potential in handling complex decisions relating to product designs, new markets, etc., can be of great value in enhancing the chances for successful implementation of the alternative chosen. The latter has been the Achilles heel for many of the rational models, in such cases.

REVIEW QUESTIONS

 1. Describe the basic characteristics of the following systems:
    (*a*) A neighborhood grocery store
    (*b*) A community hospital
    (*c*) A multinational manufacturing corporation
 2. Justify the need to understand the hierarchy in which a system belongs.
 3. Explain the meaning of the system properties (*a*) stability and (*b*) adaptation. How would the absence of each affect performance?
 4. For what purpose(s) might a management scientist develop a model for a system, such as a maintenance service facility?
 5. How are models classified in terms of their (*a*) degree of generality, (*b*) assumed information, (*c*) planning horizon, (*d*) purpose of application, and (*e*) solution method.
 6. Describe the structure of a mathematical model and illustrate with an example.
 7. What is a fundamental property that must be kept in mind when building a model?
 8. What trade-offs need to be balanced in constructing a model?
 9. Describe the steps in the model-building process.
10. State the desirable model properties according to W. T. Morris.
11. Describe the key elements of a managerial problem.
12. Using G. T. Allison's framework, which are the three ways in which a complex problem might be viewed?
13. What are the key assumptions in each of the three decision-making approaches?
14. Which are the advantages of the political approach?
15. Which of the above approaches would be most appropriate for deciding:

(*a*) How many spare parts of a machine to carry in stock

(*b*) Where to locate a new branch office of a commercial bank

(*c*) How to sequence a set of orders through a machine shop

(*d*) What country to select for building an overseas plant

(*e*) How to respond to pressure for recalling allegedly defective products

SELECTED REFERENCES

1. Ackoff, R. L.: *Scientific Method: Optimizing Applied Research Decisions*, Wiley, New York, 1962.
2. Ackoff, R. L., and M. W. Sasieni: *Fundamentals of Operations Research*, Wiley, New York, 1968.
3. Allison, G. T.: *The Essence of Decision*, Little, Brown & Co., Boston, Mass. 1971.
4. Anthony, R. N.: *Planning and Control Systems: A Framework for Analysis*, Harvard University Press, Cambridge, Mass., 1965.
5. Beer, S.: *Decision and Control*, Wiley, New York, 1966.
6. Chestnut, H.: *Systems Engineering Tools*, Wiley, New York, 1965.
7. Churchman, C. W.: *The Systems Approach*, Dell, New York, 1968.
8. Cleland, D. I.: *Systems, Organizations, Analysis, Management: A Book of Readings*, McGraw-Hill, New York, 1969.
9. Easton, Allan: *Complex Managerial Decisions Involving Multiple Objectives*, Wiley, New York, 1973.
10. Flagle, C. D., et al. (eds.): *Operations Research and Systems Engineering*. Johns Hopkins University Press, Baltimore, 1960.
11. Hall, A. D.: *A Methodology for Systems Engineering*, Van Nostrand, New York, 1962.
12. Hare, V. C.: *Systems Analysis: A Diagnostic Approach*, Harcourt, New York, 1967.
13. Hillier, F., and G. J. Lieberman: *Introduction to Operations Research*, 2d ed., Holden-Day, San Francisco, 1974.
14. Johnson, A., et al.: *Theory and Management of Systems*, 2d ed., McGraw-Hill, New York, 1967.
15. Miller, D. W., and M. K. Starr: *Executive Decisions and Operations Research*, 2d ed., Prentice-Hall, Englewood Cliffs, N.J., 1969.
16. Radford, K. J.: *Complex Decision Problems: An Integrated Strategy for Resolution*, Reston, Reston, Va., 1977.
17. Riggs, J. L., and M. S. Inoue: *Introduction to Operations Research and Management Science*, McGraw-Hill, New York, 1975.
18. Wagner, H. M.: *Principles of Operations Research*, Prentice-Hall, Englewood Cliffs, N.J., 1974.

Supplementary Chapter A

DECISION ANALYSIS

A-1   INTRODUCTION

If there is one aspect of the environment we are certain about, it is the uncertainty that surrounds it. For convenience we often assume that environmental conditions for a given planning period are known. With routine decisions such an approach might be satisfactory because the impact of uncertainty is generally limited. However, the importance of uncertainty increases with:

1. The length of the planning horizon
2. The amount of resources committed for a given course of action
3. The difficulty of reversing a decision once implementation begins

In short, environmental uncertainty is more serious with strategic decisions than tactical ones. Such decisions in operations management include the introduction of a new product, the selection of new technology, determination of desired changes in capacity, and the selection of a new location. Our focus here will be on rational methods for dealing with environmental uncertainty.

It is helpful at the outset to draw an important distinction between a good decision and a good outcome. When we introduce a new product or technology, there is no guarantee possible for a good outcome, i.e., large profits. A decision is termed "good" when it is based on adequate consideration of the outcomes of each course of action under various environmental conditions. This presumes making good use of data available at the outset plus new information obtained at a reasonable cost. Once a course of action has been selected, it is no longer possible to affect the outcome. The randomness and complexity of environmental forces play a dominant role in shaping the final result. In a way it is like choosing carefully one of several places for a weekend pleasure trip without being able to determine the weather when we get there.

A-2 EXAMPLE

Suppose that the management of a health-foods firm has decided to increase production capacity in response to rising demand in recent years. Following a preliminary study, the alternatives proposed include three plants of small, medium, and large size. The decision what plant size to select is to be based on each alternative's projected profits for the upcoming planning period. Determination of economic performance is discussed in Supplementary Chapter B. The net effect of future environmental influences in this case can be expressed by the level of future demand for the planning period.

In the absence of uncertainty about future demand, other things being equal, management would select the plant size with the largest projected profit. However, for a period of 5 or more years it is difficult to justify the assumption of known future demand. Thus, it is necessary to evaluate how each plant size will perform under different market conditions.

Figure A-1 shows that demand for the next planning period may (1) level off due to market saturation or economic recession, (2) continue to increase at about the same rate, or (3) increase at a higher rate due to improvements in the economy or opening of new markets. The projected profits for each plant size under the three possible levels of demand are summarized below:

Plant size	Demand level		
	Low	Average	High
Small	$100	$ 60	$ 20
Medium	80	100	40
Large	30	60	120

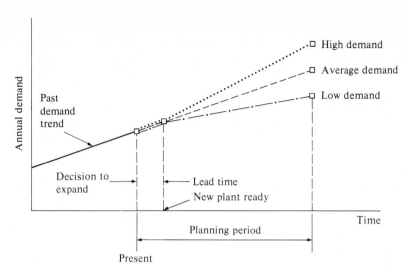

Fig. A-1 **Alternative future-demand conditions.**

It can be seen above that the attractiveness of each alternative depends on the market conditions that will prevail. For a low demand level the small plant size will yield the largest profit, thanks to a better matching between available capacity and actual demand. The same alternative, however, is the least attractive under conditions of high demand, because of higher costs incurred when operating above normal capacity and possible loss of customers from failure to satisfy orders. The situation is reversed with the large plant size, which will be underutilized if demand is low or average.

To make the choice of plant size wisely management needs some additional information specifying the degree of environmental uncertainty. This is provided by estimates of the probability with which each environmental state, i.e., demand level, will occur. Suppose management assigns a 20 percent chance for low demand, 50 percent chance for average demand, and 30 percent chance for high demand. The choice of optimum plant size will most likely vary as we change the set of values for these probabilities. Such estimates of the likelihood of each possible state must be specified in advance to reflect either past experience or management's strength of belief in the occurrence of certain environmental conditions.

The quality of decisions made rests on the accuracy of the probability estimates for different future states. For this reason, it is sometimes worthwhile to improve their accuracy by collecting further information about the environment. Such information can be obtained through special studies, surveys, consultants, or other means. The term *experiment* is often used to refer to whatever scheme is considered appropriate to refine the initial probability estimates.

In the next section we formulate our example as a decision-analysis problem and describe methods to solve it. First we use available probability estimates and then adjust them to reflect new information obtained with an experiment at a cost.

A-3   A DECISION-ANALYSIS FRAMEWORK

A description of a decision-analysis problem requires specifying the following elements:

1. *The decision maker, who is assumed to behave rationally.* For example, one who prefers X to Y and Y to Z would be expected to prefer X to Z.
2. *The set of available alternatives $a_1, a_2, \ldots, a_m$.* In our capacity-expansion example let
   a_1 = select small plant size
   a_2 = select medium plant size
   a_3 = select large plant size
3. *The set of different environmental states $s_1, s_2, \ldots, s_n$.* They must be described in a way that avoids overlaps; in other words, they must be mutually exclusive. For our example, let
   s_1 = low demand, say less than 5,000 units annually
   s_2 = average demand, say 5,000 to 10,000 units annually
   s_3 = high demand, say over 15,000 units annually
4. *The set of possible outcomes q_{ij} from taking action a_i and having state s_j,* where $i = 1, 2, \ldots, m$ and $j = 1, 2, \ldots, n$. In our example, the possible outcomes refer to the actual sales in units of output made for a given plant size and a level of demand. Thus, for a large plant size a_3 and average demand s_2 the outcome q_{32} might correspond to sales of 8,500 units.
5. *The utility function $U(q_{ij})$, by which a decision maker evaluates the importance of different outcomes to him.* Often one can use monetary values. For very large sums that might threaten a firm or an individual with disaster expressing utility in dollars may not be an accurate measure of the full impact of the outcome, say a loss exceeding a firm's total assets. Methods have been devised for specifying custom-made graphs for utility functions. They evaluate outcomes to portray the seriousness of gains or losses and the risks to the decision maker. Such graphs are especially important when the outcome cannot be measured by money, i.e., safety risks of a given technology, reliability of a product design, etc. For our example, we assume that the range of gains and losses is expressed adequately by monetary values, and so we have agreed to use projected profits in millions of dollars. For simplicity $U(q_{ij})$ or U_{ij} denotes the value to the decision maker of the outcome resulting from action a_i and state s_j. The decision matrix can be specified as follows:

	State		
Alternative	Low demand s_1	Average demand s_2	High demand s_3
Small plant a_1	$U_{11} = \$100$	$U_{12} = \$\,60$	$U_{13} = \$\,20$
Medium plant a_2	$U_{21} = \quad 60$	$U_{22} = \quad 100$	$U_{23} = \quad 40$
Large plant a_3	$U_{31} = \quad 30$	$U_{32} = \quad 60$	$U_{33} = \quad 120$

6. *The set of probability estimates for different states of nature* $p(s_1), p(s_2), \ldots, p(s_n)$, *or simply* $p_1, p_2, \ldots, p_n$. For our example, we assume that

$$p_1 = .20 \qquad p_2 = .50 \qquad p_3 = .30$$

These estimates mean that, considering current economic development s, management believes that there is a 50 percent chance the economy will stay the same (s_2), a 20 percent chance it will slow down (s_1), and a 30 percent chance it will improve (s_3).

7. *An information-gathering procedure F, that is, a market survey, or a consultant.* The outcome of such a procedure $(f_1, f_2, \ldots, f_k)$ is used to refine the accuracy of available (or a priori) probability estimates $p_1, p_2, \ldots, p_n$ to obtain adjusted (or a posteriori) probabilities $p'_1, p'_2, \ldots, p'_n$. The latter are then used in the place of the original estimates to select the best alternative. The value of additional information provided by such a procedure depends on its cost and its reliability in predicting environmental states.

A-4 EXPECTED VALUE (OR BAYES')
CRITERION

Let us assume that in our example the management of the firm is pressed to reach a decision only with the information already specified. The problem can then be represented by a decision tree, as shown in Fig. A-2. Squares correspond to decision points, and circles stand for junction points with uncontrollable environmental developments.

The relative merit of each action is expressed by its expected value, i.e., the sum of the weighted payoffs for that action for different states. The weights here corre-

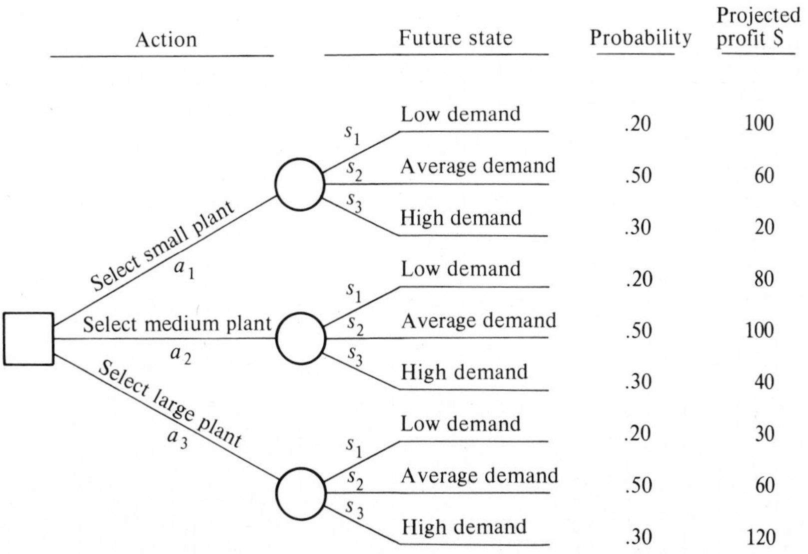

Action	Future state	Probability	Projected profit $
	Low demand	.20	100
Select small plant a_1	s_1		
	s_2 Average demand	.50	60
	s_3 High demand	.30	20
	Low demand	.20	80
Select medium plant a_2	s_1		
	s_2 Average demand	.50	100
	s_3 High demand	.30	40
	Low demand	.20	30
Select large plant a_3	s_1		
	s_2 Average demand	.50	60
	s_3 High demand	.30	120

Fig. A-2 A decision-tree representation for a problem of capacity expansion.

spond to the probabilities of occurrence for each state. Thus, for a given alternative a_i its expected value $EV(a_i)$ is calculated by multiplying the payoff entries in its row by their corresponding probabilities and summing

$$
\begin{aligned}
EV(a_i) &= p_1 U_{i1} + p_2 U_{i2} + \cdots + p_n U_{in} \quad \text{Expected value} \\
&\qquad\qquad\qquad\qquad\qquad\qquad\quad \text{of action } a_i \\
&= \sum_{j=1}^{n} p_j U_{ij}
\end{aligned}
$$

$$(A\text{-}1)$$

In our example

$$EV(a_1) = (.20)(\$100) + (.50)(\$60) + (.30)(\$20) = \$56 \text{ million}$$

$$EV(a_2) = (.20)(\$80) + (.50)(\$100) + (.30)(40) = \ 78 \text{ million} = a^{*1}$$

$$EV(a_3) = (.20)(\$30) + (.50)(\$60) + (.30)(\$120) = \ 72 \text{ million}$$

According to the *expected value, or Bayes' criterion,* management must select the alternative with the maximum expected value. In our example, this would mean capacity expansion with the medium plant size. In the decision tree this is shown by blocking off all action branches except a_2. The relevant data for this form of decision analysis are often summarized in a decision matrix, as shown in Table A-1.

TABLE A-1   Decision matrix for capacity-expansion problem

Action (plant size)	Low s_1 $p_1 = .20$	Average s_2 $p_2 = .50$	High s_3 $p_3 = .30$	Expected value $EV(a_i)$
	State (future demand)			
a_1 (small)	$100	$ 60	$ 20	$ 56
a_2 (medium)	80	100	40	78 = a^*
a_3 (large)	30	60	120	72

If the payoffs in the decision matrix refer to the cost of each outcome or other negative measure, Bayes' criterion selects the action with the minimum expected value.

A-5   THE VALUE OF PERFECT INFORMATION

Before implementing an alternative that is optimum with respect to the initial (a priori) probabilities, it is advisable to determine the value of additional information about the environment. An upper limit for this is the value of perfect information.

---

[1] Optimum values are starred.

This is the benefit to management of knowing with certainty in advance what state of the environment will occur. With the availability of such a "crystal ball" predicting with perfect reliability the future, all uncertainty about the environment is removed.

Let V = value of having perfect information on future conditions

EVPI = expected payoff of acting with perfect information

M_j = payoff corresponding to preferred alternative when we know in advance that state s_j will prevail; in other words, M_j = best payoff in decision-matrix column for s_j

that is, M_j = maximum payoff U_{ij} in column j for all actions a_i

In our example

$$M_1 = \text{maximum } \{\$100, \$80, \$30 \text{ given } s_1 \text{ will occur}\} = \$100$$

$$M_2 = \text{maximum } \{\$60, \$100, \$60 \text{ given } s_2 \text{ will occur}\} = \$100$$

$$M_3 = \text{maximum } \{\$20, \$40, \$120 \text{ given } s_3 \text{ will occur}\} = \$120$$

In the absence of any uncertainty, the long-term payoff would be the sum of the maximum payoff for each state M_j weighted by the relative frequency with which that state occurs p_j. This is known as the *expected value with perfect information* (EVPI). Thus

$$\text{EVPI} = p_1 M_1 + p_2 M_2 + \cdots + p_n M_n \qquad \text{(A-2)}$$

In our example

$$\text{EVPI} = p_1 M_1 + p_2 M_2 + p_3 M_3$$
$$= (.20)(\$100) + (.50)(\$100) + (.30)(\$120) = \$106 \text{ million}$$

The *value of perfect information V* is the difference between the long-term payoff when management knows in advance what the future holds and the expected payoff based on the initial (a priori) probabilities, i.e.,

$$V = \text{EVPI} - \text{EV}(a^*) \qquad \text{(A-3)}$$

In the example

$$V = \$106 - \$78 = \$28 \text{ million}$$

We may also consider V as the loss we incur by not being perfectly informed, i.e., the cost of environmental uncertainty. Additional information about future conditions can at times be obtained through an experiment or a survey at a cost. Such actions may reduce this uncertainty considerably, depending on the reliability of the experiment to predict the future. The higher the reliability the more we should be willing to pay to have that information. This implies, of course, that we do not exceed the limit V, which is the maximum we have to gain through perfect information. In Chap. 11 we discuss various methods for forecasting future conditions and their value to management.

A-6   DECISION ANALYSIS WITH REVISED PROBABILITIES

Sometimes the value of perfect information is large compared with the expected payoff using Bayes' decision rule $EV(a^*)$. It is then desirable to explore ways of reducing environmental uncertainty. In our example, this payoff of $78 million could be increased as much as $28 million, or about 25 percent, if management could use the perfect crystal ball. More realistic alternatives might include the conduct of a market survey or hiring a consultant, in the hope that the increase in the expected payoff by reducing uncertainty will offset the cost of such a study.

Let us assume that in the example management can hire a consulting firm to study future economic conditions and report on the economic outlook for the planning period of interest.

Let $F = (f_1, f_2, f_3) =$ study that can yield three possible results
   $f_1 =$ pessimistic economic forecast, i.e., low expected demand
   $f_2 =$ normal economic forecast, i.e., average expected demand
   $f_3 =$ optimistic economic forecast, i.e., high expected demand

Before using the results of this study, we must know how reliable the consulting firm's record is. In other words, we need estimates of the probability of having future conditions develop as predicted by the study, based on the firm's record on similar projects. This information is provided in the form of a table of conditional probabilities (see Table A-2).

To illustrate the meaning of conditional probabilities. Let us assume that the consulting firm has submitted an optimistic forecast f_3. The probability of such a prediction given that the true future state of the economy will generate low demand, $p(f_3|s_1)$, is .1, in other words quite low. On the contrary, the probability that future demand will actually be high given an optimistic prediction, $p(f_3|s_3)$ is

TABLE   A-2   Reliability   of   forecasts   expressed   as   conditional probabilities

Forecast prediction	Actual state of economy		
	Low demand s_1	Average demand s_2	High demand s_3
Pessimistic f_1	$p(f_1|s_1) = .7$	$p(f_1|s_2) = .2$	$p(f_1|s_3) = .1$
Normal f_2	$p(f_2|s_1) = .2$	$p(f_2|s_2) = .6$	$p(f_2|s_3) = .1$
Optimistic f_3	$p(f_3|s_1) = .1$	$p(f_3|s_2) = .2$	$p(f_3|s_3) = .8$
Total	1.0	1.0	1.0

.8, or quite high. The more reliable the consulting firm is in predicting the future state of the economy the closer the conditional probability of anticipating that state will be to 1.0. A perfect "crystal ball" would thus have values of 1.0 along the diagonal of Table A-2 and zero elsewhere.

Management should be willing to pay for such a forecast as long as its cost does not exceed the expected benefit which for perfect reliability has a maximum value of $28 million.

Our purpose in using the results of an experiment is to increase the accuracy of the initial probability estimates for the different future states of the environment. Therefore, we must convert the available probability estimates $(p_1, p_2, \ldots, p_n)$ to a new set of estimates that take into account the forecast f_k of the information-gathering experiment, $p'_1 = p(s_1 \mid f_k)$, $p'_2 = p(s_2 \mid f_k)$, $\ldots$, $p'_n = p(s_n \mid f_k)$. This conversion is accomplished using a relationship known as *Bayes' theorem* (see Fig. A-3).

Bayes' theorem says that if we know the initial probabilities and the experimental outcome, the improved adjusted probabilities can be computed as follows:

Bayes' theorem

$$p(s_j \mid f_k) = \frac{p(f_k \mid s_j)p(s_j)}{p(f_k \mid s_1)p(s_1) + p(f_k \mid s_2)p(s_2) + \cdots + p(f_k \mid s_n)p(s_n)} \quad \text{(A-4)}$$

In our example, if the consulting firm predicts a high future demand f_3, Bayes' theorem can be used to convert the initial estimates $p(s_1) = .20$, $p(s_2) = .50$, and $p(s_3) = .30$ into adjusted probabilities as follows:

$$p(s_1 \mid f_3) = \frac{p(f_3 \mid s_1)p(s_1)}{p(f_3 \mid s_1)p(s_1) + p(f_3 \mid s_2)p(s_2) + p(f_3 \mid s_3)p(s_3)}$$

$$= \frac{p(f_3 \mid s_1)p(s_1)}{p(f_3)}$$

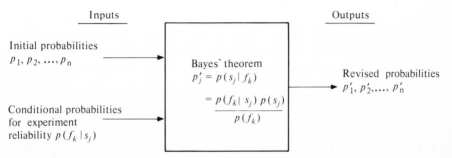

Fig. A-3 Transformation of initial probabilities with the use of additional information (from forecast f_k).

or

$$\text{Prob}\begin{pmatrix} \text{low future demand} \\ \text{given optimistic forecast} \end{pmatrix} = \frac{\text{Prob}\begin{pmatrix} \text{study yields optimistic forecast} \\ \text{in view of low future demand} \end{pmatrix}\text{Prob(low future demand)}}{\text{Prob}\begin{pmatrix} \text{study will yield an optimistic forecast} \\ \text{regardless of future conditions} \end{pmatrix}}$$

Substituting, we have

$$p'_1 = p(s_1 \mid f_3) = \frac{(.1)(.20)}{(.1)(.20) + (.2)(.50) + (.8)(.30)} = \frac{.02}{.02 + .10 + .24}$$

$$= \frac{.02}{.36} = .055$$

Here we note that in the light of an optimistic forecast f_3, the initial probability for low demand $p_1 = .20$ dropped sharply to an adjusted value of $p'_1 = .055$, or from 20 percent to less than 6 percent. If the reliability of the consulting firm were perfect, we would have $p(s_1 \mid f_3) = 0$; that is,

$$\text{Prob}\begin{pmatrix} \text{low future demand} \\ \text{given optimistic forecast} \end{pmatrix} = 0 \qquad \text{For perfect reliability in prediction}$$

The calculation of the remaining adjusted probabilities proceeds in a similar manner, as follows:

$$p'_2 = p(s_2 \mid f_3) = \frac{(.2)(.50)}{(.1)(.2) + (.2)(.50) + (.8)(.3)} = \frac{.10}{.36} = .278$$

$$p'_3 = p(s_3 \mid f_3) = \frac{(.8)(.30)}{.36} = \frac{.24}{.36} = .667$$

Again we note that the initial probability for high future demand, $p_3 = .30$, in the light of an optimistic prediction f_3 rose significantly to .667, or more than doubled. Had the consulting firm developed a perfectly reliable prediction, we would have had

$$p(s_3 \mid f_3) = 1.00 \qquad \text{while} \qquad p(s_1 \mid f_3) = p(s_2 \mid f_3) = 0$$

Now we have a complete set of estimates for the revised probabilities of future environmental conditions. We can check the numerical results by making sure that all probabilities add up to 1.00 ($.55 + .278 + .667 = 1.00$). In order to select the best plant size for future capacity expansion, we must apply Bayes' decision criterion to the same payoff matrix with the revised probabilities, as shown in Table A-3.

Thus, an optimistic forecast f_3 by the consulting firm switched the choice to a large plant size ($a^* = a_3$). The revision of the initial probabilities yielded a maximum expected value $\text{EV}(a^* \mid f_3)$ for a_3 as opposed to a_2, which would be preferred in the absence of additional information.

Had the results of the study produced a different forecast, we would have had

TABLE A-3 Decision matrix for example with revised probabilities reflecting an optimistic economic forecast

Action (plant size)	State			Revised expected value $EV(a_i\|f_3)$
	Low demand s_1 $p_1' = .055$	Average demand s_2 $p' = .278$	High demand s_3 $p' = .667$	
a_1 (small)	$100	$60	$20	$35.52
a_2 (medium)	80	100	40	58.88
a_3 (large)	30	60	120	98.37 $(a^* = a_3)$

to calculate different adjusted probabilities as follows. For a pessimistic economic outlook f_1

$$p(s_1 \mid f_1) = \frac{p(f_1 \mid s_1)p(s_1)}{p(f_1 \mid s_1)p(s_1) + p(f_1 \mid s_2)p(s_2) + p(f_1 \mid s_3)p(s_3)} = \frac{p(f_1 \mid s_1)p(s_1)}{p(f_1)}$$

$$= \frac{(.7)(.2)}{(.7)(.2) + (.2)(.5) + (.1)(.3)} = \frac{.14}{.14 + .10 + .03} = \frac{.14}{.27}$$

$$= .519$$

$$p(s_2 \mid f_1) = \frac{p(f_1 \mid s_2)p(s_2)}{p(f_1)} = \frac{(.2)(.5)}{.27} = \frac{.10}{.27} = .370$$

$$p(s_3 \mid f_1) = \frac{p(f_1 \mid s_3)p(s_3)}{p(f_1)} = \frac{(.1)(.3)}{.27} = \frac{.03}{.27} = .111$$

Thus, for a pessimistic forecast f_1

$$p_1' + p_2' + p_3' = .519 + .370 + .111 = 1.00$$

For a normal economic outlook f_2

$$p(s_1 \mid f_2) = \frac{p(f_2 \mid s_1)p(s_1)}{p(f_2 \mid s_1)p(s_1) + p(f_2 \mid s_2)p(s_2) + p(f_2 \mid s_3)p(s_3)} = \frac{p(f_2 \mid s_1)p(s_1)}{p(f_2)}$$

$$= \frac{(.2)(.2)}{(.2)(.2) + (.6)(.5) + (.1)(.3)} = \frac{.04}{.04 + .30 + .03} = \frac{.04}{.37}$$

$$= .108$$

$$p(s_2 \mid f_2) = \frac{p(f_2 \mid s_2)p(s_2)}{p(f_2)} = \frac{(.6)(.5)}{.37} = \frac{.30}{.37} = .811$$

$$p(s_3 \mid f_2) = \frac{p(f_2 \mid s_3)p(s_3)}{p(f_2)} = \frac{(.1)(.3)}{.37} = \frac{.03}{.37} = .081$$

Thus, for normal economic outlook f_2

$$p_1' + p_2' + p_3' = .108 + .811 + .081 = 1.00$$

TABLE A-4   Summary of results for different economic forecasts

Outcome f_k consulting firm study F	$p(f_k)$	Information about environment (adjusted state probabilities)			Maximum expected profit (optimum action) $EV(a^* \mid f_k)$
		$p(s_1 \mid f_k)$ p_1'	$p(s_2 \mid f_k)$ p_2'	$p(s_3 \mid f_k)$ p_3'	
f_1	.27	.519	.370	.111	$83.00 (a_2)
f_2	.37	.108	.811	.081	93.00 (a_2)
f_3	.36	.055	.278	.667	98.37 (a_3)
Initial probability		.20	.50	30	78.00 (a_2)

If we use the revised probabilities for a pessimistic forecast, with the payoff table for our example, the selected action will be a_2, that is, a medium plant size with an expected value $EV(a_2 \mid f_1) = \$83$ million (for a_1 and a_3 this would be 76.40 and 51.00, respectively). For a normal outlook f_2, the best action is again a_2 with an expected value $EV(a_2 \mid f_2) = \$93$. (For a_1 and a_3 this would be 61.20 and 61.50.) The reader should verify these values. The results of our analysis are summarized in Table A-4.

If such a problem were to come up repeatedly and management were to reach a decision based on the consulting firm's forecast, the *long-term expected value* would be be

$$LTEV(F) = p(f_1)EV(a^* \mid f_1) + p(f_2)EV(a^* \mid f_2) + p(f_3)EV(a^* \mid f_3)$$

$$= (.27)(\$83) + (.37)(\$93) + (.36)(\$98.37)$$

$$LTEV(F) = \$22.41 + \$34.41 + \$43.28 = \$100.10 \text{ million}$$

From the above we note that the long-run *expected net benefit* to management of using the services of the consulting firm will be

$$ENB(F) = LTEV(F) - EV(\text{no } F)$$

$$= \$100.10 - \$78 = \$22.20 \text{ million}$$

or

$$\begin{bmatrix} \text{Expected net benefit} \\ \text{using experiment } F \end{bmatrix} = \begin{bmatrix} \text{long-term expected payoff} \\ \text{using experiment } F \end{bmatrix} - \begin{bmatrix} \text{expected payoff} \\ \text{without experiment } F \end{bmatrix}$$

As the reliability of forecasting economic developments increases, the expected benefits from using the consulting firm approach the value of perfect information, $ENB(F) \to V$. Therefore, given the actual reliability of such forecasts, management should be willing to pay a fee C_F for the study no greater than the expected benefit from it; that is, C_F must be less than $ENB(F)$. The entire analysis of the decision problem in the example is summarized in the form of a decision tree in Fig. A-4. The relationships between the expected profit with and without a forecast and the relative magnitudes of $ENB(F)$ and V are shown in Fig. A-5.

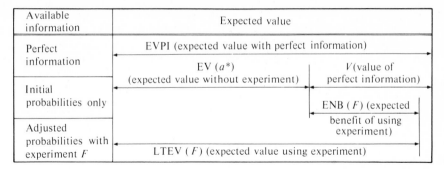

Fig. A-4 **Comparison of expected values of payoffs with and without experiment.**

A-7 BAYES' STRATEGY

When problems with considerable uncertainty arise infrequently, the preferred decision-analysis procedure is the one described previously. It involves setting up the initial decision matrix, performing an experiment, and (based on the outcome) revising the initial probabilities to select the best course of action. If a similar problem appears rather frequently, say in medical diagnosis or oil exploration, it may be preferable to compute in advance the revised probabilities for each possible outcome of the experiment. This enables management to proceed directly to select the best alternative as soon as the outcome of the experiment becomes known.

The second approach is known as a *Bayes strategy*, i.e., an automatic procedure that says "if you observe this, then do that." This is shown for an oil-exploration project in Fig. A-6. The experiment here may involve a seismic sounding test that yields information about the potential amount of oil in a given site.

A-8 RECOMMENDED PROCEDURE
FOR DECISION ANALYSIS

Having examined, with the aid of an example, the conditions under which decision analysis is desirable and some basic methods of applying it, we can visualize the entire process better using the flow diagram of Fig. A-7.

We must keep in mind that decision analysis, like all techniques or models used by managers, is limited by the quality of data available and by certain assumptions. The approach we have described is suitable when we have one decision maker, one criterion for evaluating outcomes, and a small number of actions and future states which can be described by a discrete rather than a continuous probability distribution. There are some methods that allow for continuous distributions and for multiple criteria. There are also methods for evaluating the effectiveness of different experiments, but all these are beyond the scope of this book, and the interested reader is advised to consult the Selected References. To date, decision analysis has been used successfully by many organizations for problems related to the introduction of a new product or service, the expansion of facilities, the evaluation of marketing and financial strategies, medical diagnoses, oil exploration, and many others.

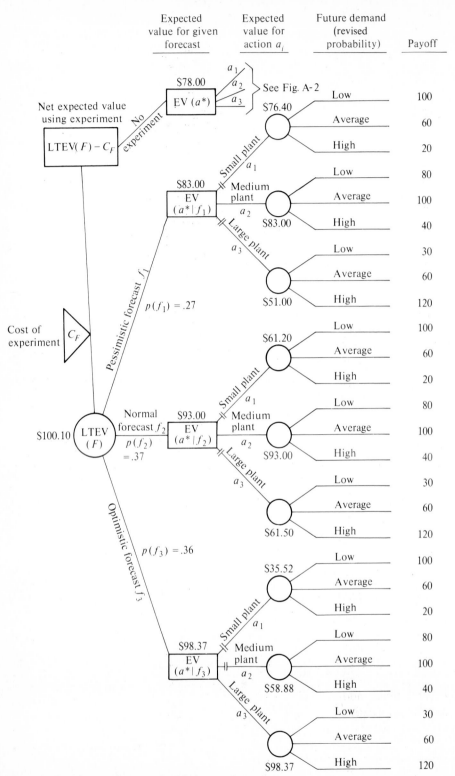

Fig. A-5 Decision tree for example with the use of experiment.

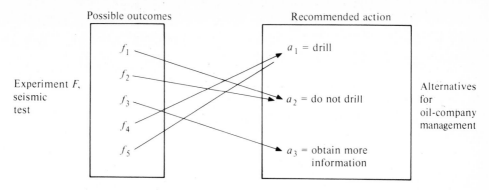

Fig. A-6   Graphical representation of a Bayes' strategy.

A-9 SUMMARY

Our discussion of decision analysis in this chapter has the objective of presenting the basic concepts and methods in the formulation and solution of relatively simple problems. For situations with uncertainty in which we can assume that the choice will be made by a single person behaving rationally, the problem structure can be portrayed by a decision table or matrix. This shows available actions, alternative future conditions, and the payoff resulting from a given action for each possible future state.

Given a set of initial probabilities for the likelihood of future states, the decision maker can use *Bayes' criterion* to select the action with the maximum expected value. Sometimes it is feasible and desirable to collect additional information about the future with the aid of an experiment (a survey, a forecast, or other procedure). If the expected net benefit from such action pays for its cost, it is possible to revise the initial probabilities on the basis of the new information from the experimental outcome. The revised estimates are then used as before, with the initial payoff table, to select the best action.

Whenever the frequency of solving certain decision problems is high, as in medical diagnosis or oil exploration, it is preferable to have revised probabilities for each outcome automatically. This defines a *Bayes strategy*, i.e., a recipe for action given the outcome of the experiment.

The use of decision analysis can contribute to our understanding both of the structure of a problem, with the help of decision trees, and also of the effects of uncertainty on different actions. (For managerial problems the methods discussed in this chapter have been applied with discounting of the sums of money occurring at different times, adding more realism to the payoffs involved.) The increasing number of applications not only in business but also in public and nonprofit organizations attests to the valuable insights decision analysis provides decision makers challenged by the need to act rationally in the presence of considerable uncertainty about the future.

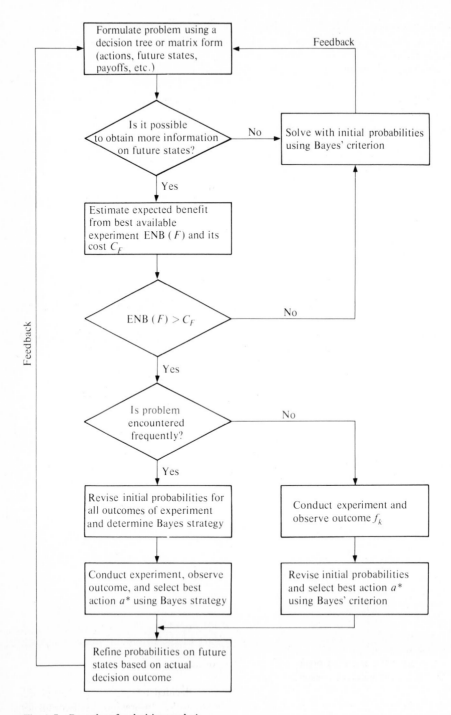

Fig. A-7 Procedure for decision analysis.

REVIEW QUESTIONS

1. Under what conditions should management account for uncertainty explicitly?
2. Explain in your own words the difference between a good decision and a good outcome. Give an example.
3. Discuss Bayes' criterion for payoffs measured in (a) profits, job satisfaction, performance reliability, etc., and (b) in costs, probability of failure, job completion time.
4. Explain the meaning of (a) expected value with perfect information (EVPI) and (b) value of perfect information V.
5. Discuss how we measure the reliability of an experiment, such as a survey or a forecast, used to gain more information about the states of nature.
6. Describe what is meant by expected net benefit of using an experiment [ENB(F)].
7. Under what conditions is it preferable to determine a Bayes strategy for a decision problem?

PROBLEMS

1. Formulate the following problems using a decision-analysis framework: (a) selecting a picnic site, (b) choosing a route for getting to work, (c) deciding on the need to operate on a patient in the absence of incomplete information about his true condition.
2. The management of Phase-Brooklyn Bank has decided to open an overseas branch and is considering alternative locations in the capitals of three Middle Eastern countries, A, B, C. The profitability of this venture will depend on the political stability of the region. For this reason the bank's planning staff has prepared a table with the projected profits for each location over a 5-yr planning period and probability estimates for alternative political futures.

Projected 5-yr profits (millions)

Country of new branch location	Political future in region	
	Stable	Unstable
A	$85	$28
B	70	42
C	60	55
Probability of future conditions	.65	.35

(a) Select the best location based on Bayes' criterion.
(b) Determine the expected profit with perfect information.
(c) Calculate the value of perfect information.

3. Refer to Prob. 2. The management of the bank has decided to hire the services of Dr. Klaus Fishinger, a political scientist and former ambassador. In previous assignments for the bank, Dr. Fishinger has had the following reliability record:

Prediction of future conditions	Political situation	
	Stable s_1	Unstable s_2
Improvement f_1	.6	.3
Deterioration f_2	.4	.7
Total	1.0	1.0

(a) Determine the optimal location for the new branch of Phase-Brooklyn if Dr. Fishinger predicts an improvement in the political situation of the region.

(b) Formulate a Bayes strategy for the location of new branches in the region.

(c) Calculate the long-term expected value of such ventures using the services of Dr. Fishinger.

(d) What is the expected net benefit from the use of Dr. Fishinger's advice?

(e) Prepare a decision tree showing the characteristics of the above problem.

4. Grapho-Tronics Corp. has completed the design of a new graphic-display unit for computer systems and is about to decide on whether it should produce one of the major components internally or subcontract it to another local firm. The advisability of which action to take depends on how the market will respond to the new product. If demand is high, it is worthwhile to make the extra investment for special facilities and equipment needed to produce the component internally. For low demand it is preferable to subcontract. The analyst assigned to study the problem has produced the following information on costs (in thousands of dollars) and probability estimates of future demand for the next 5-yr period:

Action	Future demand		
	Low	Average	High
Produce	$140	$120	$ 90
Subcontract	100	110	160
Probability	.10	.60	.30

(a) Prepare a decision tree that describes the structure of this problem.

(b) Select the best action based on the initial probability estimates for future demand.

(c) Determine the expected cost with perfect information.

5. Refer to Prob. 4. The management of Grapho-Tronics is considering hiring Dr. John Macro, an economist and head of a local consulting firm, to prepare an economic forecast for the computer industry. The reliability of his forecasts from previous assignments is provided by the following table of conditional probabilities:

Economic forecast	Future demand		
	Low	Average	High
Optimistic	.1	.1	.5
Normal	.3	.7	.4
Pessimistic	.6	.2	.1
Total	1.0	1.0	1.0

(*a*) Select the best action for Grapho-Tronics if Dr. Macro submits a pessimistic forecast for the computer industry.

(*b*) Prepare a decision-tree diagram for the above problem with the use of Dr. Macro's forecasts.

(*c*) What is the Bayes strategy for this problem?

(*d*) Determine the maximum fee that should be paid for the use of Dr. Macro's services.

6. The management of Fantastic Cruises, Ltd., operating in the Caribbean, has established the need for expanding its fleet capacity and is considering what the best plan for the next 8-yr planning period will be. One strategy is to buy a large 40,000-ton cruise ship now, which would be most profitable if demand is high. Another strategy would be to start with a small 15,000-ton ship now and consider buying another medium 25,000-ton ship 3 yr later. The planning department has estimated the probabilities for high and low demand for each period to be .6 and .4. If the company buys the large ship, the annual profit after taxes for the next 8 yr is estimated to be equal to $800,000 if demand is high and $100,000 if it is low. If the company buys the small ship, the annual profits each year will be $300,000 if demand is high and $150,000 if it is low.

After 3 yr with the small vessel a decision for new capacity will be reviewed. At this time the firm may decide to expand by adding a 25,000-ton ship or by continuing with the small one. The annual profit after expansion will be $700,000 if demand is high and $120,000 if it is low.

(*a*) Prepare a decision tree that shows the actions available, the states of nature, and the annual profits.

(*b*) Calculate the total expected profit for each branch in the decision tree covering 8 yr of operation.

(*c*) Determine the optimum fleet-expansion strategy for Fantastic Cruises, Ltd.

7. Rework Prob. 6 if revised estimates assign a probability of .7 for high demand and .3 for low demand.

8. Refer to Prob. 6. Assuming you are familiar with the contents of Supplementary Chapter B on economic analysis, determine the optimum fleet-expansion strategy if projected annual profits are discounted at the rate of 12 percent.

SELECTED REFERENCES

1. Brown, R.: "Do Managers Find Decision Theory Useful?," *Harvard Business Review*, vol. 48, 1970.
2. Hammond, J. S.: "Better Decisions with Preference Theory," *Harvard Business Review*, November–December 1967.
3. Jones, J. M.: *Statistical Decision Making*, Irwin, Homewood, Ill., 1977.
4. Keeney, R. L., and H. Raiffa: *Decision Analysis with Multiple Objectives*, Wiley, New York, 1976.
5. Raiffa, H.: *Decision Analysis*, Addison-Wesley, Reading, Mass., 1968.
6. Schlaifer, R.: *Analysis of Decisions under Uncertainty*, McGraw-Hill, New York, 1969.

Chapter 3

ANALYSIS OF ENVIRONMENTAL CONDITIONS

3-1 INTRODUCTION

Management views the environment as the source of opportunities which may advance the organization toward its objectives. At the same time, the environment imposes restrictions on whatever activities are undertaken to take advantage of recognized opportunities. Consequently, the continuous monitoring and evaluation of environmental conditions represents one of management's most important responsibilities. What is at stake here is not only success or failure but the very survival of the firm, especially in the turbulent waters of the private sector.

An analysis of the environment is undertaken with three objectives in mind: (1) an attempt is made to recognize the real boundaries between the system and its environment more clearly; (2) various environmental factors are evaluated in order to identify the most significant in terms of their present or future impact on system performance; (3) an attempt is made to determine the types of relationships between such factors and system performance.

Defining a system's real boundaries with its environment, as indicated in Chap. 2, involves identification of those variables which can be controlled by management and those not subject to control. This task is difficult to perform, but in the end it involves deciding whether technology, the economy, the social setting, or other aspect which affects performance can be controlled by management or is to be taken as given. At times an environmental factor for one firm may be a controllable variable for another. Thus, product price is likely to be outside a farmer's control, but it is a controllable variable for General Motors.

The performance of operations managers is affected considerably not only by external factors but also by the structure and function of other parts of the firm. It therefore is essential to understand the roles of marketing, finance, personnel, and engineering as well as how they interact. Failure to do so results in suboptimization with regard to higher-level objectives set for the organization as a whole.

The variety of environmental influences felt by a production system is depicted in Fig. 3-1. Factors that relate to other parts of the same organization determine the *internal environment*. The latter describes variables outside the control of operations management but controllable by top management responsible for integrating functional policies into an overall strategy. Factors that are beyond control by any management level within the firm define the *external environment*. This can be described by the state of the economy, the available technology, social and political conditions, and in some cases international relations and trade.

All facets of operations management, from the design of the system itself (products, processes, etc.) to the planning and control of actual operations, require considerable information about both the internal and external environment. The most important way the latter affects the production system is by the demand it places for its products and services. If this is interpreted as the resultant force of all factors beyond management's control, it can be treated as a statistical, i.e., random, variable. Therefore, successful interpretation of environmental conditions for most firms really affects the probability of satisfying expected demand in terms of quantity and quality of output as well as its timing and location.

3-2 INTERNAL ENVIRONMENT OF AN OPERATIONS SYSTEM

In this section we survey those parts of an organization and their interactions which form the key aspects of the internal environment. First, we examine the structure needed for the basic functions performed within most organizations. Next, we consider in more detail each function separately and discuss how it interacts with decisions made by operations management. Here we will discuss only the marketing, finance, and personnel functions. The role of R&D and engineering will be considered in Chaps. 4 and 7.

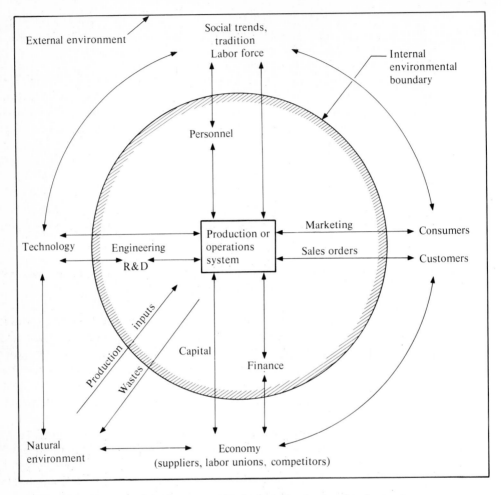

Fig. 3-1   Interactions of a production system with the internal and external environment.

Organizational Structure for Basic Managerial Functions

The functional parts of a typical profit-oriented firm and their most significant interactions are shown in Fig. 3-2. For organizations in the public sector, i.e., government agencies, educational institutions, hospitals, and others, the major difference is likely to be the substitution of marketing by a public-relations function.

All parts of an organization are connected through a continuous flow of information made possible by a management information system. The latter is comparable to the nervous system of the human body and makes possible the coordination of all managerial activity responsible for satisfying actual demand. This requires regulating the flows of customer orders, materials, energy, products, cash, and others. To extend the analogy a bit further, top management functions like the brain. Its role is to interpret the external environment, assess the firm's capabilities,

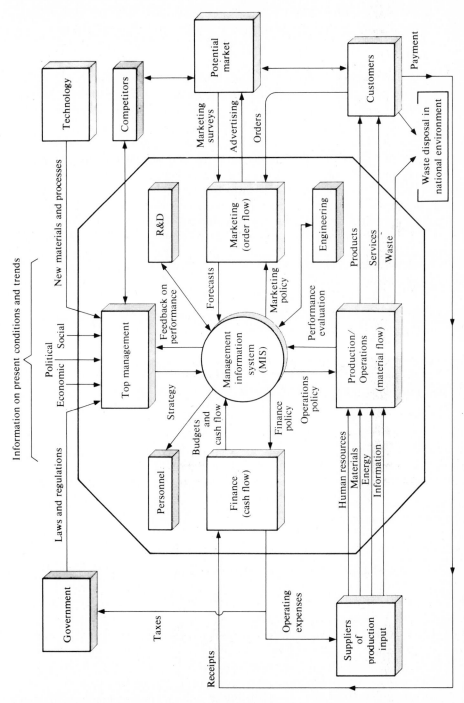

Information on present conditions and trends

Fig. 3-2 An overall view of an organization's internal and external environment.

81

and develop an overall strategy that integrates, coordinates, and evaluates all activities undertaken by the component parts.

The Marketing Function

For a private firm the profit or other objectives are achieved through the satisfaction of consumer needs for products and services. The role of the marketing system is to sense, define, and evaluate the kind and magnitude of such needs and disseminate this information to other parts of the organization for concrete action plans. For new products and services, as well as the processes needed to provide them, management draws on the talents of those in research and development (R&D) and engineering, who collaborate with marketing and production to arrive at concrete specifications. These activities are further explored in Chaps. 4 and 7. After specific products or services are developed in response to identified needs, marketing assumes the responsibility of pricing and facilitating promotion and distribution to potential consumers. Thus, *marketing is the primary link between an organization and its environment.* The information flow designed to serve the decision requirements for effective marketing is shown in Fig. 3-3. More specifically it covers the following activities:

1. *Developing organizational plans based on reliable forecasts about future demand for existing and new products or services*
2. *Pricing products and services so that they are competitive and still yield a profit*
3. *Conducting systematic market research and developing advertising programs and promotional activities to attract customers and maintain their loyalty*
4. *Providing customer assistance with the use and care of products or services*

Marketing's major responsibility to the production function is to supply it with reliable demand forecasts. Relying on such forecasts, it depends on production to (1) have sufficient available capacity to meet anticipated demand; (2) utilize suitable processes, equipment, and work methods to achieve production at a competitive cost; and (3) exercise effective quality control in order to meet the general specifications of products and services offered.

Before coming to a final decision to produce a new or redesigned product, marketing and production personnel must cooperate in the resolution of a series of common problems, including the following:

1. The general product specifications (size, styling, color, capacity, etc.)
2. The capacity and the desired configuration of necessary facilities (technology, location, etc.)
3. The appropriate level of quality control
4. The need for inventory of finished products or of skills or other forms of capacity to allow satisfactory service levels with regard to shortages
5. The ability to provide prompt customer service
6. The determination of production cost as an input to pricing decisions
7. Customer handling after the sale, i.e., customer complaints, assistance, and facilitating repair or maintenance

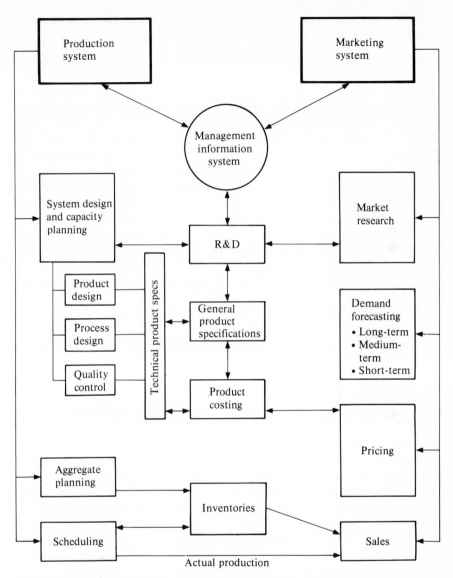

Fig. 3-3 Significant interactions between marketing and production decisions within a private firm. (*Adapted from R. Levin et al., Production/Operations Management, McGraw-Hill Book Company, New York, 1972 by permission.*)

The different criteria employed to evaluate the marketing and production functions often result in conflicts about how common problems ought to be solved. The situation may be further aggravated by the lack of a top-level strategy designed to integrate functional policies into a coherent program for achieving organizational objectives.

As indicated in Chap. 1, the production function is evaluated on the basis of unit production costs, processing times, and quality levels. Marketing, on the other hand, is evaluated by the sales volume it can generate. It is thus tempting for marketing to accept orders beyond the forecast level, which are difficult to handle with the same delivery times and production costs as regular orders. The results often take the form of poor schedules, delayed deliveries, higher costs, and even poor quality as a result of rushing orders through the system. Customer complaints, internal bickering, and poor communications are typical consequences that are detrimental to the organization as a whole.

The potential conflicts mentioned above can be resolved through an improved understanding of how each function's actions affect the others and of their impact on general rather than local objectives. With respect to order delivery times, it is possible for production to supply marketing with tables specifying the normal required time given the order type and size. If marketing wishes to expedite an order for a special customer or accept one above the planned workload, it must assume the responsibility for any delays in orders already scheduled as well as any increases in production costs. Such an approach permits problems to be handled more effectively in terms of how solutions affect total performance.

Harmonious cooperation of marketing and production requires a reliable and efficient information system for preparing updated plans and schedules and reporting indications of how they will be affected by accepting special orders. There is also a need for estimates of the economic impact of schedule rearrangements so that they can be assigned to those responsible for expediting orders above and beyond the forecast demand. Marketing is also charged with the costs related to capacity flexibility required due to the forecast error, which measures the perceived uncertainty in the environment (see Chap. 11).

Figure 3-3 shows the decisions assigned to marketing and production and how they interact in successive stages of planning. Market research and R&D determine consumer needs and propose new products and services. New product ideas in the form of general specifications and long-term forecasts provide valuable inputs for the design of the production system and its capacity.

Technical specifications, developed to meet general specifications with existing processes, provide the basis for quality-control procedures and estimation of production unit costs. The latter serve to determine prices which are competitive and consistent with the quality built into the products. Medium-term forecasts are used to determine how existing capacity will be used, especially for items with seasonal fluctuations. This is expressed in the form of aggregate production plans.

Short-term forecasts by marketing assist production management in securing sufficient worker-hours, raw materials, and parts and preparing schedules that use capacity efficiently and meet actual demand from actual production and inventories.

The Finance Function

The conduct of most activities undertaken by a firm, especially those related to production, require the availability of long- and short-term, i.e. working, capital. This is the responsibility of the finance function, which also undertakes the evaluation of present and proposed activities in order to determine the best allocation of funds. The interaction between production and finance is shown in Fig. 3-4.

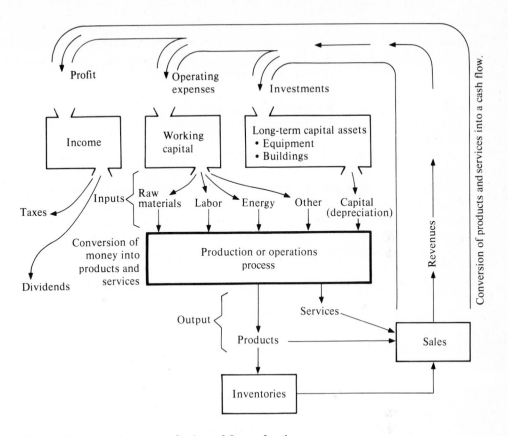

Fig. 3-4 Interactions between production and finance functions.

Long-term capital provides the necessary fixed assets (buildings, equipment, etc.), while working capital covers the cost of inputs such as materials, labor, energy (fuel, electricity, etc.), supplies, and others. The contribution of capital in each period is measured by the estimated depreciation of buildings, equipment, and other fixed assets. Thus, the production system converts funds in the form of long-term and working capital into services or products for satisfying immediate demand or into inventories for anticipated future demand.

As the output is sold, we have another transformation of products and services into a cash flow. The latter replenishes funds for long-term capital requirements, provides needed working capital to maintain productive activity, and distributes what is left after taxes to the owners of the firm.

Of all activities performed by the finance function the most significant ones are the following:

1. *Maintaining accounting records needed for external and internal purposes.* For *external reporting* we include all accounts necessary, i.e., sales, inventories, cash, receivables, etc., to prepare statements for the government (income tax and others), for stockholders (balance sheet or other), and the public. *Internal reporting* focuses on information helpful in managing the organization. It is therefore

designed to provide information on cost estimates for different products or services, their profit margins, and other types of financial information that might assist management.

2. *Evaluating proposed investments for the purchase, improvement, or expansion of buildings or equipment, training personnel, etc.* Such evaluations require an estimate of the internal rate of return, net present value of costs and revenues, or other criteria consistent with organizational objectives (see Supplementary Chapter B).

3. *Determining sources of funds for financing desirable capital projects and the optimum investment portfolios of surplus funds.* Proposed plans by the production function for capacity expansion, new products, installation of antipollution equipment, etc., cannot be implemented unless the finance function secures the necessary capital. Depending on existing management policy, sources of new capital may include:

   a. The issue of new stock
   b. Mergers
   c. The issuance of bonds
   d. Obtaining a loan
   e. Internal funds, i.e., retained earnings
   f. A combination of the above

   Alternatives *a* and *b* preserve the financial strength of the company in terms of its debts but may diffuse managerial control by expanding the ownership. The opposite would be true of alternatives *c*, *d*, and *f*, and the best approach depends on the particular circumstances of the firm and its long-term objectives. Figure 3-5 outlines the analysis of alternative sources of capital.

The Personnel Function

Of equal importance to the production, marketing, and finance functions is that pertaining to personnel. Human resources represent the most valuable input to the production process and deserve the special attention of all levels of management because of their unique role in the total system.

In most organizations *the personnel function is responsible for resolving three basic problems* related to human resources:

1. *Recruitment of a sufficient number of people with adequate qualifications for the variety of job descriptions to be filled*
2. *Effective utilization of existing personnel*
3. *Holding and improving existing personnel through sufficient tangible and intangible rewards*

The proper planning of the internal working environment and the utilization of human resources must satisfy workers in the same way as the design of products and services must satisfy the needs of potential customers.

In the past it was often assumed that employee satisfaction was mainly related to wages or salaries and other financial incentives. Today it is widely understood that to attract and maintain an effective work force requires the satisfaction of a

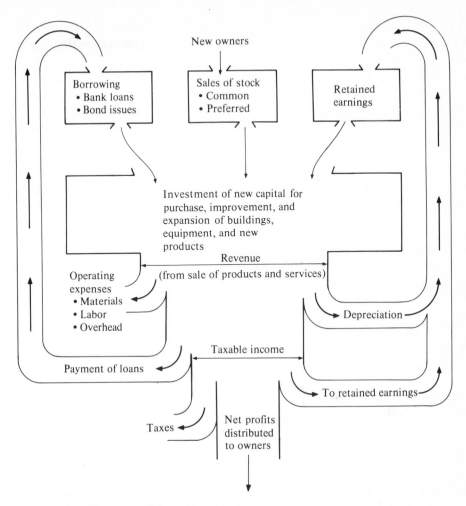

Fig. 3-5   Cash flows generated by new investments.

wider range of human needs relating to working conditions, proper motivation, and opportunity for advancement.

Drucker (Ref. 6) argues convincingly that in the design and operation of productive systems we must consider the *work* to be performed and the *working*. The first relates to the tasks needed to create a product or service and can be treated objectively, impersonally, and in a logical fashion. The second aspect, working, relates directly to the people performing the tasks and by its very nature is highly subjective and personal, defying rational analysis. An effective system is not possible only with the logical analysis of the tasks to be performed, i.e., the work, but must satisfy the needs of those working. Working is described in terms of the following dimensions:

1. The *physiological* dimension, which differentiates people from machines

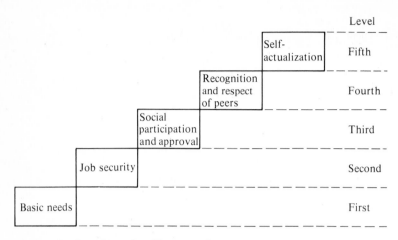

Fig. 3-6   Maslow's hierarchy of human needs.

2. The *psychological* dimension, which covers the many and often conflicting attitudes for, and needs from, work
3. The *social* dimension, which explains the need for bonds through work with others and the community at large
4. The *economic* dimension, which covers the need to earn a living with one's wages from work
5. The *power* dimension, which explains one's relationships to others in a work group and the ability to decide how rewards and punishments will be distributed

Thus, the proper utilization of human resources requires working conditions, structuring of jobs, and development of plans that contribute not only to the achievement of the organization's objectives but to the satisfaction of needs of those employed in it.

Maslow[1] developed a hierarchy of needs (Fig. 3-6) as a framework for developing effective means to motivate employees. Workers initially are motivated to satisfy basic needs, i.e., food, clothing, and shelter. Next, they seek to ensure security for themselves and their families, and this motivates them to strive for job security as a source of income. In the following stage, workers are motivated by the need to be accepted by their fellow workers and those who form their immediate social environment. With this accomplished, they shape their behavior and job performance to gain the respect and recognition of others. Having started with self- and family-oriented needs at the basic levels (1 and 2), workers proceed to satisfy psychological and social needs (3 and 4). When these have been achieved, they return to the self again, aiming for personal fulfillment in a manner consistent with the concurrent satisfaction of other needs.

We can see that a worker's behavior is a dynamic evolution initiated by the need to survive and motivated by the need for self-fulfillment. This shift in the center of gravity of a worker's motivations is very important to management.

[1] Abraham H. Maslow, *Motivation and Personality*, Harper & Row, New York, 1954.

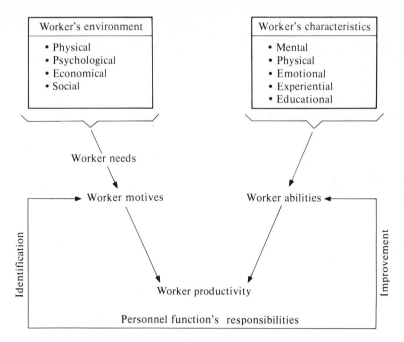

Fig. 3-7   Determining factors in workers' productivity.

Unless workers are motivated to satisfy the level of needs they have reached in Maslow's hierarchy, it is difficult to elicit from them the kind of behavior that contributes to the satisfaction of organizational objectives.

The key responsibility, then, of the personnel function is to assist in creating working conditions that improve productivity (an organization objective) while satisfying as much in the spectrum of human needs as possible. The main determinants of worker productivity are shown in Fig. 3-7.

▶ EXAMPLE 3-1
The interaction of different parts of an organization in resolving a strategic problem can be illustrated with reference to the development and selection of a new product design. Marketing will encourage or prefer new products or services with the potential for maximum sales consistent with the organization's desired image and reputation. Marketing would also like the new product to be manufactured in such a wide variety of models that it will capture as large a share of the market as possible.

Given a set of tentative general specifications, R&D is usually inclined to design a product striving for engineering excellence in terms of materials, precision in manufacture, safety, and performance. The proposed designs will probably be beyond the capability of existing processes, equipment, and skills.

Production or operations people will look at the same set of alternatives and will be attracted to the new product that will be easiest to accommodate with existing resources, known reliable suppliers, etc. Instead of being moved by the desired image of the organization in regard to quality, as visualized by marketing and R&D, they will be more concerned with the capability of the available processes and workers to meet desired specifications. As for variety in the models produced, operations people will be in favor of one or very few variations to minimize the number and complexity of setups, allow longer production runs, and reduce the amount of needed inventory. This position will also be shared by the purchasing department, which will prefer large order quantities of materials or parts to achieve price discounts and limited variety of inputs to limit the replenishment effort and avoid relying on too many suppliers.

Those representing the finance function within the organization will consider alternative product designs and concentrate on the initial costs and projected cash flows associated with each proposal. Their willingness to provide needed funds will be affected more by the rate of return or some other index of profitability than by projected sales volume, unit production costs, or other considerations. Furthermore, such measures of merit must be balanced by the more general requirements to manage the cash flows from existing products or services effectively so that the organization can maximize return from its overall investment while maintaining sufficient liquidity to cover its requirements for working capital.

In view of such conflicting parochial objectives of R&D, marketing, operations, purchasing, and finance, top management must attempt to reconcile them in the light of broader objectives and strategic considerations concerning market trends, competitors, and shifts in other environmental aspects, i.e., social, political, legal, ▶ and broader economic constraints.

▶ EXAMPLE 3-2

Another illustration of the workings of a firm's internal environment is provided by the solution to the inventory problem, a tactical but important aspect in the operation of most organizations. The inventory characteristics of interest include inventory variety, inventory levels, and order or production quantities. Marketing, motivated to maximize sales volume, prefers an inventory policy that provides a wide variety of items in stock and high inventory levels to maintain high service levels, i.e., few or no stockouts and fast deliveries. Operations people dislike large variety in inventories because numerous production setups and limited production runs increase unit costs. Furthermore, variety in output complicates the scheduling and quality-control tasks and requires greater effort to provide satisfactory maintenance. Finance takes a dim view of variety in items stocked and high inventory levels. Extreme variety results in less competitive products, due to their increased production cost, and large inventories tie up excessive amounts of capital that could be more productive elsewhere.

Here again we note how parochial objectives tend to favor different policies for the same problem. This makes it necessary for top management to develop an inventory policy that reconciles conflicting functional objectives. Similar conflicts arise between R&D and operations management when output specifications exceed process capabilities or between personnel and operations management when production plans call for layoffs and at a later time hiring of employees to achieve desired production rates. An operations manager must be familiar with the objectives and motives of other parts of the organization so that potential conflicts, foot

dragging, and other disruptive acts can be anticipated and prevented or reduced
▶ before assuming major proportions.

3-3 EXTERNAL ENVIRONMENT OF AN OPERATIONS SYSTEM

It was stated previously that in addition to the influences or restrictions imposed by other parts of the organization, the production or operations function is affected by factors outside the boundaries of the organization. Most significant among them are factors relating to:

1. The economic environment
2. The natural environment
3. The government (federal, state, and local)
4. The social and cultural environment
5. The technological environment

Operations management must be sensitive and responsive to significant changes and trends in these factors because all have direct and indirect impacts on decisions that determine performance. Table 3-1 summarizes the significant interactions between environmental influences and the decisions made in design, planning, and control of a production system.

The analysis of the external environment usually proceeds in three steps:

1. Determine the most important factors in the environment which influence performance but cannot be controlled, e.g., the GNP, disposable income, competitors, international developments, population changes, etc.
2. Identify methods that can be used to forecast future environmental conditions, prevalent trends, and their combined effect on demand for the organization's products and services. Techniques for forecasting future demand are discussed in Chap. 11.
3. Formulate alternative strategies for optimum expected performance under anticipated conditions.

Some of the environmental factors are quantitative, but others can be described only in qualitative terms. Decision analysis (see Supplementary Chapter A) has contributed important insights and methods for selecting an action, or strategy, i.e., a series of actions, in the face of uncertainty about environmental conditions, the outcome of which may or may not be evaluated in quantitative terms. In this section we focus on the economic, natural, and government environment. Social, cultural, and technological aspects are beyond our scope.

The Economic Environment

For most firms in the private sector and for many agencies in the public sector as well, the economic environment often determines the range of opportunities available and the most tangible restrictions in pursuing them.

For convenience we shall focus on the characteristics of the national economy.

TABLE 3-1 Interactions between production decisions and the environment

Production or operations decisions	Natural environment						Economic, social, and cultural environment			
	Resource use			Pollution characteristics			Economic		Social	
	Renew-able	Nonrenew-able	Energy	Air	Water	Noise and others	Inflation	Unemploy-ment	Minor-ities	Handi-capped
Design:										
Product	1	1	1	1	1	1	2	2		2
Process	1	1	1	1	1	1	2	2	2	2
Equipment selection	2	2	1				2	2	3	1
Job design			1							
Layout										
Location	1	1	1	1	1	1	2	1		2
Planning and control:										
Forecasting	2	2	2				2	2		
Aggregate planning							2	2		
Inventory										
Scheduling										
Quality control										
Maintenance	2	2	2				2	2		

KEY: 1 = critical interaction, 2 = significant interaction, 3 = limited interaction.

The reader, however, is advised to keep in mind the extensive interdependence that exists with other economic systems. International trade, multinational corporations (IBM, Shell, etc.), and international economic institutions (the International Monetary Fund and others) have brought about a web of complex interactions, especially among the economies of the West.

The state of the economy, as measured by the average income per capita and the GNP growth rate, seriously affects the level of demand for a firm's products and its pricing policy. (Remember the car or camera rebates in the recession of 1973–1975?) Similarly, the cost of production and distribution for a product depends on:

1. The regional economic development of rural and industrial areas
2. The availability of natural resources (raw materials and energy)
3. The unemployment level in the labor market from which human resources are drawn
4. The efficiency of the economy's infrastructure, i.e., the transportation and communication networks, the education system, banking system, distribution channels, etc.
5. The government's economic policy on import tariffs and export limitations. The rapid growth in imports of foreign cars, TV sets, shoes, and clothing has been a threat to the survival of many United States companies, while limits on the exports of wheat, computer technology, and other items have severely restricted American farmers and computer industries

We can see from the above list that the economic system and government economic policies affect a firm on both the input (supply of resources) and output (demand for products and services) side.

As a result of many advances in technology and an impressive economic prosperity, especially after World War II, operations systems have been confronted with expanding markets for goods and services aimed at satisfying not only human needs but an unlimited range of human wants. Such a phenomenon, especially in the industrialized countries of the West, is a consequence of a philosophy which equates prosperity with growth and progress with greater and greater quantities of everything. The trend of unlimited economic growth has begun to raise some rather disturbing issues. Many people have started voicing their concern that unguided economic growth can lead to serious problems of pollution and shortages of important raw materials and energy. Both these problems have played a key role in the increase of inflation, which reduces purchasing power despite the economic growth which was intended to improve it.

In recent years, we have been witnessing a countermovement toward quality rather than quantity and a call for selective rather than unlimited growth. Even though such a movement has taken several forms and expressions, its most concrete platform goes by the name of *steady-state economy*. Its active proponents have come from the fields of biology and ecology, which are most acutely aware of the finite limits of our planet in the resources it can provide and the wastes it can absorb. The ideas discussed and the proposals that follow are still very controversial and have met with strong resistance from all quarters with vested interests in

TABLE 3-2 Contrast between unlimited-growth and steady-state-economy approaches

Aspect of the economy	Steady state	Unlimited growth
Physical:		
Flow of resources through system	To be minimized	To be maximized
Total material stock (all products, equipment, buildings, etc.)	To be kept constant	To be increased
Population	To settle to a steady level	No clear position
Natural-resources reserves	Assumed finite	Assumed infinite
Nonphysical:		
Material standard of living, i.e., consumption habits	Given (human needs are viewed as finite and differentiated from human wants)	Variable and increasing (human needs are lumped with human wants and assumed infinite)
Material-demanding activities (production of tangible goods)	Limited	Unlimited
Time-demanding activities (education, friendships, travel, etc.)	Unlimited	Limited

old theories and the social and economic status quo. The basic differences between the new and the old economic philosophies are summarized in Table 3-2. For more on the subject see Ref. 4.

In short, the *steady-state-economy approach* takes the physical aspects of the economy as given and attempts to regulate the flow of natural resources through the system to a minimum, given the population size and the desired standard of living. Economic growth is still possible with time-intensive rather than material-intensive activities that do not require excessive amounts of natural resources as inputs and do not pollute the environment. The *unlimited-economic-growth approach* takes the nonphysical aspects of the economy as given, i.e., consumption patterns for given life styles, and attempts to increase the material flow through the system to satisfy the "infinite needs" of a given population.

Recent government policies, especially with regard to energy, seem to support the arguments advanced by proponents of the steady-state economy. However, full recognition of the implications is still lacking, and the changes will be slow and painful. Whatever the tentative form of the new economics will be, it cannot ignore the key arguments for a steady state. In any event, the impact of the transition, slow as it may be, will be felt by all those responsible in managing productive systems. Some of the implications of changing toward a steady-state economy are explored further in subsequent chapters.

Another source of pressures on operations managers is the intensifying competition from abroad (European Economic Community, Japan, etc.), where productivity growth rates in recent years have been consistently higher than those in the

United States. Coupled with the new power of countries in the Third World with oil (OPEC) and basic materials industries, these pressures present the greatest challenge for the effective design, operation, and control of productive systems.

The Natural Environment

In recent years our understanding of the natural environment has changed drastically. Both as a source of production inputs (materials and energy) and as a sink of polluting wastes, the natural environment under the severe pressures we have created is increasingly perceived as having finite capacity limits.

This shift in our view is particularly critical in planning for the future, both at the level of the national economy and that of the individual firm. It is becoming clear that the economy is embedded in a larger biophysical system with strong ecological interdependence. The emphasis on growth in economies guided by either capitalism or socialism has moved most industrialized societies closer to the threshold at which ecological constraints have become effective. As stated in Chap. 1, the rise in the capital stock and the output of the economy, population growth, and the increase in the power of technology have brought about environmental disruptions from resource depletion and pollution, both indicative of finite limits in the capacity of our natural environment.

In discussing the earth's capacity to supply us with needed materials and energy, we must be aware of the distinctions in the terms *resources* and *reserves*, which in general use are often vague and taken as synonymous.

Definitions[1]

1. *Resources* are the total quantities of ore minerals determined by the composition of the earth's crust, seas, and atmosphere. They are fixed and static.
2. *Reserves* are the quantities of ore minerals located in identified deposits that can be developed at current levels of technology and costs. They are dynamic and changing.
3. *Reserve base* represents the possible expansion of reserves through improvements in technology and higher costs to insure feasibility. This is also dynamic and variable.

Our knowledge of reserves, let alone resources, for many materials is incomplete due to limited explorations. Our estimates of reserves must take into account updated information on geologic assurance (measured, indicated, and inferred), the state of technology, and economic and political factors. The relationship of reserves to resources is shown in Fig. 3-8.

[1] Our discussion in this section draws heavily on J. N. Hartley, *World Mineral and Energy Resources: Some Facts and Assessments*, Battelle, 1974.

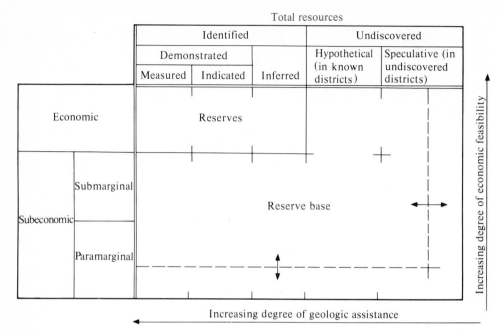

Fig. 3-8   **Classification of mineral resources.** (*From J. N. Hartley, World Mineral and Energy Resources: Some Facts and Assessments, 1974, by permission.*)

This scheme, which has been agreed upon by the U.S. Geological Survey (USGS) and the U.S. Bureau of Mines (USBM), suggests that as new technology and higher prices make it feasible to tap new mineral deposits, some resources are converted into reserves. Unless these factors are taken into account, it is possible to underestimate future supplies of raw materials and energy by extrapolating only from current reserves.[1] Figure 3-9 shows the estimates of reserves for various materials needed by an industrialized economy like that of the United States.

The seriousness of limited supplies of key minerals is further reinforced by the difficulties of United States mineral industries to keep pace with increasing demand from failure to increase capacity and introduce new technologies. This has led to an increasing dependence on imports. In 1973 the United States was self-sufficient in only 7 of 39 major minerals, 50 percent self-sufficient in 16, and completely depended on imports for 6 (the platinum metals, of critical importance as catalysts for manufacturing petroleum products). When we consider the strong international competition for such imports from the European Economic Community (EEC) and Japan, we see some of the key elements of the vicious circle of inflation.

Figure 3-10 shows the energy flows in the United States economy, and Fig. 3-11 indicates the results of unlimited and unguided growth patterns in our energy-consumption habits. Despite an oil embargo that shook the world in 1973 and considerably distorted western economies, increased demand for oil in the

---

[1] This error was made in preparing projections in Ref. 10 using 1968 reserve data; see also Ref. 11.

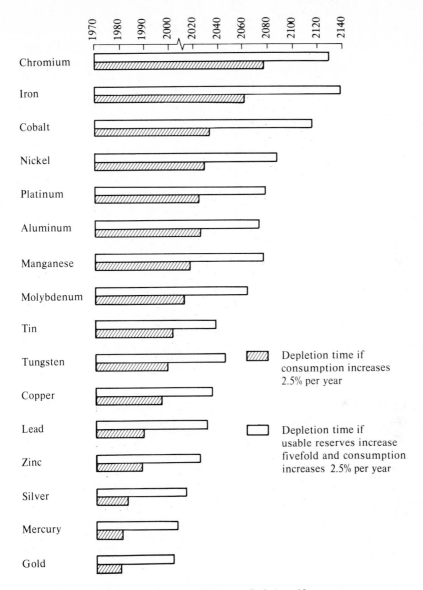

Fig. 3-9   Estimated number of years to 80 percent depletion of key resources.

United States raised oil imports from 33 percent in 1974 to 38 percent in 1975 to almost 47 percent in 1977! Such trends create not only conditions for environmental disasters, such as huge oil spills, but a dangerous economic and political interdependence that increases the country's vulnerability to external pressures. An MIT study (Ref. 13) suggests that by 1985 western societies will reach the point where expected demand for oil will start exceeding the available supply under quite general conditions, and the difference will have to be met from alternative fuels requiring large investments and long lead times.

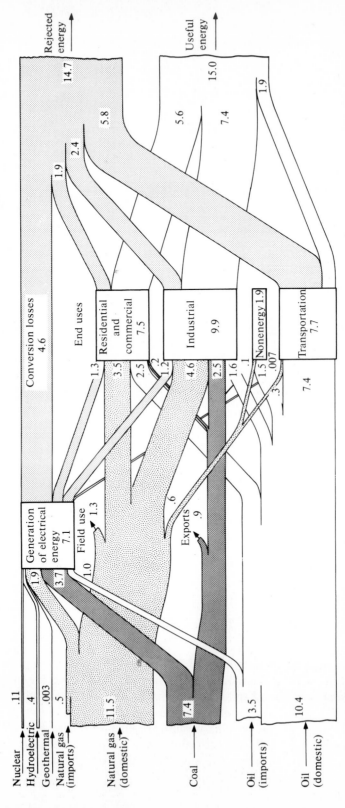

Fig. 3-10 United States energy-flow diagram for 1970, millions of barrels per day. (*Lawrence Livermore Laboratory, Energy, Uses, Sources, and Issues, UCRL-51221, May 30, 1972.*) (**Public source.**)

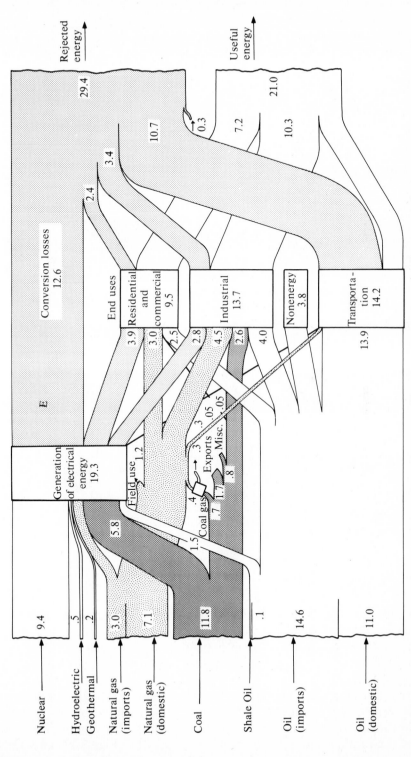

Fig. 3-11 Projected energy flow for the United States for 1985, millions of barrels per day. (*Lawrence Livermore Laboratory, Energy, Uses, Sources, and Issues, UCRL-51221, May 30, 1972.*)

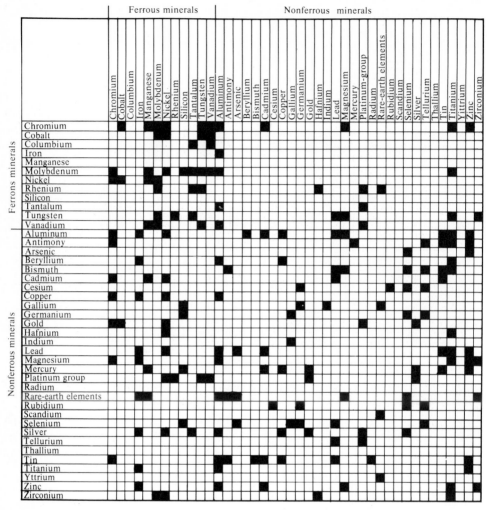

Substitution matrix worksheet

Fig. 3-12   General ferrous and nonferrous minerals substitution according to USBM commodity specialists. *(From J. N. Hartley, World Mineral and Energy Resources: Some Facts and Assessments, 1974, by permission.)*

Our changing perception of the limits of the natural environment is likely to have a considerable effect on our future material standard of living. This in turn will force a change in our priorities of human needs and wants and the demand patterns for the variety of products and services operations systems will be called upon to produce.

The environmental impacts of operations-management activities are examined in more detail in later chapters. With respect to securing adequate supplies of production inputs *substitution* is in some cases a promising approach to avoid shortages in critical materials and fuels in short supply (see Figs. 3-12 and 3-13). In

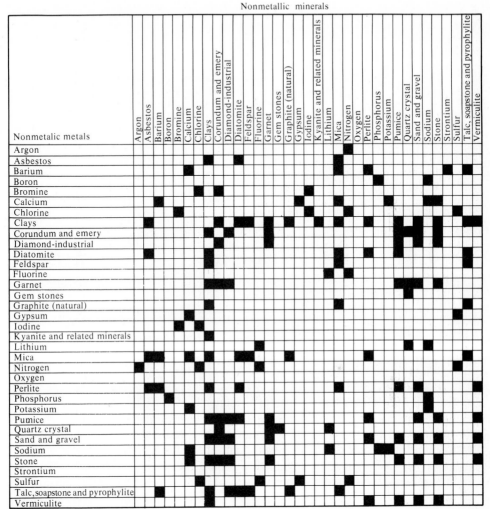

Fig. 3-13 Substitution matrix for nonmetallic materials, according to USBM commodity specialists. (*From J. N. Hartley, World Mineral and Energy Resources: Some Facts and Assessments, 1974, by permission.*)

the long run, however, *recycling* is viewed as a more effective means for reducing the pressure on nonrenewable resources. Furthermore, recycling has the advantage of reducing the amount of waste generated during the production and disposal of many products.

The Increasing Role of Government

No analysis of the environment can be complete without an evaluation of government regulations. As the size and complexity of an organization increase, so does the role of government in its multiple forms of regulation. *Newsweek* magazine

TABLE 3-3   Interfaces between a firm and the government

Type of decision	Legal requirements
Starting a business	Obtain permission and registration (corporate charter, etc.)

Developing a new product	Legal requirements to:
	    Avoid patent infringement or obtain patent protection
	    Conform to regulations about packaging, safety, and
	       pollution characteristics

Introducing a new service for an airline to fly on a new route or for a restaurant to sell liquor on the premises	Legal requirements to obtain approval of regulatory agencies, e.g., Civil Aeronautics Board, state liquor agency
Locating a new plant and building facilities	Environmental-impact statements Licensing from government agencies (building-code compliance, utilities, etc.)
Operating a production process	Labor regulations and laws on hiring, overtime, retiring, firing, etc. Safety regulation and laws (OSHA) Custom duties on imported materials and parts, clearances needed for exports Payment of taxes Compliance with pollution regulations
Closing a business	Various legal requirements concerning creditors, outstanding product warranties, availability of parts, etc.

reported that in 1978 there were 87 federal agencies regulating American business. For the same year this involved filling out some 4,400 different forms at an estimated 143 million labor-hours of clerical and executive effort per year. The total annual bill for such regulation has been estimated at $103 billion.[1]

The effect of government on a private firm is felt when starting or expanding, during its operation, and when it is terminated. Table 3-3 shows typical instances in which a business must deal with government at the local, state, or federal level.

The effects of regulations, intended to protect the consumer, the public at large, and the natural environment, take the form of increased difficulty and higher costs to do business. To comply with such regulations even small firms need expert assistance in legal and tax matters. A small dairy in Illinois with 27 employees was required to report to over 12 different agencies.[1] Much of the cost incurred to comply with government regulations is, of course, passed on to the consumer. Thus, for 1977 the regulatory costs for a typical GM car were estimated at $200 (safety rules $68, management costs $40, pollution controls $38, plant facilities $38, OSHA regulations $14, and noise abatement $2).[2]

The enforcement of new antipollution legislation in the early 1970s had a profound effect on capital budgeting activities of firms in the automobile, paper, chemical, and other industries. Requirements for new equipment to clean the air, the water, and solid waste made it difficult to expand capacity or modernize plant

---

[1] The Regulation Mess, *Newsweek*, June 12, 1978, pp. 86–88.
[2] Ibid.

facilities. Similar pressures were applied by the enactment of the Occupational Health and Safety Act (OSHA), designed to enhance safety at work. This has led in recent years to waves of protests from business, questioning both the value and the manner of implementing such regulations.

In response to such complaints, certain forms of deregulation have been attempted. For example, deregulating air fares and routes in the airline business increased air traffic in 1978 by almost 21 percent and profits for the industry by 16.5 percent. How did this affect operations managers? The lower fares increased the demand for airline capacity in passenger seats tremendously, resulted in serious scheduling difficulties, and affected flight safety due to increased air traffic. Secondary or derived effects have been felt at airports, travel agencies, and other systems in the travel industry. This example suggests a trend for government agencies to pay more attention to the trade-offs that exist. The *expected benefits from more regulation must be balanced against the tangible and intangible costs to business and the consumer.* According to the Council of Wage and Price Stability, regulation-related costs supported inflation, adding .5 to .75 percent annually to the cost of living.[1] In any event, it is imperative to remain abreast of new rulings in order to avoid curtailment of activity, high fines, or unusually large capital expenditures to conform.

3-4 FLEXIBILITY AND ADAPTABILITY

The most distinctive aspect of an operations system's environment is the change with time in the variables that define it. Changes in the economy, in relevant technologies, and in life styles are likely to have a significant effect on the activities undertaken by any organization. Its survival and success therefore depend on two related abilities: (1) a need for the ability to prepare accurate forecasts of future demand for products and services and (2) a need for flexibility and adaptation to meet the changing nature of that demand in terms of quantity, quality, timing, and location.

Since productive systems are evaluated by the cost at which they satisfy actual demand, it is necessary to operate in a mode that keeps production costs as low as possible. This often requires methods associated with mass production in order to take advantage of economies of scale. The latter in turn require a stable product design for standardized items so that it is possible to use specialized equipment and methods. For mass-production methods to pay off, it is necessary to serve a large market, so that potential economies of scale can be realized from large production volume.

With the exception of a few items so standardized and stable that all customers receive identical units of output, the pressure to satisfy a wide variety of tastes for the same product requires diversified styles and features with regard to its final form. Thus, most production systems are confronted with the conflicting pressures for low competitive cost, possible through mass-production methods, while at the

[1] Ibid.

same time they are expected to create products that are diversified enough to satisfy a wide variety of functional and psychological consumer needs.

This conflict is usually resolved by what is known as modular product design (see Chap. 4). According to this approach, a production system is set up for a small number (three to six) of different products, say home appliances or cars. Then, by using the maximum possible number of common parts it is possible to use mass-production techniques for the basic product configuration. This allows diversification in the latter stages of production by varying only a few design features such as color, engine size, accessories, etc. The number of possible combinations that will allow a customer to have a choice is so high that by this approach the production system can serve a much larger market than would be possible with one product design.

The desired ability to be flexible and adapt both to environmental changes and a wide variety of customer preferences can be achieved in a number of ways. The use of standardized parts in various combinations, the employment of human resources with training in various skills, and the utilization of flexible processing and materials-handling equipment can all be used in various configurations to provide an adaptive system responsive to a wide variety of demands placed on it (see Fig. 3-14).

3-5 SUMMARY

The purpose of understanding and attempting to predict the environment is two-fold: (1) it represents the source of opportunities that can advance the organization toward its objectives, and (2) it imposes several restrictions on whatever activities are undertaken to take advantage of the opportunities pursued.

It is helpful for an operations manager to classify environmental factors into two categories. Those not controlled by him, which can be influenced by others within the same organization responsible for marketing, finance, or other function, determine the *internal environment*. The remaining environmental characteristics

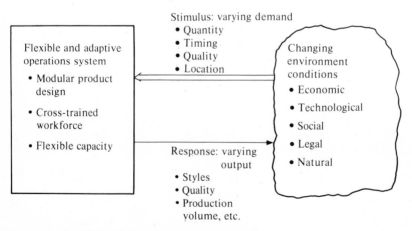

Fig. 3-14 Flexibility and adaptation in meeting demand.

that affect performance but cannot be controlled by any decisions within the organization shape the *external environment*. This includes the state of the economy, available technologies, tradition and social trends, international trade, politics, and others.

An organization responds to anticipated demand as the resultant force of all environmental factors. Since change is the most permanent characteristic of the environment, an organization must maintain flexibility in order to adapt to the dynamic changes in the type of demand that must be met in terms of quantity, quality, timing, and location.

REVIEW QUESTIONS

1. Why is the study of system's environment important, and what are the objectives in undertaking it?
2. What is the key difference between the internal and external environment of an operations system?
3. Describe marketing's basic activities within an organization.
4. What is the major responsibility of marketing to the operations function of an organization?
5. What are the responsibilities of the operation's function to the marketing function?
6. Describe important decision areas in which joint action is usually necessary by operations and marketing.
7. Explain the most significant activities of the finance function.
8. Discuss the major responsibilities of the finance and operations functions to each other.
9. Which problems related to human resources does the personnel function attend to?
10. Why is Peter Drucker's distinction between the work and the working important in operations management?
11. Discuss the levels of needs in Maslow's hierarchy that would motivate a typical worker in an economically (a) underdeveloped, (b) developing, and (c) developed society.
12. Describe the factors that seem to affect human productivity. Why should they be of interest to the personnel function?
13. Discuss which aspects of the external environment would be most influential on the operation of:
    (a) A manufacturer of medical research instruments
    (b) A military hospital
    (c) A United States automobile manufacturer in South America
    (d) A pulp and paper manufacturer
14. Explain the major differences between an unlimited-growth and a steady-state economy.
15. Explain the meaning of (a) resources, (b) reserves, and (c) reserve base.
16. Why is increasing dependence of the United States on imported materials and oil crucial to its economy and security?
17. What makes platinum especially critical for the United States economy?
18. Which are considered the most promising approaches for reducing the pressure on nonrenewable natural resources in short supply?
19. Describe which decisions, especially in operations management, are affected by government regulations.
20. Discuss the significance of flexibility and adaptability for an organization operating in a dynamic environment.

SELECTED REFERENCES

1. Ackoff, R. A.: *Concept of Corporate Planning*, Wiley, New York, 1970.
2. Ayres, R. Y.: *Technological Forecasting and Long-Range Planning*, McGraw-Hill, New York, 1969.
3. Churchman, C. W.: *The Systems Approach*, Dell, New York, 1968.
4. Daly, Herman E. (ed.): *Toward a Steady State Economy*, Freeman, San Francisco, 1973.
5. Detwyler, Thomas (ed.): *Man's Impact on Environment*, McGraw-Hill, New York, 1971.
6. Drucker, Peter: *Management: Tasks, Responsibilities, Practices*, Harper & Row, New York, 1974.
7. Hall, A.: *A Methodology for Systems Engineering*, Van Nostrand, 1962.
8. Litterer, J. A.: *Organizations: Structure and Behavior*, 2d ed., vol. 1, Wiley, New York, 1971.
9. Litterer, J. A.: *Organizations: Systems, Control and Adaptation*, vol. 2, Wiley, New York, 1972.
10. Meadows, D. H., et al.: *The Limits to Growth*, New American Library, New York, 1972.
11. Penner, S. S., and L. Icerman: *Energy*, vols. 1–3, Addison-Wesley, Reading, Mass., 1974–1976.
12. Quade, E. S., and W. I. Boucher: *Systems Analysis and Policy Planning*, Elsevier, New York, 1968.
13. WAES: *Energy: Global Prospects 1985–2000*, McGraw-Hill, New York, 1977.

Supplementary Chapter B

ECONOMIC ANALYSIS

B-1   INTRODUCTION

Managerial decision making is generally aimed at the evaluation of alternative courses of action. As indicated in Chap. 2, several factors in real life tend to increase the complexity of such decisions:

1. The *uncertainty about the future* often clouds the potential consequences from a given action
2. The need to consider *multiple criteria* (costs, safety, quality, etc.) poses serious problems in the evaluation of tangible and intangible aspects
3. The *pressure of time* to reach a decision often results in unrealistic fragmentation and oversimplification of problem components
4. The *presence of conflict* between participants creates different views of what the problem really is

Despite such difficulties management must still make many decisions, and traditional economic analysis provides methods for both tactical and strategic level problems. At the tactical level we have problems of interest to operations managers, e.g., machine replacements, accepting or not accepting new orders, make or buy decisions, and the like. At the strategic level the issues affect the whole organization, e.g., new products or processes, changing capacity or location, and others.

Pervasive in all such decisions is a satisfactory analysis of costs as they are affected by changes in output volume, technology, or product or service variety. In the study of strategic problems, management must understand the effects of costs on prices, the relationship between prices, costs, and production volume, and the impact of output variety on overall performance.

This supplementary chapter provides an introductory treatment of important cost concepts and economic analysis methods for both tactical and strategic decisions.

B-2   COST CLASSIFICATION

The ultimate value of an economic analysis can be no better than the quality of data on the costs and revenues associated with the alternatives under study. The information provided by accounting systems designed to satisfy legal requirements and stockholders is not generally suitable for decision-making purposes. Accounting costs represent out-of-pocket expenditures or valuations of assets by conventional procedures that do not usually reflect relevant costs.

From the different costs used by economists, accountants, or engineers we must select the type most appropriate for a specific application. This will normally be developed from accounting data or special studies. Common to all types of costs is the concept of giving up something of value in exchange for something else. What is sacrificed or given up may be assessed objectively or subjectively, directly or indirectly. Purchasing an office typewriter involves a cost that is objective and direct. However, a decrease in worker job satisfaction generates a cost that is subjective and indirect. Difficulties in measuring certain types of costs do not justify their exclusion from analysis. In the following sections we examine the most useful kinds of costs so that in a particular study one can select the ones that measure the effects of a proposed course of action most realistically.

Direct versus Indirect Costs

Managers must often evaluate alternatives that affect specific products or services, processes, or facilities. In such cases the ability to trace costs to such entities varies.

Direct costs are costs that can be identified directly with a particular process or its output. For example the direct materials, parts, and labor needed to make a piece of furniture or a TV set result in costs easily traceable to each unit of output. Similarly, supervision, power, and other overhead items generate costs that can be traced directly to a particular department or facility.

Indirect costs are costs that cannot be identified with a specific process or its output. The cost of heating and lighting a facility cannot be traced to a unit of output and may vary with output volume.

Fixed versus Variable Costs

For a given facility size, it is important for some decisions, such as accepting a new order, to know whether or not certain costs vary with production volume in a given period. This leads to the useful distinction between fixed and variable costs.

Certain costs associated with the operation of a facility for a given period remain constant regardless of the output volume in that period. Called *fixed costs*, they include such items as rents for buildings, insurance premiums, supervisory salaries, and others. Whether the facility is operated at 50 or 95 percent of its capacity, such costs remain constant as long as the time period is relatively short, say a month. These costs are usually determined by the size of the facility. Changes in the latter through expansion or redesign usually change the fixed costs per period.

For a given plant size the sum of all the direct costs that can be traced to a single unit of output also remains fixed. This includes costs for direct labor, materials, and packaging per unit, which taken together represent the *unit variable cost*. While the unit variable cost remains fixed for an operating period, the *total variable cost* for all units produced in that period varies with the output volume, taken as a measure of plant-capacity utilization.

When we evaluate alternative plant sizes or technologies, we seek a balance in the trade-offs of higher fixed costs for lower unit variable costs. The answer must usually rest on the expected capacity utilization. For this purpose we often rely on a break-even analysis, discussed later in this chapter.

Incremental and Marginal Costs

When one is evaluating the economic impact of a specific decision some costs may change while others remain unaffected by the proposed change. The decision must be evaluated on the basis of the net change, or incremental cost, of an alternative compared with a net change in associated revenues, i.e., in incremental revenues resulting from implementation of that alternative.

Many important decisions made by operations managers require incremental costs. Consider, for example, inventory-related decisions when no price discounts are permitted for large orders. In such cases, the cost of purchasing the total quantity to cover annual demand is not affected by the size and frequency of orders. Consequently, this cost can be omitted from further analysis. By doing so the management analyst can focus on the incremental costs for holding, replenishment, and shortages that are affected by decisions on when and how much to order. Another example is the decision to accept a new order when excess capacity is available. When such a proposal is assigned its full cost, including overhead costs not affected by the new order, it may be unattractive. From incremental costs, i.e., those and only those costs which will change if the new order is accepted, it may be advisable to accept it for a lower cost than regularly priced orders if such practice does not violate other policies. Similar considerations apply to decisions about adding new capacity, new products or services, and others.

When incremental costs are determined on a per unit change in output, we use the term marginal analysis. *Marginal cost* and *marginal revenue* refer to the incremental cost and revenue resulting from a unit change in output. This approach is a special case of incremental reasoning, especially suited for evaluating trade-offs when cost and revenue relationships are nonlinear.

Opportunity Costs

An organization's limited resources can often be assigned to alternative uses, inside or outside the organization. If a resource is allocated to an alternative other than the best, there is an *opportunity cost* equal to the net revenue foregone. For an engineering graduate who decides to continue for a M.B.A. degree, the opportunity cost of attending a 2-year graduate program would be the highest salary he could receive working as an engineer. The opportunity cost of using a machine in a furniture shop to make coffee tables is the loss of earnings that would be possible from a more profitable product, say sofas or reclining chairs currently not included in the product mix.

In evaluating alternatives management may use opportunity costs for the use of resources or incremental costs. Both approaches should yield the same answer, and the choice depends on the particular aspects of problems that must be highlighted (see Ref. 2).

Sunk Costs

At a given time the book value of an asset, say a building or machine, may be higher than its real value if it were to be traded or sold. The difference is known as a *sunk cost* and should not affect any decisions concerning its use or replacement, which must be based on true costs. For example, if a machine in its third year of use has a book value of $12,000 but its resale value is only $7,000, the $5,000 difference is a sunk cost that should not influence any decision to continue its use or replace it with a more efficient machine.

Depreciation

The value of a physical asset, such as a fork-lift truck, normally decreases with time, reflecting both physical and functional deterioration. *Depreciation* is an accounting scheme by which the initial investment for an asset is allocated to successive periods in its productive life.[1] This is done so that a part of each year's earnings, equal to the depreciation for that period, can be set aside as an expense in order to recover the initial investment, possibly for the eventual replacement of the asset.

A critical assumption in the calculation of depreciation is the asset's productive life. This may be measured by its *physical life*, i.e., the length of time the asset is capable of performing its intended function satisfactorily. However, an asset's life might be better related to its *economic life*, determined by the length of time the asset performs its intended function not only satisfactorily but also competitively compared with available alternatives. Technological innovations render many assets obsolete before they reach the end of their physical life. This, however, is hard to predict. For decision-making purposes, the depreciation of an existing asset must be based on the opportunity cost of not employing the best alternative for the specific task under study.

Since the depreciation each year becomes part of the total cost for that year, the larger the depreciation charged the smaller the gross profit (= revenue − total cost); hence the smaller the taxes that must be paid. Higher real profit, due to lower taxes, is one good reason for trying to depreciate an asset rapidly in the early years. The second reason is that such an approach protects a firm more against obsolescence in the event of unforeseen technological improvements.

Accounting depreciation methods, to be explained shortly, may or may not reflect the true decrease in the value of an existing asset. However, for the purpose of evaluating proposed investments for new assets they provide the only basis for comparing alternatives and for assessing the effect of different depreciation patterns on taxes and expected cash flows. Here we shall consider three methods of depreciation and illustrate and compare them with a numerical example in Table B-1. Our discussion requires that we specify in advance the following:

P = initial cost of asset
N = productive life of asset, yr
S = salvage (or residual) value of asset after N yr

The different depreciation methods will be illustrated with an example in which P = \$20,000, N = 5 yr, and S = \$5,000.

Straight-line depreciation method   In the simplest case, the initial investment is allocated uniformly throughout the life of the asset. The constant annual depreciation (AD) is calculated as follows:

$$\text{AD} = \frac{1}{N}(P - S) \qquad \text{for years 1, 2, ..., } N \qquad \text{(B-1)}$$

[1] The term *amortization* is used to refer to the decrease in value of intangible assets such as patents, goodwill, and others.

TABLE B-1 Comparison of depreciation methods using example with initial cost $P = \$20,000$, economic life $N = 5$ yr, and salvage value $S = \$5,000$

Depreciation method	Year	Annual depreciation	Book value	Graph†
Straight-line	0	...	$20,000	
	1	$3,000	17,000	
$AD = \dfrac{1}{N}(P - S)$	2	3,000	14,000	
$= \frac{1}{5}(\$20,000 - \$5,000)$	3	3,000	11,000	
$= \$3,000$	4	3,000	8,000	
	5	3,000	5,000	
Sum-of-digits	0		$20,000	
$AD_1 = \frac{5}{15}(15,000)$	1	$5,000	15,000	
$AD_2 = \frac{4}{15}(15,000)$	2	4,000	11,000	
$AD_3 = \frac{3}{15}(15,000)$	3	3,000	8,000	
$AD_4 = \frac{2}{15}(15,000)$	4	2,000	6,000	
$AD_5 = \frac{1}{15}(15,000)$	5	1,000	5,000	
Declining-balance for fixed per-centage, 25%	0		$20,000.00	
$AD_1 = (.25)\,(20,000)$	1	$5,000.00	15,000.00	
$AD_2 = (.25)\,(15,000)$	2	3,750.00	11,250.00	
$AD_3 = (.25)\,(11,750)$	3	2,812.50	8,437.50	
$AD_4 = (.25)\,(8,437.50)$	4	2,109.37	6,328.13	
$AD_5 = (6,328)\,(13-5,000)$	5	1,328.13	5,000.00	

† ○—— Book value, ↓ annual depreciation

or

$$\text{Annual depreciation} = \frac{\text{initial cost} - \text{salvage value}}{\text{asset life}}$$

In our example

$$AD = \frac{\$20{,}000 - \$5{,}000}{5 \text{ yr}} = \$3{,}000/\text{yr}$$

Sum-of-digits method   If we wish to write off an asset fast, one method for calculating the depreciation in a given year is based on the ratio of a digit corresponding to that year and the sum of the digits corresponding to all the years in the asset's life. The digit in the numerator is N for the first year and decreases by 1 for each successive year. The sum of the digits is $1 + 2 + \cdots + N$. These ratios are applied to the amount to be depreciated equal to the initial investment less its salvage value. Thus, we have

first year:
$$AD_1 = \frac{N}{1 + 2 + \cdots + N} (P - S)$$

second year:
$$AD_2 = \frac{N - 1}{1 + 2 + \cdots + N} (P - S)$$

$$\vdots$$

nth year:
$$AD_n = \frac{1}{1 + 2 + \cdots + N} (P - S)$$

For our example the calculations are shown in Table B-1.

Declining-balance method   Another approach that allows rapid early depreciation is the declining-balance method. In this case the depreciation in each year is a fixed percentage of the asset's current book value, defined as the difference between the initial investment and the cumulative depreciation. The fixed percentage is selected arbitrarily, but it cannot exceed a value that will result in annual depreciation greater than double the amount computed by the straight-line method. It is applied initially to the original investment and then successively to the asset's book value except for the last year, in which it cannot reduce the asset's book value below its salvage value. In Table B-1 this method is illustrated using a fixed percentage equal to 25 percent. Whenever this percentage is set equal to $2(1/N)(100)$ percent, i.e., double the straight-line percentage, the method is known as the *double-declining-balance method*.

Methods providing for a fast write-off of an asset are often preferred because, as stated earlier, they offer greater protection against early obsolescence and allow larger early cash flows due to reduced taxes. Such advantages, however, must be assessed within the broader financial policies of the firm. Thus it might be preferred to have larger cash flows postponed to compensate for declining revenues from existing product. The objective is optimum cash-flow management for all investments in the long run.

For certain cases, it may be more realistic to use a depreciation method geared to the extent of use of a given asset. Suppose the asset in our example refers to a fork-lift truck expected to run satisfactorily for 30,000 mi. If in the first year it is used for 12,000 mi, the corresponding depreciation would be $(12,000/30,000) \times (\$20,000 - \$5,000) = \$6,000$, and so on.

Effects of Different Time Perspectives

How attractive an alternative is may depend on whether it is viewed in a short-term or long-term perspective. Certain decisions that appear profitable in the short run may appear less profitable when the planning horizon stretches farther into the future. For example, laying off part of the work force due to declining demand might seem advisable when looking 2 or 3 months ahead, but if this change in demand is part of an annual seasonal cycle, it might be less costly to avoid layoffs and build up inventories during the slow periods, so that there will be no need to hire workers back when the busy season begins again.

Another important aspect of time is its effect on the true value of costs and revenues occurring at different points during the projected life of an investment. We all know that $1,000 today is worth more than the same amount 1 year later. The time value of money plays an important role in evaluating alternatives with different streams of costs and revenues. How they are converted to equivalent amounts that can be compared is discussed later. Nevertheless, under the pressure of time, managers may avoid such adjustments, especially in a preliminary analysis of the alternatives under study. One approach allowing such simplification is break-even analysis.

B-3 BREAK-EVEN ANALYSIS

General

Managers must often evaluate alternatives on proposed products, processes, or facilities under considerable time pressure and with limited relevant information. Given estimates on fixed and variable costs and on price per unit of output, one can determine the profitability of each alternative using break-even analysis. By ignoring future uncertainty and the time value of money break-even analysis quickly and inexpensively provides valuable information about the effect on profits from changes in sales and output volume.

Break-even analysis is more than determining the *break-even point*, i.e., the output volume at which total revenue equals total cost. It is a simple and versatile tool for expressing the relationships between total cost or total revenue and output volume, i.e., for different degrees of capacity utilization.

Construction of a Simple Break-Even Chart

An example of a simple break-even chart is shown in Fig. B-1. The horizontal axis shows the output volume measured in physical units of output or as a percentage of the capacity utilization for the facility or process used. The vertical axis measures

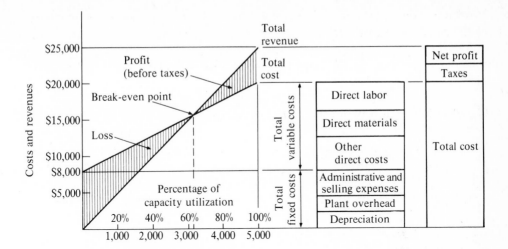

Fig. B-1   A break-even chart.

costs and revenues at different output volumes. More specifically, there is a horizontal line for fixed costs equal to $8,000 per period, say a month, covering cost items that do not vary with output volume (salaries, depreciation, insurance payments, rents, etc.). Assuming a fixed variable cost per unit for direct labor, materials, and other items traceable to each unit of output, we have a total variable cost that varies proportionally with output volume (see Fig. B-1). If the variable cost is $2.40 per unit, the total variable cost at full capacity utilization will be $(5,000) \times (\$2.40) = \$12,000$. The total cost at this output volume is $8,000 + \$12,000 = \$20,000$. If the price per unit is $5, the total revenue from sales will be $(\$5)(5,000) = \$25,000$, resulting in a total profit of $25,000 - \$20,000 = \$5,000$ per month. Similar calculations can be made for different output volumes using the following relationships:

$$\text{Profit (or loss)} = \text{total revenue} - \text{total cost}$$

$$= \begin{bmatrix} \text{Unit} \\ \text{price} \end{bmatrix} \begin{bmatrix} \text{output} \\ \text{volume} \end{bmatrix} - \left(\begin{bmatrix} \text{total} \\ \text{fixed cost} \end{bmatrix} + \begin{bmatrix} \text{total} \\ \text{variable cost} \end{bmatrix} \right)$$

$$= \begin{bmatrix} \text{unit} \\ \text{price} \end{bmatrix} \begin{bmatrix} \text{output} \\ \text{volume} \end{bmatrix} - \left(\begin{bmatrix} \text{total} \\ \text{fixed cost} \end{bmatrix} + \begin{bmatrix} \text{unit} \\ \text{variable cost} \end{bmatrix} \begin{bmatrix} \text{output} \\ \text{volume} \end{bmatrix} \right)$$

At the break-even point profit is zero, i.e., total revenue equals total cost. Therefore,

$$\begin{bmatrix} \text{Unit} \\ \text{price} \end{bmatrix} \begin{bmatrix} \text{break-even} \\ \text{output volume} \end{bmatrix} = \begin{bmatrix} \text{total} \\ \text{fixed cost} \end{bmatrix} + \begin{bmatrix} \text{unit} \\ \text{variable cost} \end{bmatrix} \begin{bmatrix} \text{break-even} \\ \text{output volume} \end{bmatrix}$$

Rearranging terms, we have

$$\left(\begin{bmatrix} \text{Unit} \\ \text{price} \end{bmatrix} - \begin{bmatrix} \text{unit} \\ \text{variable cost} \end{bmatrix} \right) \begin{bmatrix} \text{break-even} \\ \text{output volume} \end{bmatrix} = \begin{bmatrix} \text{total} \\ \text{fixed cost} \end{bmatrix}$$

Thus,

$$\begin{bmatrix} \text{Break-even} \\ \text{output volume} \end{bmatrix} = \frac{\text{total fixed cost}}{\text{unit price} - \text{unit variable cost}} \qquad \text{(B-2)}$$

The difference between the unit price and unit variable cost is called the *contribution per unit of output*. This is an important economic concept whose usefulness extends beyond break-even analysis. In the above context, the contribution per unit is the amount of revenue per unit sold that goes to cover fixed costs. Thus, an alternative interpretation of the break-even point is that level of output at which the revenue from units sold is just enough to cover total fixed cost in addition to the total variable costs. If excess capacity is available in a facility, any contribution from additional orders is better than none. Alternatively, for systems operating at full capacity, the contribution-per-unit concept can be used to select the most profitable use of limited resources by starting with activities for which the contribution per unit of resource is the highest (for additional details see Ref. 2).

The data needed to construct a break-even chart can be found by careful analysis of a single income and expense statement from a representative operating period. This method, known as the *classification approach*, requires considerable judgment in classifying costs as fixed or variable and in decomposing certain cost items, such as telephone service bills, into fixed and variable components. An alternative method, known as the *historical approach*, uses statistical regression analysis on the data from a series of income and expense statements covering periods with different output levels (Ref. 2).

Break-Even Analysis

Management can use break-even charts to answer several questions beyond the determination of the break-even volume. Typical examples include the following:

What is the effect on profits from different pricing policies? Assuming that fixed and unit variable costs remain the same, this question can be answered by plotting total revenue lines (or curves) corresponding to each price level and determining the corresponding break-even points and revised profits at the output level expected at each price.

What is the effect of changing to a new process or larger plant size assuming price remains the same? A switch to a more advanced technology or larger plant size requires higher fixed costs as a trade-off for lower unit variable costs. This in turn shifts the position of the total cost curve and yields a different, usually higher, break-even point. However, at higher output volumes, it results in greater total profits. This was the intent for many commercial airlines[1] in switching from conventional to jumbo jets in the early 1970s.

---

[1] For airlines the term used for break-even point is *break-even load factor*, describing the percentage of occupied seats in a plane for which total revenue covers total cost.

What is the effect of reducing unit variable costs for a given plant size through reductions in direct labor, materials use, scrap losses, and the like? Many programs aimed at raising productivity help decrease unit variable costs. Their impact can be evaluated using break-even analysis.

What should the output volume be for the firm to achieve desired profit objectives per period? Given the cost and price data indicated in the example, this calls for producing enough for the total contribution from units sold to be sufficient to cover fixed costs plus the desired profit

$$\begin{bmatrix} \text{Output volume for} \\ \text{desired profit target} \end{bmatrix} = \frac{\text{total fixed cost} + \text{desired profit}}{\text{unit price} - \text{unit variable cost}}. \tag{B-3}$$

All the above questions and more (see Ref. 4) can be answered by working with a set of basic relationships that can be manipulated to provide the desired answer.

Let V = output volume
  BEP = break-even output volume
  p = unit price
  c = unit variable cost
  TFC = total fixed cost
  TVC = total variable cost
  TC = total cost
  TR = total revenue

Then, for any output volume

$$\text{Total revenue TR} = pV$$
$$\text{Total variable cost TVC} = cV$$
$$\text{Total cost at break-even volume TC} = \text{TFC} + \text{TVC}$$
$$\text{TR} = \text{TC} = \text{TFC} + c\text{BEP}$$

and   Break-even output volume $\text{BEP} = \dfrac{\text{TFC}}{p - c}$

Assumptions and Limitations of Break-Even Analysis

Despite the ease and versatility of break-even analysis, its proper use requires familiarity with its assumptions and caution with its limitations. Our discussion so far has been based on linear relationships for the cost and revenue relationships. Assuming a constant price p, regardless of output volume, implies a market of pure competition.[1] Therefore, this assumption would not be correct in a market where price depends on the supply available. Similarly, the constant unit variable cost implies that there are no economies of scale realized from greater productivity at high output volume or discounts available when using large quantities of required inputs. When these assumptions are seriously violated, it is advisable to use nonlinear revenue and cost curves plotted from available data.

---

[1] A market of pure competition means that the price is not controlled by the firm, which may sell all it can within its capacity at the going rate. The price-versus-demand curve for this case is a horizontal line.

Among the most serious limitations of break-even analysis are the exclusion of taxes from consideration, the difficulties arising when the output includes multiple products[1] or services, and the inaccuracies in the estimates for costs due to errors in the data themselves or the methods of using them. As long as these limitations are recognized and adequately corrected for, break-even analysis can be extremely helpful in the economic analysis for many decisions.

B-4   ADJUSTMENTS FOR THE TIME VALUE OF MONEY

We stated earlier that an amount of $1,000 today is worth more a year later because it can be invested to earn interest. Recognizing the time value of money enables us to convert the stream of costs and revenues occurring at different points in the life of an investment so that we can compare it with competing investments having different patterns of receipts and expenditures. The result of such a conversion is known as a *discounted cash flow*.

Adjustments of costs and revenues to reduce them to an equivalent basis take the form of either compounding or discounting. *Compounding* refers to the process of determining the future value F that would be equivalent to a specified amount at the present time P. For example, the future worth of $1,000 borrowed today at 12 percent interest rate will include the principal plus the interest earned

first year:
$$F = P + Pi = P(1 + i)$$
$$= \$1,000 + (\$1,000)(.12) = (\$1,000)(1.12) = \$1,120$$

second year:
$$F = P(1 + i) + P(1 + i)i = P(1 + i)^2$$
$$= (\$1,000)(1.12)^2 = \$1,254.40$$

Nth year:
$$F = P(1 + i)^N$$
$$= (\$1,000)(1.12)^N$$

Discounting refers to the process of determining the present worth, i.e., the value now, of a specified future sum. The present worth P of a future sum F is found from the previous equation by solving for P

$$P = \frac{1}{(1 + i)^N} F$$

Thus, the present value of $1,210 at the end of 2 years from now at 10 percent interest rate will be

$$P = \frac{1}{(1 + .10)^2} (\$1,210) = \$1,000$$

---

[1] A break-even chart can be used for two or more products if they are produced in the same fixed proportions as parts of the total output.

Compounding or discounting may apply to single amounts, as indicated above, or to a series of equal amounts A that are assumed to occur at the end of each interest period for a specified time interval. The series of equal payments are referred to as *annuities*. Interest calculations for time-value adjustments are carried out with formulas appropriate for the desired conversion. The key elements needed to describe the pattern of costs and revenues for a proposed investment are defined as follows:

P = present value, referring to value of a single amount now
F = future value, referring to value of a single amount at specific time in the future
A = single annuity payment from a series of equal payments occurring at end of each interest period, starting with first
N = number of interest periods, years, months, or other time interval
i = interest rate, i.e., increase (or decrease) in value per interest period

Table B-2 summarizes six cases of compounding and discounting. In each case we specify three elements and solve for a fourth. The conversion is accomplished with an interest formula, usually abbreviated as an interest factor in which the first letter in parenthesis is the element we are solving for if values for the others are given.

The use of the interest formulas and factors in Table B-2 will be illustrated as follows assuming an interest rate of 9 percent. Values for interest factors are given in App. 6.

Question   If one borrows $5,000 at 9 percent interest compounded annually what will be the future value owed 3 years later?

Answer   For $P = \$5,000$, $i = 9$ percent, and $N = 3$

$$F = P(1 + i)^N = (5,000)(F/P, 9, 3)$$
$$= (5,000)(1.295) = \$5,475$$

Question   If the nominal value of a promissory note due at the end of 5 years is $14,500, what would be its present worth if the interest rate is 9 percent?

Answer   For $F = \$14,500$, $i = 9$ percent, and $N = 5$

$$P = F\frac{1}{(1 + i)^N} = (\$14,500)(P/F, 9, 5)$$
$$= 14,500(.6499) = \$9,423.55$$

Question   What is the future value of a series of six annual payments equal to $1,500 at the end of the sixth year from now?

Answer   For $A = \$1,500$, $i = 9$ percent, and $N = 6$

$$F = A(F/A, 9, 6) = (\$1,500)(7.523)$$
$$= \$11,284.50$$

TABLE B-2 Basic conversion types and interest formulas to include time value of money

Compounding	
Problem	Interest formula

Find the future value F
given the present value P

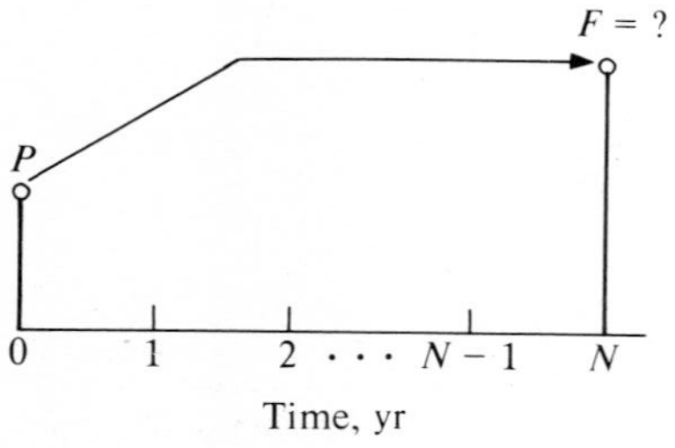

$F = P(1 + i)^N$

abbreviated as

$F = P(F/P, i, N)$
(compound-amount factor)

Time, yr

Discounting	
Problem	Interest formula

Find the present value P
given the future value of a
single amount F

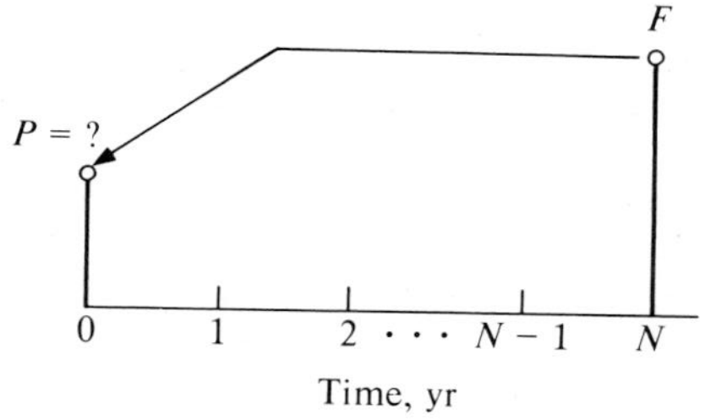

$P = F \dfrac{1}{(1 + i)^N}$

abbreviated as

$P = F(P/F, i, N)$
(present-worth factor)

Time, yr

Find the future value F given the amount of annuity payments A

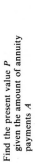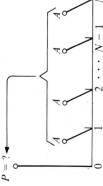

$$F = A\frac{(1+i)^N - 1}{i}$$

abbreviated as

$$F = A(F/A, i, N)$$
(compound-amount factor)

Time, yr

Find the value of annuity payments A given the present value P

$$A = P\frac{i(1+i)^N}{(1+i)^N - 1}$$

abbreviated as

$$A = P(A/P, i, N)$$
(capital-recovery factor)

Time, yr

Find the present value P given the amount of annuity payments A

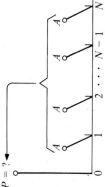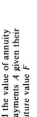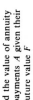

$$P = A\frac{(1+i)^N - 1}{i(1+i)^N}$$

abbreviated as

$$P = A(P/A, i, N)$$
(present-worth factor)

Time, yr

Find the value of annuity payments A given their future value F

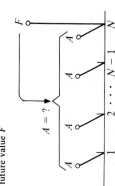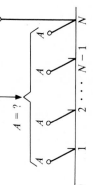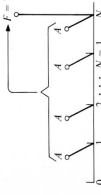

$$A = F\frac{i}{(1+i)^N - 1}$$

abbreviated as

$$A = F(A/F, i, N)$$
(sinking-fund factor)

Time, yr

B-5   METHODS FOR EVALUATING
CAPITAL INVESTMENTS

Management must periodically evaluate a variety of projects that compete for the limited capital available to the firm. These projects might be classified as cost-reducing or revenue-raising types, e.g.,

1. Proposals for new products or services or for discontinuing existing ones
2. Proposals for new facilities, new technologies, and new equipment or for shutting down old ones
3. Proposed replacements of existing equipment, processes, or facilities
4. Make or buy decisions
5. Make or lease decisions

The evaluation of capital investments usually proceeds in two phases (see Fig. B-2). First, for each proposed project there is a need to select the best of several alternatives. For example, the need to introduce a new product or service (project A) may be satisfied by one of several new designs. Similarly, the replacement of an old machine (project B) may be accomplished by one of several new machines. In the first phase, we must identify the best alternative for each project. This requires an evaluation of investments associated with the alternatives for each project using one or a combination of methods, such as payback period, present value, annual cost, or internal rate of return, discussed in the next section.

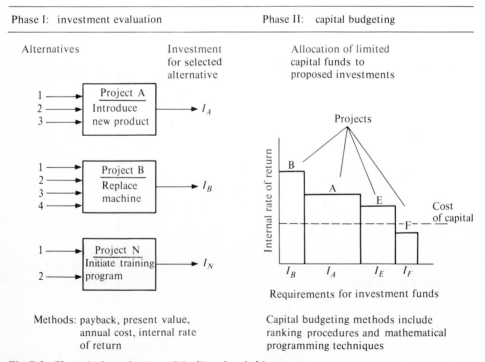

Fig. B-2   **Phases in the evaluation and funding of capital investments.**

In the second phase, each project and the investment required for the best alternative must be ranked so that management can allocate the limited capital funds available to the firm. This is the capital-budgeting problem, discussed in Sec. B-6.

The methods used in phase I, except for the payback period, rely on the analysis of discounted cash flows for each alternative. Each method offers certain advantages in certain types of applications and highlights different characteristics of the investments being evaluated. We start with the simplest, the payback method, and conclude with the internal rate of return, which is valuable not only for selecting the best alternative for each project but also for ranking investments that compete for limited capital funds.

Several aspects of proposed investments are usually fraught with uncertainty. The expected life of an asset, the assumed cost of capital, and the asset's salvage value at the end of its expected life are all subject to unpredictable changes due to technological, economic, or other environmental factors. Management should consider the potential effects of such uncontrollable changes when evaluating alternative investments by assessing their performance under various assumptions indicative of normal, favorable, and unfavorable developments. Such a sensitivity analysis helps establish whether the selected alternative is superior under general or rather restrictive assumptions about potential developments in its life cycle. Decision analysis and simulation represent two of the most powerful approaches for exploring the impact of uncertainty in such cases (see Supplementary Chapters A and D for details).

Payback-Period Method

One of the easiest methods of evaluating a proposed investment is to calculate the time it will take for net revenues to recover the initial outlay. Known as the *payback period*, this time is a measure of the speed with which the investment can be recovered for further reinvestment. Suppose, for example, that an investment of $16,000 now with zero salvage value will yield net annual revenue of $4,000 for the next 10 yr. Here we have

$$\text{Payback period} = \frac{\text{initial investment} - \text{salvage value}}{\text{net annual revenue}}$$

$$= \frac{\$16,000 - 0}{\$4,000} = 4.0 \text{ yr}$$

In words, the initial investment would be recovered from net earnings in 4.0 yr. Two drawbacks to this payback method seriously limit its appeal as the only basis for reaching a decision. (1) The method ignores the net earnings beyond the payback period, thus providing us with only part of the picture. In our example, the same initial investment for another alternative that yielded a net income of $6,000 for only 3 yr would be preferred for having a payback period of $16,000/6,000 = 2\frac{2}{3}$ yr even though its total earnings would amount to ($6,000) $\times$ (3 yr) = $18,000 compared with ($4,000)(10 yr) = $40,000 for the previous alternative. (2) The payback method ignores the time value of money, thus yielding an unrealistic measure of future earnings by failing to reduce them to an equivalent basis for all alternatives. Both these disadvantages are overcome in the methods described below, which depend on equivalent discounted cash flows.

Net-Present-Value Method

For project alternatives with an equal productive life the best method for evaluating investments is the present-value method. For each alternative the earnings (= revenues − costs) occurring at different times are discounted to the present with an interest rate equal to the cost of capital and compared with the initial investment. A measure of profitability is the amount by which the present worth of future earnings exceeds the initial cost. This difference is known as the *net present value*. Thus, we select the alternative which has the maximum net present value. For some evaluations, such as replacement studies, in which only costs are considered, the method selects the alternative with the minimum present worth of initial and future disbursements.

The major drawback in evaluating investments on the basis of their present value is the difficulty in comprehending the rather large numbers in today's dollars associated with the discounted cash flow for each alternative.

▶ EXAMPLE B-1

The management of Fine Liqueur Co. is considering which type of labeling machine to purchase for the bottling line of its new plant. Three machines that qualify in terms of capacity requirements differ in the pattern of initial and future operating costs due to varying degrees of mechanization and maintenance characteristics. The relevant data are summarized in Table B-3.

To determine the present value of each alternative management must discount the stream of costs for each machine using an interest rate of 12 percent, equal to the cost of capital that will be required.

TABLE B-3 Cost data for proposed labeling-machine alternatives

	Alternative		
Characteristic	A	B	C
Initial cost	$83,000	$87,000	$105,000
Estimate life, yr	5	5	5
Operating costs:			
Year 1	$ 8,500	$ 6,600	$ 5,000
Year 2	8,500	6,600	5,000
Year 3	10,000	6,600	5,000
Year 4	8,500	6,900	5,000
Year 5	8,500	7,200	5,000
Salvage value	9,000	10,000	12,500

Let P = initial cost

  N = estimated life of machine

  C_j = operating cost in year j ($j = 1, 2, ..., n$)

  S_N = salvage value of machine after N yr

   i = interest rate to be used equal to cost of capital

  PV = present value

Then for each alternative

$$PV = P + \left[\frac{1}{1+i} C_1 + \frac{1}{(1+i)^2} C_2 + \cdots + \frac{1}{(1+i)^5} C_5 \right] - \frac{1}{(1+i)^5} S$$

or

$$\begin{bmatrix} \text{Net present} \\ \text{value} \end{bmatrix} = \begin{bmatrix} \text{initial} \\ \text{cost} \end{bmatrix} + \begin{bmatrix} \text{sum of discounted value of all} \\ \text{annual operating costs} \end{bmatrix} - \begin{bmatrix} \text{discounted} \\ \text{salvage value} \end{bmatrix}$$

For a 12 percent cost of capital the interest factors are obtained from Appendix 6. For example, the calculations for alternative B in the example are

$$PV_B = \$87,000 + (.8929 + .7972 + .7118)(\$6,600) + (.6355)(\$6,900)$$
$$+ (.5674)(\$7,200) - (.5674)(\$10,000) = \$105,648.77$$

The results for all three alternatives are summarized in Table B-4.

Assuming that the labeling machines under study do not differ in any other respects, the management of Fine Liqueur Co. should select alternative B. With machine B the labeling operation in the bottling line will be performed at minimum cost.

When the alternatives considered differ in their expected lives, one approach might be to extend the evaluation over a planning period equal to the smallest common multiple for the life of all alternatives. Thus, if $N_A = 4$, $N_B = 6$, and $N_C = 12$ yr, we would use a planning period of 12 yr that would require the use of three machines of type A, two of type B, and one type of C with their respective

TABLE B-4 Present-value calculations for proposed labeling-machine alternatives

Characteristic	Interest factor $(P/F, 12, 5)$	Alternative A	B	C
Initial cost	1.000	$83,000	$87,000	$105,000
Operating cost:				
Year 1	.8929	$7,589.65	$5,893.14	$4,464.50
Year 2	.7972	6,776.20	5,261.52	3,986.00
Year 3	.7118	7,118.00	4,697.88	3,559.00
Year 4	.6355	5,401.75	4,384.95	3,177.50
Year 5	.5674	4,822.90	4,085.28	2,837.00
Salvage value	.5674	− 5,106.60	− 5,674.00	− 7,092.50
Net present value		$109,601.90	$105,648.77	$115,931.50

cost patterns repeating for each machine as many times as it is replaced. The assumption of equivalent service and costs for each machine poses some difficulties because it ignores technological developments, inflation, and other potential ▶ changes (for further details see Ref. 4).

Equivalent-Annual-Cost Method

One way to get around the difficulty of understanding the merit of an investment based on net present value is the method of converting all revenues and costs into an equivalent annual figure. This approach is especially attractive for assets periodically renewed to provide a service needed on a continuous basis, e.g., the selection of refrigerated trucks for a dairy company or the selection of a copier for an office operation.

If we assume that the desired activity remains the same and that projected costs are not likely to change, the equivalent-annual-cost method can also handle the difficulty of comparing alternatives with different expected lives. The basic trade-offs considered in this case are between an asset of a longer life and a higher initial cost rather than the reverse.

▶ EXAMPLE B-2

The owner of Speedy Delivery Flower Shop is considering the purchase of additional delivery vans and has received bids from two manufacturers with the following information:

Characteristic	Delivery van	
	Make X	Make Y
Initial cost	$15,000	$12,000
Estimated life, yr	7	5
Annual operating cost	$ 1,600	$ 1,850
Salvage value	$ 4,000	$ 3,200

Assuming that both types of vans provide identical service and that the cost of capital is 10 percent, the calculation of an equivalent annual cost might proceed as follows:

1. The initial cost is converted into a series of annuities using a compounding factor

$$A_1 = P(A/P, i, N)$$

Thus, for alternative X

$$A_1 = (\$15,000)(A/P, 10, 7) = (\$15,000)(.20541) = \$3,081.15/\text{yr}$$

and for alternative Y

$$A_1 = (\$12,000)(A/P, 10, 5) = (\$12,000)(.26380) = \$3,165.60/\text{yr}$$

2. The salvage is converted into another series of annuities using a discounting factor

$$A_2 = S(A/F, i, N)$$

Thus, for alternative X

$$A_2 = (\$4,000)(A/F, 10, 7) = (\$4,000)(.10541) = \$421.64/\text{yr}$$

and for alternative Y

$$A_2 = (\$3,200)(A/F, 10, 5) = (\$3,200)(.16380) = \$524.16/\text{yr}$$

3. The equivalent annual cost for each alternative is determined by adding the first annuity from the initial cost to the annual operating cost and then subtracting the annuity from the salvage value

$$EAC = A_1 + C - A_2$$

Thus, for alternative X we have

$$EAC_X = \$3,081.15 + 1,600 - 421.64 = \$4,259.51/\text{yr}$$

for alternative Y

$$EAC_Y = \$3,165.60 + 1,850 - 524.16 = \$4,491.44/\text{yr}$$

From their EAC values the owner of Speedy Delivery Flower Shop should choose the delivery van from manufacturer X. The same result could be obtained by finding the present value for each alternative and then converting it into an equivalent annuity over the life of that alternative.

Internal-Rate-of-Return Method

During its lifetime an investment is expected to generate a stream of cash flows to recover the initial cost and earn a profit. How attractive an investment is can be measured by discounting such cash flows to the present at some interest rate and then comparing their sum to the initial cost. In the previous section we noted that if the sum of all future cash flows discounted at an interest rate equal to the cost of capital is greater than the initial cost the investment is a profitable one. An alternative index of profitability is the internal rate of return.

The *internal rate of return* (IRR) is the *interest rate which makes the sum of discounted future cash flows equal to the amount of the investment.* In a sense, the internal rate of return measures the annual gain from an investment as a percentage of the initial cost.

Before we proceed to calculate an internal rate of return we must determine exactly what is to be included in the expected future cash flows. For a profit to be possible, the revenue in each period must cover total operating costs and the depreciation, which reflects the loss of value in the asset. Thus, each year we have

Gross profit = revenue − (operating cost + depreciation)

However, the gross profit overestimates the true earnings from the asset because no adjustment is included for taxes, which for many firms is almost 50 percent of the gross profit. Therefore, we need to determine

$$\text{Net profit} = \text{gross profit} - \text{taxes}$$

Each year in the life of the asset the cash flow of interest includes not only the net profit after taxes but also the amount set aside as an expense to cover annual depreciation. Thus, we have

> Annual net cash flow = profit after taxes + depreciation

This relationship suggests once again the importance of writing off an asset rapidly in the early years to generate larger cash flows, which when discounted yield a higher present value. Figure B-3 shows a stream of annual net cash flows CF; resulting from an initial investment P with no salvage value ($S_N = 0$).

For an interest rate i smaller than the IRR the sum of the discounted cash flows will be larger than the initial cost, whereas for a value of i larger than IRR the sum will be smaller than the initial cost. For this reason, the value for IRR is usually determined by interpolation between two successive values of i which bracket the IRR. An initial approximation of i is determined from the following consideration. The IRR converts the initial cost of an asset into an equivalent annuity series for the life of the asset, so that each annuity payment A is sufficient to cover depreciation and a net profit on the investment. The interest formula that makes this conversion is known as a *capital-recovery* factor ($A/P, i, N$). Thus,

$$A = P(A/P, i, N) = P \frac{i(1 + i)^N}{(1 + i)^N - 1}$$

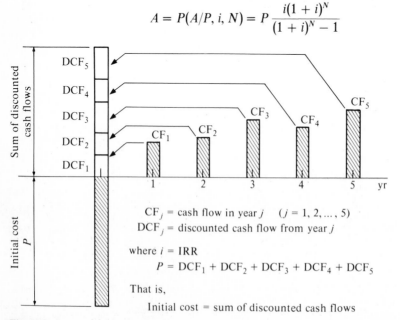

CF_j = cash flow in year j ($j = 1, 2, ..., 5$)
DCF_j = discounted cash flow from year j
where i = IRR
$$P = DCF_1 + DCF_2 + DCF_3 + DCF_4 + DCF_5$$
That is,
Initial cost = sum of discounted cash flows

Fig. B-3   Determination of internal rate of return.

or

$$\begin{bmatrix} \text{Annual net} \\ \text{cash flow} \end{bmatrix} = \begin{bmatrix} \text{initial} \\ \text{cost} \end{bmatrix} \begin{bmatrix} \text{capital-recovery} \\ \text{factor using IRR} \end{bmatrix}$$

To illustrate this, suppose an investment of \$22,000 results in an annual net cash flow of \$6,000 for 5 yr. The internal rate of return will be interpolated from values for the interest rate that yields a capital-recovery factor value for $N = 5$ equal to

$$(A/P, i, N) = \frac{\text{annual cash flow}}{\text{initial cost}} = \frac{\$6,000}{\$22,000} = .27273$$

Inspection of the interest tables for capital-recovery factor values given $N = 5$ (see Appendix 6) suggests that for $i = 12$ percent the value of $(A/P, i, 5)$ is .27741, whereas for $i = 10$ percent the value of $(A/P, i, 5)$ is .26380. The value of i corresponding to the IRR that can be found by interpolation from the above values (see Fig. B-4) is a reasonable approximation.[1]

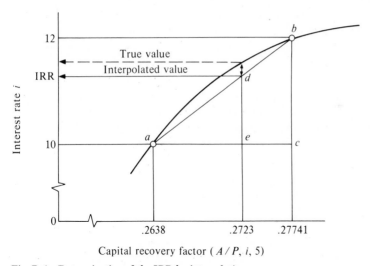

Fig. B-4   Determination of the IRR by interpolation.

In Fig. B-4 we note that from similar triangles we have

$$\frac{de}{bc} = \frac{ae}{ac}$$

or

$$\frac{\text{IRR} - 10}{12 - 10} = \frac{.27273 - .26380}{.27741 - .26380}$$

[1] The value of IRR obtained from interpolation is an approximation because it is assumed that the points a and b are connected with a straight line even though the factor $(A/P, i, N)$ is a power function with respect to i.

Thus
$$\text{IRR} = 10 + (12 - 10)\frac{.27273 - .26380}{.27741 - .26380}$$

$$= 10 + (2)\frac{.00893}{.01361}$$

$$= 10 + 1.31187 \approx 11.312\%$$

For an interest rate $i = 11.312$ percent equal to the IRR the sum of discounted cash flows of $6,000 for 5 yr will be equal to the initial investment of $22,000. By comparing the IRR with the cost of capital to finance the investment we can determine the net rate of return that measures how attractive the project is. Thus, if for this project the cost of capital is 9 percent, the net rate of return is $11.312 - 9.000 = 2.312$ percent. For a project to be profitable the internal rate of return must be greater than the cost of capital; otherwise it cannot cover the cost of capital resources needed to finance it.[1] An evaluation of alternative investments based on IRR is illustrated with the following example.

▶ EXAMPLE B-3

The manager of a firm providing duplicating services is considering the purchase of a new copier. After a preliminary analysis the choice has been narrowed to two models, A and B, whose cost characteristics are summarized in Table B-5. The expected annual revenue from either machine is estimated at $20,000, and taxes on this income will be at a rate of 50 percent. The cost of capital needed to finance this investment is assumed to be 10 percent. The manager wants to know whether the investment in either of these models is profitable and if so which one should be purchased. The firm uses a straight-line depreciation method.

TABLE B-5   Cost characteristics of copiers A and B†

Item	Model A	Model B
Initial cost	$40,000	$50,000
Operating cost (less depreciation):		
Year 1	6,000	4,000
Year 2	6,000	4,000
Year 3	6,000	4,000
Year 4	6,000	4,000
Year 5	6,000	4,000

† Both models have a salvage value equal to zero.

The annual cash flow from each alternative is estimated by calculating the net profit and adding the straight-line depreciation. Thus, we have, for model A

[1] For a more thorough discussion of the cost of capital and its determination see Ref. 2.

$$\text{Gross profit} = \text{revenue} - (\text{operating cost} + \text{depreciation})$$

$$= \$20,000 - \$6,000 + \frac{\$40,000 - 0}{5}$$

$$= \$20,000 - \$14,000 = \$6,000$$

$$\text{Net profit} = \text{gross profit} - \text{taxes at } 50\%$$

$$= \$6,000 - (.50)(\$6,000) = \$3,000$$

$$\text{Annual net cash flow} = \text{net profit} + \text{depreciation}$$

$$= \$3,000 + \$8,000 = \$11,000$$

For model B

$$\text{Gross profit} = \$20,000 - \$4,000 + \frac{\$50,000 - 0}{5}$$

$$= \$20,000 - \$14,000 = \$6,000$$

$$\text{Net profit} = \$6,000 - (.50)(6,000) = \$3,000$$

$$\text{Annual net cash flow} = \$3,000 + \$10,000 = \$13,000$$

The determination of IRR by interpolation would proceed as follows. For model A

$$(A/P, i, 5) = \frac{\$11,000}{\$40,000} = .27500$$

for $i = 12\%$: $(A/P, 12, 5) = .27741$

for $i = 10\%$: $(A/P, 10, 5) = .26380$

Thus,

$$\text{IRR}_A = 10 + (12 - 10)\frac{.27500 - .26380}{.27741 - .26380} = 10 + (12 - 10)(.8229) = 11.646\%$$

For model B,

$$(A/P, i, 5) = \frac{\$13,000}{\$50,000} = .26000$$

for $i = 10\%$: $(A/P, 10, 5) = .26380$

for $i = 8\%$: $(A/P, 8, 5) = .25046$

Thus,

$$\text{IRR}_B = 8 + (10 - 8)\frac{.26000 - .25046}{.26380 - .25046} = 8 + 1.43 = 9.43\%$$

On the basis of the IRR the firm must select copier A, with an internal rate of return of 11.646 percent. Since for copier B the internal rate of return is 9.43 percent, it does not even cover the cost of capital needed to finance this investment.

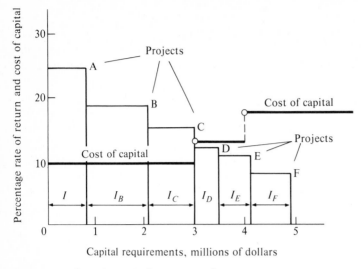

Fig. B-5   Ranking alternative investment projects.

B-6   CAPITAL BUDGETING

In the rather unusual situation where we have unlimited funds for investment the only requirement is that approved projects have a rate of return higher than the cost of capital needed to finance them. However, the more typical case is when several projects compete for the limited capital funds available to the firm. Whether such funds are available internally or can be secured from external source, there is a cost associated with their use. This cost of capital measured by the interest rate used may be fixed up to a certain volume of investments and then increase as the firm is forced to extend its credit by borrowing more from outside sources. Figure B-5 shows that the cost of capital (heavy horizontal lines) is 10 percent for funds up to $3 million. Beyond this limit, which might represent internally available capital, and up to $4 million the cost of capital jumps to 12 percent. For amounts beyond $4 million additional capital can be secured only at the higher cost of 18 percent, reflecting the increased risks assumed by borrowers or the tightness of funds in the money market.

The amounts of capital available to the firm for investment and the corresponding cost of capital at each investment level is known as a *capital inventory*. The allocation of these funds is a problem which must be examined in the framework of a firm's corporate strategy. In other words, the projects approved must be consistent with long-term objectives with regard to the type of products and services that enhance the strength of the firm, the markets that are most suitable for its long-term survival and growth, and the risks that are compatible with its current position and distinctive competence. Thus, the projects evaluated in phase I before proceeding to phase II for capital rationing must be screened to ensure that they serve the objectives of corporate strategy as formulated by top management.

In order to select which projects will be funded, the required investments are ranked, starting with the one yielding the highest rate of return. In Fig. B-5 projects A, B, and C have rates of return higher than the 10 percent cost of capital in the range of $0 to $2.5 million. The jump in the cost of capital beyond $2.5 million disqualifies project D because its rate of return does not even cover the cost of capital required to finance it. The same holds for projects E and F, which are even less attractive due to another jump in the cost of capital that would be needed if they were approved.

One difficulty in ranking projects in the order of decreasing rate of return stems from ignoring the size of the investment involved in each case. At times it is preferable to select a project with a lower rate of return on a large investment than a higher one on a small investment. The rationale here is that the larger the base to which the rate of return applies the higher the total profit from a investment. One method of avoiding this dilemma is to rank projects on the basis of their net-present value.

Care should also be exercised in capital budgeting to identify possible linkages of certain investments. For example, approving a plant in a remote area may require additional future investments for road construction, power distribution, and other projects. Thus, capital-rationing procedures should avoid the pitfall of evaluating only partially proposed investment packages. Both the evaluation of individual investments and the capital-rationing decisions can be studied and analyzed with the aid of library computer programs available in most computer facilities. Some of them allow management to study the effect of uncertainty and conduct sensitivity analysis for changes in interest rates, project costs, and so on.

B-7 SUMMARY

Despite complications due to future uncertainty, intangible factors, etc., most managerial decisions, especially in operations management, require sound economic analysis. This is true for repetitive decisions such as machine replacements or inventory control, as well as for strategic decisions about new products or services, new facilities, and others.

For both public and private organizations, economic analysis requires a clear understanding of relevant costs. For this reason we have included a detailed cost classification covering direct and indirect costs, fixed and variable costs, incremental and opportunity costs, sunk costs, and depreciation. Two fairly common approaches in economic analysis are based on incremental costs, i.e., costs affected by a given decision, or on full economic costs, making use of the concept of opportunity costs.

Another important concept in economic analysis is the time value of money. This means that an amount of money today is worth more at some time in the future and vice versa. It is therefore necessary to adjust the stream of revenues and costs for each investment under study so that all alternatives can be compared on an equivalent basis. The appropriate adjustments take the form of *discounting*, a process for assessing the present value of future amounts, or *compounding*, which does the reverse. Both adjustments are based on an assumed *interest rate* which reflects the cost of capital needed to finance a proposed investment.

One of the simplest yet most versatile tools for evaluating economic decisions is the *break-even chart*. For a given facility this chart shows how revenue, costs, and profits change with output volume or capacity utilization in each period. The break-even chart for an on-going plant can be used to answer questions about the effect(s) of changing prices, accepting a new order, improving productivity, etc. It can also be used to evaluate proposed new facilities in terms of their impact on production costs, marketing strategy, and financial planning. Despite the difficulties associated with cost and market assumptions, data collection, and ignoring the time value of money, the break-even chart can help illuminate the relationships of the above factors.

In the course of running any organization, management must evaluate numerous projects requiring sizable investments. The first screening involves the selection of projects that genuinely serve the objectives of corporate strategy, in terms of new products and services, new technologies, new facilities, and new markets. For projects judged to be consistent with corporate strategy, the next phase involves an evaluation of the alternatives for each project. At this point the evaluation might be based on payback period, net present value, equivalent annual cost, or internal rate of return. The particular choice depends on the characteristics of the proposed investment and managerial preferences and tradition.

Once the best alternative for each project has been identified, it is necessary to allocate available capital to the different competing projects. This is the problem of *capital budgeting*. It involves ranking proposed investments on the basis of their rate of return or, preferably, their net-present value. Starting from the top, projects are approved with funds from the *capital inventory*, which shows the amount of capital available at progressively higher cost to the organization, until all capital has been allocated. As a minimum requirement for project approval its rate of return must at least equal the cost of capital needed to finance the investment. Care must be exercised to account for project interdependencies, if they exist, and to consider the effect of uncertainty about an investment's economic life, the cost of capital, and market developments.

REVIEW QUESTIONS

1. Which complicating factors are generally omitted from traditional economic analysis?
2. Discuss the difference(s) between the following and give an example for each:
   (*a*) Direct versus indirect costs
   (*b*) Fixed versus variable costs
   (*c*) Out-of-pocket versus opportunity costs
   (*d*) Incremental versus marginal costs
3. Discuss the meaning of sunk costs and their treatment when evaluating alternatives.
4. What is the purpose of depreciation and its effect in evaluating alternative investments?
5. What is the significance of an asset's economic life?
6. Describe the characteristics of the following depreciation methods:
   (*a*) Straight-line
   (*b*) Sum-of-the-years
   (*c*) Declining-balance

7. How does the analysis time frame affect study results?
8. Discuss the information needed for constructing a break-even chart and the information provided by the chart.
9. What types of problems can be analyzed using break-even analysis?
10. State the assumptions behind the type of break-even analysis discussed in this chapter.
11. Describe the two basic conversions employed to adjust cash flows for the time value of money.
12. Discuss the purpose in each phase of evaluating and funding of proposed investments.
13. Discuss the conditions under which it would be most appropriate to evaluate alternative investments using:
    (*a*) The payback method
    (*b*) The net-present-value method
    (*c*) The equivalent-annual-cost method
    (*d*) The internal-rate-of-return method
14. Describe alternative methods for allocating limited capital to competing projects.

PROBLEMS

1. The manager of a duplicating services firm bought a copier with an initial cost of $30,000 and an economic life of 5 yr. The estimated salvage value after 5 yr is equal to $5,000. Determine the asset's annual depreciation and book value using.
   (*a*) The straight-line method
   (*b*) The sum-of-years method
   (*c*) The declining-balance method using fixed percentage of 18 percent
2. Refer to Prob. 1. Suppose the copier purchased is expected to need replacement after running 900,000 copies. The projected use of the machine is as shown below:

Year	1	2	3	4	5
Projected no. of copies	250,000	200,000	180,000	150,000	120,000

Determine the book value and annual depreciation of the copier based on use.
3. The success of current avant-garde magazines has led to a feasibility study for a new magazine to be called *Play Person*. It will be aimed at both male and female readers and will be a monthly magazine for all adults. The success of the proposed venture will depend on the size of future circulation. The data collected for a facility with a monthly capacity of 1 million copies are as follows:

$$\text{Fixed monthly costs (salaries, rents, depreciation, etc.)} = \$300,000$$
$$\text{Variable unit cost per copy} = \$.80$$
$$\text{Selling price per copy} = \$2.00$$

   (*a*) What is the unit contribution for this product?
   (*b*) Plot a break-even chart and identify the break-even point.
   (*c*) Determine the monthly circulation needed for *Play Person* to break even.
   (*d*) What is the loss or total profit before taxes for a monthly circulation of (i) 300,000 (ii) 800,000, and (iii) 1 million copies?

4. Refer to Prob. 3. Determine the revised break-even circulation if:
   (a) The fixed monthly costs are increased to $500,000.
   (b) The unit variable cost, due to inflation, increases to $1.20 per copy.
   (c) The selling price per copy is set at $2.50.
5. Refer to Prob. 3. Determine the circulation necessary to have a monthly profit before taxes equal to $100,000 (a) under the initial conditions and (b) under the revised conditions as stated in part (c) of Prob. 4.
6. After the Hometown basketball team won the world championship, a local manufacturer decided to introduce a beer mug with the team's insignia combined with "We're no. 1" to commemorate the occasion. This was to be sold at $4 per unit. The cost estimates obtained for the project were as follows:

Production volume	Unit variable cost	Total fixed costs
0–10,000	$1.80	$12,000
10,001–15,000	2.00	15,000
15,001–18,000	2.40	20,000

(a) Prepare a break-even chart showing the total cost and revenue in the above production volume ranges.
(b) Determine the break-even point at the initial price and the unit contribution at each production range.
(c) Calculate the profit before taxes or loss, if sales reach (i) 9,000, (ii) 12,500, and (iii) 17,000 mugs.
(d) How many mugs will the manufacturer have to sell in order for his profits before taxes to equal (i) $10,000 and (ii) $20,000?
(e) How many mugs must be sold to maximize total profits before taxes?
7. Refer to Prob. 6. Prepare a break-even chart and determine the break-even point if the unit price is (a) $3 and (b) $5.
   (c) Calculate the production volume that will result in maximum profits for a unit price of $3 and $5.
8. Charlotte De Main, the manager of Orange City's civic auditorium, is considering modernizing the theater's air-conditioning system. Following the announcement of desired technical specifications she has received proposals with the following alternatives:

Alternative	Initial cost	Economic life, yr	Salvage value	Annual operating cost
A	$750,000	10	$50,000	$11,000
B	480,000	10	35,000	25,000
C	600,000	10	40,000	15,000

Assuming that the above systems are equivalent in other respects, determine which alternative should be selected using an interest rate of 9 percent, on the basis of (*a*) present value and (*b*) equivalent annual cost.

9. The management of Elsie Dairy Co. is considering the overhaul or replacement of its refrigerated 5-ton truck with a new one of equal capacity. The book value of the truck is shown to be $18,000, but its market value, if sold in its current condition, is only $8,000. The needed overhaul will cost an estimated $12,000 and extend the truck's life for another 6 years. The data for the present and two new trucks with similar characteristics are as follows:

	Initial cost	Economic life, yr	Annual operating cost	Salvage value
Present truck	See above	6	$10,000	$2,000
New truck model A	$42,000	12	8,000	3,000
New truck model B	50,000	12	7,000	5,000

Assuming the service provided by each delivery truck to be the same and the cost of capital for Elsie Dairy Co. to be 15 percent, determine the best alternative.

10. The International Conglomerate Co. (ICC) has completed a feasibility study for the location of a new solar heater plant in one of three locations A, B, and C. The financial data for each location are summarized below.

Plant location	Initial cost (000)	Economic life, yr	Annual revenue (000)	Annual operating cost (less depreciation) (000)	Salvage values (000)
A	$2,700	12	$1,600	$700	$500
B	3,500	12	1,600	600	700
C	4,200	12	1,600	500	800

Profits at each location will be taxed at 50 percent, and the cost of capital for ICC is 12 percent. Determine where the company should build its food-processing plant if subjective, or intangible, factors are the same for all locations.

11. The president of Executive Consultants, Ltd., has completed the study of an internal report which suggests that travel expenses for the company are becoming a major cost and that the company might consider operating its own aircraft, which could be purchased outright or rented from a local firm. If an aircraft is purchased, it will cost an initial $500,000 to acquire, it will have an annual fixed cost of $20,000 for insurance, hangar rental, etc., and an operating cost of $1.25 per mile flown. Its economic life is expected to be 10 yr and its salvage value will be $80,000. A rental will cost the company $60,000 per year and the same operating cost per mile. If the average number of miles logged annually is estimated to be equal to 135,000, which alternative would be most attractive to the consulting firm?

12. Refer to Prob. 3. (This requires familiarity with the contents of Supplementary Chapter A on decision analysis.) From a preliminary survey the circulation potential of *Play Person* has been estimated as follows:

Monthly circulation level	Probability
500,000–700,000	.20
700,000–800,000	.40
800,000–900,000	.30
900,000–1,000,000	.10

From the information provided by the break-even chart and the above probability distribution of demand, calculate the monthly expected profit for the proposed publication.

SELECTED REFERENCES

1. Brigham, Eugene, and James Pappas: *Managerial Economics*, 2d ed., Dryden, Hinsdale, Ill., 1976.
2. Henri, W. R., and W.W. Hayes: *Managerial Economics*, 4th ed., Irwin, Homewood, Ill., 1978.
3. McGuigan, James R., and R. Charles Moyer: *Managerial Economics*, Dryden, Hinsdale, Ill., 1975.
4. Riggs, James L.: *Engineering Economics*, McGraw-Hill, New York, 1977.
5. Spencer, Milton H., K. K. Seo, and Mark G. Simkin: *Managerial Economics: Text, Problems, and Short Cases*, Irwin, Homewood, Ill., 1975.

Part Two

OPERATIONS
SYSTEM DESIGN

Part 2 is addressed to the strategic level decisions that are strongly affected by and have an effect upon operations management. These are decisions that commit large amounts of resources for long periods of time and are difficult to change in the short run. These decisions help define an organization's distinctive competence and display the more lasting interactions with and impacts to its environment.

Chapter 4 discusses the design of products and services offered to serve human needs and to advance an organization towards its objectives. Chapter 5 presents the methods for the determination of needed productive capacity for manufacturing systems, while Chap. 6 extends this discussion to the area of service systems. Chapter 7 examines the approach usually taken in designing a production process in terms of transformation stages, basic process types, and the elements of both. Chapter 8 focuses on man-machine systems and examines various approaches for the analysis and design of jobs and the measurement of work.

Chapter 9 discusses the issues faced in determining a layout for a facility. Chapter 10 considers the problems arising from and the methods used for determining the location of such a facility. Also included in Part 2 are Supplementary Chaps. C, D, and E which focus on linear programming (simplex and transportation methods) and simulation as general decision-making tools.

Chapter 4

WHAT TO PRODUCE? THE DESIGN OF PRODUCTS AND SERVICES

4-1   INTRODUCTION

Human needs often represent a powerful stimulus for new products and services. Combined with organizational objectives of survival and growth in the private sector, such needs initiate a chain of activities that culminates in the creation of new or improved products and services. Social needs not covered adequately by the private sector become an equally strong stimulus for new programs and services in the public sector.

Operations management, as noted previously, is responsible for the smooth and economic function of an existing productive system, the development of a new one, and at times its termination when there is no longer a need for its output. The required decisions are affected by the stage in the life cycle of a product. Both productive systems and their outputs can be described by a life cycle comparable to that of a living organism.

Life Cycle of a Product or Service

The phases in the life cycle of a product or service are shown in Fig. 4-1. As with living beings, after a product is introduced, it goes through an *infancy* stage, characterized by the presence of many risks and a high mortality rate. The numerous failures of new products are related to unforeseen product weaknesses, market conditions, or other factors beyond management's control. Demand growth in this phase is slow and can be attributed to the group of consumers willing to experiment with an unproved item.

For a new product or service that survives the infancy diseases there follows a period of rapid demand *growth*. Acceptance is now gained among wider segments of the market, through wider recognition of a need being satisfied more effectively or more economically. High rates of increase in demand often create strong pressures for additional capacity, for changing production technology, for more efficient distribution and service, and at times for important adjustments in managerial style. The importance of an accurate demand forecast in this phase is crucial.

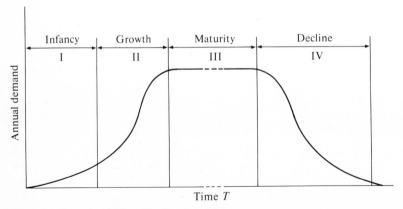

Fig. 4-1   **Phases in the life cycle of a new product.**

Undue optimism may result in unwarranted heavy investments for a scale of operation that may not materialize. The resulting high production costs per unit diminish the firm's ability to compete and create a lack of funds elsewhere. Similarly, excessive pessimism may prevent an organization from taking advantage of market opportunities and establishing a strong market position.

Once demand reaches a saturation level, a product has entered the phase of *maturity*. At this stage, the demand is related to replacements and population growth. With the market reasonably well defined there is enough profit to justify the productive resources allocated regularly to this item. Products that satisfy genuine needs remain in the maturity phase for long times. Food items, soap, books, and TV sets are just a few examples. Items directed at satisfying psychological wants, however, have a rather ephemeral existence. This may be the case with fashionable clothing, interior-decorating items, movies, hit records, and others.

After a time in the maturity phase, a product may enter a phase of *decline*. The introduction of new improved substitutes, changes in technology, changes in the economy, or other considerations bring about a drop in demand until it is no longer economical to produce the item. The introduction of pocket calculators made slide rules and desk calculators obsolete. Color TV sets replaced black and white ones by covering the same need better. The jet airplane made travel by ship less attractive and more expensive. The increasing cost of energy is making people switch to smaller, more fuel-efficient automobiles. Producing and marketing a product must be changed in each phase to achieve an optimum utilization of capacity for existing market conditions.

Phasing In New Products or Services

For an on-going concern, as current products approach the decline phase, management must be prepared to phase in new products. Otherwise, declining demand results in poor utilization of available productive capacity, with potentially disastrous effects to the organization's financial health.

The uncertainty of the marketplace makes it difficult to anticipate with great accuracy the phasing in of new products or services. Ideally, new products must be introduced so that their infancy phase coincides with the end of the maturity phase for existing ones (see Fig. 4.2). This will allow freed capacity from the decline of demand for current products to be absorbed by the rapidly expanding market for the new ones so that the firm's productive capacity will be utilized without being disrupted by long-term fluctuations.

The development of new products or services requires not only the skill to anticipate market trends and new technologies but also the capability for timely use of internal or external R & D efforts. In the presence of strong competition and rapidly advancing technology the preparation time for introducing new products or services is increasingly reduced. For this reason a number of companies, for example in detergents or pocket calculators, attempt to manipulate the degree of decline or growth in their products through promotion and pricing policies. These are aimed at smoother transitions and faster market penetration to take advantage of acquired patents or take an early lead over competitors.

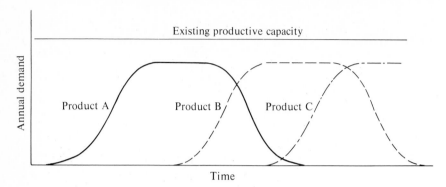

Fig. 4-2 **Phasing in new products for optimum capacity utilization.**

4-2 THE DISTINCTION BETWEEN PRODUCTS AND SERVICES

Products

We have often used "product" to include both physical goods and services. In a narrow sense, a product is defined by physical, chemical, or other attributes related in one entity that is easily recognizable. This interpretation allows an easy description of many items without paying attention to the many psychological attributes used in marketing to increase product appeal. In this sense, two small cars with the same physical and operating characteristics produced by Ford and General Motors would be examples of the same product.

In a broader interpretation the product description includes not only physical and operating characteristics, say size or power, but those psychological attributes which may affect the consumer, e.g., color, style, or packaging. Product differentiation is now possible in terms of subjective attributes designed to appeal to consumers, e.g., styling, method of retailing, and quality of service.

In the past, operations management has been mainly concerned with the more objective aspects of a product, while the psychological attributes have been considered the domain of marketing specialists. Since both types of product characteristics influence consumer choice, we must take into account both physical and psychological aspects in product design. In considering the purchase of furniture or a car, color, styling, and comfort become as important as functional characteristics. It is the combined effect of all such attributes that cover the purchaser's functional and psychological needs and project him as desired in his social environment.

Services

The distinction between a product and a service can be made on several points. A service refers to the satisfaction of human needs by facilitating certain procedures (legal defense, preparation of an income-tax statement), by caring for the maintenance and/or repair of living and nonliving systems (medical care, auto maintenance and repair, etc.), and by attendance to other needs for basics and luxuries (restaurants, cruises, etc.). Modern people also depend extensively on services relating to police and fire protection, education and entertainment, transportation, and many others.

Progress in the economic well-being of a society, as measured by income per capita, contributes to the release of free time and is coupled by increases in the standard of living. In the initial phase of such economic growth, people expend larger and larger shares of their disposable income on material things—more and better food and clothing, more comfortable houses, bigger cars, color TV sets, and stereo equipment. As consumers reach a point of saturation in the satisfaction of needs for material goods, they turn gradually to the enjoyment of more and more services, e.g., education, entertainment, or tourism.

According to Clark,[1] the economic development of a country goes through three stages. In the first, the emphasis is in the sector of *primary production*, agriculture, mining, forestry, fishing, etc. In the second stage, the emphasis shifts to the sector of *secondary production*, industry and crafts, designed to add value to the output of primary production, say food canning, metal processing, furniture making, and others. The third stage is characterized by increased activity in the sector of *tertiary production*, or profit-oriented and non-profit-oriented services (government at all levels, defense, transportation, education, communication, and others). Thus, as more and more countries develop economically, service-oriented systems assume an increasingly important role in satisfying the needs of their peoples.

The key differences between products and services can be summarized as follows:

1. Services are intimately related to the person(s) rendering them. Furthermore, they are consumed in the process of being offered (transportation by plane, medical care of a patient, etc.).
2. Services present unique distribution problems, because unlike physical products, they cannot be stored and they cannot be separated from those dispensing them. Furthermore, services are to a great extent perishable. The empty seats in an airplane flight, the unused beds in a hospital, and the idle periods of human resources and equipment all represent permanent losses.
3. Services, in general, do not lend themselves to extensive standardization, even though they are outputs of the same production system. The medical care offered by a doctor may vary in attention from patient to patient, and the same applies to service for the passengers on a plane, the customers of a car repair shop, and the students of a class. The lack of uniformity in output and defiance of standardization make it extremely difficult to enforce quality-control procedures as successfully as for products.
4. Services, like many products, display significant demand fluctuations on a seasonal, weekly, or daily basis. This calls for different approaches in the planning and control of production systems that are mainly service-oriented.

[1] C. Clark, *The Conditions of Economic Progress*, Macmillan, New York, 1957.

In practice, most operations systems offer well-integrated combinations of products and services. Systems designed for physical products, say cars or appliances, are supported by subsystems for needed services of delivery, maintenance, and repair. Similarly, most service-oriented systems require the use of numerous products and supplies, like x-ray plates for medical care or meals for airplane passengers.

4-3 CRITICAL FACTORS IN PRODUCT DESIGN

An integrative approach to product design requires the consideration of many factors with significant interactions. Most important among these are the following:

1. Materials and processing requirements
2. Determination of product specifications
3. Orientation toward modular design
4. The need for ease of use, ease of maintenance, and reliability

Converging on the most desirable values for the above factors is at best a trial-and-error process. After cycling through the various steps, successive approximations lead to the combination of product features that result in the most economical satisfaction of consumer needs. The central factor that affects most of the above decisions is the estimated level of demand. The most significant interactions are shown in Fig. 4-3.

Once specific decisions are made in product design, they determine the production cost per unit and set an upper limit to the firm's competitive position. Subsequent adjustments or improvements after the product reaches the market can

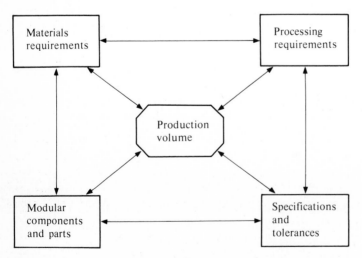

Fig. 4-3 Significant interactions between critical factors in product design.

only bring limited reductions in the production cost. Therefore, such decisions play a key role in the success of the particular product and the organization in general.

The above considerations are easier to handle in the design of services than in that of manufactured items. The design of a service is generally more flexible, requiring shorter periods for modifying various aspects of the service offered. Changes in capacity, working hours, degree of standardization, or procedures for handling customers have considerably shorter lead times and are much easier to implement in a service system than a factory.

Materials and Processing Requirements

The ability to choose among various materials to be used for a product or a service depends on the nature of the item, the available technology, and the advantages offered by certain widely available materials and parts. For some products, the range of choice is very limited or nonexistent. Thus, the designer of electronic equipment must use available transistors, while the x-ray laboratory can use only a given type of plates.

Usually, however, there is a wide choice of materials, and the selection proceeds in three stages. In the first stage attention is focused on what types of materials in the final product are most likely to appeal to the consumer. Since designers must satisfy not only functional but also psychological needs, they must consider properties beyond those relating to strength, durability, or weight. The color, texture, and other qualities of materials affect the appearance of the product and its packaging. At this point, designers need the cooperation of marketing in determining the type of consumer and market the product is addressed to. For a luxury car one is likely to select leather rather than vinyl seats but not for an economy compact. A fast-food chain may serve food in paper plates and cups and use plastic spoons or forks, but this would be out of the question in a restaurant for luxury dining.

In the second stage, having selected the most attractive materials that meet functional requirements, designers consider the various sources of supply. The objective here is to identify suppliers who offer competitive prices combined with reliability of service with regard to quality and delivery times. Management must sometimes allow for trade-offs between higher cost of materials and more reliable service from the chosen supplier.

In the third stage, selected materials are examined from the standpoint of processing cost. This calls for detailed knowledge of their properties (hardness, flexibility, etc.) and the capabilities of the production system to process them with available equipment. Steel or glass are expensive and difficult to process by machine. Wood or aluminum, however, are easier to process on various equipment.

The required processing depends on the desired tolerances. These in turn determine the precision in assembly and the quality and reliability of the product. Lenses for a Nikon camera require much closer tolerances than for a Kodak, and the same applies to automobile parts for a Porsche and a Volkswagen.

In the end, the difficult selection of materials is made in a way that achieves desired product characteristics at minimum cost for their purchase and processing.

Engineering Specification and Tolerances

Consumer satisfaction is achieved when the product or service meets certain expectations related to quality and performance. Specifications represent an ideal value for each one of the desired attributes and the degree of allowed deviations known as *tolerances*.

For manufactured products the general characteristics perceived by the consumer must be translated into engineering specifications for every part or subassembly, so that there will be no ambiguity about their processing at specific work stations. Product specifications may be very precise, like the engineering blueprints for a machined part or a formula for producing a petroleum product by an oil refinery. Thus, the specifications for a machine steel plate may be 2.540 $\pm$ 0.075 in, and a pollution-control device may not allow more than x parts per million of carbon dioxide in the air. However, specifications can be more general, as in the production of clay decorative vases for tourists, recipes for a restaurant, and so on.

Specifications for services tend to be more imprecise due to their strong dependence on human factors. The service time in a restaurant, at an airline counter, or at a commercial bank displays considerable variability from customer to customer because of their unique requirements, the pace of the server, the length of the waiting line, and so on. As a service becomes more and more standardized and people for certain operations are replaced by machines, there is a tendency for service output to become more uniform from customer to customer. Fast-food restaurants, medical laboratories, and push-button-operated bank facilities for obtaining cash on credit cards are just a few examples of services with specifications comparable in precision with manufactured products.

With advanced technologies one might expect that the values for critical product characteristics would remain the same from unit to unit. However, even though they may look the same, more detailed examination of successive units reveals variation in the dimensions of the same part or in the content of a given ingredient. As long as observed deviations from the ideal values are within specified tolerances, a product is expected to function properly; otherwise it is rejected.

Related to the tolerances for a given part, which specify the permissible variation in some critical dimension, is the *allowance*, which defines the maximum difference in the size of parts that fit together. If a motor shaft has a tolerance of 2.540 $\pm$ 0.075 in and is to fit a ball bearing whose inside diameter is 2.630 in, the allowance is $(2.630 - 2.540) - .075 = .090 - .075 = 0.015$ in.

The determination of tolerances and allowances in the development of specifications depends not only on the desired characteristics of a product but also on the capability of the production process. The latter is defined by the *natural process tolerance*, which measures the normal variation displayed by the process in successive measurements of some critical dimension, e.g., the weight of contents in a coffee can or the length of fabric or paper in a standard size roll. This concept is explored more fully in Chap. 16, where we discuss various procedures of evaluating whether or not actual output from a production system conforms to desired specifications.

Those responsible for formulating product specifications proceed in two phases.

In the first phase, key decisions are reached for those general attributes that enable consumers or users to evaluate the product. For a passenger car these refer to size, weight, engine horsepower, fuel efficiency, seating capacity, etc. Developing general specifications for a product requires a sound understanding of consumer needs with knowledge of the firm's objectives and its distinctive competence. Going from the production of large to small cars or from regular to minicomputers requires considerable technological adjustment. Similarly, deciding to service as well as manufacture a complex product involves additional managerial and technical skills.

In the second phase, appropriate parts and/or materials are selected, and the technical specifications of components are determined to satisfy the general specifications. The designer assigns to each part those dimensions that best satisfy its functional requirements and subsequently determines the largest possible, or *critical, tolerances* that will allow satisfactory product performance. Finally, within the critical tolerances, the designer chooses the tolerance values resulting in the most economical production. Generally, the economic tolerances are as large as the critical tolerances, except when smaller values result in savings in the assembly and maintenance of the complete unit. The procedure for arriving at product specifications is shown in Fig. 4-4, along with the possible relationships between production and assembly costs.

Standardization and Interchangeability

It is difficult to imagine the impact on our life styles of not having the standardization and interchangeability of parts for the thousands of products developed by modern technology. For the consumer, failure of a manufactured product would result in long waiting and much inconvenience, especially from the forced idleness of cars or buses, home appliances, elevators, heating systems, etc. Without standardized spare parts, failure of such items would require needed parts to be made by special setups not only for different products but also for different models of the same product. The cost of such repairs or replacements would be very high, in addition to the many disruptions in our working and private lives. This type of production would keep the price of many products high, thus limiting the market size.

Thanks to standardization and interchangeability, mass production has significantly lowered the cost to consumers of most of the complex products that characterize today's life styles, i.e., appliances, TV sets, cars, stereo components, etc. The standardized dimensions of many raw materials (tin and steel sheets, bricks, or lumber) and parts (nuts, bolts, washers, transistors, capacitors, etc.) allow their use in many products with a large degree of interchangeability. It is therefore desirable when designing a product to evaluate and employ as many readily available standardized materials and parts as possible. This practice lowers the cost of production, enables the firm to operate with limited inventories for each part or subassembly, makes maintenance and repair more economical, and contributes to easier and more effective quality control.

In some sectors of the economy, e.g., in the transportation or food industries, the government requires standardization of certain components and/or procedures

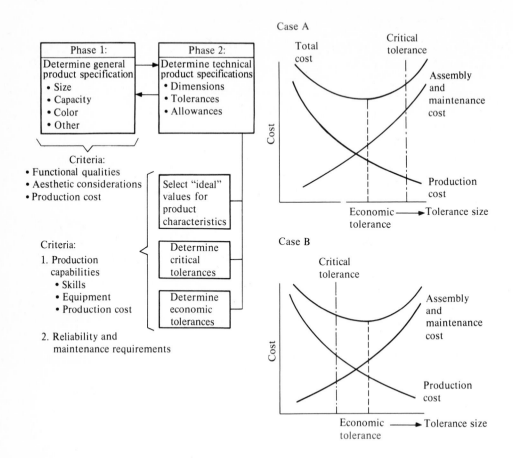

Fig. 4-4   Procedure for arriving at product specifications and relevant cost trade-offs.

to protect public safety and health, to restrict environmental pollution and to limit the use of certain resources in short supply such as energy. This has been particularly true for products ranging from aircraft and automobiles to detergents, clothing for children, and spray products for drugs or cosmetics.

Despite the above trends and restrictions for uniformity, the firm must at the same time strive to achieve innovative designs that satisfy human needs better or at lower cost and thus enhance the firm's competitive position in the market.

Persistent changes and trends in life styles, such as an increasing number of working wives, have contributed to new products and changed services. Fast-food restaurants have been able to adapt certain of the simplification and standardization techniques found in manufacturing. This applies both to the products and their processing, with the result of consistent, well-controlled quality and short service times. Partially prepared foods, permanent-press clothing, and other products aim at easing the demands on the time of people with both family and career interests.

Product Design for Human Use; Ergonomics

The improper design of new products with regard to their use by people may not only result in inferior performance but contribute to injury or even loss of life. For a long time products were designed with technical feasibility and cost as the dominant criteria. It was expected that people had to adapt to the characteristics of the product. The difficulty in operating cars, airplanes, and other devices of previous generations was at the root of many accidents. Limited visibility, hard-to-read instruments, and awkwardly placed knobs and control levers were often responsible for unsafe operation and at times loss of life.

Designing products and machines to adapt them to human characteristics is the domain of *ergonomics*, a field that has experienced impressive growth and respect since World War II. A key requirement in such an effort is the measurement and statistical analysis of the parts of the human body and their abilities and limitations on how they can be used and the load they can carry. This kind of information becomes a key input in the design of products for the consumer (cars, appliances, clothing, shoes, etc.) and equipment used in a production process.

Recent trends point to the increased importance of designing a product for ease of use, safety, ease of maintenance, and high performance. In this spirit, automobile design, as one example, has changed to allow for greater visibility, easy-to-read instruments, seats adjustable to maximize driver comfort, an interior that is pleasing and safe in the event of impact (collapsible steering wheel, padded dashboard, rounded-out handles, etc.).

Designing for optimum human use proceeds in the following steps:

1. *Determination of key characteristics of the consumer for which the product is intended.* Products for women and/or children must be operated with less muscular effort than those for men.
2. *Determination of the body members and senses that will be required to use the product.* Thus, typewriter keys must be designed according to the size and shape of human fingers; levers for gear-shifting, braking, etc., must conform to the contour of the hands; and airplane seats must be comfortable and allow for reasonable movement. Equally important is the ease and effectiveness of utilizing sensory inputs. Control panels for a chemical plant or a steel mill and instruments on the dashboard of a car or in the cockpit of an airplane are examples of products that must be designed for easy and accurate reading. Similarly, the ring of a telephone or the siren of an ambulance must elicit the required responses without disruptive and annoying stimuli.
3. *Determination from available statistical measurements of key consumer characteristics and the critical percentage of the consumer population that will be unable to use the product.* The value of the key product parameter corresponding to this critical percentage becomes the basis for determining the remaining values for other product characteristics.

Consider as an illustration the design of a bicycle frame for men. The key product parameter here might be the maximum weight the bicycle will be designed

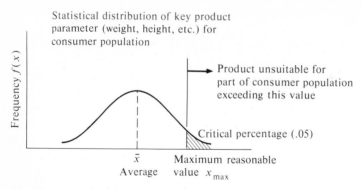

Fig. 4-5   **Determination of product-design parameters.**

to support. From a statistical distribution of men's weights, it can be seen that a realistic frame design cannot handle a certain proportion of extremely overweight consumers, say over 200 lb. If this critical percentage of the consumer population of men is set at 5 percent, the maximum weight to be handled can be used to determine the kind of metal to be used for each component and its thickness and size so that the frame will be adequate for the 95 percent of potential consumers who do not exceed 200 lb (see Fig. 4-5).

The critical percentage for many products is often set at 5.0 percent, because it is a near optimum design compromise of the expected losses from those who cannot use the product and the increased production cost required to satisfy small additional increments of the total population. This approach is applied whether one is designing shirts, shoes, airplane seats, and a wide variety of other products. Similar considerations apply to the design of various service characteristics (waiting times, allowed spaces for waiting and service, etc.). However, in the case of services the population preference characteristics are more subjective, and the design values are likely to be determined by trial-and-error adjustments rather than statistical data.

4-4   PROCEDURE FOR THE DESIGN OF PRODUCTS AND SERVICES

The development of a new product or the improvement of an existing one has as a stimulus certain ideas about the best way to satisfy perceived human needs. Potential sources of such ideas may include:

1. The results of basic research in fields such as chemistry, physics, biology, etc.
2. Technological breakthroughs that result in new processes with new or extended capabilities
3. Suggestions from an organization's personnel, e.g., the staff in R&D, production, quality control, etc.
4. Suggestions from consumers of the products for ways of improving operating features, safety, or other attributes

5. Ideas from the examination of products made by competitors
6. Recognition of existing needs without known means of satisfying them

From the above ideas management first selects those offering the greatest promise for achieving organizational objectives (profit, market share, etc.) with existing capabilities. Next, there is a preliminary analysis which examines the economic and technical feasibility on the basis of expected demand, available technologies, raw materials, and estimated production costs.

A preliminary analysis requires the close cooperation of R&D, marketing, and production. From the proposed ideas for new products, those selected are the ones with the highest probability of success. This is a subjective estimate that may be arrived at informally or with a more systematic approach, such as the Delphi approach, discussed in Chap. 11.

A detailed analysis is then undertaken for the most promising ideas on new products. These must now be evaluated in greater depth on the basis of:

1. General specifications (size, capacity, horsepower, etc.)
2. Expected market size
3. Production feasibility (availability of required materials, energy, equipment, human skills, and other inputs)
4. Estimates of production cost per unit
5. Human engineering characteristics (ease of use by consumers, maintenance requirements, safety, etc.)
6. Finance requirements (sources of funds for anticipated long-term investments and additional working capital)

For a new product, the above analysis permits an effective screening before undertaking construction of a prototype. The prototype is produced in small quantities and follows the design of technical specifications that achieve desired functional and other characteristics. A prototype thus makes it possible to evaluate and adjust alternative specifications and methods of production, as well as the ease of use and safety features.

When the required investment for new products is significant, the construction of the prototype is followed by carefully planned market trials. These are detailed experiments involving the selection of market type, geographical region, sales methods, and consumer assistance in the use of a new product. From consumer feedback from market trials it is possible to make desired changes in the specifications, in processing and quality-control methods, and in distribution and marketing strategies.

Most new ideas for products and services are discarded in the market trial stage.[1] To increase the reliability of the survey results and the demand projections made from them, it is crucial to examine the risks of distortion from competitive actions; introduction of untested products, saturation advertising, and other approaches may change market conditions.

Successful results from the market trial of a new product are often followed by

---

[1] Booz, Allen and Hamilton, Inc., *Management of New Products*, New York, 1968.

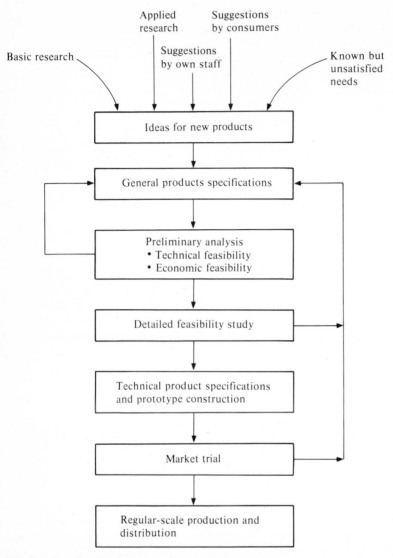

Fig. 4-6 Procedure for the introduction of new products.

production on a regular scale. This requires developing production plans, quality-control programs, and distribution procedures that can be integrated with existing ones. From this point on the responsibility for conformance to accepted specifications is entirely that of operations management. The reiterative process employed for the design and introduction of new products is shown in Fig. 4-6.

During the preliminary analysis and the detailed feasibility study the criteria employed to evaluate new ideas are as follows:

1. Is there a large enough market for the new product or service?
   a. What is the expected size?

   b. What is its geographic distribution?
2. Is production and distribution possible at a competitive cost?
   a. What are the requirements for production inputs and their estimated cost?
   b. What is the best strategy for the development of sales?
3. Is it possible to finance the research and development as well as the production and distribution of the new venture?
   a. What are the sources of finance?
   b. On the basis of the cash-flow analysis, what is the estimated rate of return?
   c. What impact will the new product have on an existing product line?
4. Are legal, environmental, and other laws or restrictions satisfied?
5. Is there available managerial and technical expertise, or can it be developed in time?
6. Does the new product blend with the existing set of organizational activities and is it consistent with the firm's market reputation?

The weight of these criteria may be different for different organizations, but unless they are adequately met by a new proposal, it is unwise to reach full-scale production.

4-5 THE CONCEPT OF QUALITY

Success or failure of a product in the marketplace is greatly determined by its quality, production cost, and competitive price. The concept of quality has different meanings for the producer and the consumer. This distinction becomes particularly crucial in the phase of product design.

A consumer rates quality subjectively according to how well a product satisfies a number of functional and psychological needs. Operations management, however, evaluates quality objectively by the extent to which actual units produced conform to the specifications of the product design.

Improvements in quality as perceived by the consumer require better materials, tighter tolerances, and more careful processing to ensure better performance and increased reliability. Packaging is sometimes an important aspect of quality. All these features tend to increase production costs, which in turn decrease the firm's competitiveness. The inherent conflict between quality and production costs means that a compromise must be made. In practice, the problem is resolved by specifying the desired quality in terms of product specifications and then striving to meet them at minimum cost.

The most frequently employed criteria for product quality relate to the following:

A. Functional quality aspects
   1. Product performance while in use
   2. Reliability during expected lifetime
      a. Accuracy during performance
      b. Expected life-span and nature of breakdowns
      c. Costs of maintenance and repair
      d. Manufacturer's warranties

3. Human factors
   a. Ease of use
   b. Safety during use and maintenance
B. Nonfunctional, i.e., psychological quality aspects
   1. Appearance and styling
   2. Consumer's psychological profile
   3. Variety of styles or models to choose from
C. Other quality aspects
   1. Packaging
   2. Timely production and distribution
   3. Service characteristics

With regard to nonfunctional quality criteria, evaluation is difficult due to the subjective interpretation specific product features receive by different consumers. Customers' social status, education, income, and life style are important factors that affect their choices and motivation.

For most consumer products the designer must be concerned with both functional and psychological characteristics. In some instances, say cosmetics, clothing, furniture, etc., the latter are even more significant than the former. In the case of producer goods, however, the dominant criteria are those pertaining to functional characteristics, i.e., performance accuracy, reliability, safety, etc. In selecting a lathe or drilling machine for a job shop, management is not likely to be affected very much by aesthetic factors such as color, shape, or styling as long as they do not interfere with satisfactory operation.

For profit-oriented organizations, the criterion for selecting the optimum quality level is profit maximization. The key relationships are shown in Fig. 4-7.

Although the same general remarks apply to the selection of optimum service quality for service organizations, for services there is a greater flexibility and ease of experimentation with various configurations, such as those found in hospitals, universities, airline travel, restaurants, and others. The more immediate the feedback from consumers in the form of preferences, complaints, etc., the easier it is to adjust to their needs rapidly. Table 4-1 summarizes some of the major differences in the design of products and services.

In certain cases, the design of a new product may contain innovations that require protection by one or more patents. It is advisable early in the development

TABLE 4-1   Differences in product and service design

Characteristic	Product	Service
Required R&D effort	Considerable	Limited or negligible
Need for preliminary testing	Considerable	Negligible
Nature of specifications	Usually precise and restrictive	Usually general and flexible
Reversibility of decisions	Time-consuming, costly, and difficult	Rapid, moderately expensive, and relatively easy

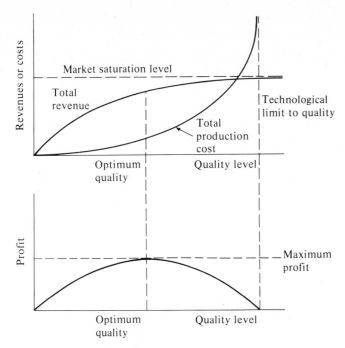

Fig. 4-7   Determination of optimum quality level.

phase to make sure that the proposed design does not infringe on exclusive rights of competitors protected by earlier patents. In both instances, there is a need for collaboration between technical and legal specialists for developing new product introduction plans that give sufficient protection to the rights for production and distribution provided by law.

4-6   GRAPHIC AND COMPUTER AIDS IN PRODUCT DESIGN

During the development of a new product design and in the later phases of its production and marketing, management relies on a number of graphic aids for facilitating communication between the different parts of an organization.

Process engineering and quality control rely heavily on technical specifications in the form of blueprints and tables. The latter show requirements for needed parts, desired grade and quantities of raw materials, and special assembly instructions to prevent damage during transportation and storage.

One of the most helpful graphic aids in product design, the *assembly*, or *gozinto* (goes-into), chart, shows in exploded form how a product is made from manufactured and purchased parts. An assembly chart identifies clearly the points in the production flow where parts or components are joined to form subassemblies and the points where purchased components are incorporated in the product. An example of an assembly chart for a simple desk lamp is shown in Fig. 4-8.

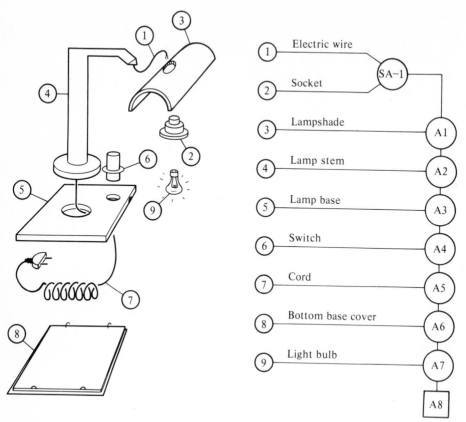

Fig. 4-8 Assembly (or gozinto) chart for a simple desk lamp.

For a number of complex products, e.g., automobiles, airplanes, ships, it has become possible to use a new approach known as *computer-assisted design* (CAD). The computer is provided with information on certain product characteristics, in the form of drawings with a light pen on a cathode-ray screen or typed-in parameter values. Direct feedback is then received by the design specialist on the specifications needed to meet operating requirements. Such feedback is also in the form of printed information or computer-produced drawings that can be manipulated to focus on specific design features. In such cases the computer has been programmed to translate input information on design parameters, e.g., weight-carrying capacity, into product specifications, such as the dimensions of the product or its parts. This powerful approach allows the designer to analyze and evaluate in detail several alternative configurations before making the product design final. The computer output often includes instructions that facilitate drafting engineering drawings and the operation of automated (or numerically controlled) machines.

For marketing purposes, it is preferable to use nontechnical descriptions that highlight the product design features most likely to attract potential customers. These include photographs, sketches, or three-dimensional models that are easily interpreted. Further information is provided concerning general specifications such as size, styling, capacity, power, or other characteristics.

4-7 PRODUCT DIFFERENTIATION
WITH MODULAR DESIGN

For most manufactured items, there is a conflict in designing a basic product to satisfy a wide range of customer options while retaining low production costs and other advantages associated with mass production. One approach to resolving this conflict is to design a product with a minimum number of standardized components and then allow product differentiation in the final assembly phase. This *modular design* is used extensively by many industries. For example, in the automobile industry, using the same chassis and standardized components and parts, it is possible to offer a large variety of cars by varying the engine size, transmission type, exterior color, and upholstery material. The inclusion of secondary accessories (radio, stereo cassette players, air conditioning, etc.) increases product differentiation even further to suit the needs of individual customers. The same applies to industries for furniture, home appliances, canned foods, sports equipment and others. Similar techniques have found their way into the operation of cafeterias, the packaging of travel tours, health care benefits, insurance, and other service systems.

The extent of product differentiation through modular design can be appreciated with the use of tree diagrams like that shown in Fig. 4-9. This method requires that we specify those attributes or parameters which when modified will result in significant product differentiation. For a manufacturer of TV sets the parameters in the product design that can be varied may include the following:

A. Picture type
B. Screen size
C. Cabinet type

Each design parameter may take different values, depending on consumer needs or preferences, current technological capabilities, availability of raw materials and parts, or other considerations. For our example, let us assume that we have the following possibilities:

A. Picture type
   1. Color
   2. Black and white

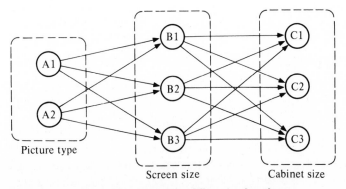

Fig. 4-9 **Tree diagram for determining differentiated products.**

B. Screen size
    1. Large (25-in diagonal)
    2. Medium (21-in diagonal)
    3. Small (17-in diagonal)
C. Cabinet type
    1. Deluxe (walnut)
    2. Regular (metal)
    3. Economy (plastic)

The tree diagram in this case is shown in Fig. 4-9. Each path through the diagram from left to right corresponds to a differentiated version of the same basic product. The number of possible combinations is determined by taking the product of the possible values of each parameter n_i. Here $n_A n_B n_C = (2)(3)(3) = 18$.

4-8   EVALUATION OF ALTERNATIVE PRODUCT DESIGNS

General

The selection of a new product design, like many other decisions in operations management, generally involves several objectives usually in conflict with each other. For example, we seek to minimize the cost of production and the cost of use and maintenance for a car while at the same time trying to maximize its safety, reliability, marketability, and other attributes. The final selection may be based on a market survey, an internal evaluation scheme, or a combination of both.

If all the several objectives we wish fulfilled could be reduced to a single scale of measurement, i.e., a cost or profit figure, the evaluation task would be easy. We would simply rank the alternatives along that scale and select the one with the highest rating. Sometimes this approach can be used for machine-replacement studies or for other situations where the alternatives under study are assumed to be equivalent in all respects (safety, quality of output, etc.) except economic performance. Most often, however, evaluation problems are quite complex because we must explicitly consider multiple objectives rated on different scales. The results must then be combined using dimensional analysis,[1] so that we shall avoid the common pitfall of adding apples and oranges.

▶ EXAMPLE 4-1
Suppose that the management of Natural Sound, Inc., a manufacturer of high-quality stereo components, is about to select one of three candidate designs for its new cassette deck model. It is felt that the three most important objectives are (1) performance in sound reproduction as measured by distortion of sound at different frequencies, signal-to-noise ratio, etc., (2) styling as measured by the layout of the

---

[1] Dimensional analysis involves expressing the measurements of different attributes in such a way that different alternatives can be compared with the same units.

various controls, ease of use, and appearance, and (3) ease of manufacture based on processing requirements, availability of parts, etc.

Each objective may be rated on a different scale. For Natural Sound, Inc., the adopted scheme is as follows:

1. Performance is rated on a scale from 1 to 10 (10 is best).
2. Styling is rated on a scale from 1 to 10 (10 is best).
3. Ease of manufacture is rated by the estimated cost of production per unit in dollars.

To reflect their different importance, each objective is assigned a certain weight w_j. For our example, the relevant data for the ratings of the alternative cassette deck designs are as shown:

Product design	Objective		
	1	2	3
A	8	10	$100
B	9	8	120
C	7	9	90
Assigned weight	$w_1 = 3$	$w_2 = 1$	$w_2 = 2$

▶

Evaluation of Alternatives with Multiple Objectives

For the general case of comparing alternatives with several objectives, we can use the following notation:

R_{ij} = rating of alternative i ($i = 1, 2, ..., m$) with respect to objective j ($j = 1, 2, ..., n$)

w_j = weight value of objective j

PM_i = preference measure or index of alternative i

It is tempting to multiply, for each alternative, the rating received for each objective by the weight for that objective. The results can then be added to obtain an overall figure of merit for that alternative. Such a procedure, however, is misleading, because it violates the principle of keeping the quantities added dimensionally consistent. By adding for each alternative terms whose values are expressed by units of different scales, we obtain a sum which as an index of merit is meaningless. A more detailed explanation requires an understanding of the properties of measurements obtained on different scales.[1] For example, an object weighing 100 lb is twice as heavy as one equal to 50 lb, but we cannot say that a room with a temperature of 120°F is twice as hot as one with a temperature of 60°F.

---

[1] For a discussion of measurement-scale properties the reader is referred to R. D. Luce et al., *Handbook of Mathematical Psychology*, vol. 2, Wiley, New York, 1965.

The correct evaluation procedure requires that the measure of preference developed for each alternative be computed as a product of the ratings after each one has been raised to a power equal to the weight assigned to that objective. This operation is needed to convert all preference measures into equivalent units. Thus

$$PM_i = (R_{i1})^{w_1}(R_{i2})^{w_2} \cdots (R_{im})^{w_m} \qquad i = 1, 2, \ldots, n \qquad (4\text{-}1)$$

The actual calculation of each PM_i can be simplified using logarithms:

$$\log PM_i = w_1 \log R_{i1} + w_2 \log R_{i2} + \cdots + w_n \log R_{in} \qquad i = 1, 2, \ldots, n \quad (4\text{-}2)$$

Before performing the calculations, we must determine whether the preference measure PM_i improves with smaller or larger values. Similarly, we must specify whether the objectives included are to be maximized, e.g., fuel efficiency for a car, or minimized, e.g., probability of a breakdown. *If PM_i improves with higher values, the ratings for objectives to be maximized are included as given, while those to be minimized are written as reciprocals of their original values.* The reverse holds true in the opposite case.

The comparison of two alternatives A and B is performed by taking the ratio PM_A/PM_B, a pure number. We select A if this ratio is greater than 1.00 or B if it is not. The use of the ratio is exactly the opposite if PM_i improves with smaller numbers. The division of the preference measures for each pair of alternatives is needed to cancel out whatever type of equivalent units resulted from the multiplication of ratings on different scales for each alternative. The above procedure is illustrated with the data of the Natural Sound, Inc., example.

▶ EXAMPLE 4-1 *(cont.)*
The calculation of the preference-measure values for the three cassette deck designs to be evaluated by management are

$$PM_A = (R_{A1})^{w_1}(R_{A2})^{w_2}\left(\frac{1}{R_{A3}}\right)^{w_3} = (8)^3(10)^1\left(\frac{1}{100}\right)^2 = .512$$

$$PM_B = (R_{B1})^{w_1}(R_{B2})^{w_2}\left(\frac{1}{R_{B3}}\right)^{w_3} = (9)^3(8)^1\left(\frac{1}{120}\right)^2 = .405$$

$$PM_C = (R_{C1})^{w_1}(R_{C2})^{w_2}\left(\frac{1}{R_{C3}}\right)^{w_3} = (7)^3(9)^1\left(\frac{1}{90}\right)^2 = .381$$

Note that since the preference measure for each deck design increases with higher ratings for performance and styling, the numerical values are used as given. However, since higher production costs reduce the preference measure, we use their reciprocal values.

Comparison of cassette decks A and B is made from the ratio $PM_A/PM_B = 1.264$. Since large numbers are desirable, design A is to be preferred to B. Following this by a comparison of B to C, the ratio $PM_B/PM_C = 1.063$ suggests that design B is preferred to C. Therefore, in order to achieve the stated objectives, the manage-
▶ ment of Natural Sounds, Inc., must select design A.

Another versatile approach that can be used for the evaluation of alternative product designs, based on multiple criteria, is the Brown-Gibson method discussed in Chap. 10.

4-9 SELECTION OF OPTIMAL PRODUCT OR SERVICE VARIETY

From a number of existing products or services and a set of promising designs for new ones, management has the challenging task of selecting which will actually be produced with the limited resources available to the organization. To solve this problem we need a knowledge not only of the profit contribution of each candidate product or service but of the resources required for each type, their availability, and the current phase in the life cycle of each product.

Determination of the optimal output variety may be based on long-term life-cycle management of different products, on economic analysis (see Supplementary Chapter B), or the use of linear programming (LP). The last represents a powerful method for this and other types of resource allocation problems and is covered separately in Supplementary Chapter C.

It must be pointed out that determination of the optimal output variety exceeds the authority of the operations-management function. It is an issue that affects marketing strategy and financial planning, with broader strategic impacts on the reputation of the firm and its competitors.

4-10 ENVIRONMENTAL IMPACTS OF PRODUCT DESIGN

General

Chapter 1 pointed out that industrialized societies have experienced pressure from the related problems of rapid depletion of natural resources and environmental pollution. Product design, as approached in a growth-oriented economy, has been a major contributing factor to these problems. It can play a significant role in reducing their impact in the future.

The specific product design selected by management and the process used to make it determine the demand for raw materials, energy, and human resources. Similarly, the technology used and how a product and its packaging will be discarded after use determine the form and extent of environmental pollution (see Fig. 1-7). Decisions reached about the design of products and processes affect not only production costs but significant social costs related to resource depletion and pollution.

Product Design in a Steady-State Economy

If future generations are to enjoy a material standard of living comparable to ours, it is imperative that the material flow through the economy be reduced to conserve scarce materials and energy and decrease the wastes and pollution in the environment. In Chap. 2 we noted that a selective growth economy adjusts the flow through the system to the level necessary to sustain a stable total stock of physical wealth, i.e., material things such as producer and consumer goods. The specific amount of physical wealth needed will depend on the size of the population and the standard of living desired.

The main conclusion is that *in order to use natural resources wisely and reduce pollution and waste what is produced must have a longer life.* The implications of this to operations management concerning product design are the following:

1. *Products must be designed with high built-in quality rather than built-in obsolescence.* This in turn will require better materials, smaller tolerances in component parts to be assembled, better workmanship, and a more thorough effort in quality control.
2. *Emphasis must be on easy and low-cost maintenance rather than easy replacement.* Since several of the production inputs (materials, parts, energy, air, water, etc.) have been undervalued for so long by failing to include the social costs that accompany their extraction or use, the prices for many products (automobiles, appliances, clothing, etc.) have been at such a level that it is preferable to replace them with new ones rather than maintain and repair them as needed. This approach contributes to economic growth, as measured by the GNP, but this indicator of prosperity is rather misleading because it fails to account for all the costs incurred and even treats some of them improperly, i.e., adds rather than subtracts costs to clean up pollution to determine GNP.
3. *Reliance must be on materials and product components and packaging that can be recycled economically.* For decades decisions relating to product design have been guided mainly by technological and economic criteria. In most cases, little thought was given to available reserves of the raw materials selected, the energy requirements imposed by the process used, and the pollution created by the disposal of wastes. It took worldwide crises in energy and key materials shortages, along with disruptive environmental pollution in cities and rivers and along coastlines to focus attention on these issues. Adjustments now appear inevitable, especially as a result of government intervention induced by public concern.
4. *A more limited range of design styles must be oriented primarily toward human needs rather than human wants.* Many problems related to the environment can be traced to the assumption of contemporary economic policies that human needs are unlimited and economic growth is the only meaningful approach to satisfy them. It is important to distinguish between human needs on one hand, which are predictable and identifiable (nutrition, clothing, housing, education, health, transportation, and other requirements), and human wants, on the other, which are psychologically motivated and truly boundless (entertainment, fashionable clothing, jewelry, etc.).

Several examples can be cited of recent attempts in the private and public sectors to modify or redesign products and services to conserve resources and control pollution. It is ironic that many of these efforts have been initiated by economic pressures, government regulations, or a combination of both. Nevertheless, they point the way of things to come and contribute in developing an awareness of environmental thresholds. Indicative cases are to be found in the following types of organizations:

1. The design of automobiles has been changing in recent years to promote higher fuel efficiency, thus conserving energy, and to reduce emissions of harmful pollutants. The incorporation of more recyclable materials, such as aluminum, lowers the pressure for raw materials while reducing solid waste.
2. The design of commercial aircraft has progressed significantly through improvements in fuel efficiency, reduction of pollutants in the atmosphere, and lowering of the noise level through retrofitting of aircraft engines. The same design objectives are pursued even more in the development of recent types of medium-range aircraft achieving 30 to 40 percent fuel savings.
3. The newspaper industry has innovated several changes designed to conserve newsprint paper and reduce solid waste. These include using reduced-basic-weight paper, changing page width and layout of columns with news, ads, etc., and limited use of recycled paper. Similar trends are also observed in the book-publishing industry, which is turning increasingly to recycled paper.

These applications and others in all areas of productive activity represent a late start toward reestablishing an environmental balance to support a population that can enjoy a respectable standard of living more equitably distributed to all nations.

4-11 SUMMARY

Products and services represent the bridges organizations use to reach public and private needs. How well this is accomplished determines how an organization will succeed in achieving its long-term objectives and even whether it will survive.

Despite its seemingly technical nature, the design of a product or service is a strategic decision that must involve the entire organization. It must reflect a firm's distinctive competence, be consistent with its reputation in the marketplace, and strive to enhance its competitive posture. In the case of a nonprofit service organization it is imperative that services provided cover genuine needs in effectively fulfilling its mission, whether it is education, health maintenance, transportation, or something else.

In the private sector, design of products and services must take into account not only functional needs but also psychological ones. This calls for diversity in the finished form of the product or service which is in conflict with the economies of scale made possible through mass producing well-standardized items. Modular design represents a successful attempt to reconcile the need for product diversification with low-cost processing.

Products and services differ in a number of respects and require varying managerial responses in all phases of system design, planning, and control. The improvement of the material standard of living in western societies has increased the pressure for a greater variety and quality of services as a consequence of changing life styles. The inherent difficulty in exercising tight quality and cost control in service systems poses some of the greatest challenges to present and future managers.

Product design assumes increasing significance due to its impact on the environment on both the input side for scarce resources and the output side affecting pollution through solid waste. The approaching of environment thresholds will encourage a greater concern for improvements in product design by emphasizing high quality and ease of maintenance to increase a product's useful life. Considerations for easy recycling may also reduce the pressure for new materials and the amount of solid waste after disposal. Product design in an environment of limited capacity will be a challenge not only as a means of economic survival but as an effort to preserve a standard of living that adequately covers human needs but not human wastefulness.

REVIEW QUESTIONS

1. Describe the different phases in the life cycle of a product. Why is it important to know what phase an actual product is in?
2. What is the difference between the narrow and broad definition of a product?
3. In what respects does a service differ from a product as a system output?
4. Which are the most critical factors in the design of a physical product?
5. Explain in your own words the following terms:
   (a) Tolerance for a machined part   (c) Natural process tolerance
   (b) Allowance for fitted parts   (d) Standardization
6. What are the usual sources of new ideas for products and services?
7. Discuss the phases in the process undertaken for the introduction of a new product.
8. What are the most frequently used criteria for specifying product quality? State how they apply in the design of the following:
   (a) A passenger car
   (b) A piece of furniture
   (c) A camera
9. Describe some of the key differences between product and service design.
10. What would be the most important criteria to you for judging the quality of services provided by:
    (a) A commercial airline
    (b) An insurance company
    (c) A mass-transit system
    (d) A community general hospital
11. Discuss the importance of product differentiation through modular design as applied to mass-produced items.
12. Describe some of the diverse environmental impacts of product design and possible ways to reduce them. Give some examples.

PROBLEMS

1. The specifications for a shaft have been set equal to $3.460 \pm .015$ in. This is to fit the inside diameter of a ball-bearing set equal to 3.500 in.
   (a) What are the ideal dimensions for the motor shaft and the tolerances to compensate for variability in production?
   (b) What is the designer's allowance for these parts?

2. Prepare an assembly chart for (*a*) a three-ring binder for 8½ by 11-in paper sheets and (*b*) an hourglass whose parts are shown in the sketch.

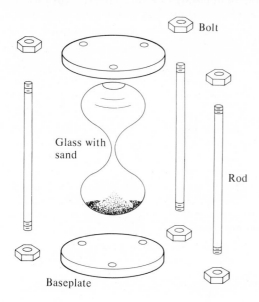

3. The R&D department of a home-appliance manufacturer has proposed three new designs for a washing machine intended to replace its current model. The criteria selected for evaluating each design include (1) ease of operation, determined by the configuration of the control panel, (2) cleaning ability for different fabrics, (3) ease of maintenance, and (4) unit cost of manufacture. Performance according to each of the first three criteria is rated on a scale from 0 to 10 with 10 best. The ratings of each proposed design for each criterion and the weights assigned to the four criteria are indicated below.

Proposed design	Ease of operation	Cleaning ability	Ease of maintenance	Unit cost of manufacture
A	9	7	10	$140
B	7	8	9	150
C	6	10	8	170
Weight	2	4	1	3

Determine the best design based on the indicated ratings for the criteria above.
4. Refer to Prob. 3. Repeat the evaluation of the proposed washing-machine designs if the assigned weights for the criteria are set equal to (*a*) 1, 3, 1, and 5 and (*b*) 4, 2, 1, and 3.
5. Refer to Prob. 3. Repeat the evaluation of the proposed designs if as a result of inflation the revised estimates for the cost of manufacture are $155 for A, $180 for B, and $190 for C.
6. Select a product or service of interest and identify the design changes brought about by environmental considerations.

†7. The Special Motors Co. has completed testing prototypes of its solar-powered automobile. Due to limited productive capacity, the company can introduce either a compact or regular-sized model but not both. Expected profits will depend on future demand for this new product. Estimates of expected annual profit for each model under conditions of low, average, and high demand are provided in the accompanying table, which also includes estimates of the likelihood of these levels of demand.

Decision payoff matrix (profit in millions)

Solar-powered automobile model	Demand level		
	Low	Average	High
Compact	$ −8	$15	$30
Regular	−12	10	50
Probability of demand level	.25	.55	.20

(a) Determine which solar-powered model should be selected according to the initial estimates of market response for the new product.
(b) Calculate the value to the company of having perfect information about future demand.

†8. Refer to Prob. 7. Special Motors, Inc., is considering hiring the services of Clairvoyant Associates, a marketing firm with the following record on past forecasts:

Demand forecast	Market response		
	Low	Average	High
Pessimistic	.7	.2	.1
Average	.2	.5	.1
Optimistic	.1	.3	.8

(a) Determine which model Special Motors Co. should introduce if the survey by Clairvoyant Associates results in an optimistic forecast.
(b) What is the expected gain from the use of the services of the marketing firm?
(c) What is the maximum fee that should be paid to the marketing firm for its services?

SELECTED REFERENCES

1. Abernathy, W. J., and P. L. Townsend: "Technology, Productivity and Process Change," *Technological Forecasting Social Change*, vol. 7, no. 4, 1975.

† Requires familiarity with decision analysis (Supplementary Chapter A).

2. Abernathy, W. J., and K. P. Wayne: "Limits of the Learning Curve," *Harvard Business Review*, September–October 1974, pp. 109–119.
3. Buffa, E. S.: *Modern Production Management*, 4th ed., Wiley, New York, 1973, chap. 9.
4. Chase, R. B., and N. J. Aquilano: *Production and Operations Management*, Irwin, Homewood, Ill., 1973.
5. Claycamp, H. J., and L. E. Liddy: "Prediction of New Product Performance: An Analytical Approach," *Journal of Marketing Research*, vol. 6, no. 4, November 1969, pp. 414–421.
6. Evans, M. K.: *Macro-Economic Activity: Theory, Forecasting and Control*, Harper & Row, New York, 1969.
7. Hahir, J. P.: "A Case Study on the Relationship between Design Engineering and Production Engineering," *Proceedings Fifth Annual Industrial Engineering Institute, University of California, Berkeley–Los Angeles, 1953.*
8. Lowrance, William W.: *Of Acceptable Risk*, William Kaufmann, Inc., Los Altos, Calif., 1976.
9. Meyers, S., and D. Marquis: *Successful Industrial Innovations*, National Science Foundation, Washington, 1969, pp. 69–70.
10. Niebel, Benjamin W., and Alan B. Draper: *Product Design and Process Engineering*, McGraw-Hill, New York, 1974.
11. Paper, G. W.: "Minimizing Manufacturing Costs through Effective Design," *Proceedings Sixth Annual Industrial Engineering Institute, University of California, Berkeley–Los Angeles, 1954.*
12. Parker, G. G. C., and E. L. Segura: "How to Get a Better Forecast," *Economic Forecasting*, Irwin, Homewood, Ill., 1961.
13. Riggs, James L.: *Production Systems: Analysis Planning and Control*, 2d ed., Wiley, New York, 1976.
14. Riggs, James L.: *Engineering Economics*, McGraw-Hill, New York, 1977.
15. Starr, Martin K., and I. Stein: *The Practice of Management Science*, Prentice-Hall, Englewood Cliffs, N.J., 1976.

Supplementary Chapter C

LINEAR PROGRAMMING: SIMPLEX METHOD

C-1 INTRODUCTION

Every organization seeks to achieve its objectives operating with limited resources. As a result, one of the most important types of problem confronting managers at all levels is the allocation of these resources to activities competing for their use. Some typical allocation problems include:

1. The allocation of productive resources (materials, machines, labor, etc.) to various products or services
2. The allocation of different types of capacity (regular time, overtime, inventories, and subcontracting) to expected demand in successive planning periods
3. The allocation of available capital to competing projects for new facilities, new equipment, worker-training programs, and others
4. The assignment of personnel or machines to different jobs, sales persons to market districts, and the like on one-to-one basis

One of the greatest achievements in approaching such managerial problems scientifically has been the development of linear programming by George Dantzig in 1947. For certain resource-allocation problems the restrictions imposed by limited resources in performing desired activities and the criterion of expressing management's objectives can be assumed to be linear. Dantzig's *simplex method* can identify those activities which will result in the optimum allocation plan. The availability of computers has led to countless applications in both private and public organizations. Linear programming today is being used routinely for problems related to diet planning, oil refining, transportation planning and scheduling, energy planning, pollution control, and many others.

In this review chapter we discuss linear programming with the use of a simple example designed to clarify the key features in the formulation of a problem for solution by a graphical method and the simplex procedure.

C-2 A TWO-PRODUCT EXAMPLE

A small toy manufacturer has recently discontinued a model for which sales had been declining. This action has freed productive capacity in three departments, and

TABLE C-1   Data on proposed new products

Production department	Production requirements, min		Available weekly capacity, min
	Rebecca R	Polly P	
A	3		180
B		5	200
C	4	6	360
Profit contribution per unit	$15	$10	

management is considering the introduction of two new dolls, Rebecca (*R*) and Polly (*P*), recently designed by the R&D group.

The data on production requirements for each new doll, its expected profit contribution, and the amounts of freed capacity in each department are summarized in Table C-1. Results from a market survey suggest that the company could sell all the dolls of either kind it can produce.

It is desired to determine the amounts to produce of each new doll with the capacity available in each department so as to maximize the total profit from the sale of these products.

C-3   LINEAR-PROGRAMMING FORMULATION AND ASSUMPTIONS

Key Concepts

Before we can formulate a resource-allocation problem, we must specify the following:

1. *The activities that can be performed to achieve the objectives of the organization.* The activity levels represent the extent to which each activity is performed and are represented by the variables $X_1, X_2, \ldots, X_n$. In our example, the activities of interest are the production of dolls Rebecca in amount *R* and Polly in amount *P*. These variables are also known as *decision variables* because they are under management's control.
2. *The limited resources available to perform the various activities.* These may refer to labor-hours, machine-hours, raw materials, warehouse space, capital, or other. In the general case we allow for *m* different types of resources in amounts $B_1, B_2, \ldots, B_m$. For the example, since the limited resources are the amounts of production time in each of the three departments, we have $B_1 = 120$ min, $B_2 = 200$ min, and $B_3 = 360$ min.
3. *The activity contribution to the objective of the organization, or the amount by which each activity helps advance the organization according to the criterion employed to evaluate different allocation plans.* For the general case with *n* activi-

ties $(X_1, X_2, \ldots, X_n)$ their unit contributions are $C_1, C_2, \ldots, C_n$. In our example, the activity contribution for each product is measured by the expected profit contribution, which is $C_1 = \$15$ per unit of R and $C_2 = \$10$ per unit of P.

4. *The production (or process) technology which specifies how much of each resource a unit of a given activity will require.* This is designated by the symbol A_{ij}, that is, the amount of resource i needed per unit of activity j $(i = 1, 2, \ldots, m$ and $j = 1, 2, \ldots, n)$.

In our example we have:

Resource type, capacity in department	Production activity	
	Rebecca R	Polly P
A	$A_{11} = 3$	$A_{12} = 0$
B	$A_{21} = 0$	$A_{22} = 5$
C	$A_{31} = 4$	$A_{33} = 6$

Linear-Programming Problem Formulation

Based on the preceding linear-programming concepts, the problem of resource allocation can be formulated by specifying (1) the objective function, which mathematically expresses the criterion for evaluating alternative allocation plans, and (2) the restrictions imposed by the process technology and resource availability.

Objective function   From the unit contribution of each activity we can calculate its total contribution for different activity levels. In our example, since each Rebecca doll contributes \$15 to profit, the production of R units will contribute a total of \$15R. Similarly, the production of P Polly dolls at \$10 each will make a total contribution equal to \$10P. The objective function Z states the combined contribution from all activities, and for our example we have

$$Z = \$15R + \$10P$$

Profit contribution of P

Profit contribution of R

In the general case, where the allocation of resources is to be made to n activities, the contribution of activity 1 at level X_1 will be $C_1 X_1$, of activity 2 at level X_2 will be $C_2 X_2$, and so on. The objective function for the general case can be stated as

$$Z = C_1 X_1 + C_2 X_2 + \cdots + C_n X_n$$

Restrictions   Given the production requirements for each activity, we can proceed to formulate the restrictions or constraints imposed by the limited availability of needed resources. In our example, resource 1 corresponds to productive capacity in department A. Since only R's require processing there, at the rate of 3 min/unit, the restriction imposed by department A can be written as

$$3R + 0P \leq 120 \qquad \text{Restriction by department A}$$

In words, the amount of time allocated to the production of R's in department A cannot exceed the limit of 120 min available per week. Similarly, for department B the time allocated to whatever number of units we produce of P's cannot exceed the 200 min available weekly. Thus, the restriction imposed by limited capacity can be stated as

$$0R + 5P \leq 200 \qquad \text{Restriction by department B}$$

Since both R's and P's require processing in department C, the sum of times allocated to each activity cannot exceed the available productive capacity of 360 min/wk. Thus,

$$4R + 6P \leq 360 \qquad \text{Restriction by department C}$$

In the general case, we have as many restrictions as we have different resources plus any special constraints imposed by market size or other considerations.

An additional type of restriction exists because only resources can be converted into activities and never the reverse. This means that all activities are allowed at positive or zero levels, but none is permitted to assume a negative value. This is also a requirement for the simplex method to work, although for special cases adjustments are possible to allow for negative values, e.g., when some decision variables represent inventory levels.

In summary, our formulation of the linear-programming problem for the toy-manufacturer example is as follows: Find values for the decision variables R and P (amounts produced of Rebeccas and Pollys) that will maximize

$$Z = \$15R + \$10P \qquad \text{Total profit contribution}$$

subject to restrictions

$$3R + 0P \leq 180 \qquad \text{Capacity in department A}$$
$$0R + 5P \leq 200 \qquad \text{Capacity in department B} \qquad \text{(C-1)}$$
$$4R + 6P \leq 360 \qquad \text{Capacity in department C}$$

and $\qquad\qquad R \geq 0 \quad$ and $\quad P \geq 0 \qquad$ Nonnegativity constraints

The problem involves two decision variables (R and P) and three independent constraints. In the general case we deal with n decision variables ($X_1, X_2, \ldots, X_n$) and m independent constraints.

The formulation of the general linear-programming problem is as follows: Find values for the decision variables $X_1, X_2, \ldots, X_n$ that will maximize

$$Z = C_1 X_1 + C_2 X_2 + \cdots + C_n X_n \qquad \text{Objective function}$$

subject to the restrictions

$$
\left.
\begin{array}{c}
A_{11} X_1 + A_{12} X_2 + \cdots + A_{1n} X_n \leq B_1 \\
A_{21} X_1 + A_{22} X_2 + \cdots + A_{2n} X_n \leq B_2 \\
\cdots\cdots\cdots\cdots\cdots\cdots\cdots\cdots\cdots\cdots\cdots\cdots \\
A_{m1} X_1 + A_{m2} X_2 + \cdots + Z_{mn} X_n \leq B_m
\end{array}
\right\} \qquad \text{(C-2)}
$$

and $\qquad X_1 \geq 0, X_2 \geq 0, \ldots, X_n \geq 0$

This standard formulation of the linear-programming problem can be adapted to handle situations where the objective function is to be minimized and the constraints are equalities or inequalities of the greater-than-or-equal-to-type ($\geq$).

Linear-Programming Assumptions

Before management attempts to solve specific problems, one must make sure that certain assumptions of linear programming hold.

1. All relationships in the problem formulation, i.e., both the objective function and constraints, must be linear. For the objective function this requirement implies no price discounts, and no economies, or diseconomies of scale as the activity level is changed. In other words, for any activity both the use of a resource and its contribution to the objective function must be proportional to the activity level. This precludes any terms with products of the variables (X_1, X_2) or variables raised to a power X_4^3.
2. The amounts of resources available ($B_1, B_2, \ldots, B_m$), the unit contributions ($C_1, C_2, \ldots, C_n$), and production requirements A_{ij} must be known and constant; i.e., they must assume specific fixed values.
3. The values of decision variables may be either whole numbers (integers) or mixed numbers ($X_2 = 4, X_3 = 5\frac{3}{4}$, etc.).

Even though linear programming may yield useful results when real conditions depart somewhat from the above assumptions, it is important to make sure that they are satisfied even approximately. Extensions of linear programming have been developed to handle cases where one or more assumptions are violated.

For problems with serious nonlinearities in the objective function or constraints *nonlinear-programming* methods exist for certain cases. When the decision variables must assume only integer values, as in determining the requirements of a region in power plants, there are techniques available known as *integer programming*. Finally, when the problem "constants" tend to change or vary as statistical variables, one can use *parametric* or *stochastic programming*.

It is important to keep in mind that linear programming usually solves a rather complex problem in a static sense, i.e., at once and completely for a given period. For some types of problems, such as budgeting or inventory-level determination, decisions over a planning horizon must be made stage by stage as the outcome of decisions in previous stages becomes known. Here linear programming is of no use, and management must resort to other approaches, such as decision analysis (Supplementary Chapter A) or dynamic programming (see Selected References).

C-4 GRAPHICAL SOLUTION OF A TWO-VARIABLE LINEAR-PROGRAMMING PROBLEM

For linear-programming problems with two or three variables it is possible (and very instructive) to use a graphical solution method. This provides significant insights into the key points of linear programming and the mechanics of the algebraic techniques used by the simplex method. The method of graphical solution consists of the following steps:

1. State the problem in mathematical form
2. Plot on a graph the problem constraints
3. Determine the area of feasible solutions
4. Plot the objective function
5. Determine the optimum solution

The procedure will be illustrated with the example of the toy manufacturer.

Step 1: State the Problem in Mathematical Form

This has been done already in the previous section, and we repeat here the formulation for convenience. Find values for R and P that will

$$\text{Maximize } Z = \$15R + \$10P \qquad \text{Objective function}$$

subject to the following constraints:

$3R + 0P \leq 180$	Capacity in department A
$0R + 5P \leq 200$	Capacity in department B
$4R + 6P \leq 360$	Capacity in department C
$R, P \geq 0$	Nonnegativity requirement

Step 2: Plot the Constraints on a Graph

We start with a graph showing the amount produced of R along the horizontal axis and the amount of P on a vertical axis (Fig. C-1). To plot each constraint we temporarily ignore the inequality sign and solve for a given variable directly, if possible, or by setting the other variable equal to zero. Next, we show how the nonnegativity constraints ($R, P \geq 0$) limit us on or to the right of the vertical axis and on or above the horizontal axis. The restriction imposed by limited capacity in department A, $3R \leq 180$, corresponds to the area on or to the left of a vertical line at $R = 60$ (see Fig. C-1). Similarly, the constraint by department B, $5P \leq 200$,

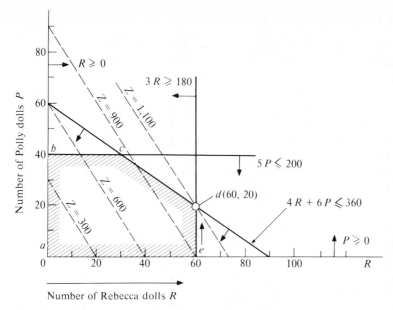

Fig. C-1 Feasible area in toy-manufacturer example.

corresponds to the area on or below a horizontal line at $P = 40$ units. For department C we have $4R + 6P \leq 360$. When $P = 0$, $R = 90$; and when $R = 0$, $P = 60$. The line for this constraint is shown in Fig. C-1, and the permissible values of R and P are on or below the line $4R + 6P = 360$.

Step 3: Identify the Area of Feasible Solutions

After plotting all constraints, we can proceed to identify the area of feasible solutions. This area, also known as the *feasible set*, corresponds to all points that satisfy all the problem constraints. In our example, it corresponds to all the combinations of Rebecca and Polly dolls that can be produced with the capacity available in each department. The feasible set, shown in Fig. C-1 by the shaded area, forms a *convex polygon*[1] and includes all points that lie along the boundary-line segments or in the interior. Sometimes no combination of products can satisfy all constraints simultaneously. This would be the case in our example if there were an additional restriction such as $R \geq 100$ or $R + P \geq 150$. This might happen if there were an error in the formulation of the constraints. In the absence of errors, the lack of any points that satisfy all constraints simply means that the linear-programming problem has no feasible solution.

---

[1] A feasible set is convex if it has no holes or recesses. This means that a line segment joining any two points of the set lies entirely within the boundaries of the polygon. Unless the area of feasible solutions is convex, linear programming cannot be used to solve the problem. The feasible set is also referred to as the *solution space* for the problem under study.

Step 4: Plot the Objective Function

Given the set of all product combinations that satisfy the capacity constraints, we next attempt to find the one yielding the largest total profit. This requires plotting the objective function to check the relative worth of alternative combinations. We can do this by selecting an arbitrary total-profit figure, for convenience a common multiple of both unit-profit contributions, say $300. Such a profit can be achieved by a combination of no P's and $R = 20$ at one extreme, or no R's and $P = 30$ at the other extreme. Between these two extreme points (shown in Fig. C-1 connected by a dotted line) there is an infinite number of combinations of P's and R's along the line all yielding the same total profit of $300. For this reason, the dotted line for $Z = 300 is known as an *isoprofit* line. Other isoprofit lines yielding a greater total profit can be obtained by moving away from the origin but staying parallel to the line for $Z = 300.

Step 5: Determine the Optimum Solution

To determine the optimum solution graphically we must move the Z line as far away from the origin as possible while staying in the feasible set and keeping it parallel to its initial position. In the example, this happens when an isoprofit line goes through corner point d with values $R = 60$ and $P = 20$.

It is a *basic property of linear programming that the optimum solution will be at one of the corner points*[1] *of the feasible set.* For a small problem the number of corner points of the convex polygon is rather small. Thus we can evaluate the objective function at each corner point and select the one yielding the highest total profit. The coordinates of the corner points are determined by the intersection of the straight lines plotted for the constraints. For corner point b $(R = 0, P = 40)$, $Z = 400; for c $(R = 30, P = 40)$, $Z = 850; for d $(R = 60, P = 20)$, $Z = $1,100$; and for e $(R = 60, P = 0)$, $Z = 900. From this enumerative approach we conclude again that point d is the optimum solution. Thus, the maximum total profit is achieved by producing 60 R's and 20 P's and it is equal to $1,100.

In minimization problems the constraints are usually stated as inequalities of the greater-than-or-equal-to type. Determination of the optimum solution for this case requires plotting the constraints and the objective function and moving the latter *toward* the origin as close as possible without leaving the feasible set.

C-5   THE SIMPLEX METHOD

For linear-programming problems with more than three decision variables the graphical method cannot identify an optimum solution. Since most realistic appli-

---

[1] In the literature, corner points are also called *extreme points* and correspond to algebraic solutions for the system of equations representing the constraints. Since the number of corner points in a convex polygon is finite, another linear-programming property states that the optimal solution, if one exists, will need a finite number of steps.

cations involve a large number of decision variables and constraints, a different approach is needed. Dantzig's simplex method is an algebraic procedure designed to identify an optimum solution, if one exists, in a finite number of stages or iterations. This is accomplished by evaluating successive corner points of the convex feasible set in manner leading to a better solution at each stage until no further improvement is possible. The sequence of steps per stage in solving a linear-programming problem by the simplex method is as follows:

Step 0: Set up the linear-programming problem in standard form, i.e., maximization of the objective function with less-than-or-equal-to inequalities.

Step 1: Determine an initial feasible solution, i.e., a starting corner point, after converting all inequalities into equalities.

Step 2: Evaluate the current solution for possible improvement. If no improvement can be made, the current solution is optimal.

Step 3: If improvement is possible, identify the incoming decision variable from those not in the current solution.

Step 4: Determine the outgoing variable from those in the current solution.

Step 5: Determine the new feasible solution resulting from the exchange of the outgoing variable for the incoming one. This corresponds to an adjacent corner point in the feasible set with a higher value for the objective function Z.

Step 6: Return to step 2.

This procedure, shown in flowchart form in Fig. C-2, will be illustrated using the simple two-variable example. In this way, the algebraic steps can be related to the graphical representation of the problem.

Step 0: Set Up the Problem in Standard Form

For our example the problem formulation is already in standard form. However, for problems involving minimization of the objective function and constraints in the form of equalities or inequalities of the greater-than-or-equal-to type, further adjustments are needed.

For our example we have

$$\text{Maximize } Z = 15R + 10P$$

subject to restrictions

$$3R + 0R \leq 180$$
$$0R + 5P \leq 200 \tag{C-3}$$
$$4R + 6P \leq 360$$

and

$$R, P \geq 0$$

Beyond this point it is not necessary to be explicitly concerned with the non-negativity constraints.

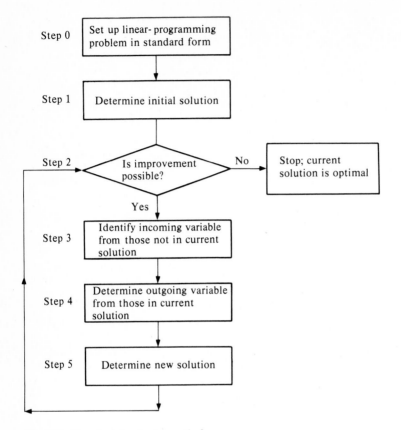

Fig. C-2   Flowchart for simplex method.

Step 1: Determine an Initial Solution

In order for the simplex to work, all inequalities except the nonnegativity constraints must be converted into equalities. This is required to enable us to use a system of linear equations to solve for the variables associated with corner points of the feasible set. The conversion into equalities is done with the introduction of *slack variables*, one for each constraint.

To illustrate the meaning of a slack variable, let us examine the constraint imposed by limited capacity in department A

$$3R + 0P \leq 120$$

In words, this states that the capacity used to produce R's in department A, $3R$, cannot exceed the capacity available, 120 min, in that department. The introduction of a new variable S_A to convert this inequality into an equality makes sense if we interpret the new variable as the unused capacity or slack in department A. Thus,

$$3R + 0P + S_A = 120 \qquad \text{For capacity in department A}$$

where S_A is the slack variable for the first constraint representing unused capacity or slack in department A. In words,

$$\begin{bmatrix} \text{Allocated capacity} \\ \text{in department A for } R\text{'s} \end{bmatrix} + \begin{bmatrix} \text{unused capacity} \\ \text{in department A} \end{bmatrix} = \begin{bmatrix} \text{available capacity} \\ \text{in department A} \end{bmatrix}$$

Similar adjustments with the same interpretation can be made to the second and third constraints

$$0R + 5P + S_B = 200 \qquad \text{For capacity in department B}$$

$$4R + 6P + S_C = 360 \qquad \text{For capacity in department C}$$

where S_B and S_C are the slack variables for the second and third constraints representing unused or slack capacity in departments B and C. Since slack variables stand for unused capacity, their contribution to total profit is zero. Thus

$$Z = \$15R + \$10P + 0S_A + 0S_B + 0S_C$$

In all other respects they are treated like the initial decision variables.

Rearranging the objective function so that all terms appear to the left of the equality sign, as in the constraints, we have

$$Z - 15R - 10P - 0S_A - 0S_B - 0S_C = 0$$

Now we can restate the linear programming problem so that we can readily identify the initial solution. Our formulation includes five variables (R, P, S_A, S_B, S_C), the objective function, and three equations. This system can be solved for only three variables at a time by setting the remaining two variables equal to zero. Here we have

$$E_0: \qquad Z - 15R - 10P - 0S_A - 0S_B - 0S_C = 0$$

$$E_1: \qquad 3R + 0P + S_A + 0S_B + 0S_C = 180 \qquad \text{(C-4)}$$

$$E_2: \qquad 0R + 5P + 0S_A + S_B + 0S_C = 200$$

$$E_3: \qquad 4R + 6P + 0S_A + 0S_B + S_C = 360$$

By arbitrarily setting R and P equal to zero an initial feasible solution can be read directly from the formulation as follows:

$$S_A = 120 \qquad S_B = 200 \qquad S_C = 360$$
$$\text{yielding} \quad Z = 0 \quad \text{for } R = P = 0 \qquad \text{(C-5)}$$

The above initial solution is interpreted as follows. If we produce no Rebecca and Polly dolls ($R = P = 0$), we shall have 120 min of unused capacity in department A, 200 min in department B, and 360 min in department C. This solution is feasible because it satisfies all constraints. It corresponds to the corner point a at the origin of the corner polygon. Since the values of the profit contributing activities R and P are zero, the total profit Z associated with the initial solution will be zero.

Trivial and unattractive as this initial solution may seem, it nevertheless allows the simplex to get a handle on the problem. It is customary to call the variables in the current solution *basic variables*, while those set equal to zero are called *nonbasic variables*. Note that there is only one basic variable associated with each constraint equation. In order to read the current solution directly, it must be expressed so that a basic variable appears with a coefficient of 1 in only one equation and 0 elsewhere. The reader can see how this holds for S_A, S_B, and S_C in the previous formulation.

Step 2: Evaluate the Current Solution for Improvement

Given that a solution must always have as many basic variables as the problem has constraints, an improvement can be achieved by trading an activity already included in the solution for a more profitable one presently excluded. In our example, an examination of the initial solution reveals that either one of the variables R and P currently out could be included in it and could be increased from zero to a positive amount to raise total profit.

Step 3: Identify the Incoming Variable

If there are several candidates that could improve the current solution, the simplex method uses the following rule to select the incoming variable:

Rule 1

When two or more variables qualify to enter the current solution, select the one that will increase the objective function at the fastest rate. For a maximization problem this corresponds to the nonbasic variable with the largest negative coefficient in the current Z row. Ties can be broken arbitrarily.

Applying this rule to the initial solution of the example, we select R because it makes the highest contribution to total profit Z at the rate of $15 per unit, as the incoming variable R will increase from zero to a positive amount. Referring to the graph of Fig. C-1, we see that this choice is equivalent to a movement away from the origin along the horizontal axis.

Step 4: Determine the Outgoing Variable

To obtain a new solution with the incoming variable, one of the variables in the current solution must be forced out. Which one will leave depends on what constraint will become binding first as we increase the value of the incoming variable.

In our example, R will force out of the initial solution one of the slack variables S_A, S_B, and S_C. To determine which one will leave we solve for the basic variable in each constraint equation and note which restriction becomes the bottleneck, i.e., the most limiting, as we increase R:

	Maximum limit on R
$S_A = 180 - 3R$	60 (bottleneck)
$S_B = 200 - 5R^0$	No limit
$S_C = 360 - 4R - 6R^0$	120

Since the capacity in department A becomes the bottleneck, it will be the basic variable in that constraint, S_A, which will reach zero first and leave the current solution. The new improved solution will therefore include R, S_B, and S_C as basic variables, with S_A and P equal now to zero. This corresponds to corner point e in Fig. C-1. The procedure for selecting the outgoing variable is governed by the following rule.

Rule 2

The outgoing variable corresponds to the basic variable in the constraint that becomes a bottleneck, as we increase the incoming variable.

Step 5: Determine the New Feasible Solution

To read out the new solution directly we must convert the objective function and the constraints so that each basic variable appears with a coefficient of 1 in only one equation and 0 elsewhere. This is done by *pivoting*, which includes two steps:

1. Select the equation in which the incoming variable will appear and adjust it so that the new variable has a coefficient of 1. This is called the *key equation* and is the one associated with the bottleneck constraint, i.e., the one which includes the outgoing variable.

   For our example, the key equation is the first constraint E_1 containing S_A

E_1: $\qquad\qquad\qquad 3R + 0P + S_A = 180$

It is changed to

E_1': $\qquad\qquad\qquad R + 0P + \frac{1}{3}S_A = 60 \qquad$ Key equation by dividing all terms by $3(E_1' = \frac{1}{3}E_1)$. The coefficient 3 of the incoming variable in the key equation is known as the *pivot*.

2. Add or subtract multiples of the key equation to the remaining equations to eliminate those terms with the new basic variable.

In the example, to eliminate the term $-15R$ in the objective function we multiply the key equation by 15 and add it to the current equation for Z $(E_0' = E_0 + 15E_1')$:

E_0		$Z - 15R - 10P - 0S_A - 0S_B - S_C = 0$
$+15E_1'$	$(+15)(R + 0P + \frac{1}{3}S_A = 60) \longrightarrow$	$15R + 0P + 5S_A \qquad\qquad = 900$
E_0'	(revised objective function)	$Z \qquad - 10P + 5S_A - 0S_B - 0S_C = 900$

In the second equation E_2 for department B there is no need for any adjustment because there is no term with the new variable P; that is, $E_2' = E_2$. It therefore remains

$$E_2': \qquad\qquad 0R + 5P + S_B = 200$$

To eliminate the term $4R$ in the third equation E_3 for department C, we multiply the key equation by 4 and subtract $(E_3' = E_3 - 4E_1')$:

E_3		$4R + 6P \qquad + S_C = \quad 360$
$-4E_1'$	$(-4)(R + 0P + \frac{1}{3}S_A = 60) \longrightarrow$	$-4R - 0P - \frac{4}{3}S_A \qquad = -240$
E_3'	(revised third constraint)	$6P - \frac{4}{3}S_A + S_C = \quad 120$

After those adjustments, all equations can be restated together as follows:

$$
\begin{aligned}
E_0': & \qquad Z \quad -10P + 5S_A && = 900 \\
E_1': & \qquad\quad R \qquad\quad + \tfrac{1}{3}S_A && = 60 \\
E_2': & \qquad\qquad 5P \qquad\quad + S_B && = 200 \\
E_3': & \qquad\qquad 6P - \tfrac{4}{3}S_A \qquad + S_C && = 120
\end{aligned}
\qquad\text{(C-6)}
$$

The new solution, read directly from these equations, is $R = 60$, $S_B = 200$, and $S_B = 120$ with $P = S_C = 0$ and $Z = \$900$. In words, if we produce 60 R's and have unused capacity equal to 200 min in department B and 120 min in department C, profits for the toy manufacturer will increase to $900.

The preceding steps complete one stage, or iteration, for the simplex method, which now returns to step 2 to evaluate the current solution for improvement.

Second Iteration

The presence of a variable outside the solution with a negative coefficient in the current Z equation suggests that further improvement is possible. Thus, the introduction of P, producing Polly dolls, will increase total profit by \$10 per unit.

In step 3 the selection of P as the incoming variable is obvious because it is the only variable that qualifies. In Fig. C-1 this corresponds to a vertical movement upward along the line $R = 60$.

To determine which variable will leave the solution in step 4, we check which of the constraints will become a bottleneck as we increase P. Solving for each of the current basic variables, we have

	Maximum limit on P
$R = 60 - S_A^{\,\,0}$	No limit
$S_B = 200 - 5P$	40
$S_C = 120 - 6P + S_A^{\,\,0}$	20 (bottleneck)

Thus, as we increase P from zero to a positive amount, the unused capacity in department C will be exhausted first, thus making S_C the outgoing variable. In Fig. C-1 the first constraint that becomes binding is the equation for department C. The new solution will therefore be point d and will consist of variables R, S_B, and P, with S_A and S_C equal to zero.

The revisions of the equations necessary before we can identify the new solution directly are summarized below. The constraint for department C becomes the key equation by dividing all its terms by 6, the new pivot: $E_3'' = E_2'/6$.

E_3'': $\qquad\qquad\qquad P - \tfrac{2}{9}S_A + \tfrac{1}{6}S_C = 20 \qquad$ Key equation

The objective function is revised by adding to it the key equation multiplied by 10 ($E_0'' = E_0' + 10E_3''$):

E_0'	$Z - 10P + 5S_A \qquad\qquad\quad = 900$
$+ 10E_3'' \quad (+10)(P - \tfrac{2}{9}S_A + \tfrac{1}{6}S_C = 20) \longrightarrow$	$10P - \tfrac{20}{9}S_A + \tfrac{5}{3}S_C = 200$
$E_0'' \quad$ (revised objective function)	$Z \qquad\quad + \tfrac{25}{9}S_A + \tfrac{5}{3}S_C = 1{,}100$

The first equation requires no adjustment because it contains no terms with the incoming variable P; that is, $E_1'' = E_1'$,

E_1'': $\qquad\qquad\qquad R + \tfrac{1}{3}S_A = 60$

The second equation is revised by adding to it the key row multiplied by -5 $(E_2'' = E_2' - 5E_3'')$:

E_2'	$5P$	$+ S_B$	$= 200$
$-5E_3'' (-5)(P - \frac{2}{9}S_A + \frac{1}{6}S_C = 20) \longrightarrow$	$-5P + \frac{10}{9}S_A$	$- \frac{5}{6}S_C = -100$
E_2'' (revised second equation)	$\frac{10}{9}S_A + S_B - \frac{5}{6}S_C =$	100

Restating all equations in their revised form after the second iteration, we have

$$E_0'': \qquad\qquad Z \quad + \tfrac{25}{9}S_A \qquad + 10S_C = 1{,}100$$

$$E_1'': \qquad\qquad R \; + \tfrac{1}{3}S_A \qquad\qquad\quad = 60$$

$$E_2'': \qquad\qquad \tfrac{10}{9}S_A + S_B - \tfrac{5}{6}S_C = 100$$

$$E_3'': \qquad\qquad P - \tfrac{2}{9}S_A \qquad + \tfrac{1}{6}S_C = 20$$

(C-7)

The new, improved solution, corner point c in Fig. C-1, is read directly as

$$R = 60 \qquad S_B = 100 \qquad P = 20$$

with

$$Z = \$1{,}100 \text{ and } S_A = S_C = 0 \qquad\qquad \text{(C-8)}$$

Examination of the current objective function E_0'' reveals that no further improvement is possible because all variables outside the solution have positive coefficients. This can be seen more easily by restating the objective function as

$$Z = \$1{,}100 - \tfrac{25}{9}S_A - 10S_B$$

If we increase either S_A or S_B from zero to a positive amount, the current total profit of $\$1,100$ will decrease.

We conclude that the above solution, corner point c, is the optimum solution yielding the highest total profit of all feasible production combinations of R and P. Even though the graphical solution method was easier for the simple two-variable example, the simplex method is the most general and most powerful for linear-programming problems with a large number of variables and constraints. In actual applications management is limited only by the size of the computer facilities available.

For problems to be solved by hand, it is more efficient to perform the necessary calculations for each iteration using a table known as the *simplex tableau*. For the example this is illustrated in Table C-2.

A simplex tableau has three main parts. The first specifies the basic variables in the solution for each iteration and their respective profit coefficients. For all iterations Z might be viewed as the basic variable in the objective function. The second part of the tableau shows at the top all the decision and slack variables. The entries in the column for each variable are the coefficients of that variable in each equa-

TABLE C-2 Simplex tableau for toy-manufacturer example

Equation	Basic variables in solution	$C_j \rightarrow$	Z	R $15	P $10	S_A 0	S_B 0	S_C 0	Right-hand constant	Bottleneck ratio
E_0	Z		1	-15	-10	0	0	0	0	
E_1 ←	S_A	0	0	3	0	1	0	0	180	$\dfrac{180}{3} = 60*$
E_2	S_B	0	0	0	5	0	1	0	200	
E_3	S_C	0	0	4	6	0	0	1	360	$\dfrac{360}{4} = 90$
E_0'	Z		1	0	-10	5	0	0	900	
E_1'	R	$15	0	1	0	$\frac{1}{3}$	0	0	60	
E_2'	S_B	0	0	0	5	0	1	0	200	$\dfrac{200}{5} = 40$
E_3' ←	S_C	0	0	0	6	$-\frac{4}{3}$	0	1	120	$\dfrac{120}{6} = 20*$
E_0''	Z		1	0	0	$\frac{25}{9}$	0	10	1,100	Not needed
E_1''	R	$15	0	1	0	$\frac{1}{3}$	0	0	60	
E_2''	S_B	0	0	0	0	$\frac{10}{9}$	1	$-\frac{5}{6}$	100	
E_3''	P	$10	0	0	1	$-\frac{2}{9}$	0	$\frac{1}{6}$	20	

tion. The third part of the tableau shows the current values assumed by the basic variables. These are the right-hand side constants in the equations that yield the solution directly at each iteration.

For each variable in solution, the reader will note that the entries in the corresponding column assume values of 1 in only one equation and 0 in all others. Thus, the current values for the basic variables can be read directly from the column with the constant values.

Interpretation of Information in a Simplex Tableau

The entries of the simplex tableau in each iteration can be interpreted in a way that adds considerably to our understanding of the allocation process. For example, the entries in the column for each nonbasic variable are known as *substitution rates*. These entries represent the amount by which each variable in the solution will be reduced per unit increase in the column variable. Consider, for example, variable R in the initial solution. In the R column the entries are 3 in E_1, 0 in E_2, and 4 in E_3. These are the amounts by which the basic variables S_A, S_B, and S_C, that is, the unused capacity in departments A, B, and C, will be reduced per unit increase in R. In this case the interpretation is straightforward because these were the specified production requirements for R. Consider next the entries in the column for S_A in the second iteration. Their values are $\frac{1}{3}$ for E_1, $\frac{10}{9}$ for E_2, and $-\frac{2}{9}$ for E_3. If we choose to increase S_A by 1 unit, i.e., free up a unit of capacity in department A, the production of R will decrease by $\frac{1}{3}$ unit, the unused capacity S_B in department B by $\frac{10}{9}$, and the production of P will be increased by $\frac{2}{9}$.

The entry for a nonbasic decision variable in the Z row (E_0) represents the effect of a unit increase of that variable on the objective function. This is known as the *marginal value*, or *cost*, of bringing that variable into solution. For R in the initial solution this entry is -15. This negative reduction is equivalent to an increase of \$15 in the objective function per unit increase in R.

For a slack variable the Z-row entry in the optimal solution represents the *shadow price* of increasing the corresponding resource by 1 unit. Thus, the entry of 10 in the Z row for S_C can be interpreted as the worth of adding one more unit of capacity in department C.[1]

B-6 VARIATIONS AND COMPLICATIONS IN LINEAR PROGRAMMING

Our discussion of the simplex has been based on a simple example especially developed to focus on the key features of the method. Real linear-programmming problems may have variations or complications that require special adjustments.

Minimization Problems

In certain cases the allocation of resources is evaluated by a minimization of a criterion such as cost (diet or blending problems). The adjustment to the objective function involves either multiplying all terms by -1 and proceeding as before or restating rule 1 so that the incoming variable is chosen according to the largest positive coefficient.

Greater-than-or-Equal-to Inequalities

For constraints of the greater-than-or-equal-to type the adjustment is more complicated. Suppose the constraint for department C in the example is stated as

$$4R + 6P \geq 360$$

To convert this into an equation we bring in a variable S_C, comparable to a slack variable, which is subtracted from the left-hand side

$$4R + 6P - S_C = 360$$

where S_C is a nonnegative *surplus variable* with zero profit contribution that shows the extent by which we fail to meet the constraint for department C.

---

[1] This assumes that the unit increase in the resource will not change the basic variables in the optimum solution.

The simplex does not allow any basic variable to assume a negative value. S_C in an initial solution, with $P = R = 0$, would be set equal to -360. Therefore, an additional variable must be introduced in this constraint to allow the simplex to get started. This is done by adding an *artificial variable* S_D, which must be discarded before reaching the optimal solution

$$4R + 6P - S_C + S_D = 360$$

where S_D is a nonnegative artificial variable needed to get the simplex started which must be eliminated at a later stage. To force the artificial variable out, it must carry a large penalty $M = \$9,999$ in the objective function, which would be written as

$$Z = 15R + 10P - MS_D$$

Degeneracy

When we try to select the outgoing variable, two constraints may become bottle-necks at the same time. With two basic variables reaching zero simultaneously as the incoming variable is increased, it may become difficult to continue with subsequent iterations. In practice, the tie for the leaving variable is broken arbitrarily with no precedents of real complications.

Infeasible Solution

At times, as a result either of an error in the formulation or of true incompatibility in the constraints, there is no feasible solution. In the simplex this is signaled by the presence of an artificial variable in the final iteration.

Multiple Solutions

When a variable outside the optimal solution has a zero coefficient in the final Z row, it is possible to exchange it for a variable already in the solution with no change in the optimal value of the objective function. This implies the existence of multiple optimal solutions, allowing management considerable flexibility in arriving at the final allocation plan. In the graphical representation this would happen if the objective function had the same slope as one of the constraints. For the example, if $Z = \$10R + \$15P$, it would coincide with the constraints $4R + 6P \leq 360$ and any point along the edge *c-d* would be optimal.

Sensitivity Analysis

In a dynamic environment, in which little remains constant for long, the value to management of an optimal linear-programming solution would be limited indeed. Variations in the availability of resources (changing B_i's), fluctuations in prices and costs (changing C_j's), improvements in technology (changing A_{ij}'s), and the development of new products continually exert pressure on management to reevaluate its allocation strategies.

Linear programming offers a powerful method for studying the sensitivity of the optimal solution when one or more changes of the above types occur individually or in combination. Thus, management can proceed to adjust the optimal solution when necessary to maximize its performance under prevailing operating conditions.

A considerable amount of sensitivity analysis is possible by the information provided in the final iteration, but for more extensive analyses it is possible to use the computer to explore a wide variety of on-going or anticipated changes. Some simple forms of sensitivity analysis are considered in the problems at the end of this supplement. For additional material see the Selected References.

C-7   SUMMARY

Whenever management is concerned with the allocation of limited resources to competing activities, linear programming may offer a powerful approach for decision making. If the objective function and the constraints of a problem are assumed to be linear, we can use the simplex method or some variation not only for a numerical solution but for a thorough analysis of what would happen under various operating conditions.

Looking back at the application of the simplex method to the two-variable example, we can summarize its main features as follows:

1. The convexity (no holes, no recesses) of the feasible set, guaranteed by the assumption of linear relationships, makes it possible to solve linear-programming problems by considering only the corner points of the convex polygon. This means that the optimum will not be an interior point, although solutions may be located along one of the edges.
2. The simplex method starts at the origin and moves to an adjacent corner determined by the most profitable direction, i.e., the largest negative coefficient for a nonbasic variable.
3. As long as improvements are possible, the simplex method moves to a new adjacent corner point at each successive iteration. When no further improvement is indicated, the simplex stops, identifying at that point the optimum solution.
4. Since the direction of movement is determined by the rate of improvement possible, the simplex does not necessarily reach the optimum in the shortest number of iterations possible. As a rule of thumb, the number of iterations is approximately equal to the number of constraints.
5. At each iteration the simplex tableau provides information about:
   a. The current values of the variables in the solution.
   b. The possibility of further improvement by inspecting the coefficients of outside variables in the Z row.
   c. The substitution rates for each variable not in the current solution.
   d. The marginal value of each outside variable.
6. At the final iteration the simplex tableau provides information about:
   a. The optimal solution by reading the values of the basic variables and Z directly from the right-hand-side constants.
   b. The marginal value or shadow price for each resource unit increase by reading the coefficients of the slack variables in the Z row.

c. The marginal cost of bringing in any decision variable not in the optimal solution.

It is the versatility and wealth of information provided by the simplex method that has made linear programming one of the most powerful tools available to modern management.

REVIEW QUESTIONS

1. What general class of management problems is linear programming appropriate for? Give three examples of typical linear-programming applications.
2. Define in your own words the linear-programming concepts of (*a*) activities, (*b*) limited resources, (*c*) activity contribution, and (*d*) process technology.
3. Describe the main parts of a linear-programming problem formulation. What assumptions are made in such a formulation?
4. What methods have been developed to handle situations where linear-programming assumptions are seriously violated?
5. What information is provided by the graphical linear-programming method?
6. State the basic linear-programming property about the location of an optimum solution.
7. Describe the standard form of a linear-programming problem formulation.
8. What is the purpose and meaning of (*a*) slack variables, (*b*) surplus variables, and (*c*) artificial variables?
9. In solving a linear-programming problem, what are the number and name of variables (*a*) included and (*b*) not included in the solution?
10. When solving a linear-programming problem with the simplex method, what is the *indication* that (*a*) an optimum solution has been reached, (*b*) several optimum solutions exist, and (*c*) the problem has no feasible solution?
11. When using the simplex tableau, what is the meaning and location of:
    (*a*) Substitution rates of nonbasic variables
    (*b*) Shadow prices
    (*c*) Marginal value and cost of certain variables

PROBLEMS

1. Jay's furniture shop makes two products, *P* and *Q*, which require processing in three departments with the weekly capacities indicated below:

Department	Product P	Q	Weekly capacity, h
Cutting	2	6	240
Assembly	9	5	450
Finishing	4	4	320

The unit profit contributions for *P* and *Q* are $8 and $12, respectively, and the shop sells all the units it can produce. Find the optimal solution using the graphical method.

2. Refer to Prob. 1. Find the optimal solution using the simplex method and relate the advance in each iteration on the graph of the feasible set. In the final iteration identify the shadow price for each additional hour of capacity in the three departments.

3. Refer to Prob. 1. What would be the optimal solution for Jay's product mix if changes in the cost of materials mean that the revised unit profit contribution is $7 for P and $3 for Q?

4. A materials-testing laboratory with more requests than it can handle specializes in two types of tests, X and Y, and would like to determine how many of each to perform each week to maximize its revenue. Each week the lab can use up to 240 technician-hours, 100 inspector-hours, and 40 testing-equipment hours. Each test X requires 4 technician-hours, 1 inspector-hour, and no equipment time. Each test Y requires 2 technician-hours, 2 inspector-hours, and 1 machine-hour. The unit profit contributions are $20 for test X and $30 for test Y.

   (a) Identify the decision variables and state the objective function and constraints for the problem.

   (b) Using the graphical linear-programming method, determine the optimal solution.

   (c) Solve the above using the simplex method.

5. Refer to Prob. 4. In the final iteration of the simplex tableau identify:

   (a) The shadow prices for an additional hour of technicians, inspectors, and testing equipment

   (b) The marginal cost (or value) for each nonbasic variable

6. The owner of a farm is considering which combination of fertilizers F_1 and F_2 will supply seasonal soil requirements in two ingredients A and B. A pound of type F_1 will supply 5 units of A and 7 units of B, while a pound of F_2 will supply 12 units of A and 3 of B. The farm acreage will require a minimum of 6,000 units of A and 4,200 units of B. The cost of the fertilizers is 30 cents per pound of F_1 and 20 cents per pound of F_2.

   (a) Identify the problem decision variables and formulate the objective function and constraints.

   (b) Using the graphical method, determine the fertilizer mix that will meet soil requirements at minimum cost.

7. Refer to Prob. 6. Adjust the constraints and objective function to prepare the problem for solution by the simplex. Explain the meaning of each variable used beside the decision variables.

8. The International Space Research Agency is about to conduct a series of experiments with satellites carrying animals. The animal in each satellite is to be fed two types of meals, L and M, in the form of bars that drop into a box from automatic dispensers. The daily nutritional requirements for the animal, in terms of nutrients A, B, and C, can be supplied with different combinations of quantities for foods. The content of each food type and the weight of a single bar are shown below.

Nutrient	Nutritional content, units		Daily requirement, units
	L	M	
A	2	3	90
B	8	2	160
C	4	2	120
Weight per bar, gm	3	2	

Using a graphical method, find the combination of food types to be supplied so that daily requirements can be met while minimizing the total daily weight of food needed to allow ample capacity for various satellite instruments.

8. A ready-to-wear manufacturer is about to mass-produce his three latest designs *A*, *B*, and *C*, for which prospective buyers during preliminary showings have indicated they would order all the firm can produce. The production data and unit profit contribution for each design are as follows:

Production department	Design style requirements, min			Weekly capacity, min
	A	*B*	*C*	
Cutting	6	2	5	2,400
Sewing	8	10	4	3,200
Finishing	12	9	3	3,600
Unit profit contribution	$15	$6	$5	

(*a*) State the objective function and constraints for the problem.

(*b*) Solve using the simplex. Is the solution unique? Why?

(*c*) In the final simplex iteration identify, (i) the shadow price per unit of capacity in each department and (ii) the marginal cost of nonbasic variables.

9. Refer to Prob. 8. Resolve the problem if:

(*a*) A new labor contract decreases the unit profit contribution by $1 for each design style.

(*b*) Power shortages reduce the capacity in cutting and sewing by 50 percent.

SELECTED REFERENCES

1 Anderson, D. R., D. J. Sweeney, and T. R. Williams: *Fundamentals of Management Science*, West, St. Paul, 1978.

2. Hillier, F., and G. Lieberman: *Introduction to Operations Research*, 2d ed., Holden-Day, San Francisco, 1974.

3. Levin, R., and C. A. Kirkpatrick: *Quantitative Methods in Management*, 4th ed., McGraw-Hill, New York, 1978.

4. Loomba, N. Paul: *Management: A Quantitative Perspective*, Macmillan, New York, 1978.

5. Wagner, H.: *Operations Research*, 2d ed., Prentice-Hall, Englewood Cliffs, N.J., 1974.

Chapter 5

HOW MUCH TO PRODUCE I: CAPACITY PLANNING FOR MANUFACTURING SYSTEMS

5-1 INTRODUCTION

General

Determination of productive capacity requirements is a key problem not only when designing a new system or expanding an existing one but also for the shorter operating periods during which the plant size cannot be changed. Decisions about capacity are thus important because they provide a unifying thread for both long- and short-term managerial planning and control.

Definition

Productive capacity, generally measured in physical units, refers either to the maximum output rate for products or services or to the amounts of key resources available in each operating period.

When the output of an operations system is fairly standardized, *nominal physical capacity* can be expressed as a maximum sustainable output rate achieved by a full complement of labor on regular time. However, for systems producing a wide variety of products or services that cannot be measured in common units, it is necessary to express capacity in terms of critical resource inputs, e.g., labor-hours or machine-hours. Examples of capacity measurement for various systems are given in Table 5-1.

Since capacity alterations are made to satisfy expected changes in demand, capacity has the same dimensions as demand. The correspondence is shown in Table 5-2.

TABLE 5-1   Typical examples of capacity measurement

Facility	Unit of measure
Class A: Uniform output characteristics:	
Steel mill	Tons of steel produced daily
Shoe factory	Pairs of shoes produced per shift
Commercial airline	Passenger-seat-miles flown per route
Bottling plant	Gallons (cases) per shift
Class B: Variable output characteristics:	
Hospital (or hotel)	Number of beds
Auto repair shop	Number of mechanic-hours per day
Machine shop	Machine hours available daily
Bank or savings and loan	Operating capital
Stadium, night club, restaurant	Seating capacity
Telephone switchboard	Number of trunklines

TABLE 5-2   Relationship between demand and productive capacity

Dimension of demand	Effect on capacity requirements
Quantity	How much capacity is needed?
Timing	When should capacity be available?
Quality	What kind of capacity is needed?
Location	Where should capacity be installed?

In this chapter, our main concern is with the quantity and timing dimensions of capacity. The kind of capacity needed to satisfy quality requirements is specified by the technology selected in the process-design phase (see Chap. 7). The question of location is treated in Chap. 10.

Aspects of Capacity Planning

Management, in general, treats capacity-related problems in three ways. First is the issue of large increments in capacity needed for changes in demand over the long term, say 5 to 10 years ahead. For most technologies, capacity increments can be made only in large chunks at a time, even though they cannot be fully utilized when installed (another shift, or steel mill, or aircraft added when demand exceeds available capacity). This involves step increases in fixed costs that cannot be absorbed immediately from the gradual increase in expected demand over a long period. This type of capacity change sets the upper limit to what a system can produce; i.e., it defines the *system design capacity*. This problem is the focus of this chapter.

Second, within the framework imposed by the system design capacity, management can make limited adjustments for periods up to a year or two in order to cover fluctuations in demand due to seasonal and business cycles. This *aggregate planning* relies on the use of inventories and changes in the size of the work force through hiring and layoffs, use of overtime, and subcontracting orders to another firm. This level of capacity planning is treated in Chap. 12.

Finally, finer adjustments in capacity may be needed to cope with short-term random fluctuations in demand. This is done on a weekly or even daily basis because by definition random fluctuations in demand are both unpredictable and uncontrollable. The methods used for this refinement in capacity planning are discussed in Chap. 15 on *operations scheduling*.

5-2   DETERMINATION OF CAPACITY REQUIREMENTS

A feasibility study is usually performed to determine how much capacity will be needed and when. The phases in long-term capacity-related studies are shown in Fig. 5-1.

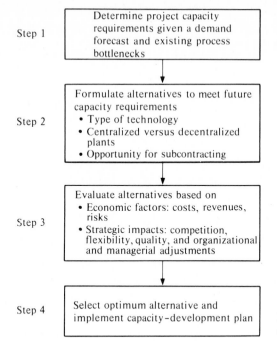

Step 1	Determine project capacity requirements given a demand forecast and existing process bottlenecks

| Step 2 | Formulate alternatives to meet future capacity requirements
• Type of technology
• Centralized versus decentralized plants
• Opportunity for subcontracting |

| Step 3 | Evaluate alternatives based on
• Economic factors: costs, revenues, risks
• Strategic impacts: competition, flexibility, quality, and organizational and managerial adjustments |

| Step 4 | Select optimum alternative and implement capacity-development plan |

Fig. 5-1 Procedure for developing a plan to change capacity.

Capacity Planning for a Single-Stage System

For simplicity we shall consider an example for an operations system as a whole. In practice, however, the analysis indicated must be carried out for each stage of the production process separately, in order to concentrate first on existing bottlenecks. Let us consider a food-processing firm which has experienced an average annual increase in demand equal to 200 units, as shown in Fig. 5-2. Its present maximum capacity is equal to 2,400 units/yr. The trend line for annual demand has been estimated from past data as $Y'_t = 600 + 200t$ (with $t = 0$ in 1974). Management is interested in adding enough capacity to cover expected demand for the next 12 yr, assuming that the linear upward trend will continue.

The minimum duration of the planning horizon is set by the lead time needed to add new capacity, i.e., engineering design, construction, equipment installation, etc., and the frequency with which top management reviews such issues. For example, if the lead time for a new facility is 2 yr and management reviews such issues 4 yr after the latest additions, the minimum planning horizon should be $2 + 4 = 6$ yr. This question is treated in Chap. 11.

For the last year in the planning horizon, i.e., in 1992, the value of t in the trend-line equation will be 18; therefore, the annual expected demand then will be $Y'_{92} = 600 + (200)(18) = 4,200$. Thus, if the present trend continues, we must provide enough capacity to produce at an annual output rate equal to $Y'_{92} = 4,200$ units. Given a current capacity limit of 2,400 units, the projected increase in capacity requirements for 1992 is equal to $4,200 - 2,400 = 1,800$ units. Whether the

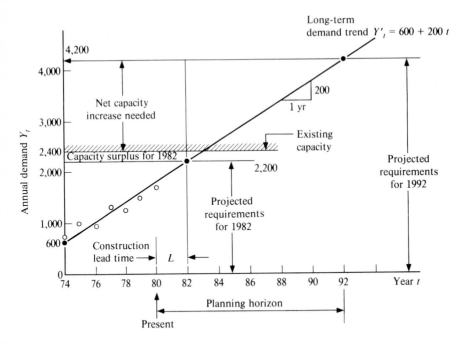

Fig. 5-2   Projected capacity requirements to handle increase in demand.

needed capacity will be added all at once or in smaller increments depends on the process technology. A shoe manufacturer might choose to build facilities for a new large plant and acquire equipment gradually as needed. A sugar refinery or a steel mill, however, is more severely restricted by the technology used to large-capacity increments. The choice depends on balancing the trade-offs between lower variable costs for large-capacity increments against high fixed costs that cannot be absorbed due to underutilization.

The above procedure does not account for the degree of uncertainty in future demand. This may be evaluated subjectively by top management planners or statistically by computing a measure of dispersion of actual demand points in the past from the trend line. An alternative approach accounting explicitly for future uncertainty in demand was illustrated in Supplementary Chapter A.

The projected estimate for net capacity requirements can be adjusted further to allow for planned shutdowns to handle preventive maintenance or for hedging against unexpected growth or decline. To illustrate, suppose that the above firm has decided to build the new plant with a capacity of 2,000 tons/yr overseas. If management wants to increase this by 15 percent for planned maintenance and another 10 percent for further growth, the capacity adjustment needed would be

$$\text{Normal plant capacity} = (2,000 \text{ units})(1.15) = 2,300 \text{ units}$$

$$\text{Adjusted plant capacity} = (2,300)(1.10) = 2,530 \text{ units}$$

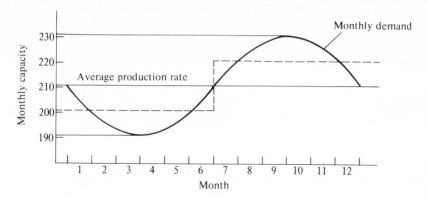

Fig. 5-3 Effect of seasonal cycle on capacity requirements.

The preceding figure still represents an average annual output rate for the overseas food-processing plant. If there are no seasonal fluctuations, the monthly rate will be 2,530/12 = 211 tons; but in the presence of a strong seasonal cycle typical of food-processing plants, actual requirements will exceed this monthly average during the peak season and in slack periods they will be less, as shown in Fig. 5-3. If management can rely on seasonal inventories, overtime, or subcontracting, the annual capacity requirements can be met by the above monthly rate.

If inventories cannot be used, the production rate must be continually changed to follow the actual demand ups and downs. Let us assume that the plant in this case can handle demand with a monthly maximum capacity equal to 230 tons. On an annual basis this corresponds to increasing capacity to 2,760 tons. Between the extremes of 2,530 tons needed for producing at a constant rate of 211 tons/month and 2,760 tons to absorb peaks of up to 230 per month, it is often possible to adopt a compromise plan, like that shown by the dashed line in Fig. 5-3. For our example, we assume we need (220)(12) = 2,640 tons/yr, a level imposed by the economics and technology of the process. Therefore, *in the determination of long-term capacity we must be aware of the feasibility of using short-range alternatives such as inventories, overtime, multiple work shifts, or subcontracting.*

Capacity Planning for a Multiple-Stage System

When the production process consists of one stage only, the determination of capacity requirements by previous methods yields the output rate for the entire new system directly (see Fig. 5-4*a*). More often, however, we must deal with multistage processes. Different equipment configurations for each stage make it virtually impossible to have all stages operate with the same maximum capacity (see Fig. 5-4*b*). In this case, the capacity requirements calculated previously apply to the bottleneck operation. This imbalance results in higher operating costs due to underutilization of facilities at other operations, but this may well be the only feasible way.

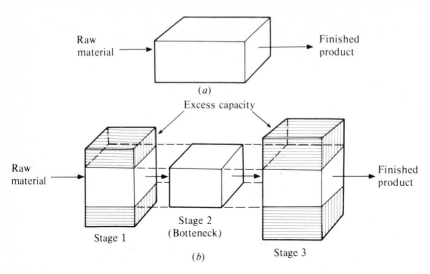

Fig. 5-4   Comparison of (*a*) single-stage and (*b*) multiple-stage, or system capacities.

5-3   EVALUATION OF ALTERNATIVE PLANT SIZES

The amount of capacity needed for a future planning period can be obtained from one or several plant sizes, each having a different maximum-capacity limit. The choice involves critical strategic decisions not only about the technology to be used but also about whether capacity will be available in one centralized or several geographically dispersed locations. Here management must consider not only production and distribution costs but the effects of such decisions on competition, the organizational structure and managerial style, and the flexibility needed to adapt to future changes in the environment. Sometimes these strategic issues have a greater influence in the final selection than the more quantifiable aspects pertaining to technology and costs.

Traditional Economic Analysis

Notwithstanding the importance of subjective factors, a proposal for capacity expansion must be able to meet sound economic criteria. Unless the investment is shown to offer a satisfactory return without excessive risks, it cannot be funded from the capital budgeting allocations. The financial-performance measures, derived from a cash-flow analysis, can take the form of a net present value (NPV) or rate of return on the required investment for new capacity. Once the revenues and costs for the project have been estimated, the calculation of such measures is routine and can be computerized so that it can be repeated for various assumptions.

Let us assume that the new capacity requirements of 2,640 units/yr, determined from the previous example, can be met from three different plant sizes with the cost

TABLE 5-3 Data for three alternative plant sizes

Annual capacity, units/yr	Initial investment	Annual fixed cost	Variable cost per unit	Average unit cost at full capacity
2,500	$ 700,000	$25,000	$50	$60
5,000	1,200,000	30,000	47	53
10,000	1,800,000	36,000	45	48.60

characteristics listed in Table 5-3 and average unit cost at different production volume shown in Fig. 5-5.

From the data in Table 5-3 we note four points of special significance in capacity studies: (1) An increase in plant size requires a large investment but can lead to significant economies of scale near the full-capacity production volume. This usually results from savings in construction and equipment per unit of capacity. The cost per square meter of floor space or per Btu for a boiler is smaller for large plants than for small ones. (2) Fixed costs per unit become smaller because items like utilities, supervision, insurance, etc., are about the same over a wide range of plant capacity. (3) Certain variable costs are also allocated over more units, thus decreasing unit variable costs. (4) Variable costs also tend to be lower in larger plants due to economies in raw-materials purchases and shipping and lower processing costs from more specialized equipment that are economical only for large production volume. In going to larger and larger plant sizes, especially through the use of more advanced technologies, we are in effect substituting capital for labor. At the same time we achieve higher organizational efficiencies through more advanced management techniques for planning and control of operations

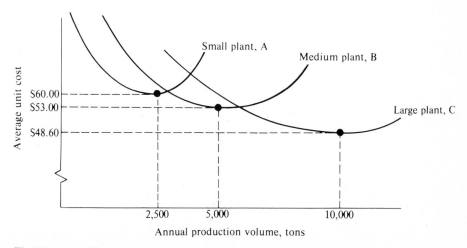

Fig. 5-5 Cost-volume curves for three plant sizes.

(computer-assisted scheduling, maintenance, inventory control, and other functions).

A closer examination of the average-unit-cost curves reveals that economies of scale for a given plant size are lost if we depart considerably from full-capacity utilization. At lower output rates with a new system there may be inefficiencies which are gradually removed as cumulative production output increases due to learning effects (see discussion of learning curves in Chap. 8). When we exceed the nominal design capacity, however, average unit costs increase. This is caused by the need for overtime, multiple shifts, extra supervision, and inefficiencies in processing and handling. The last are due to congestion from poor scheduling or additional repairs imposed by overworking workers and equipment.

Economies of scale have been a powerful force in shaping economic activities in our time, both in the private and public sector. Organizations affected include such industries as oil refining, steel, communications, and transportation and such service systems as supermarkets, giant department stores, education, and government. Despite this strong appeal, *the choice of the correct plant size must be determined not only by cost performance but also by the level of expected demand.* This requires the type of cost-volume-profit analysis discussed below.

Cost-Volume-Profit Analysis

The selection of optimum plant size given capacity requirements must be based on adequate analysis of cash flows for each alternative plant size. This in turn requires the estimation of total costs (TC) and total revenues (TR) at different production volumes for each plant size. The total costs in each case are determined from the estimates of fixed and variable costs that apply for each plant size. Total revenues are obtained from the level of expected demand and the pricing policy of the firm. Given a demand forecast for each year in the planning horizon, we select the plant size that maximizes the return on investment in new capacity. These relationships are shown by conducting a cost-volume-profit analysis for each plant size, as shown in Fig. 5-6.

Figure 5-6 shows that the profitable output range varies for each plant size. For a low demand level Y_1 plant sizes A and B result in a profit, but C's high fixed cost results in loss. However, for a high demand level Y_2 size A results in a loss, while B and C result in profits. A more detailed discussion of cost-volume-profit analysis, also known as break-even analysis, is given in Supplementary Chapter B. When the output volume in the planning horizon is known with uncertainty, i.e., in terms of a statistical distribution, it is possible to combine the method of cost-volume-profit analysis with decision analysis to determine an average or expected profit for each alternative plant size.

5-4 DETERMINATION OF EQUIPMENT REQUIREMENTS

After we estimate the design capacity needed for the system as a whole and the individual production stages, we must translate this information into requirements

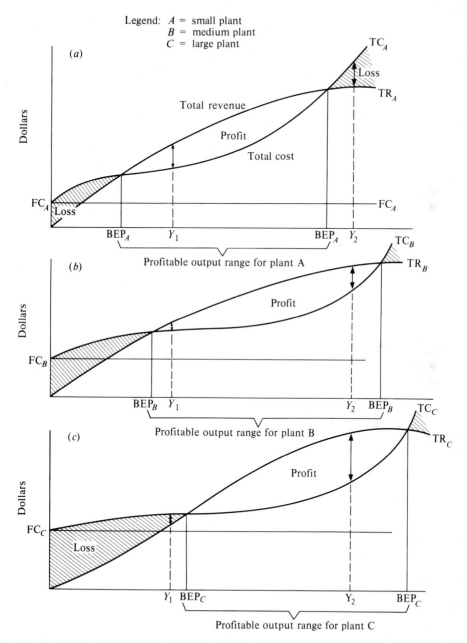

Legend: A = small plant
B = medium plant
C = large plant

(a)

Dollars

Total revenue

Profit

Total cost

TC_A

Loss

TR_A

FC_A

Loss

FC_A

BEP_A Y_1 BEP_A Y_2

Profitable output range for plant A

(b)

Dollars

Profit

TC_B

TR_B

FC_B

BEP_B Y_1 Y_2 BEP_B TC_C

Profitable output range for plant B

(c)

Dollars

Profit

TC_C

TR_C

FC_C

Loss

Y_1 BEP_C Y_2 BEP_C

Profitable output range for plant C

Fig. 5-6   Cost-volume-profit analysis for (a) small, (b) medium, and (c) large plant sizes.

for equipment and the work force necessary to operate it. We shall discuss how this is done for one stage, which may include a work station or an entire department, and then extend the analysis to include several stages.

Equipment Requirements for a Single Production Stage

In order to convert a measure of capacity into equipment requirements we require (1) an estimate of demand for each period in the planning horizon, expressed by the number of good units needed per period and obtained from a detailed demand forecast, and (2) an estimate of processing time for the work station where the equipment will be used. This is usually obtained by one of the work-measurement methods discussed in Chap. 8.

Let P = production rate of work station, units of output per period
T = processing time per unit, min
D = duration of an operating period, h (for one shift $D = 8$, for two, $D = 16$, and for three, $D = 24$)
E = efficiency of equipment expressed as percentage of running time per period (this accounts for downtime due to setups, breakdown repair, or other reasons that force idleness)
N = number of machines required by work station

The calculation of equipment requirements is based on the formula

$$N = \frac{T}{60} \frac{P}{D \cdot E} \qquad (5\text{-}1)$$

or

$$\begin{bmatrix} \text{Number of} \\ \text{machines needed} \end{bmatrix} = \begin{bmatrix} \text{processing time} \\ \text{per unit, h} \end{bmatrix} \begin{bmatrix} \dfrac{\text{Required output rate}}{\text{available time/period}} \end{bmatrix}$$

To illustrate this relationship with an example, suppose that a fabrication department must supply 3,000 good parts daily to another department for assembly. Processing time is 2.50 min/unit, and the equipment efficiency for two shifts daily is estimated at 80 percent. The equipment requirements for this case will be

$$N = \frac{T}{60} \frac{P}{D \cdot E} = \frac{2.50}{60} \frac{3,000}{(16)(.80)} = 9.77 \approx 10 \text{ machines}$$

In practice, the proposed method for determining equipment requirements must be used with caution. In particular, it is important to examine P and D more extensively. To estimate P correctly we must keep in mind that the total number of units processed at a work station include those which meet specifications and can be forwarded to the next production stage along with some defective units. Thus,

$$P = P_g + P_d \qquad (5\text{-}2)$$

where P_g are good units and P_d are defective units.

For a given operation the number of defective units can be expressed as a percentage of defective units p over the total number of units processed. Rearranging (5-2), we have

$$P_g = P - P_d = P - \frac{P_d}{P} P = P - pP = P(1 - p)$$

and

$$P = \frac{P_g}{1 - p} \qquad (5\text{-}3)$$

where p is the percentage defective output of the work station.

Returning to our example, if the number of required good parts is 3,000 daily and for the work station under study the defective output amounts to 5 percent, the output rate must be revised as follows:

$$P = \frac{P_g}{1 - p} = \frac{3{,}000}{1 - .05} = 3{,}158 \text{ units}$$

For the estimation of D, the use of 8 clock hours per shift is appropriate when the processing time T refers to an average required time per unit. If T represents a standard time developed by one of the methods discussed in Chap. 8, it includes not only the strictly productive time but allowances for operator fatigue, time for personal needs, and time for uncontrollable delays. Therefore, when using standard times for T, the duration of an operating period must also be expressed in standard working hours. For example, if we have 25 working days per month and use two shifts, we have $(2)(25)(8) = 400$ clock hours. However, if the average output rate of the work force is 110 percent of that based on standard times, possibly due to wage incentives or other factors, the 400 clock hours are equivalent to $(400)(1.10) = 440$ standard hours per month.

The revised equipment requirements for our example, assuming the standard processing time is 3 min, will be

$$N' = \frac{T_s}{60} \frac{P}{D_s \cdot E} = \frac{3}{60} \frac{3{,}158}{(440/25)(.80)} = 12.49 \approx 13$$

· where T_s = standard processing time per unit

D_s = duration of operating period in standard hours

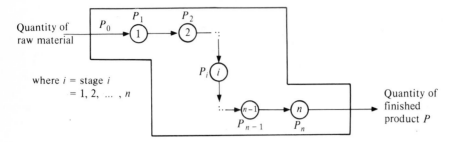

Fig. 5-7   **Flow pattern in a multistage production process.**

Equipment Requirements for Successive Production Stages

A production process often consists of several stages in series that the product must flow through in order to complete all the necessary operations. The determination of equipment requirements for each stage is accomplished by successive application of the formula (5-1), so that in each step we account for the particular operating conditions that apply to that stage. The procedure used can be explained more easily with reference to Fig. 5-7, which illustrates a multistage process.

The number of pieces flowing between stages decreases with the number of completed stages. This reflects the losses of defective units and various differences in operating characteristics for each stage, e.g., the condition of equipment, maintenance effectiveness, and training of the operators. If we examine the conversion performed in a typical stage i more closely, we have a flow pattern like that in Fig. 5-8, where stage i receives an amount of good units from stage $i - 1$ equal to $P_{g, i-1}$. After processing is completed at i, we obtain a quantity of good units equal to $P_{g, i}$ that can be advanced to the next stage and an amount of defective units $P_{d, i}$. In symbols this conservation-of-flow relationship is

$$P_{g, i-1} = P_{g, i} + P_{d, i} \qquad (5\text{-}4)$$

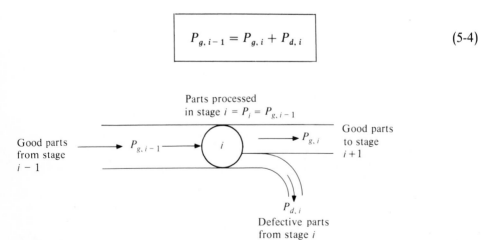

Fig. 5-8   **Product flow relationship at stage i.**

or

$$\begin{bmatrix} \text{Input to} \\ \text{stage } i \end{bmatrix} = \begin{bmatrix} \text{good output} \\ \text{of stage } i \end{bmatrix} + \begin{bmatrix} \text{defective output} \\ \text{of stage } i \end{bmatrix}$$

In order to meet an expected level of demand equal to P finished units, the flow through successive stages must satisfy the following balance equations:

Stage i	Balance equation (input = output)†
n(final)	$P_{g,\,n-1} = P_{g,\,n} + P_{d,\,n} = P_n$
$n-1$	$P_{g,\,n-2} = P_{g,\,n-1} + P_{d,\,n-1} = P_{n-1}$
. . . .	
i	$P_{g,\,i-1} = P_{g,\,i} + P_{d,\,i} = P_i$
. . . .	
2	$P_{g,\,1} = P_{g,\,2} + P_{d,\,2} = P_2$
1	$P_0 = P_{g,\,1} + P_{d,\,1} = P_1$

† $P = P_{g,\,n}$ = final demand.

For each stage, the determination of equipment requirements if defective units cannot be reworked is based on the relationship

$$N = \frac{T_i}{60} \frac{P_i}{D \cdot E_i} \qquad i = 1, 2, \ldots, n \tag{5-5}$$

When using Eq. (5-5) we assume that all stages are operating simultaneously.

For some operations it may be possible to rework some defective units, while the rest are simply discarded as scrap. If it is economically feasible to rework such units so that they will pass quality inspections, it is necessary to compute additional requirements in equipment and operators to perform this task. Rework of defectives may be done in special areas or in the same area provided for regular production. We must keep in mind that reworking defective units may require different processing times and special equipment that may operate with different efficiencies. To keep such requirements separate from regular production, we can use the modified equation

$$N_i' = \frac{T_i'}{60} \frac{P_i'}{D \cdot E_i'} \tag{5-6}$$

where i = stage where rework of defectives is feasible, say $i = 2, 6, n$

T_i' = rework time of defective unit from stage i

P_i' = number of units $P_{d,\,i}$ from defective output of stage i that can be reworked

If rework is done in the same area and with the same machines used for regular production, the total requirements in equipment for stage i will be $N_i + N_i'$.

Estimation of the Percentage Defective Output *p*

It is common practice to judge the quality level of a transformation process by the percentage of defective output *p*. This was also shown to be important in the determination of equipment requirements.

For an existing production process *p* can be estimated from samples of output collected during a base period, i.e., a period typical of future conditions, in terms of worker training, maintenance policies, quality of raw material, etc. This method is discussed in Chap. 16. More expedient methods may include consulting past work orders or other production records. Sometimes the value of *p* can be related to suppliers of materials or parts, working conditions, training and experience of work force, or maintenance effort.

For a new process the estimation of *p* may have to be derived from comparable experience in the same industry or from special studies that treat the factors mentioned previously in a more systematic fashion.

Determination of the Stage Efficiency *E*

Equally important but more difficult to assess is the efficiency measure for a given work station. Efficiency is defined as

$$E = \frac{H}{D} \tag{5-7}$$

$$= 1.00 - \frac{DT + ST}{D} \tag{5-8}$$

where E = work-station efficiency
$\quad H$ = expected running time per period, h
$\quad D$ = duration of an operating period, h
$\quad DT$ = downtime, h
$\quad ST$ = setup time for processing different orders per period, h

Even with advanced production technologies, a certain percentage of an operating period is spent in forced idleness. This may be due to the need for repair, special adjustments of machines during operation, power failures, or delays in the deliveries of raw materials and parts. The efficiency measure of a given stage depends on three factors:

1. The type of equipment used
2. How the equipment is operated (speeds, feeds, adjustments, etc.)
3. The maintenance policy used

The trend toward extensive mechanization of certain tasks or even automation of groups of operations has created complex problems in achieving reliable performance. The evaluation of a system's reliability and the crucial role of maintenance

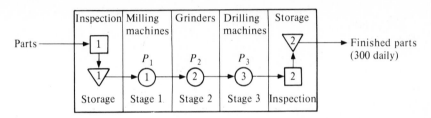

Fig. 5-9   Representation of a three-stage process for Example 5-1.

in achieving high efficiency are discussed in Chap. 17. For certain types of equipment preventive maintenance can be a most effective approach for reducing downtime due to breakdown repairs and thus increasing efficiency directly. This requires close coordination with the function of operations scheduling to minimize the combined cost from repairs, downtime, and preventive maintenance while maintaining prompt deliveries. Another approach might also emphasize the training and motivation of operators so that sources of breakdown can be sensed and corrected before costly and time-consuming failures occur.

▶ EXAMPLE 5-1
Precision Parts Co. has just signed a large contract with an automobile manufacturer for the delivery of 300 parts per day, following a trial order to determine feasibility and ability to meet quality standards. The manufacture of the part requires processing in three successive stages (milling, grinding, and drilling), as shown in Fig. 5-9, with the relevant data shown in Table 5-4.

TABLE 5-4   Processing data for Example 5-1†

Production stage	Working hours per period D	Processing time per unit T, min	Average daily downtime DT, min	Average daily setup time ST, min	Defective p, %
1	8	15	80	16	6
2	8	10	90	30	4
3	8	20	40	8	9

Note: † Defective units cannot be reworked and are discarded as scrap.

From the data in Table 5-4 we can proceed to determine the equipment requirements for each department so that Precision Parts, Inc. can meet the final demand of 300 units/day. Before applying the previous procedure in this case, we must calculate some additional characteristics of each production stage, i.e., the efficiency of each stage and the required production rate P_i to meet demand.

Determination of Production Stage Efficiency E

In general, we have

$$E = 1.00 - \frac{\text{unavailable time per period}}{\text{working hours per period}}$$

or

$$E = 1.00 - \frac{DT + ST}{D}$$

For the milling machines (stage 1)

$$E_1 = 1.00 - \frac{80 + 16}{(60)(8)} = 1.00 - .20 = .80$$

For the grinders (stage 2)

$$E_2 = 1.00 - \frac{90 + 30}{(60)(8)} = 1.00 - .25 = .75$$

For the drilling machines (stage 3)

$$E_3 = 1.00 - \frac{40 + 8}{(60)(8)} = 1.00 - .10 = .90$$

Thus, the efficiencies of production stages 1, 2, and 3 are .80, .75, and .90, respectively.

Determination of Production Rate per Stage P_i

Since processing in each stage results in both good and defective units, the total number of units processed in each department must satisfy the following relationships

$$P_i = \frac{P_{g,i}}{1 - p_i} \qquad i = 1, 2, 3$$

To determine the appropriate production rate for each department we start with the last stage and move backward.

For the drilling machines (stage 3)

$$P_{g,3} = 300 \text{ units/day} \qquad \text{Final demand}$$

and

$$P_3 = \frac{P_{g,3}}{1 - p_3} = \frac{300}{1 - .09} = \frac{300}{.91} = 329.67$$

therefore

$$P_3 \approx 330 \text{ units}$$

For the grinders (stage 2)

$$P_2 = \frac{P_{g,2}}{1 - p_2} = \frac{330}{1 - .04} = \frac{330}{.96} = 343.75$$

therefore

$$P_2 = 344 \text{ units}$$

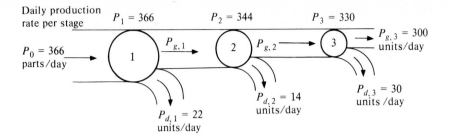

Fig. 5-10   Flow of units in a three-stage production process.

For the milling machines (stage 1)

$$P_1 = \frac{P_{g,1}}{1 - p_1} = \frac{344}{1 - .06} = \frac{344}{.94} = 365.95$$

therefore $P_1 = 366$ units

Thus, the loss of defective units in each processing stage means that in order to obtain 300 good units from the last stage we must supply the first one with 366 good parts. This is shown more graphically in Fig. 5-10.

Determination of Equipment Requirements N_i

Using the general equation (5-1), we can now proceed to calculate for each department the equipment requirements for the manufacture of the automobile part.
For the milling department (stage 1)

$$N_1 = \frac{T_1}{60} \frac{P_1}{D \cdot E_1} = \frac{(15)(366)}{(60)(8)(.80)} = 14.3$$

Thus $N_1 = 15$ milling machines

For the grinding department (stage 2)

$$N_2 = \frac{T_2}{60} \frac{P_2}{D \cdot E_2} = \frac{(10)(344)}{(60)(8)(.75)} = 9.55$$

Thus $N_2 = 10$ grinders

For the drilling department (stage 3)

$$N_3 = \frac{T_3}{60} \frac{P_3}{D \cdot E_3} = \frac{(2)(330)}{(60)(8)(.90)} = 15.3$$

▶ Thus $N_3 = 16$ drilling machines

Determination of Net Requirements for Each Production Stage

The number of machines needed per stage to meet a given output volume will be a fraction or a mixed number rather than a whole number. This can be seen from the results of applying Eq. (5-1) in the previous example. Unless these machines can be time-shared for processing other items, the computed requirements must be rounded off to the next larger integer value, as done in the example. A consequence of rounding up fractional equipment requirements is the creation of idle capacity. At this point, it might be advisable to consider subcontracting as an alternative to underutilizing expensive equipment. After making allowances for relevant subjec-tive factors (quality, reliability of delivery dates, etc.), the decision of purchasing the machine resulting from rounding up is based on the marginal cost of producing a unit with the new machine as opposed to subcontracting some units to a competitor.

When a group of similar machines is used for several products, the fractional or mixed-number requirements for each item can be added up to determine net equip-ment requirements per production stage or functional area. In practice these mini-mum requirements must be adjusted to allow for change-over or setup times in changing production runs. Therefore, feasible solutions are to be found in the range between maximum, i.e., rounded-up, and minimum requirements. The specific choice depends on the ease and versatility of equipment to be set up for different products.

▶ EXAMPLE 5-2

To illustrate the adjustments possible in arriving at equipment requirements for time-shared machines in a production stage, consider the information in Table 5-5 for a five-product system. Let us assume that in the grinding department of the Precision Parts Co. (Example 5-1) there is a need to process five different products (A, B, C, D, E). Each product requires a different grinding operation ($O_1, O_2, \ldots, O_5$). We can calculate equipment requirements by applying Eq. (5-1); the results correspond to unadjusted, i.e., fractional, requirements per product for grinders. These figures can be added up to yield minimum total requirements of 19.91. By

TABLE 5-5   Information needed for combined equipment requirements

Product	Processing operation in stage i	Unadjusted equipment requirements	Maximum equipment requirements	Feasible combinations	Total equipment requirements
A	O_1	2.68	3	O_2	3
B	O_2	4.17	5	O_1	4
C	O_3	3.51	4	O_4	4
D	O_4	4.33	5	—	4
E	O_5	5.22	6	O_3	6
Total		19.91	23		21

rounding up individual product requirements and adding we obtain a maximum total of 23 machines.

If we can identify operations which can be done on the same machines, from the feasible combinations we can add fractional values of requirements for machines that are interchangeable. For example, products A and B require operations that can be done on the same machines. Therefore, we can combine their unadjusted requirements $(2.68 + 4.17 = 6.85)$ and allocate them to O_1 and O_2 for A and B. Machines for C can also handle D, but not vice versa, so that fractional requirements of D (.33) can be added to the unadjusted figure for C to make the first equal to 4 and the second equal to 4. Proceeding as above, we can combine equipment requirements that meet processing restrictions and thus reduce the total from a maximum of 23 to 21. For expensive machinery such adjustments may result in significant savings as long as they do not create serious problems for scheduling or maintenance.

5-5 DETERMINATION OF REQUIREMENTS IN OPERATORS

Having calculated equipment requirements, we can determine the number of machine operators from our knowledge of how machine assignments are handled. If we need one operator per machine, then for stage i the number of operators will be equal to N_i. The problem, however, becomes more difficult if a machine requires a crew of specialized workers. These workers during part of the machine cycle can be assigned to similar machines or can be given additional tasks.

Effective scheduling of skilled operators working individually or in crews requires a careful matching of operator cycle times with machine cycle times where interchangeability of operators is possible. The utilization of operator time must aim not only at increasing productivity but also in providing job satisfaction by allowing the fulfillment of psychological and social needs of the worker. This issue is discussed in greater length in Chap. 8 in relationship to job and work environment design.

5-6 SUMMARY

Selection of the most desirable combination of products and/or services an organization will offer is followed by an equally critical decision concerning the amount of needed productive capacity. For specific time frames, capacity specifies the maximum sustainable output rate if the items produced can be expressed in common units; otherwise it refers to the maximum amount of available critical resources, i.e. labor-hours, machine-hours, or other.

Productive-capacity determination provides the unifying thread for long-, medium-, and short-term planning. The long-term-capacity decision considered in the phase of system design must take into account how capacity will be used in the medium term, for which the maximum is fixed but during which demand follows pronounced seasonal fluctuations. Depending on company strategy and available production alternatives, the design capacity may be less than what is needed to cover peak demand. The balance can be satisfied from inventories, work-force changes, subcontracting, or other alternatives. For the short run, available capacity must adjust to the random fluctuations in demand as estimated in a forecast. This is a problem in scheduling dealt with in Chap. 15.

The choice of an "optimum" plant size is based on economic analysis using traditional cost-volume-profit (or break-even) analysis. The objective here is to balance the potential savings from economies of scale against the increased average unit costs due to underutilization of capacity in the early years of operation. The same problem can be solved under conditions of uncertainty using a decision-tree approach, as illustrated in Supplementary Chapter A.

After the design capacity has been established, the requirements in equipment for each period in the planning horizon can be determined by a straightforward method which balances demand for capacity against equipment output rate. At this point it is important to realize that a production stage must usually process more units than estimated for final demand due to losses from defective output. Capacity requirements must also be adjusted to account for limited efficiency attributed to setup time and downtime for repairs, delays, etc. The analysis employed for one stage can be easily extended to cover several stages. Adjustments are also possible when processing times are in the form of standard times obtained from work measurement. Economies in equipment investment and operating costs are possible when machines can be shared by several items and when operators or crews can be scheduled to alternative tasks during machine-cycle idle periods.

REVIEW QUESTIONS

1. Explain the meaning of capacity for a productive system.
2. What measures of capacity would you suggest for:
   (a) A shipping company
   (b) An oil refinery
   (c) An engineering consulting firm
   (d) A private high-prestige college
3. Discuss how capacity adjustments are made for short-, medium-, and long-term planning horizons.
4. Explain the steps followed when preparing and implementing a plan to change system design capacity.
5. How is required capacity obtained from a trend relationship adjusted for the presence of a seasonal cycle in demand?
6. Is there a difference in capacity planning between single-stage and multiple-stage operations system?
7. In selecting the optimum plant size, what are the trade-offs between a single large plant and several smaller ones to obtain the same overall capacity?
8. For a given plant size, what happens when output volume deviates from its full-capacity-utilization level?
9. What information is provided by a cost-volume-profit analysis for different plant sizes?
10. Discuss the information inputs needed to translate desired productive capacity for a given stage into equipment requirements.
11. Explain the meaning of *conservation of flow* for a given production stage.
12. Explain how we determine the efficiency of a given production stage before we can calculate equipment requirements.

13. How can the gross equipment requirements be reduced when machines are time-shared by several products?

14. Explain how the requirements for machine operators can be reduced for certain production configurations.

PROBLEMS

1. The management of Elsie Dairy Co. is considering adding to the capacity of its processing plant, currently limited to 24 million gallons a year. Annual demand in 1980 has reached the level of 20 million gallons and has been steadily rising at the rate of 1.5 million gallons per year. Once a decision is reached to add new capacity, it requires 2 yr before the new facilities are operational. Management reviews capacity related issues every 6 yr from the time new additions are completed.

   (a) If the present upward trend continues, in what year will demand exceed current capacity?

   (b) If management decides now to add a new plant in a different location, what is the net annual capacity increase that will be required until the next review period?

2. Refer to Prob. 1. The company will shut down the new plant each year for maintenance, thus reducing available capacity.

   (a) What should the adjustment in the desired capacity of the new plant be to allow an increase of 8 percent?

   (b) If management wishes to hedge for a further 5 percent growth in the expectation of higher sales, what should the total adjustment in the capacity needed for the new plant be?

   (c) If there are no seasonal fluctuations, what would the monthly production rate corresponding to the adjusted capacity be?

3. In Prob. 1 the calculations for capacity in the *new plant* assumed a steady month-to-month output rate. Suppose that demand for dairy products displays a seasonal cycle. If the system must operate in some months with a production rate as much as 20 percent higher than the average, what should the adjustment in the overall capacity increase be?

4. ABC Co. manufactures small gears used for special office equipment. Production of these gears requires processing in two departments, stamping and grinding, with the respective capacities of 48,000 and 52,000 units. Current demand is 41,000 units/yr, rising at the rate of 3,000 units/yr. The lead time for adding new capacity is 2 yr.

   (a) Plot a graph showing the trend line for annual demand and indicate the existing capacity limits.

   (b) Determine when each department will run out of capacity if the present trend continues.

   (c) Estimate the net capacity increases needed to satisfy annual demand for the next 5 yr.

5. Suppose that the plant facilities of Gourmet Foods Corp. consists of three stages with the following present capacities:

Stage	Activity	Capacity tons/yr
1	Washing and preparation	132,000
2	Cooking	120,000
3	Canning	125,000

Annual demand in 1980 is 112,000 tons; large increases in export sales mean that it is expected to rise at the steady rate of 3,000 tons/yr. The required lead time to add new capacity to any stage is 2 yr. Capacity increments can be made only in amounts of 15,000, 25,000, and 40,000 tons for each stage.

(a) Plot a chart of demand versus time and specify:
  (i) The trend line for annual demand
  (ii) The capacity limit for each processing stage
  (iii) The year in which demand will exceed the capacity for each stage
  (iv) Expected demand level by 1990

(b) What are the unadjusted capacity increases for each stage to meet projected demand for 1990?

(c) How should the capacity change for each stage be adjusted to allow a 12 percent increase due to planned annual maintenance?

(d) How should management phase in the new additions so that there will be no capacity shortages at any stage until 1990?

6. Refer to Prob. 5. If capacity changes in each stage can be made in amounts of 18,000- and 30,000-ton increments, how should they be phased in to balance the system by the end of the planning horizon?

7. Grapho-Tronics, a small manufacturer of a graphic display unit for computer systems, is considering expanding its capacity to keep up with increasing demand. Expected demand may be covered by building a small, medium, or large plant with cost performances similar to the alternatives discussed in the Example 5-1 (see Fig. 5-5). If the company continues its current pricing policy, the price per unit will be $1,400 and the probabilities for different demand levels at that price along with average unit costs for each plant size are summarized below:

Annual demand, units	Probability of demand at current price	Average unit cost at given production volume		
		Small plant	Medium plant	Large plant
3,000	.3	$ 450	$740	$950
5,000	.5	620	410	580
8,000	.2	1,030	970	360

The contribution to profit per unit of output at a given production volume is the difference between the selling price and the average unit cost for that level of capacity utilization.

(a) Prepare a table showing the total contribution to profit for each plant size at the expected demand levels.

(b) Select the optimum plant size for the current pricing policy (using decision analysis).

8. The management of Grapho-Tronics (see Prob. 7) believes that a change in pricing policy involving a price increase to $1,500 per unit and a price decrease to $1,300 per unit will affect the probabilities of expected sales as follows:

Demand level	Estimated probability	
	After price increase	After price decrease
3,000	.5	.1
5,000	.4	.6
8,000	.1	.3

(a) Determine the contribution to profit and select the optimum plant size if management proceeds with a price increase to $1,500 per unit.

(b) Repeat part (a) if management decides to have a price decrease to $1,300 per unit.

(c) For which plant size and pricing policy will the management of Grapho-Tronics maximize expected profits?

9. Refer to Prob. 7. (This problem requires familiarity with Supplementary Chapter A.) The management of Grapho-Tronics has decided to use the service of a consulting firm, Decision Aids, Inc., to prepare an economic forecast before selecting the best plant size. The reliability of the consulting firm's forecasts, based on past experience, is specified by the following conditional probabilities:

Decision Aids, Inc., forecast	Future state of economy		
	Low demand s_1	Average demand s_2	Large demand s_3
Pessimistic f_1	.8	.1	.1
Normal f_2	.1	.6	.2
Optimistic f_3	.1	.3	.7
	1.0	1.0	1.0

(a) Prepare a decision tree for the Grapho-Tronics expansion problem.

(b) Determine the value of perfect information.

(c) Determine the optimal course of action, given
   (i) A pessimistic forecast f_1
   (ii) A normal forecast f_2
   (iii) An optimistic forecast f_3

(d) Specify the Bayes strategy for Grapho-Tronics.

(e) Calculate the long-term expected value (LTEV) for this problem.

(f) Determine the long-term expected benefit (LTEB) from using the services of the consulting firm.

(g) Determine the maximum reasonable fee Grapho-Tronics should pay to Decision Aids, Inc.

10. Refer to Prob. 4. The operating data for the part manufactured by ABC Company are shown below:

Process characteristic	Department	
	Stamping	Grinding
Working hours per day	16	16
Processing time, min/part	3	5
Average daily downtime, min	115	130
Average daily setup time, min	40	54
Defective output, %†	7	8

† All defectives are rejected as scrap. The company operates 250 working days per year.

If the annual demand is currently 65,000 parts, determine:
(a) The efficiency E for each department
(b) The required production rate P_i for each department
(c) The equipment requirements for each department

11. Refer to Prob. 10. What would the effect on equipment requirements be if the company were to go to one shift operation $(D = 8$ h$)$?

12. Refer to Prob. 10. If a quality-control program on incoming materials can reduce the percent defectives to 5 percent for stamping and 6 percent for grinding, what would the effect on equipment requirements be?

13. Reliable Parts Co. has signed a contract with a farm-equipment manufacturer for 100,000 parts to be delivered uniformly over 1 yr. Each part is processed in three departments (pressing, drilling, and grinding) with the following production data. The company operates 250 days/yr.

	Department		
	Pressing	Drilling	Grinding
Working hours per day	8	8	8
Processing time per part, min	4	12	8
Average daily downtime, min	20	40	30
Average daily setup time, min	5	8	7
Defective output, %	3	9	5

Determine:
(a) The efficiency E for each production department
(b) The required daily production rate for each department if all defectives are discarded as scrap
(c) The equipment requirements for each department

14. Refer to Prob. 13. What would the effect on equipment requirements be if the company were to go on two shifts $(D = 16$ h$)$?

15. Refer to Prob. 13. As a result of a recent preventive-maintenance program, the downtime in each department was reduced by 10 percent. Determine the effect on equipment requirements.

16. Refer to Prob. 13. After completing a methods-improvement program, machine operators devised, on their own, a work procedure reducing processing and setup time in each department by 25 percent. Determine the effect on equipment requirements.

SELECTED REFERENCES

1. Abramowitz, I.: *Production Management*, Ronald, New York, 1967.
2. Buffa, E. S.: *Modern Production Management*, 5th ed., Wiley, New York, 1976.
3. Gavett, J. W.: *Production and Operations Management*, Harcourt, New York, 1968.
4. Johnson, R. A., et al.: *Operations Management*, Houghton Mifflin, Boston, 1970.
5. Marshall, Paul W., et al.: *Operations Management: Text and Cases*, Irwin, Homewood, Ill., 1975.
6. Monks, J. G.: *Operations Management: Theory and Problems*, McGraw-Hill, New York, 1977.
7. Morris, W. T.: *The Capacity Decision System*, Irwin, Homewood, Ill., 1967.
8. Reed, R.: *Plant Layout*, Irwin, Homewood, Ill., 1961.
9. Spencer, M. H., et al.: *Managerial Economics*, 4th ed., Irwin, Homewood, Ill., 1975.
10. Wells, L. T., Jr.: "Don't Overautomate Your Foreign Plant," *Harvard Business Review*, January–February 1974.

Chapter 6

CAPACITY PLANNING FOR SERVICE SYSTEMS

6-1 INTRODUCTION

The methods discussed in Chap. 5 are mainly applied in manufacturing systems with a predictable, i.e., deterministic, flow of units through successive production stages. In estimating capacity requirements for such systems we assumed that the flow rate P is known and constant and so is the processing time per unit T. A large

220

number of operations systems, especially in the service sector, are characterized by considerable randomness both in the pattern of units arriving for service and in the time required to receive it. These are also known as *waiting-line* or *queueing systems*. The units may be people, semifinished products, information to be processed, machines to be repaired, and many others.

Definition

A *queueing system* is one in which we observe alternating periods of congestion, i.e., waiting lines, and idleness of the service facility due to limited capacity and randomness in the arrival of units and the time required to service them.

Examples of queueing systems abound, and we experience them daily in our working and private lives. We are part of a queueing system when we wait in line at the post office, the bank, or a theater window. For some systems the waiting line may not be observable, but congestion nevertheless exists when machines remain idle waiting for repair or when people wait for an ambulance, the police, or the fire department to take care of an emergency.

Queueing problems are of considerable interest in operations management because they appear constantly in the analysis of various private and public systems.

Definition

A *queueing problem* is one in which we seek to determine the optimum capacity for a production phase. This is measured by the number of parallel servers, or the average output rate, for which the combined cost from units waiting and the service level is a minimum.

To illustrate how a queueing problem arises consider the operation of a medical first-aid office in a large factory covered by one registered nurse. Factory employees arrive at random when involved in minor accidents or are seriously injured and require first aid before being sent to a hospital. The time required for treatment also varies at random, being quite short for most employees but occasionally taking considerably longer.

As a result of the randomness in the pattern of employee arrivals for first aid and randomness in the duration of treatment sometimes there is a waiting line in the nurse's office due to limited capacity and sometimes the nurse is idle, waiting for employees who need help. The presence of waiting lines generates waiting costs. They include not only the wages of employees for nonproductive time but also

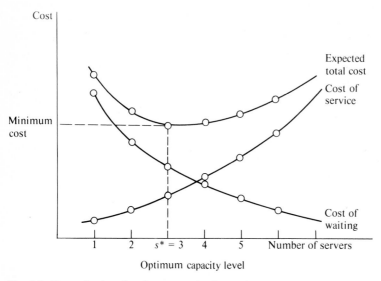

Fig. 6-1 Determination of optimum capacity for service system.

involve the loss in production output due to the forced idleness of whatever re-sources the employees in line are responsible for (machines or other facilities) and possible health-complication costs.

Let us assume that as a result of a new safety program the average rate of accidents has settled to a reduced new value. The probability that an employee may have to wait and the average waiting time can be decreased by hiring one or more additional nurses. This increase in the first-aid system capacity, however, will also raise the probability and average duration of idle periods for the nurses, thus increasing the overhead cost for the firm. In this example, the queueing problem consists of finding the optimum number of nurses to keep the variable operating costs of service and waiting to a minimum.

Similar problems arise in determining the optimum number of tellers in a bank, cashiers in a supermarket, clerks in tool crib for a large auto-repair shop, fire trucks or police cars on duty for a given city area, and the like.

The relevant trade-offs in determining optimum capacity for a queueing system are shown in Fig. 6-1, where we note that as we increase the number of servers, we raise the (variable) cost of service $E(SC)$. In doing so we decrease the cost of waiting customers $E(WC)$. Our objective in analyzing a queueing system is to find the number of servers or the average output rate that minimizes the combined cost of service and waiting customers.

In symbols, the queueing-analysis objective is to

$$\text{Minimize } E(TC) = E(SC) + E(WC) \tag{6-1}$$

where $E(TC)$ = expected total cost[1]
  $E(SC)$ = expected service cost
  $E(WC)$ = expected waiting cost

---

[1] The expected total cost $E(TC)$ is in fact an expected total variable cost for a service facility determined by the level of capacity provided in each period.

If certain assumptions about arrivals and service times can be justified, queueing analysis can be performed with mathematical models. Otherwise, we must rely on simulation using available empirical data. In either case, determination of optimum capacity requires three steps: (1) we calculate certain operating characteristics of the facility under study, i.e., the utilization rate, the average waiting, and total time in the system, etc.; (2) we estimate the costs associated with customers waiting and with different service levels; and (3) we combine the cost and performance characteristics to form an expected-operating-cost measure that we wish to minimize with respect to the capacity level. Each step is explained in detail in the following three sections.

6-2 QUEUEING-SYSTEM CHARACTERISTICS

The physical performance characteristics that could be estimated before we determine the optimum service capacity of a queueing system include:

P_n = probability of n customers in system, waiting and receiving service, when observed at random
P_0 = probability that facility will be idle when observed at random
L = average number of customers in system
L_q = average number of customers in system waiting to receive service
W = average time customer will spend in system waiting and receiving service
W_q = average time customer will spend in waiting line before service begins
ρ = utilization rate of system

These values can be calculated from our knowledge of the population of units that may arrive for service (size, arrival rate, and behavior while waiting) and of the service facility (size, structure, waiting-room size, rule of customer selection for service, etc.), as shown in Fig. 6-2 and summarized in Fig. 6-3.

To describe waiting-line systems, it is convenient to represent the relevant system parameters with the following notation:

λ = mean arrival rate at facility, units per hour or other time interval (mean time between successive arrivals = $1/\lambda$)
μ = mean service rate per channel, units served per hour or other time interval (mean service time per unit = $1/\mu$)
s = number of identical service channels or servers in parallel
ρ = utilization rate of service facility = $\lambda/s\mu$
m = maximum holding capacity for facility, including units in waiting line and those receiving service
σ = standard deviation of distribution for either interarrival times or service times

6-3 CALLING POPULATION: THE CAPACITY-DEMAND SIDE

The *calling population* is defined as the set of units that may need the service provided by a facility, e.g., the number of people that may need hospital emergency treatment, the number of buildings that may require fire protection, or the number

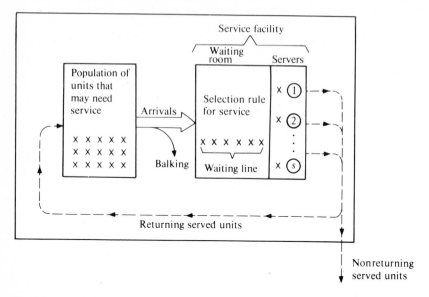

Fig. 6-2 Description of a waiting-line system.

of machines in a shop that may need repair after a breakdown. Thus, the population source in terms of its size and behavior shapes the demand placed on a service system.

Calling-Population Size

The population size may be *finite*, like machines in a shop that may need repair, or *infinite*, like users of an emergency hospital facility. The distinction is a relative one, in the sense that for the purpose of analysis "infinite" may refer simply to a large number of units, say 30 fire alarm calls for a day or 1,000 orders for a mail-order store. In general, the assumption of an infinite population simplifies the analysis, especially when using a mathematical model, because the number of units inside the facility does not affect the arrival rate of new ones.

Calling-Population Behavior

The behavior of the calling population can be described by the arrival pattern and by how units act before and after they join a waiting line.

An *arrival pattern* refers to the size of arrivals and the distribution of time intervals between successive arrivals. Units may arrive in a facility one at a time, e.g., telephone calls at a switchboard or vehicles at a toll bridge, or in batches, e.g., passengers of a charter flight going through customs or a shipment of parts requiring inspection.

The time between successive arrivals may be constant, as for semifinished parts arriving at a work station on a conveyor belt, or variable. If it is variable, it may be predictable, as in a schedule for a doctor's appointments, but usually the time

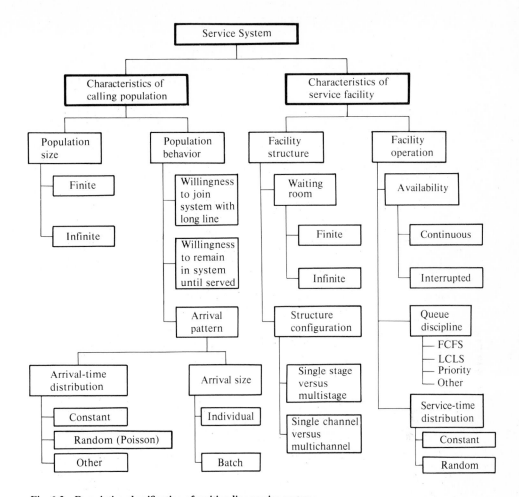

Fig. 6-3 Descriptive classification of waiting-line service systems.

between arrivals varies at random according to some probability distribution (discussed in the examples given later). For some systems we may have continuous arrivals, e.g., the flow of water into a reservoir. Our interest here, however, is on the analysis of random arrivals.

For many service facilities we can assume that units arrive for service according to a *Poisson distribution*[1] with a mean rate equal to λ. For an airline reservation desk λ may be equal to 15 calls per hour. The Poisson assumption is appropriate whenever:

1. The probability of an arrival at any instant is very small, but there are many opportunities for it to happen.

---

[1] The Poisson distribution is suitable for low-probability events (typing errors, accidents, product defects, etc.) that have repeated opportunities to occur. It is very useful in many decision areas in operations management such as inventory control, maintenance, and others.

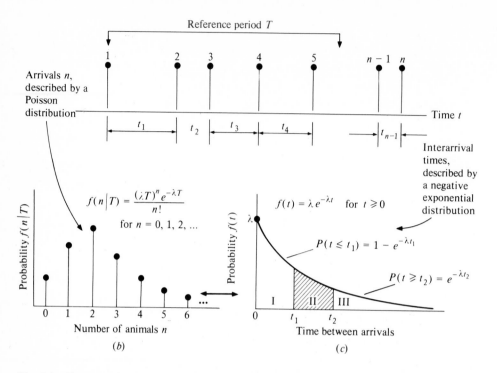

Fig. 6-4 Alternative descriptions of a hypothetical arrival pattern: (*a*) sequence of random arrivals, (*b*) Poisson distribution $f(n|T)$, and (*c*) negative-exponential distribution $f(t)$.

2. Units arrive at random independently of each other, with the same average rate λ.

3. The probability of two or more arrivals in a very short time, say 1 s, is almost zero.

For illustrative purposes, a random sequence of arrivals is shown in Fig. 6-4*a*.

The Poisson distribution (Fig. 6-4*b*) is discrete: i.e., it assumes only integer values 0, 1, 2, ... for the units that may arrive in a reference period T. For example, at an airline reservation desk at which calls arrive with a mean rate $\lambda = 15$ per hour, we are able to answer such questions as the following.

Question 1 What is the probability that the number of actual calls in 1 h will be equal to 20, less than 20, and at least 20?

Answer Using the Poisson distribution with $T = 1$, we have[1]

$$f(n|T = 1) = \frac{(\lambda T)^n e^{-\lambda T}}{n!} = \frac{\lambda^n e^{-\lambda}}{n!} \qquad \text{for } n = 0, 1, 2, \ldots \qquad (6\text{-}2)$$

---

[1] Poisson probabilities for different arrival rates can be easily determined from tabulated values in Appendix 3. For values of $\lambda \cdot T$ greater than 20, Poisson probabilities can be approximated using a normal distribution with a mean $\mu = \lambda \cdot T$ and a variance $\sigma^2 = \lambda \cdot T$.

Thus,

$$f(n = 20/h) = \frac{(15)^{20}(2.7182)^{-15}}{20!} = .0418$$

$$P(n < 20/h) = P(n = 0) + P(n = 1) + \cdots + P(n = 19) = \sum_{n=0}^{19} f(n)$$

$$= \sum_{n=0}^{19} \frac{[(15)(1)]^n e^{-15}}{n!} = .875$$

$$P(n \geq 20/h) = 1 - P(n < 19/h) = 1 - \sum_{n=0}^{19} f(n \mid T = 1)$$

$$= 1 - \sum_{n=0}^{19} \frac{[(15)(1)]^n e^{-15}}{n!} = .125$$

Question 2   What is the probability that the actual number of calls in an 8-h period will be 100 or between 100 and 160?

Answer $P(100 \text{ calls in 8-h period}) = f(n = 100 \mid T = 8) = \dfrac{[(15)(8)]^{100} e^{(-15)(8)}}{100!}$

$$P(100 \leq n \leq 160 \text{ per 8-h period}) = f(100) + f(101) + \cdots + f(160)$$

$$= \sum_{n=100}^{160} \frac{[(15)(8)^n e^{(-15)(8)}}{n!}$$

The calculation of such probabilities is facilitated by tabulated values of the Poisson for different arrival rates λT.

Important property

Whenever units arrive at a service facility according to a Poisson distribution with a mean arrival rate equal to λ, the times between arrivals follow a negative-exponential distribution with a mean equal to $1/\lambda$, and vice versa.

This property allows us to study arrivals by focusing on the interarrival times as values of a random variable described by the negative-exponential distribution (Fig. 6-4c). The negative-exponential distribution is continuous, allowing for inter-arrival times equal to or greater than zero ($t \geq 0$). It is therefore helpful in answering questions like: What is the probability that the time between successive arrivals will be (1) less than t_1, (2) greater than t_2, or (3) between t_1 and t_2? The answers correspond to the areas I, II, and III under the curve[1] in Fig. 6-4c and can also be obtained from tables (see Appendix 4).

The description of the calling population must also include information on how units behave once they arrive to receive service. Some units may be repelled by the sight of a long waiting line (balking), while others might be attracted for exactly the same reason, especially with recreational or entertainment facilities (movie theaters, pop concerts, night clubs, etc.).

Once a unit joins a waiting line, it may wait until served, may decide to leave (reneging), or join another waiting line (jockeying). The analysis is simplified if we can assume that arriving units wait until service on them is completed. Then we must also consider whether serviced units join the original calling population, like the machines in a shop after repair, or leave never to return.

6-4 SERVICE FACILITY:
THE CAPACITY-SUPPLY SIDE

A service facility must be described in terms of its structure and its operation. The two jointly determine the capacity available to meet the demand placed on the system by the calling population.

Facility Structure

A service facility's structure is specified as follows:

1. *Number of channels per stage.* The number of servers in parallel in each production stage determines its maximum capacity level as follows:
    a. Single-channel stage allows the servicing of one unit at a time.
    b. Multiple-channel stage allows the simultaneous servicing of several, say n, units at a time.
2. *Number of stages in the system.* The successive phases a unit must go through before processing is completed may have the following configurations (examples of some of these configurations are given in Table 6-1):
    a. Single-stage, single-channel
    b. Single-stage, multiple-channel
    c. Multiple-stage, single-channel (tandem arrangement)
    d. Multiple-stage, multiple-channel (separate or mixed paths)
3. *Waiting-room size.* For certain facilities the waiting room before a server may be finite (number of tables in a restaurant, seats in a barber shop, storage space for in-process inventories, etc.), in which case arrivals are blocked when it is

---

[1] For exponential probabilities we can use the following:

$$P(t \leq t_1) = 1 - e^{\lambda t_1}$$

$$P(t \geq t_2) = 1 - P(t \leq t_2) = 1 - (1 - e^{-\lambda t_2}) = e^{-\lambda t_2}$$

$$P(t_1 \leq t \leq t_2) = 1 - P(t \leq t_1) - P(t \geq t_2) = 1 - (1 - e^{-\lambda t_1}) - e^{-\lambda t_2} = e^{-\lambda t_1} - e^{-\lambda t_2}$$

TABLE 6-1 Representative examples of facility structures for service systems

Channels	Stages	
	Single	Multiple
Single	Restaurant with one hostess, one cash register	Cafeteria service line
	Emergency room with one physician	Automatic car wash
Multiple	Bank tellers for deposits or withdrawals	Processing an order through a machine shop
	Tool-crib clerks for a machine shop	Processing an insurance claim or loan application
	Supermarket cashiers	Medical treatment of patients in a hospital

completely filled up. When the size of the waiting room is assumed to be infinite (vehicles at a toll bridge or calls at an information desk or switchboard), the facility's operation does not affect new arrivals.

Facility Operation

Our description of a facility's operation must include the following details.

Availability Service may be available on a continuous basis (emergency hospital treatment, police or fire protection) or during specified hours (banks, stores, restaurants, etc.). When service is interrupted, it takes some time before reaching a state of equilibrium (transient phase), and this limits the applicability of most queueing models which describe system performance only for equilibrium conditions (steady state).

Rule for selecting the next unit to be served (queue discipline) The selection of which unit will be served next from those in a waiting line may vary from facility to facility, depending on the service offered. The following rules, or queue disciplines, are the most commonly used in practice for single-channel facilities:

1. First come, first served (FCFS) is used most extensively when there is no reason to differentiate arriving units.
2. Priority assignments may be enforced for different classes of units to reflect their relative importance or critical nature in meeting system objectives. Accordingly, orders from special customers may be processed first by a job shop, emergencies in a hospital may be treated according to their seriousness, and so on.
3. Last-come, first-serve (LCFS) selection may occur in the processing of raw materials or parts or the order in which people leave an elevator.
4. Other selection rules might apply, depending on the nature of the service or the requirements of the customers (reservations for airline travel or exclusive restaurants, shortest processing time for handling orders in a job shop, or even

random selection when it is not possible to keep track of arrival times or assign priorities).

For multiple-channel service systems the selection rules include:

1. Specialization by channel to save processing time and cost and to use specialized equipment
2. Rotation to distribute the load evenly
3. Assignment to the first free server, as applied in banks, the post office, restaurants, etc.
4. Allowing each unit to select its preferred server, e.g., patients selecting a doctor, customers selecting a salesperson, etc.

Service-time distribution   Once a unit has been assigned to a given channel, the time it takes to get served may be a constant or vary at random. Constant times are common when processing is mechanized or automated. This is true in manufacturing systems, even though certain banking transactions and fast-food service systems come close to fixed service times. *The greater the involvement of the human element in providing a service, the larger the variability in the duration of service time.* This is especially true when a unit presents unique service requirements, like a medical examination or the repair of a car or appliance.

A service-time distribution is a statistical distribution from empirical data that can at times be approximated by a well-defined probability distribution. Such an approximation requires that service times satisfy certain assumptions with respect to average service rates, the variability of individual service times, and the independence of such times for successive units.

Unlike arrival patterns, which can often be well approximated by the Poisson distribution, service times require more analysis before they can be described by some known probability distribution. For a given channel, the mean service rate μ may apply to service times that are constant and to others that vary at random. For service times with maximum variability we can use an *exponential distribution* whose mean service time per unit is $1/\mu$, similar to the one in Fig. 6-4c. Its form is

$$f(t) = \mu e^{-\mu t} \qquad \text{for } t \geq 0 \qquad (6\text{-}3)$$

This distribution has an important property that considerably limits its applicability. Accordingly, the probability that service on a unit will be completed in the next small time interval is the same, independently of how long the unit has been receiving it. In other words, the server has no memory of how long it has been working on the given unit. The probability, however, of short service times is larger than that for long ones. This condition might exist when servicing complex equipment, people at a bank or a supermarket, or in an operating room in a hospital, where most units require a relatively short processing time, but occasionally we run into one that requires much longer than average service time.

Whenever the service consists of a well-defined sequence of steps, it is not correct to describe it using the negative-exponential distribution and the variability is too significant to ignore by using constant times. For such cases, a very flexible distribution to employ is the *Erlang*, which is specified by two parameters as

$$f(t) = \frac{(\mu k)^k}{(k-1)!} t^{k-1} e^{-k\mu t} \qquad \text{for } t \geq 0 \tag{6-4}$$

where k = positive constant assuming integer values and determining spread, i.e., variability, of distribution

μ = mean service rate, as in negative-exponential distribution

The Erlang distribution, shown in Fig. 6-5, is considered important for two reasons: (1) Its flexibility makes it possible to use in describing a wide variety of service facilities. By assigning appropriate values to μ and k we can approximate

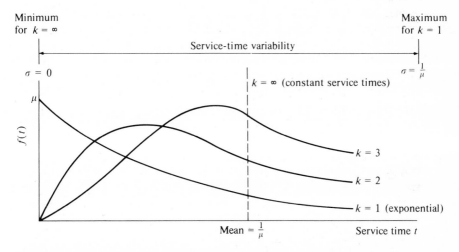

Fig. 6-5   A family of Erlang distributions with the same mean service time equal to $1/\mu$.

many empirical service-time distributions. At the extreme cases, we can obtain constant service times for $k = 1$ and negative-exponential times for $k = \infty$ (see Fig. 6-5). (2) It can give us the total service time for a process with k independent stages and the stage service time T with a mean for all stages equal to $1/k\mu$.

If we cannot use a theoretical service-time distribution, like the Erlang, we must resort to a simulation analysis using an empirical statistical distribution.

6-5 REPRESENTATIVE QUEUEING SYSTEMS

In the discussion that follows we examine some simple types of service facilities to illustrate the application of representative queueing models. The analysis indicated is needed before we can evaluate the cost performance of such systems.

Fundamental Relationships between Queueing-Performance Characteristics

The evaluation of different performance characteristics varies with each system configuration. For example, the expected number of units waiting L_q or in the system L are often easier to determine than the expected time W or time waiting W_q in the system. Therefore, knowing how these are related can prove extremely helpful in specific applications. Little[1] established that the following relationships hold under quite general conditions:

$$L = \lambda W \qquad L_q = \lambda W_q \qquad W = W_q + \frac{1}{\mu}$$
(6-5)

Poisson Arrivals and General Service Times

Let us assume that jobs arrive at a single-channel facility according to a Poisson distribution with a mean rate equal to $\lambda = 4$ units/h. All we know about service times is that they are independent, have an average equal to $1/\mu = 10$ min, i.e., an average service rate equal to $\mu = 6$ per hour, and a standard deviation equal to σ. Furthermore, the calling-population size and waiting-room capacity are large enough to be considered infinite. Service is on a FCFS basis.

A key requirement for the system's operation to remain stable is that the service rate μ be greater than the arrival rate λ; that is, $\lambda/\mu < 1$. Otherwise, the waiting line gets infinitely long and the system "explodes." Assuming that customers do not decline to join the system when the waiting line is too long (no balking) and that they do not leave the line until service is completed (no reneging), we have the general result[2]

$$L_q = \frac{(\lambda\sigma)^2 + (\lambda/\mu)^2}{2(1 - \lambda/\mu)}$$
(6-6)

In words, the average length of the waiting line depends on the utilization rate $\rho = \lambda/\mu$, and for fixed values of λ and μ it increases with the variability in service times as measured by σ. It was stated earlier that variability in service times is minimum $(\sigma = 0)$ when service time is constant and maximum $(\sigma = 1/\mu)$ when service times vary according to the negative-exponential distribution. Substituting these extreme values of σ in (6-6), we find that for exponential service times with a

---

[1] John D. C. Little, "Proof for the Queueing Formula: $L = \lambda W$," *Operations Research*, May-June, 1961, pp. 383–387.

[2] This is known as the *Pollaczek-Khintchine equation*, derived in Refs. 2 and 10.

mean equal to $1/\mu$ and $\sigma = 1/\mu$

$$L_q = \frac{\lambda\left(\frac{1}{\mu}\right)^2 + (\lambda/\mu)^2}{2(1 - \lambda/\mu)} = \frac{2(\lambda/\mu)^2}{2(1 - \lambda/\mu)}$$

that is,

$$L_q = \frac{(\lambda/\mu)^2}{1 - \lambda/\mu} \qquad \text{(Poisson-Exponential)} \quad (6\text{-}7)$$

$$= \frac{(4/6)^2}{1 - .667} = \frac{.444}{.333} = 1.333$$

and that for constant service times with a value equal to $1/\mu$ and $\sigma = 0$

$$L_q = \frac{[(\lambda)(0)]^2 + (\lambda/\mu)^2}{2(1 - \lambda/\mu)} = \frac{(\lambda/\mu)^2}{2(1 - \lambda/\mu)} \qquad \text{(Poisson-Constant)} \qquad (6\text{-}8)$$

$$= \frac{(4/6)^2}{2(1 - .667)} = \frac{.4444}{.667} = .667 \text{ units}$$

Comparing these two results, we conclude that when we reduce the variability of service times from its maximum possible value $\sigma = 1/\mu$ (in the negative exponential) to its minimum value $\sigma = 0$ (for constant service times), the average waiting-line length is reduced to one-half. This minimum average length of the waiting line is due to the randomness in the Poisson arrivals. In short,

L_q for negative-exponential service times $= 2L_q$ for constant service times

This explains the advantage of reducing service-time variability through mechanization or automation beyond any gains from economies of scale and specialization.

Using the fundamental relationships (6-5) after we evaluate L_q, we can determine the remaining performance characteristics. Thus, *for Poisson arrivals and exponential service times* $(\sigma = 1/\mu)$ we have

$$W_q = \frac{1}{\lambda} L_q = \frac{1}{\lambda} \frac{(\lambda/\mu)^2}{1 - \lambda/\mu} = \frac{\lambda^2}{\mu(\mu - \lambda)} \tag{6-9}$$

$$W = W_q + \frac{1}{\mu} = \frac{\lambda^2}{\mu(\mu - \lambda)} + \frac{1}{\mu} = \frac{1}{\mu - \lambda} \tag{6-10}$$

$$L = \lambda W = \lambda \frac{1}{\mu - \lambda} = \frac{\lambda}{\mu - \lambda} \tag{6-11}$$

From Table 6-2 we can see that for a Poisson-exponential single-channel facility half of the average waiting-line length is due to randomness in the arrivals and half to the randomness in the exponential service times $(\sigma = 1/\mu)$. Given Poisson arrivals, as we reduce the variability in service times $(\sigma < 1/\mu)$, the average waiting-line length decreases, until for $\sigma = 0$ (constant service times) it is equal to one-half its value for exponential service times. The same effect is produced by decreasing the variability in interarrival times $\sigma = 1/\lambda$.

TABLE 6-2 Average waiting-line length L_q for different single-channel queueing systems

Queueing system		Average waiting-line length L_q		Value of L_q for waiting line $(\lambda < \mu)$
Arrivals	Departures	Arrivals	Service time	
Poisson	exponential			$\dfrac{\lambda^2}{\mu(\mu - \lambda)}$
	general			$\dfrac{(\lambda\sigma)^2 + (\lambda/\mu)}{2(1 - \lambda/\mu)}$
	constant			$\dfrac{(\lambda/\mu)^2}{2(1 - \lambda/\mu)}$
Constant	exponential			$\dfrac{(\lambda/\mu)^2}{2(1 - \lambda/\mu)}$
	constant			0

When we deal with a service facility for which the average arrival rate is smaller than the overall service rate $(\lambda < s\mu)$, the performance of the system as measured by average processing time W and average waiting-room (or storage) L_q requirements can be improved as follows:

1. *Decreasing the variability in service times through mechanization or automation.* If this is not feasible, improvements can be made by having units arriving for service do by themselves one or more parts of the total service while waiting. The latter approach has been successfully tried out in supermarkets, miniservice gas stations, cafeterias, medical-exam procedures in which patient fills out needed forms, and others.
2. *Decreasing the variability in interarrival times through scheduling whenever possible.* This practice is followed for improving the utilization of physicians and operating rooms in hospitals, mechanics in an auto repair shop, and in other service systems with critical or bottleneck resources.
3. *A combination of methods 1 and 2 as allowed by economic and technical factors as well as accepted levels of service for the market under study.*

Similar results have been developed for queueing systems operating with differ-

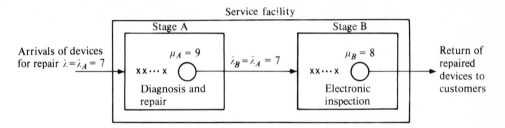

Fig. 6-6   A two-stage single-channel service facility for Example 6-1.

ent assumptions about arrivals, service times, number of channels, and size of calling population and waiting room. For convenient reference, the performance characteristics of several types of queueing systems have been summarized in Tables 6-6 and 6-7 at the end of this chapter. The tedious calculations involved often make it preferable to use appropriate nomographs (see Ref. 2) or computer programs derived from the model equations for each system.

▶ EXAMPLE 6-1   DETERMINATION OF PHYSICAL-PERFORMANCE CHARACTERISTICS
In order to see how two models shown in Table 6-6 apply to real situations, let us consider a facility for the maintenance of air-pollution control devices, as shown in Fig. 6-6. Arrivals to the system occur at random, as the devices fail according to a Poisson distribution with an average rate $\lambda = 7$ units/wk. This becomes the input rate to stage A for diagnosis and repair, or $\lambda_A = \lambda = 7$. Some devices need only minor adjustments, but since occasionally a unit may require a long time to diagnose the trouble and fix it, service times in stage A are assumed to follow a negative-exponential distribution with a mean rate $\mu_A = 9$ units/wk.

After repair has been completed, units are advanced to stage B to be inspected on an electronic machine. Inspection time is constant at the rate $\mu_B = 8$ units/wk and includes any fine adjustments before the devices are returned to customers.

We shall assume that all units go through both stages and are serviced on a FCFS basis. The number of customers served is so large that the calling population is considered infinite. Furthermore, the devices are so small that the waiting-room capacity is infinite. The determination of the performance characteristics of this system can now begin.

Stage A   Here we have a system with Poisson arrivals and exponential service times for which we can use the equations for the basic model. Thus, since $\lambda_A/\mu_A = 7/9 < 1$, the percentage of idle time and stage utilization is

$$P_0 = 1 - \frac{\lambda_A}{\mu_A} = 1 - \frac{7}{9} = .222$$

Therefore,

$$\rho = 1 - P_0 = 1 - .22 = .778$$

The probability of having n devices in stage A is

$$P_n = P_0\left(\frac{\lambda_A}{\mu_A}\right)^n = (.222)(.778)^n$$

The average number of devices in stage A is

$$L = \frac{\lambda_A}{\mu_A - \lambda_A} = \frac{7}{9 - 7} = \frac{7}{2} = 3.500 \text{ units}$$

The average number of devices waiting to be repaired is

$$L_q = \frac{\lambda_A^2}{\mu_A(\mu_A - \lambda_A)} = \frac{(7)^2}{9(9 - 7)} = \frac{49}{18} = 2.722 \text{ units}$$

The average time a device will be in stage A is

$$W = \frac{1}{\mu_A - \lambda_A} = \frac{1}{9 - 7} = \frac{1}{2} = .500 \text{ wk}$$

The average time a device will wait before it is repaired is

$$W_q = \frac{\lambda_A}{\mu_A(\mu_A - \lambda_A)} = \frac{7}{9(9 - 7)} = \frac{7}{18} = .389 \text{ wk}$$

The probability that the actual time T_A for a device in stage A will exceed a given time t, say 2 wk, is

$$P(T_A > t = 2) = e^{-\mu_A(1 - \rho_A)t} = 2.7182^{-9(1 - 7/9)2}$$

$$= 2.7182^{-4} = .0183$$

Stage B   According to an important property for input and output rates in a system with a series of stages, the arrival rate λ_B in stage B will be equal to the arrival rate λ_A in stage A, or $\lambda_B = \lambda_A = 7$ units/wk. Thus, for the electronic-inspection phase of the process we have Poisson arrivals and constant service times equal to $1/\mu_B = \frac{1}{8}$. From the general relationship for L_q [Eq. (6-6)] and the equi-valence relationships (6-5) the average number of units waiting for inspection is

$$L_q = \frac{\lambda_B^2 \sigma_B^2 + \rho_B^2}{2(1 - \rho_B)} = \frac{(7)^2(0)^2 + (7/8)^2}{2(1 - 7/8)} = \frac{.7656}{.250} = 3.06 \text{ units}$$

From $L_q = \lambda W_q$, the average time a repaired device will wait for inspection is

$$W_q = \frac{L_q}{\lambda_B} = \frac{3.06}{7} = .437 \text{ wk}$$

The average time a repaired device will be in the inspection department is

$$W = W_q + \frac{1}{\mu_B} = .4375 + \frac{1}{8} = .562 \text{ wk}$$

The average number of units that will be in the inspection department is

$$L = \lambda_B W = (7)(.562) = 3.93 \text{ units}$$

It must be emphasized, once again, that the use of the model equations to determine physical performance characteristics is based on the assumption that the utilization rate ρ for each stage is less than 1:

$$\rho = \begin{cases} \dfrac{\lambda}{\mu} < 1 & \text{for single-channel stage} \\[2ex] \dfrac{\lambda}{s\mu} < 1 & \text{for stage with } s \text{ channels} \end{cases}$$

If this condition is not satisfied, the length of the waiting line increases without limit $(L_q \rightarrow \infty, W_q \rightarrow \infty, \text{etc.})$, and the ensuing congestion forces the system to close ▶ or break down.

6-6 COST-PERFORMANCE ANALYSIS

The determination of optimum capacity in service systems requires two kinds of information input: (1) we must determine the measures of physical performance, namely, P_0, P_n, ρ, L, L_q, W, and W_q, and (2) we need an explicit treatment of costs associated with operating at a given capacity level and costs resulting from waiting due to the limited capacity.

Waiting costs are often difficult to estimate, especially for customers external to the service facility, e.g., bank customers and hospital patients, but ignoring waiting costs and solving capacity-related problems only on the basis of explicit service costs may lead to the wrong conclusions.

The capacity-determination problem can take several forms, depending on the structure of the service facility. For a given stage of the system, we usually deal with two possible arrangements. In the single-channel case $(s = 1)$ we may wish to determine the capacity level as one of several values for the service rate μ. For example, we may wish to choose the size of the repair crew in a production department, one of several man-machine systems for a specific job type (excavator, cash-register, materials-handling truck, etc.), or one of several employees with different output rates. This case is treated in Example 6-2. In the second case we assume that the service rate is fixed. Here the optimum capacity is determined by the number of service channels (s is variable) for the facility, say the number of windows at the post office. This situation is treated in Example 6-3.

Service Costs

When analyzing service-related costs using queueing models, we are generally concerned with variable costs. For the single-channel case the expected service cost is

$$E(\text{SC}) = c_s \mu \tag{6-12}$$

where μ = channel service rate, i.e., number of units served per hour, day, etc.

c_s = the marginal cost of increasing service rate μ by 1 unit

For a multichannel facility the expected service cost is

$$E(\text{SC}) = c_s' s \tag{6-13}$$

where s = number of channels assigned to facility

c'_s = marginal cost of adding one more server (person, machine, or man-machine system) per unit time

For example, adding another cashier in a supermarket may have an incremental cost of $5 per hour, adding another metal detector for security inspections in an airport may have an incremental cost of $50 per day, and so on. Estimating c'_s can be done from accounting records, manufacturer's specifications, or better from a special study.

Waiting Costs

The expected cost incurred when units wait for service, regardless of the facility structure, is

$$E(\text{WC}) = c_w L \tag{6-14}$$

where L = average number of units in service facility

c_w = cost of 1 unit or customer waiting per unit time

For example, the cost of an operator waiting in line to get service at a tool crib may be estimated to be $25 per hour ($8.50 per hour for operator's wage plus $16.50 per hour for loss of productive output of operator's idle machine).

The difficulty in estimating waiting costs depends on whether the unit serviced is internal or external to the organization. Machine operators needing tools or semifinished parts waiting to be processed for inventory represent units internal to a firm. The cost of waiting for them may be sometimes difficult to estimate, but it can be approximated reasonably well.

The task is much more complex when units are external, e.g., customers waiting in line at a bank, a supermarket, or an auto-repair shop, patients waiting to be admitted to a hospital, or passengers waiting to board a commercial flight. Tempting as it may be for management to avoid assessing such costs, their explicit estimation is important. Otherwise, capacity is determined subjectively, and the imputed cost values implied by a given policy or decision may be much higher than with a more approximate but explicit estimate. As we shall see in Chap. 13, management faces a similar dilemma with the estimation of shortage costs when orders cannot be met from existing supplies. Failure to consider shortage costs explicitly may result in excessively high costs for holding too much inventory as an insurance against shortages. Similar considerations hold in the estimation of waiting costs to determine desirable service-capacity levels.

Expected Total Cost

By combining the expected cost of service $E(\text{SC})$ and the expected cost of waiting $E(\text{WC})$ we can arrive at a cost measure for a service facility that we can use to determine optimum capacity. This is the expected total cost $E(\text{TC})$ defined as

$$
E(\text{TC}) = E(\text{SC}) + E(\text{WC}) = \begin{cases} c_s\mu + c_w L & \text{single-channel facility} \\ c_s's + c_w L & \text{multichannel facility} \end{cases} \tag{6-15}
$$

Our objective in solving the general queueing problem can be related to minimizing $E(\text{TC})$ with values of μ or s restricted by available technology, capital budget, existing physical space, or other constraints. The procedure for combining physical-performance characteristics with cost data for service and waiting at different capacities is shown in Fig. 6-7.

▶ EXAMPLE 6-2 DETERMINATION OF OPTIMUM REPAIR-CREW SIZE
The knitting department of Electra Co., a ready-to-wear manufacturer, operates a large number of identical machines in its production floor. They break down at the rate of 9 per hour, following a Poisson distribution. A repair crew of three men is responsible for servicing these machines at the rate of 12 per hour, the service time following a negative-exponential distribution. Here the repair crew functions as a single-server facility.

Even though the present repair crew has some idle time (crew utilization rate $= \rho = \lambda/\mu = 9/12 = .750$), management wishes to investigate the effect of speeding up the average repair time per machine. This requires increasing the size of the repair crew to achieve savings from improved machine utilization by reducing machine waiting time and related costs. A preliminary study reveals that each repair crew member is paid $10 per hour and each idle knitting machine results in a cost of $20 per hour.

The operations manager for the knitting department assumes that as the size of the repair crew is increased, there will be a proportional decrease in the average

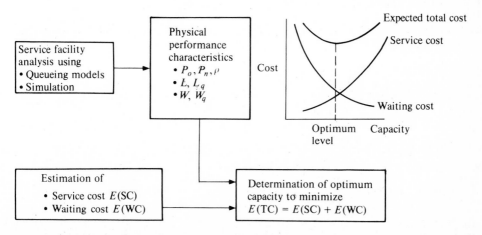

Fig. 6-7 **Procedure for determining optimum service capacity.**

TABLE 6-3   Repair-system characteristics for knitting department

	Repair-crew size k			
Performance measure	3	4	5	6
Average repair rate μ, machines/h	12	16	20	24
Crew utilization rate $\rho = \lambda/\mu$	.750	.562	.450	.375
Prob (crew is idle) P_0	.250	.438	.550	.625
Prob (crew is busy) P_w	.750	.562	.450	.375
Average number of machines in system L	3	1.286	.818	.600
Average number of machines waiting L_q	2.25	.723	.368	.225
Average time a machine spends in system W, h	.3333	.1429	.0909	.0667
Average time a machine spends waiting W_q, h	.2500	.0804	.0409	.0250
Average repair time $\bar{t} = 1/\mu$, h	.0833	.0625	.0500	.0417

repair time. If the three-man crew repairs an average of 12 machines per hour, the average repair time per machine will be $1/12 = .0833$ h. If the crew size is taken into account, this means that the average repair requirement per machine is equal to $(3)(.0833) = .25$ labor-hour. For a crew of size $k = 2, 3, 4, \ldots$ the average repair time per machine is thus equal to $.25/k$ h.

Similarly, if a crew size of three can repair 12 machines per hour, each man can be assumed to be responsible for 4 machines per hour. Therefore, increasing the crew size to 4 will result in a service rate of 16 machines per hour, to 5 in 20 machines per hour and so on.

Following the procedure outlined in Fig. 6-7, the operations manager of the knitting department must first determine the physical performance measures (ρ, P_0, L, W, etc.) using the single-channel queueing model. For $k = 3$ the calculations are shown below. For $k = 3, 4,$ and 5 they are summarized in Table 6-3.

Given $\lambda = 9$ machines per hour and $\mu = 12$ machines per hour for a crew size of 3, the average repair time per machine is

$$\bar{t} = \frac{1}{\mu} = \frac{1}{12} = .0833 \text{ h} = 5 \text{ min}$$

The crew-utilization rate is

$$\rho = \frac{\lambda}{\mu} = \frac{9}{12} = .750 = 75\%$$

The probability the crew will be idle is

$$P_0 = 1 - \frac{\lambda}{\mu} = 1 - \frac{9}{12} = .250 = 25\%$$

The probability a machine that breaks down will have to wait is

$$P_w = 1 - P_0 = 1 - .250 = .750 = 75\%$$

The average number of machines in the repair system is

$$L = \frac{\lambda}{\mu - \lambda} = \frac{9}{12 - 9} = 3 \text{ machines}$$

The average number of machines waiting to be repaired is

$$L_q = \frac{\lambda^2}{\mu(\mu - \lambda)} = \frac{9^2}{12(12 - 9)} = \frac{81}{(12)(3)} = 2.25 \text{ machines}$$

The average time a machine will be in the system is

$$W = \frac{L}{\lambda} = \frac{3}{9} = .333 \text{ h} = 20 \text{ min}$$

The average time a machine will wait before repairing starts is

$$W_q = \frac{L_q}{\lambda} = \frac{2.25}{9} = .250 \text{ h} = 15 \text{ min}$$

Since the average time in the system includes the average waiting time plus the average repair time, we also have as a check that

$$W = W_q + \tfrac{1}{12} = .250 + .0833 = .333 \text{ h}$$

Another check is provided by the relationship

$$L = L_q + \frac{\lambda}{\mu} = 2.25 + .75 = 3.00 \text{ machines}$$

Inspection of Table 6-3 shows the proportional improvement in average repair times from .0833 h (5 min) per machine for a crew size of 3 ($k = 3$) to .0417 h (2.5 min) per machine for $k = 6$. At the same time we also note an increase in idle time for each crew size from 25 percent with $k = 3$ to 62.5 percent with $k = 6$.

Determination of optimum service rate must account for both service and waiting costs using the relationship

$$E(\text{SC}) = c_s k + c_w L \qquad (6\text{-}16)$$

where c_s = marginal cost per hour of increasing crew size by one worker = $10 per worker-hour

k = repair-crew size
c_w = waiting cost per machine per hour = $20 per machine-hour
L = average number of machines in repair system

For the original crew size ($k = 3$) we have

$$E(\text{TC}) = (\$10/\text{worker-hour})(3 \text{ workers}) \quad \text{Service cost}$$

Total expected variable cost

$$+ (\$20/\text{idle machine-hour})(3 \text{ idle machines/h}) \quad \text{Waiting cost}$$

$$= \$30 + \$60 = \$90/\text{h}$$

The remaining results are summarized in Table 6-4.

TABLE 6-4   Total expected hourly cost for repair-crew system

Crew size k	Hourly repair-crew cost $c_s k$	Hourly idle-machine cost $c_w L$	Total hourly repair cost $E(TC)$
3	$(10)(3) = \$30$	$(20)(3) = \$60.00$	$90.00
4	$(10)(4) = 40$	$(20)(1.286) = 25.72$	$65.72 \leftarrow k^* \ (\mu^* = 16)$
5	$(10)(5) = 50$	$(20)(.818) = 16.36$	$66.36
6	$(10)(6) = 60$	$(20)(.600) = 12.00$	$72.00

From Table 6-4, the operations manager of the knitting department realizes that the optimum repair-crew size is 4. For $k = 4$ the expected total cost attributed to repair service and waiting costs is at a minimum. This corresponds to a service rate of 16 machines per hour, or $\mu = 16$. The reader will note that when one more worker is added to the crew $(k = 5)$, the total cost increase of 64 cents per period might be a small price to pay for the substantial improvements in performance indicated in Table 6-3. It is therefore important to evaluate the trade-offs in changing the optimum configuration with the help of the above type of sensitivity ▷ analysis.

▷ EXAMPLE 6-3: A MULTIPLE-CHANNEL SINGLE-STAGE SYSTEM
Decision Aids, Inc., a large management consulting firm, is considering the installation of several computer terminals for use by systems analysts and other highly trained technical staff. A preliminary study has revealed that during an 8-h workday job requests arrive at random with a Poisson distribution and a mean rate equal to 36 per day. Terminal times can be approximated by a negative-exponential distribution with an average of 30 jobs per day using a FCFS queue discipline.

The incremental cost per computer terminal is equal to $120 per day, and the cost of having a user wait is estimated at $40 per job-hour (including loss of personal time and other productive resources forced to idleness). The problem here is to determine the number of terminals to be installed that will minimize the combined cost of providing computing service through terminals and the cost of having highly paid technical staff wait.

This situation can be viewed as a multichannel single-stage queueing system with computer terminals as the servers and job requests by the technical staff as the units arriving to get served. Converting all parameters to a daily basis, we have

$$\lambda = 36 \text{ job requests arriving per day}$$

$$\mu = 30 \text{ jobs handled by each terminal per day}$$

$$c_s' = \$100 \text{ per terminal daily}$$

$$c_w = \$320 \text{ per job request waiting per day}$$

The structure of the service facility is similar to that shown in Fig. 6-2. Using the equations for a multichannel queueing system, we can calculate the physical-performance characteristics for different values of s, as follows. For $s = 3$

$$P_0 = \frac{1}{\left[\displaystyle\sum_{n=0}^{s-1} \frac{1}{n!}\left(\frac{\lambda}{\mu}\right)^n\right] + \frac{1}{s!}\left(\frac{\lambda}{\mu}\right)^s \frac{s\mu}{s\mu - \lambda}}$$

$$= \frac{1}{\left[\frac{1}{0!}\left(\frac{36}{30}\right)^0 + \frac{1}{1!}\left(\frac{36}{30}\right)^1 + \frac{1}{2!}\left(\frac{36}{30}\right)^2\right] + \frac{1}{3!}\left(\frac{36}{30}\right)^3 \frac{(3)(30)}{(3)(30) - 36}}$$

$$= \frac{1}{1 + 1.2 + 0.72 + 0.48} = \frac{1}{3.40} = .294$$

$$L_q = \frac{(\lambda/\mu)^s(\lambda/s\mu)}{s!(1 - \lambda/s\mu)} P_0$$

$$= \frac{(36/30)^3[36/(3)(30)]}{(3!)[1 - 36/(3)(30)]} 0.294 = \frac{.6912}{2.400} .294 = .0847 \text{ job}$$

$$L = L_q + \frac{\lambda}{\mu} = .0847 + \tfrac{36}{30} = 1.285 \text{ jobs}$$

$$W = \frac{L}{\lambda} = \frac{1.285}{36} = .0357 \text{ day}$$

$$W_q = \frac{L_q}{\lambda} = \frac{.0847}{36} = .0024 \text{ day}$$

To avoid such complex calculations, it is possible to use nomographs or computer programs developed for this and other queueing models (see Ref. 2). For our example the relevant data are shown in Table 6-5, where we can see that the expected total variable cost is a minimum when the consulting firm uses three computer terminals.

TABLE 6-5 Performance characteristics for different computer-terminal capacities†

Number of computer terminals	Idleness P_0, %	Average number of jobs in system L	Expected cost		
			Service $c_s s$	Waiting $c_w L$	Total $E(TC)$ $= c_s s + c_w L$
1	0	∞	$100	∞	∞
2	.250	1.877	200	$600.64	$800.64
3	.294	1.294	300	414.08	714.08
4	.300	1.216	400	389.12	789.12

† Optimum computer capacity corresponds to three computer terminals ($s^* = 3$).

TABLE 6-6 Formulas for selected single-channel models with Poisson arrivals

	Exponential service times			General†	Erlang†	Constant†
	Basic model	Finite waiting room	Finite calling population			
P_0	$1 - \dfrac{\lambda}{\mu}$	$\dfrac{1-\rho}{1-\rho^{N+1}}$	$\dfrac{1}{\displaystyle\sum_{n=0}^{m}\left[\dfrac{m!}{(m-n)!}\rho^n\right]}$			
P_n	$\left(1-\dfrac{\lambda}{\mu}\right)\left(\dfrac{\lambda}{\mu}\right)^n$	$\rho^N P_0 \quad$ for $n \le N$	$\dfrac{m!}{(m-n)!}\rho^n P_0$ for $n < m$			
L	$\dfrac{\lambda}{\mu-\lambda}$	$\dfrac{\rho}{1-\rho} - \dfrac{(N+1)\rho^{N+1}}{1-\rho^{N+1}}$	$m - \dfrac{1}{\rho}(1-P_0)$	λW	$\dfrac{\lambda}{\mu} + \dfrac{1+k}{2k}\dfrac{\lambda^2}{\mu(\mu-\lambda)}$	$\dfrac{\lambda}{\mu} + \dfrac{\lambda^2}{2\mu(\mu-\lambda)}$
L_q	$\dfrac{\lambda^2}{\mu(\mu-\lambda)}$	$L - (1-P_0)$	$m - \dfrac{(\lambda+\mu)(1-P_0)}{\lambda}$	$\dfrac{(\lambda\sigma)^2 + \lambda/\mu}{2(1-\lambda/\mu)}$	$L - \dfrac{\lambda}{\mu}$	$\dfrac{\lambda^2}{2(1-\lambda/\mu)}$
W	$\dfrac{1}{\mu-\lambda}$	$\dfrac{L}{\lambda(1-P_N)} + \dfrac{1}{\mu}$	$\dfrac{m}{\mu(1-P_0)} - \dfrac{1}{\lambda}$	$W_q + \dfrac{1}{\mu}$	$\dfrac{L}{\lambda}$	$\dfrac{L}{\lambda}$
W_q	$\dfrac{\lambda}{\mu(\mu-\lambda)}$	$W - \dfrac{1}{\mu}$	$\dfrac{1}{\mu}\left(\dfrac{m}{1-P_0} - \dfrac{\lambda+\mu}{\lambda}\right)$	$\dfrac{L_q}{\lambda}$	$\dfrac{L_q}{\lambda}$	$\dfrac{L_q}{\lambda}$
Remarks	$0 < \rho < 1$	$0 < \rho < \infty$	$0 < \rho < \infty$		k = Erlang parameter	$\sigma = 0, k = \infty$

† No queue discipline assumed.

TABLE 6-7 Formulas for selected multiple-channel model with Poisson arrivals and exponential service times[1]

	Basic model	Finite waiting room	Finite calling population
P_0	$\dfrac{1}{\displaystyle\sum_{n=0}^{s-1}\left[\dfrac{(\lambda/\mu)^n}{n!}\right] + \dfrac{(\lambda/\mu)^s}{s!}\dfrac{1}{1-\lambda/s\mu}}$	$\dfrac{1}{1 + \displaystyle\sum_{n=1}^{s}\dfrac{(\lambda/\mu)^n}{n!} + \dfrac{(\lambda/\mu)^s}{s!}\sum_{n=s+1}^{N}\left(\dfrac{\lambda}{s\mu}\right)^{n-s}}$	$\dfrac{1}{\displaystyle\sum_{n=0}^{s-1}\dfrac{m!}{(m-n)!\,n!}\left(\dfrac{\lambda}{\mu}\right)^n + \sum_{n=s}^{m}\dfrac{m!}{(m-n)!\,s!\,s^{n-s}}\left(\dfrac{\lambda}{\mu}\right)^n}$
P_n	$\dfrac{(\lambda/\mu)^n}{n!}\,P_0\quad$ for $0 \le n \le s$ $\dfrac{(\lambda/\mu)^n}{s!\,s^{n-s}}\quad$ for $n \ge s$	$\dfrac{(\lambda/\mu)^n}{n!}\,P_0\quad$ for $0 \le n \le s$ $\dfrac{(\lambda/\mu)^n}{s!\,s^{n-s}}\quad$ for $n \ge s$	$\dfrac{m!}{(m-n)!\,n!}\left(\dfrac{\lambda}{\mu}\right)^n P_0\quad$ for $0 \le n \le s$ $\dfrac{m!}{(m-n)!\,s!\,s^{n-s}}\left(\dfrac{\lambda}{\mu}\right)^n P_0\quad$ for $s \le n \le m$
L	$L_q + \dfrac{\lambda}{\mu}$	$\dfrac{(\lambda/\mu)^{s+1}}{(s-1)!\,(s-\lambda/\mu)^2}\,P_0 + \dfrac{\lambda}{\mu}$	$\displaystyle\sum_{n=0}^{s-1} n P_n + L_q + s\left(1 - \sum_{n=0}^{s-1} P_n\right)$
L_q	$\dfrac{(\lambda/\mu)^s}{s!(1-\rho)^2}\,P_0$	$L - \dfrac{\lambda}{\mu}$	$\displaystyle\sum_{n=s}^{m}(n-s)P_n$
W	$W_q + \dfrac{1}{\mu}$	$\dfrac{L_q}{\lambda} + \dfrac{1}{\mu}$	$\dfrac{L}{\lambda}$
W_q	$\dfrac{L_q}{\lambda}$	$\dfrac{L_q}{\lambda}$	$\dfrac{L_q}{\lambda}$
Remarks	$0 < \rho < 1$	$0 < \rho < 1$	$0 < \rho < \infty$

[1] There are extensive tables available with computational results for both single-channel and multichannel models with finite calling population in L. G. Peck and R. W. Hazelwood, *Finite Queueing Tables*, Wiley, New York, 1958.

A variety of queueing-cost models enable the analyst to take into account the following:

1. Servers whose performance is affected by pressure from a waiting line
2. Linear and nonlinear cost functions for service-capacity increments
3. Traveling time for customers for different working-area shapes

▶ For these and other models consult Refs. 2, 3, and 11.

6-7 SUMMARY

Our purpose in this chapter is to show how queueing models can be used to determine capacity requirements for a service facility. For most operations systems providing services both the times between successive arrivals of customers and the service times per customer vary randomly. When we can make some simplifying assumptions concerning the probability distributions of such times and how the facility operates, queueing models can determine a number of physical-performance characteristics, such as utilization rates, average time in the system, etc. Combined with data about service and waiting costs, these models help management determine the optimum capacity needed for various processing stages of the system.

In approaching the capacity problem using waiting-line models it is helpful to keep in mind the following points:

1. For a service facility with random customer arrivals and random service times, it is not desirable to achieve 100 percent utilization ($\rho = \lambda/s\mu = 100$ percent). When this occurs, the length of the waiting line L_q and the waiting time W_q become infinitely long. This requires extremely large waiting (or storage) space and excessively long delivery times.
2. The use of simple rules of thumb to make decisions instead of careful analysis usually leads to wrong actions. The oversimplification of waiting-line problems cannot account for the complex interaction of corrective measures on the operating aspects of a service facility.
3. Congestion of customers at the various service points results in a waiting cost. This involves not only the idle time of units in the waiting line but also all the productive resources controlled by those waiting.
4. All physical-performance measures of a facility (average length of the waiting line, average time in the system, etc.) can be improved by reducing the variability in both service and arrival times. On the service side this is an incentive to mechanize (or automate) one or more aspects of the operation (automatic car washes, blood-testing machines, fast-food restaurants, etc.). On the arrival side this is an incentive for scheduling arrivals (doctor's or lawyer's appointments, scheduling of hospital operating rooms, courts of justice, construction crews, and so on).
5. Even though queueing theory by itself does not provide optimal answers to capacity-determination problems, it is helpful in conceptualizing many operating problems. As has been said, life is nothing but a series of queues.

When the required assumptions approximate real conditions satisfactorily, some of the models yield useful results directly. In most cases, operations management can combine a waiting-line formulation with the powerful method of simulation to handle a wide variety of operating situations.

NOTATION

For Selected Queueing Models in Steady-State Condition

n = number of units in system
λ = mean arrival rate, units per time period
μ = mean service rate, units per time period
s = number of channels (or servers)
ρ = utilization rate (or traffic intensity) = $\lambda/s \cdot \mu$
N = number of units allowed in system (waiting-area capacity)
m = number of units in calling population
P_0 = probability service facility is idle
P_n = probability of having n units in system
L = average number of units in system
L_q = average number of units in waiting line
W = average time in system
W_q = average time in waiting line

REVIEW QUESTIONS

1. Describe in your own words the meaning of
   (*a*) queueing system and (*b*) queueing problem.
2. Describe the characteristics of a queueing system with reference to:
   (*a*) A bank
   (*b*) A hospital emergency room
   (*c*) A factory tool crib
   (*d*) A police patrol car
3. Why do different types of service facilities employ different queue disciplines, i.e., customer selection rules?
4. Discuss how the calling-population characteristics determine the demand for capacity in a service facility.
5. Discuss the effects of variability in arrival and service times on the performance of a service facility.
6. How can performance be improved for a queueing system?
7. Under what conditions is simulation preferred to queueing theory as an approach to studying service systems?
8. What must the analyst keep in mind when estimating waiting costs for a service facility?

PROBLEMS

In the following problems, unless stated otherwise, the customer selection rule is FCFS.

1. The mayor's office in Green City maintains a desk with a phone to handle calls during working hours with citizens' complaints. Phone calls arrive according to a Poisson distribution with a mean rate equal to 5 per hour ($\lambda = 5$ per hour)

(a) What is the probability that the number of calls received in any hour will be (i) 0, (ii) 1, (iii) 2, (iv) 3?

(b) What is the probability that the number of calls received in any hour will be (i) more than 3, (ii) less than 10, and (iii) between 4 and 9?

2. Refer to Prob. 1. If the time to handle each complaint follows an exponential distribution with a mean rate equal to 7 per hour ($\mu = 7$ per hour), what is the probability that a call will take (a) more than 10 min, (b) less than 2 min, (c) anywhere between 2 and 10 min? Draw a graph for this distribution and show above events.

3. A European international airport operates a 24-h foreign exchange bank. Customers arrive at the window according to a Poisson distribution with a mean rate of 15 per hour. Service time, with a single teller on duty, follows a negative-exponential distribution with a mean service rate of 18 customers per hour. Determine:

(a) The probability a customer will get served immediately upon arrival

(b) The probability a customer will have to wait

(c) The percentage utilization of the teller for foreign-exchange transactions

(d) The expected number of customers in the system

(e) The expected number of customers waiting in line

(f) The average time a customer will spend in the system

(g) The average time a customer will have to wait in line

4. Rework Prob. 3 if service time follows a general rather than exponential distribution, with the same mean service rate and a standard deviation equal to $\sigma = 0.02$ h.

5. Refer to Prob. 3. As a result of recent foreign-exchange regulations to control the country's trade deficit, each transaction at the bank must get an OK from the branch auditor. The forms that are filled out by the teller for each transaction are now taken to the desk of the auditor, who can check them at the rate of 20 per hour according to an exponential distribution.

(a) Repeat parts (a) to (g) in Prob. 3 for the auditor's desk.

(b) Determine the expected time a customer will take to go through the teller-auditor system.

6. The maintenance department of Sunrise Airlines receives components associated with reported malfunctions according to a Poisson distribution with a mean rate of 8 per day. These components are first subjected to x-ray tests by a technician; then they are repaired by an expert mechanic or a report is filled out for their replacement. The service time in the first stage for x-ray tests is constant at the rate of 12 per day, while the repair service is exponential with a mean rate equal to 10 per day.

(a) Determine P_0, ρ, P_n, L, L_q, W, and W_q (i) for the x-ray technician and (ii) for the expert mechanic.

(b) What is the expected total time before a component is returned?

7. Dr. Goodheart, a psychiatrist for the Robinson Social Services Center, is responsible for assisting the six social workers of the center with special problems as they arise in their casework. Requests for the doctor's assistance arrive at the rate of 8 per day according to a Poisson distribution and he can handle them at the rate of 12 per day with consultation times following an exponential distribution. Determine:

(a) The percentage utilization of Dr. Goodheart

(b) His average daily case load

(c) The average time a social worker must wait before consulting with the psychiatrist

8. The management of Reliable Navigation Instruments Co. submits all units to a final inspection before they are packaged for shipment. If a unit does not operate properly, it is returned to a special testing station. There it is subjected to a set of diagnostic tests (stage 1) and is then repaired for any defects (stage 2). The service time for each stage is

exponential with a mean equal to 1 hr. Defective units arrive at the special testing section at a rate of three per 8-h shift. Determine:

(*a*) The average number of units in the special testing section per day

(*b*) The average number of units waiting to be serviced per day

(*c*) The average time a unit will have to wait before service begins on it

9. A garage providing emergency road service operates two tow trucks. Calls for assistance arrive at the mean rate of 8 per hour according to a Poisson distribution. Service times follow an exponential distribution with a mean equal to 12 min. Determine:

(*a*) The probability a person calling for assistance will have a tow truck sent out immediately

(*b*) The probability a caller will have to wait before a truck is dispatched

(*c*) The percentage utilization of the tow trucks

(*d*) The expected number of callers waiting for road assistance

(*e*) The expected time a person will have to wait before a tow truck reaches the location of the disabled car

10. Refer to Prob. 9. Determine the performance of the garage if management decides to add another tow truck to the existing two.

11. Company trucks with fresh produce arrive at the receiving dock of a food-processing plant according to a Poisson distribution with a mean rate equal to 5 per hour. A crew of two workers is responsible for unloading them at the rate of 6 per hour. Unloading times follow an exponential distribution. Each member of the unloading crew costs the company $12 per hour. However, an idle waiting truck costs the company $36 per hour. Management would like to increase the size of the unloading crew on the assumption there will be a proportional decrease in unloading times for the purpose of reducing spoilage and improving truck utilization. Determine the optimum size of the unloading crew.

12. At Gentletone Mills Co. machine operators are responsible for the repair of minor breakdowns which occur according to a Poisson distribution with a mean rate of 12 per hour. Following a machine breakdown, an operator goes to the plant tool crib for the necessary tools and parts. Service times follow an exponential distribution with a mean of 6 min per operator. The cost of waiting for each operator in line is $20 per hour. A tool crib clerk costs $10 per hour. Determine the optimum number of tool-crib clerks, assuming the number of machines is large enough to treat it as an infinite calling population.

SELECTED REFERENCES

1. Cooper, R. B.: *Introduction to Queueing Theory*, Macmillan, New York, 1972.
2. Hillier, F. S., and G. T. Lieberman: *Introduction to Operations Research*, Holden-Day, San Francisco, 1974.
3. Lee, A.: *Applied Queueing Theory*, St. Martin's New York, 1966.
4. Morse, P. M.: *Queues, Inventories and Maintenance*, Wiley, New York, 1958.
5. Newell, G. F.: *Applications of Queueing Theory*, Chapman & Hall, London, 1971.
6. Panico, J. A.: *Queueing Theory: A Study of Waiting Lines for Business, Economics and Science*, Prentice-Hall, Englewood Cliffs, N.J., 1969.
7. Plane, D. R., and G. A. Kochenberger: *Operations Research for Managerial Decisions*, Irwin, Homewood, Ill., 1972.
8. Prabhu, N. U.: *Queues and Inventories*, Wiley, New York, 1965.
9. Riordan, J.: *Stochastic Service Systems*, Wiley, New York, 1965.
10. Saaty, T. L.: *Elements of Queueing Theory with Applications*, McGraw-Hill, New York, 1961.
11. Taha, Hamdy A.: *Operations Research: An Introduction*, 2nd ed., Macmillan, New York, 1974.

Supplementary Chapter D

SIMULATION

D-1   INTRODUCTION

The value of an approach for decision making is greatly enhanced by its flexibility. In this regard, simulation assumes a special significance as one of the most versatile methods available to operations management. Its range of application covers the widest variety of problems inside and outside an organization, from inventory analysis to world-dynamics modeling.

D-2   NATURE OF SIMULATION

The means by which managers reach a decision concerning the design or operation of a system include pure judgment or intuition, experience with similar situations, analysis with the help of analytical models, experimentation with the real system, and experimentation with a model of the real system. Simulation is associated with the last approach.

Definition

Simulation is an approach which uses a model of a situation or a system and manipulates it with the help of a computer in order to imitate the system's behavior over time for the purpose of evaluating alternative operating decision rules.

In the above definition the simulation model may be *physical* (wind-tunnel model of an airplane), *analog* (hydraulic representation of a supply system), or *mathematical* (inventory or scheduling model of a private firm). The situations studied vary in complexity from the operation of a hospital emergency room to that of an entire sector of the national economy.

The manipulation of the model refers to the conduct of experiments to test assumptions about the system design or evaluate alternative decision rules or policies for its operation. Simulation may be *static* when system performance is time-independent, but most often it is *dynamic*. Similarly, the relevant system variables may be deterministic, although the most interesting applications are those in which such variables are stochastic, i.e., governed by such probabilistic or statistical relationships as the random demand for spare parts or the uncertain duration of service time in a bank.

Purpose of Simulation

A simulation study may be undertaken for any of the following purposes:

1. The desire to understand the structure and operation of a system so that we can explain its behavior
2. The need to predict the behavior of a real system as it evolves in time

3. The need to evaluate the effects of changing the structure or operating policies; from the insights obtained through experimentation with a dynamic model of the system, one can influence or control future behavior in the real system

Note that these are similar to the reasons for building models in general as aids for decision making.

Reasons for Using Simulation

Compared with other approaches, simulation becomes attractive under the following conditions:

1. *The real system of interest is too complex to be represented with analytical models.* Complexity may arise from the large number of interacting components, e.g., in representing an industry or an urban region. For smaller systems complexity may be excessive because of the large number of variables and interactions that must be accounted for, e.g., in the development of corporate planning models or in behavioral models of human learning.
2. *Analytical models can be constructed but are difficult to solve.* Sometimes it is possible to state a relationship mathematically but very difficult to derive a solution from it. One example is the inventory situation where both the demand and the lead time vary at random according to some statistical distribution.
3. *Direct experimentation with the real system is expensive, time-consuming, or dangerous.* Of course when dealing with a system that does not yet exist such as a new facility or a new distribution system this option is not even available.

Types of Simulation

Simulation methods may be classified by one or more criteria.

The degree of abstraction of the simulation model   The most popular approach is simulation with the aid of a mathematical model, as in inventory or waiting-line problems. However, nonmathematical simulations are possible with the use of physical and analog models or with descriptive models such as case studies.

The extent of human involvement   Depending on the situation under study, the human involvement may be negligible, as in the case of a physical system, e.g., a cruise missile, or considerable, with one or more people present, as in a simulated space flight. When the presence of more than one person is significant, it is important to specify whether the interaction is *cooperative*, as in group problem solving, or *competitive*, as in business games.

The role of computers   By far the most widely used form of simulation relies on digital computers. The Monte Carlo method, which is employed when system variables are stochastic, depends heavily on the computer for the replication of the system's behavior for several runs. However, there have been successful efforts to simulate competitive situations as well as problems related to logistics and others without a computer.

D-3   MONTE CARLO SIMULATION

Our main interest here is with the Monte Carlo method as a tool for simulating systems with dynamic behavior. With the aid of a digital computer and a quantitative model and with less restrictive assumptions than most analytical models, the Monte Carlo method attempts to imitate the behavior of the real system by generating random values for key model variables that obey the same probability laws as the corresponding system variables. By conducting numerical experiments on the model, it is possible to observe the system's behavior over time and evaluate certain of its design characteristics or different decision rules for its operation.

Key Concepts Concerning the System Description

Our main objective in simulation is to predict and evaluate the real system's behavior. For this we need an accurate description of its key features and the rules by which management exercises control over it. The following concepts are intended to provide such a description.

System (or state) variables   These are the attributes of the system that change with time. There are two types. *Independent* (or input) *variables* are determined outside the model (exogenous), e.g., the demand experienced by an inventory system or the rainfall in a given watershed. *Dependent* (or output) *variables* are those whose values are generated within the model (endogenous), e.g., the size and timing of inventory replenishments.

System parameters   These refer to the attributes of the system which remain unchanged during the time covered by a simulation run. In an inventory system the parameters may refer to unit costs, supply lead times, budget limit, etc.

System decision rules   These represent the predetermined response of the system, through the controllable variables, to the values assumed by the uncontrollable variables.

In simulation studies the usual focus of investigation is on the decision rule(s) by which a system is operated. We evaluate alternative rules so that we can select the one that yields the "best" performance.

Procedure Employed in Simulation

The use of simulation follows a procedure similar to that discussed in Chap. 2 for model building. However, certain adaptations are necessary to allow for the extensive experimentation needed with the computer. Thus, typical Monte Carlo simulation studies go through the following steps:

1. Problem formulation in quantitative form
2. Construction of simulation model
3. Experimental design for data collection and analysis
4. Writing and testing the computer program
5. Running and validating the simulation model
6. Evaluation of simulation results

D-4   A SIMPLE INVENTORY-SYSTEM SIMULATION

To illustrate some of the key features of the simulation process, we shall first examine a simple inventory example with probabilistic demand. (An analytical solution for this problem is discussed in Chap. 13.) The owner of the Edelweiss Bakery Shop wishes to find a decision rule for how many special cakes to make each weekend so that long-term profit will be maximized. To keep matters simple we shall assume that there is no cost associated with shortages.

   The problem description for the Edelweiss Bakery Shop, using simulation language, includes the following:

State variables   *Exogenous* y_t is the actual demand for fresh cakes in period t with the following experience from past sales:

Demand y	0	1	2	3	4	5
Probability $f(y)$	.05	.15	.20	.25	.20	.15

Endogenous

$$Q_t = \text{quantity prepared in period } t$$

System parameters

$$B = \$8 = \text{price per fresh cake}$$

$$C = \$5 = \text{cost per cake}$$

$$S = \$3 = \text{salvage value per day-old cake}$$

Performance measure   *This is the same as profit per week Z.*

Case 1   demand less than or equal to supply $(y \le Q)$

$$Z = (B - C)y - (C - S)(Q - y)$$
$$= (\$8 - \$5)(y) - (\$5 - \$3)(Q - y) = \$3y - (\$2)(Q - y)$$

or

$$\begin{bmatrix} \text{Weekly} \\ \text{profit} \end{bmatrix} = \begin{bmatrix} \text{unit} \\ \text{profit} \end{bmatrix}\begin{bmatrix} \text{number of fresh} \\ \text{cakes demanded} \end{bmatrix} - \begin{bmatrix} \text{unit} \\ \text{loss} \end{bmatrix}\begin{bmatrix} \text{number of} \\ \text{leftover cakes} \end{bmatrix}$$

Case 2   demand greater than supply $(y > Q)$

$$Z = (B - C)Q$$
$$= (\$8 - \$5)Q = \$3Q$$

or

$$\begin{bmatrix} \text{Weekly} \\ \text{profit} \end{bmatrix} = \begin{bmatrix} \text{unit} \\ \text{profit} \end{bmatrix}\begin{bmatrix} \text{number of} \\ \text{cakes prepared} \end{bmatrix}$$

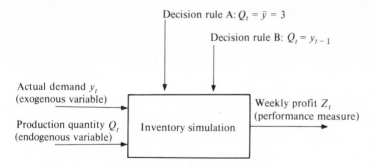

Fig. D-1   Representation of Edelweiss Bakery Shop problem.

Suppose that in the absence of any knowledge (from an analytical model) of the optimal decision rule the owner has been considering two alternatives:

Decision rule A: Prepare three cakes, i.e., the closest integer value to the average demand.

Decision rule B: Prepare as many cakes as the number demanded the previous week.

Thus
$$Q_t = \begin{cases} \bar{y} = 3 & \text{rule A} \\ y_{t-1} & \text{rule B} \end{cases}.$$

The preceding formulation is summarized graphically in Fig. D-1.

To evaluate alternative decision rules using simulation, we must replicate, i.e., imitate, the operation of the bakery shop for several weeks. This is done by generating a sequence of values representing demand and then calculating the resulting profits for each decision rule. *It is important that the values generated for demand occur with the same relative frequency experienced in the past.* Thus, a value of 2 should occur 20 percent of the time, a value of 3 should occur 25 percent of the time, and so on. One could use 100 folded slips of paper, 5 of which have the number 0, 15 of which have the number 1, 20 of which have the number 2, etc. These could be mixed thoroughly in a bowl each time before drawing a slip. The number on the slip of paper is recorded and returned to the bowl before the next draw. Another procedure might be to use a device like a roulette wheel subdivided into 100 slots. With this scheme, if the ball stops in slots 1 to 5, the value for demand would be 0, if in 6 to 15 the value would be 1, and so on.

Procedures like these are attractive for instructional purposes. In practice, however, they are awkward because of the large number of random values needed in a typical simulation run. Instead, it is preferable to obtain random numbers (RN) either from a random-number table (Appendix 1) for use with hand simulations or from a digital computer for the majority of realistic applications.

To generate a value for demand with the same relative frequency as in real life, we must assign a range of random numbers to that value so that numbers in that range occur with the same probability as the relative frequency of the selected value for demand.

Suppose the demand for cakes could only assume values of 0, 1, and 2 with frequencies 20, 50, and 30 percent. Then we could employ one-digit random numbers so that the range 1 to 2 corresponds to zero demand, the range 2, 3, 4, 6, 7 to demand for one cake, and the range 8, 9, 0 to demand for two cakes. Since in our example the relative frequencies are specified with two digits, it is necessary to use two-digit random numbers to simulate actual demand as indicated below.

Range of random numbers	Relative frequency	Corresponding value of demand	Probability of demand	Cumulative probability of demand
01–05	.05	0	.05	.05
06–20	.15	1	.15	.20
21–40	.20	2	.20	.40
41–65	.25	3	.25	.65
66–85	.20	4	.20	.85
86–00	.15	5	.15	1.00

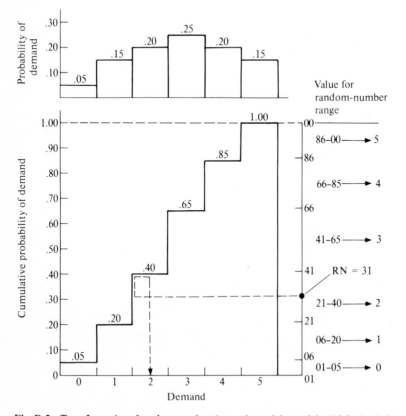

Fig. D-2   Transformation of random numbers into values of demand for Edelweiss Bakery Shop example.

The random numbers chosen for each value of demand correspond to the appropriate range in the cumulative probability distribution for demand (see Fig. D-2). Suppose the random number chosen is 31. The dotted line in Fig. D-2 is shown to transform the random number 31 into a value of demand equal to 2 from the cumulative-probability graph. The transformation of a random number into a specific value for the random variable of interest is a key step in the formulation of a simulation model.

Before the simulation we must decide on the length of the simulation run, i.e., the number of periods covered, and the initial values for parameters and certain state variables. In our example, the unit costs have been specified, but we need an initial value for demand to evaluate decision rule B. For the sake of illustration, we have selected a 15-wk interval and have set the initial value of demand equal to 3 ($y_0 = 3$), which is its average value. In practice these decisions are critical in the interpretation of results and the amount of computer time needed.

For a 15-wk simulation run we shall need 15 random numbers to drive our inventory model by providing representative values of demand. These are obtained from a random-number table by reading the first two of five-digit numbers across a row or down a column (see Table D-1).

For each simulation trial we have the following steps:

1. Obtain a random number from a random-number table.
2. Determine the range in which the random number belongs.
3. Identify the value of demand y corresponding to the selected random-number range. Here we use the transformation indicated in Fig. D-2.

TABLE D-1 Simulation of Edelweiss Bakery Shop operation

Week number t	Random number	Corresponding demand value y_t	Decision rule A $Q_t = \bar{y} = 3$ Q_t	Z_t	Decision rule B $Q_t = y_{t-1}$ Q_t	Z_t
0	—	3				
1	18	1	3	$ -1	3	$ -1
2	37	2	3	4	1	3
3	08	1	3	-1	2	1
4	61	3	3	9	1	3
5	88	5	3	9	3	9
6	76	4	3	9	5	10
7	44	3	3	9	4	7
8	40	2	3	4	3	4
9	11	1	3	-1	2	1
10	70	4	3	9	1	3
11	32	2	3	4	4	2
12	79	4	3	9	2	6
13	54	3	3	9	4	7
14	62	3	3	9	3	9
15	62	3	3	9	3	9
Total profit				$93		$73
Weekly profit = (total profit)/15				$6.00		$4.87

4. Calculate the weekly profit from the appropriate equation

$$Z_t = \begin{cases} \$3y_t - \$2(Q_t - y_t) & \text{if demand is less than or equal to supply} \\ & (y_t \leq Q_t) \\ \$3Q_t & \text{if demand is greater than supply } (y_t > Q_t) \end{cases}$$

These steps are repeated 15 times to cover the desired 15-wk simulated period. Table D-1 summarizes the results of a hand simulation.

From the results in Table D-1, decision rule A, preparing three cakes each week, yields a higher weekly profit than decision rule B, for which the quantity prepared equals last week's demand. The owner might examine other decision rules, such as setting Q_t equal to a four-period moving average. The above conclusion might not be the same if the simulation run were longer, if the initial value for demand were different, and, of course, if the parameters were changed. All these issues in well-designed simulation studies require careful consideration.

Our inventory example is too simple compared with more realistic simulation applications. Nevertheless, it is useful for bringing out some of the issues that arise in practice. The inventory problem in which both demand and lead time are specified, with empirical frequency distributions, represents an interesting case where simulation has been employed successfully to evaluate alternative decision rules. The same holds true for job-shop scheduling and maintenance problems in which job arrivals occur at random and we wish to evaluate several priority rules for their sequencing.

D-5 PROCEDURE EMPLOYED FOR A SIMULATION STUDY

As stated previously, the steps involved in a simulation study follow the same sequence as in the problem-solving process described in Chap. 2. Our interest in this section relates mainly to points that require special care in the conduct of a simulation study.

Problem Formulation

Successful problem formulation requires an accurate assessment of management objectives accompanied by a description of the real system. This involves the specification of (1) criteria of performance by which alternative decision rules will be evaluated, (2) all significant state variables, and (3) all the necessary system parameters. In our inventory example the relevant criterion was profit maximization, while the important state variables included demand (exogenous) and production quantity (endogenous). Relevant parameters in this case included the unit price and cost and the salvage value.

Construction of a Simulation Model

Unlike analytical models, such as linear-programming or queueing models, which apply to rather general problems like the allocation of limited resources or the behavior of a service facility, simulation models are restricted to specific situations.

Consequently, their results cannot be generalized for the analysis of similar problems.

When building a simulation model we are concerned with the following:

	Inventory-system application
Specification of state variables:	
Uncontrollable variables and their statistical distributions	Demand for units (empirical), supply lead time (normal), etc.
Controllable variables	Production or order quantities, reorder points, reorder time intervals
Specification of parameters	Unit holding, ordering, and shortage costs and unit prices
Specification of performance criteria	Minimization of total inventory cost
Specification of system relationships and constraints	Reorder quantity = (maximum desired level) − (inventory level during review time); inventory investment, inventory budget

An important advantage of simulation is the flexibility possible in the formulation of assumptions. This allows more realistic representation of system behavior because there is no need to force relationships to take a linear or other form usually required for analytical solutions. Thus, one can use empirical statistical distributions for state random variables that do not follow the usual normal, Poisson, or other well-defined distribution. If a relationship can be approximated with an analytical expression, it is very convenient to do so. Using certain statistical tests, it is possible to determine how well a theoretical distribution approximates an empirical set of data.

As with analytical models, it is better to start out with a few key variables and relationships that focus satisfactorily on the problem. If the simple model can predict well, it can be enriched with additional variables for further refinement. Starting with a simple model is crucial in simulation because of the added costs of writing a computer program, validating it, and conducting numerical experiments with a computer. The objective here is to balance the costs from inaccuracy (insufficient system representation) against the costs of developing and using the model.

Experimental Design for Data Collection and Analysis

Within the conceptual framework of the simulation model, it is necessary to have an experimental design which will provide guidelines for the collection of data, their analysis, and how the simulation results will be used to answer the questions the study was undertaken to solve. Since simulation relies on sampling to test certain hypotheses concerning the behavior of the real system, it is essential to observe certain statistical procedures before interpreting the simulation results.

The data to be collected must be sufficient to give an adequate description of the stochastic variables employed in the model. This is a time-consuming task, aimed at specifying the form and parameters of the statistical distribution for each such variable. Even though their form may be sometimes assessed subjectively, assuming, for example, that arrivals of repair jobs in a shop follow a Poisson distribution, the simulation of a system is more reliable when based on empirical data from records or direct observation.

From data analysis we can determine whether simulation will be run with empirical distributions (histograms) based on observed relative frequencies or from some theoretical approximation which considerably streamlines many calculations at subsequent steps. For this purpose a *chi-square* or a *Kolmogorov-Smirnov* statistical test is usually most helpful.

The experimental design also attempts to answer questions with respect to:

1. The initial values to be assigned to state variables and parameters
2. The simulation-run length
3. The procedures for the evaluation of alternative decision rules

Specification of initial values for state variables and parameters is an important issue in simulation because it affects how long it will take the model to reach a steady state, i.e., a condition of equilibrium. Since we wish to interpret simulation data from a steady rather than the preceding transient state, we must either assign initial values typical of equilibrium conditions or discard the results from the early phases.

Similarly, deciding the length of the simulation run is crucial because it determines the sample size on which experimental results will be evaluated and influences how long the system will be observed in a steady state. In practice, there are procedures for handling these problems so that the evaluation of simulation results will meet certain statistical requirements.

Writing and Testing a Computer Program

Since the use of a computer is indispensable for any realistic application, it is necessary to write and test a computer program for the simulation model. Assembler computer languages are too dependent on the manufacturer's hardware for easy and general use. The more general programming (compiler) languages such as FORTRAN, PL1, BASIC, and others work well for simulating a wide variety of problems.

To reduce the programming effort a number of special-purpose simulation languages have been designed that simplify this task even more. These include SIMSCRIPT, GPSS, GASP, and DYNAMO, in which simple instructions are equivalent to complete subroutines in other languages. As more analysts develop the skill to use special-purpose languages and their availability with commercial computer systems increases, the requirements for writing simulation programs will not restrain the use of this powerful approach for the solution of more problems.

**Running and Validating the
Simulation Model**

Before simulation results can be evaluated, it is necessary to have a few trial runs in order to validate the simulation model. Validation covers both program correction and model suitability. First, we must ensure that the program written correctly instructs the computer to perform the desired operations. Testing the program may be done with hand calculations, programs traces, or some other technique. Second, we must be satisfied that the computer output of the simulation model is a satisfactory representation of the real system's behavior.

For example, if actual inventory demand for a spare part follows a Poisson distribution with a mean equal to 20 units/wk, the values of demand generated at random by the simulation model must also follow a Poisson distribution with the same mean. This can be tested by the same statistical techniques employed to see whether a theoretical distribution used in the simulation model accurately represents an empirical distribution.

One way to validate a simulation model is by comparing its output with historical data. Another method is to have experienced managers review its structure, especially its computer output, and comment on its ability to imitate the behavior of the real system. If no significant differences emerge from these comparisons, using either statistical or subjective tests, the model is acceptable for predicting behavior under conditions prevailing when the model was built.

Evaluating Simulation Results

Two conditions that must hold before we can evaluate the results of simulation are the validity of the model and the correct design of the experiments that will be performed on the model. Since simulation is a sampling process, the results must be evaluated using statistical techniques (hypothesis testing, analysis of variance, or other). By formulating and testing different assumptions concerning the system's behavior we can evaluate proposed policies or decision rules so that management can choose the one that best meets organizational objectives.

**D-6   CHARACTERISTICS OF
SIMULATION**

Before undertaking a simulation study on some managerial problem, it is important to keep in mind some characteristics of the process. The *major advantages* of simulation are as follows:

1. Simulation is a versatile approach for studying the behavior of very complex and dynamic systems with no advanced mathematics.
2. Simulation makes it possible to compress real time (years or months of operation into minutes or seconds) and evaluate alternative policies or decision rules based on imitated rather than actual behavior.
3. Simulation allows experimentation in situations where direct experimentation with the real system would be dangerous, time-consuming, or expensive.

4. Simulation requires the close cooperation of experienced managers and analysts. This leads to more realistic representation of actual problems and easier implementation of adopted decision rules after testing and evaluating alternative "what if" proposals.

The *major disadvantages* of simulation are as follows:

1. Simulation is an expensive method for solving decision problems. In addition to the cost of building and validating a model we have the significant cost of experimentation with the computer.
2. Simulation results may suffer from sampling errors in the output. This makes their evaluation difficult. Increases in the length of simulation runs and statistical refinements to reduce sampling errors add considerably to the cost.
3. Simulation is a descriptive rather than an optimization process. It can select, subject to sampling errors, only among proposed alternatives.
4. Simulation results apply only to the specific application for which the model was built. Changes in the structure or operating conditions of the system are likely to invalidate the results, with limited transfer of decision rules to similar problems.

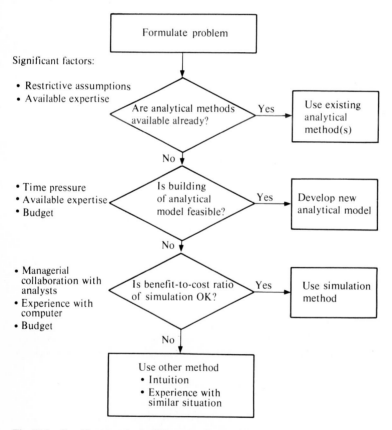

Fig. D-3   Considerations in deciding to use simulation.

5. Simulation studies often suffer from faults or omissions in the experimental design. This is associated with the difficulty of having all the necessary skills in the few persons usually assigned to a simulation study.

In the light of the above characteristics, the decision to use simulation may be handled as suggested by the flowchart in Fig. D-3.

D-7 SIMULATION APPLICATIONS IN OPERATIONS MANAGEMENT

Simulation has found a number of significant applications in several decision areas of operations management. In the design of a new production or operations system simulation has been used to evaluate:

1. Alternative investments for new products, new technologies, or new facilities
2. Various configurations of the capacity of service facilities (waiting-line problems)
3. Alternative facility layouts
4. Alternative facility locations

With respect to the planning, operation, and control of an existing system, simulation has been used to evaluate:

1. Inventory-control policies
2. Aggregate planning with heuristic methods
3. Scheduling policies for job shops with random arrivals
4. Scheduling policies of projects with random duration of individual activities
5. Maintenance policies for equipment subject to random breakdowns

For some interesting descriptions of successful applications see the Selected References, especially Ref. 7. The Selected References also provide detailed examination of the different issues arising in simulation, and efficient computer simulation languages and methods for conducting a simulation study. These subjects go beyond the scope of this book.

D-8 SUMMARY

Our purpose in this brief chapter has been to highlight the key features of simulation, especially the Monte Carlo method, as a decision-making approach. Under certain conditions, simulation provides a powerful method for studying the behavior of systems that are too complex to analyze with analytical models. Inability to experiment directly with such systems, because of the time, cost, or danger involved, makes simulation the last resort for the effective evaluation of proposed policies or operating decision rules.

Nevertheless, simulation represents a rather expensive and difficult undertaking if one is to use it properly. The usual reliance on the computer and the requirement for a careful design of the statistical experiments to be performed impose two of the most critical limitations of simulation in terms of its cost and needed expertise. Management must thus view its use on the basis of a benefit-cost analysis comparing it with judgmental or analytical approaches to the same problem.

REVIEW QUESTIONS

1. Describe in your own words the meaning of simulation.
2. What types of models can be employed in a simulation study?
3. Discuss the main reasons for using simulation.
4. Describe the basic types of simulation.
5. Outline the procedure employed in a simulation study.
6. What are the distinctive features of Monte Carlo simulation?
7. Explain the difference between exogenous and endogenous variables in a simulation model.
8. Describe a few methods for generating random numbers.
9. Discuss the similarities and differences in the development of a simulation and an analytical model.
10. Why is the experimental design for data collection and analysis especially critical in simulation?
11. Discuss the effect of initial conditions and the length of the simulation run on simulation results.
12. What computer languages are appropriate for digital simulation?
13. Discuss what must be done when validating a simulation model.
14. State the major advantages and disadvantages of simulation.
15. Discuss the differences in the use of solutions obtained from a simulation model, as opposed to those obtained from an analytical model.

PROBLEMS

1. Billy Joe operates a news stand in the downtown open mall and wishes to develop an ordering policy for *City Life*, a weekly magazine covering the city's cultural activities. Each copy sells for $1 and costs Billy Joe 60 cents. Leftover copies are purchased back at 30 cents per copy. From the records of the last 50 wk Billy Joe has developed the following information:

Magazines sold per week	20	21	22	23	24
Weeks	3	12	18	15	2

   (a) Prepare a relative frequency distribution for weekly sales of *City Life* magazine.
   (b) Identify the ranges of random numbers corresponding to each demand value.
   (c) Perform a simulation for 20 days and estimate average weekly sales.

2. Refer to Prob. 1. Billy Joe wishes to check whether it will be more profitable for him to order (a) a quantity equal to 22 copies per week or (b) a quantity equal to actual sales from the previous week. From a simulation run of 20 wk estimate which decision rule would be preferred. For rule B assume $y_0 = 22$.

3. Refer to Prob. 1. On rainy days Billy Joe moves his stand to a different location, and for such days the relative frequency distribution for the sales of *City Life* magazine is different, as shown below:

Magazines sold per week	20	21	22	23	24
Relative frequency	.25	.45	.15	.10	.05

For the upcoming season the records of the National Weather Bureau indicate rain for 40 percent of the time.

(*a*) Prepare a simple flowchart for a simulation model to estimate weekly sales and profits, accounting for weather fluctuation.

(*b*) Perform a new simulation run of 20 wk to evaluate the decision rules (1) for ordering 22 copies per week and (2) for ordering a quantity equal to actual sales in the previous week. For rule B assume $y_0 = 22$.

4. United Builders Corp., a housing development firm, can complete work on a new site either by doing it all or subcontracting part of it to another firm with estimated completion times as shown in the figure. Several other sites have already been approved for

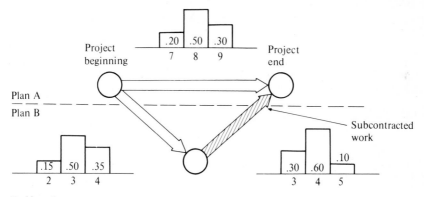

Problem 4

similar housing-development projects to begin after the current project. Assuming costs and construction quality would be the same by either plan, the management of United Builders Corp. would like to select the method that would result in the shortest completion time.

(*a*) Prepare a simulation model flowchart that will evaluate project-completion time.

(*b*) Perform a simulation with 15 trials and evaluate the two alternative plans.

5. At Northwestern Mills Corp. machine operators are responsible for repairs of minor breakdowns. For this task they need tools and parts, which they obtain at a central tool crib. Because of the randomness in both the occurrence of breakdowns and the service time of operators, one might observe a line of operators at the tool crib waiting to get served or idle tool crib clerks. Concerned about this problem, management directed a preliminary study which produced the following data on times between successive arrivals of operators to the tool crib and their service times:

Relative frequency of service times

Interarrival time, min	4	5	6	7	8	9
Relative frequency	.10	.30	.25	.20	.10	.05

Relative frequency of interarrivals times

Service time, min	3	4	5	6	7	8
Relative frequency	.10	.40	.20	.15	.10	.05

(a) Assuming that the tool crib operates with one clerk, perform a simulation for 20 arrivals, starting out with no operators in the system.

(b) From the results of the simulation, estimate (i) the average number of machine operators in the waiting line, (ii) the average waiting time per operator, and (iii) the average time a machine operator will spend in the tool crib waiting and getting served.

(c) Discuss the significance for this problem of (i) initial system conditions, and (ii) length of simulation run.

6. Refer to Prob. 5. The estimated cost for an operator waiting in line is $30 per hour whereas for each clerk working in the tool crib the cost is $12 per hour.

(a) Prepare a flowchart for a simulation model that will evaluate the average length of the waiting line and the total cost of the tool-crib operation for one and two tool-crib clerks.

(b) Perform a simulation with 20 arrivals using one, two, and three tool-crib clerks and select the alternative that minimizes the sum of waiting and service costs.

7. Louise Marchant is the owner of the Moulin Rouge West, a small French restaurant. The menu each day includes three choices, the evening special, priced at $18 per couple, the gourmet selection, priced at $22 per couple, and the Parisian treat at $30 per couple. Louise has observed that her customers include local college students, out-of-town tourists, and other local people fond of French food. The relative frequency of menu selections by customer group is shown below.

Menu selection	College students	Tourists	Others
Evening special	.60	.20	.10
Gourmet selection	.30	.30	.70
Parisian treat	.10	.50	.20
Percentage of total customers	.25	.30	.45

The number of couples served varies from day to day, but from past records, Louise has developed the following information:

Number of couples	3	4	5	6
Relative frequency	.15	.30	.35	.20

(a) Prepare a flowchart for a simulation model intended to estimate daily revenue for Louise's restaurant.

(b) Perform a simulation for 10 days and show the day-by-day revenue and the total revenue for that period.

8. Prepare a library report on the development and actual application of:

(a) A simulation model for an operations management problem

(b) A simulation model for an entire firm (cash flows, etc.)

(c) A simulation model for a complex system at the community, regional, or higher level

SELECTED REFERENCES

1. Carlson, J. G., and M. J. Misshauk: *Introduction to Gaming: Management Decision Simulations*, Wiley, New York, 1972.
2. Forrester, Jay W.: *Industrial Dynamics*, Wiley, New York, 1961.
3. Forrester, Jay W.: *World Dynamics*, Wright-Allen, Cambridge, Mass., 1971.
4. Hertz, D. G.: "Risk Analysis in Capital Investment," *Harvard Business Review*, January-February, 1964, p. 102.
5. McMillan, C., and R. F. Gonzalez: *Systems Analysis: A Computer Approach to Decision Models*, 3d ed., Irwin, Homewood, Ill., 1973.
6. Meier, R. C., W. T. Newell, and H. L. Pazer: *Simulation in Business and Economics*, Prentice-Hall, Englewood Cliffs, N.J., 1969.
7. Naylor, T. H., J. L. Balintfy, D. S. Burdick, and K. Chu: *Computer Simulation Techniques*, Wiley, New York, 1968.
8. Wagner, J., and L. J. Pryer: "Simulation and the Budget: An Integrated Model," *Sloan Management Review*, vol. 12, no. 12, Winter 1971, pp. 45-58.
9. Wiest, J. R.: "Heuristic Programs for Decision Making," *Harvard Business Review*, September-October 1966, pp. 129-143.
10. Wyman, F. P.: *Simulation Modeling: A Guide to Using Simscript*, Wiley, New York, 1970.

Chapter 7

HOW TO PRODUCE I: PROCESS DESIGN

7-1   INTRODUCTION

The conversion of inputs (human resources, raw materials, etc.) into desired outputs (products and services) requires a set of operations in successive stages. The technology, equipment, and work methods used for the necessary operations make up the production process of the system.

Sound process design requires that those in management and engineering responsible for it understand the output product characteristics and the pattern of projected growth in the demand for the product. The problems of product design and process design are therefore closely interrelated, requiring successive adjustments in the product specifications to adapt them to the capabilities and cost characteristics of known feasible technologies.

We may classify production processes according to the nature of the output, the type of transformation involved, or the flow within the process. Figure 7-1 summarizes the main distinctions, which are significant in that they affect the design as well as the methods used for planning and control of the system.

At this point it is necessary to draw an important distinction between the content and form of a production process. The *content of a process* refers to the specific technology, equipment, and materials employed, as determined by the nature of its output(s) or input(s). This requires empirical knowledge of the particular industry and is of limited use in applications to other industries. However, the *form of a process*, which refers to the type of flow in it, provides valuable insights into its management, its strengths, and its limitations. For present and future managers such an understanding is extremely important and can be transferred regardless of the industry where it will be used. The basic forms of a process are related to the type of flow of units through successive conversion stages.

Also important during the phase of process design are certain issues related to energy requirements and pollution characteristics because both affect performance in the long and short run. These are discussed in detail in later sections.

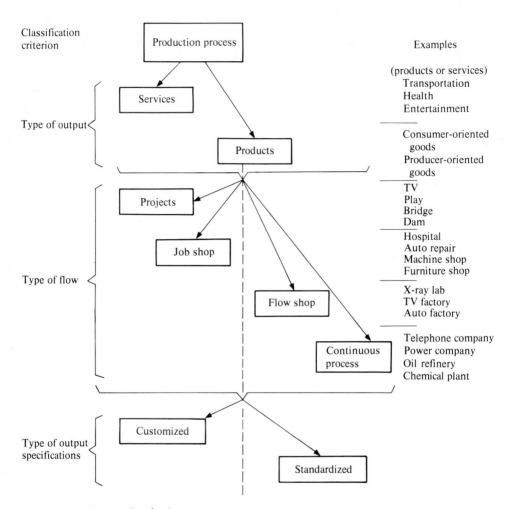

Fig. 7-1 Classification of production processes.

7-2 TYPES OF PRODUCTION PROCESSES

The great diversity of human needs for products and services has brought about an equally impressive variety of production processes. Thus, processes for products range in complexity and size from a craft shop for jewelry to a huge oil refinery or General Motors. Services may require as simple a process as the corner dry-cleaning shop or as large and complex an entity as the federal government.

Process Types by Flow Pattern

In product design our concern is with *what* is to be produced. In process design the emphasis is on *how* it is to be produced. The latter may often prove more critical to the success of an organization than the former. The most important criterion for classifying production processes is the type of flow of units through successive conversion stages. We recognize three basic types known as *flow shop*, *job shop*, and *project*. Management's choice of a particular flow type is a decision of profound importance. It will affect the technology to be used, the human skills to employ, the methods for planning and control of operations, the marketing strategy, and the extent and complexity of the necessary financial planning.

The flow shop For products or services with a basic design that remains stable over time and is intended for a large market, it is necessary to arrange the production process as a flow shop which normally produces for stock.

Definition

A *flow shop* is a conversion process in which successive units of output undergo the same sequence of operations with specialized equipment, usually positioned along a production line.

An extreme form of a flow shop, sometimes treated as a separate case, is the *continuous process*, in which there is a constant flow of materials. Examples include oil refining, chemical processing, and others in which there is no way to identify successive units of output.

Ordinary flow shops might be further subdivided into continuous and intermittent types. In the *continuous flow shop* the process goes on producing the same type of output, e.g., cigarettes or boxes of cereal. In the *intermittent flow shop* the process is periodically interrupted to set it up to handle different specifications of the same basic design. In each run, however, all units follow the same sequence. This is often the case with canning factories, bottling plants, mass-produced clothing items, etc.

For a product to reach a wide market the price must be quite low and competitive with similar or substitute products. This in turn requires a low production cost per unit, which is possible through economies of scale from large and specialized facilities and equipment. To reach high output rates the specialized equipment for each stage must be arranged in sequence to allow relatively rapid movement through the system. For such an operation, workers need have only limited skills to perform those repetitive tasks which cannot be assigned to machines. This contributes to high uniformity in quality. The rapid movement of units through successive stages reduces in-process inventories but places a premium on prompt supply deliveries and reliability of system components to avoid forced idleness of entire production lines due to the breakdown of individual equipment.

With most of the planning and control of the flow shop built into the production line, the challenging tasks for management focus on the development of marketing strategies that will sustain and enhance high output volume, on financial planning to purchase and periodically replace expensive specialized equipment, and on personnel policies designed to motivate a work force employed in a way that provides limited job satisfaction. The natural target for flow shops are the almost infinite varieties of consumer goods (auto, TV sets, appliance, clothing, detergents, toys, etc.) and services for which there are large markets to support the essential high volume of the same basic design.

The specialized expensive equipment and facilities needed for flow-shop operations tend to limit the flexibility of a firm with respect to other market opportunities. However, for the successful organizations it is possible to achieve high productivity, impressive growth, and large profits.

The job shop   For products and services that must be flexible to handle specialized customer needs, the rigidity of the flow shop must be replaced by a more flexible and responsive conversion process. This is the job-shop arrangement, which normally produces to order.

Definition

A *job shop* is a conversion process in which units for different orders follow different sequences through the resource centers grouped by function to satisfy special customer needs for products or services.

The need for flexibility to handle a wide variety of product designs requires the use of versatile human resources and equipment. This means highly skilled workers and general-purpose equipment grouped by function that can be adapted to the special requirements of different orders. The price for flexibility includes longer processing times due to frequent equipment setups; a greater need for in-process inventories of materials, parts, and components; and a formidable task in scheduling different orders through the various processing centers in which resources must be time-shared. All these result in longer delivery times, more variable quality, and higher costs than in a flow shop.

A job-shop organization is more concerned with its reputation for quality and technical excellence than for effective marketing strategies to sustain high output volume. The employment of highly skilled workers with considerable responsibility for the planning and control of their jobs offers greater job satisfaction and higher morale than the flow shop. However, their effective utilization requires more competent engineers and managers to plan and control operations than the flow shop with its routine procedures.

The project   Most organizations are frequently challenged by the need to create a product or service that is a unique one-shot undertaking. This calls for a large number of tasks that must use limited resources in a highly coordinated manner because of the strict sequencing requirements.

Definition

A *project* refers to the process of creating a rather complex one-of-a-kind product or service with a set of well-defined tasks in terms of resource requirements and time phasing.

Many of the functions affecting production, such as planning, design, purchasing, marketing, hiring personnel and/or equipment, which are usually kept separate in flow-shop or job-shop systems, must now be integrated in a carefully time-phased sequence to ensure prompt and economic completion.

The need to manage projects does not arise only in project-oriented organizations, such as movie studios, research institutes, and construction firms. It is a very important concern of flow-shop and job-shop systems whenever they must plan for new facilities or technologies and whenever there is a need to design, evaluate, and introduce a new product or service.

Processes for Products

The tangible output of a production process may be a raw material, say timber, to be used as the input for another process, e.g., a piece of furniture. Some products, like a drill press, may be used as part of another production process. In general, most products are made for the final consumer, e.g., a TV set, a box of cereal, or a pair of shoes.

Processes with a tangible output are classified according to the type of physical transformation required to convert the required inputs. We generally distinguish five such types, which are found individually or in various combinations. They include *extraction, chemical change, preparation, fabrication*, and *assembly*. In Fig. 7-2 the conversion types are related to the basic forms of a process classified according to the flow of the product.

Processes for Services

With the rise in a society's standard of living there is an increase in the consumption not only of products but also of services. Today we have come to depend on a multitude of service systems that may cover new needs (credit reporting) or old ones in a better way (jet transportation). In fact, the percentage of gross personal consumption expenditures for services has increased steadily since World War II and in 1970 exceeded that for consumer nondurable goods.

In contrast to the majority of products, for which it is possible to use mass production, service systems often involve a process that is affected by the unique requirements of customers and the characteristics of the person(s) rendering the service. The variety of service processes are designed to cater to individual human needs from the cradle to the grave. There exist, furthermore, service systems to

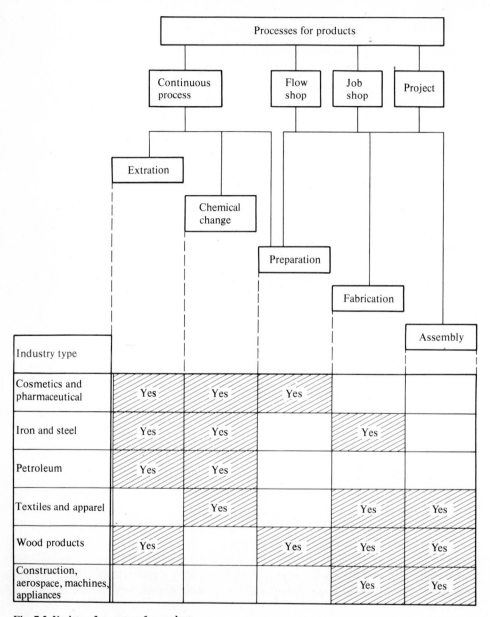

Fig. 7-2 Variety of processes for products.

274

TABLE 7-1   Types of private and public service systems

Private	Public	Quasi-public
Transportation	Defense	Telephone services
Banking	Education	Water supply
Commerce	Welfare	Electricity and gas supply
Medical care	Transportation networks	Research
Legal assistance	(waterways, highways, etc.)	
Technical assistance	Police and fire	
Maintenance and repair	protection	
Entertainment	Local, state, and	
Education	federal government	
Research	Research	

cover needs of groups, cities, the nation, or even the whole globe. An indicative list of such systems is provided in Table 7-1.

The rapidly increasing costs of medical care, education, transportation, and others require that the design of processes for service systems be given the same thorough attention as systems producing physical goods. It is ironic that although our times have developed the technology to land a man on the moon, average people spend a significant part of their lives simply waiting for service in systems for transportation, medical care, education, and even entertainment.

7-3 METHODOLOGY FOR PROCESS DESIGN

Process design as an activity goes through a series of successive approximations, starting with a rather tentative set of product specifications which are to be matched to the characteristics of various production methods. The general procedure is outlined in Fig. 7-3 and described in more detail in the sections that follow. Here we assume that before we proceed with process design for specific components or parts, an economic *make-or-buy analysis* has been completed to justify such action.

Phase 1: Determination of Production Stages

The preparation of any product or service requires a series of operations or tasks which can be meaningfully grouped to form successive stages, as the following examples show:

1. In a factory for ready-to-wear clothing the production process consists of cutting the fabric into the necessary pieces that form the item, joining them by sewing, adding zippers, buttons, etc., inspecting them as part of quality control, and placing them in appropriate boxes for shipment.

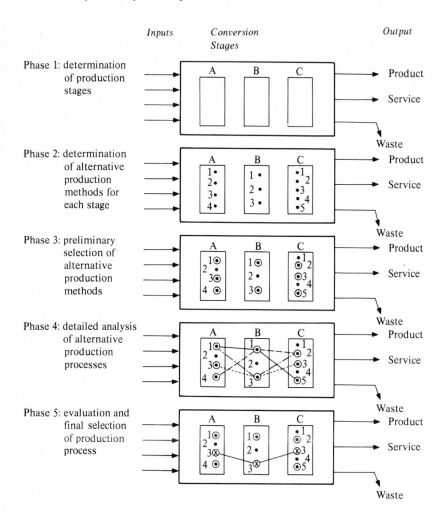

Fig. 7-3 Phases in production process design.

2. For a passenger traveling by plane from New York to Paris the procedure consists of the stages of ticket checking and luggage weighing, personal and hand-luggage security clearance, boarding the aircraft, being transported with the appropriate amenities (drinks, meals etc.), landing and disembarkation, and then passport and customs control. Note that the stages involved would be different if one were analyzing the process for the plane. Here the stages would include ground maintenance and refueling, pretakeoff checks by the pilot, takeoff, etc.

3. In a data processing system for inventory control, the procedure would involve data collection, data processing, analysis on the basis of an established procedure for the desired inventory policy, and then storing and reporting the desirable course of action for management concerning stock replenishment.

Phase 2: Determination of Alternative Production Methods for Each Stage

Having defined the appropriate stages of a production process, one next attempts to identify the alternative methods or technologies available, or to be developed, to perform the necessary operations that belong to that stage. Alternative production methods usually involve different patterns of distributing the necessary tasks between people and machines. *Labor-intensive* methods rely heavily on the human element for most of the tasks involved, while *capital-intensive* methods make extensive use of machines for the desired transformations. In the ready-to-wear factory cutting fabric may be done by hand or by an automatic machine. In the data processing system for inventory control, data collection, analysis, storage, and reporting may be handled using a manual system or an electronic computer.

The number of alternative production methods for each stage depends on the nature of the required operations and the state of the art for the relevant technology (testing a blood sample can be done by a machine; surgery cannot). In order to avoid overlooking important alternatives, it is essential at this point to have the advice of technical experts in the area involved. In Fig. 7-3 the alternatives for each stage are shown with dark circles.

When for one or more stages there are no satisfactory technologies, it may be desirable to consider changing the product specifications. If this is not possible, there is simply no way the proposed product can be made. In such an event, we must either cancel the product or postpone its production until a technological breakthrough is made as a result of internal or external R&D efforts.

Phase 3: Preliminary Selection of Alternative Production Methods

The alternative methods identified for each production stage in the previous step are generally given without detailed study of their capabilities, requirements, or limitations. Furthermore, there is no analysis of how they will be coupled with methods of other stages to form a complete production process. The main reason for this approach is the wish to include as many candidate solutions for evaluation as possible. Omitting a promising technology from consideration at this point might later impose a serious penalty in the development of a competitive process.

During the preliminary selection, each proposed method for a given stage is analyzed in greater depth and is rejected if it fails to meet the product specifications or is unable to reach the output rate necessary to satisfy the expected level and timing of future demand. Occasionally, an alternative which is acceptable on these grounds may be rejected because it can only be coupled with methods in other stages that do not satisfy the above requirements.

Phase 4: Detailed Analysis of Alternative Production Processes

The alternative methods screened for each stage in phase 3 are shown with double circles in Fig. 7-3. At this point it is necessary to interrelate them with the methods screened in the remaining stages, so that we can obtain complete alternative production processes. If each stage is independent of all others, thus allowing complete freedom of choice, the task of determining compatible combinations is unnecessary and each alternative method is analyzed individually rather than as part of an integrated process.

For the example shown in Fig. 7-3, in the case of complete independence for all stages the number of processes that require analysis is $(4)(3)(5) = 60$. If because of technological or other constraints the permissible combinations are those shown by connecting the compatible methods with straight lines, we are left with only four integrated processes that require analysis. In particular, we have

$$a_1: \quad A_1, B_1, C_5$$
$$a_2: \quad A_1, B_3, C_2$$
$$a_3: \quad A_3, B_3, C_3$$
$$a_4: \quad A_4, B_1, C_2$$

These processes satisfy product specifications, demand requirements, and compatibility requirements.

In the present phase, we must now analyze each solution in detail on the basis of physical performance, economic performance, and qualitative criteria. In particular it is necessary to have management and the technical specialists evaluate the characteristics of each solution summarized in Table 7-2.

Phase 5: Evaluation and Final Selection
of Production Process

The preceding detailed analysis of the physical and economic performance, along with the qualitative characteristics of each candidate solution, provides the information on which management can perform a quantitative as well as a qualitative evaluation.

Evaluation of physical and economic characteristics   The data collected concerning the physical-performance characteristics and the fixed and variable costs for each solution can be used for a discounted-cash-flow analysis to determine the best process based on economic criteria. Such methods are discussed in Supplementary Chapter B. This approach, however, requires knowledge of the projected future demand and the pricing policy for the product, so that we can estimate the stream of future revenues. Without an estimate of revenues the evaluation of the proposed solutions can be based only on costs using a diagram like Fig. 7-4.

Let us assume that solution a_4 is rejected because it does not satisfy budget restrictions. In the absence of any qualitative differences in the alternatives a_1, a_2, and a_3, the cost comparisons shown in Fig. 7-4 suggest that if the production volume will be less than V_1, a_1 is the best. For output volume in the range between V_1 and V_2 solution a_2 yields a lower total cost. If the projected production volume exceeds V_3, a_3 is the preferable solution.

TABLE 7-2   Process characteristics requiring analysis before evaluation

Process characteristics	Example
Physical	
Productive capacity in physical units for maximum output rate: Pieces per hour Tons per hour Passenger seats per trip Other	Cutting machine Y-1 for stage A can cut 250 pieces per hour Packaging method X can handle 1,200 cases per 8-h shift X-ray lab in a hospital can handle an average of 180 tests per day
Economic	

Purchase cost
Installation cost
Startup cost
Depreciation pattern
Production cost per unit
  Direct costs:
    Labor
    Materials
    Other
  Indirect costs:
    Supervision
    Energy
    Maintenance
    Other
	Oil refineries, sugar mills, etc., do not start at full capacity and experience startup costs beyond those for the purchase of equipment and installation
	The operation of an automated data processing inventory-control system beyond the purchase cost for equipment and installation costs will also incur startup costs due to the slow and erratic initial performance (inexperienced personnel, programming errors, etc.)

Qualitative	

Operating flexibility:
  Product-design flexibility
  Output-rate flexibility
Safety
Maintainability and reliability
Managerial requirements
Expandability
	An organization with an increasing demand that displays seasonal fluctuations, e.g., a canning factory, must not only have a process that is safe, reliable, and easy to maintain but must permit flexibility in the output rate and allow for capacity expansion or contraction

Differences in the cost characteristics of alternative processes are a result of the trade-offs obtained when we substitute capital for labor. More specifically, as we increase production volume, labor-intensive processes that have a low fixed cost and high variable cost per unit, such as a_1, tend to become less competitive than capital-intensive ones. As stated earlier, the latter require a significant initial investment and operate with a low variable cost per unit, which is imperative for high-volume production. The effect of technological improvements on costs is illustrated with a technology curve for a particular industry (Fig. 7-5).

Evaluation of qualitative factors   An evaluation of alternatives based only on costs is seldom sufficient for the final selection of a production process. In most cases there is a need to consider along with costs a number of qualitative but nevertheless

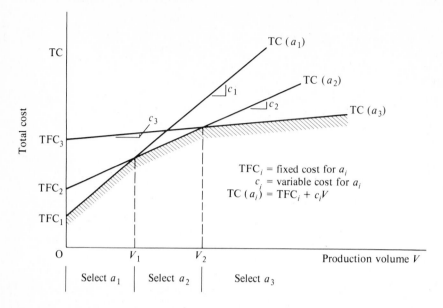

Fig. 7-4 Economic evaluation of alternatives based on total cost.

important factors. Among them it is desirable to include safety, reliability, maintainability, flexibility with regard to output rate or use, and the ability to expand or even contract capacity as required. Another set of increasingly important qualitative factors relates to the impacts of the process on the environment, i.e., pollution characteristics (for water, air, etc.), and the local economy. These are discussed in more detail in subsequent sections.

Since the evaluation of qualitative factors is at best subjective, it is desirable to use an ordinal scale by assigning ratings based on a scale from 1 to 10, with 10 being best, as was done with the evaluation of product designs in Chap. 4. A versatile approach for combining objective and subjective factors is the Brown-Gibson method discussed in Chap. 10 for location problems. Here, again, it is important to avoid the pitfalls of combining into one index values that involve different units. The above methods provide preference measures for alternatives that meet this criterion.

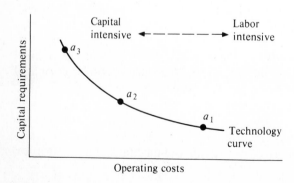

Fig. 7-5 Capital-intensive versus labor-intensive processes.

TABLE 7-3   Evaluation of production-process characteristics

	Criterion				
Alternative	Purchase and installation cost (millions)	Unit production cost	Safety†	Flexibility†	Reliability†
a_1	$ 8	$17	7	8	6
a_2	12	14	8	7	8
a_3	15	12	9	5	9

† Subjective ratings are assigned on a scale from 1 (worst) to 10 (best).

The performance and cost information for each alternative along with assigned ratings for qualitative factors can be conveniently summarized in a table for easy comparison. For our example, the relevant data are summarized in Table 7-3.

Final process selection   Before making a final choice we examine each one of the candidate solutions for feasibility in a general sense. If an alternative does not satisfy certain financial, legal, environmental, or other restrictions not examined before, we must reject it at this point. In our example, if it is determined that a_3 results in greater water pollution than allowed by law, it is rejected.

Next we eliminate any alternatives that are inferior on all counts to some dominant one, so that we can limit the number of candidates further. If a_1 and another alternative a_4 have the same costs and ratings on qualitative factors and a_1 is superior to a_4 in performance, a_4 will be dropped because it is dominated completely by a_1.

The strategic impacts associated with a new process are often subject to varying interpretations by the participants in the decision-making process. This calls for extensive reliance not only on rational models, based on economic or decision analysis, but on organizational and political models taking into account tradition, company reputation, and existing centers of power in the organization that will be affected by future outcomes.

The design procedure described above is appropriate for new products and services as well as for the improvement of old ones. In the sense that operating conditions change in terms of new technologies, new materials, better methods, etc., the process-design activity must be repeated periodically to ensure that new developments are incorporated to increase competitiveness of the production process.

7-4   GRAPHIC AIDS FOR PROCESS DESIGN

The description of a process during the phase of analysis and after the final selection is greatly assisted by using certain graphic aids. The simplest of these are used in the preliminary phases, and the more complex are reserved for the detailed analysis. The most widely used graphic aids in order of increasing detail are:

1. A process block diagram
2. An operations chart
3. An operations (or route) sheet
4. A process flow diagram
5. A process chart

Process Block Diagram

In order to visualize the changes required to convert raw materials into a finished product, it is necessary to specify the basic transformations that define the production process. The same is true in representing the major steps involved in offering a service.

Each of the basic transformations corresponds to a stage in the process and can be accomplished in a variety of ways, depending on technologies available and the economic and other restrictions to the problem. A block diagram displays the structure of the process in the broadest possible terms. The number of stages depends on the complexity of the product and the extent of vertical or horizontal integration in the organization. Two indicative examples describing a one-way communication process and a furniture-making process are shown in Fig. 7-6.

Operations Chart

Given the structure of a process in the form of a block diagram, further analysis involves looking at the productive or value-adding tasks that are combined to achieve the desired transformation(s) for each stage.

An operations chart provides a comprehensive picture of the production process by including the following information:

1. The required raw material(s) and supplies (*horizontal arrows*)
2. The necessary operations on each component or piece of raw material (*a circle on a vertical line*)

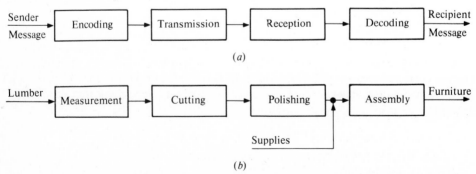

(a)

(b)

Fig. 7-6 Illustrations of block diagrams for representing the production process: (*a*) stages in a one-way communications process and (*b*) stages in a simplified furniture-manufacturing process.

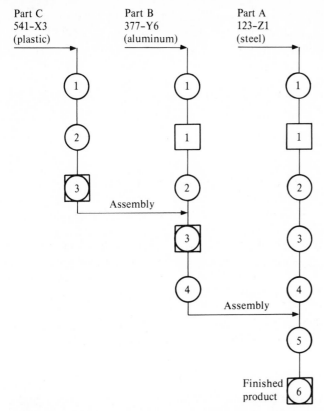

Fig. 7-7 Representative example of an operations chart for a simple product.

3. The various parts needed at their point of use (*horizontal arrows*)
4. The assembly operations for items 1 and 3 to prepare the final product or its main components (*circles*)
5. The inspections to be performed at different points of the production process (*squares*)
6. Combined tasks, e.g., a concurrent assembly and inspection of a component (*circles in squares*)

An illustration of an operations chart is shown in Fig. 7-7. In addition to making it easier to visualize the entire process, an operations chart is valuable in the following activities:

Selection of appropriate equipment

Development and evaluation of different layouts for the process

Scheduling and procurement of raw materials and parts

Planning production

Training new personnel unfamiliar with the process

Operations (or Route) Sheet

After the selection of the best production process, an operations chart must be supplemented with additional information to relate specific operations and inspections to the characteristics of available machines and tools.

For each component of the final product corresponding to a branch of an operations chart, we prepare a route sheet which includes:

1. Identifying information
   a. Product name and code number
   b. Part name and code number
   c. Order number
   d. Quantity desired, date wanted, etc.
2. For each operation or inspection
   a. Code number
   b. Description of operation or inspection
   c. Equipment with output rates and tools to be used
   d. Requirements by type and quantity of raw material, parts, and supplies

In computer-assisted production systems the above information can be punched in cards or kept in some other form. In any event, copies of an operations (or route) sheet are distributed for the processing of all products requiring the particular part or component.

Process Flow Diagram

In addition to the essential productive tasks and inspections, a process may include activities for the transportation and storage of materials and components, as well as some delays. The latter increase the cost of processing, sometimes significantly, without usually adding anything new to the characteristics of the final product. For this purpose, in a new process we strive to keep them to a minimum.

In order to have a complete picture of a production process, especially for a system already in existence, it is helpful to prepare a diagram that includes the following information represented with the symbols shown on the right.

Process element	Symbol†
Operation (fabrication, assembly, etc.): intentional change in form, shape, content, information	○
Inspection: comparison of actual versus desired quality, quantity, color, etc.	□
Transportation: an intentional movement that is not part of 1 or 2	⇒
Storage: holding an item before starting next step	▽
Combined activities: simultaneous performance of different elements	◻
Delay: unintentional idleness between successive steps	D

† These symbols were established by the American Society of Mechanical Engineers (ASME) and have been used extensively.

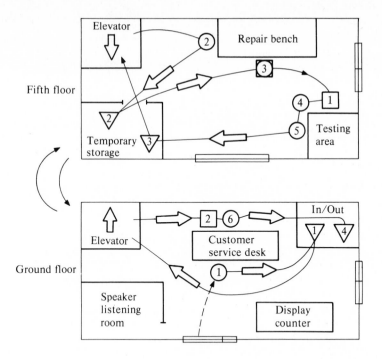

Fig. 7-8 Process flow diagram for the Top Hi-Fi Shop repair-service procedure.

The information can be displayed graphically in the form of a process flow diagram. This may be developed by following the flow of the product itself, say a unit processed in a manufacturing facility, or by following a person doing the work, e.g., a medical lab technician. In such a diagram we include data on the duration of each activity, the distances traveled, the equipment used for transportation, and so on.

A process flow diagram is valuable in the design of a new process or in the redesign for the improvement of an old one. It can be used to determine the process needs for materials handling, storage, and other supporting facilities. An illustration of a process flow diagram is given in Fig. 7-8. The detailed information included is usually recorded in a form known as a process chart (see Fig. 7-9).

Our example covers the proposed process of handling repairs of stereo units at the downtown Top Hi-Fi Shop in Rose City. The analysis begins at the point where a customer brings in a unit for repair at the customer service desk on the ground floor. It ends when the repaired unit is returned to the desk for customer pickup. Figure 7-8 shows the plan of the ground floor and the repair shop on the fifth floor of the same building. Marked on the floor plans are the elements of the process and the flow of a unit from receipt to customer delivery. Figure 7-9 shows a more detailed description of the same process in the form of a process chart, which includes a summary of the process and remarks that may help improve it. This is done by challenging the what, when, how, where, by whom, and why aspect of each

FLOW PROCESS CHART	Page 1	Present ☐	Proposed ☑

Study no. 329 Analyst N.S.0. Date 8/10/79	Summary	Number	Time
Subject description: Stereo receiver unit for repair	Operations	6	65
	Inspections	3	8
Chart begins: With unit received at customer service desk	Transports	9	–
	Storages	4	–
Chart ends: With repaired unit ready for pickup	Delays	–	–
	Total distance	303 ft	

Step	Symbol	Time, min	Distance, ft	Description
1		5		Unit received for repair by clerk, who fills out repair request form
2			20	Transported manually to in-out shelf
3				Until picked up for repair shop
4			80	Taken by elevator to repair shop on fifth floor by store assistant
5		2		Assigned priority rating by repairman
6			23	Taken to temporary stage area
7				Until ready for repair work
8			28	To repair bench
9		48		Disassembled, inspected, and repaired
10			12	To testing area by cart
11		5		Electronic inspection
12		7		Repair form filled out for labor and parts and attached to unit
13		1		Call service desk for pickup
14			40	Taken to temporary storage area
15				Until ready to be carried downstairs
16			80	Taken by elevator to ground floor by store assistant
17		3		Clerk inspects attached repair form and forwards one copy to cashier
18		2		Clerk calls customer for pickup
19			20	Unit taken to in/out shelf for customer
20				Until picked up by customer

Fig. 7-9 **Flow process chart for the Top Hi-Fi Shop proposed repair-service procedure.**

step. The objective here is to eliminate unnecessary activities, to simplify or combine required operations, and to reduce storage and movement. By superimposing multiple-flow paths (preferably on color transparencies) it is possible to study the simultaneous flow of several items in the same facility. For an existing process the process chart would also include all delays observed in following the product or worker being studied.

7-5 PROCESS DESIGN AND ENERGY CONSIDERATIONS

General

Energy is defined as the capacity to do work. In its various forms (electricity, coal, oil, etc.) energy probably represents the most critical input of a production process. As such it affects material-transformation processes from the extraction of raw materials to their processing for manufacturing and their use and disposal. Equally significant is energy in the operation of service systems such as transportation.

Our interest in energy here is twofold: (1) As a process input energy affects the cost of products and services. Furthermore, its availability determines the effectiveness and reliability not only of individual organizations but of whole sectors in the economy. (2) The production and use of energy itself is associated with some of the most critical environmental problems of our times. In this section we shall discuss some aspects of energy as a process input. Later we shall examine some of the environmental problems related to power generation.

Energy as a Process Input

Our material standard of living has so far been strongly correlated with our use of energy. Table 7-4 presents the changes in per capita energy consumption for societies at different stages of technological development.

An examination of worldwide consumption patterns reveals serious imbalances in the rate of per capita consumption. In 1970 industrially developed countries, with 20 percent of the population, consumed 63 percent of the total energy, whereas developing countries, with 48 percent of the population, used only 8.3 percent of the total energy. Converting these figures to a per capita basis suggests that a person living in a developed country consumes 18 times more energy than one of a developing country.

The spectacular increase in energy consumption in industrialized societies reflects modern reliance on energy-intensive products and processes. Many pro-

TABLE 7-4   **Daily energy consumption per capita for different stages of technological development**

Type of society	Daily energy consumption per capita kcal
Primitive	2,000
Hunter-gatherer	5,000
Early agricultural	12,000
Advanced agricultural	26,000
Early industrial	70,000
Advanced industrial	230,000

SOURCE: Adapted from Tyler W. Miller, *Living in the Environment: Concepts, Problems and Alternatives*, Wadsworth Publishing Co., Belmont, Calif., 1975, p. 216.

ducts are energy-intensive both in their production and their use. For example, the "average" automobile (3638 lb, or 1637 kg), one of today's prime symbols of material well-being, requires for its production about 23,000 kWh, or the amount of fuel needed to drive the car for 12,000 mi (19,300 km).[1]

The shift from labor-intensive to capital-intensive production processes which accompanies industrial development contributes further to the consumption of huge amounts of energy. Mining primary raw materials also demands more energy-intensive processes. Recycling can help relieve some of that pressure, as we shall see later, but does not solve the energy problem.

In Chap. 3, where we discussed various aspects of the natural environment, we examined the sources and uses of energy in the United States economy and the projected flows for 1985. A greater reliance on imported oil to cover increasing demand for energy is bound to increase the uncertainty of energy availability and pressures for higher prices and political readjustments and risks. The large price increase of oil from $3.95 per barrel in 1973 to $30 in 1980, following the 1973 energy crisis, strained Western economies, contributed to double-digit inflation for several of them, and brought about significant changes in political alliances to secure the uninterrupted flow of oil as a key energy input. The recent crises in Iran and Afghanistan in 1979 and 1980 and the resulting drastic changes in U.S. foreign policy further demonstrate the critical importance of importing oil to cover energy needs.

Potential Impacts of Energy Trends on Process Design

Energy-related problems will present a serious challenge to operations managers in many decision areas, but nowhere will the impact be felt more strongly than in process design. Many of our present energy conversion systems operate at low efficiencies. In 1970 50 percent of the total energy produced in the United States was lost. For the world energy flow in 1964 67 percent of the total energy was lost. Power plants using conventional fossil fuels are on the average 33 percent efficient. Automobiles have an overall efficiency of 5 percent. Of all the energy input only 25 percent is converted into work in the engine and from this only 2 percent is transmitted to the road (Ref. 5). Table 7-5 presents the energy-consumption figures for typical manufacturing industries. It is apparent that one of the approaches needed to cope with decreasing energy reserves at increasing prices is to press for technologies that use energy more efficiently. Recent design improvements of auto-mobiles, airplanes and many machines are part of this effort. The $35 million cost of a Boeing 767 197-seat passenger plane is attributed to its advanced technology for reducing fuel consumption by about 30 percent. This is large when compared to the $50 million cost of the Boeing 747 jumbo jet, which seats 340 passengers with conventional technologies. Included in this approach is the development of processes with reduced energy-transfer chains, i.e., fewer energy-conversion stages that limit the amount of dissipated or wasted energy.

[1] J. C. Branard and C. Portal, *Energy Expenditures Associated with the Production and Recycling of Metals,* ORNL-MIT-132, Oak Ridge, Tenn., May 26, 1971.

TABLE 7-5   Energy consumption, 10^{12} Btu, for various manufacturing industries in the United States, 1972

Industry	Coal	Natural gas	Petroleum products	Thermal equivalent of electrical energy	Total energy
Primary metals	2,838	863	306	1,291	5,298
Chemical and allied products	666	1,219	1,426	1,626	4,937
Petroleum refining and related indus.	na†	1,012	1,589	225	2,826
Food and kindred products	263	593	134	338	1,328
Paper and allied products	467	341	211	280	1,299
Stone, clay, glass, and concrete products	406	449	87	280	1,222
All other industries	976	4,781	721	1,572	8,050
Total	5,616	9,258	4,474	5,612	24,960

† Included in all other industries, na = not available.
SOURCE: *Chemical and Engineering News*, Sept. 18, 1972.

A second approach to improved energy utilization is the use of *industrial secondary energy* (ISE), i.e., energy emitted as a by-product of an industrial process. For 1970 the estimated ISE was equivalent to 182 million metric tons (t) of coal. The cumulative energy savings by the year 2000 of utilizing ISE could amount to 20 billion metric tons of coal equivalent. Related to this is the development of the so-called *energy-optimized industrial-park* concept, in which different types of manufacturing plants are located in the same area so that some can make optimum use of the waste energy from the others as regulated by an energy-control center (Fig. 7-10).

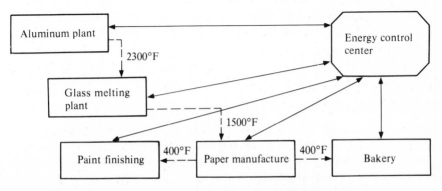

Fig. 7-10 An energy-optimized industrial park. (*From R. Seamans, "Energy Systems and Technology Development," paper presented at Energy and Community Development International Conference, Athens, Greece, July 1978.*)

TABLE 7-6   Energy expended for 1 gal of soft drink in 12-oz cans

Operation	Btu/gal
Mining (2.5 lb of ore per pound of finished steel)	1,570
Transportation of ore (1,000 mi by barge)	560
Manufacture of finished steel from ore	27,600
Aluminum lid (11.9% of total can weight; 4.7	
times the unit steel energy)	12,040
Transportation of finished steel (392 mi average)	230
Manufacture of cans (4% waste)	3,040
Transportation to bottler (300 mi average)	190
Transportation to retailer	6,400
Retailer and consumer	—
Waste collection	110
Total energy for can-container system†	51,740
Total energy for 12-oz returnable-glass system	17,820
Ratio of total energy expended by can-container	
system to that expended by 12-oz returnable glass	2.90

† The aluminum-can system consumes 33% more energy than the bimetal (steel and aluminum) can system.
SOURCE: B. M. Hannon "Bottles, Cans, Energy," *Environment*, vol. 14, no. 2, March 1972, p. 20.

A third approach might attempt a reevaluation of labor-intensive and capital-intensive technologies by accounting more explicitly for the environmental costs associated with energy generation and use. Such an approach must be encouraged with appropriate government tax policies, which today leave out such environmental costs, thus favoring energy-intensive technologies.

Since the type of process we select depends heavily on the product design, important energy savings are indirectly associated with appropriate adjustments in the latter. These might include simplified operations, substitution of materials, different packaging, etc. Table 7-6 presents data on the energy expended in Btu for 1 gal of soft drink in 12-oz cans.

A fourth approach to energy savings in operations management is through *recycling*. This issue, however, is so important that we discuss it in considerable detail in a later section.

7-6   PROCESS DESIGN AND ENVIRONMENTAL POLLUTION

In Chap. 1 we stated that along with needed products an operations system also generates unwanted wastes or conditions that often pollute the environment. Pollution is further aggravated by what remains of a product after consumption.

The significance of environmental pollution for operations managers stems from recent federal and state laws that set limits on the extent of pollution a particular plant may cause in the air, water, and other parts of the natural environment. The enforcement of such laws has slowed down programs for plant moderni-

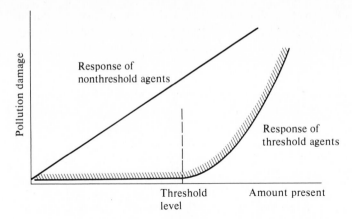

Fig. 7-11 Response patterns of threshold and nonthreshold pollutants.

zation because of the severe demands on capital budgets for pollution-related equipment. In certain cases failure to comply with such laws has forced the shutdown of existing facilities until corrective action has been taken to reduce polluting wastes.

Types of Pollutants

A process generates a pollutant as a waste material or as a set of conditions that disrupt normal environmental conditions. How much of a pollutant can be tolerated depends on the types of organisms affected, the phase in their life cycle, and the type of pollutant.

Some pollutants, called *nonthreshold agents*, are dangerous even in small amounts. This group includes some heavy metals (mercury, lead, and cadmium) and various types of radiation. *Threshold agents* are substances that pollute when present above a certain level. In this category we include chemical compounds (pesticides, sulfates), organic wastes, and certain plant nutrients (phosphorus, carbon, nitrogen). The distinction between the two groups is illustrated in Fig. 7-11.

Sometimes the combined damage of two pollutants is greater than if they were acting individually and their effects added. In such cases we say that the pollutants are *synergistic*. Occasionally, however, different pollutants are *antagonistic* in that the effect of one neutralizes that of the other.

In the following sections we take a closer look at the various forms of environmental pollution (water, air, solid waste, and noise) and examine how operations management can contribute to their abatement and control.

Water Pollution

Water pollution can be caused by several types of effluents. According to the Environmental Protection Agency (EPA), they can be grouped in the following eight categories.

Oxygen-demanding wastes   These are biodegradable organic materials that can be oxidized by bacteria to form carbon dioxide and water. Biodegradable wastes are found in domestic sewage and in certain industrial effluents, e.g., paper pulp mills, and canneries.

When discharged in a stream of water, such wastes are decomposed by absorbing large amounts of dissolved oxygen. Pollution increases with the amount of absorbed oxygen. This depends mainly on the quantities of effluent discharged, the temperature of the water, and the speed of the stream. The usual measurement of this type of pollution involves the BOD (biochemical-oxygen-demand) test. Such measurement indicates the amount of oxygen removed over a 5-day period at a temperature equal to 20°C. If the dissolved oxygen (DO) content in the receiving water becomes low, it can threaten the survival of fish and other aquatic life. Paper-pulp plants, usually located near woodlands, discharge large quantities of effluents, which may be especially harmful to the natural wildlife.

Restoration may take place naturally or artificially. *Natural restoration* of oxygen in the receiving water occurs through water aeration, especially in a fast-moving stream, and through photosynthesis as water plants release oxygen during the day. Oxygen for the degradation of organic materials can also be obtained *artificially* from dissolved nitrates and sulfates. The latter results in disagreeable-smelling gases such as hydrogen sulfide.

The variation in the oxygen content of a polluted area of a stream is usually specified through the delineation of three zones or by an oxygen-sag curve (Fig. 7-12).

Disease-causing agents   These are pathogenic microorganisms present in the waste water of municipalities, sanitoriums, tanneries, slaughterhouses, and other sources. Such agents can cause disease in human beings, livestock, and other animals. Epidemics like cholera and typhoid, which can result in heavy death tolls, have been caused by organisms transmitted by water.

Synthetic organic compounds   These include many poisonous wastes that are not biodegradable and do not settle out easily. This group includes certain detergents, pesticides, herbicides, phenols from coke ovens, and pickling liquor, a by-product of steelmaking. Such substances require special facilities for treatment that involve chemical neutralizers.

Plant nutrients   These include the nitrogen and phosphorus washed off fertilized lands as well as the effluent of most sewage-treatment plants.

Inorganic chemicals and mineral substances   This group includes acids formed from water drainage in abandoned mines. Mercury, cadmium, and excessive chloride content in water wastes are toxic and have aroused considerable public concern in recent years.

Sediment   Inert wastes that enter the water as solids and are not changed by chemical reactions consist of particles of soils, sands, metal filings, and dust and silt

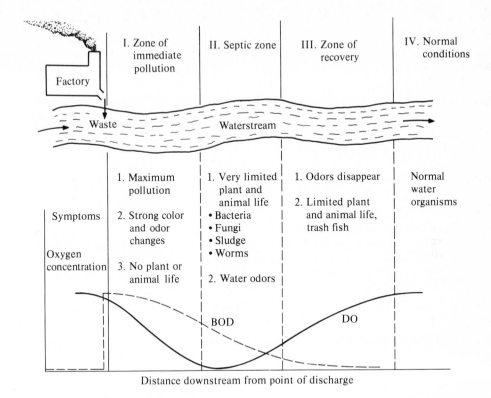

	I. Zone of immediate pollution	II. Septic zone	III. Zone of recovery	IV. Normal conditions
Symptoms	1. Maximum pollution 2. Strong color and odor changes 3. No plant or animal life	1. Very limited plant and animal life • Bacteria • Fungi • Sludge • Worms 2. Water odors	1. Odors disappear 2. Limited plant and animal life, trash fish	Normal water organisms

Distance downstream from point of discharge

Fig. 7-12 Variation in dissolved oxygen.

from soil erosion. Unless they are removed or filtered, these substances eventually settle to the bottom of the stream and block the sunlight. Since the result is often harmful to plant life, it may mean that fish and other animal life die from lack of adequate food supply. Strip mines are frequent offenders of water pollution through inert wastes.

Radioactive substances   Mining and processing of radioactive ores, nuclear-power-plant operations, medical facilities, and nuclear-weapon testing may be responsible for the release of radioactive substances as wastes in bodies of water. The resulting radioactivity, like DDT, is likely to concentrate in the food chain. The nuclear reactor accident which took place at Three-Mile Island, Pennsylvania, in 1979 has forced a serious review of nuclear energy as an alternative source of power. An immediate result has been to delay construction of new such plants and reexamine critically their design and operating features.

Thermal discharges   The discharge in a stream of hot noncontaminated water used for cooling purposes may be as harmful as organic oxygen-demanding wastes. This is due to the decrease in the oxygen-holding or oxygen-absorbing capacity of the water as its temperature rises. Breweries, steel mills, oil refineries, and electric utilities rely on large quantities of water for cooling. Even though such water is clean in other respects, its discharge at a high temperature in a stream of water or a lake may be very destructive to the fish population. Beyond lowering the oxygen content of the water, the thermal pollution makes it difficult for many organisms with restricted temperature adaptability to adjust their metabolism rates to the temperature fluctuations. The resulting growth of blue-green algae, the least desirable food for aquatic life, is most responsible for the taste and odor problems in the water and may be toxic for some organisms. Overall, thermal pollution may bring about serious environmental disruption through both direct and the subtle long-term effects influencing the ecological balance.

Measurement of water pollution   Any effort to prevent or control water pollution rests on our ability to measure the degree to which polluting wastes change the environment. Ideally, the measurement method needed is one that applies to several pollutants and is accurate, easy to use, and inexpensive. Unfortunately, our methods and technology for such measurements are not yet as refined and inexpensive as required. Sometimes we are not aware of the inflicted harm to the environment until we can smell the strong odors, see the changes in color of the water, or observe hundreds or thousands of dead fish as evidence of the damage.

The type of measurement used to detect pollution may be physical, biochemical, or biological. *Physical methods* are currently used to determine the level of dissolved salts in the water by inserting a meter that measures electrical conductivity. The BOD 5-day test represents the most common approach today. This is a *biochemical method* of measurement of the amount of molecular oxygen required to decompose an organic material through aerobic biochemical action. A *biological method* may involve putting a number of fish in various dilutions of an effluent to determine what percentage will die and how fast.

Treatment of water pollution   The most common types of industrial waste undergo sewage treatment that is usually simple and considerably standardized. Such treatment may involve one, two, or three stages. The types used by most municipalities are shown in Fig. 7-13.

Primary treatment is simple and is performed at low cost. It involves screening the solid waste and gravity settling of the particulates in the effluent. This is done mechanically through a wire-mesh screen for the large floating objects, through a grit chamber for sand, grit, cinders, and small objects, and through a sedimentation tank for particulates suspended in the solution. If discharged to a stream the effluent is treated with chlorine for bacteria and odors.

Primary treatment results in the removal of one-third of the BOD, 60 to 80 percent of the sedimentation, and small amounts of nitrogen and phosphorus. As might be expected, this is hardly sufficient for preventing most forms of water pollution.

Secondary treatment begins where primary treatment ends. It relies on biological and bacterial action to achieve the desired degree of oxidation of the screened primary waste. The biological action may involve either a biological filter or an activated-sludge process. The filter method consists of a bed of rocks with bacteria that oxidize, i.e., consume, the organic matter in the sewage as it moves through, while air is circulated through the filter. The activated-sludge process consists of

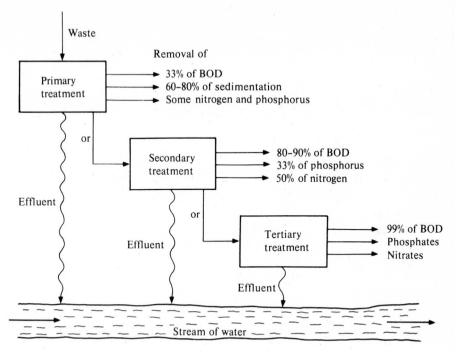

Fig. 7-13 Types of water waste treatment.

forcing compressed air through tanks containing sewage and activated sludge. The latter interacts and oxidizes the impurities.

A satisfactory secondary treatment removes 80 to 90 percent of the BOD, one-third of the phosphorus, and one-half of the nitrogen. Both methods above attempt to imitate the natural self-cleansing process of streams.

Tertiary treatment, when employed, is intended to remove the phosphates and nitrates that are not adequately handled through biological methods in the previous stage. Furthermore, there is an additional removal of BOD, usually up to 99 percent.

Tertiary treatment is carried out through extensive aeration of the water. Instead of aeration this stage sometimes involves filtration over a bed of natural rocks and sand or even charcoal.

The above types of treatment usually provided by a municipal installation do not guarantee pollution control and may need to be supplemented by further processing for certain industrial uses. Treated water which is potable may contain too many minerals for industrial use, such as steelmaking.

Air Pollution

Many people are under the impression that the atmosphere around the earth is almost infinite in thickness, but actually the air surrounding our planet represents only a thin layer.

In some important respects, air and water pollution have certain similarities. Both result because the impurities discharged are not absorbed adequately and rapidly enough. One difference, however, is that *water is self-purifying while air is not.* Air pollution in the form of disruptive elements, exhaust gases, and particulates can be cleaned either by being blown away to another area or by the particulates settling out, thus polluting the ground. An example of the first case is the air pollution of New York City, which has no heavy industry, by the polluted air of the industrialized New Jersey blown by the prevailing winds.

Major air pollutants and their sources   Among the most harmful air pollutants are carbon monoxide, sulfur oxides, nitrogen oxides, hydrocarbons, and particulates. All appear in different amounts in the emissions of power plants, industry, motor vehicles, space heating, and refuse disposal. Table 7-7 shows the content in different air pollutants measured.

Effects of air pollution   Air pollution has been associated with a number of harmful effects on human, plant, and animal life. In particular, human health has been threatened by air pollutants occurring individually or in various combinations, and the evidence is massive even though there are still some arguments about the extent of the danger.

Carbon monoxide reduces the oxygen supply carried by blood to the cells. This causes the respiratory system and the heart to work much harder as the concentration of carbon monoxide increases. With badly jammed traffic the content of carbon monoxide in the air may approach the fatal limit of 400 parts per million.

TABLE 7-7   **United States air pollution emissions in 1970, 10^6 tons/yr**

Pollution source	Pollutant				
	Carbon monoxide	Particulates	Nitrogen oxides	Sulfur oxides	Hydro-carbons
Fuel burned for transportation	111.0	0.7	11.7	1.0	19.5
Fuel burned in stationary sources†	0.8	6.8	10.0	26.5	0.6
Other industrial processes‡	11.4	13.1	0.2	6.0	5.5
Burning solid waste	7.2	1.4	0.4	0.1	2.0
Agriculture burning, forest fires, and others	16.8	3.4	0.4	0.3	7.1
Total	147.2	25.4	22.7	33.9	34.7

† Includes electrical generators, industrial process heat, and space heating of homes, commerce, and industry.
‡ Major contributors include pulpmills, smelters, refineries, and cement plants.
SOURCE: Council of Environmental Pollution, 1972.

Poisoning symptoms include loss of vision, headache, decreased muscular coordination, and nausea. Nitrogen oxides seem to have the same effects as carbon monoxide.

Sulfur dioxide has been considered responsible for higher rates of such respiratory diseases as chronic asthma, bronchitis, and emphysema. Sulfur compounds are extremely irritating to the respiratory system and are viewed as the major cause of death in smog disasters, such as that of London in 1952 (4,000 deaths).

Hydrocarbons and particulates are almost certainly involved in the increasing death rates from cancer.

In addition to the serious threat of air pollution to human life, there is evidence of considerable damage to plant and animal life even at relatively great distances from the sources of pollution, such as that observed hundreds of miles east of Los Angeles (Ref. 4, p. 125).

Treatment of air pollution   The main approaches for treatment of air pollution are (1) improving the combustion process, (2) filtering, (3) scrubbing, and (4) chemical treatment of the emissions. Overall the state of the art is still rather primitive.

Combustion-process improvement represents an attempt to reduce air pollution before it is created. The aim here is to decrease the incompletely burned dust and ashes contained in the emitted smoke. Certain devices for pollution control required on recent car models are intended to ensure a more complete combustion of the gasoline.

Filtering of the emissions after they have been generated from combustion may involve a mechanical device such as a screen or a *gravity process*. The latter requires particulate matter to go through several settling chambers before reaching the chimney flue. In order to attract the dust and ashes that would fly into the open air, it is possible to use an *electrostatic precipitator*. This is constructed with a mesh of electrically charged wires placed at different points along the chimney stock. Electrostatic precipitators are very expensive (they run into several million dollars) and are effective only with coal fires. Their use with oil fires is questionable, since the high voltage on the wires has no effect on oil. The Energy Act of 1978, however, has put a stop to the use of oil for new power plants in order to decrease the nation's dependence on imported oil.

Oil or water *scrubbing* results in the most effective treatment of air pollution. Here most of the ash and some of the gases are washed quite clean. On the negative side, scrubbing is an expensive method, even more so than electric precipitation. Furthermore, the air is cleaned at the expense of increased water pollution.

Under certain conditions, it may be desirable to remove certain air pollutants before combustion, such as sulfur from oil. It may also be necessary to subject the smoke from factories to *chemical treatment* by neutralizing it or even forming some valuable by-product.

Solid Waste

Much of the physical output of a production system after its intended use or consumption ends up as solid waste. In 1972, when the GNP in the United States reached $1,152 billion, only a small fraction of this output, valued at $2.4 billion,

TABLE 7-8   Classification of solid waste

Source	Per capita distribution, lb
Direct, urban:	
Household	
Commercial	
Paper and paper products	580
Metal cans	300
Bottles and jars	280
Plastics	38
Rubber	20
Metal squeeze tubes	6
Total	1,224
Municipal	
Indirect:	
Agriculture	20,000
Mining	17,000
Industry	1,100
Total	38,100

SOURCE: Council on Environmental Quality, Washington, 1970.

was recycled or reclaimed. The rest contributed to solid waste equivalent to 2.1 billion tons (20,000 lb per capita), excluding animal and crop waste. This corresponds almost to one-half of the 4.4 billion tons of new raw materials used as production inputs at a cost of $50 billion.[1] Any way we look at these figures, the conclusion is that our economy is a waste machine. The enormous costs involved for collection and disposal of solid waste ($6 billion in 1971 for urban wastes only) combined with the resulting pollution make this an important societal problem that has attracted considerable public attention in recent years.

Types and sources of solid waste   Of the possible ways we can classify solid waste, the most useful one from an operations-management point of view, is that shown in Table 7-8. Even though on a weight basis agricultural, mining, and mineral wastes account for the bulk of total solid waste, the residential or domestic waste is becoming the most serious problem because of the great cost of its collection and disposal ($6 billion in 1970 and estimated to increase roughly 5 percent annually).

Problems related to solid waste   Solid waste is responsible for several problems which can be grouped as pollution-oriented or resource-depletion-oriented. Both uncollected solid waste and waste that is collected and disposed of may threaten human life by polluting the air through incineration and the land and the water through improperly designed landfills. Furthermore, they may pose fire hazards or breed disease-causing germs.

[1] Data from U.S. Department of Interior.

Our failure to include external, or spillover, costs in the price of raw materials and products has prevented large-scale recycling of valuable minerals in wastes from becoming economically feasible. Thus, we are wasting resources whose known reserves are rapidly declining. The situation is aggravated further by our general rather than selective economic-growth philosophy, which encourages maximizing the flow of natural resources (materials and energy) through the economy. Since this stimulates greater waste, the costs of waste collection and disposal are increasing exponentially. One promising idea of using garbage to generate energy, if feasible, would do much to reduce both aspects of the solid waste problem.

Operations-management decisions that can reduce solid waste   Even though the solid-waste problem is complex and will require a combination of approaches, operations management can genuinely assist in its solution in several ways. In the product-design phase we noted how recycling could reduce solid waste by making ecologically sound decisions with regard to the selection of raw materials, modular-component design, and packaging materials. The decision to switch to throwaway bottles, cans, and other containers has contributed immensely to the increase of solid waste.

Good process design can considerably reduce scrap losses and industrial wastes. Through improvements in manufacturing processes and quality control it is possible to make products having improved built-in quality and a longer life, so that it will not be necessary to replace an item as often as it is now with the emphasis on built-in obsolescence.

Noise Pollution

Noise pollution can be a serious problem both inside and outside the working environment. It has been estimated that industrial noise results in an annual cost of $4 billion attributed to hearing-loss compensation claims, absenteeism, reduced productivity, and accidents.[1] Furthermore, the number of people in the United States with hearing problems is between 10 and 16 million and increasing.

Noise generally refers to sound that is unwanted because it is loud, unpleasant, or sudden. Because sound is due to the presence of mechanical waves in matter (gaseous, liquid, or solid), noise is measured by the intensity (or amplitude) and the pitch (or frequency) of these waves. High-pitched tones are given more weight because they are the most annoying.

The most common yardstick for measuring noise is the A scale (dB A) based on the decibel as a unit. The A scale matches the effect of sound on the human ear closely, and a given value in decibels is the logarithm of the ratio of the sound-intensity level to the threshold of audible sound as a reference point (0 dB = .0002 dyn/cm^2). Each increment of 10 decibels corresponds to a tenfold increase in sound intensity.

---

[1] A. Bell, *Noise: An Occupational Hazard and Public Nuisance*, World Health Organization, Geneva, 1966.

TABLE 7-9   Noise levels for different sources

Noise source	Relative sound intensity†	dB	Likely effects of prolonged exposure
Jet takeoff (nearby)	10^{15}	150	Rupture of eardrum
City warning siren, aircraft carrier deck	10^{14}	140	Threshold of pain
Hydraulic press (at 3 ft)	10^{13}	130	
Jet takeoff (at 200 ft), riveting (at 4 ft)	10^{12}	120	
Circular saw, live rock music	10^{11}	110	
Power mower, jackhammer, printing plant	10^{10}	100	Serious hearing loss from prolonged exposure
Diesel truck	10^9	90	Limit for industrial exposure
Noisy office with machines, average factory, freight train, heavy traffic	10^8	80	Annoying
Freeway traffic, vacuum cleaner	10^7	70	
Usual office, light traffic	10^6	60	Intrusive
Private business office	10^5	50	Quiet
Library	10^4	40	
Quiet rural area at night	10^3	30	Very quiet
Whispering conversation	10^2	20	Barely audible
Broadcast studio	10	10	Threshold of hearing
Rustling leaves	0	0	

† 10^{15} = 1 followed by 15 zeros, etc.

Sources of noise   Almost everyone is exposed daily to noise from a number of sources. At work it is industrial noise, and in the community at large we may be exposed to noise related to *construction or repair* work; *transportation* vehicles such as trucks, motorcycles, cars, and airplanes; and a variety of *machines and appliances* such as power saws, power lawn mowers, and others. Table 7-9 gives the noise level of several familiar sources.

Effects of noise   Working or living with excessive noise, which is a form of stress, may cause both psychological and physical health problems. The effects of noise may take the form of annoyance, disruption of activity, various degrees of hearing loss, and even physical or mental deterioration. The long-run effects depend on the noise level and the length of exposure.

Medical experts are in agreement that continuous exposure to levels above 90 dB (busy city street or diesel trucks) results in hearing damage, which gets serious above 100 dB (power mower or motorcycle). A number of industries in metal products, automobiles, iron and steel, printing and publishing, heavy construction, lumbering, and wood products operate under conditions that pose severe hearing-loss problems. Furthermore, sudden noises below the level of hearing damage cause constriction of blood vessels, increased heartbeat, tensed muscles, and stomach spasms that contribute to fatigue, nervousness, and reduced performance at work.

Noise-pollution control methods   The increasing impact of noise pollution from both occupational and community sources can be considerably reduced. It is argued that noise control is technologically and economically feasible[1] and that the only problem is political. The Soviet Union and several countries in Western Europe are considerably ahead in noise-pollution control. It has been accomplished through the development of quiet machinery (air compressors, jackhammers, etc.), whose cost is little higher than the noisy types, and appropriate regulation concerning maximum allowable noise levels and daily periods during which noise is permitted. Noise control is usually accomplished with three different approaches.

1. *Reduction of the noise at the source.* This is done by redesigning equipment or processes, as indicated above, and proper maintenance. Softer city auto horns for cars, rubberized wheels for heavy vehicles, etc., may also serve the purpose.
2. *Creating barriers between noise source and people.* Europeans muffle construction-equipment noise using tents or small sheds. The Frankfurt airport in West Germany has 50-ft concrete barriers to reduce sideline noise to adjacent neighborhoods. One of the best natural barriers for absorbing noise from sounds is growing trees.
3. *Providing protective devices, such as ear muffs or ear plugs.*

Whether the noise source is in the workplace or the community at large, noise control can bring about considerable reduction in the effects from noise pollution and help increase productivity at work and the enjoyment of other activities the rest of the time.

Approaches to Pollution Control

Pollution as a societal problem can be tackled with an input approach, an output approach, or both. Viewing the economy as a giant production system, the *output approach*, relied upon almost exclusively, attempts to reduce pollution as an output of this system mainly after it has already been generated. On the other hand, the *input approach* focuses on the amount of matter and energy flowing into the economy and attempts to reduce this flow by the elimination of wasteful production activities. According to Watt,[2] the input approach is far more effective because by concentrating on the input side we not only reduce pollution but also ensure the wise use of scarce natural resources, especially the nonrenewable types. Transportation by private cars and jet aircraft are cited by Watt as prime examples of wasteful

[1] See Ref. 8, p. E49.
[2] Kenneth E. F. Watt, *The Titanic Effect*, Dutton, New York, 1974, p. 66.

TABLE 7-10   Areas of pollution control for a production system

Inputs	Process	Output
Elimination of wasteful inputs, reducing flow of matter and energy through system	Design of a process that minimizes the generation of pollutants: • New automobiles • New aircraft engines	Removal of pollutant or reduction of its concentration at emission source Sewage system Smokestack Exhaust pipes
Selection of inputs that contain or produce less pollutant: • Low-sulfur oil for power plants • Degradable or recyclable packaging materials • Natural gas for energy	Replacement of existing process with less polluting one	Removal of pollutant or reduction of its concentration in the environment (air, water, or soil)
Removal of pollutants from the inputs before use, e.g., sulfur from coal or oil	Modernization of process to increase thermodynamic efficiency for improved energy utilization	Treatment of pollutant to make it less harmful
		Scheduling discharge of effluents to minimize pollution impact

activities using up natural resources (iron, aluminum, and especially energy) and polluting the environment (air, noise, solid waste).

Adaptation of the input approach will require serious gradual adjustments in our value system, our habits, and the structure of our economy. The output approach will therefore continue to figure prominently in the foreseeable future. With reference to a production system, Table 7-10 summarizes some of the steps that can be taken with regard to pollution control at the input, process, and output levels.

Assuming that pollution control for the next 20 to 30 years will be mainly based on the output approach, it is important to identify what policies may be followed.

In order to control the various forms of pollution, it is necessary to establish a set of standards to specify the levels of effluents that can be tolerated without causing serious environmental disruption. The responsibility for setting standards is assigned to a *regulatory agency*. This agency is also given the authority to maintain the quality of the environment by enforcing whatever program is in effect for pollution control. Individual firms affected by such programs may attempt to abate pollution by changes in the design of their products and/or processes and by treatment of wastes that exceed the imposed standards.

A managing agency can enforce pollution control by one of three strategies, *regulation* of the polluters, *subsidies* to municipalities and firms for waste-treatment equipment and pollution-control devices, and *charges* reflecting the amount of damage caused by disposed wastes. These strategies can be implemented *across the*

TABLE 7-11   Characteristics of pollution-control strategies in output approach

Control strategy	Implementation scheme		Impact on taxpayer
	Across the board	Point by point	
Regulation: Licenses, permits Zoning Registration	Regulations imposed; all polluters treated equally for damage caused by their wastes	Degree of regulation depends on amount of waste produced by each pollutant	Consumers of product(s) bear burden of waste-disposal costs; expensive strategy
Subsidies: Direct payments Accelerated depreciation Lower taxes	Equal sum is paid to all polluters to reduce their wastes by a given amount, say 10%	Subsidies paid only to polluters who can reduce their wastes efficiently	All taxpayers pay for waste disposal costs; inequitable sharing of cost
Charges		Charge is levied reflecting amount of waste discharged and its damage to environment	Cost of pollution absorbed by consumer of product(s); may be self-supportive; most economical strategy
Characteristics of implementation scheme	Inefficient, unfair	Very costly administration	

board for all firms regardless of their polluting characteristics or on a *point-by-point* basis which directly reflects the amount of waste disposed and associated damage to the environment.

These strategies for pollution control, their means for implementation and other characteristics are summarized in Table 7-11.

7-7   RECYCLING

General

Recycling is the recovery of material from wastes created in manufacturing and consumption, for reuse in the production of new items. The idea of recycling is not new; it has been practiced in some industries such as metal processing for some time. However, under the strong pressure from current environmental problems recycling has assumed new prominence and is looked upon with great hope for alleviating these problems. As we shall see, recycling promises to contribute a great deal, but it cannot be relied upon as the single or most effective approach.

Recycling is important because it can accomplish two things at the same time: (1) by removing reusable materials from wastes it reduces environmental pollution due to solid waste, and (2) by utilizing recoverable materials as a production input it helps conserve both nonrenewable resources and energy. However, *recycling itself requires considerable energy, and it is this factor that seriously limits the extent of its use.*

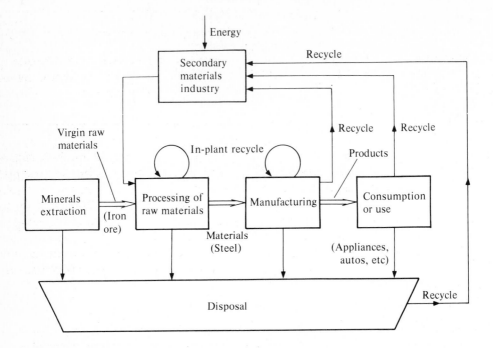

Fig. 7-14 Basic types of recycling in successive stages of materials conversion and use. (*Adapted from J. N. Hartley, World Mineral and Energy Resources; Some Facts and Assessments, 1974.*)

Types of Recycling

The waste created during materials processing, manufacturing, and consumption cannot be recovered entirely because the change in the form of some materials and the degree of their dispersion does not allow recycling. The sequence of material conversions shown in Fig. 7-14 shows two basic types of recycling.

In-plant recycling   It is possible at several stages of production to recycle certain materials within the same manufacturing facility. This is common practice in steel mills, which remelt their scrap from the forming process and reuse it as raw material, sometimes as much as 30 percent of the gross input. This is known as *in-plant recycling*. When feasible, this type has the advantage of lower costs due to reduced handling.

Recycling (or secondary-materials) industry   When in-plant recycling is not feasible, it may be possible to recover certain materials from wastes by organizations in the recycling business, i.e., a secondary-materials industry consisting of dealers, scrap processors, and brokers. These people are responsible for the collection, transportation, processing, and marketing of the scrap recovered from manufacturing and consumption. The materials handled include paper, glass, metals, plastics, and others. Table 7-12 shows the amount of recycling for several materials as a percentage of total consumption.

TABLE 7-12 Extent of recycling of major materials in the United States in 1967

Material	Total consumption, 10^6 t	Total recycle, 10^6 t	Recycling as percentage of consumption
Copper	2.65	1.32	49.7
Lead	1.15	0.57	49.6
Iron and steel	96.3	30.12	31.2
Paper	48.3	9.21	19.0
Aluminum	3.6	0.66	18.3
Zinc	1.45	0.18	12.6
Glass	11.7	0.55	4.7
Textiles	5.16	0.23	4.3
Rubber	3.59	0.23	4.3
	174.00	43.8	25.2

SOURCE: Environmental Protection Agency, *Salvage Markets for Materials in Solid Waste*, Washington.

Estimating the Effect of Recycling on Resource Depletion

To appreciate the importance of recycling, it is helpful to examine how it affects the depletion rate of nonrenewable resources. First we must assume that a certain material standard of living implies a desired level of physical stock, i.e., an inventory of a material to cover human needs for the products and services using it. Next, if we are given the expected wearout time in years of this material and the percentage of it recycled annually, we can determine the annual requirements in virgin raw material that must be met by depleting available reserves.

Suppose we must maintain a stock of 1 million metric tons (t) of lead, which we assume has a wearout time of 50 yr and can be 50 percent recycled. Then we need 10,000 t/yr in primary material, the depletion rate of lead reserves, to maintain the constant inventory of 1 million metric tons in our system. This is shown in Fig. 7-15, where we note that given a wearout time and level of inventory, the depletion rate for resource decreases as we increase the percentage of recycle. Similarly, for a fixed recycle rate the depletion rate decreases as we lengthen the wearout time. These benefits can be achieved by improvements in both process and product design that extend a product's life and facilitate the recycling of basic materials used to manufacture it.

Benefits of Recycling

When it is feasible, recycling can contribute in the following ways:

1. Recycling can retrieve valuable material from wastes, thus reducing the need for primary materials. According to one estimate, the percentage of material requirements for manufacturing in the United States that could be covered from recycling is 40 percent. For some industries, such as copper and lead, the recycled material has reached 50 percent (see Table 7-13).

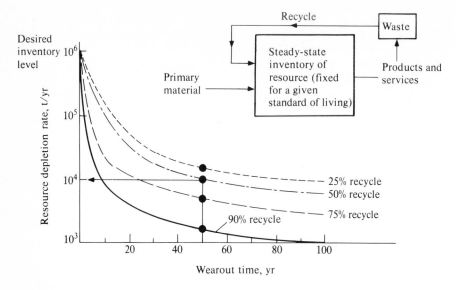

Fig. 7-15 Determination of resource depletion rate given wearout time and recycle rate. (*Adapted from J. N. Hartley, World Mineral and Energy Resources; Some Facts and Assessments, 1974.*)

2. Recycling can reduce manufacturing energy requirements. For a number of industries processing recycled material requires less energy than for primary material. Table 7-13 shows the energy savings from processing several recycled materials.
3. Recycling can considerably reduce the problems associated with solid waste, e.g., health hazards, land deterioration, and waste disposal.

Limitations of Recycling

Considering the substantial benefits that can be realized from recycling, one wonders why there is no more of it. The present limitations of recycling are related to existing technologies, economies, and public policies.

TABLE 7-13   Energy savings from the use of recycled materials

Material	Total production, 1970, 10^6 t	Percentage from recycled scrap 1970	Energy consumption for production processes, 10^6 Btu/t	
			Primary material	100% recycled scrap
Steel	132.0	26	23	8
Aluminum	4.0	4	218	9
Paper	52.5	18	28	21

SOURCE: E. Hirst, *Energy Implications of Several Environmental Quality Strategies*, ORNL-NSF-EP-53, Oak Ridge, Tenn., 1973.

1. Today's technology for recycling is not sufficiently developed to allow this approach to be used competitively. This means higher costs for both recycling equipment and recycled materials. For example, it is more expensive to produce pig iron from iron scrap ($39.90 per metric ton) than from iron ore ($39 per metric ton). The same holds true for other materials, such as paper.
2. With current economic criteria it is cheaper to use primary materials than recycled ones. One reason is the omission of environmental costs associated with the production of virgin materials. Another reason pertains to transportation costs, which are higher for recycled material.
3. An important cause of rapid depletion rates for nonrenewable resources has to do with public tax policies, which through depletion allowances encourage the extractive industries to use primary rather than secondary materials. This is further reinforced by insisting on product specifications that restrict the use of recycled materials, especially paper.

Unless new policies are set that will provide tax and other incentives for using recycled materials, the present discrimination in favor of primary materials will continue. This aggravates even more the environmental problems of natural-resource depletion and excessive pollution from solid waste. Recycling can go a long way to convert operations systems from parts of open conversion systems into components of more effective and less polluting closed ones.

7-8 SUMMARY

Decisions about process design must be examined in conjunction with product design and facilities layout. One of our objectives in this chapter has been to highlight these crucial interactions.

Processes can be classified in several ways, i.e., in terms of their output (product or service), by the type of conversion accomplished, or other criteria. The most useful way to group production processes, however, is by the nature of the flow of what is being worked on inside a system. In this scheme we recognize flow patterns that can be described as a flow shop, a job shop, and a project. In practice these basic types are combined. Each flow pattern is most appropriate under different operating conditions specified by production volume, flexibility of product or service design, or other restriction. Once a choice has been made, however, it sets a general framework within which operations management will resolve long-term problems about system design and repetitive ones arising during planning and control. Increase in productivity becomes possible when a process is designed in a way that emulates flow-shop and continuous processes.

The problems arising in process design can be effectively attacked by a methodology consisting of five phases. The underlying idea here is the same as that in the problem-solving process. It is important to start with a sound formulation of the transformations needed by specifying the various production stages. This is followed by a broad examination of available methods for each conversion stage in a way that will not eliminate promising technologies. With the widest variety of methods per stage, an elimination process is set into action by introducing known constraints on product specifications, production volume, compatibility with other stages, and other parameters of the specific situation. This elimination continues with more detailed technical, economic, and general analysis of both quantitative and qualitative aspects until a well-integrated process has been selected.

The procedures for describing, analyzing, and evaluating a process can be assisted by a number of useful graphic aids such as an operations chart or a flow process chart. Each of these aids can be used to emphasize the most relevant aspects of the process for each occasion. Such graphic aids are also very effective for communication and personnel training.

Of extreme importance in process design are considerations relevant to energy as an input and to various forms of pollution. In the context of recent developments, the difficulties of managing an operations system with more costly and less plentiful energy and with increased antipollution regulation are discussed. Such trends present a challenge to both designers and managers of such systems by adding more costs and complexity. In a similar vein, we discussed the methods and potential of recycling as a means of conserving nonrenewable resources and limiting pollution due to solid waste.

REVIEW QUESTIONS

1. State the criteria used for classifying production processes and list the basic types for each criterion.
2. Discuss the major physical transformation processes for products and give some examples for each type.
3. State a useful criterion for classifying processes for services and give some examples of its application.
4. Describe the phases in the design of a production process.
5. Describe information contained in the following graphic aids for process design:
   (*a*) Block diagram
   (*b*) Operation chart
   (*c*) Operation (or route) sheet
   (*d*) Process flow diagram
   (*e*) Process chart
6. Why are energy considerations important during process design?
7. Discuss some approaches that might be used in process design to cope with increased energy costs and demand.
8. How are pollutants classified in terms of their effects?
9. State some types of water-polluting effluents.
10. Give the meaning of the following terms:
    (*a*) Biochemical oxygen demand (BOD)
    (*b*) Dissolved oxygen (DO)
    (*c*) Natural and artificial restoration
11. What methods are employed to measure water pollution?
12. How can water pollution be treated?
13. Which are the major air pollutants and their sources?
14. What are the most important effects of air pollution?
15. How can air pollution be treated?
16. Describe the major types of solid wastes and their sources.

17. How can solid waste be controlled?
18. What are the sources of noise pollution, and how is it measured?
19. What are the effects of noise pollution, and how can it be controlled?
20. Discuss the major approaches for pollution control in general.
21. What are the characteristics of control strategies related to the output approach?
22. What types of recycling are possible?
23. How is the depletion rate of a nonrenewable resource affected by recycling?
24. Discuss the benefits and limitations of recycling.

PROBLEMS

1. State how you would apply the process-design methodology in the following cases:
   (a) The high-volume production of a canned vegetable soup
   (b) The deployment of a rescue mission to a snowed-in mountain top for a stranded hiking party
   (c) The transportation service by ship for a trip from New York to Naples, Italy, for freight in containers
   (d) The "processing" of a criminal case from police arrest to court sentencing
2. In what ways have the following service organizations used new technologies and/or methods to increase or improve their output?
   (a) Grocery store to supermarket
   (b) Hospitals
   (c) Commercial banks
   (d) Commercial airlines
3. Consider a company making ready-to-wear clothes or shoes in a *developed* country, such as the United States or West Germany. How would its factors of production differ for each production stage compared with a similar system in a *developing* country such as Spain or South Korea?
4. Prepare a flow process chart for:
   (a) A hospital admission procedure for surgery
   (b) Processing an auto insurance claim for an accident
   (c) Handling an application for admission to your university
   (d) Processing a book returned to the university library
5. Select a system that you can easily obtain reasonably complete information about, e.g., a university or private company mail room. Specify the system in terms of output(s), input(s), production stages, control variables, and criteria for performance evaluation.
   (a) Prepare a process chart for a typical item.
   (b) Analyze the process for possible improvements.
   (c) Prepare recommendations for redesigning the system.
6. Read Theodore Levitt, "Production-Line Approach to Service," *Harvard Business Review*, September–October 1972, pp. 41–52. Could this approach be applied to other service processes?
7. Identify a company in your area that is considered to be a polluter and arrange an interview to find out about the development and implementation of their pollution-control program. Prepare a class report with your findings.
8. Select an organization that you are familiar with and determine what measures, if any, have been taken to respond to increasing energy costs and potential shortages with respect to product design or process design. Prepare a class report.
9. Identify an organization in your city that has developed and implemented a recycling

program. Arrange an interview to discuss their experience with recycling (costs, savings, people's attitudes, etc.). Prepare a class report.

10. A chemical-products company is considering three alternative process designs for its new plant. The relevant aspects to be evaluated for each design include objective factors summarized by annual operating costs and subjective factors related to (1) safety, (2) flexibility, and (3) expandibility. Following extensive discussion the subjective ratings of each process design, the cost data, and the relative weights for each factor were estimated as follows (ratings were made on a scale from 1 to 10 with 10 being best):

	Process design			Assigned weight
Criterion	A	B	C	
Annual operating cost C	$5†	$7	$6	$w_1 = 4$
Evaluation:				
Safety	7	9	8	$w_2 = 3$
Flexibility	9	6	4	$w_3 = 2$
Expandibility	5	8	7	$w_4 = 1$

† In millions

Using the method of evaluating alternatives with multiple objectives or criteria, discussed in Chap. 4, select the "best" process design for the new chemical plant.

11. Refer to Prob. 10. Determine the "best" process design if due to revisions:
(a) The annual costs are $C_A = \$8$, $C_B = \$15$, $C_C = \$9$.
(b) The weights for the criteria are $w_1 = 3$, $w_2 = 2$, $w_3 = 3$, $w_4 = 2$.

12. True Sound, Inc., a manufacturer of high-quality stereo products, has been purchasing the motors used in its record player sets at a cost of $18 per unit. Next year's production volume for the record player has been estimated at 3,000 units. A recent proposal to make the record-player motors internally indicates that this would result in the following additional costs.

	Costs
Labor	$21,600
Materials	10,800
Overhead	15,900
Other administrative	6,300

Determine whether the proposal would be profitable if the company's annual production volume is expected to be (a) 2,000, (b) 3,000, (c) 4,000 units.

13. Refer to Prob. 12. The probability estimate for each level of annual production volume is as follows: 20 percent for 2,000 units, 45 percent for 3,000 units, and 35 percent for 4,000 units. Determine whether True Sound, Inc., should continue to buy or switch to making the motors internally if the same costs continue for the next 5 years.

SELECTED REFERENCES

1. Abernathy, W. J., and P. L. Townsend: "Technology, Productivity and Process Change," *Harvard Business School, Division of Research, Working Paper* 73-30, June 1973.
2. Buffa, Elwood S.: *Modern Production Management*, 5th ed., Wiley, New York, 1977.
3. Chase, Richard B., and Nicholas J. Aquilano: *Production and Operations Management*, Irwin, Homewood, Ill., 1973.
4. Ehrlich, Paul, et al.: *Human Ecology*, Freeman, San Francisco, 1972.
5. Hartley, J. N.: *World Mineral and Energy Resources: Some Facts and Assessment*, Battelle, Richmond, Wash., 1974.
6. Holstein, W. K., and W. L. Berry: "Work Flow Structure: An Analysis for Planning and Control," *Management Science*, February 1970, p. 324.
7. Masters, Gilbert: *Introduction to Environmental Science and Technology*, Wiley, New York, 1974.
8. Miller, W. Tyler: *Living in the Environment*, Wadsworth, Belmont, Calif., 1975.
9. Niebel, B. W., and A. B. Draper: *Product Design and Process Engineering*, McGraw-Hill, New York, 1974.
10. Olsen, R. A.: *Manufacturing Management: A Quantitative Approach*, International, Scranton, Pa., 1968.
11. Skinner, Wickham: "Manufacturing: Missing Link in Corporate Strategy," *Harvard Business Review*, vol. 47, no. 3, May–June 1969.
12. Starr, Martin K.: *Production Management, Systems and Synthesis*, Prentice-Hall, Englewood Cliffs, N.J., 1964.
13. Timms, Howard L., and Michael F. Pohlen: *The Production Function in Business*, Irwin, Homewood, Ill., 1970.

Chapter 8

HOW TO PRODUCE II: WORK ANALYSIS, DESIGN, AND MEASUREMENT

**8-8   THE EFFECT OF LEARNING ON STANDARD TIMES;
          LEARNING CURVES**

8-9   SUMMARY

8-1   INTRODUCTION

Despite the rapid pace of technological developments in our time, the human element still remains the most significant component of a production system. The ability to subject certain operations to mechanization or automation has resulted in substituting machines for people either as sources of energy or control. Nevertheless, in both manufacturing and service organizations men and women play vital roles as components of the production process.

As noted previously, one of the major tasks in designing a production system is to specify a sequence of operations for the conversion of inputs (raw materials, labor, etc.) into desired products and services. For each operation needed in the above sequence, it may be possible to employ only people, only machines, or a combination of both, better known as a *man-machine system*[1] (see Fig. 8-1). The man-machine system is responsible for a well-defined microconversion or microprocess. In other words, its role in the total production process is similar to that of an organ, e.g., lungs or heart, in the human body.

The object of work design is to determine the best method of performing the set of operations that define the entire production process. As such, work design is one of the most critical stages of the design of a new production system. Furthermore, the development of cost-reducing technologies, the introduction of new products or services, and the need for adapting to a dynamic and competitive environment

---

[1] This is a generic term that includes both men and women as components of the process.

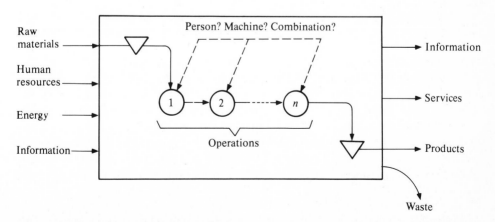

Fig. 8-1 Determination of a production process.

make work redesign a vital part of any effort to improve a system's performance. Before addressing the issues related to work design, it is necessary to break the entire process down into its component parts at whatever level of detail is necessary to identify objectives and process requirements. From the analysis of these parts we can then proceed with the synthesis involved in the design phase.

In general, the purpose of work design or redesign is to enhance the productivity of the entire organization, accomplished through:

1. The development of effective work methods for the necessary operations
2. The creation of a comfortable physical, psychological and sociological work environment
3. The full utilization of the organization's human resources through careful matching of employees' abilities and experience to job requirements.

Work design is usually carried out in two successive stages, known as *job design* (or methods study) and *work measurement* (or time study). In job design the required operations are carefully analyzed to determine their content in terms of component tasks. Following the analysis of tasks, a decision is reached about the distribution of those tasks between people and machines or the appropriate man-machine system in terms of work stations. Job design is completed with the layout of individual work stations in a way that contributes to the safety, efficiency, motivation, and comfort of the worker.

How well a job is designed or how much it has been improved can be assessed through work measurement. This is the second stage of work design that provides management with an estimate of the time required to perform an operation. The precision of the appropriate measurement technique depends on management's needs for planning future production, for evaluating employee performance, and for measuring and improving overall productivity. When wage incentives are considered desirable, their use is based on some kind of individual or group time standard.

8-2 WORK ANALYSIS

The variety of operations within a production system can be analyzed in different degrees of detail. The recommended approach in each case depends on the production volume, the frequency of change in the product specifications, and the time and funds available for the analysis.[1] The reader may recall that the first two factors are the dominant considerations in the selection of the production process type, i.e., flow, job shop, or project.

For a flow shop engaged in mass production, the production volume is large and the product specifications stable for extended periods. Here the opportunity to reduce the time of a critical operation by even a fraction of a minute may lead to impressive savings since it affects the cost of thousands of units. In this case, the

---

[1] An alternative way of viewing this choice is to consider the product of the potential improvement per cycle times the number of cycles performed per time period.

work analysis may be quite detailed at each work station, even to the point of individual hand or eye movements.

In a job shop producing according to customer specifications, the order size per customer is usually limited, and the product specifications are subject to frequent change. As a result, the desired detail in work analysis is considerably reduced, since the production volume is small and does not allow savings from small improvements to pay off. In a job shop the opportunities for improvement are to be found in the layout of work areas to minimize materials handling and in the effective scheduling and follow-up of orders to reduce delays and allow for smooth flow and timely deliveries.

For projects the uniqueness of the items produced and the complexity of the tasks and their interrelationships do not permit the type of work analysis considered in the previous two cases. Productivity improvement in projects depends on effective scheduling of the tasks and careful coordination of materials deliveries and crew assignments.

The various levels of analyzing productive work, the objective of the analysis for each level, the component parts considered, and methods for their representation and improvement are summarized in Table 8-1. Each level of analysis is determined by the duration and intensity of the work performed. Thus, a production system is described in terms of the processes, i.e., transformations, involved in delivering a product or service. A process is decomposed into productive, i.e., economic-value-adding, and nonproductive activities, such as transportations or inspections. An operation can be further subdivided into elements performed by person or machine, the former classified according to the part of the body involved. *A job refers to the set of tasks normally assigned to a worker with given skills.*

8-3 PEOPLE OR MACHINES?:
A COMPARATIVE EVALUATION

For each of the required operations in a production process management can decide to use a person, a machine, or a combination of them. Making the choice wisely requires knowledge of the abilities and limitations for each alternative.

In general, a person is preferred when the content or the conditions of work performed are highly variable or uncertain. Machines, on the other hand, are selected over people when the work is standardized within predictable limits and highly repetitive. Despite the trend of substituting machines for people in many work situations, there are significant differences between the two.

Limitations of People as Productive Elements

Compared with machines, people as a component of a production process are known for the following limitations:

1. They cannot apply large amounts of physical force or pressure, e.g., that needed to cut metals.
2. They cannot use their muscular power with a fixed intensity or high accuracy.

TABLE 8-1 Work analysis: levels, objectives, tools, and procedures

Analysis level	Analysis objectives	Component parts: Symbol	Component parts: Description	Graphic aids for description and analysis	Analysis procedure
System	To improve the system's effectiveness in satisfying human needs for products and services		Inputs (materials, labor, etc.) Outputs (products, services) Conversion mechanism Control mechanism	Block diagram 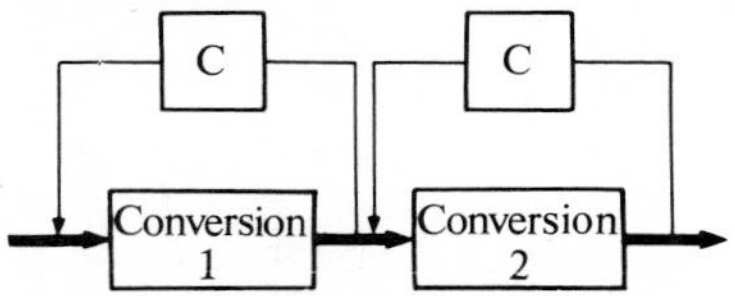	Eliminate unnecessary conversions Modify system structure Change process technology Change system objectives
Process	To improve the flow of: Materials Energy Information	○ □ ⇒ D ▽	Operation Inspection Transportation Delay Storage	Operations chart Process chart Process flow diagram Trip frequency chart† Precedence diagram‡	Eliminate unnecessary operations Change sequence of operations Combine two or more operations Simplify necessary operations by asking what, how, where, who, when Why
Work station (man-machine system operation)	To increase the productivity of human and nonhuman resources at man-machine level To enhance job satisfaction, safety, and comfort	Set up Do Put away	(prepare machine for work and load unit of work) operate machine (unload machine)	Man-machine chart Multiple-activity chart Movies Work-sampling studies	Reduce idle time for people and machines on basis of cost analysis for each resource
Physical tasks involving micromovements	To balance the work load on both hands To improve the utilization of other parts of the body	Get Place Use Hold Assemble	Reach, Grasp Transport, Position, Release A tool A part Two or more components	Left- and right-hand chart Movies (regular and slow-motion)	Reduce idle time for left and right hand by combining micromotions or changing their sequence Eliminate nonproductive movements

† See Chap. 9 on layout methods.
‡ See Chap. 15 on operation scheduling.

3. They cannot perform rapidly simple and repetitive movements without fatigue, boredom, and mistakes.
4. They cannot perform complex calculations rapidly and accurately.
5. They cannot carry out several different tasks simultaneously.
6. They cannot store and recall a large number of unrelated data rapidly.
7. They cannot respond rapidly to frequently changing control signals.
8. They cannot function satisfactorily in a working environment in which conditions relating to heat, cold, noise, etc., go beyond natural limits.

Whenever an operation of the type described above is necessary, we generally select a machine.

Limitations of Machines as Productive Elements

In comparison with people, machines as a general rule are limited in the following respects:
1. They cannot respond to a wide range of stimuli beyond strictly predetermined limits.
2. They cannot respond to unpredictable events.
3. They cannot "think" inductively, i.e., generalize from the particular to the general.
4. They cannot "think" creatively, i.e., develop new patterns of operation.
5. They cannot act with flexibility, i.e., use new alternatives not allowed for previously.
6. They cannot function properly beyond their normal loading or capacity limits.

Even though it has been possible to build certain computers or robots that can function without some of the above limitations, for the majority of production systems where the above limitations are undesirable, people are usually selected as the most suitable alternative. Even in space flights and lunar missions using the most advanced technologies, a significant part of the mission is under human control, whether in the space capsule or in the mission control center on Earth.

People as an Element in the Production Process

In their role as a component for one or more operations in the production process, people are generally responsible for three basic functions:

1. Receiving information through sensory organs for seeing, hearing, etc.
2. Making decisions on the basis of information received through the senses and stored in the memory
3. Acting according to their decision(s) by performing various physical or other mental tasks

It appears from the above that people come in contact with their work in two ways, through the stimuli that provide them with information and through their activity in performing desired tasks based on available information (see Fig. 8-2).

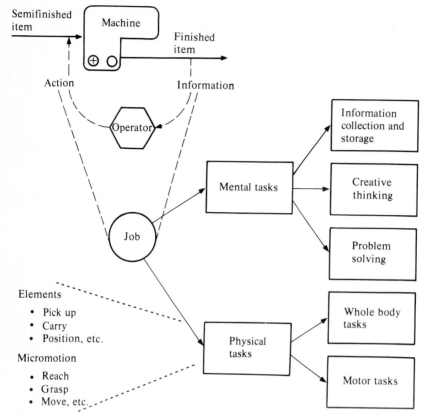

Fig. 8-2 Levels of aggregation of work content.

The development and use of machines is desirable to assist people as an information-processing and decision-making element and to aid or substitute for people as a source of physical energy. In this regard, the use of certain devices such as a microscope, a loudspeaker, or a thermometer assists a person in receiving stimuli through sensory organs limited in range or capacity. Similarly, such tools and machines as levers, hydraulic lifts, drilling machines, etc., amplify or replace the muscular force needed to perform a task. The phenomenal growth of computers, pocket calculators, magnetic tapes, and disks represents ways of helping people make decisions and store information.

Ergonomics and human engineering continuously add to our knowledge of the abilities and limitations of human beings as an element of a production process either alone or as part of a man-machine system. By studying a number of characteristics, e.g., the speed of movement or the accuracy and the reliability in performing various tasks, ergonomics seeks to compile information that will make the selection between people and machines easier. Furthermore, information collected on human mental activities (recall speed, memory capacity, memory reliability, etc.) can assist in the assignment of mental tasks. In a similar vein, the performance of people under various environmental conditions relating to heat, light, noise, etc., has been studied in order to develop optimum working conditions.

8-4   WORK-CONTENT DETERMINATION

The effective utilization of a person as a productive component requires the careful design of jobs in every phase of the production process. Such a design effort consists of specifying for each job the content of work, in terms of related tasks to be performed and the responsibility for planning and control of these tasks. To accomplish this, management must determine existing constraints and appropriate criteria for performance.

The work content of a job performed by an individual consists of mental and physical tasks. *Mental tasks* vary from simple activities of collecting and storing information as input to more complex activities of problem solving and creative thinking (see Chap. 2). *Physical tasks* require the use of the human body as a source of power and can be classified on the basis of their scope and the parts of body involved (see Fig. 8-2).

The best approach for determining the optimum work content for a job requires recognition and study of the factors that permit a combination of tasks in a well-integrated sequence. Among these factors one must consider production volume, the variety of products made, and the stability of their design.

For a new operation the work content can be determined empirically or through a special study. However, for many skilled operators or craftsmen the work content is often established by tradition. We can describe the *work content* of a job in terms of two aspects, the *number of tasks* a worker is normally expected to perform and the *amount of responsibility* assigned the worker for how these tasks are performed, i.e., for their planning and control. The second aspect enables us to view a worker not just as a machine but as a manager of a particular work assignment. It is this dimension which provides the key for motivating employees more effectively and thus enhancing overall productivity as measured by both economic criteria and employee job satisfaction.

Job Specialization

Since the first industrial revolution the most significant trend in determining the work content of a job has been that of specialization. Adam Smith (1776), the famous classical economist, argued that through job specialization it is possible (1) to reduce the learning time for the task(s) involved, (2) to economize through reduced setups or change-overs, (3) to allow for mechanization of simple repetitive tasks, and (4) to make it possible to manage the work force with less supervision. Furthermore, with job specialization Charles Babbage argued in 1832 that one can use wage incentives that raise productivity. The pressures leading to reduced work content for a job are shown in Fig. 8-3.

Even though many of the improvements in our material standard of living can be traced to mass-production methods made possible through specialization, there is convincing evidence that the trend has passed the optimum point. The picture of the automobile assembly worker positioning and tightening a nut to a wheel for each passing car dramatizes the extreme to which specialization has been carried. Similar situations, however, exist in many other types of factories and offices, e.g., insurance and finance companies. Increased productivity through specialization has

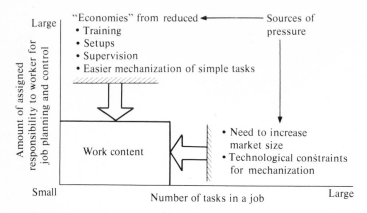

Fig. 8-3 Existing pressures for job specialization.

often materialized at the high price of low employee morale (high turnover and absenteeism), sometimes poor quality, and often dissatisfaction from the job due to boredom, fatigue, and frustration. One reason for the misuse of this approach has been the lack of sound criteria for determining the optimum degree of specialization.

Job Enlargement and Job Enrichment

To counteract the excessive trend for specialization, a number of psychologists and sociologists since the 1920s have pointed out forcefully the need for making work more satisfying. The result has been an opposite trend toward job enlargement and job enrichment. Accordingly, the content of work for a single person is expanded to maintain his interest and afford a sense of accomplishment for his contribution in the production of a finished product or service. Job enlargement, as can be seen in Fig. 8-4 may be horizontal, vertical, or both. *Horizontal job enlargement* requires increasing the number of similar physical tasks a worker is expected to perform. *Vertical job enlargement*, for a set of tasks, involves giving the worker more respon-

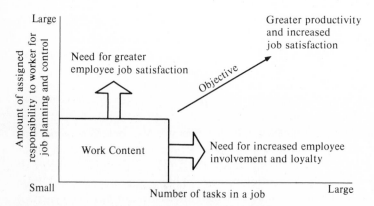

Fig. 8-4 Forces at work for job enlargement and enrichment.

sibility in planning the work, controlling output quality, helping with maintenance of equipment, and so on. *By using both vertical and horizontal job enlargement a job is enriched.* The purpose of job enrichment is to make the job more interesting, to relate it to the larger picture for the whole organization, and through increased job satisfaction to improve productivity, morale, and loyalty. In this sense, it is more effective than *job rotation* which usually reassigns a worker to alternative similar jobs of comparable complexity.

Unfortunately, even for job enlargement there are no criteria for determining when the optimum enlargement has been achieved. Thus, the major accomplishment of the job-enlargement trend was to limit excessive specialization.

A Sociotechnical Systems Approach

According to Davis (Ref. 4), both trends (for specialization and job enlargement) allow technology to play a dominant role as a source of constraints in determining the work content and the role of people in the production system. As a result, job design involves adapting human beings to product, process, and equipment design as key constraints in maximizing job satisfaction.

An emerging approach for balancing the conflicting pressures in determining work content starts by recognizing the existence of both technological and sociopsychological constraints. According to this point of view, a person at work is an element of a system that must satisfy psychological and social needs as well as the requirements imposed by the technology used. In arriving at a satisfactory work content for a job we must satisfy both types of constraints, as shown in Fig. 8-5. A work-content configuration, such as point *A*, satisfies the technological requirements of the process but may be extremely boring or frustrating or result in extreme fatigue. Another configuration, such as point *B*, may be interesting, satisfying, and comfortable for the worker but may not meet technical requirements relating to output rate, quality, equipment operation, etc. The acceptable solutions are the points in the area where both constraints overlap. From this set we can select that configuration which maximizes a criterion for both productivity and job satisfaction.

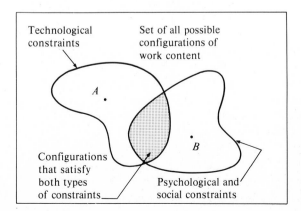

Fig. 8-5 A sociotechnical systems approach to work-content determination. (*Adapted from E. S. Buffa, Operations Management: The Management of Productive Systems, John Wiley & Sons, Inc., New York, 1976, p. 211, by permission of the publisher.*)

In a study made by Scoville (Ref. 22) to develop a general model for determining the optimum work content or job breadth, it was shown that the answer is not to be found at the regions near the extremes of job specialization or job enlargement. For workers the optimal job content includes more tasks and responsibility compared with what is most desirable from the manager's point of view. Nevertheless, the Scoville framework provides a rationale for balancing the conflicting pressures that are present. The specific work content of a job varies with the kind of production process used, tradition, and union contract provisions.

In a flow shop the work content for each work station is affected by the desired production rate. Suppose a system assembles typewriters using an 8-h shift daily, i.e., 480 min. If the daily demand rate is 240 units, we must produce one typewriter every 2 min. Therefore, the entire assembly process must be decomposed into a series of work stations none of which can exceed 2 min. For a job shop or a project, the work content is heavily influenced by the specifications for the product or service design, the equipment used, and the plant layout.

The criteria for determining the optimum work content are both economic and qualitative. The strong interaction between productivity, as an economic criterion, and other considerations, such as employee satisfaction, safety, and comfort, make the work-content problem a challenge to both management and specialists.

8-5 WORK-METHODS DESIGN

Having determined the work content for a job, the next step is to develop appropriate methods for performing the necessary tasks. The depth of analysis at this point increases with production volume and product design stability.

For certain jobs it is possible to use a microsystem where the dominant element may be the worker or the machine. In most cases, however, we use a man-machine system whose capabilities match the requirements of the tasks that define the job. Typical responses to the problem of work-methods design are shown in Fig. 8-6.

Choosing the appropriate work method is equivalent to deciding which type of man-machine system is best suited to the tasks specified in the work content. At one extreme we have an operator-dominated, or *manual, man-machine system*, in which a worker assisted only by tools is responsible for all physical and mental tasks involved in the operation as well as its control. At the opposite extreme is a machine-dominated, or *automatic, man-machine system* responsible for the transformation involved and its control. The operator's role in this case is to monitor the system periodically to ensure that critical process characteristics (temperature, pressure, voltage, etc.) do not exceed desirable limits for safe and economic operation. Between the two extremes, which are usually uneconomical for most applications, we have a large variety of mechanized or *semiautomatic man-machine systems*. For this category a machine is generally responsible for the desired conversion or microprocess while the operator functions as a source of control.

Work-methods design is undertaken with two major objectives: (1) to achieve a productivity rate high enough to make the organization competitive and to maximize employee job satisfaction as an element of the production process. These objectives are accomplished by taking into account the following:

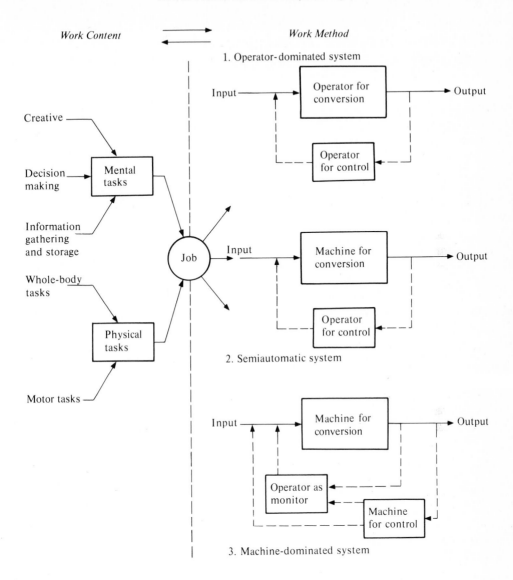

Fig. 8-6 Alternative types of man-machine systems as work methods for a job.

A. *Factors pertaining to the worker*
   1. The physiological limits of the human organism
      a. Anthropometric data (range and speed of movement of eyes, hands, and feet, typical body measurements for women and men, etc.)
      b. Muscular abilities and fatigue limits
      c. Abilities and limitations of sensory organs
      d. Others
   2. The psychological impact of the nature of the work performed
   3. The sociological impact on group relationships, communication, etc.

    4. Certain work-design principles
B. *Factors pertaining to technological constraints*
    1. Product or service design specifications
    2. Process technology and characteristics of equipment used
    3. Production-system layout
C. *Factors related to economic constraints*
    1. Required capital investments for work stations
    2. Working capital needed for operating work stations

These factors are determined after estimating the production volume and the life-span of the product. Thus, work stations and methods are designed differently for mass production of transistor radios than for the production of a limited series of expensive jewelry or high-fashion dresses.

For large companies work methods are designed by specialists such as industrial engineers or systems and procedures analysts. In many cases, however, it is the production-management staff, the foreman, and the operators themselves who are responsible for the methods used. Valuable in the design of work methods are several of the graphic aids discussed in Chap. 7 for representing the process and its elements, including information on processing times, distances for transportation, and other relevant facts.

Work-Design Principles

As a result of extensive studies of different work situations and ergonomic research, we have developed a set of practical rules known as work-design principles. Like the familiar advice for recovering from a cold ("drink plenty of fluids, take some aspirin, and get enough rest") the "principles" combine popular wisdom and present knowledge to guide us in the design of new processes or the improvement of old ones. They refer to the appropriate use of the parts of the body involved, the machines needed, and the layout of the work-station area (see Table 8-2).

Shaping the Working Environment

The impact of the working environment on worker productivity is one of the most significant factors that must be studied in the phase of the production-system design. This is best accomplished by considering the effect of both physical and psychological aspects of the environment.

Physical environment   Among the most significant variables that define the physical environment we include the layout of the work station, the heating and lighting of work areas, the humidity and pollution in the air, noise levels, and others. Research in ergonomics has contributed a great deal toward understanding the effects of these variables for a variety of tasks. Thus, for specific jobs we can determine optimum distances for bodily movements, appropriate heights of desks, chairs, etc., optimum lighting and heating arrangements, maximum allowed noise levels, etc. Neglecting to take such findings into account can be detrimental both to productivity and to employee job satisfaction.

TABLE 8-2 Principles of motion economy (checksheet for motion economy and fatigue reduction)

Use of the human body	Arrangement of the work place	Design of tools and equipment
1. The two hands should begin and end their motions at the same time	10. There should be a definite and fixed place for all tools and materials	18. The hands should be relieved of all work that can be done more advantageously by a jig, a fixture, or a foot-operated device
2. The two hands should not both be idle except during rest periods	11. Tools, materials, and controls should be located close to the point of use	19. Two or more tools should be combined wherever possible
3. Motions of the arms should be made in opposite and symmetrical directions and should be made simultaneously	12. Gravity-feed bins and containers should be used to deliver material close to the point of use	20. Tools and materials should be prepositioned whenever possible
4. Hand and body motions should be confined to the lowest classification with which it is possible to perform the work satisfactorily	13. Drop deliveries should be used wherever possible	21. Where each finger performs some specific movement, as in typewriting, the load should be distributed in accordance with the inherent capacities of the fingers
5. Momentum should be used to assist the worker wherever possible and should be reduced to a minimum if it must be overcome by muscular effort	14. Materials and tools should be located to permit the best sequence of motions	22. Levers, crossbars, and handwheels should be located in such positions that the operator can manipulate them with the least change in body position and with the greatest mechanical advantage
6. Smooth, continuous curved motions of the hands are preferable to straight-line motions involving sudden and sharp changes in direction	15. Provision should be made for adequate conditions for seeing; good illumination is the first requirement for satisfactory visual perception	
7. Ballistic movements are faster, easier, and more accurate than restricted or "controlled" movements	16. The height of the workplace and the chair should preferably be arranged so that alternate sitting and standing at work are easy	
8. Work should be arranged to permit easy and natural rhythm wherever possible	17. A chair of the type and height to permit good posture should be provided for every worker	
9. Eye fixations should be as few and as close together as possible		

SOURCE: Ralph M. Barnes, *Motion and Time Study*, John Wiley & Sons, Inc., New York, 1968, p. 220, reprinted by permission of the publisher.

Psychological and social environment   In addition to the variables that describe the physical environment, it is important to consider factors that determine the psychological and social climate of the work situation. The development of an environment that contributes to higher employee motivation and loyalty can have only positive effects on productivity. This is accomplished whenever workers can take initiatives to improve work methods, whenever easy communication and cooperation with management is encouraged to handle work-related problems, and whenever management acknowledges and rewards superior performance through economic and other incentives.

8-6   WORK MEASUREMENT

Once a recommended method for an operation has been developed (by the workers themselves, a group of specialists, or a combination of both), determination of time estimates to perform each task is necessary for two basic reasons: (1) they are needed to plan future production and (2) without such estimates or standards it is not possible to evaluate performance for workers individually or the production system as a whole.

The need for time estimates in planning future production arises in the following cases:

1. Estimating personnel requirements of a plan
2. Estimating equipment requirements of a plan
3. Selecting the most effective plant layout and balancing work flow
4. Deciding on whether to make a part internally or buy it from outside suppliers
5. Determining a schedule to estimate delivery time
6. Estimating the production cost per unit as an input to selling price
7. Establishing production budgets

The use of such time estimates enables management to decide what activities it can undertake profitably and how best to schedule and perform them.

The need of time standards for the evaluation of performance is recognized in the following cases:

1. The evaluation of workers individually in order to determine their pay rate and to select them for promotion or effective job assignment
2. The evaluation of productivity for individual work stations, production lines, or the entire production system
3. The development of a standard cost system for easier and more effective preparation of budgets
4. The development of individual or group incentive systems based on economic or other rewards for above-average performance

Here it is important to emphasize that each of the above applications of time estimates or standards requires different types of work times. Thus, planning future production requires time estimates that apply to available workers under existing conditions. However, the evaluation and control of individual worker performance or system productivity must be based on standard times for each operation.

Types of Work-Measurement Times

Depending on the intended use, there are different types of times to perform a task, a selected time, a normal time, and a standard time.

Selected time Suppose that for a given work station we record the times for the duration of a series of work cycles and form their statistical distribution. The mean or average of such a distribution provides us with the best estimate of the expected time to perform the operation under study. Thus,

$$\text{Selected time } T = E(t) = \frac{1}{n} \sum_{j=1}^{n} t_i \tag{8-1}$$

where t_j = recorded time for cycle j $(j = 1, 2, \ldots, n)$
  n = number of observed cycles

The selected time of an operation is calculated by observing actual performance times for a specific worker under standard conditions and work methods. The major application of this time estimate is found in the preparation of production requirements under similar conditions.

Normal time T_n The normal time for an operation is computed from the selected time to perform the work, assuming that the worker uses the recommended method, in the appropriate work area, following a regular, i.e., normal pace. Developing a *normal time requires that three conditions be met:*

1. There must be a description of the best way to do the work. Such a description results from the work-methods design phase and implies worker acceptance, individually or based on a union contract.
2. There must be a set of specifications for the layout of the work station, position of incoming materials, tools, illumination, etc.
3. It must be possible to rate, i.e., evaluate, the actual pace of the observed worker, given certain assumptions about what is considered to be a normal pace for the type of work performed.

Whenever the worker's pace is judged to be normal, the adjustment coefficient is taken as 100 percent. For faster than normal this coefficient is above 100 percent, say 115 percent, while for a slower pace the coefficient is given values under 100 percent, say 90 percent.

The calculation of normal time is performed as follows:

$$\text{Normal time } T_n = T \cdot R \tag{8-2}$$

where T = selected time, i.e., observed representative time
  R = observed rate of worker

According to the above method, it is possible to observe two or three operators working at different paces and through appropriate ratings of their selected times to obtain the same normal time for the common task performed. To illustrate this point suppose that for an assembly operation we have the data shown below in the first three columns. The normal time is given in the fourth column:

Operator	Selected time T per piece, min	Rating R, %	Normal time T_n
X	9.0	110	9.9
Y	9.9	100	9.9
Z	11.0	90	9.9

It can be seen that the accuracy in estimating the normal time for an operation depends heavily on the observer's ability to assign accurate ratings. This ability can be developed through experience or through suitable training relying on films showing typical operations performed at different rates.

Normal times are computed so that 90 to 95 percent of all sufficiently trained workers can do that well or better. Their main use is in the design of mass-production systems, i.e., flow shops, where we seek to assign the required tasks to successive work stations in a way that will achieve a steady output rate.

Standard time T_s The time to perform a job must include not only the necessary productive time but also time for rest, personal needs, and idleness due to uncontrollable factors. In other words, the correct evaluation of a worker's performance must account not only for required productive tasks, as measured by normal time, but for the working conditions as well. This is accomplished through the use of standard times.

Definition

The *standard time* for an operation is the time for one complete cycle of the operation using the recommended method, after assigning an appropriate rating and making allowances for rest, personal needs, and delays beyond the worker's control.

The standard time is thus obtained from the normal time by adding an allowance for rest and uncontrollable delays. The allowances are estimated as a percentage k of the normal time and reflect the effect of working conditions on performance. The more uncontrollable and adverse these conditions are with regard to fatigue from lifting heavy objects, high temperatures, uncertainty in delivery time, etc., the larger the percentage for allowances k. Thus

$$T_s = T_n + kT_n = (1 + k)T_n \tag{8-3}$$

or   Standard time = normal time + allowance time

Standard times have three major applications: (1) they are used for performance evaluation of individual workers or groups; (2) they are appropriate in scheduling productive activities characterized by significant idle time and delays, such as the time to produce and deliver an order for a custom-made item; and (3) whenever management wishes to use standard costs for planning and control, it must first develop the standard times for the appropriate operations.

Comparison of Different Work Times

The key managerial functions relating to production-systems design and operations planning and control depend on estimates of the times needed to perform necessary operations. It is important that observed times for such operations be adjusted to provide the most reliable information for the type of decisions under consideration.

Thus, in order to arrive at a selected time from a series of observed times, it is necessary to achieve a certain degree of standardization in the method(s) used and the layout of the work station. To remove significant variations due to the pace followed by different workers, selected times for production tasks are adjusted by rating factors to obtain normal times. Next, it is necessary to make allowances for the effect of working conditions. Thus, in addition to the normal time for a task we allow time for rest and personal needs as well as delays and idle time beyond the operator's control. This adjustment yields the standard time for an operation.

The various estimates for work times, the assumptions in calculating them, and their major applications are summarized in Table 8-3.

8-7 WORK-MEASUREMENT METHODS

The measurement of work times can be approached with informal and practical methods that yield approximate answers or with more refined techniques. In the first group we obtain estimates without any special study from managers, industry experts, supervisors, employees, and historical data. In the group of systematic work measurement methods we include the following:

1. Stopwatch time study

TABLE 8-3 Comparison of various work-measurement time estimates

Work time	Assumptions	Major applications
Observed time t	None	Limited
Selected time T	Standardization of work methods and work stations	Planning future production with existing work force
Normal time T_n	Adoption of concept of normal pace	Production line scheduling
Standard time T_s	Allowing for effects of working conditions	Scheduling production for flow shops by line-balancing: Scheduling production in job shops Evaluating performance Standard cost systems

2. Work sampling
3. Synthetic estimates of work times
4. Predetermined time standards

The major differences in the above relate to the precision of the estimates obtained and the cost in obtaining them. Consequently, for a given application we must select that method which provides the necessary precision at minimum cost. Even though most of the above methods are general, in practice they have been mainly used for physical tasks requiring bodily movements. Their usefulness is limited when applied to work with mental tasks. The choice of the most suitable approach to work measurement depends on a cost-benefit analysis.

Practical Work-Measurement Methods

The fastest and most economical method of work measurement is the use of estimates made by people most familiar with the type of work performed, i.e. operators, supervisors, and industry experts. As long as working procedures and conditions remain reasonably stable, one can also develop time estimates from records kept on completed orders.

Whenever management is aware of changes in work methods, equipment, or other aspects, the above estimates may be adjusted to reflect the effects of such changes. The major disadvantage of time estimates obtained by practical methods is that they cannot be evaluated for their accuracy. It is thus possible to experience large and sometimes costly errors when using subjective estimates to plan or control production by projecting the past into the future unjustifiably.

Stopwatch Time Study

Historically, the first systematic and most widely used work-measurement approach is timing through direct observation, performed using a stopwatch or a movie camera. The purpose of using this or any other refined method is to develop standard times for the operations under study. It is thus necessary to develop first the best method for the job, either by the workers themselves, by specialists, or both.

Before timing an operation through direct observation, it is important to have the approval of the worker(s) to be studied and the supervisor for that department. Furthermore, it is necessary to make a careful examination of the work-station layout, the condition of the equipment used, and such other factors as the illumination, heating, etc., of the working area that may affect performance. The operator chosen must be properly trained, experienced, and capable of average or better performance.

Breakdown of work into elements for timing   Once an operation is selected for measurement, its content is subdivided into elements that lend themselves to accurate observation and timing. For this purpose it is necessary to have clearly distinguishable starting and ending points for each element, using distinct sounds, pressure changes, or other cues. The breakdown of an operation is made easier if the work elements can be classified as follows:

Operator- versus machine-controlled elements. For the first type, say positioning a part for drilling, it is necessary to rate the operator's pace. The duration of machine-controlled elements, such as drilling a hole in a part, however, depend on operating specifications for optimum quality and maintenance.

Regular versus irregular elements. Certain elements that repeat in every cycle are considered regular, whereas those required periodically, such as cleaning or replacing a cutting tool, are irregular.

Constant- versus variable-duration elements. At times the duration of an element changes with variables such as the size, shape, weight, or other feature of the item worked on. Other elements such as stamping or labeling a container are constant in duration.

Foreign or accidental elements. These differ from irregular elements which are predictable. They refer to possible occurrences that may stretch the duration of the cycle such as a power failure, breaking a tool, a defective part, an incorrect entry in an insurance claim, and others.

After classifying the elements to facilitate their timing, a detailed description for each is provided in a special form used for the time study.

Determination of number of cycles to be timed   Before completing a time study, we must determine the number of work cycles to be observed. The objective is to balance the cost of errors resulting from insufficient accuracy in the estimates against the cost of conducting the time study itself. More observations increase the accuracy of time estimates, thus reducing possible errors from their use, but also increase the cost of making the time study.

The desired degree of accuracy in the time estimates is dictated by their intended use. Thus, the application of time standards for a high-volume assembly task requires considerably more accuracy than time estimates needed for quick development of a production schedule for a job-shop operation.

Because of the difficulty of assessing relevant costs, the desired number of cycles to be timed is determined on the basis of the allowable error in the estimates. For a conservative estimation of the number of cycles we select the element in the cycle with the largest variation in t.

Let t = observed time for work element with largest variation in cycle

$\quad k$ = number of standard deviations for t that specifies minimum acceptable confidence level (assuming a normal distribution for t, for a 90 percent confidence level $k = 1.65$, for 95 percent $k = 2.00$, and for 99.7 percent $k = 3.00$)

$\quad s$ = desired degree of accuracy in estimate of t, specified as maximum acceptable percentage deviation from its true value (for $s = .05$ we set allowable error in t_j at true value $\pm.05$; the ratio k/s is known as the *confidence-precision ratio* for the time study)

$\quad n$ = initial number of observed times for selected work element

N = number of work cycles to be observed in order to keep the maximum percentage error in estimating t equal to s

Using statistical sampling theory, we have

$$N = \left[\frac{(k/s)\sqrt{n(\sum t) - (\sum t)^2}}{\sum t} \right]^2 \qquad (8\text{-}4)$$

Thus, if we wish 95 percent of the observed times t for a work element to be in a confidence interval with an accuracy of ± 2 percent of the true value for t, the confidence-precision ratio k/s (for a normal distribution of t) will be

$$\frac{k}{s} = \frac{2}{.02} = 100$$

The specific steps for this method are illustrated in the example that follows. Table 8-4, as an alternative approach, gives the minimum number of cycles that must be included in a time study as a function of cycle duration and its annual frequency f.

▶ EXAMPLE 8-1
The various types of time estimates and the stopwatch method can be understood better with an example taken from a machine-shop situation and considerably simplified to bring out the important points. However, the procedure followed is

TABLE 8-4   Recommended minimum number of cycles for a time study

Minimum cycle duration, h	Minimum number of cycles to be timed		
	Annual frequency over 10,000	Annual frequency 1,000–10,000	Annual frequency under 1,000
8.000	2	1	1
3.000	3	2	1
2.000	4	2	1
1.000	5	3	2
.800	6	3	2
.500	8	4	3
.300	10	5	4
.200	12	6	5
.120	15	8	6
.080	20	10	8
.050	25	12	10
.035	30	15	12
.020	40	20	15
.012	50	25	20
.008	60	30	25
.005	80	40	30
.003	100	50	40
.002	120	60	50
Under .002	140	80	60

SOURCE: Benjamin W. Niebel, *Motion and Time Study*, 6th ed., Richard D. Irwin, Inc., Homewood, Ill., 1976, p. 325, © 1976 by Richard D. Irwin, Inc.

very useful for any operation that has been or can be standardized in a hospital laboratory, in a bank, or elsewhere.

In our example suppose that an operator receives semifinished steel plates which require two holes to be drilled. The finished part is used to mount the alternator to the engine block of an automobile. The operation studied has been broken down into the following work elements:

1. Take a plate from tray A with semifinished parts, place it in the fixture for drilling, and start the machine.
2. Wait for machine to drill $\frac{3}{8}$-in hole.
3. Stop machine, move and position plate to drill second hole, and start machine again.
4. Wait for machine to drill second $\frac{3}{8}$-in hole.
5. Stop machine, remove plate, and drop it in tray B for finished parts.
6. Replace drilling tool on machine with new one and check fixture setting after every 400 parts.

We can see that work elements 1, 3, 5, and 6 are operator-controlled. This requires rating the operator for pace. Elements 2 and 4, however, are machine-controlled, and no rating is necessary. Element 6 appears once every 400 work cycles, i.e., is irregular, while the others are regular since they appear in every cycle.

The supply of semifinished plates deposited in tray A and the removal of finished parts from tray B are the responsibility of materials handlers paid by hourly wages. Similarly, the cleanup of the work-station and the maintenance of the drilling machine are performed by others in the machine shop. The irregular element 6, replacing the drilling tool, has been timed extensively before this operation and has a standard time of 16 min, allowing for any special adjustments needed.

The allowances provided for this type of work include:

Allowance	%
Personal allowance for all machine-shop employees	7
Fatigue allowance for drilling operations	6
Uncontrollable-delay allowance due to lack of materials, random inspection visits, etc.	3
Total	16

The information from a stopwatch time study is customarily recorded in a special work sheet known also as an *observation sheet*. This includes data on the operator observed, the method used, a sketch of the work-station layout and, of course, the recorded times for each work element. Observed times can be obtained with either the *snap-back* or the *continuous timing* method. In the first the stopwatch hand is snapped back to zero after each element, and in the second we allow the stopwatch to run continuously as we record consecutive readings at the end of each element. Continuous timing is more accurate, especially for work elements of short duration, but requires more clerical work.

Table 8-5 summarizes the information collected for timing the drilling operation of the example. The accumulated time readings at the end of each element are recorded for 10 parts and the elemental times are then determined by successive subtractions. The foreign elements due to a power failure and a defective part are ignored, and selected times are computed by taking the average of observed times for each element.

Suppose that we desired a 95 percent confidence level ($k = 2$) that our estimate of average cycle time would not exceed the true cycle time value by more than 10 percent ($s = 0.10$). In other words, we want 95 percent of the sample observations to be in the range of two standard deviations from the mean. For the 10 percent desired accuracy this range will correspond to the interval between $t_{min} = t - (0.1)t$ and $t_{max} = t + (0.1)t$. Using the observed values of element 5, which has the largest variation as measured by their range, we have

$$\frac{k}{s} = \frac{2}{.10} = 20$$

$n = 10$ cycles for observed values

$$\sum t = .10 + .09 + \cdots + .08 = 1.01 \text{ min}$$

$$\sum t^2 = (.10)^2 + (.09)^2 + \cdots + (.08)^2 = .1041$$

Thus

$$N = \left[\frac{(k/s)\sqrt{n \sum t^2 - (\sum t)^2}}{\sum t} \right]^2 = \left[\frac{(2/.10)\sqrt{10(.1041) - (1.01)^2}}{1.01} \right]^2$$

$$= \left(\frac{20\sqrt{.021}}{1.01} \right)^2 = \left(\frac{2.898}{1.01} \right)^2 = 8.23 \text{ cycles}$$

For the desired confidence-precision ratio we already have observed enough cycles.[1] Therefore, we can proceed to calculate normal and standard times for the above operation. Normal times for operator-controlled elements are determined by applying the rating factors given during observation.

The normal time for all regular elements of the operation and the prorated normal time for element 6 (tool replacement every 400 parts) will be

$$T'_n = .234 + .250 + .115 + .250 + .111 + \frac{22.00}{400} = 1.015 \text{ min}$$

and the standard time for the same elements with $k = 16$ percent is

$$T'_s = \text{normal time} + \text{allowance} = T'_n + kT'_n = 1.015 + (.16)(1.015) = 1.117 \text{ min}$$

Thus, the standard time for the entire operation, based on the above stopwatch time study, is 1.117 min per part.

From this estimate we can compute the daily output for one operator per 8-h shift to be $(480 \text{ min}) \div (1.117 \text{ min per part}) = 430 \text{ parts}$.

---

[1] If we knew that the frequency of this operation with a selected cycle time for 0.924 min was 18,000 per year, we could use Table 8-4 to determine the desired number of cycles as 6.

TABLE 8-5   Observation sheet used for stopwatch time study

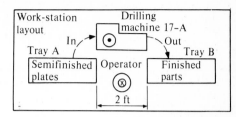

TIME-STUDY OBSERVATION SHEET

Operation: Drilling of two $\frac{3}{8}$-in holes in steel plate
Operator: John Elias, 5 yr experience
Part no.:   SP-X1012 made of steel
Equipment: Drilling machine 17-A
Analyst: Chris Ben   Date: 2-15-80

Work element	Rating R, %	Observed time per part, min										Selected time T	Normal time $T_n = T \cdot R$
		1	2	3	4	5	6	7	8	9	10		
1	120	.18 .18	.20 1.10	.19 2.01	.35† 3.08	.17 3.99	.21 4.94	.22 5.90	.42‡ 7.06	.19 7.98	.20 33.38	.195	.234
2	100	.25 .43	.25 1.35	.25 2.26	.25 3.33	.25 4.24	.25 5.19	.25 6.15	.25 7.31	.25 8.23	.25 33.63	.250	.250
3	90	.12 .55	.13 1.48	.11 2.37	.14 3.47	.15 4.39	.13 5.32	.14 6.29	.12 7.43	.13 8.36	.11 33.74	.128	.115
4	100	.25 .80	.25 1.73	.25 2.62	.25 3.72	.25 4.64	.25 5.57	.25 6.54	.25 7.68	.25 8.61	.25 33.99	.250	.250
5	110	.10 .90	.09 1.82	.11 2.73	.10 3.82	.08 4.72	.11 5.68	.10 6.64	.11 7.79	.13 8.74	.08 34.07	.101	.111
6	90									24.44 33.18		24.44	22.00

† Power failure.   ‡ Defective plate (observed times omitted).

Work Sampling

For certain activities the work cycle may be quite long, or the tasks may be required at unexpected times. This is true, for example, with equipment repairs. In such cases, the cost of determining time estimates using a stopwatch time study can be very high. There are also other occasions where work measurement using a stopwatch is either impossible or unacceptable to the workers or their union.

Whenever continuous direct observation is not feasible or appropriate, we can develop time estimates through work sampling. The method consists of a series of instant observations of the activity under study taken at random intervals. From the outcome of such observations we can use statistical methods to arrive at estimates of the duration of the elements of the activity.

The statistical validity of work sampling rests on two assumptions. According to the first, when a sample of instant observations is representative of the entire work cycle, the proportion of time an element is observed in the sample can be used to estimate the duration of the work element. Suppose, for example, that we are interested in the percent of idle time per day for an expensive piece of equipment, a maintenance crew, or a hospital operating room. After taking a sample of instant observations of the activity of interest, we can estimate the daily idle time from the percentage of observations in the sample corresponding to idleness of the people or facility observed. In order for the sample to be representative, it must be selected so that the timing of the observations reveals the underlying structure of the activity observed. Representativeness is generally assured through the use of random, stratified random, or other types of samples appropriate for the activity under study.

The second assumption in work sampling is that the accuracy of an estimate increases with the number of instant observations in the sample. The recommended sample size is determined by reasoning similar to that used to specify the number of work cycles to be timed with a stopwatch. Thus, we are again faced with the problem of balancing the costs arising from lack of sufficient accuracy against the costs of making the observations. The desired sample size is determined using Eq. (8-5).

Performing a work-sampling study, an example   Having selected work sampling as the most appropriate method of work measurement, it is necessary to break down the activity of interest into its component elements, or tasks. They must be defined clearly so that one can readily identify the beginning and end of each element. Let us assume that the administration of a metropolitan hospital is concerned with the utilization of a computerized brain-scanning device, representing an important recent investment for its neurology department. It is felt adequate to describe the elements of this activity as follows:

State 1: Scanning device is in use

State 2: Scanning device is idle

To determine the desired number of instant observations, it is necessary to have a preliminary rough estimate of the machine's idle time as a percentage, based on past experience or experience in similar hospitals. For the above hospital, a subjective estimate of the percentage of idle time is 25 percent ($p = 0.25$).

For a given confidence level and degree of precision in the estimate, the desired number of observations can be determined statistically. For our example, the probability of various outcomes from our observations is described by the *binomial distribution*.[1] Thus, the necessary sample size N can be determined from the formula

$$N = \left(\frac{k}{s}\right)^2 \frac{1-p}{p} \tag{8-5}$$

---

[1] The binomial distribution is appropriate when a random outcome of a process can be classified in one of two ways (idle or busy, present or absent, success or failure, etc.). If the probability of success in any trial is p and we have n trials, then

$$\text{Prob}(x \text{ successes}) = \binom{n}{x} p^x (1-p)^{n-x} \qquad x = 0, 1, 2, \ldots, n$$

where

$$\binom{n}{x} = \frac{n!}{x!\,(n-x)!}$$

where p = preliminary estimate of percent of idle time or other activity element

k = number of standard deviations implied by desired confidence level in estimate

s = desired degree of precision in estimate of p expressed as maximum allowed percentage deviation from true value of p

Suppose for the hospital study we need an estimate of p that can differ no more than 10 percent of its true value ($s = 0.10$) and we wish to have a 95 percent confidence level that our precision interval includes the true value of p ($k = 2$). The appropriate sample size in this case is computed as follows:

$$N = \left(\frac{k}{s}\right)^2 \frac{1-p}{p} = \left(\frac{2}{.10}\right)^2 \frac{1.00 - .25}{.25} = (20)^2(3) = 1,200 \text{ observations}$$

These may be distributed equally over a series of working periods (50, 100, or more observations daily) based on the sequence of selected random numbers.

Preparation of the random sampling plan   In order for the sampling results to be representative of the activity under study, it is necessary for the instantaneous observations to be made at random intervals to avoid undue coincidence with regular rest periods, machine setup times, or prescheduled maintenance.[1]

The selection of random times for the observations can be made with the help of random-number tables (see Appendix 1). Such tables contain several columns of numbers called random because they are formed so that in each position there is an equal probability of selecting any digit from 0 to 9. Thus, for a sample size equal to N we select N random numbers, one for each observation.

Each random number is transformed into a random time for making an instantaneous observation during a working period of one or more shifts daily. For our hospital example we shall assume one 8-h shift from 8 A.M. to 5 P.M. with an interruption of 1 h at noon for lunch. For our purposes we need to use three-digit numbers, with the first digit specifying the hour after the beginning of the shift and the remaining two specifying the minutes in that hour. Starting at a randomly selected row and column of a table suppose we obtain the three-digit random number 026. This can be interpreted as an observation made .26 h after the start of the shift. This is $(.26)(60) = 15.6$ min after 8:00 A.M., or at 8:15 A.M. Similarly, a second random number 789 corresponds with a time 7.85 h after work begins, i.e., at 4:43 P.M.

After determining N observation times, it is necessary to specify their chronological sequence as part of the sampling plan. The method for converting random numbers into random observation times and arranging them in a sampling schedule is illustrated in Table 8-6. In general, it is important to take every precaution so that the act of observation will not affect the activity being observed.

---

[1] Whenever the activity studied takes place at random intervals, e.g., repair work or emergency aid in a hospital, it may be possible or even desirable to time the observations at regular intervals. This case requires a special statistical analysis to determine the sample size.

TABLE 8-6 Determination of schedule for instant observations in a work-sampling study

Random number	Hours after start†	Observation time	Time-ordered observation schedule
317	3.17	11:10	(1) 08:27
884	8.84	Ignored‡	(2) 10:05
309	3.09	11:05	(3) 10:17
228	2.28	10:17	(4) 11:05
782	7.82	16:49	(5) 11:10
418	4.18	13:11	(6) 11:52
926	9.26	Ignored‡	(7) 13:11
573	5.72	14:43	(8) 14:43
208	2.08	10:05	(9) 15:31
386	3.86	11:52	(10) 16:49
045	0.45	08:27	
652	6.52	15:31	
		etc.	

† Not counting lunch hour.
‡ Falls outside working period.

Suppose the results of the study were as follows:

State	Condition	Number of observations	%
1	Device in use	888	74.0
2	Device idle	312	26.0
	Total	1200	100.0

It can be seen that the actual figure for the percentage of idle time is greater than the original estimate of 25 percent; therefore the 1200 observations suffice. Had it been smaller, say 20 percent, we would have to compute a revised number of observations N' based on $p = .20$ and determine the additional number of required observations $N' - N$. Thus,

$$N' = \left(\frac{2}{.10}\right)^2 \frac{1.000 - .20}{.20} = (20)^2(4) = 1{,}600 \text{ observations}$$

Therefore $N' - N = 1{,}600 - 1{,}200 = 400$ additional observations.

We can interpret the results of the above work sampling study as follows. For regular working conditions we can be 95 percent confident that the true proportion of idle time for the scanning device is in the interval

$$26.0 \pm (26.0)(.10) = 26.0\% \pm 2.6\%$$

Had the same study been repeated a large number of times, the estimate of p obtained in 95 percent of these attempts would be in the range 23.4 to 28.6 percent.

Since p is quite large, it is advisable for the hospital administration to delve deeper into the causes of the observed idleness. This would help identify and perhaps remove some of the controllable factors of idleness. The recommended analysis would require a finer breakdown of the operation of the device:

State	Description	Proportion
1	Device in use	p_1
2	Device idle, waiting for test requests	p_2
3	Device idle, waiting for repair service	p_3
4	Device idle, repair being performed	p_4
5	Device idle, lack of materials needed	p_5
6	Device idle, uncontrollable events such as power failure, operator absence due to illness, etc.	p_6

Note that the sum $p_1 + p_2 + \cdots + p_6$ must always add to 1.

Excessive values for p_2 may point out poor scheduling procedures or the opportunity to accept test requests from other hospitals. High values for p_3 and p_4 might suggest improvements in the maintenance program or point the need for additional operator training. On the other hand, a high value for p_5 may indicate poor performance of the purchasing department or unreliable suppliers.

Determination of normal and standard time from work sampling, an example
Whenever we want normal- and standard-time estimates for elements of an activity performed by a worker or a crew, during each observation it is necessary to evaluate the pace through an appropriate rating. Suppose that in a job shop processing a metal part on a machine requires careful setting of the machine. The normal time for this task can be estimated from the percentage of observations during which the operator was seen to perform machine setups. Suppose a work-sampling study produced the following results:

$$p = 15\% \text{ (for setups)}$$

$$D = 480 \text{ min (shift duration)}$$

$$n = \text{average daily output} = 30 \text{ pieces}$$

$$R = \text{average rating of observed operator} = 110\%$$

We can proceed to calculate the normal time for a machine setup before processing each piece as follows:

$$T_n = p\frac{D}{n}R = (.15)\frac{480}{30}1.10 = 2.64 \text{ min/setup}$$

If the allowance for fatigue, delays, personal needs, etc., for this type of work is 12 percent, we can determine a standard time as follows:

$$T_s = T_n + .12T_n = 2.64 + (.12)(2.64) = 2.96 \text{ min/setup}$$

Recommended applications for work sampling   Work sampling for time estimates can be used for tasks that lend themselves to direct observation. As a rule, it is most appropriate for activities of rather long duration, with rather limited frequency, and unpredictability in the time of occurrence.

Work sampling is most widely employed to determine the utilization rate of various productive resources, and it is particularly valuable for determining the allowances used due to uncontrollable factors in stopwatch time studies. Furthermore, it can be used to estimate normal and standard time when a stopwatch time is too expensive or inadvisable for other reasons.

Work sampling can be useful for providing labor-requirement inputs to a production plan, assist in developing standard costs, and evaluating nonrepetitive activities with long cycles. Thus, it can be used for studying work methods in office procedures, repair and maintenance activities, hospital operations, retail-store operations, banks, courts of justice, research institutions, and government agencies.

Synthetic Times

When designing a new system, it may be necessary to develop standard times for various tasks without the benefit of direct observation. In other situations where direct observation is possible, the nature of the work and its frequency might make stopwatch time study and work sampling very expensive.

Whenever the work performed involves the same elements in different combinations and the tasks are repeated with high frequency, it is possible to employ synthetic times. *The synthetic time for a job is determined from the normal times of the component elements.* Thus,

$$T_n = T_{n,1} + T_{n,2} + \cdots + T_{n,r} = \sum_{j=1}^{r} T_{n,j} \qquad (8\text{-}6)$$

where $T_{n,j}$ = normal time for element j $(j = 1, 2, \ldots, r)$
    T_n = synthetic time for a given task

The normal time of each element can be expressed as a function of one or more variables. For example, the time to paint a surface or to clean a floor depends on the area measured in squared feet. Similarly, the time to drill a hole in a metal plate depends on the diameter and depth of the hole and so on. In general, the normal time for an element is determined from an empirical equation after specifying the values of the determining variables. Thus,

$$T_{n,j} = f(x, y, \ldots)$$

where $x, y, \ldots$ are the independent work variables, i.e., diameter and depth of a hole to be drilled, area to be cleaned or painted, etc.

The set of empirical equations employed to compute the normal times for the

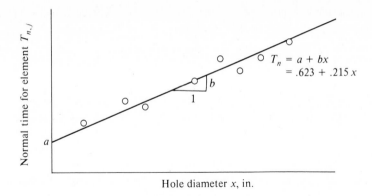

Fig. 8-7 Regression line for developing synthetic times for drilling $\frac{1}{4}$-in-deep holes in metal plates.

elements that define a task can be derived by statistical techniques. These usually include regression and multivariate analysis of data on elemental performance times obtained through direct observation. The normal time for drilling a $\frac{1}{4}$-in-deep hole in a metal plate of specified hardness will vary with the hole diameter, the relationship specified by a regression line of the form shown in Fig. 8-7. Standard times can be calculated from synthetic normal times by adding the usual allowance for fatigue, personal needs, and uncontrollable delays.

Work measurement using synthetic times has become quite well accepted in a variety of production systems. In the service sector, the method is used to estimate repair or maintenance times, times for office procedures (typing, filing, etc.), and for information processing systems (programming, auditing, and others). In manufacturing, synthetic times are used for tasks related to fabrication, assembly, and packaging as well as quality control and other functions.

Predetermined Standard Times

For mass-production systems in which the tasks performed at each work station can be broken down into small movements (reach, grasp, etc.), it may be preferable to use work-measurement techniques based on predetermined times. Several commercially available systems contain tables with predetermined times for each type of elementary movement. Such times are a function of key parameters or determining factors for each work element. For example, the time to transport an object from one position to another depends on its weight, the distance traveled, the required hand pressure, etc.

Using predetermined times has been an effective method for over 30 years for industries in which we need standard times for tasks with short duration cycles that are highly repetitive. The major advantages claimed are the following:

1. The ability to determine time standards without direct observation or before the actual operation of the production system

2. Avoiding the need to rate the pace of the operator, a most difficult aspect of direct observation methods, as well as other errors related to the time analysis or the observed worker
3. The increased accuracy of predetermined times due to the extensive data base used from direct timing methods

The most widely used commercial systems for predetermined times include MTM (Methods and Time Measurement), BMT (Basic Motion Timestudy), and Work Factors. In order to use any of the commercial systems the tasks under study must be analyzed with great care to determine the work content in terms of elementary movements. This requires experience and the ability of analyzing in detail tasks for nonexisting operations. The above systems differ in the classification of basic movements, and the selection depends on the nature of the tasks the predetermined times will be applied to. Additional considerations include the cost of buying the system and the assistance provided to the user with regard to training suitable personnel to apply it correctly.

The normal time for a contemplated or existing task is equal to the sum of the elemental normal times as obtained from appropriate tables for each basic motion. This procedure assumes that the sequences of elements that define a task are independent of each other. After summing the predetermined times for the component elements to obtain the normal time for a task, we add the recommended allowance to obtain a standard time.

Comparison of Work-Measurement Methods

In comparing the various work-measurement techniques, it is necessary to consider the number and the nature of tasks for which we need time standards.

Predetermined and synthetic time standards require a large initial cost to adapt or develop for a particular organization. However, once the method is in use, time standards for new operations can be determined at low cost. The opposite is true with direct-observation methods (stopwatch and work sampling). They are not expensive to setup but require considerable effort and cost for each additional application (see Fig. 8-9).

As we can see in Fig. 8-8, for a large number of similar repetitive tasks the methods of synthetic and predetermined times are preferred over stopwatch and work-sampling techniques. Furthermore, management must take into account that the implementation of predetermined times, when appropriate, requires 3 to 6 months.

8-8   THE EFFECT OF LEARNING ON STANDARD TIMES; LEARNING CURVES

In the development and use of standard times it is important to take into account the effects from learning and experience. For example, in assembly operations that require considerable manual dexterity it has been noted that production time

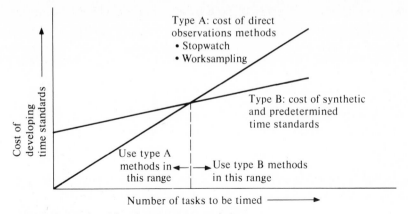

Fig. 8-8 Comparison of work-measurement techniques.

decreases with experience due to improved learning of the tasks and use of more efficient methods. The same phenomenon is observed for the construction of complex products (airplanes, tankers, weapon systems, etc.) and complex services (surgical operations, maintenance of intricate equipment, etc.).

Learning effects are most pronounced in work situations with a significant input of human resources, i.e., in labor-intensive systems. Whenever the work elements are controlled mainly by machines and in mass-production systems where the accumulated experience is excessive, the effects of learning on production times are limited or negligible. The reductions in the time required to produce successive units of output can be shown with a learning curve (see Fig. 8-9). When plotted on a regular graph, the learning curve is exponential; i.e., there is a fast reduction at first gradually becoming smaller as cumulative production increases. When plotted on logarithmic scale, the learning curve appears as a straight line with negative slope. The gains in productivity portrayed by a learning curve summarize performance improvements attributed not only to labor but to other aspects of work,

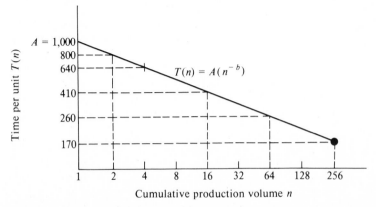

Fig. 8-9 Example of a learning curve using logarithmic scales for $l = .80$, that is, 80 percent learning rate ($b = .322$).

such as methods and layout, equipment utilization, and managerial effectiveness to plan, coordinate, and control.

To illustrate the concept, let us assume that the number of units produced so far is equal to n and that the production time for the last unit is $T(n)$. On the basis of a learning curve, we can predict that when the production volume reaches the level of $2n$ units, i.e., double the present cumulative output, the production time will be decreased by a fixed percentage l, known as the *learning rate*

$$T(2n) = l \cdot T(n) \qquad \text{for } n = 1, 2, \ldots \tag{8-7}$$

$$0 < l < 1$$

Suppose that the first unit of a new small aircraft requires 1,000 h of labor. If there is an 80 percent learning rate ($l = .8$), the second unit will require $(.8)(1,000) = 800$ h, the fourth unit $(.8)(800) = 640$ h, the eighth $(.8)(640) = 512$ h, and so on (see Fig. 8-9).[1]

In the above relationship n may assume any value whatsoever, and the learning rate l depends on the kind of operations performed. The general equation specifying the time required for the nth unit is

$$\boxed{T(n) = A(n^{-b})} \tag{8-8}$$

where $T(n)$ = time, required to produce nth unit, labor-hours
$\qquad A$ = time required to produce first unit, labor-hours, i.e., $A = T(1)$
$\qquad b$ = index whose value depends on learning rate

For $l = .8$, for example, $b = .152$; for $l = .9$, $b = .322$. The learning-curve equation can be derived using regression analysis on data for production times for successive units with previous orders.

The validity of the learning curve has been demonstrated in various industries. For example, in the steel industry the value of l for the work hours required per unit is .60 (60 percent learning rate), while for petroleum products for the work time per barrel the value of l is .75 (75 percent learning rate). Learning curves are extremely useful in preparing work-force plans, estimating unit costs, and submitting bids for special items or projects. In such applications, a significant percentage of the costs are for labor, and the amount required depends on the order size, due to a decreasing production time per unit resulting from learning.

8-9 SUMMARY

In order to place in proper perspective the different parts of work design either for a new production system or for the improvement of an existing one, the material discussed in this chapter is summarized in the diagram in Fig. 8-10.

---

[1] The times for successive units as a proportion of the time for the first unit have been tabulated in Appendix 5 for different learning rates l.

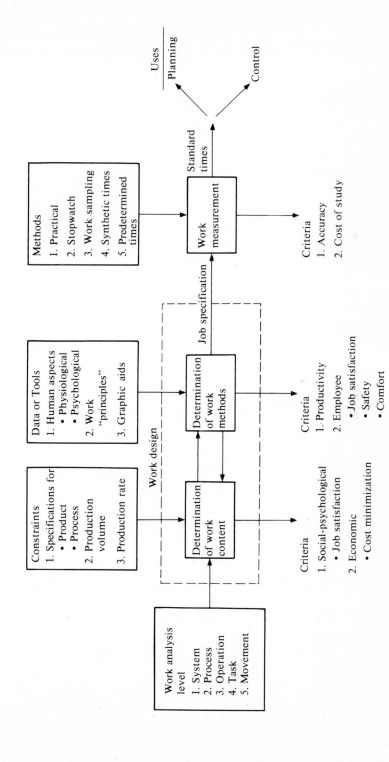

Fig. 8-10 The phases in a work study.

345

REVIEW QUESTIONS

1. What is the main purpose for undertaking a work study?
2. What are the objectives for each level of work analysis?
3. How is work subdivided, and what is the procedure for analysis at the level of (*a*) process, (*b*) work station, and (*c*) micromovements?
4. In choosing between people and machines as parts of a production process, what limitations arise with each alternative?
5. What are the interfaces between workers and their work, and how can machines be employed to assist them?
6. Which are the levels of aggregation for the work content of a processing center?
7. What are the two aspects (or variables) that determine work content in a given situation?
8. Describe briefly the advantages and limitations of the following approaches for the determination of work content: (*a*) job specialization and (*b*) job enlargement (vertical, horizontal).
9. Which are the distinctive features of the sociotechnical system approach to work content?
10. State the objectives in the design of work methods.
11. Which man-machine types can be employed in the design of work methods given the specification of work content?
12. What factors must be taken into account in the selection of a work method?
13. Select a simple work situation and after a preliminary study indicate which work-design principles have been incorporated and which others could apply to improve productivity. Examples might include a secretary's working area, a watch repairman's bench, a bartender's work area, etc.
14. Discuss aspects of the working environment that are pertinent in work design and give an example of successful design configuration from your experience.
15. Describe the most important uses of time estimates for (*a*) operations planning and (*b*) performance evaluation.
16. Define carefully the following types of time estimates and specify what operating conditions must be satisfied before they can be used:
    (*a*) Selected time
    (*b*) Normal time
    (*c*) Standard time
17. Which is the most controversial part of developing a normal time for a job?
18. Discuss the relevant trade-offs when developing a time estimate for a task.
19. When is a practical work-measurement approach preferable to the more systematic methods?
20. Discuss the conditions under which it is most desirable to develop time standards using:
    (*a*) Stopwatch time study
    (*b*) Work sampling
    (*c*) Synthetic estimates
    (*d*) Predetermined time standards
21. What is the general attitude of a labor union in the development of a time standard?
22. What are the most important reasons for the limited use of time standards in the service sector?
23. Give an example of an application for each work-measurement method and justify your choice.

24. For the following applications, which work-measurement method would you recommend and why?

(*a*) Determination of a time standard for the assembly operation of a desk lamp for a medium-sized manufacturing company

(*b*) Determination of the allowances for the assembly of a high-volume oil pump

(*c*) Determination of the standard time for the assembly of a newly designed quartz wrist watch not yet in production

(*d*) Determination of the standard time for street-cleaning operations in the city's downtown area

(*e*) Determination of the utilization rate for a new spectral-analysis machine in a food-technology lab

25. Discuss the effect of learning on time standards and the type of industry most likely to be affected by it.

PROBLEMS

1. The main office of Continental Bank, Ltd., wished to develop a time estimate for typing draft notes for routine international transactions. The following data were collected by studying the operation:

Day	Employee-hours	No. of notes processed
1	60	153
2	56	137
3	72	190

(*a*) Determine an average time for typing a draft note.

(*b*) Under what conditions would this qualify as a selected time T?

(*c*) If the employees for this operation are paid $5 per hour, what is the average typing cost per draft note?

(*d*) Can this be used as a standard cost per draft note? Why?

2. Vanessa and Philip Jourden operate Contemporary Fashions Co., a ready-to-wear clothing establishment. They have recently completed a new design for women's skirts about to be put into production. Each skirt consists of three precut pieces of fabric (front, back and waistband). The front and back pieces are sewn together by the two side seams at one work station, a zipper and waistband are placed at a second work station, and the hemming is done at a third work station. The work elements at the first work station include the following:

1. Take precut front and back pieces and align for sewing
2. Position pieces in sewing machine
3. Sew first side seam
4. Reposition pieces for second side seam
5. Sew second side seam
6. Remove semifinished skirt from sewing machine and place on a cart for moving to second work station
7. Change spool with thread every 100 units

After a stopwatch time study based on 10 cycles, the following results were recorded:

Work element	Rating, %	Sum of 10 observed times, min	Work element	Rating, %	Sum of 10 observed times, min
1	90	9.35	5	100	22.0
2	105	5.74	6	120	2.36
3	100	22.00	7	110	3.68
4	110	4.87			

(a) Determine the normal time for each work element
(b) Determine the standard time for the operation if a 12 percent allowance is appropriate for this type of work.
(c) Determine the standard daily output rate of this work station for an 8-h shift.

3. Refer to Prob. 2. How many cycles should be timed at work station 1 in order to have a 90 percent confidence level in an estimate of a selected time for the entire operation with a ± 10 percent precision?

4. Refer to Prob. 2. Suppose that the Jourdens have estimated that the standard time to make a skirt is 12.80 min (total time in all three stations). The operators are paid $7 per hour, the cost of material and supplies per skirt is $33, and overhead has been estimated at 60 percent of direct labor and material cost. Determine (a) the standard labor cost per skirt and (b) the standard cost per skirt.

5. After completing a methods study of a work station where an operator places a time mechanism on a home-appliance frame, the following data in minutes were recorded from a stopwatch time study:

Observed cycle	Work element†					
	1	2	3	4	5	6
1	.25	.20	.41	.19	.30	.52
2	.23	.20	.40	.18	.30	.88‡
3	.24	.20	.42	.20	.30	.51
4	.24	.20	.41	.19	.30	.54
5	.26	.20	.43	.19	.30	.52
6	.23	.20	.43	.21	.30	.53
7	.24	.20	.41	.20	.30	.52
8	.63§	.20	.42	.21	.30	.54
9	.25	.20	.42	.22	.30	.51
10	.27	.20	.44	.21	.30	.53

† The operator for this job was rated at 115 percent for elements 1, 3, 4, and 6. Elements 2 and 5 were machine controlled. The allowance for this type of work is 12 percent.
‡ Lights went off temporarily.
§ The time-mechanism housing unit was bent and would not fit, so it had to be replaced.

(a) Determine the selected time for the entire operation following the improvement of work methods and work-station layout.

(b) Determine the normal time for this operation.

(c) Calculate the standard time for this operation.

(d) What is the daily standard output rate for this operation if the plant operates two 8-h shifts?

6. Refer to Prob. 5. How many cycles should be timed in order to have a 95 percent confidence level in an estimate of selected time of the whole operation with a 5 percent precision?

7. The manager of Medical Lab Services Co. has received customer complaints on turn-around times for the results of medical tests. The latter require the OK of the chief lab technician, who complains frequently of work overloads. From a study over 12 work days based on 80 random observations per day, the manager has obtained the following results:

Day	1	2	3	4	5	6	7	8	9	10	11	12
Observations of chief lab technician being idle	11	8	14	9	10	12	11	7	10	12	14	9

(a) Determine an estimate of the percentage idle time of the chief lab technician.

(b) Are his complaints of work overloads justified?

(c) How many observations need the manager make to have a 90 percent confidence that the above estimate of idle time is accurate within 10 percent?

(d) Repeat part (c) for 95 percent.

8. Refer to Prob. 7.

(a) What was the preliminary estimate assumed on the percentage idle time for the chief lab technician for the manager to arrive at 960 $[= (80)(12)]$ observations for the study expecting a 90 percent confidence level in an estimate with ± 10 percent precision?

(b) What is the actual precision of the study results at the 90 percent confidence level, and what would be the implied confidence interval for the percentage idle time?

9. The Downtown Continuing Education Center sends out brochures on new offerings to 1,500 people on its mailing list. The job of typing an address, placing the brochure in an envelope, and sealing it is done by Sally Devine. After a 10-week period, the section manager who keeps a tally of the outcome of random observations on Sally has compiled the following data:

$$\text{Sally working} \quad = 2,500$$

$$\text{Sally not working} = \quad 500$$

The number of letters sent out for the above period was equal to 1,500. The manager has rated Sally at 110 percent of normal, compared with other office jobs, and allowances for such jobs are 9 percent. Determine (a) the normal time per letter and (b) the standard time per letter.

10. Refer to Prob. 9. For what initial estimate of the percentage idle time would Sally's manager arrive at 3,000 observations if he wanted a 90 percent confidence level and 10 percent precision in the estimate of p?

11. The assistant manager of the High View Towers office building has been studying floor-cleaning times T_c for different office complexes and has developed the following regression equation:

$$T_c = 10.50 + 3.40X \qquad \text{min}$$

where X = number of square meters (m^2) of floor space to be cleaned.
   (a) Determine the synthetic floor-cleaning time for the following companies in the eighteenth floor:
      (i) The International Finance Corp., $X = 964$ m^2
      (ii) Allied Aluminum Products, Ltd., $X = 732$ m^2
      (iii) Environmental Consultants Co., $X = 558$ m^2
   (b) Repeat for the entire building if all 18 floors have the same office-space area as the layout of the eighteenth.
   (c) Estimate the cost for (a) and (b) if the cleaning personnel are paid $5 per hour.
12. Refer to Prob. 11. The regression equation for the time to wax office floor space T_w has been estimated as

$$T_w = 12.60 + 5.30X \qquad \text{minutes}$$

where X = number of square meters to be waxed.
   (a) Repeat parts (a) and (b) with reference to waxing time.
   (b) Estimate the waxing costs for (a) and (b) if the work is done by the same personnel as office floor cleaning.
13. The John Brandock Co. specializes in small aircraft and has just received an order for 16 two-engine patrol planes for the Coast Guard of an African country cracking down on the smuggling of illegal arms. From similar experience Brandock Co. estimates that the learning rate on this type of aircraft is 90 percent and that the labor for the first plane will be 3000 h.
   (a) Set up a table showing the production time for successive units of the patrol plane and plot the learning curve on regular graph paper.
   (b) The contract provides for delivery of four planes at the end of each quarter, starting from the date of signing the agreement. Specify the labor requirements in hours per quarter.
   (c) If each person on the work force puts in twenty-one 8-h days per month, determine the work-force requirements per quarter for this contract.
   (d) How could the delivery schedule for each quarter of the coming year be rearranged to meet requirements with a fixed-size work force?
14. Refer to Prob. 13. Suppose the cost of materials per plane is $18,000 and overhead is assumed to be 50 percent of the labor cost. If wages in the labor contract provide for $9 per hour, determine the average cost per plane.
15. Refer to Prob. 13. Repeat parts (a) through (d) assuming an 80 percent learning rate.
16. Refer to Prob. 13. The foreign government is willing to accept a simplified model of the original aircraft design (less electronic gear), for which the first unit will require 2,000 labor hours. Determine:
   (a) The revised learning curve (for 90 percent learning rate)
   (b) The revised labor requirements for a uniform delivery schedule, i.e., four planes per quarter
   (c) The revised average cost per plane if the cost of materials now is $12,000 per unit and overhead is 50 percent of labor cost with wages at $9 per hour.

SELECTED REFERENCES

1. Adernathy, W. J., and P. L. Townsend: "Technology, Productivity and Process Change," *Harvard Business School, Division of Research, Working Paper* 73–30, June 1973.
2. Barnes, R. M.: *Motion and Time Study: Design and Measurement of Work*, 6th ed., Wiley, New York, 1968.
3. Chapanis, A.: *Man-Machine Engineering*, Wadsworth, Belmont, Calif., 1965.
4. Davis, L. E.: "Job Satisfaction Research: The Post-Industrial View," *Industrial Relations*, vol. 10, 1971, pp. 176–193; also in L. E. Davis and M. C. Taylor (eds.), *Design of Jobs*, Penguin, Middlesex, England, 1972.
5. Davis, L. E.: "The Coming Crisis for Production Management," *International Journal of Production Research*, vol. 9, 1971, pp. 65–82; also in L. E. Davis and M. C. Taylor (eds.), *Design of Jobs*, Penguin, Middlesex, England, 1972.
6. Davis, L. E., and R. R. Canter: "Job Design Research," *The Journal of Industrial Engineering*, vol. 12, no. 6, November-December 1956.
7. Davis, L. E., and A. B. Cherns (eds.): *Quality of Working Life: Cases*, vol. II, Free Press, Glencoe, Ill., 1975.
8. Davis, L. E., and J. C. Taylor (eds.): *Design of Jobs*, Penguin, Middlesex, England, 1972.
9. Davis, L. E., and J. C. Taylor: "Technology Effects on Job, Work and Organizational Structure: A Contingency View," chap. 12 in L. E. Davis and A. B. Cherns (eds.), *Quality of Working Life: Problems, Prospects, and State of the Art*, vol. I, Free Press, Glencoe, Ill., 1975.
10. Elliot, J. D.: "Increasing Office Productivity through Job Enlargement," *The Human Side of the Office Manager's Job*, American Management Association, Office Management Series 134, New York, 1953, pp. 5–15.
11. Every, F. E., and E. L. Trist: "Socio-Technical Systems," in C. W. Churchman and M. Verhulst (eds.), *Management Science, Models and Techniques*, Pergamon, London, 1960.
12. Fogel, L. J.: *Biotechnology: Concepts and Applications*, Prentice-Hall, Englewood Cliffs, N.J., 1963.
13. Francis, R. L., and J. A. White: *Facility Layout and Location: An Analytical Approach*, Prentice-Hall, Englewood Cliffs, N.J., 1974.
14. Krick, E. V.: *Methods Engineering*, Wiley, New York, 1962.
15. Marks, A. R. N.: "An Investigation of Modifications of Job Design in an Industrial Situation and Their Effects on Measures of Economic Productivity," unpublished Ph.D. dissertation, University of California, Berkeley, November 1954.
16. Maynard, H. B., G. J. Stegermerten, and J. L. Schwab: *Methods-Time Measurement*, McGraw-Hill, New York, 1948.
17. McCormick, E. J.: *Human Factors Engineering*, 3d ed., McGraw-Hill, New York, 1970.
18. Mundel, M. E.: *Motion and Time Study*, 3d ed., Prentice-Hall, Englewood Cliffs, N.J., 1960.
19. Nadler, G.: *Work Design*, rev. ed., Irwin, Homewood, Ill., 1970.
20. Niebel, B. W., and A. B. Draper: *Product Design and Process Engineering*, McGraw-Hill, New York, 1974.
21. Quick, J. H., J. H. Duncan, and J. A. Malcolm: *Work-Factor Time Standards*, McGraw-Hill, New York, 1962.
22. Scoville, J. G.: "A Theory of Jobs and Training," in *Industrial Relations, Design in Jobs*, Penguin, Middlesex, England, 1972.
23. Turner, A. N., and P. R. Lawrence: *Industrial Jobs and the Worker*, Harvard Business School, Boston, 1965.
24. Woodson, W. E.: *Human Engineering Guide for Equipment Designers*, 2d ed., University of California Press, Berkeley, 1966.

Chapter 9

HOW TO PRODUCE III: LAYOUT AND SAFETY

9-1 INTRODUCTION

In developing a layout for an operations system we seek the optimum allocation of space to the components of the production process. More specifically, we try to determine the best arrangement of facilities and equipment capable of satisfying anticipated demand (quantity, quality, and timing) at lowest cost. This is the step when all elements of a process must be integrated. Therefore, special care must be taken to create an environment conducive to high productivity and the satisfaction of social and psychological needs of people at work. The layout of a facility plays an important role in the formulation of groups of people and communication links with peers, superiors, and subordinates. In this sense it sets the framework for much of the human interaction at the workplace.

Some General Considerations

The study of the layout problem requires specific information about the product(s) or service(s) to be offered, the process to be used, and the expected level of demand. In addition, it requires knowledge of the constraints imposed by legal, technical, or other factors for new facilities. For existing systems the proposed layout must satisfy constraints from existing buildings, docks, and other physical structures that form part of the production process and the transportation network it is integrated with.

The layout problem presents a challenge to management because of the complex interactions of several key factors and the difficulty in assessing their impact on system performance. Although the methods available fall short of a comprehensive approach, they can provide good solutions to several layout subproblems. Therefore, rather than seeking an optimum solution to the general layout problem, we rely on experience, good judgment, and a few quantitative techniques to produce a satisfactory overall solution.

At times, difficulties encountered in the plant layout phase make it necessary to revise previous decisions on product and process design so that in an iterative fashion management can arrive at an "optimum" combination of decisions for all facets of the system-design problem.

Layout Objectives

In general, the plant-layout problem is approached with the following objectives:

1. The greatest possible simplification of the production process, accomplished by:
   a. Placing equipment in a position resulting in its maximum utilization
   b. Reducing congestion in the flow of materials or people through successive stages in the process
   c. Providing easy access for equipment maintenance and repair
2. The largest possible reduction in the processing time with the aid of:
   a. Efficient production lines for a smooth and rapid product flow
   b. Suitable means for fast and safe materials handling
3. The best utilization of space (floor space or three-dimensional)

4. The best utilization of human resources by providing a comfortable and safe working environment

Since a particular solution to the plant-layout problem is very costly and difficult to change, it is desirable to maintain adequate flexibility, so that the operations system can be adapted to new conditions. Changes in the level of demand, in the design of product(s) or services, and in technology often result in layout adjustments that can be achieved only with flexibility in the existing configuration.

9-2 DEPENDENCE OF LAYOUT ON PRODUCTION FLOW

When viewing a process as a value-adding transformation of inputs to outputs, the concept of production flow becomes essential to understanding such a transformation. From experience we often associate operations systems with the flow that occurs inside them. Thus, we have a flow of oil through a refinery, a flow of home appliances along an assembly line, a flow of paper forms in processing an insurance claim, etc. Such a flow may be continuous or intermittent. In certain cases, the item being produced does not move. Instead, we observe a flow of various production inputs (human resources, materials, equipment and others) to it.

In general, *a flow is a sequence of events in space and time*. The subject of flow may be *materials* in a factory, *energy* in a power plant, *information* in a decision process, or *people* in a service system such as a hospital. The appropriate layout in a given case is influenced by the type of flow associated with the transformation process of production. We distinguish the following three types of layout:

1. Product (or line) layout, generally used in flow shops
2. Process (or functional) layout, used in job shops
3. Fixed-position layout, used primarily for projects

In practice, most operations systems use a combination of the "pure" types. A

TABLE 9-1   Examples of operations systems using various layout combinations

Operations system	Component(s) using product layout	Component(s) using process layout	Component(s) using fixed position layout
University	Registration procedure Grade-report preparation	Classes for instruction Laboratory instruction	Selection of new research projects, new faculty, dean, etc.
Hospital	Supporting services for laundry, food, admission, etc.	Laboratory tests Preparation before surgery	Surgery Special intensive care
Automobile manufacturing	Assembly lines for specific models	Fabrication of needed parts	R&D for new models, for pollution and energy-saving devices, etc.

manufacturer of appliances may use a functional layout for the fabrication of parts, a product layout for the assembly of specific items (refrigerators, washers, etc.), and a fixed-position layout for the R&D of a new product. This idea is further illustrated by the examples in Table 9-1.

The selection of the most appropriate layout for a given production process is based on the following factors:

1. The level and variability in demand, as indicated by long-term forecasts
2. The degree of standardization and stability in the product design
3. The availability and reliability of suppliers of raw materials and parts

In the following sections we shall discuss the characteristics of each type of layout, the conditions under which it should be used, and its requirements in equipment for processing and materials handling.

9-3 PRODUCT (OR LINE) LAYOUT

In an era of mass production for most consumer goods, product layout is a common form for the arrangement of facilities and equipment. Since successive units of a product follow the same sequence of operations, as specified by the operations route sheet, equipment must also be arranged in the same sequence to provide for a smooth and fast flow.

Definition

A *product layout* is the arrangement of facilities and equipment in the same sequence as that of the operations needed to complete each unit of the product or service offered. Successive units follow the same path through the system.

Examples of product-layout applications are numerous in the manufacturing of home appliances, cars, TV sets, bottling, food packaging, etc. In the service sector, the opportunities for product layout are more limited, but we can find them in cafeterias, insurance claim processing, procedures for issuing passports and driver's licenses, and boarding and disembarkation phases in airplane travel, etc.

Conditions Favoring Product Layout

With regard to the factors affecting the selection of product layout, the most favorable conditions exist when:

1. *The product mix is limited to a few basic types.* Some minor variations may be possible, such as changing the size of bottles in a bottling line, but the range of variation is quite small. In rigid mass production, all units produced are identical (boxes of cereal, cans of food or oil, etc.).

2. *There is a stable product design for the items produced with a high degree of standardization of parts.* Since the equipment used in series tends to be quite specialized, variation in the product design may result in disruptive delays and costly setup arrangements. In flexible mass production combining a minimum number of standardized parts or components (engine size, accessories, etc.) makes it possible to achieve considerable product differentiation (auto industry, stereo, and appliance manufacturers).
3. *There is a high production volume with limited variability in demand.*

The heavy investment required for special-purpose equipment which can be used only when the product design is stable can be justified only when the demand is large. Otherwise, the high fixed costs absorbed by a small volume result in a prohibitive production cost per unit. This suggests a tendency for a product layout to be used in capital-intensive systems. However, it may also be appropriate for a labor-intensive system, e.g., that encountered in assembly line or air travel. The need to maintain a smooth and rapid flow through the system requires careful study of the arrangement of work stations in series to avoid excessive bottlenecks and make high productivity rates possible.

Advantages and Disadvantages of Product Layout

Whenever product layout satisfies the above conditions, a number of significant *advantages* are associated with its application.

1. Materials-handling times and costs can be reduced through the use of mechanized or automated devices (conveyors, chutes, etc.).
2. In-process inventory requirements are reduced due to the smooth and relatively fast movement of units through the various processing stages.
3. Space utilization is increased due to the elimination or reduction of the need for in-process storage requirements and for flexible materials-handling equipment (fork-lift trucks, carts, etc.), which require special access routes to work stations.
4. Planning, scheduling, and control of operations are simplified since these functions have largely been incorporated in the design of the production line. This significantly reduces the need for information processing and decision making.

All the above features of product layout contribute directly in decreasing the production cost per unit and thus strengthen the firm's competitive position in the market.

Along with the advantages mentioned, however, product layout has some important *disadvantages* that may limit its potential usefulness.

1. Lack of flexibility is a key problem when the need arises for adjustments in the line to accommodate desired changes in product characteristics. This often means costly and time-consuming setups or even replacement of expensive equipment.
2. Duplication of identical special-purpose equipment for different production lines often requires considerably higher investment than would be necessary if such equipment could be shared by similar products.

3. A breakdown of any one of the several machines on a production line usually forces idleness on the entire line, with costly delays, high maintenance costs, or both.
4. Highly simplified and repetitive tasks and a fast production pace create serious psychological problems with the work force, expressed in the form of low morale and high absenteeism and worker turnover rates.

Again, all the above tend to limit the effectiveness of such an arrangement and contribute to higher operating costs than would be necessary with a more flexible arrangement.

Solution Methods for Product Layout

For a given product, the line-layout problem consists of assigning the required tasks, in the desired sequence, to a series of work stations. The specific form of the assignment depends on the desired output rate. For example, if we want the line output to be equal to 960 units/day, using one 8-h or 480-min shift, we must assign the required tasks so that each work station can produce 1 unit in $\frac{1}{2}$ min or less $[(480 \text{ min})/(960 \text{ units}) = 0.5 \text{ min/unit}]$. Our objective here would be to have all stations work at the same rate; i.e., we seek an assignment of tasks that results in a balanced production line. If the cycle time for any station is less than the maximum allowed to achieve the desired output rate, we say that the line is *out of balance*. This means less than optimum utilization of human resources and equipment.

The line-balancing problem occurs both in the system-design phase and in the scheduling of actual operations. This is due to the dependence of a particular product layout on the desired output rate, which, as we shall see in Chap. 12, may have to be changed in order to satisfy demand at minimum cost. Line balancing is discussed in Refs. 1 and 7.

9-4 PROCESS (OR FUNCTIONAL) LAYOUT

Whenever facilities and equipment must be shared by various products, depending on the unique requirements of different orders, we employ a process, or functional, layout.

Definition

A *process layout* is the arrangement of facilities and equipment in groups according to the function performed. Different orders follow different paths through the system, depending on their special processing requirements.

Examples of process layout can be found in both the manufacturing and service sector. Hospitals, universities, research organizations, insurance companies, police departments, and banks are organized so that their resources are grouped according to the different functions performed. Similarly, machine shops for the fabrication of parts, foundries, repair shops, and other product-oriented firms are set up so that their equipment and skilled personnel are grouped according to their specialization (mechanics, electricians, etc.).

Conditions Favoring Process Layout

The selection of a process or functional layout is appropriate under the following conditions:

1. *When there is a need for flexibility to handle a large variety of products or services.* The variety may be due to changes in shape, size, materials used, and processing requirements. In a sense, the product mix here is almost infinite. Since this condition considerably reduces the opportunity for the effective utilization of specialized equipment, process layouts make extensive use of general-purpose machines which call for a highly skilled work force.
2. *When there is little or no standardization of components or parts.* Unlike flexible mass production, in which different combinations of parts can be used to create a large variety of similar products without changes in the order of processing, in process layout the lack of standardization results in highly variable routing arrangements.
3. *When volume for each order is low, even though the overall volume handled by the firm may be quite large.* This condition reduces the attractiveness of special-purpose equipment even further since in the absence of high production volume its use becomes extremely uneconomical.

Advantages and Disadvantages of Process Layout

When properly used, process layout can result in several *advantages* which strengthen a firm's competitive position and ability to adjust to a dynamic environment:

1. High utilization rates for human resources and equipment, since disruptions due to breakdowns or lack of supplies tend to be localized and easily bypassed.
2. Well-motivated work force due to the relative independence from an unpaced work flow, pride in the application of considerable skill and experience, and considerable freedom for satisfying personal needs at work beyond the earning of wages.
3. Lower investment in equipment due to the flexibility and interchangeability of general-purpose machines.

On the negative side process layout is characterized by certain *disadvantages:*

1. High production cost per unit due to the need for special setups and processing requirements with each order
2. Large in-process inventories
3. Relatively long processing times

4. Need for flexible materials-handling equipment (fork-lift trucks, cranes, etc.) to handle numerous product types, shapes, and sizes with increased space requirements for travel routes and access to work stations
5. Complex requirements for scheduling and control since each order must be handled individually.

Solution Methods for a Process Layout

The advantage of flexibility in routing different orders through functionally grouped work centers is gained at the price of extreme complexity in the process-layout problem. In the absence of any constraints on the relative position of different departments, the number of possible solutions for the process layout increases rapidly with the number of departments:

Number of work centers k	1	2	3	4	5	6	7	8	$\cdots$	n
Number of possible layouts	1	2	6	24	120	720	5,040	40,320	$\cdots$	$n!$

For many actual systems we may have to deal with a large number of departments, say 20, 50, or even 100. It is obvious that the task of identifying, let alone evaluating, the huge number of possible layout solutions presents a great challenge to management, even with the assistance of large computers. After eliminating most of these solutions due to constraints imposed by technology, existing buildings, safety rules, etc., we are still left with an exceedingly large number of alternatives. Thus, the best we can do is to determine satisfactory or good solutions rather than some elusive optimum.

Since different layouts result in different patterns of movement (processing costs are assumed to remain the same), a widely used criterion for evaluating alternative solutions is some indicator related to the amount of materials handling for each layout. Such an indicator may take the following form:

1. Total distance traveled between departments per day
2. Total physical flow, in volume, weight, or other units between departments per day
3. Total materials-handling cost per day

The first two cover only physical dimensions of the materials-handling characteristics of a layout, while the third incorporates the transportation costs as well. Naturally, we seek a layout that satisfies production-volume requirements and other constraints at minimum cost.

The methods available for solving the process-layout problem range from simple charts, similar to mileage charts often included in maps, to quite sophisticated computerized procedures. The choice is a matter of benefit-cost analysis, i.e., matching the cost of using a method to the savings potential from its application. Representative methods are described briefly below in order of increasing sophistication and cost.

Distance, Trip-Frequency, and Load Charts

Using a matrix format, we can list the various departments in rows and columns to represent the origin and destination of possible movements within the system. An entry in a cell may specify the distance, the number of trips, or the load moved between the corresponding departments of origin and destination on a daily or weekly basis. This is illustrated in Table 9-2, where we have combined data on loads and distances (shown in circles) between six departments. Sometimes it is preferable to use materials-handling costs rather than distances for cell entries. Data for these charts are developed from route sheets, which indicate sequences, and master schedules, which indicate production rates and parts requirements.

TABLE 9-2   An example of a load and distance chart† (distances circled)

	1 Receiving and shipping	2 Lathes	3 Drills	4 Grinders	5 Assembly	6 Packaging
1 Receiving and shipping		⑳ 20	㉚ 10	㊵ 5		
2 Lathes			⑩ 40	⑩ 40	⑩ 50	
3 Drills		⑩ 30		⑮ 40	⑩ 50	
4 Grinders					⑳ 40	
5 Assembly						⑩ 60
6 Packaging	⑳ 60					

† Distances between the same departments may vary with routing to reflect variation in movement.

We can gain a better understanding of the flow patterns specified in a distance-load chart by drawing a flow graph, in which the nodes represent work centers and the numbers on the arcs represent the volume of work flow. The latter is measured by the product of loads times distance for each pair of nodes corresponding to a matrix cell. For our example this is shown in Fig. 9-1.

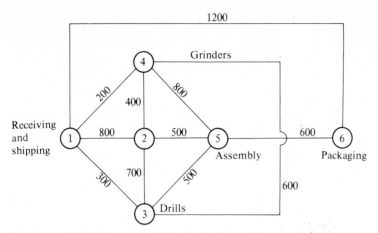

Fig. 9-1 Flow graph displaying load movements between various departments in a process layout.

Both these forms of conveying information about movement patterns can be used for conveniently summarizing large masses of data. Subsequently, different layouts can be examined by trial and error, so that from the sample generated one can select a layout that satisfies various constraints with a minimum amount of materials-handling volume or cost.

The general idea is to bring departments with a high volume of traffic between them closer together, but since a seemingly desirable adjustment initiates a chain reaction of other changes, the net result may be a more costly layout than the previous one.

Systematic Layout Planning

Sometimes qualitative factors about the relative position of departments may be more dominant than any data available on materials-handling distances, loads, or cost. An effective technique for developing a process layout under such conditions is known as SLP (systematic layout planning).

SLP makes use of a *priority code* for the need to place two departments closely and a *justification code* specifying the reason for the desired proximity. Priorities are indicated by letters and reasons for them by numbers. Whereas the priority code is fixed, the justification code may vary depending on the particular application. For example, in a machine shop the reasons for closeness may derive from the need to share skills or equipment, while for a hospital or a bank it may be the need for ease of communication or access to records. Both codes are shown in Table 9-3.

A facilities-relationship chart is a matrix similar to the load chart discussed previously, but instead of distances or loads each cell has an entry that specifies the qualitative factors of the layout problem, as expressed by a priority rating placed at the top half of the cell and a justification rating at the bottom half. This chart is illustrated for a small hospital with six functional areas in Table 9-4. Notice the need to have the administration office away from the intensive and regular care

TABLE 9-3   Information needed for developing a facilities-relationship chart

	Priority code		Justification code	
Symbol	Need for closeness	Graphical representation	Symbol	Reason
A	Absolutely necessary	≡≡≡≡	1	Type of work
E	Especially important	≡≡≡	2	Ease of supervision
I	Important	═══	3	Use of common skills
O	Ordinary closeness OK	──	4	Use of common equipment
U	Unimportant		5	Need for easy access
X	Undesirable	⋁⋀⋁⋀⋁⋀	6	Need for easy communication

units for patients (X), and the desirability of having the laboratory near the operating room (A).

On the basis of the facilities-relationship chart, it is now possible to develop first a graph showing the recommended spatial relationships (Fig. 9-2*a*) and an initial layout ignoring at first any constraints due to space and size of existing site

TABLE 9-4   Facilities-relationship chart using priority and justification codes

From functional area	To					Space requirements, m²
	2	3	4	5	6	
1. Administrative offices (admission, etc.)	I / 5, 6	O /	U /	X /	X /	200
2. Doctor's office		I / 6	U / 5	I / 5, 6	I / 5, 6	200
3. Laboratory (x-ray, etc.)			A / 1, 5, 6	O / 6	U / 6	100
4. Operating room				E / 1, 5, 6	O / 6	100
5. Intensive-care unit					O / 1	200
6. Regular-care rooms						400

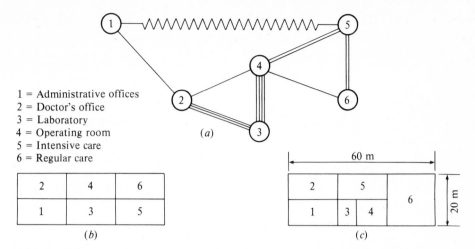

1 = Administrative offices
2 = Doctor's office
3 = Laboratory
4 = Operating room
5 = Intensive care
6 = Regular care

Fig. 9-2 Successive stages in developing a process layout for a small hospital using SLP: (*a*) graph showing relationship of facilities, (*b*) initial layout, and (*c*) final layout.

or building (Fig. 9-2*b*). This is successively adjusted to conform to existing constraints, as shown in Fig. 9-2*c*.

Computerized Heuristic Methods

Whether relying on a load chart, which quantifies a given flow pattern, or on SLP, which highlights the more dominant qualitative factors, we are limited by the great simplification of the real layout problem and the lack of an efficient computational procedure for evaluating alternatives. Therefore, neither of the previously discussed methods is capable of handling the immense complexity due to the multiple flow patterns and the variety of constraints imposed by the size, shape, and configuration of buildings and transportation routes.

A significant step for coping with the complexity of the process-layout problem has been the development in recent years of four computerized methods that use heuristic, i.e., commonsense, rules for generating alternatives and then evaluating them. These methods are known by the names ALDEP, CORELAP, CRAFT, and PREP.

Computerized layout techniques are similar in that they all rely on some type of reasoning similar to the previous simple methods. However, they provide an improved formulation and solution approach by specifying more refined criteria of effectiveness and by handling a wide variety of constraints which can be adjusted to fit different building configurations. By relying on the power of computers they can generate and evaluate a much larger sample of layout patterns than would otherwise be possible.

The techniques differ in the measure of effectiveness used, in the input information requirements, in the form of the selected layout, and the size of problem each can handle. Therefore, the selection of the most suitable one depends on the particular layout problem to be solved. The specific characteristics of each computerized method are discussed alphabetically below.

A. ALDEP (Automated Layout DEsign Program).[1]
1. *Measure of effectiveness.* Maximization of an overall preference score derived from a preference scale for department relationships similar to that used in systematic layout planning (SLP).
2. *Information inputs.*
    a. A preference matrix specifying the need or desirability of relative department locations. A priority code similar to that for SLP is used with letters assigned numerical weights in order of preference (A = 4, B = 3, etc.).
    b. A list of departments to be included in the layout each specified by number and size.
    c. A description of the building for the layout in terms of dimensions and special features such as elevators, aisles, etc.
3. *Program capacity.* A maximum of 63 departments can be arranged in a layout for a building with a maximum of three floors.
4. *Program operation.* Starting with a department selected at random a complete layout is developed by examining preference relationships with other departments. Several random layouts may be generated and evaluated to select the one with the maximum overall preference score. Alternatively, the program may generate only one random layout, which is then improved upon by successive exchanges of two departments at a time. This method is especially well suited to revisions of existing layouts. The program can be used in an interactive mode by a layout planner who may adjust the layout as it evolves.
5. *Output format.* Each layout pattern is plotted to include departments, aisles, and its respective preference score. However, the computer printouts require manual adjustment.
B. CORELAP (COmputerized RElationship LAyout Planning) (see Ref. 6).
1. *Measure of effectiveness.* Maximization of an overall closeness rating similar to that used in ALDEP.
2. *Information inputs.* Similar to those for ALDEP, except that the building description is given by a maximum length-to-width ratio and the departments can be formed by combining area modules of specified size.
3. *Program capacity.* A maximum of 70 departments allowing for over 1,000 interdepartmental relationships and flexibility in building shapes.
4. *Program operation.* Starting with a department at random, a complete layout is developed by the use of the preference matrix for selecting the next department to be added and its relative location. The procedure is repeated to generate a predetermined number of complete random layouts and their overall closeness rating, so that the one with the maximum rating can be identified and printed out.
5. *Output format.* The computer printout is in the form of a numerical layout

---

[1] See M. Jarrold and Wayne O. Evans, "Automated Layout Design Program," *Journal of Industrial Engineering*, vol. 18, no. 12 pp. 690–695, December 1967.

matrix, which must be subsequently smoothed out by hand to produce an acceptable solution.

C. CRAFT (Computerized Relative Allocation of Facilities Techniques) (see Ref. 2).

1. *Measure of effectiveness.* Minimization of total materials handling cost. This is estimated by measuring distances between the department centroids and costs proportional to distances.

2. *Information inputs.*

   a. An initial feasible layout developed by the user.

   b. A load matrix showing traffic volume between departments.

   c. A materials-handling cost matrix.

3. *Program operation.* Starting with a feasible initial layout, the program seeks to reduce costs by exchanging the relative position of *three* departments at a time. This exchange is repeated until the savings achieved are negligible. The final solution thus depends greatly on the quality of the initial layout provided by the user.

4. *Program capacity.* A maximum of 40 departments restricted to a single-story building.

5. *Output format.* The computer printout specifies a block layout that conforms to initial building description and its respective materials-handling cost. Since the final solution is a heuristic one, its cost is not guaranteed to be the minimum possible for the specific layout problem.

In terms of computational efficiency, the relative performance of the above procedures on an IBM 7090 computer was .62 min for 22 departments using CRAFT, 2.46 min for 27 departments using a digital plotter with CORELAP, and 1.03 min per layout using 11 departments with ALDEP. The reader must keep in mind, however, the fact that these methods differ significantly with respect to assumptions, performance criteria, and information inputs needed by the user.

9-5 FIXED-POSITION LAYOUT

Sometimes the nature of the product or service needed is such that instead of a product flow through the resource centers it is technologically and/or economically preferable to have the required resources flow to the item being worked on. This situation corresponds to what was defined in Chap. 7 as a project. The desired arrangement for facilities and equipment in this case is known as a fixed-position layout.

Definition

A *fixed-position layout* is the arrangement of facilities and equipment so that resources needed, in the form of workers, equipment, materials, etc., flow to the item being produced or serviced.

TABLE 9-5 Summary of characteristics for "pure" layout types

Characteristic	Product layout	Process layout	Fixed-position layout
Product or service design	Limited in number and stable over time	Unlimited in number and variable over time	One of a kind
Production flow path	Successive units follow same path with same sequence of required operations	Different orders follow different paths to comply with variable processing requirements	Unit worked on usually remains stationary and resources flow to it as needed
Human skills	Semiskilled workforce suitable for repetitive routine tasks; limited work content and uncontrolled work pace	Skilled employees assigned jobs with considerable work content, responsible for work pace and results	Skilled personnel with well-defined task assignments
Equipment	Special-purpose machines restricted to few specialized operations suited for high output rates	General-purpose machines for variety of similar operations restricted to low output rates	Mostly general-purpose equipment needed to allow versatile employment
Materials handling	Fixed materials-handling loads and paths with considerable mechanization (conveyors, chutes, etc.)	Variable materials-handling loads and paths with need for more space (carts, fork-lift trucks, etc.)	General-purpose equipment needed to fit project or job-site requirements

Resource utilization	Limited due to need for duplication and vulnerability to break-downs for several components	High, due to equipment versatility and relative independence of work centers	Limited, due to the tight requirements for scheduling and coordination
Inventory requirements	Limited due to high turnover of raw materials and work in process	Considerable, due to the low turnover of materials and semifinished components	Low, materials and supplies ordered as needed to meet schedule requirements
Cost relationships	High fixed costs and low variable costs due to special-purpose production and materials-handling equipment	Low to medium fixed costs and high variable costs, due to specialized skills, high inventories, and slow throughput rates	Low fixed and high variable costs, due to specialized skills and materials needed
Solution procedures	Line balancing for paced or unpaced production with heuristic methods	Trial and error with distance or load charts and SLP; heuristic computerized methods; ADEL, CORELAP, CRAFT	Trial-and-error methods

Examples of this type occur in heavy construction (dams, bridges, skyscrapers), aircraft and ship building, critical surgical operations, political conventions, musical concerts, forest-fire fighting, and others.

Conditions Favoring Fixed-Position Layout

The selection of a fixed-position layout is often dictated by the complexity, the size, or some other unique feature of the task performed. The size and weight of a ship or jumbo jet do not allow any other alternatives. Similarly, the maintenance of a steel mill, a power plant, or a building dictate that resources be moved where the work must be performed.

The crucial aspect in the application of this type of layout is the requirement for effective scheduling, coordination, and control of the productive activities involved and the resources used in the process. The appropriate project-scheduling techniques are discussed in Chap. 15.

Table 9-5 provides a summary of the key characteristics of each layout type and the solution methods employed to develop a plan for a specific application.

9-6 SAFETY CONSIDERATIONS AND OSHA

General

Concern for safety is essential inside and outside an operations system. Safety affects not only the workers who make a product but also consumers who use it. As such, safety is pervasive in several phases of managing an organization, from the birth of a product as an idea to its full development, production, packaging, shipping, use, and eventual disposal. During the plant-layout phase we have a comprehensive view of safety problems that are examined more closely as they relate to each design aspect.

Decisions about safety are baffling, not only because of the multitude of physical factors and their interaction that determine whether a product or process is safe but also because of the inherent conflict of satisfying high objectives for perfect safety with limited resources at our disposal. To reach some answers we usually accept the view that accidents are caused by some factors that are controllable, such as equipment and methods, and others that are mainly uncontrollable (weather, workers' moods, etc.). So we proceed to formulate safety-related decisions based primarily on acceptable levels of risk.

The Safety Problem

A token effort for safety usually results in accidents with a variety of measurable and intangible costs to both employer and employee. To the worker the cost is related to the mental and physical suffering from an injury, the loss of earnings, and (for major injuries) the inability to satisfy a wide range of human needs off and on

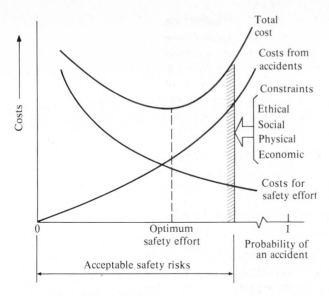

Fig. 9-3 A general relationship for safety and accident (tangible and intangible) costs.

work. To the employer accidents translate into tangible costs for medical, legal, and compensation expenses and intangible ones caused by lost productive capacity, increased training effort, equipment and facilities damage, and a bad reputation as an employment establishment.

On the other hand, unreasonably intensive efforts to increase safety contribute little in reducing the risk of accidents while depriving the organization of badly needed resources to pursue legitimate long-term objectives. We might call this the "Howard Hughes syndrome." The general nature of relationships we have described can be approximated by the curves in Fig. 9-3 where the term "costs" is used in a broad sense.

Safety Considerations for Different Operations-Management Decisions

The pervasiveness of safety considerations in operations management can be seen from Table 9-6.

Sources of Accidents and Safety Programs

Accidents are usually traced to hazardous working conditions, unsafe working habits, or a combination of both. An employer has considerable control over both these factors, and, as we shall see in the next section, the law places the major responsibility for safety on him rather than the worker. A safety program represents an organized attempt to solve the safety problem as stated previously. The role of

TABLE 9-6 Safety aspects in various operations-management decision areas

Decision area	Safety considerations
Product design	Safe materials and parts Safety in operation or use Safety during maintenance and repair Safe disposal when worn out
Process design and installation	Safety in processes and equipment by eliminating hazards (1) during construction and equipment installation (safe wiring, plumbing, etc.) and (2) during operation (mechanical hazards, noise, radiation, toxic substances, uncluttered working areas and aisles, etc.)
Work analysis	Safety in the design of man-machine systems (guarded power equipment, goggles for the eyes, earplugs for noise, etc., proper spacing of equipment controls, safe working methods)
Plant layout	Safety in overall working conditions relating to: Materials-handling equipment and storage facilities Lighting and heating of buildings, fire-protection devices Noise and pollution control
Maintenance	Safety when equipment failures occur and during equipment testing and repair

the safety program within a firm can be understood better with reference to Fig. 9-4.

A safety program cannot function well without adequate support by top management. However, its ultimate success rests with the first-line supervisors who can detect hazards and enforce safety rules on a day-to-day basis. Safety can be increased by improved process and equipment design, by improving working conditions (lighting, heating, ventilation, etc.), by training employees in using safe methods and helping to identify and remove new hazards, and by rewarding good employee safety records. Unless employees can be motivated to participate in reducing or removing hazardous conditions, the safety program becomes a mechanical routine that assumes significance only when people suffer serious injuries.

Occupational Safety and Health Act (OSHA)

Since the advent of the industrial revolution, impressive development in technology coupled with an increase in the size, scope, and complexity of business firms has

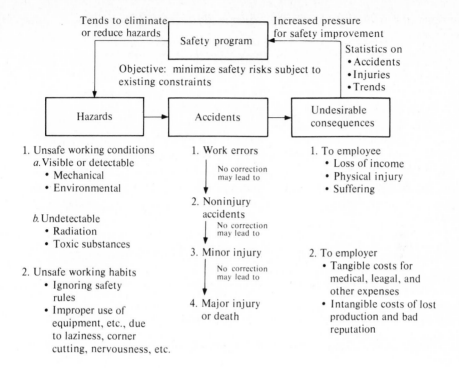

Fig. 9-4 The safety improvement cycle.

created problems that led to a series of important laws affecting management-labor relations. One of the most significant pieces of legislation of this type in recent years has been the Williams-Steiger Act of 1970, better known as the Occupational Safety and Health Act (OSHA). Despite the controversy that at times accompanies its implementation in specific cases, OSHA is destined to play a dominant influence in the shaping of future management-labor relations. The president of the Steel-workers Union, I. W. Abel, has called this act "a Magna Carta for the workers of America." Comparable are the ways it has impressed safety specialists.

Objectives and scope It is the intent of OSHA to ensure that working conditions are safe, insofar as possible, for every employee in the United States. The law covers every employer, in all 50 states and other United States territories, whose business affects commerce. It does not include public employees covered by state laws and working conditions, such as mining, whose safety is regulated by other federal occupational safety and health laws.

Implementation procedure The major responsibility for the administration and enforcement of OSHA is assigned to the Secretary of Labor. The implementation of the law involves:

1. Establishment of occupational safety and health standards
2. Inspections of business establishments to establish compliance

3. Citations for violating or failing to provide a safe and healthy working environment
4. Review procedures for cases contested by employers or employees

An important feature of this act is the right given to employees and their union to monitor the Secretary of Labor in the administration and enforcement of existing or needed standards for a safe and healthy working environment.

The law also provides for the establishment and supervision of programs that will teach employers and employees to recognize, avoid, and prevent unsafe conditions. This is accomplished with the assistance of the Secretary of Health, Education and Welfare, who is also required to conduct relevant research and develop criteria for what constitutes unhealthy conditions (toxic or harmful substances, safe exposure levels to radiation, noise, etc.), which are communicated to affected business firms.

Duties of employers and employees   OSHA assigns to those employers covered by the act a specific and a general duty. It is the employer's *specific duty* to comply with occupational safety and health standards covered by the act. The *general duty*, which is equally significant, extends the employer's responsibility beyond compliance. It requires that the place of employment be free from recognized hazards that may cause serious injury or death to employees. The general duty thus aims at keeping the employer vigilant for hazardous conditions that may not be covered by existing standards but clearly affect the safety and health of those working in his establishment.

An employee has the duty to comply with OSHA standards, rules, and regulations as they apply to the conduct of his work. However, there are no penalties for the employee who fails to comply, as there are for the employer. This lack of symmetry places the major responsibility for safety on the employer in terms of his own compliance and persuasion of employees to do likewise.

Rights of employees and employers   To administer the law for improving working conditions OSHA empowers both employees and employers with certain rights that are destined to influence management-labor relationships in a number of ways.

Accordingly, the employees in a given establishment have the right, under OSHA, to call for inspections of suspected violations, to accompany the compliance officers during the inspection of the premises, to be informed in detail of all hazards they are exposed to on their jobs, and of the steps taken by their employer to comply.

To permit a more realistic and fair implementation of the law, OSHA also gives an employer the right to apply for temporary or permanent variance from standards, the right to know the reason for an inspection, the right to request proper identification from compliance inspectors and accompany them in their walk-around inspection, and the right to file notice and contest any citation and/or penalty imposed by the OSHA area director for alleged violations.

Types of OSHA standards for safety and health   The mandatory safety and health standards to be observed by employers covered by the act fall into three categories, interim, permanent, and emergency temporary standards.

Interim standards These represent requirements developed by existing federal standards and by national consensus standards. The latter are issued by the American National Standards Institute (ANSI) and represent a broad consensus of industry, labor, professional organizations, and insurance companies. Existing federal standards are those established before the enactment of OSHA by other agencies or acts of Congress. Interim standards were required by the Secretary of Labor within 2 years from the date OSHA was enacted and were viewed as stopgap measures.

Permanent standards These revoke or modify the interim standards and are based on information from the Secretary's own investigation and inspections, recommendations from ad hoc committees set up for this purpose, and information submitted to the secretary in writing by various public or private sources. The promulgation, modification, or revoking of a permanent standard follows a procedure that allows interested parties to submit within 30 days written comment or file objections and request public hearings.

Emergency temporary standards When the Secretary of Labor determines that employees in certain occupations are exposed to grave danger from new or existing hazards (toxic or harmful substances) and an emergency standard is needed to protect them from these sources, the Secretary is required to issue emergency temporary standards. They take effect immediately while the procedure for normal standard development is initiated to produce a permanent standard within 6 months.

    Variances from standards may be allowed to an employer upon application to the Assistant Secretary of Labor for OSHA. Such variances may be temporary or permanent. At times they are justified for national defense purposes. Granting a variance, however, cannot be justified by lack of economic ability to comply. It must be based on the lack of needed resources (personnel, equipment, or materials). If an employer feels adversely affected by a new standard, he may file a petition for a judicial review with a U.S. Court of Appeals within 60 days after its promulgation.

Compliance inspections To enforce the provisions of the act, the Secretary of Labor is authorized to have the workplace of any employer covered by the act inspected for compliance by specially trained and experienced men and women. These are known as compliance safety and health officers and industrial hygienists.

    Compliance inspections are performed unexpectedly. They include an inspection of relevant safety and health records kept by the employer, a walk-around tour of the establishment, in which the compliance officer is accompanied by an employer representative and an employee representative for unionized workers, and a closing conference with the employer to discuss probable violations. During the walk-around tour the OSHA officer takes notes of working conditions and discusses them with the representatives. He is allowed to take photographs and samples as evidence of unsafe conditions, with an obligation to respect the privacy of trade secrets and security arrangements. After the closing conference with the employer the officer prepares a report for the OSHA area director for further action when necessary.

The purpose of such an inspection is twofold: (1) the OSHA officer is interested in whether or not the employer inspected is in compliance with standards already specified by the act, (2) he is concerned with how well the employer satisfies the general-duty clause of the act. The latter requires each employer to provide safe and healthy working conditions with respect to recognized hazards for which there are no standards yet. This is a controversial point that has resulted in several disputes. In general, a *recognized hazard* is a condition that causes serious injury or illness and can be detected by the senses, is common knowledge in the industry in which it occurs, and can be determined by accepted tests if not detectable by the senses.

The compliance inspector in his report may include violations of different degrees of seriousness: The following types are in decreasing order of importance:

Imminent danger. A condition almost certain to cause serious injury or death if not removed immediately

Repeated violation. Failure to comply with previously reported violations of standards, or the general-duty clause

Willful violation. The intentional and knowing, rather than inadvertent, violation of OSHA provisions or the failure to exercise reasonable effort to remove known hazardous conditions

Serious violation. The existence of working conditions with a high probability of causing death or serious injury of which the employer knew or should have known

Nonserious violation. A condition affecting directly worker safety and health but not likely to cause serious injury or death (several such conditions may combine to produce a serious violation)

De minimis violation. A condition with no direct impact on safety or health.

The types of violations invoked under the general-duty clause usually range from limited to alleged serious violations and to nonserious violations that are willful and/or repeated.

OSHA citations and penalties   Based on the report prepared by a compliance officer, after inspection of an employer's establishment, a citation must be issued promptly (no later than 6 months) reflecting the nature of the violation observed. The employer upon receipt must post the citation, along with any notice of intent to contest it, until the violation has been abated or for three working days, whichever is later. OSHA provides for follow-up inspections to ensure that cited violations have been corrected.

Following an inspection, the OSHA area director must notify the employer of the type of penalty proposed if any. *Civil penalties* must be imposed for any serious violation of OSHA requirements, the amount not to exceed $1,000 for each violation including failure to post a citation. Any willful violation of any standard which results in the death of an employee requires the assessment of *criminal penalties* including a fine and/or imprisonment. For a more detailed description of civil and criminal penalties see Ref. 5.

Employer's review rights under OSHA   Upon notification of a citation and/or penalty for violations reported after a compliance inspection, the employer can either request an informal hearing with the OSHA area director or legally contest the citation within 15 working days. Otherwise, the citation becomes a final order which cannot be appealed. For notices received on time, the review commission assigns the case to an administrative law judge. If the judge's decision is unfavorable to the employer, he may appeal first to the review commission itself and if needed after that to the U.S. Circuit Court of Appeals.

Status of OSHA implementation   As noted previously, the enactment and implementation of OSHA since 1970 has resulted in major readjustments for the management of over 4 million firms and 60 million employees. The considerable amount of controversy surrounding the new law from management's point of view centers on three main issues.[1] (1) There are complaints about the standards which business firms at times consider arbitrary and confusing. In the absence of anything comparable in its scope before OSHA, this may be attributed to the somewhat rapid pace necessary to cover so many kinds of business activity. (2) There are allegations that the cost for safety improvements to achieve compliance ($3.56 billion estimated for 1976) may adversely affect a firm's competitive position. However, on this point others argue the savings due to OSHA from reductions in injuries and lost time make the improvements pay for themselves. (3) By far the most complex issue concerning OSHA is the changing pattern of management-labor interactions. Here the law strengthens labor's position in safety matters, as other laws did on collective bargaining. The limited ability of collective bargaining to handle safety issues has prompted labor unions to establish safety departments to exercise employees' rights as provided by the act, much in the same way they established time-study departments to negotiate wages.

Over the long run, the major effects of OSHA are likely to be productive in creating a safer and healthier working environment. At present, the penalties for noncompliance are relatively low and the probability of inspection rather limited due to the small number of inspectors available. Both management and employees in the transition period can work constructively to make the necessary adjustments for safe and healthy conditions in most human productive activities.

9-7   SUMMARY

In the system-design phase of plant layout, management attempts to determine the best arrangement of facilities, work stations, and equipment. The result is a flow pattern for resources (materials, energy, information, etc.) through transformation

[1] Fred K. Foulkes, "Learning to Live with OSHA," *Harvard Business Review*, November–December 1973, pp. 58–64.

centers, so that expected demand in products and services can be met at minimum cost. The plant-layout problem must be solved under a multitude of technical, social, economic, and legal constraints. The number of possible solutions is usually extremely large, so that the final solution is a result of economic analysis seasoned by experience and subjective judgment.

The dominant influence in selecting the best layout is the type of flow dictated by the process used. This in turn is based on output volume, product design, and its stability. The major layout types are three: (1) product (line) layout for a flow-shop process, (2) process (functional) layout for a job shop, i.e., variable product-design specifications which require different processing sequences, and (3) fixed-position layout, in which the item worked on remains stationary and needed resources are taken to it. In practice, most operations systems rely on a combination of the "pure" types, each of which has special advantages and limitations with regard to processing times and costs, flexibility, resource utilization, and effects on worker productivity, motivation, and morale.

In all aspects of system design, but especially in plant layout, management is concerned with safety. Inside the system, safety concerns the employee and employer because accidents due to hazardous conditions generate high tangible and intangible costs to both. Outside the system, safety affects the use, maintenance, and disposal of a firm's products with potential consequences to the consumer and the firm's reputation.

The Occupational Safety and Health Act (OSHA) is the most recent and influential legal framework affecting safety within a private business. It places most of the responsibility for safe working conditions on the employer. According to OSHA provisions, an employer is expected not only to comply with existing safety standards (specific duty) but also to be vigilant for hazardous conditions not covered by the act (general duty). The procedures employed to enforce the act have had a controversial impact on managers, both in terms of required investments for increased safety and in terms of the changing management-labor relationships.

REVIEW QUESTIONS

1. What are some common restrictions in the design of a facility layout?
2. Discuss some of the practical objectives pursued in layout studies.
3. What kinds of flow occur in a productive system? Which are the most important in the development of layout?
4. Which are the basic layout types, and what flow pattern is each type associated with?
5. Discuss what conditions favor each of the following layout types:
   (a) Process layout
   (b) Product layout
   (c) Fixed-position layout
6. State the layout format you would recommend and why, for:
   (a) A chemistry lab
   (b) A university cafeteria
   (c) An airline maintenance shop at an international airport

(*d*) The processing of mail at the post office

(*e*) A department store

7. What kinds of materials-handling equipment are appropriate for each layout format?
8. Which are the most important advantages and disadvantages of (*a*) product layout and (*b*) process layout?
9. Describe the line-balancing problem and the layout type it is associated with.
10. Why is the problem of designing a process layout more complex than for product layout?
11. Describe the method of systematic layout planning (SLP).
12. Discuss the information inputs and outputs, the assumptions, and the measure of effectiveness for the following computerized layout techniques: (*a*) ALDEP, (*b*) CORELAP, and (*c*) CRAFT.
13. Why are the computerized layout techniques called heuristic?
14. Explain why safety problems are extremely complex to solve objectively.
15. Which types of costs do we attempt to balance when we approach a safety problem?
16. Discuss some of the safety problems of interest in decisions related to:
    (*a*) Product design
    (*b*) Process design
    (*c*) Work design
    (*d*) Plant layout
17. Define the various categories of accidents in order of increasing seriousness of their consequences.
18. What kinds of costs result from accidents for (*a*) the worker and (*b*) the employer?
19. Discuss the significance of OSHA.
20. Define clearly the meaning of the following OSHA terms:
    (*a*) An employer's specific duty to comply with OSHA
    (*b*) An employer's general duty to comply with OSHA
21. Describe briefly the following types of OSHA standards:
    (*a*) Interim standards
    (*b*) Permanent standards
    (*c*) Emergency temporary standards
22. What types of violations may a compliance inspector include in his report?
23. Which kinds of penalties may be imposed on an employer due to confirmed OSHA violations?

PROBLEMS

1. The Safe Appliance Co. operates an assembly line for electric refrigerators with eight stations. The line has been set up for a daily output of 240 for one 8-h shift.
   (*a*) What is the allowed maximum cycle time per work station for this assembly line?
   (*b*) What is the efficiency of the third work station responsible for a set of tasks requiring 1.5 min?
   (*c*) What will be the effect on the allowed maximum cycle time per work station if the output rate is increased to 360 units/day?
2. Refer to Prob. 1. Work parts (*a*), (*b*), and (*c*) if the company operates two 8-h shifts a day.
3. The Safe Appliance Co. also operates an assembly line for electric toasters set up for 10 tasks A to L. They must be performed in alphabetical order, and they are grouped in five work stations, shown below, manned by one worker each.

Work station	Assembly tasks	Task times, min
1	A	3.5
2	B, C	1.2, 2.1
3	D, E, F	0.9, 1.8, 1.3
4	G, H, I	1.7, 1.4, 0.6
5	J, K, L	1.1, 2.0, 0.7

(*a*) Which work station is the bottleneck in the assembly line?

(*b*) What is the minimum cycle time, i.e., the shortest possible time to complete one toaster?

(*c*) What is the daily output rate of this assembly line if the plant operates one 8-h shift daily?

(*d*) What is the percentage utilization of the operator at each work station?

(*e*) If the efficiency of a production line is equal to the ratio of productive versus available time per day, calculate the efficiency of the assembly line for toasters.

4. A laboratory for testing materials consists of five sections in a row, each requiring the same area in square feet.

(*a*) How many alternative layouts are possible in the absence of any relationship constraints?

(*b*) How many alternative layouts are possible if two of the testing sections must be arranged adjacent to each other?

5. The figure shows the present layout and load movements for the six work centers of a

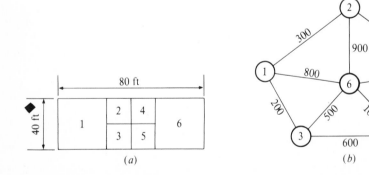

Prob. 5 (*a*) **Present machine-shop layout and** (*b*) **flow graph, showing intercenter load movements.**

machine shop. Suggest how the current layout can be revised to minimize materials-handling.

6. Ingrid Johanson, the owner and manager of Lobster Grill, has requested her architect to develop a layout for the kitchen of the new building for the restaurant. The plans provide for a kitchen with 25 by 40 ft ($= 1{,}000$ ft^2), and Ingrid and her architect have arrived at the sections indicated in the following relationship chart:

Section	2	3	4	5	6	7	Area requirement, ft^2
1. Fish and seafood	A	E	I	O	X	E	300
2. Sauces		I	I	O	I	E	50
3. Soups			E	O	O	E	150
4. Vegetables				A	O	I	100
5. Salads					O	I	100
6. Desserts						I	100
7. Clean-up							200
							1,000

(a) Using systematic layout planning, develop a relationship diagram that satisfies the above requirements.

(b) Prepare a layout based on (a) that would fit the 25 by 40-ft area allocated to the restaurant kitchen.

7. Consider the main floor of a typical open-stock library. In addition to any bookshelves or magazine racks, we normally find:

1. A desk for the librarian on duty
2. A table with references for books in print and dictionaries
3. A cabinet with a card-index catalog for books by author
4. A cabinet with a card-index catalog for books by title
5. A counter for checking books out, special services, and miscellaneous inquiries
6. A check counter for those leaving the library

(a) Prepare a diagram showing the desired relationships of these centers using systematic layout planning.

(b) Develop a layout plan for a rectangular 100 by 200-ft floor area with the main entrance at the center of one of the long sides.

8. The engineering consulting firm of Dick and Harry Associates is preparing to move to a new 6,000-ft^2 one-story building in the suburb of New Chelsea. The firm consists of three technical departments (civil, electrical, and mechanical engineering), an administrative office, business office, a duplicating center, and a computer center. The work flow within departments is measured by the number of project files moving from one section to another per month. Specified in the chart below are the interdepartmental work flows and the closeness ratings using SLP notation.

(a) Prepare a flow graph which shows work flows between departments.

(b) Draw a diagram for a desired layout based on the desired relationships using SLP.

(c) Prepare a layout from (b) to fit an area of 60 by 100 ft ($= 6000$ ft^2) for the new one-story building.

Department	2	3	4	5	6	7	Area requirement, ft^2
1. Administrative office	E / 40	E / 36	E / 32	I / 180	I / 4	A / 245	1,000
2. Civil engineer		E / 24	E / 38	I / 25	O / 15	I / 180	1,500
3. Electrical engineer			A / 36	I / 21	O / 12	I / 140	1,500
4. Mechanical engineer				E / 26	E / 27	I / 152	1,000
5. Business office					O / 42	E / 275	500
6. Computer center						O / 81	200
7. Duplicating							300

SELECTED REFERENCES

1. Buffa, E. S.: *Operations Management*, 3d ed., Wiley, New York, 1972.
2. Buffa, E. S., G. C. Armour, and T. E. Vollmann: "Allocating Facilities with CRAFT," *Harvard Business Review*, March–April 1964, pp. 136–158.
3. Buffa, E. S., and William H. Taubert: *Production Inventory Systems: Planning and Control*, rev. ed., Irwin, Homewood, Ill., 1972, pp. 303–366.
4. Francis, R. L., and J. A. White: *Facility Layout and Location: An Analytical Approach*, Prentice-Hall, Englewood Cliffs, N.J., 1974.
5. Grimaldi, V. John, and R. H. Simonds: *Safety Management*, 3d ed., Irwin, Homewood, Ill., 1975.
6. Lee, Robert S., and James M. Moore: "CORELAP: Computerized Relationship Layout Planning," *Journal of Industrial Engineering*, vol. 18, no. 3 pp. 195–200, March 1967.
7. Moore, James: *Plant Layout and Design*, Macmillan, New York, 1962.
8. Muther, Richard: *Practical Plant Layout*, McGraw-Hill, New York, 1955.

Chapter 10

WHERE TO PRODUCE: FACILITY LOCATION

10-1　INTRODUCTION

Our discussion of different aspects of a production system design has so far assumed as given the location of the physical structure, whether we deal with new facilities or the expansion of existing ones. The selection of location, however, is one of the most far-reaching top management decisions for the following reasons:

1. It involves the long-term investment of large amounts of capital under conditions of considerable uncertainty.
2. It determines a rather permanent framework of operating constraints (legal, labor, community, etc.) that may be difficult and costly to change.
3. It has significant consequences on the competitive position or viability of an organization by setting a minimum limit on the cost for production and distribution to desired markets. This is especially true for service systems that must be near the customers they serve, e.g., restaurants or movie theaters.

In addition, the final solution interacts strongly with other critical decisions considered in systems design such as facilities layout. It is therefore important to consider thoroughly all the economic, technological, social, and legal factors that will influence the choice of location.

10-2　THE LOCATION PROBLEM

Briefly, the location problem consists of selecting a site for new facilities that will minimize the production and distribution cost of products and/or services to potential customers. Such a problem may arise under different conditions which prompt management to consider alternative solutions. The final decision is usually based on the evaluation of both objective and subjective factors for each alternative site.

Reasons for Considering Location Problems

For a new firm selecting a location is an inevitable decision in the phase of system design. Here the options include the selection of a site for building new facilities or the rent or purchase of existing ones. For an existing organization, the motivation to consider the location problem may be attributed to economic, technological, social, or political factors.

The most important reasons for the need to change or expand to a new location are the following:

1. Significant changes in the level of demand
2. Significant changes in the geographical distribution of demand
3. Changes in the costs or quality requirements of critical production inputs (labor, raw materials, energy, or other)
4. Significant increases in the real-estate value of existing or adjacent sites or in their taxation
5. Need to change as a result of fire or flood or for reasons of prestige or improved public relations

Even though the selection of a new location represents a serious planning effort, for well-organized firms it is advisable to review location problems periodically, in the light of significant changes in environmental conditions.

Alternatives to New Location

Of the reasons listed above, the most common is an upward trend in the level of demand. Before undertaking a detailed study for selecting a new location, however, it is advisable to examine some alternatives for meeting the expected increase in demand, which include:

1. The increase of existing capacity by additional shifts or overtime, especially for capital-intensive systems
2. The use of seasonal inventories to reduce the need for maintaining capacity for peak demand
3. The use of subcontractors
4. The purchase of new equipment for the present location with a less expensive facilities expansion

For limited or temporary changes in demand, the above alternatives, usually considered in aggregate planning (see Chap. 12), represent more economical means of expanding capacity. Otherwise, the location problem is a very real one and a feasibility study is usually undertaken by a team of specialists or external consultants.

Significant Factors in Location Studies

As already suggested, the factors considered in location problems may relate to key production inputs, to the process technology, or to the environment.

Production inputs   The incentive to move or expand to a new location may derive from the need to secure a larger quantity or different quality inputs such as labor, raw materials, energy, or other. These considerations are related to the markets of such inputs.

Raw materials   For many firms, especially in manufacturing, a dominant factor in plant location is the need to be near the sources of raw materials. This is especially true when processing results in significant weight reduction, e.g., firms engaged in mining iron ore, copper, or marble and firms processing forest products. Proximity to the source of raw materials is also important for industries that process or package perishable items (dairy products, fresh fruit, or vegetables, etc.).

In general, industries using an *analytic process*, in which raw material is broken down in successive stages to produce different products, say a lumber mill, tend to locate near the source of such an input (see Fig. 10-1a). On the other hand, for a *synthetic process*, which combines a variety of materials, components, and parts in successive stages to assemble a finished product, there is a tendency to locate near the market (see Fig. 10-1b).

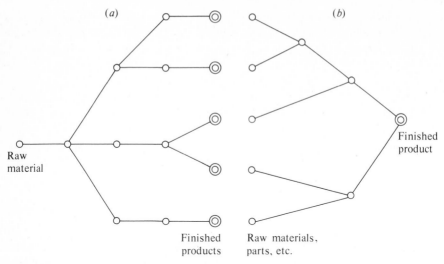

Fig. 10-1 Structure of (*a*) analytic and (*b*) synthetic processes.

Services in the private sector show a strong tendency to locate near the market of potential customers. This would be true of a bank, a restaurant, a theater, or an auto-repair service. For the public sector, however, the location of services is affected both by the geographical distribution of the need for a service (schools, hospitals, fire or police stations) and by budget limitations on the degree of desired decentralization (courts, internal revenue offices, etc.).

Human resources For many firms with unique or very large labor requirements, proximity to the appropriate labor market becomes a dominant factor in the selection of a location. Accordingly, labor-intensive organizations like large assembly-line factories or large insurance companies tend to locate in or near large metropolitan areas. Similarly, technical consulting firms gravitate to large universities for securing the needed expertise more easily. In addition to prevailing wages and salaries, location also determines the attractiveness of a firm according to the time required to commute to work. In some cities, this may be so long and tiresome that it may discourage potential employees.

The importance of labor may be reduced when it is possible to automate or mechanize one or more stages of the production process. This represents a substitution of capital for labor which is possible through technological advances. Numerically controlled equipment in manufacturing, printed circuits in electronics, and computers for data processing in large office companies are just a few examples of this possibility. The same result is possible when management can draw on a mobile or seasonal labor market, as in harvesting farms or operating tourist resort areas.

At times the wish to reduce labor costs places unwarranted emphasis on alternatives for location in a foreign country where wages are quite low. The cost of labor as an input, however, must be examined together with labor productivity, because despite low wages in some foreign locations, the accompanying low productivity results in higher overall production costs.

Process technology   For some firms the technology used may restrict the number of locations to sites that provide an abundant low-cost supply of some critical input, such as water for pulp and paper mills or electrical energy for an aluminum plant or electrochemical plating process. Occasionally, in addition to large amounts of certain inputs there is an added requirement for meeting strict quality specifications. For example, water that may be suitable for human consumption may not be appropriate for certain industrial uses, such as steel manufacturing.

Environmental factors   Beyond the consideration of factors related to the production process and its critical inputs, the location decision depends on several factors that define the external environment:

1. *The availability and reliability of supporting systems*, including public utilities for power and water, fire protection, easy transportation routes to suppliers and consumers, rapid and reliable communication, etc. Examination of these factors is especially important for the location of a new plant in a foreign country, whose economic infrastructure may lag significantly behind that of industrialized countries. Foreign investors have been discouraged from establishing new facilities in certain countries because long-distance calls may take 3 to 5 days to place, delivery of supplies is unreliable due to poor transportation, and other difficulties.

2. *Social and cultural conditions* may at times discourage the selection of a location that could pass any economic- and technical-feasibility criterion. It is thus necessary to understand the local population not only in terms of demographic variables (size, distribution, age, migration shifts, etc.) but also in terms of their attitudes toward domestic or foreign new industry and the quality, availability, and reliability of potential employees. Certain traditions and customs, especially abroad, may interfere with known ways of doing business. In several countries, for example, informal communication networks and personal relationships play a more dominant role than formalized procedures and plans.

3. *Legal and political considerations* represent a wide variety of restrictions or opportunities and must be studied very carefully before making a final choice. In some locations there are very strict laws pertaining to pollution standards, zoning codes, construction specifications, or import regulations. These restrictions may make it difficult to operate with existing technologies at a profit. Also, certain states or communities provide a wide variety of incentives to attract new employers. These may include reduced taxes, purchase discounts for construction sites, and less elaborate licensing procedures for new installations. One cannot overemphasize the importance of competent legal advice before making any final decisions on locating new facilities.

Formulation of the Location Problem

In order to formulate the location problem more precisely, it is helpful to view the operations system under study in relationship to its market and its sources of supply, i.e., its economic environment. This is shown in Fig. 10-2, where some of the most important costs that must be estimated for alternative location sites include:

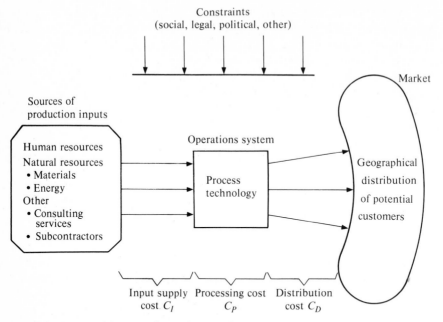

Fig. 10-2   Certain of the costs affecting location choice.

1. The cost of procurement of needed production inputs C_I, that is, the cost of raw materials, labor, energy, etc. (mainly variable costs)
2. The cost of processing the inputs given the technology C_P, that is, the overhead cost (mainly fixed costs)
3. The distribution cost involved in shipping product(s) or making services available to customers C_D (mainly variable costs)

These costs are tangible; i.e., they can be estimated for different locations using standard economic analysis. In addition, we must take into account certain intangible costs related to the quality of the labor available in each location, the degree of cooperation and the attitudes of the local government and community, possible relocation adjustments, and others. Finally, there is an opportunity cost for each location resulting from failure to select the best site possible if time and money impose no restrictions in the search for alternatives.

Our formulation of the *location problem* can now be made more complete and precise. Management has the *task of selecting among candidate locations the one that satisfies existing technological, legal, and other constraints and minimizes the combined cost of the relevant tangible, intangible, and opportunity costs.* In practice, intangible costs can be estimated only subjectively for each location, whereas opportunity costs are likely to be ignored in most studies.

10-3   A PRACTICAL SYSTEMS APPROACH TO LOCATION SELECTION

As we have seen, the problem of selecting a location is characterized by numerous factors with complex interrelationships. Several of these factors can be evaluated only qualitatively at best. Furthermore, the information needed is often incomplete due to the inherent difficulty of predicting future conditions. Various sophisticated techniques developed to solve parts of the total problem include linear programming and heuristic and simulation models based on some dominant objective, such as minimizing distribution costs.

Management, however, needs an approach that looks at the whole problem and allows for the careful evaluation of both quantitative and qualitative factors. This can be attempted within the framework of a systems analysis, which must cover the components shown in Fig. 10-3.

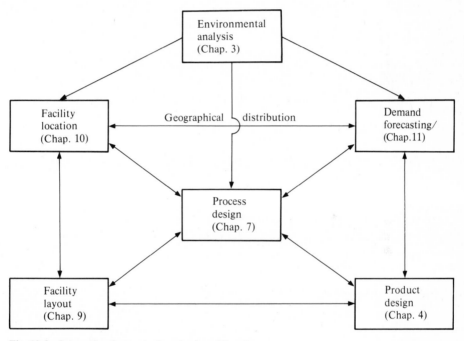

Fig. 10-3   Interacting factors in the selection of location.

In practice, it is often useful to study the location problem in two phases, as shown in Fig. 10-4. First, there is a *preliminary feasibility study*, whose purpose is to determine whether the environmental changes are important enough to warrant a more detailed analysis. Thus, phase one is mainly concerned with the study of trends in the level and geographical distribution of aggregate demand to determine whether they justify the minimum economical addition to capacity obtained by building new facilities.

Along with demand, the preliminary study focuses on other environmental factors such as the availability of critical production inputs, their current and projected costs, and any demographic changes that may affect the distribution of demand and/or the availability of labor or other resources. If the results of phase one justify the need for a more detailed analysis, management can proceed with phase two, which is conducted in three successive stages, as explained below.

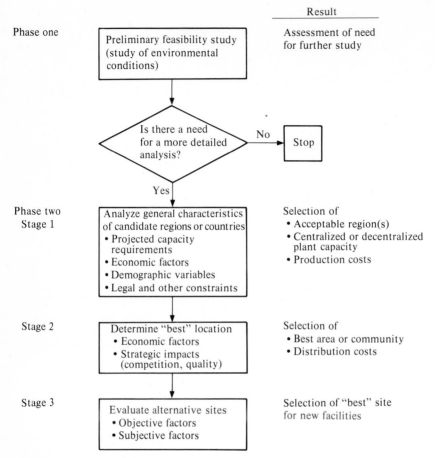

Fig. 10-4 **Procedure for selecting a location for new facilities.**

Stage 1: Analysis and Evaluation of Alternative Regions (or Countries)

In stage 1 of phase two we examine a number of general characteristics for different geographic regions or countries as they relate to the scope of the firm's present and/or proposed activities. The purpose here is to select the most suitable region and to determine the capacity needed for the new facilities.

First, the marketing-research department or a special group for this task must prepare estimates of the expected increase in demand for each region of the market, using a 5 to 10-yr forecast. These estimates are then translated into requirements for new or additional productive capacity. Given an estimate of future capacity requirements, we proceed to identify alternative regions for which profits or other measure of effectiveness will be maximized for the proposed capacity. For specific demand levels and prices, profits are determined from the analysis of costs for production and distribution. Thus in stage 1 we must consider the alternatives of meeting new capacity requirements from one centralized large installation or two or more smaller-capacity facilities geographically dispersed to reduce transporta-

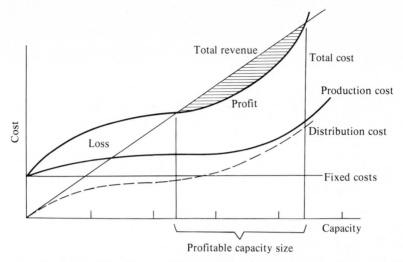

Fig. 10-5 **Relationship of production and distribution cost curves and revenue curve for facilities of different capacity.**

tion costs. Figure 10-5 shows the relevant trade-offs. To obtain lower production costs we must achieve economies of scale made possible by larger-capacity plants. This pressure for capacity concentration, however, results in larger distribution costs due to the larger distances for product deliveries, compared with several small plants geographically dispersed. The optimum configuration is selected from an economic analysis aimed at identifying the minimum production-distribution cost alternative combined with other considerations for greater flexibility and reliability usually in favor of decentralized arrangements.

The data needed to select the most suitable region(s) and the new capacity requirements include the following:

A. Future increase in demand by region translated into productive-capacity requirements
B. Cost relationships for production and distribution
C. Identification of sources of needed production inputs:
   1. Raw materials (quality, quantity, cost, reliability)
   2. Labor market (available skills, wages, supply levels)
   3. Supporting systems, i.e., economic infrastructure, for supplying
      a. Energy (sources, adequacy, cost)
      b. Water (quality, quantity, cost)
      c. Transportation and communication networks (adequacy, reliability, cost)
   4. Legal, social, and political factors
   5. Environmental considerations (pollution, climate, quality of life)

According to Yasseen,[1] almost all elements contributing to cost can be affected up to 10 percent of the total for production and distribution by the selection of the geographic region.

---

[1] L. C. Yasseen, *Plant Location*, American Research Council, Citadel Press, New York, 1960.

Stage 2: Determination of Optimum Area for Location

After selecting the most suitable geographical region (or foreign country) and the optimum-capacity plant, the analysis continues at the level of specific areas within the region. If our criterion for selecting the best area is profit maximization, then with production costs already determined in stage 1 the maximization of profit can now be achieved by minimizing the cost of distribution.

Consider the case of a new firm about to select the location for its new facilities. First, we subdivide the market to be served by the new plant into different sections and estimate for different areas the distances and projected requirements to cover future demand. For a given location let

n = number of market sections to be covered by new plant from that location
D_j = amount of monthly deliveries to section j $(j = 1, 2, \ldots, n)$
r_j = distance of section j from plant location
c_j = unit shipping cost per unit distance to destination j

Then
$$c_j r_j D_j = \text{monthly distribution cost to cover expected demand for market section } j \text{ from given location}$$

$$\sum_{j=1}^{n} c_j r_j D_j = \text{total monthly distribution cost for entire future market and given location}$$

This measure can be evaluated for each alternative location to choose the one which minimizes the total annual distribution cost.

For an existing firm which operates one or more facilities, the situation is more complicated in that demand for various market sections can be met from the old as well as the new location(s). This type of problem has been solved by the transportation method of linear programming (see Supplementary Chapter E). To illustrate it with a simple example, let us assume that the firm under study has an old plant and is considering building a new one with capacity equal to 60 units/month in location A, B, or C. The data needed are summarized in Table 10-1.

By substituting the cost values for c_{2j} that apply to the three areas A, B, and C and solving the transportation problem repeatedly, we can determine which of the three locations results in the minimum transportation cost per week.

Whether the area selection is made by straightforward economic analysis or a mathematical model, it is important to conduct a sensitivity analysis to determine whether the area selected maintains its relative advantage over other locations under different operating conditions or changes in market characteristics.

Stage 3: Community and Site Selection

Within the area chosen in stage 2 it is desirable to consider alternative sites for the construction of the new facilities. At this point, it is important to secure detailed economic and demographic data, but most factors that must be analyzed in area and site selection relate to technical, social, and legal considerations.

The factors that must be considered in the selection of a community and a site for a new location can be classified as follows:

TABLE 10-1 Data needed for new plant location†

Source	Market section			Capacity available, units/month
	1	2	3	
Old plant	$c_{11} = 5$ X_{11}	$c_{12} = 3$ X_{12}	$c_{13} = 8$ X_{13}	$S_1 = 40$
New plant	c_{21} X_{21}	c_{22} X_{22}	c_{23} X_{23}	$S_2 = 60$
Projected demand, units/month	$D_1 = 30$	$D_2 = 20$	$D_3 = 50$	100 100

† Where c_{ij} = cost of shipping 1 unit from plant i ($= 1, 2$) to market
 section j ($= 1, 2, 3$)
  X_{ij} = number of units shipped monthly from plant i to j
  D_j = amount of monthly deliveries needed for market section j
  S_i = capacity available per month in plant i

A. Projected requirements in production inputs
   1. Human resources (skills, amounts, quality)
   2. Raw materials, parts, semifinished components
   3. Energy, water, and other services
   4. Transportation and communication facilities
   5. Physical space for planned facilities and future expansion
B. Objective factors that will affect the cost and profits of new installation
   1. Projected levels of annual demand
   2. Projected annual operating costs
      a. Costs for purchase and transportation of raw materials
      b. Costs for wages of required skills
      c. Costs for requirements in energy (electricity, oil, etc.), water, telephone, etc.
      d. Taxes (on sales, income, property, inventories, etc.)
   3. Cost for construction of new facilities
   4. Estimates of annual profits for successive years
   5. Cost of purchasing construction site
C. Subjective factors that will influence the community and site selection
   1. Existing laws that will affect the firm's activities
   2. Labor-market characteristics
   3. Transportation networks
   4. Supporting infrastructure systems (power, telephone, water, waste treatment, or other)
   5. Community characteristics
      a. Population makeup, attitudes, traditions
      b. Financial institutions
      c. Cultural activities, schools, recreation

  d. Quality of life (noise, congestion, air pollution, etc.)
  e. Housing
  d. Services

  Evaluation of these factors is difficult because of the problems of (1) estimating objective factors with accuracy, (2) assigning priorities to subjective factors that defy measurement, and (3) coping with the uncertainty about the future impacts of present decisions when the stakes are so high.

  An effective method for making so complex a choice is discussed in the following section.

10-4 THE BROWN-GIBSON APPROACH FOR SITE SELECTION

Suppose that after stage 2 we have identified three alternative sites for a new plant location. We wish to develop for each site a measure of preference that combines both objective and subjective factors. For this purpose we might use the method for evaluating alternative product designs discussed in Chap. 4. A versatile approach especially designed for the location-selection problem is a model developed by Brown and Gibson (Ref. 2); its key features are displayed in Fig. 10-6. In applying the Brown-Gibson approach, outlined in Fig. 10-6, we go through the following sequence of steps:

1. Eliminate any site that does not meet certain basic requirements. This may be a technical requirement, e.g., the availability of abundant cheap electricity for an aluminum plant, or a budget constraint for the purchase of the site.
2. Compute an objective-factor measure of performance OF_i for each site. Usually we estimate all relevant costs to compute the total annual cost for each site C_i. Next we determine the objective-factor measure OF_i by multiplying C_i by the sum of the reciprocal site costs $\sum (1/C_i)$ and taking the reciprocal.
3. Determine key subjective factors and estimate their subjective-factor measure SF_i for each site by
  a. Deriving a factor rating w_j for each subjective factor $(j = 1, 2, ..., n)$ using a forced-choice pairwise comparison procedure. Accordingly, one factor is selected over another, or they are rated equal.
  b. Ranking each site for each subjective factor separately R_{ij} $(0 \le R_{ij} \le 1,$ $\sum_i R_{ij} = 1)$.
  c. Combining for each site the factor rating and site ranking, $SF_i = w_1 R_{i1} + w_2 R_{i2} + \cdots + w_n R_{in}$.
4. Combine for each site the objective-factor measure OF_i and subjective-factor measure SF_i by assigning weights k and $1 - k$, respectively, to obtain a *location preference measure* (LPM), i.e.,

$$LPM_i = k(OF_i) + (1 - k)(SF_i) \qquad 0 < k < 1$$

If the site selection is going to be based entirely on costs, $k = 1.0$ and the subjective factors are ignored. If objective factors are going to count 4 times as much as the subjective ones, then $k = .8$ $(.8/.2 = 4)$, etc. The preference measure

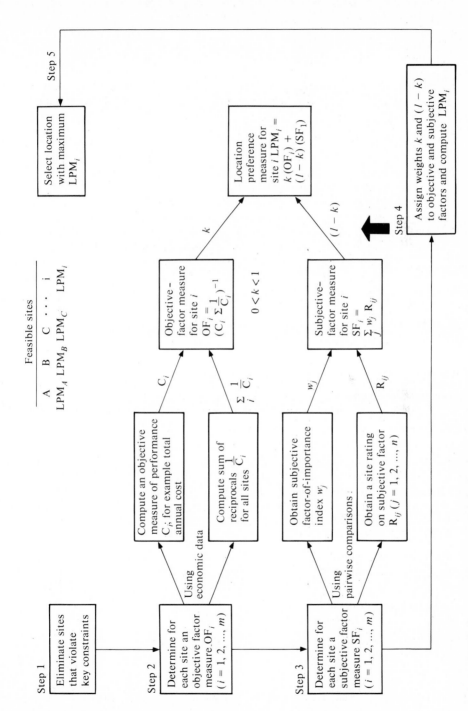

Fig. 10-6 The Brown–Gibson approach for evaluating locations.

for a given site can be tested under different assumptions concerning costs and the importance of various subjective factors.

5. Select the site with the maximum LPM.

This procedure will be illustrated with an example. Note, however, that it is quite general in nature and can be used not only for site selection but also for many complex decision problems where it is necessary to combine subjective and objective factors into an overall measure of preference for each alternative. The Brown-Gibson method would be equally suitable for the evaluation of alternative product designs, processes, or layouts of facilities, to name a few potential applications.

▶ EXAMPLE 10-1

Miranda Pacific, Inc., a pulp and paper company, has just completed a feasibility study (phase one) for the construction of a new plant to cover future increases in demand, as evidenced by a steady upward trend during recent years. The study has concluded that the expected increase in demand justifies the minimum economic plant size needed for a paper mill, since capacity changes for this industry can be made only in large increments.

In stage 1 of phase two the study of market changes and pulp and paper manufacturing characteristics for different geographic regions has shown that the most suitable region for a new plant is the Pacific Northwest (Idaho, Oregon, Washington) because of its proximity to the raw material (wood chips converted into paper pulp and then various types of paper) and good transportation networks (waterways and rail and highway systems).

In stages 2 and 3 for the selection of the best area and sites, a detailed analysis of requirements has indicated that four sites along the Columbia River would be satisfactory in terms of the large quantities of water required for pulp and paper processing. Let us call these sites A, B, C, and D near different towns along the river. The application of the Brown-Gibson approach for this case is illustrated below.

Step 1   Site D is eliminated early because real estate in that area is prohibitively expensive and the sum needed to purchase the required number of acres exceeds the amount allowed in the capital budget.

Step 2   In the remaining sites all annual costs for production inputs (raw materials, energy, etc.) are the same except for labor, distribution, and taxes:

Site i	Annual costs (millions)				Total C_i	Reciprocal $1/C_i$
	Labor	Distribution	Taxes	All others		
A	$3.62	$2.08	$ .25	$4.00	$9.95	.100503
B	3.40	2.75	.30	4.00	10.45	.095694
C	3.75	2.90	.40	4.00	11.05	.090498
				Total		.286695

The objective rating factor for each site is obtained by substitution in the formula

$$OF_i = \left[C_i \sum \left(\frac{1}{C_i} \right) \right]^{-1} \quad \text{so that} \quad \sum_i (OF_i) = 1 \quad \text{(10-1)}$$

Thus, the objective rating factors for alternative sites are

$$OF_A = [(9.95)(.2867)]^{-1} = (2.8526)^{-1} = .35056$$

$$OF_B = [(10.45)(.2867)]^{-1} = (2.9960)^{-1} = .33378$$

$$OF_C = [(11.05)(.2867)]^{-1} = (3.1680)^{-1} = .31566$$

$$\overline{1.00000}$$

Step 3   With climate, recreation opportunities, city services, and labor being the same in all areas, the key subjective factors in the selection of a site have been identified as (1) housing, (2) education, and (3) community attitudes.

These must now be evaluated using a *forced-choice procedure* which compares each factor with the others by considering one pair at a time. Repetitive application of the forced-choice procedure yields two results: (1) we obtain a subjective factor importance index w_j, which simply measures the relative weight given to each subjective factor, and (2) for each subjective factor separately we obtain a ranking of each site R_{ij}.

Suppose that the special group assigned to select a site responded to paired comparisons as follows:

1. Education (1) versus housing (2): both judged equally important
2. Education (1) versus community attitudes (3): choose community attitudes as more important
3. Housing (2) versus community attitudes (3): choose community attitudes

This information can be summarized in a table in which we can compute the subjective-factor importance index w_j:

Factor j	Pairwise comparisons			Sum of preferences	Relative-importance index w_j
	1	2	3		
Education (1)	1	0		1	$\frac{1}{4} = .25$
Housing (2)	1		0	1	$\frac{1}{4} = .25$
Community attitudes (3)		1	1	2	$\frac{1}{2} = .50$
Total				4	$\overline{1.00}$

In the column for each pairwise comparison possible[1] we assign 1 to the factor preferred and 0 to the other, while for the case of equivalence both factors are assigned a value of 1. It is important in using such a procedure to check preferences for consistency. Thus, if factor 1 is preferred to 2 and 2 is preferred to 3, 1 must be preferred to 3; otherwise the responses are inconsistent.

Next, for each subjective factor separately we repeat the same pairwise comparisons with sites to determine their relative ranking R_{ij}. For the sites considered by Miranda Pacific, Inc., the results of this procedure are shown in Table 10-2.

TABLE 10-2   Results of pairwise comparisons for rating location sites

	Education (factor 1)					Housing (factor 2)			
	Pairwise comparison response			Site ranking R_{i1}		Pairwise comparison response			Site ranking R_{i2}
Site i	1	2	3		Site i	1	2	3	
A	1	1		$\frac{2}{4}$ = .50	A	0	1		$\frac{1}{4}$ = .25
B	0		1	$\frac{1}{4}$ = .25	B	1		1	$\frac{2}{4}$ = .50
C		0	1	$\frac{1}{4}$ = .25	C		1	0	$\frac{1}{4}$ = .25
Total				1.00	Total				1.00

	Community attitudes (factor 3)					Summary of subjective factors evaluation			
	Pairwise comparison response			Site ranking R_{i3}		Site rating R_{ij}			Relative importance index w_j
Site i	1	2	3		Factor, j	A	B	C	
A	0	0		$\frac{0}{3}$ = 0	1	.50	.25	.25	.25
B	1		0	$\frac{1}{3}$ = .33	2	.25	.50	.25	.25
C		1	1	$\frac{2}{3}$ = .67	3	0	.33	.67	.50
Total				1.00	Total				1.00

---

[1] The number of possible pairwise comparisons for n subjective factors is the number of combinations of n items taken 2 at a time, i.e.,

$$\binom{n}{2} = \frac{n!}{2(n-2)!}$$

Thus

For $n = 3$: $\binom{3}{2} = \frac{3!}{2(3-2)!} = \frac{3 \cdot 2 \cdot 1}{2 \cdot 1} = 3$

For $n = 5$: $\binom{5}{2} = \frac{5!}{2(3!)} = \frac{5 \cdot 4 \cdot 3!}{2 \cdot 3!} = 10$

To determine the subjective factor measure for a site SF_i we must multiply the site rating for a given factor R_{ij} by the relative importance index w_j of that factor and sum over all the subjective factors included in the analysis

$$SF_i = R_{i1}w_1 + R_{i2}w_2 + \cdots + R_{in}w_n = \sum_{j=1}^{n} R_{ij}w_j \tag{10-2}$$

In our example the subjective rating factors for alternative sites are

$$SF_A = (.50)(.25) + (.25)(.25) + (0)(.50) \quad = \quad .1875$$
$$SF_B = (.25)(.25) + (.50)(.25) + (.33)(.50) = \quad .3525$$
$$SF_C = (.25)(.25) + (.25)(.25) + (.67)(.50) = \quad .4600$$
$$\overline{1.0000}$$

Step 4   Having completed the evaluation of both objective and subjective location factors, we can now proceed to combine the results and determine an overall location-preference measure LPM_i for each site. This synthesis requires a crucial decision, the weight that will be assigned to each category of factors. If the weight given to the objective factors is k $(0 < k < 1)$, the subjective factors receive a weight $1 - k$. Thus, for a given site we have

$$LPM_i = k(OF_i) + (1 - k)(SF_i) \tag{10-3}$$

For our example, management considers the weight of objective factors 4 times as important as that of subjective ones; that is, $k = 4(1 - k)$. This is true when $k = .8$. The location-preference-measure values for the sites considered will be

$$LPM_A = (.8)(.35056) + (.2)(.1875) = \quad .3179$$
$$LPM_B = (.8)(.33378) + (.2)(.3525) = \quad .3375$$
$$LPM_C = (.8)(.31566) + (.2)(.4600) = \quad .3446 \quad \text{(preferred location site)}$$
$$\overline{1.0000}$$

Step 5   According to the Brown-Gibson approach, Miranda, Inc., must choose site C, since this receives the highest value for a location measure. We note that even though it is the least attractive alternative based on objective factors, its superiority in subjective-factor rating puts it at the top, despite a high weight value for cost factors. The sensitivity of the preference-location measures for each site with respect to the weight assigned to objective and subjective factors can be shown with a diagram (Fig. 10-7). For our example, only for a value of k near 1.0, for which ▶ subjective factors are essentially ignored, does the choice switch to site A.[1]

---

[1] A potential weakness of the Brown-Gibson approach is in the use of pairwise comparisons. These may oversimplify a choice by failing to reveal the strength of a stated preference.

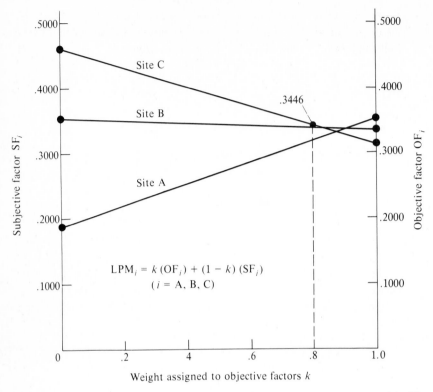

Fig. 10-7   **Sensitivity of location-preference measure for each site with respect to weight (k).**

10-5   ENVIRONMENTAL-IMPACT STATEMENT

General Background

In an unending search for ways to improve their standard of living, people until recently evaluated their ongoing or proposed productive activities on the basis of the direct benefits and costs. As noted in Chap. 7, failure to perceive or anticipate the environmental impacts of "productive" systems gradually brought industrialized countries close to destroying the ecological balance of the larger system within which they operate. The increased awareness of potential environmental threats, if past trends continue, has prompted in recent years the passing of new laws to control pollution and improve the use of scarce natural resources (energy, land, wildlife, etc.).

The effect of antipollution legislation has been limited in its scope and controversial in its implementation. This applies to the Federal Water Pollution Control Act (1972), the Clean Air Acts with several amendments, and various Pesticide Acts (1972). Problems related to formulation of acceptable definitions of what constitutes water or air pollution, difficulties with measurement methods, and disputes over the costs and rate of cleanup have slowed down enforcement of antipollution laws in most affected areas. These laws are aimed at controlling pollutants from a variety of sources, say the wastes disposed of in a city sewage system, or the specific impact of pollution from a single source, such as a steel mill. A serious omission in past and present attempts to control pollution is the failure to include more than one kind of impact from a single source and the lack of proposed alternatives to the pollution source before it is approved, constructed, and made operational.

The National Environmental
Policy Act (NEPA)[1]

In order to strengthen the effort to protect the environment as a whole, Congress passed the National Environmental Policy Act in 1972. NEPA aimed at evaluating not one but all significant environmental impacts of a proposed project. The requirement for an environmental-impact study (EIS) is more closely related to benefit and-cost analysis[2] than to pollution-control laws. Its main purpose is to assist decision makers involved in evaluating and approving large and complex projects.

Who Is Affected by NEPA

For any organization proposing a new large project, NEPA's requirement for preparation of an EIS is judged (1) by the need for project approval or some form of license and (2) the need for funding. Thus, a public agency proposing the construction of a new highway, a dam, an airport, or a recreation area must submit an EIS. A private organization, e.g., a power company, is required to prepare the equivalent of an EIS for such projects as building a new plant with significant impacts on the environment (noise, air or water pollution, destruction of wildlife, etc.). The same holds true when expanding the sewage system of an existing plant, developing a resort area in the mountains, drilling for offshore oil, etc. One of the best known EIS studies was that prepared for the Alaskan pipeline.

In conclusion, the law affects both public and private organizations requiring public funding and/or licensing at the federal, state, and at times the local government level. The EIS may be contracted out to a consulting firm, but ultimate responsibility for its contents rests with the agency required to approve a project.

EIS Contents

Although the specific form may vary for different studies, the typical content of an EIS includes:[3]

---

[1] NEPA as proposed by Representative John D. Dingel of Michigan and Senator Henry M. Jackson of Washington (as H.R. 6750) drew many of its elements from Sen. Doc. 97 (1962) for reviewing water-resource projects.

[2] For details of benefit-and-cost analysis, see James L. Riggs, *Engineering Economics*, McGraw-Hill, New York, 1977, chap. 13.

[3] Ruthann Corwin, Impact Assessment: "Origin, Operation Outlook" in P. H. Heffernan and R. Corwin (eds.), *Environmental Impact Assessment*, Freeman, Cooper, San Francisco, 1975, p. 37.

1. Description of the proposed action, including its objectives
2. Description of the project environment before the proposed changes
3. Identification and forecasting of significant project impacts
4. Description of alternatives to the proposed action
5. Evaluation of the impacts (benefits, adverse effects, irreversible commitments, or other aspects as required by law) and trade-offs between alternatives
6. Comments by concerned citizens
7. Comments by other agencies

For our purposes, the most important part is item 2, which is discussed in more detail in the following section.

A Framework for Forecasting Environmental Impacts

Until recently the evaluation of large projects was based mainly on the economic and technical factors directly associated with the proposed activities. One of the key features of NEPA is the requirement of utilizing an interdisciplinary approach to study the numerous factors, such as the distribution of impacts among different population groups; impacts on community services, employment, incomes, land use, recreation, noise, pollution, and congestion; and effects on historic or archaeological sites. In short, NEPA added to each agency's responsibilities the task of forecasting and evaluating the impacts of proposed actions on the total environment, i.e., the economic, natural, social, and cultural dimensions of the affected area. For the purpose of forecasting significant environmental impacts, it is helpful to have a framework, as shown in Fig. 10-8.

Affected Processes in Project Environment

Once a proposed project, say the location of a large new plant in a community, is specified and the goals defined, the first step in preparing an EIS involves identifying those processes which will be affected in the project environment. They may include regional economic processes, community social processes, and ecological processes. In most cases, the larger the project in scope (plant capacity, distribution network, etc.) the greater the number of affected processes and the more complex the mode of interaction.

Regional economic processes   The economic system of a region performs two types of activities: (1) The set of *basic economic activities* undertaken to bring income to the region by exporting products or services to other regions is known as the *economic base*. For the Detroit area this would include the manufacture of automobiles, for Florida it would be tourism and orange growing, and for a campus town its university educational activities. (2) The set of *nonbasic activities* aimed at providing goods and services bought with money within the region includes food, housing, transportation, entertainment, and others. Knowing the proposed changes in basic economic activities, we can proceed to estimate the impacts on nonbasic

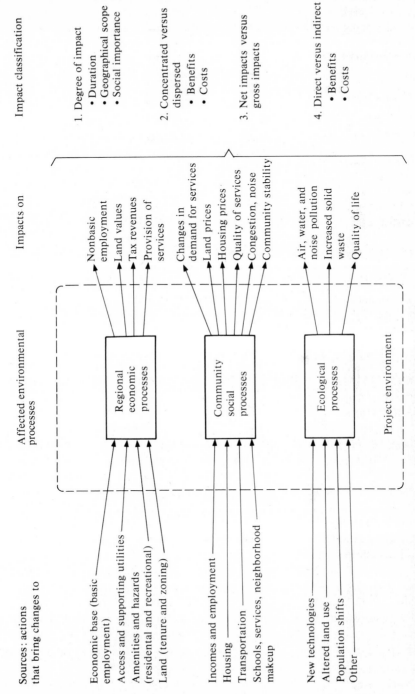

Fig. 10-8 A framework for the analysis and assessment of environmental impacts.

Impact classification

1. Degree of impact
   • Duration
   • Geographical scope
   • Social importance

2. Concentrated versus dispersed
   • Benefits
   • Costs

3. Net impacts versus gross impacts

4. Direct versus indirect
   • Benefits
   • Costs

Impacts on

Nonbasic employment
Land values
Tax revenues
Provision of services

Changes in demand for services
Land prices
Housing prices
Quality of services
Congestion, noise
Community stability

Air, water, and noise pollution
Increased solid waste
Quality of life

Affected environmental processes

Regional economic processes

Community social processes

Ecological processes

Project environment

Sources: actions that bring changes to

Economic base (basic employment)
Access and supporting utilities
Amenities and hazards (residental and recreational)
Land (tenure and zoning)

Incomes and employment
Housing
Transportation
Schools, services, neighborhood makeup

New technologies
Altered land use
Population shifts
Other

activities, say secondary jobs, increased demand for housing, etc., by well-developed methods of regional and urban planning analysis.[1] This usually is done by extrapolating from the present economic structure. According to economic-base theory, in a given region there is a balance between basic and nonbasic employment (1 to 1 for small towns, 1 to 2 for large cities) and between jobs and housing. Changes in the economic base can thus be translated into demand for housing. The number and income level of new jobs determine the amount and quality of the new housing.

Economic theories of location suggest methods for estimating the impacts of improvement in access (new roads, bridges, mass transit, etc.) and utilities (water, power, etc.) and can forecast which lands will develop and when and how as a result of such changes. The sources of information for such studies include local development agencies, bank-loan officers, university research centers, and private sources (realtors, developers, etc.).

Another source of impacts on the regional economic processes is related to the elimination of hazards, e.g., dams for flood control, and the creation of amenities, e.g., state parks, beaches, access roads to remote wilderness areas, and others. The creation of airports often results in conflicting impacts, i.e., improved access at the expense of noise, air pollution, and drastic effects on land use.

Equally important in their long-term effects on the economic processes are federal, state, and local government decisions on the ownership and zoning of land. The Bureau of Land Management and the Forest Service at the federal level have made far-reaching decisions through their land-trade and disposal practices, such as permit issues for logging, grazing, and mining. Such activities usually bring about significant ecological changes due to soil erosion. Regional and urban growth is similarly affected by land zoning. At the state level the different use of coastal resources has brought about different development patterns. For example, in Oregon the coast, most of which is publicly owned, represents a valuable recreational resource, whereas the California coast, which is mostly privately owned, offers no comparable opportunities to the public. At the city level, land zoning by local government controls the growth and pollution patterns by designating different areas as open for residential, industrial, or mixed use.

Community social processes   Significant impacts affecting the social fabric of a region or a community result not only from large-scale projects but also from policies, programs, and projects of a more limited scope. Such impacts may arise from activity changes related to the interaction of several regions undergoing structural economic changes.

The sources of social impacts at the level of a community or neighborhood can be traced to actions affecting incomes and employment, transportation, housing policies, and community services (schools, police, fire protection, etc.). Depending on the action, social impacts take the form of changes in the level of demand for various community services, changes in the prices of land and housing, and changes in the cohesiveness of the community and its quality of life as measured by noise, pollution, congestion, crime rate, or other yardsticks.

[1] See Walter Isard, *Methods of Regional Analysis*, MIT Press, Cambridge, Mass., 1960.

Ecological processes   The nature and extent of changes brought about in the economic and social processes of a region or community result in impacts that also affect the ecological balance in that area. Very often a proposed activity aimed at generating favorable economic and social changes may result in serious disturbances to the natural environment. The location of a new plant in a town may strengthen the community economically and improve its social aspects by the attraction of higher-quality housing, schools, and other community services, but the price may be high in terms of environmental pollution of the air or water, solid waste, or increased noise and congestion of areas that were previously valuable recreational resources. One of the basic objectives of the EIS is to bring out those impacts explicitly and allow all affected parties (citizens, local business, and government) to understand the trade-offs and explore mitigating measures or alternatives for reducing the adversity of environmental impacts. An outstanding example of what happens in the absence of such a study is the Aswan Dam in Egypt, which along with economic benefits brought about serious flooding by the Nile of many fertile stretches and important archaeological sites.

Classification of Environmental Impacts

Independently of the process affected by a particular project, the resulting impacts can be discussed according to various classification criteria. The following is considered general enough to allow the preparation and evaluation of an EIS to be complete and balanced.[1]

Degree of impact   The degree of impact can be evaluated on the basis of its duration, its geographical scope or scale, and its importance to those that feel it.

Duration   A specific impact of a project may be instantaneous, indefinite, or have a duration of 1, 5, or 20 years.

Geographical scope   The scale of an impact can be very limited, i.e., on site or off site nearby (factory or airport noise). In some cases, however, the impact may affect an entire community or region (air-shed or watershed pollution). Less frequently, the scale of the impact may be national (coastal pollution) or hemispheric or global (open atomic explosions).

Social importance   The ranking of an impact in terms of social significance may be minor (short and infrequent inconvenience), major (prolonged over a period to affect life-styles), or critical (dangerous to health or threatening to survival). An even more explicit ranking is possible by using the levels in the hierarchy of needs proposed by Maslow (see Fig. 3-6). According to the above scheme, the 1965 and 1977 New York power blackouts were of limited duration (several hours), regional in scope (several communities affected), and major in social importance.

---

[1] This classification scheme has been adapted from Robert A. Johnstone, "Assessing Social and Economic Impacts," in P. H. Hefferman and R. Corwin (eds.), *Environmental Impact Assessment*, Freeman, Cooper, San Francisco, 1975.

Concentrated and dispersed impacts   The various impacts produced by a project, whether they are benefits or costs, may affect people or geographical areas in a concentrated or dispersed manner. This is a crucial distinction because it determines how the issue will be treated politically by affected parties and what corrective measures may be used to reduce adverse impacts costs.

Concentrated impacts   The higher the concentration of an impact on people or geography the easier it is to identify the elements of the environment that will be affected more seriously. This allows management to anticipate project opponents, i.e., people affected by concentrated costs, say people whose land value declines from airport noise or those who will be displaced. Similarly strong project supporters can be identified with all those receiving concentrated benefits (land owners, local businessmen, etc.). By knowing the participants in the political battles that may follow, those proposing the project can anticipate likely reactions and propose early corrective measures.

Dispersed impacts   Dispersed costs are associated with the taxpayers who may be called upon to pay for a project and the environment that will absorb the induced natural and social disturbances. Dispersed benefits normally take the form of improved community services (transportation, water, etc.) or reduced taxes, subsidies or increased opportunities for recreation, travel, employment, education, etc.

In most cases, projects tend to produce concentrated benefits and dispersed costs. To improve the distribution of benefits those proposing a new project may have to provide incentives in addition to those mentioned above.

Net versus gross impacts   The size and scope of a project is the main criterion for deciding whether the EIS will include net or gross impacts.

Net impact   For small projects having a limited variety and range of impacts, it is adequate to consider only the net impact. This ignores the secondary impacts by taking them for granted. This method forecasts the future environment only with and without the project.

Gross impact   Large projects must take into account not only the impact of the project itself but also other changes induced by the construction and operation of the proposed plant. In other words, they must estimate the future environment with the project minus the present environment without the project. Construction of the Alaska pipeline is an example where gross impacts extended to economic, social, and ecological processes widely dispersed in that region.

Direct versus indirect impacts   The larger the scope of a project the more difficult it becomes to separate the direct from the indirect impacts due to the numerous and complex interactions that occur between parts of the environment.

Direct impacts   Direct impacts, also known as primary impacts, are those readily perceived to occur as an immediate result of a proposed change, e.g., the increase in employment and incomes that follow when a new firm moves into a region.

Indirect impacts These are the induced changes in the social and economic processes that follow as secondary results of a project or policy. Thus, opening a new road for access to a newly created ski resort may have as a direct impact the increase in recreational resources for the area but may also induce other economic activity along the road (motels, restaurants, gas stations) and may change the pattern of wildlife in the affected region.

In order to avoid arbitrary or unwarranted classification of impacts into direct and indirect types, it is preferable to develop a network showing the various impacts and how they interact in space and time.

Effects of Environmental Legislation on Private Business

At present the attitude of private business toward legislation to protect the environment is negative for several reasons: (1) The need to comply with such laws considerably lengthens the time required to implement decisions for large projects. For example, the time needed to build a nuclear power plant is close to 10 years, while for coal-fired plants it is 5 to 6 years. (2) The cost of such projects increases significantly due to the added expense for environmental studies and special equipment to comply with existing standards and because of the effect of inflation on delayed construction. (3) The added bureaucratic red tape is said to absorb too much time and cost at the expense of higher productivity that would strengthen the organization's standing and the national economy. There is considerable validity in these arguments. However, the numerous horror stories about environmental abuses by private business in the absence of such laws provide usually strong arguments that environmental protection is too serious a business to be left entirely to free enterprise.

With more experience, better measurement methods, and improved implementation procedures the pendulum will probably swing to a more balanced position that will enhance productivity while retaining sufficient control to limit environmental disruptions and threats.

10-6 SUMMARY

Decisions about the location of new facilities become important milestones for an organization because of their strategic significance. The impact of such decisions is felt by operations management by determining the costs of production inputs and their processing. These decisions also affect marketing because they determine the ease, time, and cost of distribution to the market. Those in charge of finance must consider the effect of the large investment required for a new location, and top management must consider the effect of a new location on its competitors and its strategy for future growth or diversification.

Methods available for selecting a new location draw heavily on economic analysis with regard to the tangible or objective factors of different alternatives, costs of materials and energy, costs for processing, taxes, etc. However, management must also cope with several subjective considerations, such as community attitudes toward new employers, quality of housing and education, and many others. Approaches like the one suggested by Brown and Gibson attempt to combine both objective and subjective factors for each alternative into an overall preference rating which forms the basis for ranking different location sites. This represents an effective rational model for the location problem, but the complexity of the issues involved and the need for consensus by several influential participants require that we also view location problems through the lens of the organizational and political models discussed in Chap. 2.

In recent years concern with environmental aspects of new large public or private projects has prompted new legislation affecting federal and often state and local agencies that must license or fund such projects. The National Environmental Protection Act (NEPA) requires such agencies to prepare an environmental-impact statement (EIS), which identifies significant impacts on the economic, social, and ecological processes of a proposed location. Using an interdisciplinary approach, the EIS is expected to consider serious effects of large projects, opposing views from other agencies and citizens, and a discussion of alternatives.

It will thus be necessary in the future to evaluate a new facility location not only on the basis of the direct costs and benefits associated with it but also in terms of its impact on various aspects of the environment in the proposed location.

REVIEW QUESTIONS

1. What reasons usually prompt an existing organization to seek a new location?
2. How can management avoid the problem of considering a new location?
3. How is the plant-location choice affected by critical production inputs? Give some examples.
4. When is the plant-location problem dominated by the technology of the operations system? Give some examples.
5. What factors encourage the clustering of similar industries in certain regions? Give some examples.
6. Is the facilities-location problem for services different from that for manufacturing and in what respects? How does this apply to (a) a department store, (b) a fire department, and (c) a law firm?
7. Discuss the importance of environmental factors in the selection of a plant location.
8. Specify the major cost types that influence the selection of a new location.
9. What reasons prompt certain companies to consider foreign locations?
10. Under what conditions might foreign locations be preferred to domestic ones?
11. What are the key factors that interact with the plant-location decision?
12. It is usually necessary to conduct a preliminary feasibility study before going into a more detailed analysis for selecting a new location. Why?
13. Why must capacity-related issues be resolved before focusing on a plant-location study?
14. What conditions must be satisfied in a location study before we can evaluate alternative sites?
15. Which quantitative methods are useful in the evaluation of different locations?
16. What are the information input requirements of the Brown-Gibson algorithm?
17. In the Brown-Gibson algorithm what is the meaning of the location-preference measure, and how is it determined?
18. In the Brown-Gibson algorithm how can we test the sensitivity of a location choice with respect to subjective factors?

19. Who is required to prepare an environmental-impact statement (EIS)?
20. What is an EIS supposed to include?
21. What types of processes are affected by proposed large projects?
22. Discuss how environmental impacts for an EIS are classified and illustrate with the case of a new airport.

PROBLEMS

1. After sales for PEROVEN, a popular soft drink imported from France, soared in recent years, the company's headquarters in Paris decided to build a new bottling plant in the United States to cover nationwide distribution. Following a feasibility study three locations were identified because of the purity of their water, and the relevant data were summarized:

Location	Market section†					
	Region 1		Region 2		Region 3	
	r_1	c_1	r_2	c_2	r_3	c_3
A	2,500	0.012	800	0.016	1,500	0.010
B	1,200	0.018	1,100	0.012	300	0.011
C	1,600	0.015	1,400	0.017	700	0.008
Projected monthly deliveries, cases	10,000		12,000		15,000	

† r_i = distance to region i in miles, c_i = shipping cost per case per mile.

Assuming that production costs and other subjective factors are the same for all three alternatives, determine the location that minimizes the expected monthly distribution cost.

2. Refer to Prob. 1. Suppose that the annual operating costs for each location that meets water-quality criteria are:

Location	Annual fixed costs	Variable unit costs
A	$760,000	$ .83
B	580,000	.96
C	690,000	.87

Assuming the proposed plant capacity is 900,000 cases/yr:

(a) Which location results in the smallest annual production costs per year for the projected demand level?

(*b*) Which location will have the smallest annual production cost if demand has doubled by the time plant construction is completed?

3. Refer to Probs. 1 and 2. Which location will minimize the production-distribution cost (*a*) for the projected level of demand and (*b*) for double the level of projected demand?

4. The management of Grapho-Tronics, Inc., has decided to build a new plant, and the special group assigned to evaluate alternative locations has proposed three sites A, B, and C. Services and quality of life have been identified as the most important subjective factors that differ in these sites. Annual operating costs C_i have been estimated as follows:

Site	A	B	C
Annual cost C_i (millions)	$10	$9	$8

Management feels that services (factor 1) are as important as the quality of life (factor 2). The results from a forced pairwise comparison of sites for each subjective factor are as follows:

	Factor 1: services, pairwise comparison			Factor 2: quality of life, pairwise comparison		
Site	1	2	3	1	2	3
A	1	1	0	0	1	
B	0	1		1		1
C			1	1	1	0

Furthermore, management considers objective factors to be twice as important as subjective factors.

(*a*) Determine the objective-factor measure for each site.
(*b*) Determine the subjective-factor measure for each site.
(*c*) Select the optimum location for the new plant.

5. Refer to Prob. 4. Which is the optimum site if objective and subjective factors are equally important to management?

6. The Second National City Bank, following the civil war in Lebanon, decided to relocate its Beirut branch office to another city in the region. In order to be close to its customers, the bank's planning group suggested relocating to one of three cities: Ankara, Turkey; Athens, Greece; or Cairo, Egypt. The annual operating costs for the relocated branch including rents for office space, wages, taxes, etc., were estimated as follows: Ankara $5.8 million, Athens $6.2 million, and Cairo $4.9 million. The management of the Second National concluded that for its business the most important subjective factors were (1) government bureaucracy, (2) services available (telex, telephone, etc.), and (3) political stability (government changes, riots, strikes, etc.). All these were viewed as being equally important. Management in this case felt that objective factors were equally important to relevant subjective factors. Following responses to forced pairwise comparison, the following results were obtained:

	Government bureaucracy, pairwise comparisons			Services, pairwise comparisons			Stability, pairwise comparisons		
Site	1	2	3	1	2	3	1	2	3
Ankara	0	1		1	1		0	0	
Athens	1		1	1		1	1		0
Cairo		0	0		0	0		1	1

(a) Determine the objective-factor measure for each relocation city.

(b) Determine the subjective-factor measure for each relocation city.

(c) Select the best relocation city if objective and subjective factors are equally important.

7. Refer to Prob. 6. Select the optimum city if political stability is judged to be twice as important as government bureaucracy or available services.

8. Refer to Prob. 6. Select the optimum city if as a result of rampant inflation in the three countries the annual costs are projected to be $8 million in Ankara, $10 in Athens, and $7 in Cairo.

9. Refer to Prob. 6. Prepare a diagram showing how the location preference changes for different values of k; that is, specify for what range of k values each alternative is superior to the others.

10. AlumCo Ltd. plans to set up a new aluminum-products plant and has selected three sites with the following characteristics (for projected 75 percent capacity utilization equal to 300,000 tons/year):

Site	Annual fixed costs (millions)	Variable costs/ ton
A	8.2	$452
B	10	290
C	7.5	530

	Rating R_{ij}			Relative importance index w_j
Relevant subjective factors	A	B	C	
Housing	.25	.50	.25	.50
Community attitudes	.25	.25	.50	.25
Services	.50	.25	.25	.25

Determine the optimum location site if objective factors weigh twice as much as subjective factors.

11. Refer to Prob. 10. Determine the optimum location site if services rather than housing are twice as important as the other subjective factors.
12. Refer to Prob. 10. Prepare a diagram showing how the location preference changes for different values of *k*.
13. Refer to Prob. 10. As a result of increased use of aluminum by the automobile industry to increase auto efficiency, the expected capacity utilization of the proposed plant is expected to be 95 percent. This increases fixed costs by 20 percent and reduces variable unit costs by 5 percent. Determine the optimum location site for the revised estimate of capacity utilization.

SELECTED REFERENCES

1. Beckman, M.: *Location Theory*, Random House, New York, 1968.
2. Brown, P. A., and D. F. Gibson: "A Quantified Model for Facility Site Selection Application to a Multiplant Location Problem," *AIIE Transactions*, vol. 4, no. 1, pp. 1–10, March 1972.
3. Buffa, E. S.: *Operations Management: Problems and Models*, 3d ed., Wiley, New York, 1972, chaps. 10 and 11.
4. Easton, A.: *Complex Managerial Decisions Involving Multiple Objectives*, Wiley, New York, 1973, p. 288.
5. Hoover, E. M.: "Some Programmed Models of Industry Location," *Land Economics*, vol. 18, no. 3, pp. 303–311, August 1967.
6. Magee, J. F.: *Industrial Logistics*, McGraw-Hill, New York, 1968.
7. Reed, R., Jr.: *Plant Location, Layout and Maintenance*, Irwin, Homewood, Ill., 1967.
8. Riggs, J. L.: *Production Systems: Analysis Planning and Control*, 2d ed., Wiley, New York, 1976.
9. Weston, F. C., Jr.: "Quantitative Analysis of Plant Location," *Industrial Engineering*, vol. 4, no. 4, pp. 22–28, April 1972.

Supplementary Chapter E

LINEAR PROGRAMMING TRANSPORTATION METHOD

E-1   INTRODUCTION

A number of important problems in operations management can be solved by the transportation method. This is a special case of the simplex method developed for the general linear-programming problem of allocating scarce resources to competing demands. Typical applications of the transportation method in this context include:

1. The determination of a minimum-cost (or maximum-profit) shipping schedule to satisfy requirements at several destinations from a number of sources with available supply. This is known as the *distribution problem*.
2. The selection of a location for a new facility (a plant or warehouse) in a way that will satisfy projected market requirements from existing and future capacity at minimum cost. This is called the *location problem*.
3. The assignment of different forms of productive capacity in successive periods to meet forecast demand in such periods so as to minimize total production costs. This is known as the *aggregate-planning problem*.

For the above types of problems the transportation method provides a versatile tool for evaluating alternatives, especially when used with computers. This section provides a brief review of the key features of this method and explains the conditions that must be met for its application. A simple example will be used throughout to explain the formulation and solution procedure.

E-2   AN EXAMPLE

SunRays Co., a commercial airline in the resort island of Saint Michel, operates flights connecting the island's four largest cities. Fuel for the four airports $(A_1, A_2, A_3,$ and $A_4)$ is supplied from three sources $(F_1, F_2,$ and $F_3)$ located near the island's three major ports. Weekly fuel requirements at each airport, available fuel supplies at each source, and unit shipping costs for each route are specified in Table E-1. The management of the airline wishes to determine how much fuel to ship from each source to each airport to satisfy fuel requirements from available supplies at minimum cost.

E-3   KEY CONCEPTS AND NOTATION
FOR THE TRANSPORTATION PROBLEM

In order to formulate a problem so that it can be solved by the transportation method, we must specify the following:

1. *Sources* with available supplies or capacity to be allocated in each planning period. The number of sources is m (in our example $m = 3$), and it is equal to the number of rows in the transportation matrix. The available supply at each source is S_i $(i = 1, 2, \ldots, m)$. In our example, $S_1 = 2,400$, $S_2 = 4,000$, and $S_3 = 3,600$ tons of fuel per week.
2. *Destinations* with specified requirements for each period. The number of destina-

TABLE E-1 Transportation matrix for airport-refueling example

From	To				Weekly fuel supplies (tons)
	A_1	A_2	A_3	A_4	
F_1	$10	$8	$5	$6	2,400
F_2	$5	$2	$6	$3	4,000
F_3	$9	$7	$4	$7	3,600
Weekly fuel requirements, tons	2,300	3,400	2,500	1,800	10,000 / 10,000

tions is n (in our example $n = 4$), and it is equal to the number of columns in the matrix. The requirement or demand for each destination is D_j ($j = 1, 2, ..., n$). In our example, $D_1 = 2,300$, $D_2 = 3,400$, $D_3 = 2,500$, and $D_4 = 1,800$ tons of fuel per week.

3. *Unit shipping cost for each route* C_{ij} measures the cost of shipping 1 unit from source i to destination j. In our example we have $m \cdot n = (3)(4) = 12$ shipping routes and the corresponding costs are shown in the matrix; for F_1 to A_1, $C_{11} = \$10$; for F_1 to A_2, $C_{12} = \$8$; ... ; for F_3 to A_4, $C_{34} = \$7$.

4. *Amount shipped per route* X_{ij} is a variable whose value we seek to determine. When multiplied by the unit cost for a given route $C_{ij}X_{ij}$, it provides the total cost of that particular shipment.

5. *Total transportation cost* Z is the criterion for evaluating alternative shipping schedules which satisfy supply and demand restrictions. In other words, Z is the index of performance of feasible solutions to the transportation problem.

E-4 FORMULATION OF THE TRANSPORTATION PROBLEM

Our formulation of the transportation problem must specify an objective function and the set of constraints that must be met by our shipping schedule. The objective function here is the total transportation cost Z, and the constraints relate to the need to meet the requirements for each destination from the supply available at each source.

This type of formulation is similar to that used for the simplex method (see Supplementary Chapter C). For our example, we seek to determine values for the possible shipments from the fuel sources to the airports (X_{11}, X_{12}, ..., X_{34}) that will minimize the objective function

$$\text{Total shipping cost } Z = C_{11}X_{11} + C_{12}X_{12} + \cdots + C_{34}X_{34}$$

subject to a set of $m = 3$ supply and $n = 4$ demand constraints.

Each *supply constraint* states that the sum of all shipments out of a particular source must equal the total amount available at that source. For fuel source F_1, this is specified as

$$\begin{bmatrix} \text{Amount shipped} \\ \text{to } A_1 \end{bmatrix} + \begin{bmatrix} \text{amount shipped} \\ \text{to } A_2 \end{bmatrix} + \begin{bmatrix} \text{amount shipped} \\ \text{to } A_3 \end{bmatrix} + \begin{bmatrix} \text{amount shipped} \\ \text{to } A_4 \end{bmatrix}$$

$$= \begin{bmatrix} \text{amount available} \\ \text{at } F_1 \end{bmatrix}$$

or
$$X_{11} + X_{12} + X_{13} + X_{14} = S_1 = 2,400 \text{ tons}$$

Similar additional constraints are imposed by supply availability at fuel sources F_2 and F_3.

Each *destination constraint* states that the sum of all shipments received at a destination must equal the requirements of that destination. For airport A_2 this is specified as

$$\begin{bmatrix} \text{Amount received} \\ \text{from } F_1 \end{bmatrix} + \begin{bmatrix} \text{amount received} \\ \text{from } F_2 \end{bmatrix} + \begin{bmatrix} \text{amount received} \\ \text{from } F_3 \end{bmatrix} = \begin{bmatrix} \text{amount required} \\ \text{at } A_2 \end{bmatrix}$$

or
$$X_{12} + X_{22} + X_{32} = D_2 = 3,400 \text{ tons}$$

Similar further constraints are imposed by fuel requirements at airports A_1, A_3, and A_4.

E-5 CONDITIONS REQUIRED FOR USING THE TRANSPORTATION METHOD

Before we can apply the transportation method to solve a specific problem, it is necessary to satisfy the following conditions:

1. *Supplies and requirements must be expressed in the same units.* This condition means that shipments received at any destination from different sources must be indistinguishable. In other words, all shipments must be measured in homogeneous units (bushels of wheat, gallons of paint, etc.). In the example, supplies and requirements are all expressed in tons of fuel.
2. *Total supply must equal total demand.* If this condition is not met, we proceed as follows:
    a. If total demand exceeds total available supply, $\sum_{j=1}^{n} D_j > \sum_{i=1}^{m} S_i$, we must add a *fictitious source*. The capacity assigned to this dummy source will be the total demand minus total supply, so that the problem is balanced. If total requirements for all airports in our example were 12,000 tons/wk, with available supplies still equal to 10,000, we would have to include a fictitious source F_4 with a capacity of 2,000 tons to supply the extra demand. Since this

quantity does not exist and will not have to be shipped, the unit shipping costs in the fourth row F_4 will all be zero.

b. If total available supply exceeds total demand, $\sum_{i=1}^{m} S_i > \sum_{j=1}^{n} D_j$, we must add a *fictitious destination*. The requirements for this dummy destination are set equal to the difference between total supply and total demand so that, again, the problem is balanced. Suppose that the total capacity at the three fuel sources in our example is increased to 11,500 tons/wk while airport requirements are still 10,000 tons/wk. In this case, we would have to add a fictitious destination, a dummy airport A_5, whose requirements would be set at 1,500 tons/wk. The unit shipping costs in the column for A_5 will all be zero, since all shipments to A_5 will never have to be made.

The requirement that total supply equal total demand in effect creates an additional constraint which makes any one of the original supply and demand constraints redundant. In the example, if we know only 6 constraints from a total of 7 $(m + n = 3 + 4)$, we can determine the missing constraint from the requirement that total demand equal total supply. Therefore, *the number of effective independent constraints in a balanced transportation problem equals the number of rows m plus the number of columns n minus 1*. For our example, this is $m + n - 1 = 3 + 4 - 1 = 6$.

3. All the assumptions that must hold in the general linear-programming case must also hold in the special case of the transportation problem.

The transportation problem, already represented in matrix form as in Table E-1, can be shown in graphical form as a network (Fig. E-1). Sources and

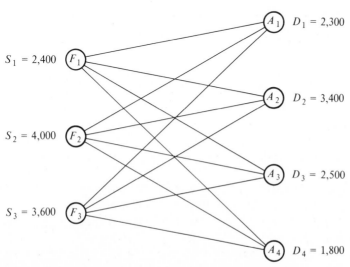

Fig. E-1   **Graphical network representation of transportation problem.**

destinations here are shown as circles, while shipment routes are shown as connecting links. A link corresponds to a cell in the matrix formulation. *Each solution evaluated by the transportation method includes as many positive shipments as there are effective independent constraints, or m + n − 1.* For the example this number is $3 + 4 − 1 = 6$. Therefore, the alternative shipping schedules to be evaluated will make use of only 6 links at a time out of 12 $[m \cdot n = (3)(4)]$ possible routes. If we visualize the links as pipelines, we seek to find which six pipelines to use and the amounts of fuel that will be shipped through each one of them so as to minimize the total weekly shipping cost. In the next section we describe a solution procedure designed to find the optimum feasible shipment schedule if one exists. The method is illustrated with our example, recognizing that for more realistic applications, one must resort to a computer.

E-6 TRANSPORTATION SOLUTION PROCEDURE

The procedure used to solve the transportation problem is similar to the one followed in the simplex method. Figure E-2 summarizes the basic steps, which are explained and illustrated below, using the airport-fuel-supply example.

Step 1   Obtain an Initial Solution

After a transportation problem has been balanced (total supply equals total demand), the first step is to obtain a starting solution. This is equivalent to getting a handle on the problem before an iterative procedure for possible improvements can be applied. For an existing transportation problem the current solution may be used as an initial one. Other methods are also available, and two of them, the northwest-corner rule and VAM, will be explained in detail shortly.

For any initial solution to be acceptable, it must meet three conditions:

1. It must be feasible; i.e., it must satisfy all the supply and demand constraints.
2. It must have a number of allocations, i.e., occupied matrix cells, equal to the sum of all constraints minus 1 $(m + n − 1)$.
3. The above allocations must be in positions that do not form a closed path.[1]

Any solution that satisfies the above conditions is known as a *basic feasible solution.*

Northwest-corner rule   A simple but inefficient way to obtain an initial solution is the northwest-corner rule. Starting with the cell at the upper left (or northwest) corner of the matrix and using available supply at the first source, we make all feasible allocations in the first row until this is exhausted. Next, we drop to the second row and continue with allocations from the second source until its supply is also depleted. This is continued with remaining rows until all destination require-

---

[1] A closed path, or loop, is formed by a group of occupied cells if one can start from any occupied cell and with right-angle (90°) turns at other occupied cells return to the starting point.

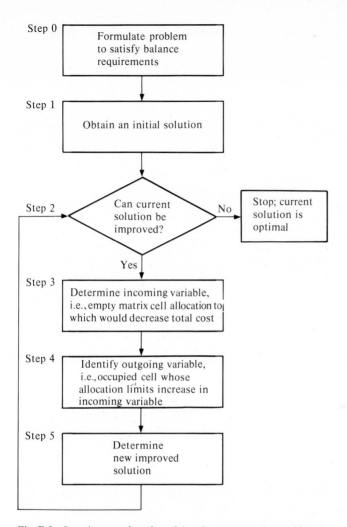

Fig. E-2   Iterative procedure for solving the transportation problem.

ments have been met from existing supplies. The initial solution for our example using the northwest-corner rule and its total transportation cost is shown in Table E-2.

By moving horizontally and vertically as successive demand and supply requirements are met, we ensure that the solution is feasible, that there are no loops, and that the number of positive allocations is equal to the number of rows and columns minus 1 ($m + n - 1 = 3 + 4 - 1 = 6$). A complication arises when following an allocation both a supply and a demand constraint are satisfied simultaneously. Since no diagonal movements are permitted, the procedure cannot continue. This condition is known as *degeneracy* and may also occur in later steps. One way to remove the degeneracy at this point is to rearrange the sequence of rows and columns in the matrix. Another approach will be described in a later section.

TABLE E-2   Initial solution for example using northwest-corner rule

From	To A_1	A_2	A_3	A_4	Available weekly supply
F_1	10 ⟨2,300⟩	8 ⟨100⟩	5	6	2,400
F_2	5	2 ⟨3,300⟩	6 ⟨700⟩	3	4,000
F_3	9	7	4 ⟨1,800⟩	7 ⟨1,800⟩	3,600
Weekly requirements	2,300	3,400	2,500	1,800	10,000 / 10,000

Total cost = 2,300($10) + 100($8) + 3,300($2) + 700($6)
+ 1,800($4) + 1,800($7) = $54,400

The advantages of simplicity and speed of the northwest-corner rule are often offset by the inferiority of the derived initial solution as measured by its total cost. This occurs because the rule ignores the unit cost value in each cell as the allocations are made. Another method that makes use of this valuable information and is often preferred for obtaining an initial solution is described next.

Vogel's approximation method (*VAM*)   In order to produce an improved initial solution, VAM utilizes the unit-cost information for alternative routes to make the most desirable allocation at each stage. The steps in VAM are as follows:

1. Calculate the difference between the two smallest unit-cost values for each row.
2. Repeat 1 for each column.
3. Select the row or column with the largest difference and proceed to make the largest feasible allocation in the cell with the smallest unit-cost value. Any ties in the values for differences or unit costs can be removed arbitrarily. At this point either a row or a column restriction is satisfied and is eliminated from further consideration.
4. Using the reduced matrix, return to step 1 and repeat the above procedure until all $m + n - 1$ allocations have been completed.

The row and column differences in each iteration represent the minimum penalty of failing to make the best allocation at that stage. By making use of this information VAM produces an initial solution which is often near the optimum or is itself the optimum. For this reason in certain applications, management may wish not to seek any further improvements.

The use of VAM is illustrated with our example in Table E-3, which shows the successive iterations separately to simplify the explanation of the procedure. After some practice, all the relevant calculations can be performed on an extended form of the initial matrix with added rows and columns for listing the VAM differences. The VAM initial solution is shown in Table E-4 with the allocations circled in the appropriate cells and the total cost at the bottom of the matrix.

TABLE E-3 Successive iterations for VAM initial solution in example

First iteration

From	To A_1	A_2	A_3	A_4	Supply	Row differences
F_1	10	8	5	6	2,400	1
F_2	5	2 ③,400	6	3	4,000	1
F_3	9	7	4	7	3,600	0
Demand	2,300	3,400	2,500	1,800		
Column differences	4	5*	1	3	Allocate 3,400 to F_2-A_2	

Second iteration

From	To A_1	A_3	A_4	Supply	Row differences
F_1	10	5	6	2,400	1
F_2	5 ⟨600⟩	6	3	600	2
F_3	9	4	7	3,600	3
Demand	2,300	2,500	1,800		
Column differences	4*	1	3	Allocate 600 to F_2-A_1	

(continued)

Table E-3 (*continued*)

Third iteration

From	To			Supply	Row differences
	A_1	A_3	A_4		
F_1	10	5	6	2,400	1
F_3	9	4 2,500	7	3,600	3*
Demand	1,700	2,500	1,800		
Column differences	1	1	1	Allocate 2,500 to F_3-A_3	

Fourth iteration

From	To		Supply	Row differences
	A_1	A_4		
F_1	10	6 1,800	2,400	4*
F_3	9	7	1,100	2
Demand	1,700	1,800		
Column differences	1	1	Allocate 1,800 to F_1-A_4	

The initial solution by VAM with a total cost of $43,800 represents a significant improvement over the one produced by the northwest-corner rule, for which the total cost was $54,400. It also satisfies all the requirements for an initial solution having $m + n - 1 = 3 + 4 - 1 = 6$ positive allocation without any closed path.

Step 2: Evaluate Initial Solution

Once an initial solution is available, the next step is to check it for possible improvement. Since the number of occupied cells must always remain equal to $m + n - 1$, the only way an improvement can come about is by switching allocations from an occupied to an empty cell. In other words, we try to see whether a reduction in total cost can be made by switching one of the current shipments to an unused route.

Testing an empty cell is done by making a trial allocation of 1 unit to it and

TABLE E-4   Initial solution produced by VAM for the example

From	To A_1	A_2	A_3	A_4	Supply
F_1	10 600	8	5	6 1,800	2,400
F_2	5 600	2 3,400	6	3	4,000
F_3	9 1,700	7	4 2,500	7	3,600
Demand	2,300	3,400	2,500	1,800	

Total cost = 600($10) + 1,800($6) + 600($5) + 3,400($2)
             + 1,700($9) + 2,500($4) = $43,800

calculating the net effect this will have on total cost. Such an allocation always creates a unique closed path in the transportation matrix. This in turn identifies the occupied cells at the corners of the closed path that will be affected by the new unit allocation. We must keep in mind that the trial allocation of 1 unit in an empty cell must not disturb the feasibility of the new solution. For this to happen, the occupied cells at the corners of the closed path must be adjusted by adding or subtracting 1 unit so that supply and demand constraints are again satisfied.

Using the northwest-corner-rule initial solution, let us see whether an improvement is possible by allocating 1 unit to cell F_2-A_4. The unique closed path formed by this allocation is

$$F_2\text{-}A_4 \rightarrow F_2\text{-}A_3 \rightarrow F_3\text{-}A_3 \rightarrow F_3\text{-}A_3 \rightarrow F_3\text{-}A_4$$

shown with dashed lines in Table E-5. Sometimes the resulting unique closed path is more roundabout. This is shown with solid lines for a trial allocation in cell F_3-A_1.

The steps taken to evaluate an empty cell, such as F_2-A_4, are as follows:

1. Identify the occupied cells on the corners of the resulting closed path that will be affected by the unit trial allocation.
2. Determine the type of allocation adjustment necessary to maintain feasibility. This involves subtracting or adding 1 unit to the occupied corner cells.
3. Measure the cost changes caused by the necessary allocation adjustments.
4. Calculate the net effect from such cost changes representing an improvement index for the empty cell being tested.

To illustrate this procedure with cell F_2-A_4, the above steps are summarized in Table E-6. For each unit allocated to cell F_2-A_4 the total cost will be reduced by $6. Therefore, switching shipments from one of the routes indicated in the initial solution to the unused route F_2-A_4 represents an improvement.

TABLE E-5   Trial allocation in cell F_2-A_4 and resulting unique closed path for northwest-corner initial solution

From	A_1	A_2	A_3	A_4	Supply
			To		
F_1	10 — (2,300) ←	8 + (100)	5	6	2,400
F_2	5	2 — (3,000) ←	6 + (700) ← —	3 — (+1)	4,000
F_3	9 (+1)	7	4 — (1,800) — —	7 — (1,800)	3,600
Demand	2,300	3,400	2,500	1,800	

TABLE E-6

Affected occupied cells	Allocation adjustment	Total cost change	Improvement index for F_2-A_4 per unit
F_2-A_4	+1	+\$3	Increase:
			$+3 + 4 = \$ +7$
F_2-A_3	−1	−\$6	Decrease:
			$-6 - 7 = -13$
F_3-A_3	+1	+\$4	———
F_3-A_4	−1	−\$7	$= \$ -6$

Step 3: Determine the Incoming Variable (or Empty Cell for New Allocation)

The question at this point is whether other empty cells might allow greater improvements than F_2-A_4. This can be answered by evaluating the remaining empty cells in the same manner. Let us consider cell F_3-A_1, for which the resulting closed path is shown in Table E-7 with solid lines. An allocation to cell F_3-A_1 would increase total cost by \$7 per unit (see Table E-8). Thus, F_3-A_1 is disqualified as an alternative shipping route. Similar evaluations for other empty cells are shown in the initial-solution matrix repeated as Table E-7. The reader is asked to verify them.

The empty cell selected to be used in an improved solution corresponds to the unused route with the largest negative value for the improvement index. This is known as the *incoming variable*. Inspection of Table E-8 reveals that cell F_1-A_4 has the largest negative value and would thus result in the greatest cost reduction per unit allocation to it.

TABLE E-7 Northwest-corner-rule initial solution with improvement-index values for empty cells

From	To A_1	A_2	A_3	A_4	Supply
F_1	10 (2,300)	8 (100) —	5 → (+1)	6 −9	2,400
F_2	5 +1	2 + (3,300) ←	6 — (700)	3 −6	4,000
F_3	9 +7	7 +7	4 + (1,800) ←	7 — (1,800)	3,600
Demand	2,300	3,400	2,500	1,800	

TABLE E-8

Affected occupied cells	Allocation adjustment		Total cost change	Improvement index for F_2-A_4 per unit
F_3-A_1	+1		+$9	Increase:
F_1-A_3		−1	−$4	$+9 + 6 + 8 = \$\ \ 23$
F_2-A_3	+1		+$6	Decrease:
F_2-A_2		−1	−$2	$-4 - 2 - 10 = \ \ -16$
F_1-A_2	+1		+$8	
F_1-A_1		−1	−$10	$\$ \ +7$

Rule 1

The incoming variable selected to improve the current solution is the empty cell, or unused route, with the largest negative value for an improvement index.[1]

Inspection of Table E-7 reveals that cell F_1-A_4 has the largest negative index value and would thus result in the greatest cost reduction per unit allocation to it.[2]

---

[1] When the cell entries represent unit profits and we seek to find the distribution pattern that maximizes total profit, the improvement index for an empty cell corresponds to the *net increase* by a unit trial assignment in that cell.

[2] There is a more efficient procedure based on the simplex which evaluates all empty cells in one step. This however requires a lengthier explanation (see Ref. 2 in supp. chap. C).

Step 4: Identify the Outgoing Variable (or Occupied Cell to Exclude from New Solution)

To maintain the number of occupied cells in the improved solution equal to $m + n - 1$, an allocation to cell F_1-A_4 must force out an occupied cell from the current solution. In other words, the decision to incorporate a new shipping route F_1-A_4 implies the simultaneous elimination of an existing route. But which one?

The transportation method, as we have seen, requires only positive shipments. However, as we increase the allocation to cell F_1-A_4, we must simultaneously reduce the allocations on some of the affected occupied cells to maintain feasibility. These cells at the corners of the unique closed path, F_3-A_4, F_2-A_3, and F_1-A_2, are shown in the matrix in Table E-8 with a negative sign. From these, the cell with the smallest allocation (F_1-A_2, with 100 units) will be the first to reach zero as more and more units are assigned to F_1-A_4. Therefore, the outgoing shipping route in the present evaluation will be F_1-A_2, because it imposes the tightest limit, 100 units, on the allocation that will be made to F_1-A_4.

Rule 2

The outgoing variable in the current solution is the occupied cell in the unique closed path whose allocation will reach zero first as more units are assigned to the empty cell corresponding to the incoming variable.

Step 5: Determine New Improved Solution

The new improved solution resulting by allocating 100 units to the shipping route F_1-A_4 and eliminating route F_1-A_2 is shown in Table E-9. The total cost reduction from this change is $(100)(\$9) = \$900$.

TABLE E-9 Improved solution for example following first iteration with northwest-corner-rule initial solution

From	\multicolumn{4}{c}{To}	Supply
	A_1	A_2	A_3	A_4	
F_1	10 (2,300)	8	5	6 (100)	2,400
F_2	5	2 (3,400)	6 (600)	3	4,000
F_3	9	7	4 (1,900)	7 (1,700)	3,600
Demand	2,300	3,400	2,500	1,800	

Potential further improvements in the new solution can be determined by returning to step 2 and calculating new values for the improvement index of empty cells. If one or more empty cells have negative values, suggesting further total cost reductions, the transportation method repeats steps 3 and 4 in successive iterations until all such values are positive or zero.

The presence of only positive values for the improvement index means that the use of any of the empty cells will only increase total transportation costs. However, having one or more zero index values means that it is possible to employ alternative shipping routes without affecting total cost. This implies flexibility for management, so that the choice can be made with criteria other than costs, such as the safety or reliability of alternative routes.

In Prob. E-1 the reader is asked to verify that the VAM initial solution is an optimal one and to check whether alternative optimal solutions exist offering flexibility in covering the fuel requirements of airports A_1, A_2, A_3, and A_4 from sources F_1, F_2, and F_3.

E-7 DEGENERACY

One instance of degeneracy may occur when in developing an initial solution we obtain fewer than $m + n - 1$ allocations. It is also possible for this complication to arise in step 4, when we determine the outgoing variable in the current solution. Suppose that from the cells whose shipments must be reduced two will reach zero first simultaneously instead of one. In other words, there are two cells with the same smallest allocation. Then as the incoming variable reaches its maximum value, the two occupied cells will both be forced to lose all their allocations. When this happens, the number of the remaining occupied cells becomes less than $m + n - 1$ and the transportation method cannot continue; in other words, the problem solution is degenerate.

One approach to removing this degeneracy is to pretend that one of the two outgoing variables remains in the solution with a very small allocation, designated by the Greek letter epsilon ε. This permits the number of occupied cells in the new solution to be equal to $m + n - 1$ even though in reality the assignment in one of them is negligible. In determining the new solution, in evaluating it for improvement, and in subsequent steps, the ε allocation is treated like a regular occupied cell until we reach the optimum. At that time we drop it, so that the matrix will show only the legitimate allocations.

E-8 SUMMARY

Certain important problems related to the distribution of goods from existing facilities, the location of a new plant or warehouse, and aggregate production planning can be formulated for solution by the linear-programming transportation method. This special case of the simplex method enables management to reach a solution efficiently and conduct valuable sensitivity analysis with widely available computer programs. The general objective in this type of problem is to satisfy the demand at different destinations from sources with available supplies (or capacity) at minimum cost.

Application of the transportation method requires that supply and demand constraints be expressed in common units and that all relationships satisfy the more general linear-programming assumptions (linearity, divisibility, and determinacy). Furthermore, it is necessary that total supply equal total demand; i.e., the problem should be balanced. If this is not initially the case, a fictitious source or destination is introduced to absorb the difference at zero cost.

With the problem balanced and in matrix form, the first step is to find an initial solution, preferably with a method that takes into account the unit cost of each shipping route, such as Vogel's approximation method (VAM). The transportation method then proceeds, like the simplex, to evaluate the initial solution for improvement by calculating a performance index for unused route (empty cells). Negative index values suggest further reduction in transportation costs achieved by switching shipments to a new route after eliminating a current one. The process is repeated until no further improvements are possible.

It is important in successive iterations for the number of occupied matrix cells in the current solution to equal the sum of the supply and demand constraints minus 1 $(m + n - 1)$. Otherwise the solution is degenerate, and special adjustments are necessary before we can continue.

REVIEW QUESTIONS

1. Explain the meaning of the requirement that the transportation problem be balanced.
2. What adjustment is necessary if total demand is greater than total supply?
3. What adjustment is necessary if total supply is greater than total demand?
4. Why is one of the supply m and demand n constraints redundant?
5. Why is the northwest-corner rule inefficient in yielding an initial solution?
6. What makes VAM an efficient procedure?
7. What is the meaning of row and column differences in VAM?
8. When is an initial or intermediate solution called degenerate?
9. How can the degeneracy be removed?

PROBLEMS

1. Refer to chapter example. Prove that the initial solution obtained by VAM is an optimal one.
2. Find the minimum-transportation-cost solution for the following problem:

From plant	To warehouse			Supply
	W_1	W_2	W_3	
A	$8	$7	$4	36
B	$3	$5	$2	42
C	$2	$6	$5	58
Requirements	45	20	71	

3. A wheat wholesaler has signed contracts for the purchase of wheat from growers in cities X, Y, and Z. The amounts purchased are to be shipped to food processing plants in cities A, B, and C with unit shipping costs as shown below. Determine the minimum-cost-shipping schedule using the northwest-corner-rule initial solution.

From	To food processing plant			Amount purchased, 1,000 bushels
	A	B	C	
X	$45	$37	$61	30
Y	$52	$65	$43	70
Z	$27	$48	$39	50
Demand, 1,000 of bushels	60	20	40	

4. A large beer company operates three breweries which must supply five marketing areas. The relevant supply and demand data including unit shipping costs in thousands are as shown. Determine the distribution plan that will minimize the total transportation cost.

From brewery	To market					Brewery capacity, 1,000 gal/wk
	M_1	M_2	M_3	M_4	M_5	
B_1	$12	$11	$13	$17	$18	640
B_2	$22	$16	$14	$15	$19	860
B_3	$14	$23	$21	$25	$12	920
Demand, 1,000 gal/wk	380	730	520	430	650	

5. An oil consortium wishes to determine how weekly capacity from its four oil fields should be allocated to three European countries so as to maximize total profit.

From oil-field	To country			Oil-field capacity, 1,000 bbl/wk
	A	*B*	*C*	
F_1	$120	$135	$125	2,200
F_2	$131	$122	$128	1,500
F_3	$125	$130	$143	1,400
F_4	$111	$118	$115	1,100
Demand, 1,000 bbl/wk	4,700	2,500	3,800	

6. Find the minimum-cost distribution plan to satisfy demand for cement at three construction sites from capacity at three cement plants using the northwest-corner-rule initial solution.

From	To construction site			Capacity, tons/month
	1	2	3	
P_1	$60	$72	$85	600
P_2	$78	$68	$62	300
P_3	$51	$59	$55	1,000
Demand, tons/month	400	500	800	

SELECTED REFERENCES

See list for Supplementary Chapter C.

Part Three

OPERATIONS
PLANNING
AND CONTROL

Part 3, "Operations Planning and Control," focuses on decisions required in medium- and short-term planning. Here, it is assumed that productive capacity is relatively fixed and aimed at its optimum utilization with existing resources.

In Chap. 11, the forecasting system and the vital role it plays as a link with an organization's environment is examined. Forecasting as an activity seeks to estimate future demand in terms of quantity, timing, quality, and location for products and services. This is accomplished with both subjective and objective methods of varying complexity for different lengths of planning horizons. Chapter 12 looks at aggregate planning, which links long-term planning with short-term planning, i.e., scheduling decisions. With capacity assumed fixed, aggregate planning attempts to determine the best utilization of inventories, work force, and subcontracting to satisfy demand with a minimum total production cost. Chapters 13 and 14 address the inventory problem in both its conceptual and practical aspects. Of the two chapters the first discusses certain inventory models that highlight the key issues, while the second describes the most common systems for managing inventories under the assumptions of independent and dependent final demand. Chapter 15, which focuses on operations scheduling is the last and most detailed step before any plans are translated into action. Different scheduling methods are presented for flow shop, job shop, and project type systems.

Chapter 16 focuses on the various approaches employed to control the performance of an organization. Most control efforts whether directed on quality, costs, job completion times, or other aspects rely on statistical sampling. Specific programs are designed so as to minimize the expected costs that may arise from poor performance going undetected (type II error) and unwarranted inspection(s) when things are going well (type I error). Chapter 17 looks at the maintenance function for both human and nonhuman resources. Here we survey typical problems calling for a policy of preventive maintenance versus repair, group versus individual replacement of parts and desired standby capacity. The chapter also examines certain key concepts in assessing the reliability of a system under various design configurations.

Part 3 concludes with Chap. 18 which provides a synthesis of the entire field of operations management, assesses current trends, and projects these trends into the future.

Chapter 11

DEMAND FORECASTING: SYSTEM AND METHODS

11-1   INTRODUCTION

Most managerial decisions, at all levels of an organization, are based explicitly or implicitly on some form of a forecast concerning the future. In a sense, a forecast becomes the connecting link between an organization and its environment, especially insofar as changes in the latter affect the organization's sphere of present and future activities.

> **Definition**
>
> *Forecasting* is the process of estimating future demand in terms of the quantity, timing, quality, and location for desired products and services.

In a stable environment with little or a predictable rate of change the need for a forecast is nonexistent. As the environment becomes more complex and dynamic, however, a forecast of future conditions becomes indispensable. Whereas a few centuries ago one expected only minor changes to occur in one's entire lifetime, nowadays the social, economic, political, and technological aspects of our environment are changing at such a pace and in such diverse ways that forecasting even for the near future becomes a challenge. Hence, forecasting has become a vital function that pervades every planning effort in most spheres of human activity, especially that of producing to satisfy an enormous variety of needs for products and services.

The discussion in this chapter focuses on the importance of forecasting as an activity, the forecasting system within an organization, and various forecasting methods for different applications.

11-2   IMPORTANCE OF DEMAND FORECASTS

Even though forecasting may not always take the form of a formal or explicit activity, it is responsible for the most valuable input to planning decisions. In this regard, it is useful to top management and all functions within an organization, especially marketing, finance, and production. Forecasts can thus be classified in terms of the user of the information.

In the context of operations management there is a need for different types of

TABLE 11-1   Types of decisions affected by different forecasts

Future planning period	Organization decisions	Individual decisions
Long-term (2–10 yr)	Types of products and services to offer Types and sizes of markets to serve Processes and technologies to employ Plant location and plant size	Types of activities to engage in (work, social, sports, etc.) Selection of form of employment Type and level of education to pursue Choice of a spouse Selection of area to work and live in, house to buy or rent
Intermediate-term (1–24 months)	Size of work force to employ Kinds and amounts of inventories to maintain Amount of desired subcontracting when needed Amount of desired overtime	Attendance of a special education course or conference Scheduling a medical checkup Painting the house Selection of a place for summer vacation
Short-term (1–5 wk)	Assignment of orders to specific facilities and personnel Dispatching to meet delivery times	Arrangement of work-related and social appointments Weekly diet Selection of a place for a weekend trip Choice of entertainment (movies, concerts, other)

forecasts based on the length of the planning period of interest. Table 11-1 summarizes the types of decisions affected by forecasts of different planning horizons. Whereas for most types of personal decisions the forecasts for the future may not be clearly spelled out or approached in a systematic manner, forecasts for organizations tend to be articulated in concrete terms.

Forecasting is at best an art. This is due to the inherent uncertainty about the future and the complex nature of processes in the environment that generate the demand for an organization's products and services. However, today's production manager can be assisted by many powerful techniques that can be combined with sound managerial judgment to advance the state of the forecasting art considerably.

11-3 THE DEMAND FORECASTING SYSTEM

As an activity within an organization, forecasting is expected to provide relevant information concerning the future to marketing, finance, production, and others that require it for planning purposes. This function is performed by a system which, like any other system, can be analyzed in terms of its key components:

1. Forecasting-system outputs, information provided by a forecast
2. Forecasting-system inputs, information needed to prepare a forecast
3. Forecasting constraints, factors limiting the method(s) used
4. Forecasting-system decisions
5. Forecasting-system performance criteria
6. Forecasting methods, for converting inputs to outputs

These components specify an information-processing system which is an important part of the organization's nervous system (Fig. 11-1).

Forecasting-System Outputs

From the production manager's point of view, what is needed to plan for different periods in the future is a forecast of expected demand rather than future sales. *Demand relates to orders received from customers, while sales refer to shipments made.* Demand thus may sometimes differ from sales in amount, due to limited capacity (thus lost sales) or in the timing of shipments due to production lead times. When

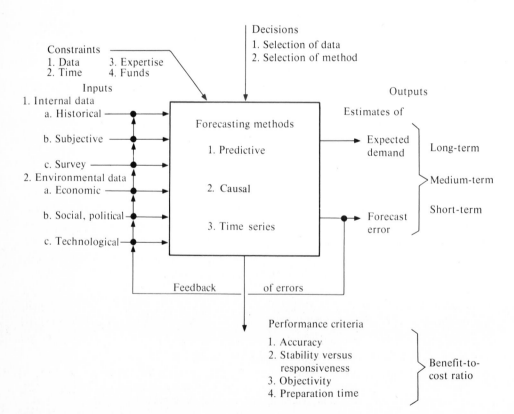

Fig. 11-1   The forecasting system.

there is no record of customer orders, it may be necessary to rely on sales data only, but it should be recognized that the resulting forecasts may not relate exactly to future demand for the reasons stated.

The output of a forecasting system is expressed in whatever form is most valuable to the user of the information. Thus, to formulate a marketing strategy it may be necessary to have the estimate of future demand expressed in dollar sales broken down by region or by some customer attribute such as age, sex, education, or other. Finance, on the other hand, requires a forecast that can easily be translated into capital requirements for new capacity, working capital, or funds for other purposes such as energy conservation equipment.

Before a forecast can be used for production planning, we must translate demand for output units into requirements for various production inputs. Thus, an estimate in physical units of future demand for a product or service must be converted into a set of requirements for materials or parts needed, labor-hours of desired skills, machine-hours on different types of equipment, energy, and others (see Fig. 11-2).

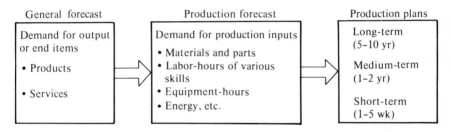

Fig. 11-2   Translation of demand into production input requirements.

The conversion of demand in final products into demand for input requirements depends mainly on the stability of the product design. If the product characteristics remain relatively stable from period to period, historical data can be used to develop statistical relationships, e.g., regression equations, relating output volume to input requirements, as shown in Fig. 11-3. Given a forecast for the end items, we can go back to the regression lines and estimate the input requirements that correspond to this production volume.

For products or services whose designs change often due to fashion trends, technological improvements, or other factors, this method of statistical extrapolation is not applicable. In this case, the conversion is carried out using a *bill of materials*, which has the input requirements for each design style in matrix form. Once a general forecast for a given design is obtained, the input requirements are computed in a straightforward method from the table. A simplified case for three designs *A*, *B*, and *C* is illustrated in Table 11-2.

When considering the length of the planning horizon for a forecast, we need to know the system's reaction time, or lead time, to changes in some key characteristic and the frequency with which such decisions are considered, i.e., the management review time.

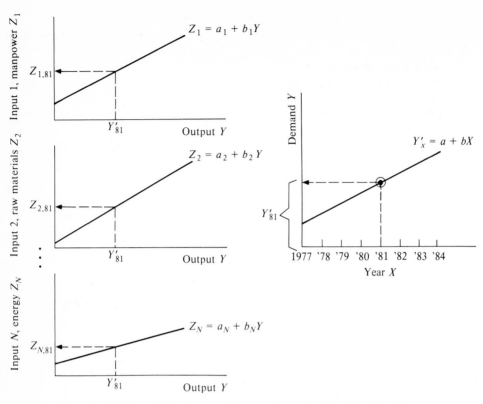

Fig. 11-3 Converting final demand into input requirements for products(s) with stable design.

The *lead time* includes the time to reach a decision whether a certain type of change is needed and the time to implement the decision. Different production inputs require different lead times to be changed. For example, adding a new wing to a hospital may require 2 years (time for reaching a decision, completing engineering plans, constructing the building, installing equipment, etc.), but hiring more medical doctors may take 6 months to a year.

TABLE 11-2 Converting final output demands into input requirements when product design is unstable

Design style	Input requirements per unit				General forecast Y'
	1	2	$\cdots$	N	
A Deluxe	3	2	$\cdots$	4	$100 = A_{81}$
B General	2	2	$\cdots$	6	$150 = B_{81}$
C Economy	2	1	$\cdots$	3	$200 = C_{81}$
Total requirements	1,000	700		1,900	

Review time depends on managerial policy about how often certain changes may be desired. The hiring of unskilled hospital personnel may be reviewed on a weekly or even daily basis, but decisions related to capacity expansion may be considered 2 or 3 years after the most recent addition.

General rule

The length of the period covered by a forecast must be at least equal to the lead time plus the review time for the production input or capacity change(s) under consideration.

Thus, if the lead time for capacity changes is 2 years and the review time is equal to 1 year after the most recent change, the forecast for capacity requirements must look at least 3 years into the future. Replenishment of parts used in an assembly, however, where the lead time is 1 week and the inventory level is reviewed biweekly, require a forecast of requirements at least 3 weeks into the future.

Forecasting-System Inputs

The data needed to prepare a demand forecast can be obtained from internal and/or external sources. Historical data in the form of a time series on previous sales or orders, expert opinions of an organization's personnel, and results of special surveys are the most frequently used information inputs that can be generated within the organization.

External sources may provide valuable information in the form of economic, social, political, and technological forecasts. Additional sources may include industry experts, private consulting firms, and government agencies.

For a short- and medium-term forecast in a relatively stable environment, one usually relies on internal sources, often supported by some type of economic forecast. However, as an organization looks further into the future in order to formulate long-term strategies on new products, processes, and markets, information from external sources concerning competitors, new trends in technology, and likely developments on the social, political, and international scene become extremely valuable.

Forecasting-System Constraints

The selection of the forecasting method and the value of the forecasts prepared depend heavily on the constraints imposed on the forecasting system. Most important among these are the following:

1. The time available to prepare a forecast
2. The lack of relevant data from internal and external sources

3. The quality of available data
4. The expertise within the organization
5. The available computing facilities

It can be seen that constraints 1 to 3 can seriously limit the quality of the forecast, while 4 and 5 can be relaxed by increasing the budget allocated to the forecasting system.

Forecasting-System Decisions

In operating a forecasting system, management must make decisions with respect to the data and the method(s) that will be used to develop a forecast. The data may be in the form needed or may require adjustment or aggregation. If there is a long history of demand, care must be exercised with regard to "how far back to go."

The choice of method to prepare the forecast will depend on the amount and quality of data available, the time needed, and the expertise that can be secured.

Forecasting-System Performance Criteria

The effectiveness of the forecasting system in serving the organization can be evaluated on the basis of four criteria:

1. Accuracy
2. Stability versus responsiveness
3. Objectivity in the treatment of historical data
4. Time required to prepare forecast

Accuracy of the forecast   By far the most important attribute of a forecasting system is the accuracy of its forecasts. The difference between actual demand and forecast demand for a given period, i.e., the forecast error, is always translated into costs. Therefore, any persistent bias in preparing a forecast, whether optimistic or pessimistic, can be a source of serious difficulty for the organization. Any time actual demand is less than forecast demand, we are left with idle capacity or surplus inventory that cost money (tied-up capital, etc.). Similarly, when actual demand is greater than forecast, we suffer the consequences of shortages in the form of forgone profits, expediting expenses, and possible loss of good will.

Management cannot expect perfect performance, but an attempt should be made to have enough accuracy in the forecasts for the combined cost of surpluses and shortages of inventory and capacity to be minimized.

Stability versus responsiveness   The immense complexity and inherent uncertainty in the organization's environment is responsible for random fluctuations in actual demand from period to period. Such variations may conceal an underlying pattern due to a long-term growth trend or seasonal influences. A good forecasting system is expected to smooth out such random fluctuations so that subsequent forecast(s) will not be unduly affected by such irregular changes. In doing so the system displays *stability*.

However, we also expect the forecasting system to be sensitive enough to the fluctuations observed to reveal any genuine changes in the process that generates demand for products or services. Thus, the forecasting system should sense a jump in the average level of demand due to a recent market expansion rather than smooth it out. This property we call *responsiveness*.

It is obvious that we are attempting an important compromise. It is therefore desirable to have the forecasting system operate in two modes. The *stable mode* is employed when the environment changes slowly, while the *responsive mode* is called on when there are significant developments that affect the process that generates demand.

Objectivity   Sometimes current conditions reflect changes in the environment that are not incorporated in the historical data used to prepare a forecast. Rather than being subjective in the treatment of the data, it is preferable to treat the data objectively first and then adjust the resulting forecast to account for the more recent developments. Any arbitrary selection or manipulation of data distorts reality to the point where it is difficult to evaluate the final estimate.

Time required to prepare a forecast   For a forecasting system to be effective, it is necessary to make needed forecasts available on time for the decisions that rely on them. Anything else becomes an academic exercise at the expense of the organization's success.

Benefit-to-cost ratio   If one were to use a single criterion of performance for the forecasting system, it should be a benefit-to-cost ratio, i.e., the ratio of the benefits derived to the costs of developing and operating it. This is easier said than done, but an attempt can be made to assess the improvement in the quality of decisions made with a given forecast (measured by cost savings) and to compare this with the cost of installing and maintaining the forecasting system. A critical trade-off for top management is to remove as much as feasible of the environmental uncertainty through more accurate forecasts or to provide the desired flexibility to cope with that uncertainty.

Organizational Position and Responsibilities

Of the different functions within the organization, marketing is the most suitable home for the forecasting system, thanks to marketing's multiple contacts with the organization's environment and the sensitivity of its personnel to existing trends and recent developments.

To reduce the conflict between marketing and production, the latter assumes the responsibility to produce within the limits of the forecast. However, when demand exceeds the forecast maximum level, any increases in production costs or delays in delivery time are charged to marketing. Costs arising from the forecast error, a measure of the environment's uncertainty, are generally charged to the marketing function which is responsible for anticipating future events.

If the above arrangement is not desirable, forecasting should be an independent staff function reporting directly to top management.

11-4   FORECASTING METHODS

It has previously been suggested that an organization needs several kinds of forecasts to plan for the future. In each case the forecast to be used depends on the activity being planned and the length of the planning horizon. Selection of the appropriate method will be influenced by the constraints that exist when preparing the forecast, e.g., the availability and quality of relevant data, time, expertise, and computational facilities. Existing forecasting techniques fall into three major categories, subjective (or predictive), causal, and time series, discussed in detail in the following sections.

11-5   SUBJECTIVE (OR PREDICTIVE) FORECASTING METHODS

Subjective, or predictive, methods refer to the variety of techniques that rely primarily on the experience and opinions of people inside or outside the organization. Such techniques are generally employed either when there is little time or no past relevant data or when available data may not be enough to cover possible developments in the more distant future.

Introducing a new product, say an electric car, or a new service, such as a new supersonic commercial flight, represents activities with limited or nonexisting historical data. The second major application of subjective forecasting methods is for long-range strategic planning. The sophistication of subjective forecasting methods may vary considerably, but all of them are difficult to evaluate in terms of accuracy in the final estimates.

Subjective-Estimates Survey

For many companies a widely used approach for developing a demand forecast draws on the experience, knowledge, and "sixth sense" of their own people. In a typical case, individual salesmen are asked to submit estimates of anticipated demand in their areas for a future period. These figures are then pooled at the regional level and adjusted to take into account regional economic, demographic, and other factors not previously considered. The revised regional estimates are then combined at headquarters with further adjustments related to the economy, international trade, competitors, and other developments. The final estimate for total demand is the sum of subjective inputs from a variety of sources that summarizes the whole organization's expectations of future demand.

Such an approach can produce a forecast rather quickly, at low cost, and without any need for special expertise. At the same time, however, it suffers from a few drawbacks: (1) there is a tendency to allow recent experiences to play a more dominant influence than they should; (2) dominant personalities can produce estimates that depart seriously from the more general consensus, and (3) the lack of any measure of accuracy in the estimate makes it difficult to plan how to cope with large errors.

Subjective forecasts can be supplemented by using the results of consumer surveys, customer surveys, distributor surveys, or more carefully planned studies such as marketing research and market trials. The use of these procedures depends on the value of the information obtained and the time and funds available to secure it.

The Delphi Method

An increasingly popular method relying on subjective opinions but utilizing them more effectively is the Delphi method. This approach uses a panel of experts that respond to a questionnaire about future demand. Individual estimates are summarized and returned to the panel members so that if they wish, they can revise their original guesses. This critical feedback mechanism makes it easier to arrive at an estimate of demand most people will accept. It is possible to have several rounds that will aid in converging to some form of consensus, even though maverick opinions are not ignored. The cost of this method is generally medium to high, depending on the panel composition and the number of rounds used.

The Delphi method, originally applied in technological forecasting, has been used for a variety of long-term predictions in operations management for which historical data are insufficient. It may also be helpful in developing new products, acquiring new capacity, penetrating new markets, and making other strategic decisions.

11-6 CAUSAL FORECASTING METHODS

It is sometimes possible, especially for short- and medium-term forecasting, to assume that the demand-generating process will remain stable. It may then be helpful to construct a forecasting model that relates demand to the internal or environmental variables believed to cause changes in the observed demand level. A model attempting to unveil the structure and operation of a process (social, economic, or other) that determines demand for our products or services takes the form of one or more equations, usually statistical in nature.

In building a causal forecasting model we proceed in three steps:

1. *Identify one or more variables that can be assumed to influence demand.* Changes in such factors as GNP, disposable income, births, marriages, construction permits, and others are frequently responsible for increases or decreases in the demand for many items. The type and number of variables to be included requires experience and insight. Furthermore, we must consider the degree of accuracy necessary in our forecasts for effective planning.
2. *Select the form of the relationship(s) that link the causation variables with demand.* Even though computations are easier with linear relationships, if the implied assumptions do not hold, we can use certain transformations, e.g., logarithms, to convert some nonlinear forms into linear ones.

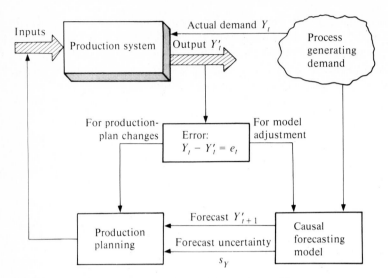

Fig. 11-4   Development and use of a causal forecasting model.

3. *Validate the forecasting model so that it will satisfy both commonsense and statistical tests as an adequate representation of the process it describes.* The approach taken is summarized in Fig. 11-4. Causal models can be classified as (1) regression- and correlation-analysis models, (2) econometric models, (3) input-output models, (4) systems dynamics models, and others.

Regression-Analysis Models

Demand can often be linked to one or more causes in the form of an equation in which demand is the dependent variable and the causative factors are viewed as independent variables. This type of forecasting model can be developed using regression analysis. The usefulness of the regression equation is evaluated by the standard error of the estimate s_Y and the coefficient of determination r^2. The first measures the expected uncertainty, or range of variation in a future forecast, while the second indicates the proportion of variation in demand explained by the independent variable(s) included in the model.

In the service sector, an airline's demand on a given route may depend on scheduled flights, types of aircraft used, GNP, prices of other transportation modes, etc. The demand, however, of a durable consumer item such as an electrical appliance or a piece of furniture may be related to disposable income, new housing starts, new marriages during the year, or other.

It is often advisable to start with a simple model that makes common sense and enrich it, if needed, for increased accuracy. Such an approach facilitates acceptance and implementation by management, while keeping the data collection and processing costs low. Relevant data can be found in government and industry publications or provided by time-sharing companies that maintain extensive data banks on a wide variety of economic, social, demographic, and other statistics. Data processing has also become easier and less costly with the availability of many commercial computer programs for regression analysis with the accompanying statistical tests.

Two-variable regression models The simplest possible regression model is one in which demand is related to one independent variable only

$$Y = f(X)$$

where Y = level of demand
  X = causative factor

In the examples cited, a commercial airline may select as the most important factor to estimate weekly demand per route the number of flights scheduled per week. Producers of home electrical appliances, however, may believe that in their case the most significant factor is disposable income or new housing starts 1 year ago, to allow for construction lead time.

The form of a two-variable, or bivariate, regression equation may be linear

$$Y = a + bX \tag{11-1}$$

exponential

$$Y = ab^X \tag{11-2}$$

parabolic

$$Y = a + bX + cX^2 \tag{11-3}$$

or other.

In Eqs. (11-1) to (11-3), a, b, and c represent the unknown parameters that must be specified from the pairs of observed values of X and Y. Conceivably, in different years the same values of X, say new housing starts, may be associated with different values of Y, demand for appliances. The forecast value of Y derived from the regression equation by specifying the value of X thus represents only an expected or average estimate of demand.

For any specific pair of observed values of X_t and Y_t the appropriate relationship is

$$Y_t = a + bX_t + e_t \tag{11-4}$$

or

$$\begin{bmatrix} \text{Actual demand} \\ \text{level in period } t \end{bmatrix} = \begin{bmatrix} \text{forecast in period } t \\ \text{using regression equation} \end{bmatrix} + \begin{bmatrix} \text{error} \\ \text{term} \end{bmatrix}$$

Here the error term e_t measures the difference between the actual value of Y and that which we would have predicted from the regression equation given the value of X.

The presence of the error term is due to the many possible sources of variation in demand which are left out of the model, such as the influence of demographic variables, competitor's prices, etc. Even though an equation can be approximated by drawing a smooth curve through the data, it is best determined by the method of least squares, as explained in Sec. 11-7.

Multivariate regression models   The reliability of forecasts obtained from a simple regression equation may be poor, as evidenced by a large value for the standard error s_Y and a large proportion of unexplained variation suggested by low values in the coefficient of determination r^2. Such a model can be improved by including additional independent variables that describe the process more realistically. The new model is known as a *multiple* or *multivariate regression model*

$$Y = f(X_1, X_2, \ldots, X_n)$$

In the home-appliance example, a multivariate model can be built by linking demand not only to new housing starts but also to other variables, such as disposable income, advertising, new marriages, and price. For an example, see Ref. 10.

The form of multivariate regression equations may be linear

$$Y = a_0 + a_1 X_1 + a_2 X_2 + \cdots + a_n X_n \tag{11-5}$$

or nonlinear, which in turn may be polynomial

$$Y = a_0 + a_1 X + a_2 X^2 + \cdots + a X^n \tag{11-6}$$

or other.

Both simple and multiple regression models require certain important assumptions about the error term to be satisfied. In particular:

1. The errors e_t are normally distributed with a mean value equal to zero and constant variability.
2. The errors observed in successive periods are independent of each other; i.e., there is no autocorrelation.
3. The equation(s) used in the original formulation or after suitable transformations must be linear.

Unless the consequences of violating these assumptions are understood, the use of this powerful class of models will be seriously limited and perhaps dangerously misleading.

The application of regression-analysis models has been increasing in the last 10 years and will continue to increase (1) as more managers realize the potential these models offer for producing accurate forecasts and (2) with the decreasing costs in the collection and processing of the extensive data required. Thus, such models, through the insight they provide into the environment and the key variables that shape demand, will be valuable for long-term forecasting to aid in strategic decisions on new product introduction, capacity expansion, and facility location.

Econometric Models

An econometric model consists of a system of statistical equations that interrelate the activities of different sectors of the economy and help assess their impact on the demand for a product or service. In this regard, it is an extension of regression analysis. Such models are employed for intermediate forecasts of changes in the economy's GNP in terms of many other (mostly time-lagged) variables interrelated in a set of 30 to 60 structural equations. *The need for econometric models is most pronounced when the causative factors that could be used in a regression equation are interdependent.* Available econometric models have been used at the industry, regional, and national levels.

Input-Output Models

An input-output table for the national economy or a geographic region displays in matrix form the flows from one sector to the others. By summing the elements of a row for a sector we have its output, while summing the elements of a column for a sector gives the inputs received from itself and other sectors. Using this highly versatile representation of the economy's structure, developed by W. Leontief, we can estimate the impact of a change in the output of one sector to the activities of other sectors as a series of chain reactions.

It can be seen that causal forecasting models require a considerable amount of data, expertise, and computations to be set up and produce estimates of future demand in a given industry. Therefore, their cost is medium to high, depending on the complexity of the model. Since we assume a relatively stable process for generating demand, causal models are mainly limited to existing products, services, and technologies.

11-7 TIME-SERIES FORECASTING METHODS

Time-series data refer to a set of values of some variable of interest measured at equally spaced time intervals. Thus, values of monthly inventory levels, quarterly sales, or annual production volume represent time-series data that we may wish to analyze for forecasting future activity levels.

Our interest here is on time series relating to demand (or sales) experienced in the past. In making a time-series analysis the objective is to reveal an underlying pattern in the process generating demand. Knowledge of such a pattern, we hope, will enable us to make more accurate forecasts of future demand, assuming of course that the process remains basically the same. Our attitude when selecting a time-series forecasting approach is that future demand will be largely determined by what happened in the past. If significant changes have occurred in the environment, such as an economic recession or an oil embargo, which are not reflected in our historical data, a forecast obtained from a time-series analysis can always be adjusted subjectively to portray current conditions.

Time-Series Components

In a time-series analysis, we assume that demand experienced in a given period is the result of four interacting factors, or *time-series components*. These factors refer to a trend, a business-cycle influence, possible seasonal fluctuations, and a random or irregular residue.

The trend component T   Complexity and uncertainty in the environment imply that it is natural to expect random fluctuations in the actual level of demand over time. Thus, it is preferable to study the average level of demand over a number of periods, rather than the specific demand in any one period. Experience with many products and services suggests that the average level of demand may remain the same or change with time as a result of a long-term or secular growth or decline.

Definition

In a time series, the *trend* refers to the long-term growth or decline in the average level of demand.

The cycle component C   The actual level of demand in one or more years may significantly differ from what one might expect on the basis of an existing long-term trend. This departure of actual demand from an assumed trend line is viewed as the result of a business cycle. The latter represents the combined effect of economic, social, technological, and other environmental forces on the demand we wish to estimate.

Definition

In a time-series, the *business cycle* refers to the large deviation of actual demand values from those expected on the basis of a trend, due to complex environmental influences.

Business cycles do not have repeatable patterns in terms of amplitude and duration. They may extend from one to several years. Since they cannot be predicted or controlled, our interest in forecasting is in developing an awareness of what phase of the business cycle we are in, so that our plans can be adjusted accordingly.

The seasonal component S   Unlike business cycles, which cannot be predicted, the demand for many products and services displays certain fluctuations whose pattern has a duration of 1 year and is repeated annually. This type is known as *seasonal variation* and may depend on the weather, e.g., ice-cream sales, tradition, e.g., greeting cards, or managerial policy, e.g., introduction of new car models.

Definition

In a time series, the *seasonal component* refers to the annually repetitive demand fluctuations that may be caused by weather, tradition, or other factors.

The random component R   The actual demand in a given period usually differs from what one might expect based on an understanding of the underlying trend, the current phase of the business cycle, and the prevailing seasonal pattern. Such discrepancy is attributed to the uncertainty of the environment, i.e., the "noise" in how we perceive the process generating demand to operate. This irregular, or random, residual is always unpredictable and as a result uncontrollable.

Definition

In a time series, the *random component* is the irregular residual in the demand due to the many complex random forces in the environment.

The four components of a time series are shown in Fig. 11-5. For long-term forecasts (2 or more years) seasonal and random factors are usually ignored, so that we can focus on the dominant trend component with minor emphasis on the business cycle. For medium-term forecasts (1 to 24 months), the trend factor becomes less important, and the focus shifts to the seasonal and cyclic factors, making allowance for the random component. For short-term forecasts (1 to 5 weeks) we are primarily concerned with the random fluctuations and any short-duration regular movements (daily or weekly patterns). Of course, the above types of forecasts must be interrelated and a distinction made on the basis of the type of productive activity requiring planning.

Interaction of time-series components   Having identified the compònents of a time series, it is necessary to make an important assumption about how they interact. Two time-series models have been proposed. In the *additive model* actual demand is viewed as the sum of each of the components

$$Y = \underbrace{T + C + S}_{\text{Pattern}} + \underbrace{R}_{\text{Noise}} \tag{11-7}$$

In such a formulation all components must be expressed in the same units, and the assumption of additivity creates both practical and theoretical difficulties. The *multiplicative model* assumes that actual demand can be expressed as the product of the

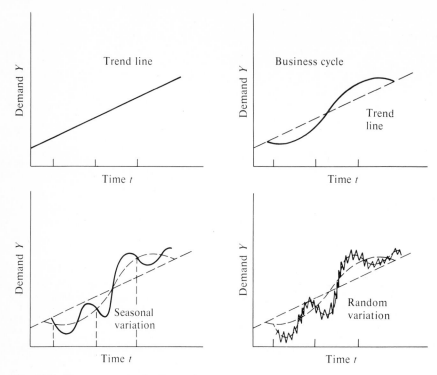

Fig. 11-5   The components of a time series.

time-series components:

$$T = \underbrace{T \cdot C \cdot S}_{\text{Pattern}} \cdot \underbrace{R}_{\text{Noise}} \tag{11-8}$$

Here, demand is expressed in physical units or dollars for the trend value, and the effects of the cyclic, random, and seasonal fluctuations are shown as percentage adjustments.

Trend Analysis

In order to get a feeling for the type of trend relationship that may exist, it is always advisable to plot several points for the demand levels experienced in the past. After inspecting these points, we can draw a smooth curve through them and then try to specify the form (linear, exponential, or other) by a freehand or statistical method that best fits the historical data. Both approaches allow a trend projection to be made for future periods.

The freehand method is quick, easy, and inexpensive but offers no measure of accuracy in a projection or the goodness of fit of the assumed relationship. The statistical approach requires more effort, money, and expertise but yields estimates for the forecasting error and the degree to which the selected trend pattern fits the historical data.

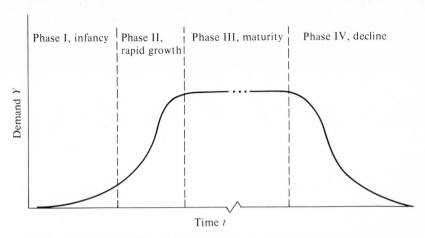

Fig. 11-6   Different forms of trend relationships for successive phases in product life cycle.

Fitting a particular trend line or curve to a set of points in order to forecast demand requires much more than statistical skills or a steady hand. Here it is crucial to understand the nature of the market served and the current phase in the life cycle of the product or service planned for. Figure 11-6 shows that different forms of trend relationships may apply for each phase in the life cycle.

▶ EXAMPLE 11-1

For the last 7 years the Hermes Paint Manufacturing Co. has experienced the quarterly demand shown in Table 11-3. This history of demand will be used to illustrate some key points of time-series analysis as employed in forecasting.

Time-series analysis normally requires data covering 10 to 15 years with demand expressed quarterly or monthly. In the example the period covered is shorter than advisable to keep the calculations simple.

After plotting the points for annual demand in Fig. 11-7, we recognize an upward trend that we assume to be linear. The trend component in the time series

TABLE 11-3   Demand data for Hermes Co., thousands of gallons of paint

Year	Q_1 Winter	Q_2 Spring	Q_3 Summer	Q_4 Fall	Annual total
1974	289	410	301	213	1,213
1975	212	371	374	333	1,290
1976	293	441	411	363	1,508
1977	324	462	379	301	1,466
1978	347	520	540	521	1,928
1979	381	594	573	504	2,052
1980	444	592	571	507	2,114

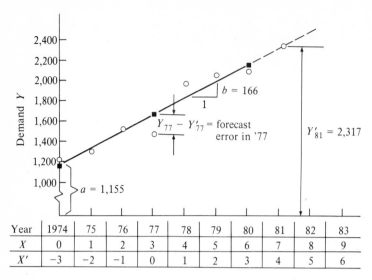

Year	1974	75	76	77	78	79	80	81	82	83
X	0	1	2	3	4	5	6	7	8	9
X'	−3	−2	−1	0	1	2	3	4	5	6

Fig. 11-7 A least-squares trend line for the historical data of Hermes Co.

can now be specified by a straight line of the form $Y' = a + bX$. The assumption in using a linear relationship is that the increase (or decrease) in the average level of demand in each period is constant. To specify a straight line for the trend we must agree on the base period, i.e., the origin in our data (for which $X = 0$) and the time increment over which we measure the slope b, that is, the amount of change per unit time.

Freehand methods and refinements   To obtain a quick trend projection we can fit a line to the points freehand, so that we balance the deviations of actual points above and below the trend line. As indicated previously, this is not a reliable approach because of its highly subjective character.

A refined freehand method involves computing the average actual demand $\bar{Y}$ for all periods and having a straight line pass through $\bar{Y}$ placed at the center of the time series $\bar{X}$. This guarantees that the sum of all the deviations will be zero since the positive ones cancel out the negative ones; that is, $\sum (Y - Y') = 0$. However, one can still be quite arbitrary and this can be reduced with the *method of semi-averages*. With this method the historical data are divided chronologically into two groups, and a mean is computed for each one and positioned at the center of each subperiod. A line drawn through the two semiaverages must pass through the mean of all the data, again making the sum of all the deviations equal to zero.

Least-squares method   For all lines passing through the point $(\bar{Y}, \bar{X})$ the sum of deviations equals zero. To identify which one fits the data best, it is preferable to examine the sum of their squared deviations. The line with the smallest sum of squared errors fits the data better than any other and is known as the *line of least squares*. It is unique and represents a reasonably objective approach for fitting a trend relationship to a set of actual points.

TABLE 11-4 **Calculation of trend-line parameters for Hermes Co. with basic year** $(X = 0)$ **in 1974**

Year	Demand $Y = $ TCSR	Time X	XY	X^2	Forecast Y'	Error $Y - Y'$	Squared error $(Y - Y')^2$
1974	1,213	0	0	0	1,155	58	3,364
1975	1,290	1	1,290	1	1,321	−31	961
1976	1,508	2	3,016	4	1,487	21	441
1977	1,466	3	4,398	9	1,653	−187	34,969
1978	1,928	4	7,712	16	1,819	109	11,884
1979	2,052	5	10,260	25	1,985	67	4,489
1980	2,114	6	12,684	36	2,151	−37	1,369
Total	11,571	21	39,360	91		0	57,477

$$\sum Y = Na + b \sum X \quad \bigg| \quad 11,571 = 7a + 21b \quad \bigg| \quad a = 1,155$$
$$\sum XY = a \sum X + b \sum X^2 \bigg| \rightarrow 39,360 = 21a + 91b \bigg| \rightarrow b = 166$$

Thus, $\qquad Y' = a + bX = 1,155 + 166X \qquad X = 0$ for 1974

Determining a least-squares line using data from N periods requires specifying its unknown parameters a and b, or intercept and slope. This is done by solving a set of two linear equations, known as *normal equations*, in two unknowns:

$$
\begin{array}{ll}
\sum Y = Na + b \sum X & \text{Normal equations for a} \\
\sum XY = a \sum x + b \sum X^2 & \text{least-squares trend line}
\end{array}
\qquad (11\text{-}9)
$$

For the data of Hermes Co. determination of such a trend line requires preparing Table 11-4 to show the computation of the terms $\sum X, \sum Y, \sum X^2$, and $\sum XY$ from the data of N periods. Also included are the steps for the solution of the normal equations and the values of a and b. The procedure can be simplified considerably if the base year is placed at the center or midpoint of the time series,[1] making $\sum X = 0$. The shift in the origin changes the intercept value a while the slope b remains the same, as can be seen in Table 11-5.

Using the least-squares trend line derived for the Hermes Co. example, our forecast of expected annual demand for 1981 can be computed as follows: Using 1974 as a base year (for 1981: $X = 7$), we have

$$Y' = 1,155 + 166X$$

$$Y'_{81} = 1,155 + (166)(7) = 2,317 \text{ gal}$$

---

[1] When N is even the values of X around the midpoint would be $\ldots, -2\frac{1}{2}, -1\frac{1}{2}, -\frac{1}{2}, 0, +\frac{1}{2}, +1\frac{1}{2}, +2\frac{1}{2}, \ldots$

TABLE 11-5 Calculation of trend-line parameters for Hermes Co. with base year $(X = 0)$ in 1977

Year	Demand $Y = $ TCSR	X	XY	X^2	Forecast Y'
1974	1,213	-3	$-3,639$	9	1,155
1975	1,290	-2	$-2,580$	4	1,321
1976	1,508	-1	$-1,508$	1	1,487
1977	1,466	0	0	0	1,653
1978	1,928	1	1,928	1	1,819
1979	2,052	2	4,104	4	1,985
1980	2,114	3	6,342	9	2,151
Total	11,571	0	4,647	28	

$$\sum Y = Na + b \sum X \quad \Big| \quad 11,571 = 7a + 0 \quad \Big| \quad a = 1,653$$
$$\sum XY = a \sum X + b \sum X^2 \Big| \rightarrow \quad 4,647 = 0 + 28b \Big| \rightarrow b = 166$$

Thus, $Y' = 1,653 + 166X \qquad X = 0$ for 1977

Using 1977 as a base year (for 1981: $X = 4$), we have

$$Y' = 1,653 + 166X$$

$$Y'_{81} = 1,653 + 166(4) = 2,317 \text{ gal}$$

Actual demand for the future period in question is assumed to follow a normal distribution with the projected value as its mean (see Fig. 11-8). If we wish to have 95 percent confidence in our forecast of future demand we must allow for values within two standard errors of the least-squares estimate.

For the Hermes Co. example we have[1]

$$s_Y = \sqrt{\frac{\sum (Y - Y')^2}{N - 2}} = \sqrt{\frac{57,477}{7 - 2}} = \sqrt{11,495.40} = 107.22$$

Thus, the 95 percent confidence interval for the 1981 demand forecast will be[2]

$$Y'_{81} \pm 2s_Y = 2,317 \pm (2)(107.2) = 2,317 \pm 214.4 \text{ gal}$$

Seasonal-Component Analysis

To determine the best utilization of existing productive capacity when demand is seasonal, we must determine the relative share of activity for each month or quarter in the planning horizon. This is done by isolating the seasonal component S present

---

[1] The denominator under the radical is known as the *number of degrees of freedom*. This is equal to the number of independent observations N minus the number of unknown parameters (2) of the linear equation, a and b, that must be estimated from these data.

[2] For N less than 30 one must use the t distribution for which the value of s_Y would be larger. For $N = 7$, i.e., $N - 2 = 5$ degrees of freedom, $s_Y = 2.57$ for 95% confidence level.

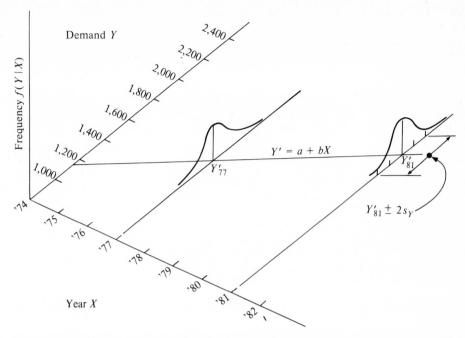

Fig. 11-8 Trend line for Hermes Co. data showing normal distribution of demand for a given year.

in the actual data by month or quarter for the time series $Y = \text{TCSR}$. Consider the quarterly data of Hermes Co. for the years 1974 and 1975 as plotted graphically in Fig. 11-9.

Moving averages For a time series, a simple moving average of n periods represents a dynamic average that smoothes out the fluctuations observed in the N

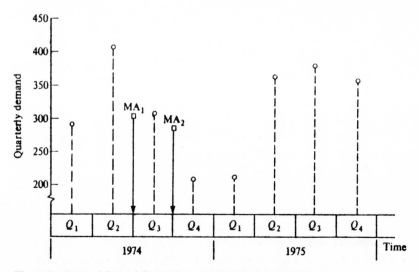

Fig. 11-9 Seasonal demand fluctuations suggested by quarterly data.

periods. Thus, a four-quarter average for Q_1, Q_2, Q_3, and Q_4 of 1974 is

$$\text{MA}_1 = \frac{289 + 410 + 301 + 213}{4} = 303.25$$

This value of MA_1 is a deseasonalized quarterly demand in 1974, i.e., an average without reference to any specific quarter. For an actual quarter in 1974 with a demand greater than 303.25, the value for S will exceed 1.00, while for another, with demand less than 303.25, the value of S will be less than 1.00. The sum of all the S values for 1 year will be 4.00 when using quarters or 12.00 if demand is given monthly.

When the actual demand for Q_1 of 1975 becomes known, a new moving average is computed by dropping the oldest quarterly demand 289 and including the most recent one 212

$$\text{MA}_2 = \frac{410 + 301 + 213 + 212}{4} = 284.00$$

If the time-series data were expressed in monthly figures, the moving average representative of a single period's deseasonalized demand would be based on 12 months.

Key property

A moving average based on as many periods as required to cover a full year has the property of removing the seasonal influence on demand. Thus, it provides a deseasonalized measure of demand for such a period accounting mainly for the trend and cyclic effect.

Seasonal as ratio of demand to centered moving average   The values for MA_1 and MA_2 are defined at the midpoint of the time interval covered. Thus, MA_1 is between Q_2 and Q_3 of 1974 and MA_2 is between Q_3 and Q_4 of 1974 (see Fig. 11-9). Therefore, neither one is representative of any of these quarters. In order to associate a moving average with a particular quarter we need to compute a centered moving average by adding two simple moving averages at a time:

$$\text{CMA}_1 = \frac{\text{MA}_1 + \text{MA}_2}{2} = \frac{303.25 + 284.00}{2} = 293.63$$

This is also a deseasonalized measure of quarterly demand, but it can now be associated with Q_3 of 1974. As such it includes the effect on quarterly demand of the long-term trend T and the business cycle C. To isolate the seasonal effect for Q_3

of 1974 we can divide the actual demand $Y_{Q_3, 74}$ by CMA_1:

$$(SR)_{Q_3, 74} = \frac{Y_{Q_3, 74}}{CMA_1} = \frac{TCSR}{TC} = \frac{301}{293.63} = 1.025 \quad \begin{array}{l}\text{Specific}\\ \text{seasonal}\\ \text{index}\end{array}$$

The ratio of actual demand in a given period by the centered moving average for the same period is known as the *specific seasonal index*. Its value determines the seasonal effect and some random influences of that quarter for the particular year it is computed. Next we compute the specific seasonal values for all quarters in the years covered, as shown in the last column of Table 11-6.

By averaging the values of the specific seasonal index for the same quarter in successive years, we can now smooth out the remaining random influence and thus isolate the seasonal effects. This is done in Table 11-7. Thus, a typical seasonal index is

$$S_{Q_3} = \frac{(SR)_{Q_3, 74} + (SR)_{Q_3, 75} + \cdots + (SR)_{Q_3, 79}}{6}$$

The value for the *typical seasonal index* of each quarter provides a measure of the share of activity expected for that quarter.

TABLE 11-6 Computation of specific seasonal-index values

Year	Quarter	Actual demand $Y = TCSR$	Four-quarter moving average	Centered moving average TC	Specific seasonal index SR
1974	Q_1	289			
	Q_2	410			
	Q_3	301	303.25	293.63	1.025
	Q_4	213	284.00	279.00	.763
1975	Q_1	212	274.00	283.25	.748
	Q_2	371	292.50	307.50	1.207
	Q_3	374	322.50	332.63	1.124
	Q_4	333	342.75	351.50	.947
1976	Q_1	293	360.25	364.88	.803
	Q_2	441	369.50	373.25	1.182
	Q_3	411	377.00	380.88	1.079
	Q_4	363	384.75	387.38	.937
1977	Q_1	324	390.00	386.00	.839
	Q_2	462	382.00	374.25	1.234
	Q_3	379	366.50	369.38	1.026
	Q_4	301	372.25	379.50	.793
1978	Q_1	347	386.75	406.88	.853
	Q_2	520	427.00	454.50	1.144
	Q_3	540	482.00	486.25	1.111
	Q_4	521	490.50	499.75	1.043
1979	Q_1	381	509.00	513.00	.743
	Q_2	594	517.00	515.00	1.153
	Q_3	573	513.00	520.88	1.100
	Q_4	504	528.75	528.75	.953
1980	Q_1	444	528.75	528.25	.841
	Q_2	592	527.75	528.13	1.121
	Q_3	571	528.50		
	Q_4	507			

TABLE 11-7 Computation of typical seasonal-index values from specific seasonal values

Year	Q_1	Q_2	Q_3	Q_4	Total
1974			1.025	.763	
1975	.748	1.207	1.124	.947	
1976	.803	1.182	1.057	.937	
1977	.839	1.234	1.079	.793	
1978	.853	1.144	1.111	1.043	
1979	.743	1.153	1.100	.953	
1980	.841	1.121			
Total	4.827	7.041	6.496	5.436	
Average	.8045	1.173	1.083	.906	3.9665
Adjusted average	.811	1.183	1.092	.914	4.000

For the Hermes Co. these values are obtained from Table 11-7 after adjusting the averages by a factor equal to $1.0084 = 4.000/3.967$ to account for the rounding errors. Thus, we have the typical seasonal index values

Winter	$S_{Q_1} = .811$
Spring	$S_{Q_2} = 1.183$
Summer	$S_{Q_3} = 1.092$
Fall	$S_{Q_4} = \dfrac{.914}{4.000}$

To determine how the forecast annual demand for 1981 will be distributed quarterly we can take the trend projection Y'_{81}, divide it by 4 to get the average quarterly demand, and then adjust it to account for seasonal effects:

$$Y'_{Q,\,81} = \frac{Y'_{81}}{4} = \frac{2,317}{4} = 579.25 \quad \begin{array}{l}\text{Deseasonalized}\\ \text{quarterly}\\ \text{demand for '81}\end{array}$$

Using the typical seasonal index values, we have

		Demand in 1981
	$Y'_{Q_1} = (579.25)(\ .811) = 469.77$	Winter
	$Y'_{Q_2} = (579.25)(1.183) = 685.25$	Spring
	$Y'_{Q_3} = (579.25)(1.092) = 632.54$	Summer
	$Y'_{Q_4} = (579.25)(\ .914) = 529.44$	Fall
Total	Y'_{81} 2,317.00	

Before using these typical seasonal index values, it is important to satisfy ourselves that the seasonal pattern from year to year is stable. This would not be so if we observe a trend in the values of the specific seasonal index for one or more quarters. The latter would suggest a gradual shift of activity in that quarter with compensating changes in other quarters. In the Hermes Co. example these values seem to vary at random, around their average value for each quarter, as they should for a stable pattern.

Cyclical-Component Analysis[1]

Since the duration and intensity of a business cycle cannot be predicted, isolating the cyclical component is useful in making us aware of the phase of business cycle we are likely to operate in, so that a trend projection can be adjusted accordingly.

When our data for demand are given annually, the time series includes only the trend and cyclical components, $Y = TC$. Compared with the cyclical fluctuations, the random influences are often negligible. In this case, the cyclical fluctuations are viewed as departures from the trend values which represent the normal growth or decay in demand. The cyclical component can be isolated by dividing actual demand by the trend value

$$C = \frac{T \cdot C}{T} \tag{11-10}$$

Demand, however, is often measured quarterly or monthly, in which case, in addition to the trend, we must remove seasonal variations. The necessary calculations proceed in four steps and for the Hermes Co. example are illustrated in Table 11-8.

Step 1: Deseasonalize quarterly (or monthly) original data by first dividing by the typical seasonal index values S determined previously

$$\frac{\text{Actual demand } Y}{\text{Seasonal index } S} = \frac{T \cdot C \cdot S \cdot R}{S} = T \cdot C \cdot R$$

Step 2: Obtain for each year an average of the deseasonalized quarterly values and fit a regression line to them for estimating the trend T in quarterly demand (see Table 11-9).

Step 3: Divide the deseasonalized values by T thus obtaining the CR components for each quarter. These values are frequently adequate for isolating the business cycle since the random fluctuations R are considered minor when compared to the cyclical ones. If this is not so, we proceed.

Step 4: Smooth the CR values using a three-quarter moving average which measures C and then divide the previous CR values by C to obtain R.

---

[1] This section is optional.

TABLE 11-8   Calculation of the cyclical and random variations in the Hermes Co. example

Year	Quarter	Actual demand $Y = TCSR$	Seasonal index S	Deseason- alized demand TCR	Trend T	CR	Cyclical component C	Random component R
1974	Q_1	289	.812	355.9	271.8	1.309		
	Q_2	410	1.186	345.7	282.3	1.224	1.160	1.055
	Q_3	301	1.087	276.9	292.8	.946	.979	.966
	Q_4	213	.915	232.8	303.3	.768	.849	.905
1975	Q_1	212	.812	261.1	313.7	.832	.855	.973
	Q_2	371	1.186	312.8	324.2	.965	.942	1.024
	Q_3	374	1.087	344.1	334.7	1.028	1.016	1.012
	Q_4	333	.915	363.9	345.2	1.054	1.032	1.021
1976	Q_1	293	.812	360.8	355.7	1.014	1.028	.986
	Q_2	441	1.186	371.8	366.1	1.016	1.011	1.005
	Q_3	411	1.087	378.1	376.6	1.004	1.015	.989
	Q_4	363	.915	396.7	387.1	1.025	1.011	1.014
1977	Q_1	324	.812	399.0	397.6	1.003	.994	1.009
	Q_2	462	1.186	389.5	408.0	.955	.930	1.027
	Q_3	379	1.087	348.7	418.5	.833	.852	.978
	Q_4	301	.915	328.9	429.0	.767	.857	.895
1978	Q_1	347	.812	427.3	439.5	.972	.904	1.075
	Q_2	520	1.186	438.4	450.0	.974	1.008	.966
	Q_3	540	1.087	496.8	460.8	1.079	1.087	.992
	Q_4	521	.915	569.4	470.9	1.209	1.088	1.111
1979	Q_1	381	.812	469.2	481.4	.975	1.067	.914
	Q_2	594	1.186	500.8	491.9	1.018	1.014	1.004
	Q_3	573	1.087	527.1	502.4	1.049	1.047	1.002
	Q_4	504	.915	550.8	512.8	1.074	1.056	1.017
1980	Q_1	444	.812	546.8	523.3	1.045	1.018	1.026
	Q_2	592	1.186	499.1	533.8	.936	.982	.953
	Q_3	571	1.087	525.3	544.3	.960	.965	1.001
	Q_4	507	.915	554.1	554.8	.999		

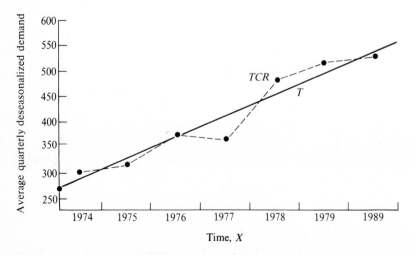

Fig. 11-10   Business-cycle influence in the demand for Hermes Co.

TABLE 11-9   Calculation of quarterly-demand trend line for Hermes Co.

Year	$Y = TCR$	X	XY	X
1974	302.83	−3	−908.49	9
1975	320.48	−2	−640.96	4
1976	376.86	−1	−376.86	1
1977	366.54	0	0	0
1978	482.99	1	482.99	1
1979	512.00	2	512.00	4
1980	531.34	3	531.34	9
Total	2,893.04	0	1,173.71	28

$$a = \frac{\sum Y}{N} = \frac{2{,}893.04}{7} = 413.29 \qquad b = \frac{\sum XY}{\sum X} = \frac{1{,}173.71}{28} = 41.92$$

Thus, $Y' = 413.29 + 41.92X$ (origin in 1977; unit time 1 yr)

Quarterly-demand trend line:

$$Y' = 271.81 + 10.48X \text{ (origin } Q_1 \text{ for 1974; unit time 1 quarter)}$$

Thus, for Q_1 1981

$$Y' = 271.81 + 10.48(X = 28) = 565.25 \text{ gal}$$

Identifying the cyclical factor is the most difficult phase in the decomposition of a time series. The availability of a sufficiently long demand history enables us to see the broad pattern of the business cycle, so that we can determine the changes most likely to follow. This can be seen by drawing a graph like that in Fig. 11-10.

The broad pattern of the business cycle can be seen after we plot the values of the column for C in Table 11-8 (see Fig. 11-11). For the years covered in the Hermes Co. example the effect of the cyclical component is quite mild. Combined

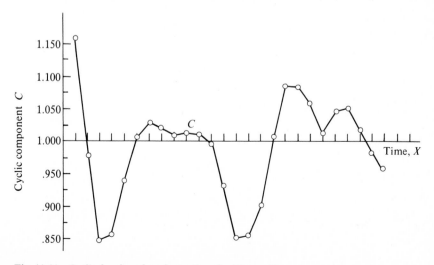

Fig. 11-11   Cyclical and random fluctuations for Hermes Co.

with the business cycle for the thousands of other products and services, it results in the overall business cycle that describes the state of the national economy and is regarded as a reference cycle for planning purposes. In the Hermes Co. example the trend projection must be adjusted mildly downward ($C < 1.00$) to account for the start of a downward trend of the business cycle unique to this product.

Random-Component Analysis[1]

The random fluctuations R, calculated in the last column of Table 11-8, are caused by unpredictable and irregular occurrences related to weather, strikes, new discoveries, and other factors not accounted by the trend, seasonal, and cyclical influences. It can be seen that such variations occur at random above or below the axis and are considerably smaller than the cyclical fluctuations. Under normal circumstances, the random-component values have an average of 1.000.

The presence of a pattern for R and the occurrence of exceptionally large values often suggest the need for further investigation. Possible reasons behind such symptoms may be related to improper selection of a time-series model (additive rather than multiplicative interaction of components), a poor fit of the trend equation, or unusual cyclical fluctuations besides the business cycle.

Assuming that for the Hermes Co. the time-series model built is satisfactory, the forecast for Q_1 of 1981 can be determined as follows:

$$Y'_{Q_1, 81} = T \cdot C \cdot S = (565.25)(.940)(.812) = 431.4 \text{ gal}$$

11-8   ROUTINE SHORT-TERM FORECASTING

Forecasting by time-series analysis is most appropriate for planning periods of several years (to assess the need for capacity changes) or for periods of several months (to maximize existing capacity utilization). In both cases we deal with aggregate demand measured in units common to all products or services. When preparing operating plans and schedules for the weeks ahead, it is necessary to have short-term forecasts related to specific products and facilities. The use of any of the previously discussed methods for routine forecasting covering hundreds or thousands of products, say biweekly or monthly, would be both cumbersome and expensive.

For the short term, therefore, we need a forecasting method that uses one or very few standard models relying on historical data. This must be easily programmed for a computer so that management can receive frequent updated forecasts to be used in scheduling and inventory control.

Simple and Weighted Moving Averages

One approach we can use to forecast next period's demand is a simple moving average. There may be objections to the equal weight given to each of the n periods

---

[1] This section is optional.

used or to the considerable requirements for computer memory storage, especially when the number of products is very large. The use of weights so that demand in more recent periods is given more emphasis than in distant ones alleviates the first problem but not the second one.

In using moving averages, we must keep in mind the following points:

1. The larger the number of periods n used to compute a moving average the greater will be the smoothing out of previous fluctuations. Equivalently, the smaller n is the more sensitive will be the forecast to recent changes in demand.
2. A moving average will lag behind any change in the level of demand due to a trend or other reasons. It is therefore best when the level of demand changes slowly.
3. A moving average can be used to forecast demand only one period ahead.

In Fig. 11-12 we can see how a simple and a weighted four-period moving average can be used to forecast next quarter's demand for the Hermes Co. example.

Exponential Smoothing

An important method for short-term forecasting that overcomes the disadvantages of moving averages is exponential smoothing. In a sense, this is a refinement in the concept of a weighted moving average in a way that permits discounting the effect of old data and reduces the requirements for data storage to a minimum.

In order to prepare next period's forecast we take a weighted average of actual demand in the last period and our forecast for that period.

Let Y'_{t+1} = forecast of demand for next period $t + 1$

$\quad\quad Y'_t$ = forecast of demand for the current period t

$\quad\quad Y_t$ = actual demand experienced in the current period t

$\quad\quad \alpha$ = smoothing constant (alpha)

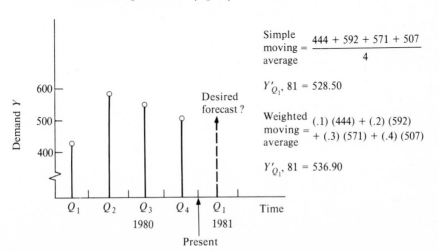

$$\text{Simple moving average} = \frac{444 + 592 + 571 + 507}{4}$$

$$Y'_{Q_1}, 81 = 528.50$$

$$\text{Weighted moving average} = \frac{(.1)\,(444) + (.2)\,(592)}{+ (.3)\,(571) + (.4)\,(507)}$$

$$Y'_{Q_1}, 81 = 536.90$$

Fig. 11-12   Using a simple and a weighted moving average to forecast next period's demand.

Then

$$Y'_{t+1} = \alpha Y_t + (1 - \alpha)(Y'_t) \qquad 0 < \alpha < 1 \qquad (11\text{-}11)$$

or

$$\begin{bmatrix} \text{Forecast for} \\ \text{next period} \end{bmatrix} = [\text{alpha}] \begin{bmatrix} \text{actual demand} \\ \text{for current period} \end{bmatrix} + [1 - \text{alpha}] \begin{bmatrix} \text{forecast for} \\ \text{current period} \end{bmatrix}$$

An alternative way of looking at the above equation for exponential smoothing is possible by multiplying out the second term and rearranging

$$Y'_{t+1} = Y'_t + \alpha(Y_t - Y'_t) \qquad (11\text{-}12)$$

or

$$\begin{bmatrix} \text{Forecast for} \\ \text{next period} \end{bmatrix} = \begin{bmatrix} \text{forecast for} \\ \text{current period} \end{bmatrix} + [\text{alpha}] \begin{bmatrix} \text{forecast error} \\ \text{in current period} \end{bmatrix}$$

When actual demand is not known for the current period, the exponential smoothing equation can be modified to adapt to the existing information time lag of one or more periods. For example, if t represents the most recent period for which we have data, say March of 1980, and the period for which we need a forecast is three periods later, i.e., June of 1980, the equation becomes

$$Y'_{t+3} = \alpha Y_t + (1 - \alpha)Y'_t \qquad \text{Three-period time lag} \qquad (11\text{-}13)$$

or $\qquad Y'_{\text{June}} = \alpha Y_{\text{March}} + (1 - \alpha)Y'_{\text{March}} \qquad$ 3-month time lag

Returning to the formulation $Y'_{t+1} = \alpha Y_t + (1 - \alpha)Y'$, we realize that to prepare a forecast in this manner we need a numerical value for α and a previous forecast. The value of α is determined by trial and error to minimize some measure of forecast error. This is illustrated in Table 11-10. It can be seen that the larger the value of α the more responsive the forecast to recent actual demand and vice versa. To initiate the calculations, the numerical value for the previous forecast is by convention set equal to the actual demand for the first period, that is, $Y'_1 = Y_1$.

By restating Y'_t in terms of actual and forecast demand in period $t - 1$ and continuing with similar successive substitutions for the remaining periods we come to the forecast for the first period in our data Y'_1. By definition this is taken to be equal to the actual demand for that period Y_1. Thus we have

$$Y'_{t+1} = \alpha Y_t + (1 - \alpha)Y'_t$$
$$= \alpha Y_t + \alpha(1 - \alpha)Y_{t-1} + \alpha(1 - \alpha)^2 Y_{t-2} + \cdots + \alpha(1 - \alpha)^{t-1}Y_1 + (1 - \alpha)^t Y_1$$
$$= \sum_{i=0}^{t-1} \alpha(1 - \alpha)^i Y_{t-i} + (1 - \alpha)^t Y_1 \qquad (11\text{-}14)$$

It can be seen that Y'_{t+1} is a weighted moving average of previous demand data with the weights decreasing exponentially with the age of the data. Hence the name

TABLE 11-10 Comparison of forecasts prepared by the naïve method, a moving average, and exponential smoothing

Time period t	Actual demand Y_t	Naïve method $Y'_{t+1} = Y_t$	Moving average $n = 3$	Exponential smoothing $\alpha = 0.2$†	Exponential smoothing $\alpha = 0.4$	Exponential smoothing $\alpha = 0.7$
1979 Q_1: 1	381					
Q_2: 2	594	381	$\cdots$	381.00	381.00	381.00
Q_3: 3	573	594	$\cdots$	423.60	466.20	530.10
Q_4: 4	504	573	516.00	453.80	508.92	560.13
1980 Q_1: 5	444	504	557.00	463.84	506.95	520.84
Q_2: 6	592	444	507.00	459.87	481.77	467.05
Q_3: 7	571	592	513.33	486.30	525.86	554.52
Q_4: 8	507	571	535.67	503.24	543.92	566.06
1981 Q_1: 9	?	507	556.67	503.99	529.15	524.72

† The forecasts for a value of $\alpha = 0.2$ are obtained as follows:

$$Y'_2 = \alpha Y_1 + (1 - \alpha)Y'_1 = (.2)(381) + (1 - .2)(381) = 381 \quad \text{since } Y'_1 = Y_1 = 381$$

$$Y'_3 = \alpha Y_2 + (1 - \alpha)Y'_2 = (.2)(594) + (1 - .2)(381) = 423.6$$

....

$$Y'_9 = \alpha Y_8 + (1 - \alpha)Y'_8 = (.2)(507) + (1 - .2)(503.24) = 503.99$$

of the technique. Using the quarterly data for 1979 and 1978 in the Hermes Co. example, Table 11-10 shows the necessary computations to produce an exponential smoothing forecast and to evaluate various values of α. These forecasts are also compared with the methods of moving averages and naïve forecasting in which the next period's forecast equals this period's actual demand ($\alpha = 1$).

Measurement and Control of Forecast Errors

A forecast cannot be complete for planning purposes unless accompanied by an estimate of the expected error. This is as valid for short-term forecasting methods as it is for medium- and long-term ones. The measures of accuracy when using a moving average or an exponential smoothing technique are similar to the standard error used in regression analysis. The most commonly used ones are the mean squared error, the mean absolute deviation, and the tracking signal.

The *mean squared error* (MSE) is determined by calculating the sum of the squared forecast errors and dividing by the number of periods N:

$$\text{MSE} = \frac{\sum (Y_t - Y'_t)^2}{N} = \frac{\text{sums of squared errors}}{\text{number of periods}} \qquad (11\text{-}15)$$

By taking the squares of the deviations of actual from forecasted demand, the MSE gives much greater weight to larger errors than to small ones. This may be appropriate when the costs of being in error, i.e., the costs of surplus or shortage of inventory or capacity, increase rapidly with the size of the error.

A simpler and often more useful measure of accuracy is the *mean absolute deviation* (MAD). This is simply the average of the observed forecast errors ignoring their sign:

$$\text{MAD} = \frac{\sum |Y_t - Y_t'|}{N} = \frac{\text{sum of absolute errors}}{\text{number of periods}} \qquad (11\text{-}16)$$

where $|Y_t - Y_t'|$ is the absolute value of the forecast error in period t. It can be seen that the MAD depends on the total forecast error. As such it is best suited to systems for which the costs of forecast deviations depend on their cumulative effect regardless of whether the MAD is attributed to several small errors or a few large ones. The standard deviation of the same errors is related to the MAD as follows:

$$S_Y = 1.25\text{MAD} \qquad (11\text{-}17)$$

In addition to its simplicity, the MAD can be used to determine the tracking signal, an indicator of a forecasting method's bias, computed as follows:

$$\text{Tracking signal} = \frac{\text{RSFE}}{\text{MAD}}$$
$$= \frac{\text{running (algebraic) sum of forecast errors}}{\text{mean absolute deviation}} \qquad (11\text{-}18)$$

Whenever the forecast tracks actual demand well, the errors observed are random with a normal distribution and an average equal to zero. Thus, for an ideal forecasting model the running, or algebraic, sum of forecast errors (RSFE) must equal zero because positive errors tend to cancel out negative ones. The presence of a bias in the forecast creates an additional source of errors. A succession of large positive values for the tracking signal means a tendency for the forecast to be too pessimistic, $Y_t - Y_t' > 0$, while large negative values imply an optimistic bias, i.e., actual demand consistently below the forecast. Such a bias may be related to a poor forecasting model and can result from omitting key variables, assuming wrong relationships for included variables, or from drastic changes in the environment that generates demand, e.g., economic disruptions, energy shortages, and political crises.

According to Wight,[1] the tracking signal is also a very useful indicator of

---

[1] Oliver W. Wight, *Production and Inventory Management in the Computer Age*, Cahners, Boston, 1974.

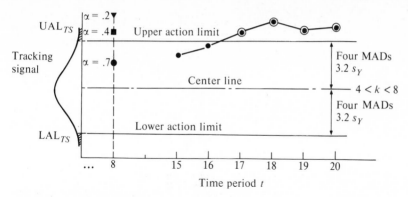

Fig. 11-13 Typical control chart for monitoring forecast tracking signal (plotted points do not correspond to example data).

trends that deviate from the forecast. As such it can be easily combined with a simple exponential forecasting model to produce more useful forecasts than the complex exponential smoothing models that have been adjusted for trend.

To enable management to monitor the accuracy of their forecasting method, it is advisable to set up a control chart for the tracking signal similar to those developed for quality control (see Chap. 16). The action (or control) limits are placed four to eight MADs from the centerline at zero.

Suppose that the action limits for the tracking signal have been set at four MADs ($k = 4$), as shown in Fig. 11-13. These limits correspond to $4/1.25 = 3.2$ standard deviations. The probability that the value of the tracking signal will fall in the ± 4-MAD interval if the forecasting method has no bias is 99.8 percent. Thus, if we observe a series of tracking-signal trips outside these limits, the probability that it might have occurred by chance is less than 2 out of 1,000. It is therefore more reasonable to assume that there is a bias in the forecasting system and proceed to inspect it for needed correction.

The objective in setting the action limits in the tracking-signal control chart is to minimize the total expected cost of possible errors. This includes inspecting unnecessarily the forecasting system when the tracking signal is by chance outside the action limits and the costs from forecast errors resulting from an undetected bias. The latter would be associated with surpluses or shortages in inventories or productive capacity. Since the effectiveness of this control procedure depends on the position of the action limits, it is important that their values be based on frequently updated values for MAD. This can be done easily using an updating method similar to exponential smoothing. Thus,

$$\text{MAD}_{t+1} = \alpha(Y_t - Y_t') + (1 - \alpha)\text{MAD}_t \qquad (11\text{-}19)$$

where α is a smoothing constant (usually $.05 \le \alpha \le .15$).

TABLE 11-11   Calculation of forecast errors and values for MAD, MSE, and tracking signals

Time period t	Forecast error = actual demand − forecast $(Y_t - Y_t')$				
	Naïve method	Moving average	Exponential smoothing		
			$\alpha = .2$	$\alpha = .4$	$\alpha = .7$
1					
2	213.00		213.00	213.00	213.00
3	−21.00		149.40	106.80	42.90
4	−69.00	−12.00	50.20	−4.92	−56.13
5	−60.00	−113.00	−19.84	−62.95	−76.84
6	148.00	85.00	132.13	110.23	124.95
7	−21.00	57.67	84.70	45.14	16.48
8	−64.00	−28.67	3.76	−36.92	−59.06
Sum (RSFE)	126.00	−11.00	613.35	370.38	205.30
Sum of absolute values of errors	596.00	296.34	653.03	579.96	589.36
MAD	90.86	59.26	93.29	82.85	84.19
Tracking signal = RSFE/MAD	+1.39	−.19	+6.55	+4.47	+2.44
Sum of squared errors	80,612	24,285	95,248	76,312	75,636
MSE	11,516	4,857	13,605	10,901	10,805

The different measures of forecast errors are used to evaluate different forecasting models, to assign values to smoothing constants, and to exercise control of the forecasting system used. Table 11-11 illustrates how different models compare on the basis of MAD and MSE. Here we also see how we might proceed to select a value for α if an exponential smoothing model had been chosen. In the example a moving average with $n = 3$ seems to provide the greatest accuracy (smallest MAD and MSE values). This is due to the greater responsiveness of the moving average for low values of n in the presence of a trend and a seasonal pattern. Figure 11-13 illustrates how a tracking signal might be monitored using a control chart.

11-9   SUMMARY

The importance of forecasting for an organization is comparable to that of the senses for the human body. Both serve to provide vital information about the environment that forms the basis for any future activity.

Forecasting as a function is performed by the forecasting system. Its key mission is to provide estimates of what the environment will demand of the organization in products and services. Such estimates about future demand cover aspects of quantity (how much?), timing (when?), location (where?), and quality (what kind?). The forecasts produced can be classified by the length of the planning horizon covered (long-, intermediate-, and short-term) and by the user of the information for planning purposes (marketing, operations, finance, other).

Developing a forecast requires information both internal and external to the organization; the former are relied upon mostly for short-term forecasts, and both are valuable for medium- and long-term forecasts. Along with estimates for future demand, a forecasting system must also provide estimates of the error in the forecast. Large errors mean poor forecasting methods, a very uncertain and volatile environment, or a combination of both.

The true value of a forecasting system is measured by some benefit-to-cost ratio. Benefits here take the form of savings realized by the reduction of undesired surpluses and shortages of inventories and/or production capacity. The larger the forecast error the greater the need for operating flexibility through inventory, extra capacity, or other means, which translates into greater operating cost. Thus, management must search for the optimum allocation of its resources directed to reducing forecast errors through better methods versus increasing operating flexibility and responsiveness through more effective utilization of productive capacity.

Improving forecasting methods may result in a change from practical and intuitive approaches to more systematic and sophisticated models. Depending on the length of the planning horizon and the availability of data, time, and expertise, management has a choice from a wide variety of techniques. These are grouped in three major categories known as subjective (or predictive), causal, and time-series methods. The last two are most appropriate for medium- and short-term forecasting when numerous data are available and the environment of the organization remains reasonably stable. For long-range forecasts and new activities there is a tendency to rely strongly on predictive methods.

In the final analysis, forecasting is and will remain more of an art than a science. It is crucial to realize that good forecasts require much more than refined statistical techniques and fast computers. The key contribution to good forecasting comes from an understanding of the complex process that generates demand for a firm's products and services and how this process evolves with time.

NOTATION

Time Series Components: $Y = TCSR$

X or t = a given period in a time series
Y = actual level of demand in a given period
Y' = estimated level of demand in a given period
s_Y = standard error of the estimate of demand
T = underlying long-term trend of growth or decline in demand
C = effect of business cycle on demand
S = seasonal effect on demand in a given period
R = residual or random effects on demand
MA = a moving average for demand
CMA = a centered moving average

SR_t = a specific seasonal index value for period t
N = total number of periods in a time series
n = number of periods used for a moving average

Exponential Smoothing

Y_t = actual level of demand in period t
Y'_t, Y'_{t+1} = estimated level of demand in periods $t, t + 1$
α = smoothing constant $(0 < \alpha < 1)$
MSE = mean square error
MAD = mean average deviation
RSFE = running (algebraic) sum of forecast errors

REVIEW QUESTIONS

1. Discuss the areas of application of demand forecasting in operations-management decisions.
   (a) In the short run   (1 to 5 weeks)
   (b) In the medium run   (1 to 12 weeks)
   (c) In the long run   (2 to 10 years)
2. Describe the operation of a demand forecasting system in terms of information outputs and inputs, decision variables and constraints, and criteria of performance.
3. Contrast a general demand forecast with a production forecast. How can the latter be obtained from the former?
4. Explain how the length of the period covered by a forecast is determined.
5. Describe the conditions under which it is appropriate to employ:
   (a) Subjective forecasting methods (executive surveys, Delphi)
   (b) Causal forecasting methods (regression, input-output models, etc.)
   (c) Time-series forecasting methods (time-series decomposition, moving averages, etc.)
6. In what respect do routine executive surveys differ from the Delphi approach?
7. What time-series components are most influential in long-term, medium-term, and short-term operations management decisions?
8. Outline the main similarities and differences between exponential smoothing and time-series decomposition methods for demand forecasting.
9. From articles or books in the literature obtain a description and fields of application of forecasting techniques such as (a) the Box-Jenkins method, (b) systems dynamics, and, (c) spectral analysis.
10. Indicate the most appropriate medium-term forecasting method(s) for the following:
    (a) A local department-store chain
    (b) A regional power utility
    (c) A large national company (U.S. Steel, GM, AT&T)
    (d) A multinational company (IBM, Ford, Shell, etc.)

PROBLEMS

1. Which forecasting method would you recommend, and what type of data would you collect for the following applications:
   (a) Estimating the demand for electricity in an industrial city for the next 5 yr
   (b) Estimating the unskilled labor requirements next season for a summer-resort complex (hotels, restaurants, etc.)

(c) Estimating the requirements for passenger-cabin personnel (stewardesses, etc.) of a commercial airline with transatlantic routes

2. A cement company operates a plant with a maximum capacity of 160 million tons per year. From past years, the typical seasonal index values have been estimated as

$$S_{Q_1} = .85 \qquad S_{Q_2} = 1.05 \qquad S_{Q_3} = 1.20 \qquad S_{Q_4} = .90$$

At present management feels that sales are increasing at a fixed amount per year. A regression line developed for forecasting sales is

$$Y' = a + bX$$

$$= 127.35 + 4.68X$$

and $\qquad\qquad S_Y = 1.25$

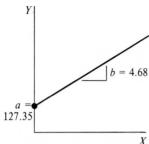

X **Problem 2**

where Y' = forecast annual sales millions of tons
$\qquad X$ = year in which sales are forecast

The base year for the time series is 1976.
(a) Using this regression line derive a forecast for sales in 1981.
(b) Specify a 99 percent confidence interval for sales in 1981.
(c) Using the given seasonal index values, obtain a forecast for each quarter in 1981.
(d) How much should be added to the existing plant capacity to cover projected annual sales increases in the period 1982–1987?

3. Suppose that in Prob. 2 management believes that due to increasing export sales a more appropriate trend line is specified by the modified exponential equation

$$Y' = c + ab^X = 127.35 + (2.0)^x$$

and $\qquad\qquad s_Y = 1.25$

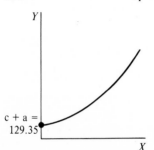

X **Problem 3**

where Y' and X are defined as before, with the base year for the time series in 1976. Solve parts (a) to (d) with the new trend equation.

4. Refer to Prob. 2. If management believes that a saturation point is reached in the cement sales the market can absorb, a more accurate trend equation may be specified by a *logistic curve* as follows:

$$Y' = \frac{1}{c + ab^X} = \frac{1}{.0056 - (.0023)(.80)^X}$$

and $S_Y = 1.25$

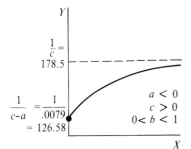

X   **Problem 4**

Solve parts (a) to (d) with the new trend equation, where Y' and X are as defined above and the base year for the time series is 1976.

5. The Co-op Bookstore manager of Green Valley State University believes that the annual sales volume of pocket calculators is strongly related to the number of new students enrolled in the schools of engineering and business administration. Data collected over the last several years on relevant new student enrollments and calculator sales are shown below.

Year	New student enrollment in engineering and business administration	Pocket calculator sales
1971	1,000	290
1972	700	280
1973	300	140
1974	600	220
1975	1,200	400
1976	700	330
1977	500	210
1978	1,000	390
1979	800	280
1980	500	200

(a) Plot the points corresponding to calculator sales Y for the given enrollment levels X.
(b) Find the least-squares regression line.
(c) How many calculators should the bookstore expect to sell in 1981 if the anticipated enrollment of new engineering and business administration students is 2,500?
(d) Give a 95 percent confidence interval for next year's demand estimate.

6. The number of housing units built annually in the island of the Coconut Republic, a resort paradise in the South Pacific, is as shown below:

Year	Quarter Q_1	Q_2	Q_3	Q_4	Total
1	53	97	80	60	290
2	50	91	84	72	297
3	69	112	98	86	365
4	66	105	111	102	384
5	73	117	112	91	393

(a) Obtain a least-squares trend line with 3 as the base year and calculate the standard error of the estimate S_Y.

(b) Using the regression line above, obtain an estimate of sales for year 6 and specify a 95 percent confidence interval.

(c) If the Coconut Republic has just enough capacity to cover the projected increase in years 6 and 7, what will be the new capacity requirements for the 5 yr period years 8 to 12?

(d) Using the ratio–to–moving-average method, determine the values for the typical seasonal indexes and use them to obtain an estimate of demand for each quarter in years 6 and 7.

7. The sales volume of the Golden Lager Brewery for the last 7 yr is given below by quarters.

Year	Sales by quarter, 1,000 gal Q_1	Q_2	Q_3	Q_4	Total
1974	258	370	392	303	1,323
1975	265	382	401	312	1,360
1976	292	387	424	325	1,428
1977	299	412	448	329	1,428
1978	304	419	463	351	1,537
1979	310	438	486	367	1,601
1980	337	449	490	372	1,648

(a) Obtain a least-squares trend line with 1977 as the base year and calculate the standard error of the estimate s_Y.

(b) Using the regression line above, obtain an estimate of sales for 1981 and specify a 95 percent confidence interval.

(c) If Golden Lager Brewery has enough capacity to cover the projected increase in 1981 and 1982, what will the new capacity requirements be for the 5-yr period 1983–1987?

(d) Using the ratio–to–moving-average method determine the values for the typical seasonal indexes and use them to obtain an estimate of demand for each quarter in 1981 and 1982.

(*e*) Using the method described in this chapter, determine the influence of the business cycle on the sales of Golden Lager Brewery.

(*f*) Is there any pattern in the random component of the time series?

8. The demand for office furniture sold by Office Designs, Ltd. for a period of 16 wk is shown below:

Week *t*	Furniture sales Y_t thousands
1	$151
2	145
3	142
4	146
5	145
6	153
7	167
8	162

Calculate the demand values that would be obtained with exponential smoothing and estimate the demand for period 9 (*a*) for $\alpha = .1$, (*b*) for $\alpha = .4$, and (*c*) for $\alpha = .8$.

9. (*a*) In Prob. 8 calculate the forecast errors for the given values of α and select the best one based (i) on MSE and (ii) on MAD.

(*b*) Is the forecasting systems under control if the action limits are set at ± 4 MAD?

10. The Camera-Shack downtown store has recorded monthly sales for its most popular 35-mm model as shown below:

Month	1	2	3	4	5	6
Units sold	43	36	34	51	48	52

(*a*) Using exponential smoothing, develop a forecast for demand in month 7 using, (i) $\alpha = .2$ and (ii) $\alpha = .9$.

(*b*) Determine the forecast error based on MAD and MSE for (i) $\alpha = .2$ and (ii) $\alpha = .9$.

(*c*) Calculate the tracking signal and suggest whether the forecasting system is under control if action limits were placed at ± 3 MAD, (i) $\alpha = .2$ and (ii) $\alpha = .9$.

SELECTED REFERENCES

1. Benton, W. K.: *Forecasting for Management*, Addison-Wesley, Reading, Mass., 1972.
2. Berry, W. L., and F. W. Bliemel: "Selecting Exponential Smoothing Constants: An Application of Pattern Search," *International Journal of Production Research*, vol. 12, no. 4, pp. 483–500, July 1974.
3. Brown, R. G.: *Smoothing, Forecasting and Prediction*, Prentice-Hall, Englewood Cliffs, N.J., 1963.
4. Brown, R. G.: *Statistical Forecasting for Inventory Control*, McGraw-Hill, New York, 1959.
5. Chambers, J. C., S. K. Mullick, and D. D. Smith: *An Executive's Guide to Forecasting*, Wiley, New York, 1974.
6. Draper, N. R., and H. Smith: *Applied Regression Analysis*, Wiley, New York, 1966.
7. Jantsch, E.: "Forecasting and Systems Approach: A Frame of Reference," *Management Science*, vol 19, no. 12, pp. 1355–1367, August 1973.

8. Johnston, J.: *Econometric Methods*, McGraw-Hill, New York, 1963.
9. Nelson, C. R.: *Applied Time Series Analysis for Managerial Forecasting*, Holden-Day, San Francisco, 1973.
10. Parker, G. C., and E. L. Segura: "How to Get a Better Forecast," *Harvard Business Review*, March–April 1971, pp. 99–109.
11. Wheelwright, S. C., and S. Makridakis: *Forecasting Methods for Management*, Wiley, New York, 1973.
12. Whybark, D. C.: "A Comparison of Adaptive Forecasting Techniques," *The Logistics and Transportation Review*, vol. 8, no. 3, pp. 13–26, 1972.

Chapter 12

AGGREGATE PLANNING

474

12-1 INTRODUCTION

The key decisions for system design determine an organization's basic character, i.e., its distinctive competence and capacity to satisfy certain human needs in products and services. Operations planning has the objective of making the best use possible of this distinctive competence and of the available capacity while satisfying demand over a period during which neither of these characteristics can be drastically changed.

Preparing a production plan would be a very simple matter if the demand rate were constant or if the production time for any order were negligible. In real life, both these conditions are rare. Thus, management has a difficult task in coping with significant production times and a host of uncertainties surrounding the estimates for demand, supplier's lead times, and internal production rates.

Demand for most consumer goods (food items, clothing, TV sets, etc.), and services (hospital beds, airplane seats, etc.) displays significant fluctuations from one period to another. Some of these changes may be part of a long-term trend, others are due to seasonal factors, and some are simply random variations that cannot be traced to any particular cause. The changes related to an underlying growth or decline trend, in the average level of demand, are usually handled through adjustments in the levels of capacity available by expanding the production system or contracting it. The random variations, as we shall see when we discuss inventory-management systems, are absorbed by buffer stocks. Our primary concern in aggregate production planning is the remaining seasonal fluctuation. The above types of demand changes are approached through different types of production plans, as explained below.

12-2 TYPES OF PRODUCTION PLANS

Selecting the right planning method for an organization depends on several factors. Some of these are external (type of market served, structure of the economy, etc.), while others are internal (management's ideas about the future, available expertise on the staff, etc.). Often the most significant consideration in how a plan is prepared is the length of the planning horizon. Accordingly, we have long-, medium-, and short-term production plans. Each type differs on the basis of the information it requires, the range of restrictions taken into account, and the number of variables controlled by management. As we reduce the length of the planning horizon, we need more specific information, we must conform to more restrictions, and we can control fewer variables. In short, we move from the strategic to the tactical decision-making level (see Table 12-1).

Long-Term Production Plans

Even though there is no widely accepted upper limit for the length of the planning horizon, a long-term plan generally looks 5 or more years into the future. The minimum time span is determined by how long it takes to change the capacity available. This includes time to complete the design for any new buildings and

TABLE 12-1 Types of production plans

Planning inputs	Decision variables			Planning outputs
	Long-term capacity Resource allocation for: Products Processes Markets	Levels of use for available production alternatives: Work-force size Production rate Inventory Subcontracting	Size of work force Production rate Sequencing of orders	
Basic purpose General objectives General forecasts: Economic Technological Other Available capital Competition	Long-term production planning (5–10 yr)			Plans for capacity expansion (or contraction) Plans for: New products New technologies New markets New plants and their location

Inputs

- Long-term plans
- Limits on present capacity
- Period-by-period annual demand forecast
- Feasible production alternatives and costs

- Aggregate production plan
- Orders received
- Desired delivery times

Processes

→ Medium-term, or aggregate, planning (1–24 months) →

→ Short-term production planning or scheduling (1–30 days) →

Outputs

- Aggregate production plans specifying how demand will be met from existing productive resources

- Production schedule assigning orders received to specific:
  Departments
  Shifts
  Personnel
  Equipment

Planning objectives

- To achieve specific organization objectives
- To enhance long-term viability and development

- To make the most effective use of available capacity through existing resources

- To ensure customer satisfaction through prompt delivery times
- To achieve maximum effectiveness from the use of production factors

equipment, construction, installation, and the debugging necessary until new facilities are operational. In effect, then, long-term production plans refer to decisions related to the design of the system.

A long-term production plan relies heavily on general economic and demographic forecasts and evaluates their projected impact on the organization's productive activities. At the same time, management examines the effects of probable changes in the political and social aspects of its environment as well as the development patterns of its competitors. Quite significant in this activity is the study of projected technological changes that may affect the system's technology with regard to the quality and cost of present and planned products. Adequate study of the above factors becomes especially critical for facilities to be located in foreign countries.

In short, long-term production plans are concerned with what effect the future will have on the system's objectives, its distinctive competence, and the adjustments that may be necessary to survive and grow through changes in its products, services, processes, or location.

Medium-Term, or Aggregate, Production Plans

For a planning horizon of 1 to 24 months we develop aggregate (or medium-term) production plans within the framework established by the long-term ones. For this type, capacity is assumed as relatively fixed. An aggregate plan relies on an annual month-by-month forecast of demand and existing productive resources (labor, inventories, current operating costs, suppliers, and subcontractors). Since this kind of plan is the subject of this chapter, we shall discuss it in detail in the following sections.

Short-Term Production Plans or Production Schedules

For times less than 1 month, operations management prepares short-term plans which are equivalent to production schedules. The objective of a production schedule is to match actual demand, as expressed through orders received, to available current resources (departments, shifts, operators, inventories and equipment), within the restrictions imposed by aggregate planning. The scheduling problem and methods for resolving it for different types of production systems are discussed in detail in Chap. 15.

12-3 PHASES OF AGGREGATE PLANNING

The development of an aggregate plan follows a procedure consisting of four phases, as shown in Fig. 12-1. After this procedure has been applied a few times and the issues involved in phases 2 and 3 have been resolved, management may proceed from phase 1 to phase 4 directly. It is desirable, however, to cover all four phases periodically to ensure adequate consideration of all options.

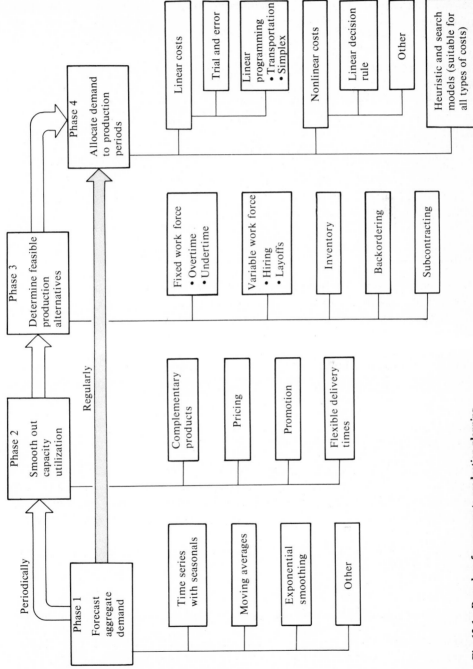

Fig. 12-1 Procedure for aggregate production planning.

479

Phase 1: Preparation of an Aggregate Demand Forecast

An aggregate demand forecast specifies the expected demand for each period in the planning horizon in units common to all products or types of services offered. For a soft-drink bottling plant the aggregate demand might be expressed in gallons, regardless of its distribution by bottle size. A government agency such as the court system or an IRS auditing department may wish to express its forecast in the form of cases to be handled. A hotel or a hospital may express its demand in terms of bed-days required, independently of whether people will be accommodated in single-, double- or multiple-bed rooms. Knowing the demand for specific product or service types becomes essential mainly for scheduling purposes when actual orders are to be assigned to specific departments or shifts.

　　Aggregate demand can be forecast using time-series analysis, moving averages, or other techniques.

Phase 2: Specification of Organization Policies for Smoothing Capacity Utilization

In the second phase, management attempts to identify promising policies that can smooth out expected aggregate demand as forecast in the previous phase. The combination of the most desirable policies represents the best strategy for absorbing future demand with its inherent seasonal and random fluctuations.

　　Before considering alternatives available only to the production function, top management with the cooperation of the marketing and production departments surveys the possible options open to the organization as a whole. Among the candidate policies considered, the following are often the most promising:

1. Introducing *complementary products or services* whose annual demand cycle peaks during the slow season for the regular product(s) or service(s) offered, for example:
   a. Use of a summer tourism facility or resort area for conventions or conferences during the fall and winter
   b. Introducing a product that peaks in the winter, e.g., heating units, when the main product, e.g., air conditioners, peaks in the summer[1]
2. Influencing the level and timing of demand through a *flexible pricing policy*, especially when demand displays significant price elasticity. This approach has been used effectively by:
   a. Commercial airlines offering lower rates during slow seasons and for night flights
   b. Hotels offering lower room rates during fall, winter, and spring compared with summer rates
3. Influencing the level and timing of demand through *advertising* or other promotional campaigns

---

[1] In Greece, an interesting application of this idea is the use of luxury buses, needed during the summer months for tourists, to transport students to their private schools during the regular school year.

4. Offering special arrangements with customers to obtain *flexibility in delivery deadlines* in exchange for reduced prices so that production can be scheduled more evenly

Sometimes it is possible for organizations of the same type to cooperate in absorbing total peak demand through some prearranged method of distribution as long as there is no conflict with existing laws. Typical examples include power utilities in different areas or cities who help each other during peak periods to absorb demand more evenly and transportation carriers who cooperate in absorbing peak demand for passenger transportation or freight on certain routes.

Phase 3: Determination of Feasible
Production Alternatives

Within the framework set by the strategy for smoothing demand, which goes beyond the authority of the production function, it is now possible to identify feasible production alternatives that enable operations management to satisfy demand at minimum cost. At this level of decision making, we include the following alternatives.

Changing the production rate with the same work force According to this method, during peak demand periods the production rate is increased through *overtime*. Similarly, during slow periods the production rate is reduced through *undertime*. Undertime here may take the form of the entire (or part of) the labor force working at slower pace with regular pay, which can be quite costly, or by the use of shorter workdays or workweeks with corresponding reductions in compensation. The latter approach turned out to be especially popular during the 1973–1975 economic recession.

This alternative is limited by the amount of change it can achieve in the production rate. One reason for this is the maximum overtime allowed by existing laws. Another relates to the higher wages necessary for overtime work, combined with additional costs for supervision or other types of overhead. The result is a higher cost per unit produced on overtime, denoted by v, whereas a unit produced on regular time costs a smaller amount r.

Changing the production rate by changing the size of the work force When demand fluctuates beyond the limits that can be handled using overtime or undertime, one of the alternatives may be to change the size of the work force through hiring or layoffs. Both these tactics also involve a variety of extra costs and are subject to restrictions.

Hiring usually includes costs related to locating, interviewing, testing, selecting, and training new employees. We assume that the cost of increasing the production rate by 1 unit through hiring can be estimated and is denoted by h. Similarly, reducing the production rate through layoffs involves costs related to severance pay, increased unemployment contributions, and detrimental loss of goodwill in the community. The cost of reducing the production rate by 1 unit through layoffs or firing can be estimated, and we denote it by f. Both unit costs for hiring h and layoffs f may vary from period to period, depending on the conditions of the local labor market and the state of the economy.

Changing the size of the work force is most appropriate when those hired or laid off have limited or no special skills (hotels, restaurants, farms, some factories, etc.) and where the labor market provides an ample supply. For organizations requiring highly skilled employees, this alternative is hardly applicable. Highly qualified workers expect and can usually get steady and secure employment. Such workers are likely to desert an employer who hires and fires workers according to seasonal demand fluctuations.

Absorbing demand through inventories   For certain organizations it is possible to absorb demand in busy periods through inventories accumulated in slow ones. The cost of this production alternative is equal to the inventory holding cost c_H, discussed in Chap. 13. This approach is not helpful when we deal with fashion items like women's clothing, perishable products, very expensive complex equipment, or other items whose storage life is limited. For service organizations (transportation, health, education, etc.) this option is not feasible because service output cannot be stored in the form of inventories.

Absorbing demand by backordering   Whenever demand exceeds the productive capacity of the system and there is no surplus inventory, it may be possible to accept orders to be satisfied at a later time. This is called backordering. It is assumed, of course, that the customer placing such an order is willing to accept a delay in delivery time.

Backordering is common for mail-order stores or companies that manufacture complex or expensive products such as special-purpose machines, computers, commercial aircraft, ships, etc. The same is true for specialized services such as difficult repairs, consulting services, doctor's appointments, elective surgery, and others. This practice would be hardly feasible for most consumer items such as food, drugs, clothing and others or routine services rendered by restaurants, theaters, x-ray laboratories, urban transportation, etc.

Whenever demand is met through backordering, we experience a shortage cost per unit per period c_S, also discussed in Chap. 13.

Absorbing demand through subcontracting   Actual demand sometimes cannot be met using the above production alternatives that are feasible. In such a case management may have the option of subcontracting part of the demand rather than refusing the orders it cannot satisfy. This course of action may be chosen to avoid losing important customers. It is assumed here that the subcontractor(s) considered can meet accepted quality standards and satisfy desired delivery deadlines; otherwise there is a risk for greater losses in goodwill than if the orders had been refused.

Subcontracting an order results in a higher cost per unit. The gain equals the difference between the subcontractor's price per unit and what it would cost to produce an additional unit internally, i.e., the marginal cost at the existing plant-capacity utilization level. The price charged per unit is denoted by u. Subcontracting was used extensively in the space program of the 1960s and is an attractive option for companies in the aircraft, automobile, and other industries.

The above production alternatives apply to systems whose maximum built-in capacity is not adequate to cover the peak demand for their output. Certain public-utility systems, such as power, telephone, and water companies, however, have enough capacity to handle peak loads. For slower periods their management simply reduces the degree of capacity utilization to adjust to current demand.

In practice, most organizations rely only on one or two production alternatives. A sample of different companies studied indicated that inventory was relied upon by a shoe company and a container company, the first because it faced a critical labor supply and the second because mechanization made it difficult to change the work-force size. A chocolate company in the same sample chose to vary the work-force size because of the limited shelf life of its products and an abundant supply of low-skilled labor (see Ref. 3, p. 150).

Careful analysis may show that for most companies the best strategy involves using a combination of the feasible production alternatives. The determination of the optimal strategy, i.e., that which minimizes the production cost of satisfying a given demand, is the objective of aggregate planning.

Phase 4: Determination of Optimal Production Strategy

Once the feasible production alternatives have been identified and their unit costs estimated, we can proceed to determine an optimal strategy. This involves allocating forecast demand by using the combination of alternatives in each period that minimizes the total cost for the entire planning horizon.

Aggregate planning methods for allocating demand to production periods vary in the assumptions made about feasible alternatives and their costs. Such methods also vary depending on whether they guarantee an optimal answer given the assumptions made. Thus, some of them are rather crude and rely on trial and error, while others depend on highly developed mathematical formulations. Available aggregate planning methods can be classified as shown in Table 12-2.

TABLE 12-2   Aggregate planning methods classification

Aggregate planning method	Cost relationships	
	Linear	Nonlinear

Not yielding optimal plan	A. Trial and error:
	    Using table
	    Using graph
		C. Heuristic models and
		    computer search models

Yielding optimal plan	B. Linear programming:
	    Transportation method
	    Simplex method
		D. Linear decision rule
		    Dynamic programming

In later sections we shall discuss the most representative types in each category. The dynamic-programming method is beyond the scope of this book. The interested reader can study the methods in greater detail by consulting the Selected References.

The availability of computers permits the use of the most powerful of the methods in categories B, C, and D to evaluate several strategies, i.e., production plans, under a variety of assumptions concerning future demand, cost relationships, and the operation of the production system. This gives management added flexibility along with the knowledge of the sensitivity of a production plan to environmental and internal changes.

12-4   THE AGGREGATE PLANNING PROBLEM

It was stated previously that, given a relatively fixed capacity, aggregate planning seeks to achieve the best utilization of available productive resources. This is done by allocating capacity in various forms to each production period in the plan so that forecast demand can be met at minimum cost.

Operations management can develop an aggregate plan using any one or a combination of the alternatives shown in Table 12-3.

▶ EXAMPLE 12-1
The forecast aggregate monthly demand data of the Apollo Company in Table 12-4 will be used to illustrate some of the methods used for aggregate planning. Let us assume that according to one production plan the expected demand in May ($Y'_5 = 700$) can be met as follows:

Source	Amount, units	Cost per unit
Regular production	300	$ 5
Overtime production	120	8
Inventory built up in March	200	1 per period
Subcontracting	80	12
Total	700	

TABLE 12-3   Potential production alternatives, their unit costs, and limits

Production alternative	Cost per unit of production	Amount used in period t	Capacity limit in period t
Regular-time production	r	P_t	L_t
Overtime production	v	Q_t	M_t
Inventory †	c_H	I_t	No limit
Backordering	c_S	B_t	No limit
Hiring	h	H_t	No limit
Layoffs	f	F_t	No limit
Subcontracting	u	S_t	N_t

† Not available for systems providing services.

TABLE 12-4   Forecast aggregate monthly demand for Apollo Company

Period		Forecast	Period		Forecast
t	Month	Y'_t	t	Month	Y'_t
1	January	500	7	July	1,200
2	February	400	8	August	1,100
3	March	300	9	September	900
4	April	500	10	October	800
5	May	700	11	November	700
6	June	900	12	December	600

† Initial inventory $I_0 = 0$; final inventory required $I_f = 200$.

It is also assumed that no hiring or layoffs were necessary to reach this production rate; that is, $P_5 = P_4 = 300$; this is shown graphically in Fig. 12-2. We note that for period 5 the forecast demand of 700 units was met at a certain cost, computed by adding the individual costs for each production alternative employed

$$C_5 = rP_5 + vQ_5 + 2c_H I_5 + hH_5 + fF_5 + uS_5$$

$$= (5)(300) + (8)(120) + (2)(1)(200) + 0 + 0 + (12)(80)$$

$$= \$3,820$$

▶

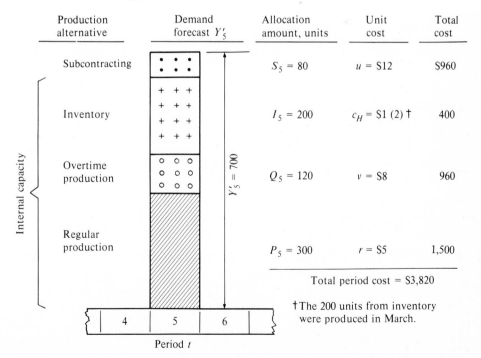

Production alternative	Demand forecast Y'_5	Allocation amount, units	Unit cost	Total cost
Subcontracting		$S_5 = 80$	$u = \$12$	$960
Inventory		$I_5 = 200$	$c_H = \$1\ (2)$ †	400
Overtime production		$Q_5 = 120$	$v = \$8$	960
Regular production		$P_5 = 300$	$r = \$5$	1,500

Total period cost = $3,820

† The 200 units from inventory were produced in March.

Fig. 12-2   One plan for satisfying expected demand in period 5 (May) and its total cost for Apollo Co. example.

In general, the cost for period t will be

$$C_t = C_R + C_O + C_I + C_B + C_H + C_F + C_S$$
$$= rP_t + vQ_t + c_H I_t + c_s B_t + hH_t + fF_t + uS_t \qquad (12\text{-}1)$$

or

$$\begin{bmatrix} \text{Production cost} \\ \text{in period } t \end{bmatrix} = \begin{bmatrix} \text{cost of regular} \\ \text{production} \end{bmatrix} + \begin{bmatrix} \text{cost of overtime} \\ \text{production} \end{bmatrix} + \begin{bmatrix} \text{cost of units used} \\ \text{from inventory} \end{bmatrix}$$

$$+ \begin{bmatrix} \text{cost of} \\ \text{backordering} \end{bmatrix} + \begin{bmatrix} \text{cost of} \\ \text{hiring} \end{bmatrix} + \begin{bmatrix} \text{cost of} \\ \text{firing} \end{bmatrix} + \begin{bmatrix} \text{cost of} \\ \text{subcontracting} \end{bmatrix}$$

Satisfying the demand for the planning horizon will result in a total production cost which is the sum of the period costs

$$\text{TPC} = C_1 + C_2 + \cdots + C_{12} = \sum_{t=1}^{12} C_t \qquad (12\text{-}2)$$

where TPC = total production cost for planning horizon
  C_t = production cost for period t as defined in (12-1)

The total cost TPC will vary according to the production plan used, depending on the extent each production alternative is employed to satisfy the forecast demand for each period.

Definition

The *aggregate-planning problem* consists of determining how feasible production alternatives must be employed in each period to satisfy expected demand at minimum total production cost.

The aggregate-planning decision system is shown in Fig. 12-3. Its complete description requires specifying the desired input and output information, existing capacity constraints, decision variables, and the measure of performance.

12-5 ALLOCATING DEMAND TO PRODUCTION PERIODS ASSUMING LINEAR COST RELATIONSHIPS

Many aggregate-planning applications assume that all cost relationships are linear. Thus, the cost of using any production alternative varies proportionally with the number of units of demand covered by that alternative. The linear-cost methods developed for solving the aggregate-production-planning problem vary from simple and somewhat crude trial-and-error procedures to very powerful linear-programming models. Here we shall discuss the simple ones first and then proceed with the more elaborate types.

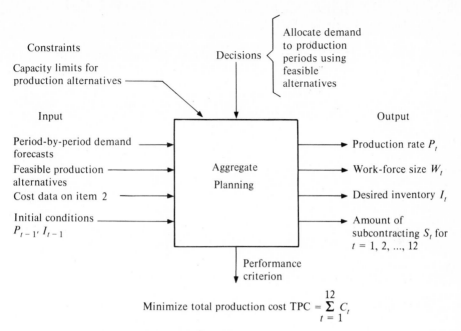

Fig. 12-3 The aggregate-production-planning system.

Trial-and-Error Method Using a Table

In order to work with the data for the Apollo Co. example we must secure additional information on feasible production alternatives, their unit costs, and capacity limits. Let us assume that the company can meet forecast demand with a combination of the alternatives shown in Table 12-5.

We can proceed to develop a production plan by trial and error after setting up a table with the monthly demand data (see Table 12-6). This is completed period by period so that demand in each period is met by selecting the minimum-cost combination of available production alternatives. Care must be taken in each step, of course, to ensure that the capacity restrictions are not violated.

Let us assume that in January we have zero starting inventory ($I_0 = 0$). In period 1 we have a demand of 500 units, which can be met entirely from regular-time production. This is shown by the entry in the table in the row for period 1 and

TABLE 12-5 Feasible alternatives and related data for Apollo Co. example

Production alternative	Unit cost	Maximum monthly capacity, units
Regular production	$ 5	650
Overtime production	8	150
Inventories	1	No limit
Subcontracting	12	100

TABLE 12-6   Trial-and-error method for aggregate-production plan of the Apollo Co. example

			Feasible production alternatives		
Period	Month	Demand	Regular production (650)	Overtime production (150)	Subcontracting (100)
1	Jan.	500	500(1)		
2	Feb.	400	400(2), 50(7), 200(8)		
3	Mar.	300	300(3), 150(6), 200(7)		
4	Apr.	500	500(4), 50(5), 100(6)		
5	May	700	650(5)	100(8)	
6	June	900	650(6)	150(7)	
7	July	1,200	650(7)	150(7)	
8	Aug.	1,100	650(8)	150(8)	
9	Sept.	900	650(9)	150(9)	100(9)
10	Oct.	800	650(10)	150(10)	
11	Nov.	700	650(11)	50(11)	
12	Dec.	600	650(12), 50(I_f)	150(f)	

the column under regular production, 500(1). The number in parentheses refers to the period for which this amount is intended. The same remarks apply for the months of February through April.

In May, however, the demand of 700 units cannot be met entirely from regular production. Now we must choose the next least expensive combination of alternatives. We can use overtime in the same period at $8 per unit or go back one period and produce enough to carry in inventory for use in May. Thus, we produce 50 units in April at a cost of $6 per unit ($5 per unit for regular time production plus $1 per unit to carry it in stock for one period).

In June demand is estimated at 900 units. We can produce 650 on regular time, then go back to April and produce 100 units remaining on regular time at a cost of $7 per unit ($5 + $2). This leaves a balance of 150 units, which can be produced on overtime in June at $8 per unit or on regular time in March and carried in stock for three periods at a cost of $8 per unit. We choose to produce in March for June so that we can retain some flexibility for later periods and smooth out the utilization of regular-time capacity. The entries for the remaining periods have been completed and shown in Table 12-6.

The trial-and-error method used for this example is straightforward. In each period we start with the most economical alternative and use it as much as needed unless we reach the limit of its capacity. When this happens, we switch to the next most desirable alternative, and so on. To calculate the cost for the above production plan we must add the period-by-period cost as determined by the alternatives used. For example, the cost for period 6 is

$$C_6 = (\$5)(650) + (\$5 + \$2)(100) + (\$5 + \$3)(150) = \$5,150$$

From June   From April   From March

TABLE 12-7   Final production plan with period and total costs

Period	Demand	Regular production	Overtime production	Subcontracting	Period cost C_t
1	500	500			$ 2,500
2	400	650			2,000
3	300	650			1,500
4	500	650			2,500
5	700	650	100		3,550
6	900	650	150		5,150
7	1,200	650	150		8,100
8	1,100	650	150		7,750
9	900	650	150	100	5,650
10	800	650	150		4,450
11	700	650	150		3,650
12	600	650	150		4,450
Total					$51,150

In words, each amount is multiplied by the unit cost of the production alternative used plus any inventory charge when produced before it is needed. The final plan and its cost are shown in Table 12-7.

One can raise several objections to this approach: (1) There is no guarantee that the final plan is the most economical. Perhaps, through further rearrangements one might identify additional improvements. For example, the availability of starting inventory may sometimes result in significant cost reductions by lessening the need for overtime or subcontracting in later periods. (2) By necessity the range of production alternatives included must be small, otherwise the calculations become hopeless. (3) Even though the production plan in Table 12-7 suggests changes in the regular production rate, e.g., a 150-unit increase from January to February, there is no way of estimating the hiring costs resulting from changes in the size of the work force. Despite these limitations and the fact that linear cost relationships may not hold for some organizations, this approach may yield significant improvements over an arbitrarily prepared production plan. Another trial-and-error procedure uses a graph showing how for different production rates in each period cumulative production compares with cumulative demand in that period. This allows for the inclusion of buffer stocks and production lead times showing the amount of inventory graphically at each stage.[1]

Aggregate Planning Using the Transportation Method

Under certain assumptions, it is possible to formulate an aggregate-planning problem in such a way that if there is a solution, it can be shown to be optimal. Thus, in

[1] For a detailed description of the trial-and-error aggregate-planning method using a graph see J. F. Magee and D. M. Boodman, *Production Planning and Inventory Control*, 2d ed., McGraw-Hill, New York, 1967.

contrast with the preceding trial-and-error methods we now have the assurance that the "best" production plan is prepared. One technique used for this purpose is the transportation method in linear programming (see Supplementary Chapter E). This approach allows for the use of regular production, overtime, inventory, backordering, and subcontracting.

In order to employ the transportation method we must formulate the aggregate-planning problem so that

1. Productive capacity (supply) and demand are expressed in the same units.
2. Total capacity for the planning horizon equals total forecast demand. If this condition is not met, we can create artificial capacity sources or demand requirements, at zero cost per unit, so that the system is balanced.
3. All cost relationships are treated as being linear.

To illustrate how the transportation method is applied we shall use the example data of the Apollo Co. However, to keep the size of the problem manageable, we shall use four periods by converting monthly demands into quarterly figures. For simplicity in calculations we shall assume that inventory carrying charges are still computed at $1 (rather than $3) per unit per period. Furthermore, we shall assume that backordering is allowed at $c_s = \$4$ per unit per period. Now the data of the example can be restated as shown in Table 12-8.

Before we set up the above problem in matrix form, we must check whether all conditions for using the transportation method have been satisfied. For the Apollo Co. example:

1. Capacity and demand are both expressed in units of production.
2. The total capacity available, including starting inventory is

$$(4)(1,950) + (4)(450) + (4)(300) + 0 = 10,800 \text{ units}$$

while total projected demand, including final inventory requirement, is

$$(1,200 + 2,100 + 3,200 + 2,100) + 200 = 8,800 \text{ units}$$

Here, total capacity exceeds total demand by 2,000, so an additional fictitious

TABLE 12-8   Data on Apollo Co. for use in transportation method

Period t	Expected demand	Limits on sources of capacity		
		Regular time	Overtime	Subcontracting
1	$Y'_1 = 1,200$	$L_1 = 1,950$	$M_1 = 450$	$N_1 = 300$
2	$Y'_2 = 2,100$	$L_2 = 1,950$	$M_2 = 450$	$N_2 = 300$
3	$Y'_3 = 3,200$	$L_3 = 1,950$	$M_3 = 450$	$N_3 = 300$
4	$Y'_4 = 2,100$	$L_4 = 1,950$	$M_4 = 450$	$N_4 = 300$
Ending inventory $I_f = 200$				

Initial inventory $I_0 = 0$

Unit production costs: $r = \$5$ $v = \$8$ $u = \$12$
Inventory carrying cost: $c_H = \$1$ per unit per quarter
Backordering cost: $c_S = \$4$ per unit per quarter

source of demand must be introduced to absorb the excess capacity. This in a matrix will be shown as a slack column with zero cost coefficients since the excess units do not have to be produced. In the opposite case, if total demand exceeded total capacity, we would introduce a fictitious source of capacity as a matrix row with zero cost coefficients since those units would never be really produced.

3. All cost relationships are linear, since no mention is made in the problem statement of any economies or diseconomies of scale for any of the production alternatives. Thus, the cost of 1,000 units produced by any particular method will be 1,000 times as large as the cost of 1 unit.

Now the aggregate-planning problem can be represented conveniently in matrix form as shown in Fig. 12-4. The first and last columns of the matrix refer to the production alternatives in each period and their maximum capacities. Here the symbols RP_t, OT_t, SC_t refer to regular time, overtime, and subcontracting capacity in period t, while L_t, M_t, and N_t denote their maximum limits. Each source of capacity, i.e., each production alternative in each period, is shown as a separate row. Initial inventory I_0 can be viewed as another source of capacity, and final inventory I_f is equivalent to an additional demand period.

Each of the intermediate columns represents a demand period in the planning horizon. Here the entry in the intersection of a row and a column is the cost of satisfying 1 unit of demand in that period using the production alternative corresponding to the row. For example, satisfying 1 unit of demand in period 2 from regular-time production in period 1 would cost $r + c_H$. The same unit satisfied from overtime production in period 4 would cost $v + 2c_s$.

When a unit is produced in the same period it is demanded, its cost depends only on the production alternative employed, r, v, or u. However, producing a unit ahead of the period it is needed (cells above the crosshatched diagonal) includes an additional carrying charge per period. Similarly, when a unit is produced at a later period than it is demanded (cells below the crosshatched diagonal), then beyond the production cost there is a backordering cost per period. If no backordering were allowed ($c_s = \infty$), all cells under the diagonal would be assigned a high cost penalty, say 99,999, to avoid using them.

The numerical data for the example of the Apollo Co. are represented in matrix form in Fig. 12-5. The reader is encouraged to verify the validity of the cost entries in the cells.

Once the aggregate-planning problem has been formulated as shown in Fig. 12-5, it can be solved by the linear-programming transportation method. For this matrix size or larger, it is best to use a computer. Longhand methods are laborious, time-consuming, and subject to computational error. Most computer systems include in their library streamlined standardized LP programs. Thus, not only can one get a solution quickly and economically but one has the opportunity of checking the effect on the production plan of various changes in forecast demand, cost data, and other conditions such as beginning and ending inventory.

The optimum production plan for the example is shown by the circled entries in Fig. 12-5. By adding these values for each column the reader can easily verify

| | Demand period | | | | Final inventory | Fictitious demand | Productive capacity |
Production source	1	2	3	4			
Initial inventory	0	c_H	$2c_H$	$3c_H$	$4c_H$	0	I_0
Period 1 — RP$_1$	r	$r+c_H$	$r+2c_H$	$r+3c_H$	$r+4c_H$	0	L_1
OT$_1$	v	$v+c_H$	$v+2c_H$	$v+3c_H$	$v+4c_H$	0	M_1
SC$_1$	u	$u+c_H$	$u+2c_H$	$u+3c_H$	$u+4c_H$	0	N_1
Period 2 — RP$_2$	$r+c_S$	r	$r+c_H$	$r+2c_H$	$r+3c_H$	0	L_2
OT$_2$	$v+c_S$	v	$v+c_H$	$v+2c_H$	$v+3c_H$	0	M_2
SC$_2$	$u+c_S$	u	$u+c_H$	$u+2c_H$	$u+3c_H$	0	N_2
Period 3 — RT$_3$	$r+2c_S$	$r+c_S$	r	$r+c_H$	$r+2c_H$	0	L_3
OT$_3$	$v+2c_S$	$v+c_S$	v	$v+c_H$	$v+2c_H$	0	M_3
SC$_3$	$u+2c_S$	$u+c_S$	u	$u+c_H$	$u+2c_H$	0	N_3
Period 4 — RT$_4$	$r+3c_S$	$r+2c_S$	$r+c_S$	r	$r+c_H$	0	L_4
OT$_4$	$v+3c_S$	$v+2c_S$	$v+c_S$	v	$v+c_H$	0	M_4
SC$_4$	$u+3c_S$	$u+2c_S$	$u+c_S$	u	$u+c_H$	0	N_4
Forecast demand	Y'_1	Y'_2	Y'_3	Y'_4	I_f	R	

Fig. 12-4 General formulation of aggregate-planning problem for solution by transportation method.

Below is the content of the transportation tableau. In each cell the small boxed number is the unit cost; a **bold** number is the quantity allocated.

Production source	\(1\)	\(2\)	\(3\)	\(4\)	Final inventory	Fictitious demand	Productive capacity
Initial inventory	0 **1,200**	1	2	3	4	0	1,200
RP_1	5	6 **750**	7	8	9	0	1,950
OT_1	8	9	10	11	12	0 **450**	450
SC_1	12	13	14	15	16	0 **300**	300
RP_2	9	5 **1,350**	6 **600**	7	8	0	1,950
OT_2	12	8	9 **200**	10	11	0 **250**	450
SC_2	16	12	13	14	15	0 **300**	300
RT_3	13	9	5 **1,950**	6	7	0	1,950
OT_3	16	12	8 **450**	9	10	0	450
SC_3	20	16	12	13	14	0 **300**	300
RT_4	17	13	9	5 **1,750**	6 **200**	0	1,950
OT_4	20	16	12	8 **350**	9	0 **100**	450
SC_4	24	20	16	12	13	0 **300**	300
Forecast demand	1,200	2,100	3,200	2,100	200	2,000	10,800

Row groups: Period 1 = RP_1, OT_1, SC_1; Period 2 = RP_2, OT_2, SC_2; Period 3 = RT_3, OT_3, SC_3; Period 4 = RT_4, OT_4, SC_4. Columns \(1\)–\(4\) are the Demand period.

Fig. 12-5 Formulation of Apollo Co. aggregate-planning problem as a transportation linear-programming problem.

that they satisfy projected demand. Similarly, added for each row, these entries also satisfy the imposed capacity constraints. The total cost of this plan is $48,750.

The most serious criticism of the transportation method is that it does not account for any changes in the production rate. The latter normally involve hiring or layoff costs, which may be quite significant. Other than that, the method is suited very well to applications where the assumptions fit the situation.

Aggregate Planning Using the Simplex Method

Whenever the costs for all relevant production alternatives can be assumed linear, a very general and powerful approach to the aggregate-planning problem is the simplex method of linear programming. The simplex, unlike its special case, the transportation method, accounts for the costs of changing the size of the work force and the production rate through hiring and layoffs.

Using the data of the Apollo Co. example, aggregated over four periods to keep the formulation simple, we have the following:

Decision Variables Relating to Production Alternatives

P_t = number of units produced on regular time in period t ($t = 1, 2, 3, 4$)
Q_t = number of units produced on overtime in period t
S_t = number of units subcontracted in period t
I_t = number of units of inventory available at end of period t
H_t = number of units production rate was increased in period t through hiring
F_t = number of units production rate was decreased in period t through firing

Capacity Restrictions on Production Alternatives

L_t = maximum numbers of units that can be produced on regular time in period t
M_t = maximum numbers of units that can be produced on overtime in period t
N_t = maximum numbers of units that can be produced on subcontracted time in period t

Unit Costs of Production Alternatives

r = cost of producing 1 unit on regular time = $5 per unit
v = cost of producing 1 unit on overtime = $8 per unit
u = cost of subcontracting 1 unit = $12 per unit
c_H = inventory holding cost per unit per period = $1 per unit per period
h = unit cost of hiring = $20 per unit
f = unit cost of firing = $10 per unit

Demand Forecasts for Planning Horizon

$Y'_1 = 1,200$ units
$Y'_2 = 2,100$ units
$Y'_3 = 3,200$ units
$Y'_4 = 2,100$ units

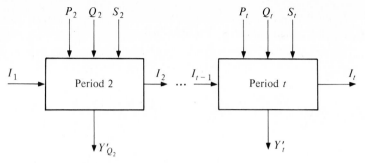

Fig. 12-6 Inventory constraints for each production period.

Initial and Final Conditions

I_0 = initial inventory = 0 units
I_f = ending inventory = 200 units
P_0 = initial production rate = 1,900 units

The formulation of the simplex model for aggregate planning consists of specifying for the planning horizon existing capacity constraints and the total production cost. For the general case and the example the formulation is shown in Fig. 12-6. An alternative representation of the example which highlights the interdependence of decisions in successive periods is shown in Fig. 12-7 and Table 12-9. Solution of the problem involves the determination of values for the decision variables resulting in a production plan that satisfies existing constraints at minimum cost.

The formulation of the restrictions is quite straightforward. The use of a specific production alternative to satisfy demand in a given period must not exceed the capacity limit for that alternative in the period of interest.

Thus, for period 2 in the example:

$P_t \leq L_t$	becomes	$P_2 \leq 1{,}950$	Regular-time production
$Q_t \leq M_t$	becomes	$Q_2 \leq 450$	Overtime production
$S_t \leq N_t$	becomes	$S_2 \leq 300$	Subcontracted production
$H_t \leq P_t - P_{t-1}$	becomes	$H_2 \geq P_2 - P_1$	Hiring
$F_t \leq P_{t-1} - P_t$	becomes	$F_2 \geq P_1 - P_2$	Firing

Similar constraints are in effect for all other periods. The inventory restriction requires a more detailed explanation. In this case, for each period the following relationship must hold true (see Fig. 12-6):

$$\begin{bmatrix} \text{Starting inventory} \\ \text{in period 2} \end{bmatrix} + \begin{bmatrix} \text{units produced on} \\ \text{regular time, overtime} \\ \text{and subcontracting} \\ \text{in period 2} \end{bmatrix} = \begin{bmatrix} \text{forecast demand} \\ \text{for period 2} \end{bmatrix} + \begin{bmatrix} \text{inventory at end} \\ \text{of period 2} \end{bmatrix}$$

Aggregate – planning decision variables

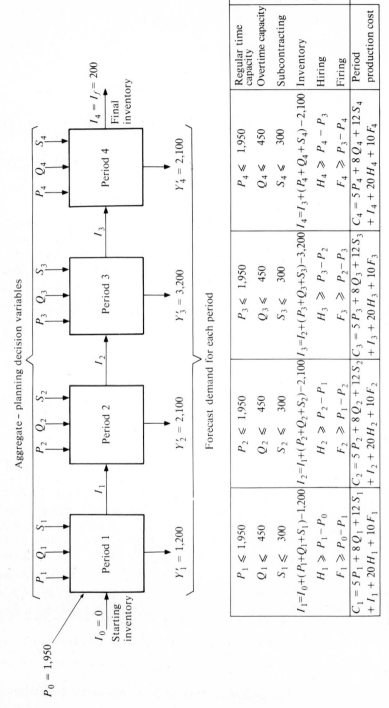

Constraints	Period 1	Period 2	Period 3	Period 4
Regular time capacity	$P_1 \le 1,950$	$P_2 \le 1,950$	$P_3 \le 1,950$	$P_4 \le 1,950$
Overtime capacity	$Q_1 \le 450$	$Q_2 \le 450$	$Q_3 \le 450$	$Q_4 \le 450$
Subcontracting	$S_1 \le 300$	$S_2 \le 300$	$S_3 \le 300$	$S_4 \le 300$
Inventory	$I_1 = I_0 + (P_1 + Q_1 + S_1) - 1,200$	$I_2 = I_1 + (P_2 + Q_2 + S_2) - 2,100$	$I_3 = I_2 + (P_3 + Q_3 + S_3) - 3,200$	$I_4 = I_3 + (P_4 + Q_4 + S_4) - 2,100$
Hiring	$H_1 \ge P_1 - P_0$	$H_2 \ge P_2 - P_1$	$H_3 \ge P_3 - P_2$	$H_4 \ge P_4 - P_3$
Firing	$F_1 \ge P_0 - P_1$	$F_2 \ge P_1 - P_2$	$F_3 \ge P_2 - P_3$	$F_4 \ge P_3 - P_4$
Period production cost	$C_1 = 5P_1 + 8Q_1 + 12S_1 + I_1 + 20H_1 + 10F_1$	$C_2 = 5P_2 + 8Q_2 + 12S_2 + I_2 + 20H_2 + 10F_2$	$C_3 = 5P_3 + 8Q_3 + 12S_3 + I_3 + 20H_3 + 10F_3$	$C_4 = 5P_4 + 8Q_4 + 12S_4 + I_4 + 20H_4 + 10F_4$

Fig. 12-7 A multistage representation of aggregate-planning problem for the example.

TABLE 12-9 Restrictions and objective function for aggregate planning with simplex

Restrictions

Period	On regular-time production $P_t \le L_t$	On overtime production $Q_t \le M_t$	On subcontracting $S_t \le N_t$	On inventory $I_{t-1} + P_t + Q_t + S_t \ge Y_t$	On hiring $H_t \ge P_t - P_{t-1}$	On firing $F_t \ge P_{t-1} - P_t$
1	$P_1 \le 1,950$	$Q_1 \le 450$	$S_1 \le 300$	$I_0 + P_1 + Q_1 + S_1 \ge 1,200$	$H_1 \ge P_1 - P_0$	$F_1 \ge P_0 - P_1$
2	$P_2 \le 1,950$	$Q_2 \le 450$	$S_2 \le 300$	$I_1 + P_2 + Q_2 + S_2 \ge 2,100$	$H_2 \ge P_2 - P_1$	$F_2 \ge P_1 - P_2$
3	$P_3 \le 1,950$	$Q_3 \le 450$	$S_3 \le 300$	$I_2 + P_3 + Q_3 + S_3 \ge 3,200$	$H_3 \ge P_3 - P_2$	$F_3 \ge P_2 - P_3$
4	$P_4 \le 1,950$	$Q_4 \le 450$	$S_4 \le 300$	$I_3 + P_4 + Q_4 + S_4 \ge 2,100$	$H_4 \ge P_4 - P_3$	$F_4 \ge P_3 - P_4$

Furthermore, $P_t, Q_t, S_t, H_t,$ and F_t must be nonnegative (≥ 0) for $t = 1, 2, 3, 4$

Objective function:

Minimize TPC $= C_1 + C_2 + C_3 + C_4$ = total production cost

where $\quad C_t = rP_t + vQ_t + uS_t + c_H \left| \sum_{j=1}^{t} (P_j + Q_j + S_t - Y_j) \right| + hH_t + fF_t \quad$ and $\quad t = 1, 2, 3, 4$

For $t = 2$: $\quad C_2 = 5P_2 + 8Q_2 + 12S_2 + (1)\{[I_0 + (P_1 + Q_1 + S_1) - Y_1] + (P_2 + Q_2 + S_2 - Y_2)\} + 20H_2 + 10F_2$

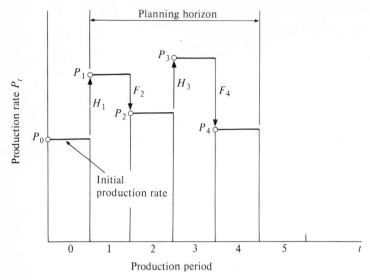

Fig. 12-8   Production-rate fluctuations in typical production plan.

In our example we have

For period 1: $I_0 + P_1 + Q_1 + S_1 = Y'_1 + I_1$

or $\qquad\qquad\qquad I_1 = P_1 + Q_1 + S_1 - Y'_1 \qquad$ since $I_0 = 0$

For period 2: $I_1 + P_2 + Q_2 + S_2 = Y'_2 + I_2$

or $\qquad\qquad\qquad I_2 = I_1 + P_2 + Q_2 + S_2 - Y'_2$

Obtaining a solution for the above formulation of the aggregate-planning problem usually requires the use of a computer. Efficient linear-programming computer programs are available today with most commercial installations.

Figure 12-8 shows typical production-rate fluctuations necessary to yield the desired minimum-cost production plan.

12-6 ALLOCATING DEMAND TO PRODUCTION PERIODS USING ALTERNATIVES WITH NONLINEAR COSTS

For some organizations the cost relationship that applies when using a specific production alternative cannot justifiably be assumed to be linear. Consider as an example changing the size of the work force. If what is needed is one or two additional workers, many of the costs associated with hiring, such as announcing the openings, interviewing, testing the applicants, training them, etc., can be absorbed with existing personnel at little extra cost. However, if we need 20 or 50 more workers, the magnitude of the task of hiring at this level requires additional costs (running an advertisement in the paper instead of calling the unemployment agency, assigning specific people and other resources to handle the interviewing, testing, training, etc.). As a result, hiring 20 people costs more than 20 times the cost to hire 1. In this case, we say that hiring costs are nonlinear, their specific form depending on the organization and its environment, i.e., the labor market. Similar arguments could be made for the costs of using other alternatives, such as overtime, inventory, and others.

Whether it is one or more production alternatives that are described with nonlinear costs, the total cost for a given production plan is nonlinear and the methods described previously do not apply. In this case, we may use the so-called linear decision rule (LDR), certain heuristic methods based on commonsense rules, or computer-search methods. Of these, only the linear-decision-rule approach guarantees an optimal production plan.

The Linear-Decision-Rule (LDR) Method

The first successful effort to deal with nonlinear costs in solving the aggregate-planning method was made by Holt et al. in 1955 (Ref. 5). Using a paint company as an actual example, they considered that the aggregate-production plan could be set up based on four production alternatives: (1) regular payroll (reflecting regular-time production), (2) hiring and layoffs, (3) overtime, and (4) inventory.

The team viewed as independent (decision) variables in each period the production rate P_t and the aggregate work force size W_t. Assigning to them specific values to satisfy forecast demand Y'_t in each period required using the production alternatives at different levels. The cost generated by each alternative, except for payroll, was assumed to be nonlinear, in this case quadratic. Thus, there is a cost for each period equal to the sum of the costs of production alternatives employed to meet demand.

The objective here is to determine a pair of values for the decision variables P_t and W_t for each period that satisfy projected demand during the planning horizon at minimum total cost. Since the cost for each period is quadratic, the total cost for the planning horizon is also quadratic. The aggregate planning problem can be formulated as a quadratic programming problem. In the process of finding the optimal values for P_t and W_t we derive a set of two decision rules that have a linear form. Hence, the name linear decision rule for the method.

The production alternatives considered by Holt et al., with their general and specific forms in the paint company example, after unknown parameters were estimated from actual data, are shown in Table 12-10.

In the LDR method the form of the cost relationship for each production alternative is quite general and can be applied to a wide variety of applications. These costs are shown in Fig. 12-9, which can be explained as follows.

Payroll cost. For each period, payroll costs represent the regular time wages due to those working at the beginning of the month W_t.

Hiring and layoff cost. These reflect the costs associated with changing the size of the work force. Cost curves for hiring and firing do not have to be symmetrical: i.e., hiring might be more expensive than firing or vice versa.

TABLE 12-10   Production alternatives in the LDR and their costs†

Production alternative	Type of cost relationship	General form	Specific form for paint company
Regular payroll	Linear	$c_1 W_t$	$340 W_t$
Hiring and layoffs	Quadratic	$c_2(W_t - W_{t-1})^2$	$64.3(W_t - W_{t-1})^2$
Overtime	Quadratic	$c_3(P_t - c_4 W_t)^2$ $+ c_5 P_t - c_6 W_t$	$0.20(P_t - 5.67 W_t)^2$ $+ 51.2 P_t - 281 W_t$
Inventory, backorders	Quadratic	$c_7(I_t - c_8 - c_9 Y'_t)^2$	$0.0825(I_t - 329)^2$

† LDR decision variables: production rate P_t and work-force size W_t in period t.
SOURCE: See Ref. 5.

Overtime and undertime cost. For a constant work force the production rate may be increased with overtime or decreased with undertime. The latter results in cost of idle labor at regular payroll rates.

Inventory and backorder costs. The inventory level here reflects net inventory, i.e., the difference between inventory and backorders. Optimal inventory levels are determined by the sum of optimal average safety stocks plus one-half the optimal economic order quantity. This cost also involves machine-setup costs.

Using the LDR, we seek to minimize the total production cost over the planning horizon (usually a year). The problem stated in general form is as follows: find values for P_t and W_t ($t = 1, 2, ..., 12$) that will minimize the total production cost TPC, where

$$\text{TPC} = \underbrace{C_1 + C_2 + \cdots + C_{12}}_{\text{Sum of period costs}} = \sum_{t=1}^{12} C_t$$

where

$$\begin{bmatrix} \text{Period cost} \\ C_t \end{bmatrix} = \begin{bmatrix} \text{regular} \\ \text{payroll cost} \end{bmatrix} + \begin{bmatrix} \text{hiring and} \\ \text{layoff cost} \end{bmatrix} + \begin{bmatrix} \text{overtime} \\ \text{cost} \end{bmatrix} + \begin{bmatrix} \text{inventory} \\ \text{cost} \end{bmatrix}$$

as specified in Table 12-10, subject to the restriction

$$I_{t-1} + P_t - Y'_t = I_t \quad \text{for } t = 1, 2, ..., 12$$

or

$$\begin{bmatrix} \text{Starting} \\ \text{inventory} \end{bmatrix} + \begin{bmatrix} \text{current} \\ \text{production} \end{bmatrix} - \begin{bmatrix} \text{demand for} \\ \text{current period} \end{bmatrix} = \begin{bmatrix} \text{ending} \\ \text{inventory} \end{bmatrix}$$

Solving the above problem yields a set of two linear decision rules for the production rate P and the work-force size W for the current period. These are based on initial conditions (starting inventory and work-force size) and the projected forecasts for the remaining periods in the planning horizon (see Ref. 5).

Whenever the cost relationships of relevant production alternatives are quadratic, as assumed in the LDR, the method offers the advantage of specifying an

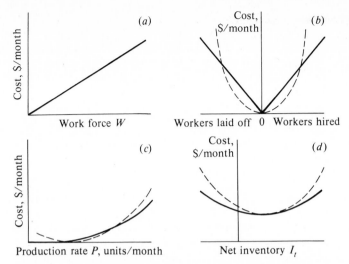

Fig. 12-9 Cost relationships for LDR method: (*a*) regular payroll cost, (*b*) cost of change in size of work force, (*c*) expected cost of overtime, and (*d*) cost of inventory, backorders, and setups.

optimal production plan. Furthermore, after the arduous task of estimating the parameters its implementation can be quick and easy. However, the method is severely limited by the assumption of quadratic costs. Even in cases where this holds, the lack of constraints on several variables such as inventory, work-force size, allowed overtime, etc., may produce plans that are not feasible.

To avoid the restrictive assumptions inherent in linear or quadratic programming formulations, alternative approaches have been developed that can portray the decision variables and cost relationships involved more realistically. Most prominent among these are the methods based on heuristic decision rules[1] and on computer-search decision rules. The price paid for their flexibility, however, is the lack of a guaranteed optimal plan.

Heuristic Methods

The motivation in developing heuristic methods for management problems in general and aggregate-production planning in particular has been to incorporate in a model those decision variables and criteria of choice which managers are most sensitive to and have the most insights into. The specific form of proposed decision rules can be determined by careful analysis, and any unknown parameters involved can be estimated by regression analysis or simulation.

A heuristic method for aggregate planning, developed by Bowman (Ref. 1), is based on the assumption that managers are sensitive to the same decision variables

---

[1] Heuristic methods are trial-and-error procedures that move to successively improved solutions. Ordinary trial-and-error methods may move to better or worse solutions at each step, depending on the direction of change.

TABLE 12-11   Bowman's heuristic decisions rules

Decision variable	General form	Specific form for a brewery (Gordon study)
Production rate P_t	$a_1 W_{t-1} - b_1 I_{t-1} + c_1 Y'_{t+1} + d_1$	$1.66 W_{t-1} - 0.12 I_{t-1} + 0.44 Y'_{t+1} + 6.98$
Work-force size W_t	$a_2 W_{t-1} + c Y'_{t+1} + d_2$	$0.63 W_{t-1} + 0.17 Y'_{t+1} + 4.20$

SOURCE: E. S. Buffa, *Production Inventory Systems*, rev. ed., Richard D. Irwin, Inc., Homewood, Ill., 1972, p. 230.

and criteria that are present in mathematical methods such as the simplex or the LDR. However, their actual decision may produce inferior results because of the tendency to apply such rules erratically. What is needed to improve performance, according to Bowman, is an increase in the consistency with which decision rules are applied.

For example, when considering the production rate P_t for period t, a manager will intuitively assume that it depends on the expected demand for the next period Y'_{t+1} and the starting conditions for period t, that is, the work force W_{t-1} and ending inventory I_{t-1} of the preceding period. Similarly, in examining the desired work force for period t, common sense would also suggest that it depends on the forecast for the next period Y'_{t+1} and the work force size in the preceding period W_{t-1}. Aggregate-planning decision rules are developed from past decisions on production rates, inventory, and work force by analyzing data with multiple-regression techniques. The equations that were used as a best fit to the data on the operation of a brewery, studied by Gordon (Ref. 4), are shown in Table 12-11. Compared with actual cost performance during the test period, those heuristic decision rules resulted in noticeable improvements.

Another heuristic method that compared favorably with analytical methods such as the LDR was the *parametric production-planning method* developed by Jones (reported in Ref. 2). This one, too, incorporates two decision rules for P_t and W_t that are now interrelated. The rules are based on four unknown parameters, and the values for them that form the best combination are determined from the estimation of the firm's cost structure in a way similar to the LDR approach but without the quadratic restrictions.

The preceding heuristic methods rely on appropriate historical data so that one can estimate the necessary parameters. Furthermore, they assume that the underlying conditions that generated such data remain reasonably stable. The undisputed advantage of heuristic approaches is their close relationship to the actual decision-making behavior of the managers involved.

Computer-Search Methods

A more recent and promising approach for aggregate planning is the so-called computer-search method, consisting of a procedure that seeks through a predetermined computer-search decision rule (SDR) those values of the decision variables which will yield the optimum, i.e., minimum-cost, production plan.

Unlike analytical models, such as linear programming or LDR, the computer-search method relies on a cost or profit model that gives a realistic picture of the cost structure of the organization under study. This cost model can be expressed by a computer subroutine that determines the cost corresponding to any set of values for the production rate and work-force level. A search routine implemented with the aid of a computer is applied, starting with a point representing some feasible set of values for the decision variables. Once the cost criterion is evaluated at the initial point, a heuristic rule is used to determine the next move to another point. The latter is specified by the direction and size of the increment in the values of the production rate and work force. The more recent point is evaluated, and the procedure is repeated until a solution is encountered which cannot easily be improved any further. The search pattern is specified by the search decision rule. As originally formulated by Taubert,[1] the method relied on the Hooke-Jeeves program in order to produce the lowest total cost for the aggregate plan over the entire planning horizon.

Even though the computer-search method does not guarantee an optimum solution and is still in an early stage of development, this approach for aggregate planning offers a number of important advantages: (1) it allows adjustments in the cost model for successive periods to accommodate the introduction of new products and/or equipment, raises in wages, or other changes; (2) it provides the planner with information concerning decisions for the current period and future ones, along with their projected impact on cost performance; (3) it is possible to allow for sensitivity analysis to check a proposed solution or obtain alternatives for changes in some or all parameter values; and (4) the method can assist in obtaining decisions for complex situations, in terms of cost relationships, multiple objective functions, or constraints, for which there is no way of applying known analytical procedures such as LDR or linear programming.

Taubert tested the SDR technique with LDR using the data of the same paint company studied to develop the latter. It was found that SDR can practically duplicate the results of the LDR when the assumption of quadratic costs is appropriate. For more complex cost structures the SDR offers greater flexibility.

12-7 COMPARISON OF AGGREGATE-PLANNING METHODS

The characteristics of the aggregate-planning methods discussed in this chapter are summarized in Table 12-12. In a special study aimed at evaluating their relative performance for the same company it was concluded that all methods yielded higher profits than the procedures used by company managers (see Table 12-13).

The company that was studied operated a manufacturing facility for capital goods in a job shop where the final product was assembled from parts that had

---

[1] William F. Taubert, "A Search Decision Rule for the Aggregate Scheduling Problem," *Management Science*, February 1968, pp. B343–B359.

TABLE 12-12 Summary of aggregate-planning methods

Method	Assumptions	Solution procedure	Advantages	Limitations
Trial and error	Linear cost relationships	Does not guarantee optimum plan	Easy to understand and use because of its intuitive appeal	Depends heavily on the judgment of manager or analyst using it; cannot be generalized
Linear programming	Linear cost relationships; constant value for costs, capacity, and demand	Yields an optimum plan	Can be used for large problems with aid of computers; allows sensitivity analysis for changes in costs, capacity, and demand	Does not account for economies of scale, i.e., large production runs, due to linear cost relationships
Linear decision rule	All cost relationships except for payroll assumed to be quadratic, i.e., second-degree equations	Yields an optimum plan	Easy to use once the cost parameters have been estimated and decision rules are available	Very difficult to set up; quadratic assumptions for cost relationships may be unrealistic, creating serious errors
Heuristic methods	Past data can be relied on to reveal good decision rules for the future	Do not yield an optimum plan; rely on regression analysis or simulation to derive rules for more consistent good decisions	Reflect more realistically the way managers respond to a problem; easier to accept than mathematical methods; not limited to linear costs	Past data for decisions by a manager may not reflect good decisions; personnel conditions may change; statistical analysis may result in errors in explaining human performance
Computer-search decision rule	Very flexible	Does not yield an optimum plan; uses computer-assisted technique to evaluate alternative plans	Can be used for complex cost relationships; permits sensitivity analysis; allows adjustments for new products, equipment, etc.	Requires skill in representing organization cost structure and in searching to evaluate different plans to reach the lower region of total-cost curves

504

TABLE 12-13 Comparative evaluation of aggregate-planning methods

	Profit	
Method	Imperfect forecast	Perfect forecast
Company decisions	$4,420,000	
Linear decision rule	4,821,000	$5,078,000
Management coefficient model	4,607,000	5,000,000
Parametric production planning	4,900,000	4,989,000
Search decision rule	5,021,000	5,140,000

SOURCE: W. B. Lee and B. M. Khumawala, "Simulation Testing of Aggregate Production Planning Models in an Implementation Methodology," *Management Science*, vol. 20, no. 6, p. 907, February 1974.

been previously produced for inventory. Based on a simulation of the company's operation, the methods shown in Table 12-13 were tested and compared.

Evaluated against an imperfect forecast, the computer-search model (SDR) performed the best, showing a 14 percent improvement over company decisions. Bowman's heuristic method, also known as the management coefficient model, was the least effective, with only a 4 percent improvement. The increased profits using a perfect forecast clearly reflect the value of having perfect information. This in turn provides a measure of the benefits possible through better forecasts.

12-8 IMPLEMENTATION OF AGGREGATE PLANNING

From the studies by Buffa and Lee and Khumawala, cited previously, it appears that few companies employ well-integrated aggregate-planning methods despite the evidence that these methods contribute to more profitable performance. Some of the difficulties in accepting and using such methods may be due partly to their quantitative nature and partly to the requirement they impose for greater coordination of different units within an organization.

With the assistance of analysts, especially in the formulation stage, it is possible to overcome the reluctance to use quantitative procedures. The experience of sorting out essential information from masses of useless and irrelevant data enables managers to understand the nature of the aggregate-planning problem better. Furthermore, the recognition of the interdependence of planning decisions in different parts of the organization (personnel, purchasing, maintenance, scheduling, etc.) fosters the development of an organizational climate that makes coordination easier.

The importance of aggregate planning in operations management stems from its role as a link between long- and short-term decisions. Capacity and work-design decisions are intended to achieve desired output rates and satisfying jobs. Unless these decisions can be translated into smooth and steady work schedules, performance will suffer.

Aggregate planning affects not only the utilization of physical facilities and equipment but even more significantly the morale and motivation of the entire organization. Thus, management must be aware of the trade-offs that exist between the economies from a fluctuating work force and the more subtle losses in productivity from the low morale and diminished job satisfaction created by frequent lay-offs. Aggregate plans balanced by human judgment and experience are to be used as a flexible framework for action rather than as static prescriptions for elusive profit maximization, despite changes in the firm's environment.

12-9 SUMMARY

The role of aggregate planning is especially important in most organizations because it links long-term capacity commitments with short-term scheduling decisions. The purpose here is to make the best use of available resources so that while design capacity is fixed demand will be satisfied at minimum cost.

As a decision system aggregate planning requires inputs in the form of (1) period-by-period forecasts for at least one seasonal cycle, (2) feasible production alternatives and their unit costs, and (3) specification of initial conditions (work force and inventories). Under the constraints of existing capacity limits, the decision variables relate to the extent each production alternative will be used in each period to satisfy expected demand. The evaluation of an aggregate plan is usually made on the basis of total production cost for the planning horizon.

The preparation of aggregate plans requires the coordination of several parts of an organization (production, personnel, purchasing, and others). Available methods range from simple trial-and-error procedures to sophisticated computer-assisted models. These can handle situations with linear or nonlinear costs and some guarantee an optimal plan if one exists.

Effective implementation of aggregate plans requires more than participation of all affected parts of the organization. It calls for a view of productivity that is based not only on economic performance but on a well-motivated work force by providing job security through steady employment and job satisfaction through effective job design.

NOTATION

Projected Requirements

Y'_t = estimated amount needed in period t $(t = 1, 2, ..., N)$
I_f = final inventory required at the end of planning horizon

Planning Variables for Production Alternatives

P_t = regular time production in period t in physical units
Q_t = overtime production in period t in physical units
I_t = surplus inventory in period t in physical units

B_t = backordering (shortage inventory) in period t in physical units
H_t = hiring (for increase in production) in period t in physical units
F_t = layoff (for reduction in production) in period t in physical units
S_t = subcontracting in period t in physical units

Costs for Employing Production Alternatives

r = cost per unit made on regular time production
v = cost per unit made on overtime production
c_H = cost per unit carried in inventory per planning period
c_S = cost per unit of shortage per planning period
h = cost of increasing production by one unit through hiring
f = cost of decreasing production by one unit through firing (or layoffs)
u = cost per unit made through subcontracting
C_t = production cost for period t $(=rP_t + vQ_t + uS_t + hH_t + fF_t + c_H I_t + c_S B_t)$
TPC = total production cost for planning horizon $(= C_1 + C_2 + \cdots + C_N)$

Capacity Limits for Production Alternatives

I_0 = amount in inventory at the beginning of planning horizon
L_t = amount that can be produced on regular time in period t
M_t = amount that can be produced on overtime in period t
N_t = amount that can be subcontracted in period t

REVIEW QUESTIONS

1. What aspects in the operation of a firm make it necessary or desirable to prepare production plans?
2. Describe the information requirements and decision (or control) variables for long-, medium-, and short-term production plans. What information does each type of plan provide, and how are they evaluated?
3. What are the usual organization policies for smoothing out capacity utilization when the demand for a firm's output is seasonal? At what level are they formulated?
4. What are the usual production alternatives employed to absorb unavoidable seasonal demand fluctuations? Why must they be considered after specifying appropriate policies for smoothing capacity?
5. Indicate which production alternatives might not be feasible in the following cases:
   (*a*) An electronics firm
   (*b*) A ski-resort complex
   (*c*) A dairy farm
   (*d*) A hospital
   (*e*) An engineering consulting firm
   (*f*) A commercial airline
6. Backordering might be a feasible alternative only under certain conditions. What are they?
7. Classify the aggregate-planning methods discussed on the basis of cost relationships assumed and ability to determine an optimal plan.
8. Discuss the advantages and disadvantages of aggregate-planning methods based on linear programming.
9. What are the limitations of the LDR and SDR methods?

10. What might be the reasons for the differences in performance of the models summarized in Table 12-11?
11. Under what conditions is the usefulness of aggregate planning limited (compared with product-oriented planning)?
12. What is the meaning of the term *productive capacity* in long-, medium-, and short-term production plans?

PROBLEMS

1. The bottling plant manager of the Fine Liqueur Co. has received the following month-by-month demand forecast for the coming year.

Month	Demand, cases	Month	Demand, cases
January	140,000	July	240,000
February	130,000	August	220,000
March	120,000	September	190,000
April	150,000	October	180,000
May	190,000	November	170,000
June	260,000	December	160,000

The feasible production alternatives, capacity limits, and unit costs are:

	Unit cost	Monthly capacity limit, cases
Regular production r	$30	165,000
Overtime production v	$40	30,000
Subcontracting u	$56	20,000

Inventory holding charge is $c_H = \$36$ per case annually. Starting inventory $I_0 = 0$. Using the trial-and-error method:

(a) Determine an aggregate production plant for next year.
(b) Calculate the monthly and total cost for part (a).
(c) Suggest some organizational policies to smooth out capacity utilization.

2. Refer to Prob. 1. Monthly capacity has been reduced due to construction work, and the cost of subcontracting has increased as follows;

$$L_t = 150,000 \qquad M_t = 20,000 \qquad N_t = 10,000 \qquad u = \$70$$

(a) Determine a revised aggregate-production plan.
(b) Calculate the monthly and total cost.
(c) Can demand be met for all periods if no backordering is allowed ($c_S = \infty$).
(d) What is the minimum required starting inventory in order to satisfy demand in all months?

3. The Alpha Airline Co. operates charter flights internationally. Based on next year's planned flights, the estimated requirements for stewardesses are given below:

Month	Requirement, h	Month	Requirement, h	Month	Requirement, h
Jan.	24,000	May	35,000	Sept.	36,000
Feb.	20,000	June	40,000	Oct.	30,000
March	25,000	July	42,000	Nov.	27,000
April	32,000	Aug.	43,000	Dec.	30,000

The maximum available hours each month with current regular stewardesses is 30,000 at a cost of $20 per hour. An additional 4,500 h can be obtained from the above personnel on overtime at a cost of $25 per hour. During busy periods (summer months, Christmas holidays, etc.) the airline can call on standby stewardesses, i.e., former regular employees willing to work part time. Standby personnel can cover up to 13,000 h at a cost of $35 per hour. It is also possible to increase the number of regular hours by recruiting and training more girls in groups of eight 2 months before needed at a cost of $36,000. If each girl works 50 h each month, this alternative adds 400 h per group after training for the remainder of the planning period.

(a) Determine an aggregate operations plan to cover stewardess requirements with currently available personnel including standby help.

(b) Determine the period by period and the total cost for part (a).

(c) Is a cost reduction possible by recruiting and training one group in February to be used from April on?

(d) Is further cost improvement possible by recruiting and training two groups, one in February and one in April?

4. Refer to Prob. 3. As a result of a new union contract, the maximum number of hours worked by stewardesses per month on regular time and overtime has been reduced by 10 percent. This changes the available hours from current, standby, and new stewardesses by 10 percent. The cost, however, remains the same. Rework parts (a) to (c).

5. Refer to Prob. 3. As a result of deregulation in the airline industry and lower air fares, the management of the Alpha Airline Co. expects a 20 percent loss in passengers to regular airlines in each month for the year ahead. Assuming proportional reductions in the requirements for stewardess hours, develop a revised aggregate plan (a) with current and standby help and (b) with new stewardesses, if needed.

6. The quarter-by-quarter demand forecast for microwave ovens manufactured by Victory Inc. is specified below, along with data on feasible production alternatives.

		Capacity limits, production units		
Quarter	Demand, units	Regular production	Over-time	Sub-contracting
1	80,000	80	15	10
2	70,000	60	10	10
3	100,000	70	15	5
4	90,000	80	20	10
Starting inventory $I_s = 10$		final inventory required $I_f = 30$		
Unit cost:		$r = \$90$	$v = \$100$	$u = \$130$

The company has an estimated inventory carrying cost of $5 per set per quarter and a backordering cost of $10 per set per quarter.

(a) Formulate the aggregate-production-planning problem using an optimizing method.

(b) What might be viewed as disadvantages in this approach?

(c) Solve the above if a computer program is available.

7. The Soft-Touch Typewriter Co. produces three models (deluxe, regular, and economy) each with different labor content depending on assembly requirements. The demand for each model for next year is specified below on a quarterly basis.

Demand by model type, units

Quarter	Deluxe	Regular	Economy
1	3,000	10,000	5,000
2	4,000	11,000	8,000
3	7,000	15,000	10,000
4	6,000	12,000	9,000
Assembly standard time per unit, h	2.5	2.0	1.8

Feasible production alternatives along with capacity limits and unit costs have been estimated as follows:

Alternative	Unit cost			Capacity limit per quarter, standard hours
	Deluxe	Regular	Economy	
Regular-time production	$ 87.50	$50.00	$36.00	42,000
Overtime production	120.00	72.00	54.00	10,000
Quarterly inventory holding charge per unit	5.00	4.00	3.60	

No backordering or subcontracting is allowed.

(a) Assuming there are no starting inventories, formulate the aggregate-production-planning problem using the transportation model of linear programming. Remember that for this technique to work the demands and (capacity) supplies must be in the same units.

(b) If there is a computer program available, solve this problem to obtain the optimum aggregate production plan.

8. Reformulate Prob. 3 if backordering is allowed at a cost of $10, $8, and $7.2 per unit per quarter for deluxe, regular, and economy models, respectively.

9. The following data pertain to demand forecasts, production alternatives, and costs for the XYZ Co., which manufactures a cleaning fluid used in hospitals.

| | Capacity limit, tons | | | |
Quarter	Estimated demand	Regular production	Overtime production	Unit cost per ton
1	210	210	15	$r = \$50$
2	200	210	15	$v = \$75$
3	170	180	10	$C_H = \$\ 5$ per period
4	230	210	15	

Furthermore, the cost of hiring is $120 per unit increase in output ($h = \$120$ per unit) while the cost of firing is $180 per unit decrease in output ($f = \$180$ per unit). The starting regular production rate is $P_0 = 220$ tons from the work-force level of the previous period.

(a) Formulate the aggregate-planning problem as a linear programming problem using the simplex method.

(b) Solve the above if there is a computer program available.

10. Suppose that recent agreements between the management of the XYZ Co. (in Prob. 9) and the labor union provide for contract changes and other economic developments will have the following impacts:

1. A $1 increase per quarter in regular and overtime production costs based on last year's estimates; that is, $r_1 = \$51$, $r_2 = \$52$, $r_3 = \$53$, $r_4 = \$54$
2. A 20 percent initial increase in inventory carrying costs due to higher prices for raw materials
3. A 10 percent initial decrease in hiring costs due to increased general unemployment

(a) Set up a revised aggregate-planning problem.

(b) Solve the problem if a computer program is available.

SELECTED REFERENCES

1. Bowman, E. H.: "Consistency and Optimality in Managerial Decision Making," *Management Science*, vol. 9, no. 2, pp. 310–321, January 1963.
2. Buffa, E. S.: *Operations Management: Problems and Models*, 3d ed., Wiley, New York, 1972, chap. 13.
3. Buffa, E. S., and W. H. Taubert: *Production-Inventory Systems: Planning and Control*, rev. ed., Irwin, Homewood, Ill., 1972, chaps. 5 to 7.
4. Gordon, J. R. M.: "A Multi-Model Analysis of an Aggregate Scheduling Decision," unpublished Ph.D. dissertation, Sloan School of Management, MIT, Cambridge, Mass., 1966.
5. Holt, C. D., F. Modigliani, J. F. Muth, and H. A. Simon: "Cost Structure and Equations for Cost Components in the Linear Decision Rule," *Management Science*, pp. 8–13, October 1955.
6. Lee, W. B., and B. M. Khumawala: "Simulation Testing of Aggregate Production Planning Models in an Implementation Methodology," *Management Science*, vol. 20, no. 6, pp. 903–911, February 1974.
7. Vergin, R. C.: "Production Scheduling under Seasonal Demand," *Journal of Industrial Engineering*, vol. 17, no. 5, May 1966.
8. Zimmerman, H. J., and M. G. Sovereign: *Quantitative Models for Production Management*, Prentice-Hall, Englewood Cliffs, N.J., 1974.

Chapter 13

INVENTORY
SYSTEMS AND
MODELS

13-1   INTRODUCTION

Because of their indispensable functions, inventories have been considered as important to an organization as blood is to the human body. Furthermore, the sizable investment in inventories, most apparent in manufacturing activities, warrants particular care in their planning and control.

Definition

In operations management, *inventory* refers to any scarce resource that remains idle in anticipation of satisfying a future demand for it.

In the above sense, the term covers not only materials in various stages of processing one is likely to see in a factory but all the human and nonhuman resources maintained but not currently used by an organization in order to meet anticipated demand for its product(s) or service(s). Table 13-1 gives illustrative examples of the kinds of inventories held by various organizations. Because the output of service organizations cannot be stored for later use, the concept of inventory for them is associated with various forms of productive capacity.

In a given period the available inventory of a resource is reduced in the process of satisfying actual demand. Therefore, it becomes necessary to replenish it in order to continue to cover new demand in subsequent time periods.

The Inventory Problem

An operations system's performance is affected directly by the size of inventories held. There is generally a penalty associated with having either too much inventory or too little.

Consider the situation of a TV manufacturer who has overestimated demand and is now stuck with numerous unsold sets in the warehouse. This undesirable

TABLE 13-1   Types of inventories maintained by various organizations

System	Inventories
Factory	Raw materials, parts Semifinished goods Finished goods
Commercial bank	Cash reserves Tellers
Hospital	Number of beds Specialized personnel Stocks of drugs, etc.
Airline company	Aircraft seat miles per route Parts for engine repairs Stewardesses, mechanics, etc.

surplus represents capital tied up that could be invested more profitably elsewhere. In addition, there is reason for concern with other costs related to storage, insurance, depreciation, taxes, etc. Similar situations may be faced by a commercial bank that has overestimated its demand withdrawals and is keeping excessive cash reserves or by an airline that flies its planes on a certain route half empty. The penalties from holding too much inventory may be serious enough to undermine an organization's financial health.

This, however, describes only one side of the coin. If the above situations were reversed and instead of overestimating demand management had underestimated it, there would be equally serious penalties for failure to maintain adequate inventory. The TV manufacturer in the example would be forgoing all the profits that would be possible from the lost sales and might lose much of his good will for not supplying his wholesalers adequately. Similarly, the bank without adequate cash reserves would have to secure funds at an increased cost to avoid embarrassment, and an airline without a sufficient number of seats on a given route would lose favor with the public because it is unable to satisfy actual demand for travel.

The conclusion here is that there must be a happy medium with regard to inventory levels. If we accept the total cost incurred to operate the inventory system as an adequate measure of performance, then for best performance inventory levels must be set so that this cost is minimized. Sometimes it is preferable to analyze inventory with a profit maximization objective.

Since management under normal conditions cannot control demand, the only way to affect inventory costs relates to the time and size of new orders to replenish existing inventories.[1]

---

[1] In operations management we are not in general concerned with *what* should be held in inventory. This, however, may be an important decision for a department store or maintenance shop, etc.

Definition

The *inventory problem* involves the formulation of decision rules that answer two important questions:

1. *When* is it necessary to place an order (or set up for production) to replenish inventory?
2. *How much* is to be ordered (or produced) for each replenishment?

The decision rules must aim at satisfying anticipated demand at minimum cost or maximum profit.

Before attempting to provide answers to these questions, it is necessary to have a forecast for demand that covers all periods in the inventory-planning horizon. In all subsequent discussions, *it is assumed that a demand forecast is available*, including, of course, a measure of the forecast error.

The Need for Maintaining Inventory

The existence of inventories at successive stages of the production process serves a number of important purposes. In general, *through inventories we attempt to achieve a smooth and economical operation of the production-distribution system.* The particular functions served are described in more detail below.

Pipeline (or transit) inventories When the producer is geographically removed from suppliers and consumers, it takes time to supply the amounts ordered at different points of the production-distribution network. Therefore, in order to satisfy demand without disruption, it is necessary to hold extra stock at various points to handle demand while replenishments are in transit from the preceding stage. These quantities are known as *pipeline* or *transit inventories*. Their amounts depend on the time required for transportation and the rate of use.

Economic order quantities As inventory is used up to cover actual demand and there is a need for replenishment, it is important to decide on how much to order at a time. It is desirable to order in quantities that will balance the costs of holding too much stock against that of ordering in small quantities too frequently.

Safety (or buffer) stocks In the real world there may be random departures from what management expects in the level of demand, the production rate, the replenishment time, or other factors. To protect against such reasonable but nevertheless random, i.e., uncontrollable, occurrences it is necessary to maintain additional inventory beyond what is needed for normal requirements. Such extra quantities are known as *safety* or *buffer stocks* because they provide a buffer, or a safety margin, against the unpredictabilities of the external environment.

Decoupling inventories   If two successive production stages operate so that when the first breaks down, the second remains idle for lack of material to work on, the existing degree of dependence is both costly and disruptive for the entire system. It is often possible to make the stages more independent by providing for in-process inventory between them. Under this arrangement, even if the first stage fails, the second can continue to function for some time, and this is possible for other stages that may follow.

Decoupling inventories are those used to reduce the interdependence of various stages of the production system. Thus, raw materials are used to decouple the producer from the supplier(s), in-process inventories to decouple successive production stages, and finished goods to decouple the consumer from the producer.

Seasonal inventories   Demand for many products or services displays significant seasonal fluctuations (agricultural products, fashion items, etc.). If an adjustment in the production rate were necessary each time demand changed, the result might be a very poor capacity utilization. Assuming that the item(s) are not perishable, one can produce more than demanded in slack periods to build up inventories that can be used when demand peaks and exceeds available capacity. These stocks are known as *seasonal inventories* and help smooth out undesirable fluctuations in the production rate.

Economic Significance of Inventories

Our motivation in studying inventories is twofold: (1) we need to develop a smooth physical operation of a production system, and (2) we seek to find more economical methods for its management.

For many organizations inventories represent large amounts of tied-up capital, usually 15 to 40 percent of total assets. Even a small decrease in the amount of inventories held, resulting from careful analysis, may represent impressive savings without any detrimental effects on the service level provided by the system.

The analysis of inventory problems has always depended on the processing of huge quantities of data. Originally, this requirement made inventory studies extremely expensive, but the development and wide use of computers today makes such studies not only feasible but worth extending to other closely related areas. Thus, the installation of management information systems can contribute effectively to the planning, operation, and control not only of inventory systems but of a greater spectrum of integrated productive activities.

13-2   SPECIFICATION OF AN INVENTORY SYSTEM

Inventory System: An Input-Output Description

In order to arrive at the best inventory policy, i.e., the best decision rules for when and how much to order, it is necessary to have a clear picture of the inventory

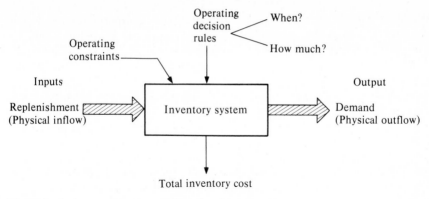

Fig. 13-1   An input-output representation of an inventory system.

system. It is only through an adequate description of such a system that we can proceed to analyze its operation and effectiveness.

Regardless of the items held in stock, an inventory system requires specification of the components shown in the input-output representation of Fig. 13-1.

These include:

1. The demand pattern for items held in stock (usually a physical outflow)
2. The replenishment pattern (usually a physical inflow)
3. The operating constraints
4. The decision-making mechanism concerning inventory replenishment
5. The total (or incremental) inventory cost that reflects system performance

Demand: the system output   The demand side is the most critical yet uncontrollable component, for without demand there would be no need for maintaining inventory. The nature of demand can be described by the following:

y = quantity removed from inventory during reorder cycle, i.e., between successive replenishments, to satisfy demand of the subsequent stage (another production department, a wholesaler, or final consumer)

For a given period y may be known with certainty, or it may be specified by a statistical distribution $f(y)$. For some items y may be a *continuous* variable (oil, cash, wheat grain, etc.); for others it is *discrete* (carburetors, TV tubes, etc.). The analysis is more difficult for inventory items for which y is statistical in nature and/or discrete.

D = demand rate = amount of stock removed from inventory per unit time (say 2,400 TV tubes annually, 15,000 barrels of oil daily, etc.)

The demand rate may remain constant throughout the cycle or variable. For a service station the demand for gas during the week may change slowly at first and fast toward the weekend, or vice versa.

Replenishment: the system input   The replenishment side represents the controllable component of the physical flow through an inventory system. It is specified by the following:

t = reorder cycle time = time interval between successive decisions to replenish

Q = lot size = order quantity for replenishment of inventory (amount added to existing stocks during replenishment cycle)

t_p = replenishment or production period (time required to add lot size to inventory)

L = replenishment lead time (time that elapses from the moment an order is placed until quantity ordered arrives)

p = replenishment rate = rate at which lot size Q is added to inventory (p may be constant or variable throughout cycle time)

Suppose a service station operates from a gas tank holding 30,000 gal. The replenishment of the station from its supplier would be described as follows:

t = time between successive decisions to replenish tank

Q = amount of gas ordered from supplier for each delivery

L = time between placing order by phone or other means and start of putting gas in station tank

t_p = time required to place quantity Q in station tank

p = rate at which gas is added to tank, e.g., gal/min

Decision-making mechanism   We have seen that demand for the items in inventory is usually uncontrollable, being generated externally. Decisions relating to the management of the inventory system must therefore be made with reference to the replenishment side. The decision-making mechanism is designed to respond to (1) *when* inventory must be replenished t and (2) *how much* must be ordered (or produced internally) for each replenishment Q.

These two questions are answered in one of two ways: (1) replenishment may take place at fixed time intervals (t = constant), by placing orders of variable size (Q = variable) to bring inventory to a desired level; (2) management may order a fixed amount (Q = constant) when inventory drops to a certain reorder level, an event which may happen at variable cycle times (t = variable). Our discussion assumes that for an operations system the decision of what items to hold in stock has already been made. For a retail store this may well be another important aspect of the inventory policy.

Operating constraints   Generally the range of options for making the decisions to operate an inventory system is limited by a number of restrictions, relating to limited warehouse space, limited budget available for inventory, etc. Occasionally, replenishment may be limited by the supplier's policy to certain times or quantities. Unless such constraints are taken into account explicitly, it is difficult to arrive at an optimum feasible inventory policy.

Total or incremental inventory cost: the system's measure of performance   The result of operating an inventory system with certain decision rules is reflected in the total (or incremental) inventory cost TC (or TIC) necessary to satisfy forecasted demand under given restrictions. This cost is made up of the following components:

C_H = holding cost = cost incurred from having surplus inventories
C_S = shortage cost = cost incurred from shortages or lack of inventories
C_R = replenishment cost = cost of setting up production to replenish existing stocks or placing an order with an outside supplier
C_B = purchase cost = cost of buying items placed on inventory

Since the performance of an inventory system is evaluated in terms of the total inventory cost, our objective is to provide a set of decision rules, i.e., an inventory policy, that minimizes such a cost while satisfying expected demand under existing constraints. The inventory problem can now be restated as follows: find values of the decision variables (1) when to order t and (2) how much to order Q that will satisfy an anticipated demand rate D subject to constraints and minimize

$$TC = C_H + C_S + C_R + C_B \tag{13-1}$$

or

$$\begin{bmatrix} \text{Total inventory} \\ \text{cost} \end{bmatrix} = \begin{bmatrix} \text{holding} \\ \text{cost} \end{bmatrix} + \begin{bmatrix} \text{shortage} \\ \text{cost} \end{bmatrix} + \begin{bmatrix} \text{replenishment} \\ \text{cost} \end{bmatrix} + \begin{bmatrix} \text{purchase} \\ \text{cost} \end{bmatrix}$$

13-3 DETERMINATION OF INVENTORY-RELATED COSTS

Since the required decisions (when?, how much?) relate to physical quantities, we must express the total inventory cost in terms of such controllable variables. To do so we must analyze each cost component separately.

Holding Cost

The holding cost is associated with carrying surplus inventory. In symbols,

$$C_H = c_H I_H \tag{13-2}$$

or

$$\begin{bmatrix} \text{holding} \\ \text{cost} \end{bmatrix} = \begin{bmatrix} \text{cost of holding} \\ \text{1 unit per unit time} \end{bmatrix} \begin{bmatrix} \text{average amount of} \\ \text{inventory held per unit time} \end{bmatrix}$$

The cost of carrying 1 unit in stock per unit time c_H is calculated by considering all types of costs related to holding inventory. Suppose that the annual costs of maintaining an average stock of 5,000 units of an item priced at \$120 are as follows:

Element	Cost	Percentage of inventory investment of \$600,000
Capital tied up in inventory	\$90,000	15
Storage	30,000	5
Insurance	15,000	2.5
Depreciation or obsolescence	9,000	1.5
Taxes	6,000	1.0
Total	\$150,000	$25.0 = f$

It is common to calculate the unit holding cost c_H by multiplying the value or price per unit of inventory b by a fixed percentage f reflecting the inventory related costs. For our example, with a cost of capital equal to 15 percent and the other carrying costs for storage, insurance, taxes, etc. equal to 10 percent of the value invested in inventory, we would have

$$c_H = fb = (.25)(\$120) = \$30/\text{unit per unit time}$$

The average amount of inventory held per unit time is determined as follows:

$$I_H = \frac{I_{max} + I_{min}}{2} l_1 \qquad (13\text{-}4)$$

$$\begin{bmatrix} \text{Average surplus} \\ \text{inventory} \end{bmatrix} = \frac{\left(\begin{matrix}\text{maximum surplus} \\ \text{during cycle}\end{matrix}\right) + \left(\begin{matrix}\text{minimum surplus} \\ \text{during cycle}\end{matrix}\right)}{2} \begin{bmatrix} \text{percentage of cycle} \\ \text{time surplus exists} \end{bmatrix}$$

Suppose during a typical cycle the maximum inventory is 600 units and the minimum is 200 units; i.e., there are no shortages (see Fig. 13-2a). The average inventory then is

$$I_H = \frac{600 + 200}{2} 1.00 = 400 \text{ units}$$

If during the reorder cycle starting with 600 units the surplus exists only two-thirds of the time (Fig. 13-2b), the average inventory will be

$$I_H = \left(\frac{600 + 0}{2}\right)\left(\frac{2}{3}\right) = 200 \text{ units}$$

Shortage Cost

The shortage, or stockout, cost in an inventory system arises when actual demand cannot be met from existing stock. Here we shall assume that unsatisfied demand

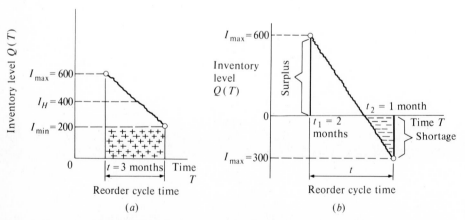

Fig. 13-2   Graph representation of inventory-level fluctuations for determining (a) average surplus I_H and (b) average shortage I_S inventory.

can be backordered, i.e., no lost sales. It is, of course, realistic that in the event of shortage sales may be lost. There are models to analyze this situation (see Refs. 8 and 10). In symbols we have

$$C_S = c_S I_S \qquad (13\text{-}3)$$

or

$$\begin{bmatrix} \text{Shortage} \\ \text{cost} \end{bmatrix} = \begin{bmatrix} \text{cost of being short} \\ \text{1 unit per unit time} \end{bmatrix} \begin{bmatrix} \text{average amount of shortage} \\ \text{per unit time} \end{bmatrix}$$

The cost of being short of stock 1 unit per unit time c_S is determined by estimating the cost incurred when demand cannot be satisfied for lack of inventory:

1. The extra expenses (administrative, clerical, etc.) for expediting an order
2. Possible loss in goodwill resulting from failure to satisfy customer
3. The forgone profits from lost customers
4. Other

Since the impact of shortages usually cannot be measured accurately, the resulting costs are difficult to estimate in practice. However, it is better to work even with rough estimates than choose to pretend that the costs do not exist or are prohibitive.

The average amount of shortages per unit time I_S is determined in the same manner as the average surplus inventory I_H. Thus,

$$I_S = \frac{I^-_{\min} + I^-_{\max}}{2} l_2 \qquad (13\text{-}5)$$

or

$$\begin{bmatrix} \text{Average shortage} \\ \text{inventory} \end{bmatrix} = \frac{\left(\begin{array}{c} \text{minimum shortage} \\ \text{during cycle} \end{array} \right) + \left(\begin{array}{c} \text{maximum shortage} \\ \text{during cycle} \end{array} \right)}{2} \begin{bmatrix} \text{percentage of cycle} \\ \text{time shortages exist} \end{bmatrix}$$

Suppose that in an assembly department shortages exist for a given part during the last third of the cycle time, maximum shortages reaching 300 units (see Fig. 13-2b). In this case, the average stockout will be

$$I_S = \frac{I^-_{\min} + I^-_{\max}}{2} l_2 = \left(\frac{0 + 300}{2} \right) \left(\frac{1}{3} \right) = 50 \text{ units}$$

Replenishment Cost

Replenishment may take place by ordering from outside suppliers or by producing the items needed internally with the appropriate setups of equipment. Here

$$C_R = c_R I_R \qquad (13\text{-}6)$$

or

$$\begin{bmatrix} \text{Replenishment} \\ \text{cost} \end{bmatrix} = \begin{bmatrix} \text{cost per order or} \\ \text{per setup} \end{bmatrix} \begin{bmatrix} \text{average number of orders or} \\ \text{setups per unit time} \end{bmatrix}$$

The cost per order c_R is determined by considering only the incremental or variable costs of placing orders or setting up equipment, as opposed to the overhead of the purchasing or production departments. The *ordering costs* generally include:

1. The cost of making a requisition
2. The cost of mailing, telephone calls, etc.
3. The cost of any follow-up action
4. The cost of receiving and storing the quantities included in the order

Whenever replenishment of inventories takes place internally through production, we incur *a setup* cost, which may include:

1. The cost of cleaning and adjusting production equipment
2. The cost of any materials or supplies used for item 1
3. The cost of inspection of equipment before production.

The number of orders (or setups) per unit time is determined by the ratio of the demand rate D and the lot size Q. Thus, if we must satisfy a demand of 2,400 units annually by ordering (or producing) in amounts of 600 units, the number of orders (or setups) will be

$$I_R = \frac{D}{Q} = \frac{2,400}{600} = 4$$

Cost of Purchase

If the price per unit b is the same regardless of the size of the order Q, the purchase cost is

$$C_B = b \cdot D \tag{13-7}$$

or

$$\begin{bmatrix} \text{Purchase} \\ \text{cost} \end{bmatrix} = \begin{bmatrix} \text{price per} \\ \text{unit} \end{bmatrix} \begin{bmatrix} \text{demand per} \\ \text{unit time} \end{bmatrix}$$

However, some suppliers offer discounts for large orders to encourage their customers to buy in greater amounts. Here, the price, which depends on the lot size Q, becomes smaller as Q exceeds certain values. The purchase cost now is variable and depends on the inventory decision of how much to order. Thus,

$$C_B = b(Q) \cdot D \tag{13-8}$$

or

$$\begin{bmatrix} \text{Purchase} \\ \text{cost} \end{bmatrix} = \begin{bmatrix} \text{price per unit when} \\ \text{lot size is } Q \end{bmatrix} \begin{bmatrix} \text{demand per} \\ \text{unit time} \end{bmatrix}$$

Total Inventory Cost

When the price per unit depends on the lot size, it is important to determine an inventory policy that takes into account the purchase cost of the items held in stock. Here we wish to minimize total inventory cost; i.e.,

$$TC = c_H I_H + c_S I_S + c_R I_R + b(Q)D \tag{13-9}$$

or

$$\begin{bmatrix} \text{Total inventory} \\ \text{cost} \end{bmatrix} = \begin{bmatrix} \text{holding} \\ \text{cost} \end{bmatrix} + \begin{bmatrix} \text{shortage} \\ \text{cost} \end{bmatrix} + \begin{bmatrix} \text{replenishment} \\ \text{cost} \end{bmatrix} + \begin{bmatrix} \text{purchase} \\ \text{cost} \end{bmatrix}$$

Total Incremental Inventory Cost

When no price discounts are offered, the purchase cost remains constant regardless of how we decide on when and how much to order. Here it is simpler to consider the total incremental inventory cost, which includes only those costs which are affected by the inventory decisions. Thus,

$$TIC = c_H I_H + c_S I_S + c_R I_R \tag{13-10}$$

or

$$\begin{bmatrix} \text{Total incremental} \\ \text{inventory cost} \end{bmatrix} = \begin{bmatrix} \text{holding} \\ \text{cost} \end{bmatrix} + \begin{bmatrix} \text{shortage} \\ \text{cost} \end{bmatrix} + \begin{bmatrix} \text{replenishment} \\ \text{cost} \end{bmatrix}$$

13-4 INVENTORY MODEL BUILDING

Solutions to the inventory problem can be reached in several ways. Available methods range from crude trial-and-error procedures to powerful mathematical and simulation models. The analysis of real inventory systems can be carried out most effectively with simulation models because they are more versatile in the assumptions made about operating conditions.

Sometimes the item in inventory will be produced or ordered only once during the planning period. The remaining decision of how much to stock when demand is known statistically can be made by minimizing expected costs. This case is discussed in Sec. 13-9.

In the following sections we examine a few quantitative models that reveal the underlying logic of inventory-system analysis. Real-life applications vary in complexity, but the basic approach remains the same. The purpose in using such models is to arrive at decision rules that suggest how to minimize the total (or incremental) inventory cost or how to minimize expected cost.

Before constructing a model, it is necessary to have an adequate description of the inventory-system components. Here we include information about the demand, the replenishment, the decision variables, and the relevant costs that are affected.

First, we examine a number of deterministic inventory models. These are appropriate for inventory systems in which we can assume that the demand, the lead time, and other relevant variables and cost parameters are known and constant. In Sec. 13-9 and the next chapter we consider inventory situations where one or more aspects are statistically described. In all cases, the *general approach* is the same and consists of the following steps:

1. Specify the inventory-system assumptions through an adequate description of system components.
2. Formulate the appropriate relationships of key system variables in algebraic or graphical form. This includes the determination of the system objective, i.e., the total (or incremental) inventory cost.
3. Determine the optimal decision rules that must be used to minimize inventory costs.

The above approach for each type of model is illustrated with examples.

13-5   ECONOMIC-ORDER-QUANTITY (EOQ) MODEL

The first inventory model, formulated by Harris[1] in 1915, focused on a simplified case that attempted to capture the main features of the typical inventory problem.

Inventory-System Specification

The operation of the system can be described in terms of the following assumptions:

1. *Demand*

   D = demand rate is known and constant throughout the reorder cycle time

2. *Replenishment*

   p = replenishment (or production) rate is infinite (entire quantity ordered Q is added to existing stock all at once)

   L = lead time is known and constant

   b = price per unit is constant [no discounts offered; thus, $b(Q) = b$ for all order quantities Q]

3. *Costs*

   c_H, c_R = unit costs of holding inventory and ordering are known and constant

   c_S = unit cost of shortage is infinite (system operates without shortages; that is, $I_s = 0$)

4. *Decision variables*

   Q = order quantity replenishment size

   t = reorder cycle time, i.e., time between successive decisions to replenish

Inventory-System Relationships

Given the above assumptions, we can establish the relationship

$$Q = D \cdot t \tag{13-11}$$

---

[1] F. W. Harris, *Operations and Costs*, A. W. Shaw Co., Chicago, 1915.

In words, the amount ordered Q must be enough to satisfy the demand date D during the cycle time t. This also means that we need to determine only one of the decision variables, say Q, and the other is given by (13-11).

At the beginning of the cycle time we start with a maximum amount of inventory equal to the order quantity ($I_{max} = Q$). As this amount is used up, the inventory level drops at a fixed rate equal to the demand rate D. When it reaches a reorder point R, we have enough inventory to cover expected demand during the lead time ($R = D \cdot L$). At this point an order is placed equal to Q, which arrives at the end of the lead time, when the inventory level reaches zero. This amount is placed in stock all at once, and the inventory level goes up to its maximum value (see Fig. 13-3).

Considering the total inventory cost needed to operate this system we realize that the shortage cost C_S will be zero since we do not allow for any shortages and the purchase cost C_B will remain constant regardless of Q because we are not allowed any discounts. Thus, we can concentrate on the total *incremental* inventory cost

$$\text{TIC} = C_H + C_R$$

or

$$\begin{bmatrix} \text{Total} \\ \text{incremental cost} \end{bmatrix} = \begin{bmatrix} \text{holding} \\ \text{cost} \end{bmatrix} + \begin{bmatrix} \text{ordering} \\ \text{cost} \end{bmatrix}$$

Since we seek to find the value of Q that makes TIC a minimum, we must express C_H and C_R in terms of Q. Here we note that

$$C = c_H I_H = c_H \frac{I_{max} + I_{min}}{2} = c_H \frac{Q + 0}{2} = c_H \frac{Q}{2}$$

and

$$C_R = c_R I_R = c_R \frac{D}{Q}$$

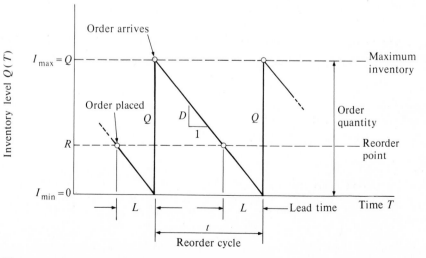

Fig. 13-3 **Inventory-level fluctuations for the EOQ model.**

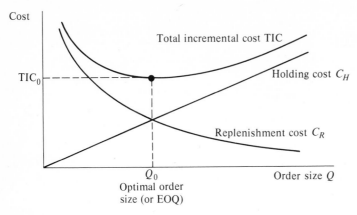

Fig. 13-4   Cost relationships in the EOQ model.

Thus

$$\text{TIC} = c_H \frac{Q}{2} + c_R \frac{D}{Q}$$

(13-12)

In words, the holding cost increases linearly, while the ordering cost decreases almost exponentially with the order quantity[1] (Fig. 13-4). The objective is to determine the order quantity that balances holding versus ordering costs.

To illustrate, suppose that annual demand for an item is 2,400 units. This can be met with one order only of $Q = 2,400$, with two orders of $Q = 1,200$, four orders of $Q = 600$, and so on. With larger values of Q we have higher holding costs because of larger average inventories but lower replenishment costs because of fewer orders (see Fig. 13-5).

An important characteristic of many inventory systems is that in the area of the optimum order quantity Q_o the total incremental-cost curve is quite flat (see Fig. 13-4). This means that considerable deviations from Q_o, attributed to errors in estimating the demand rate D, the holding and ordering costs, or other reasons, will not increase the total cost significantly.

Optimal Inventory Decision Rules and Minimum Cost

Having obtained an equation that relates total incremental cost (TIC) to the order quantity, we wish to find the value of Q that minimizes TIC. This can be done using a table that lists increasing values of Q with the respective values of C_H, C_R, and TIC. Such a method is limited in precision. An improvement involves plotting these values to obtain a graph for the TIC curve (see Fig. 13-4). Undoubtedly, the best

---

[1] Strictly speaking, the form of the ordering cost $C_R(D/Q)$ is that of a rectangular hyperbola.

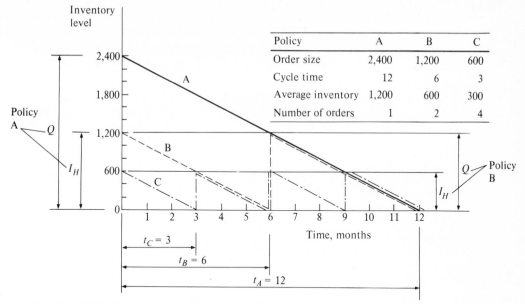

Fig. 13-5   Variation in order frequency and average inventory with changes in order size.

approach in this case is to use calculus and find the value of Q that makes the derivative (slope) of TIC equal to zero (see Ref. 11). The results yield the desired decision rules. Thus,

$$Q_o = \sqrt{\frac{2c_R D}{c_H}} \qquad \text{How much to order?} \qquad (13\text{-}13)$$

Q_o is the economic order quantity (EOQ) or optimal lot size. The optimal replenishment cycle t_o can be determined from the relationship $Q = D \cdot t$. Thus,

$$t = \frac{Q_o}{D} \qquad \text{When to order?} \qquad (13\text{-}14)$$

With these decision rules the minimum incremental inventory cost is obtained by substituting Q_o in the equation for TIC. After solving we obtain

$$\text{TIC}_o = \sqrt{2c_H c_R D} \qquad \begin{array}{l}\text{Minimum incremental} \\ \text{inventory cost}\end{array} \qquad (13\text{-}15)$$

The application of the above results can be illustrated with an example.

▶ EXAMPLE 13-1

The maintenance department for a large university requires 3,600 gal of paint annually for the scheduled maintenance of its buildings and grounds. It has been estimated that the cost of placing an order is \$16 and the cost of holding inventory is 25 percent of the investment in inventories. The price is \$8 per gallon. The manager of maintenance wishes to determine an ordering policy for this item.

This is a case where the assumptions of the EOQ model seem quite reasonable. Thus, we have

$$Q_o = \sqrt{\frac{2c_R D}{c_H}} = \sqrt{\frac{(2)(16)(3,600)}{(.25)(8)}} \qquad \text{How much to order?}$$

$$= \sqrt{57,600} = 240 \text{ gal/order}$$

The optimal spacing of the orders is determined by computing the reorder cycle time corresponding to Q_o

$$t_o = \frac{Q_o}{D} = \frac{240}{3,600} = .07 \text{ yr}$$

$$\qquad\qquad\qquad\qquad\qquad\qquad\qquad \text{When to order}$$

$$= (.07)\,(250 \text{ working days/yr}) = 17.5 \text{ working days}$$

The minimum annual incremental cost for this item will be

$$TIC_o = \sqrt{2c_H c_R D} = \sqrt{(2)(2)(16)(3,600)}$$

$$\qquad\qquad\qquad\qquad\qquad \text{How much will it cost?}$$

$$= \sqrt{230,400} = \$480/\text{yr}$$

The minimum annual total cost in this case will be

$$TC_o = TIC_o + bD = \$480 + (\$8/\text{gal})(3,600 \text{ gal})$$

▶ $$= 480 + 28,800 = \$29,280/\text{yr}$$

13-6   ECONOMIC-PRODUCTION-ORDER (EPQ) MODEL

In practice, one of the most restrictive assumptions of the EOQ model is the one about the instantaneous addition to our stock of the lot size upon arrival. This implies that the replenishment rate is infinite ($p = \infty$). Such an assumption is unreasonable in the case where replenishment occurs through setting up and operating internal production facilities. In such a case the production rate is limited, i.e., finite ($p < \infty$), and this must be accounted for explicitly in our analysis.

Inventory-System Specification

The assumptions concerning the operation of a system where replenishment is gradual are as follows:

1. *Demand*

$$D = \text{known and constant}$$

2. *Replenishment*

p = finite, known, and constant, i.e., gradual inventory buildup

L = known and constant

$b(Q) = b$ (no price discount allowed)

t_p = production period (to be determined)

3. *Costs*

$$c_H, c_R = \text{known and constant}$$

$$c_S = \infty \text{ (no shortages allowed)}$$

4. *Decision Variables*

$$Q = \text{size of each production run}$$

$$t = \text{reorder cycle time}$$

Inventory-System Relationships

The operation of an inventory system with a finite production rate is shown in Fig. 13-6. Here we note again that the amount produced each time must be enough to cover the demand during the reorder cycle time

$$Q = D \cdot t$$

If we assume that the time required to produce the amount Q at a rate p is t_p, we also have

$$Q = p \cdot t_p \qquad (13\text{-}16)$$

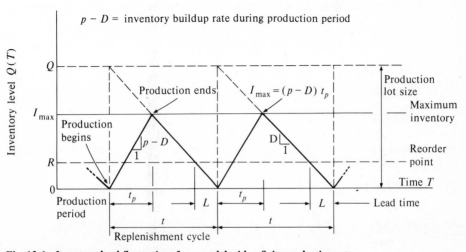

Fig. 13-6 **Inventory-level fluctuations for a model with a finite production rate.**

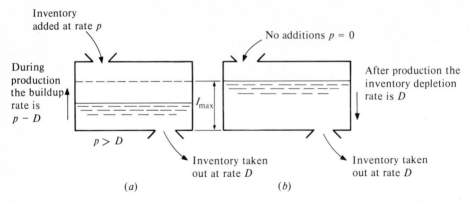

Fig. 13-7   Inventory-level fluctuations during cycle time interval: (*a*) rise during t_p and (*b*) drop after production stops.

If we think of the lead time as being equal to the setup time, then when inventory drops to the reorder point R, we begin the setup of our production facilities to replenish our stock for the next cycle time. At the end of the setup time we begin actual production at a rate p which lasts as long as necessary to produce the desired amount Q.

During the production period t_p, inventory is increased at a rate p through production and decreased at a rate D to satisfy demand. The net inventory buildup rate is $p - D$ (see Fig. 13-7). If inventory builds up at a rate of $p - D$ during production, the maximum level reached at the end of t_p will be

$$I_{max} = (p - D)t_p$$

or

$$\text{Maximum inventory level} = (\text{buildup rate})(\text{production period})$$

Now, considering the total inventory cost for operating such a system, we conclude that the only costs affected by our decisions will be those for holding inventory and setting up for production, i.e., the same as in the EOQ model. Thus we wish to minimize

$$\text{TIC} = C_H + C_R$$

or

$$\begin{bmatrix} \text{Total incremental} \\ \text{inventory cost} \end{bmatrix} = \begin{bmatrix} \text{holding} \\ \text{cost} \end{bmatrix} + \begin{bmatrix} \text{setup} \\ \text{cost} \end{bmatrix}$$

To minimize TIC we must express the component costs in terms of the decision variable Q. Here we have

$$C_H = c_H I_H$$

where

$$I_H = \frac{I_{max} + I_{min}}{2}$$

Since, $I_{max} = (p - D)t_p$ and $Q = pt_p$, we obtain

$$I_{max} = (p - D)\frac{Q}{p} = \left(1 - \frac{D}{p}\right)Q$$

Thus, $I_H = \frac{(1 - D/p)Q + 0}{2} = \left(1 - \frac{D}{p}\right)\frac{Q}{2}$

We note that if p becomes too large ($p \to \infty$), $1 - D/p$ approaches 1 and $I_H = Q/2$, or the same as in the EOQ model. The holding cost then in this case is

$$C_H = c_H\left(1 - \frac{D}{p}\right)\frac{Q}{2}$$

and the setup cost is

$$C_R = c_R I_R = c_R\frac{D}{Q}$$

Adding the above costs, we have

$$\boxed{\text{TIC} = c_H\left(1 - \frac{D}{p}\right)\frac{Q}{2} + c_R\frac{D}{Q}}$$
  (13-17)

The graphical representation of the total and component costs is similar to the EOQ model shown in Fig. 13-6.

Optimal Inventory Decision Rules and Minimum Cost

The determination of the optimal values for Q and t, given the total-incremental-cost equation, is similar to the EOQ model. Using calculus, we obtain the following results (Ref. 11):

$$\boxed{Q_o = \sqrt{\frac{2c_R D}{c_H(1 - D/p)}} \quad \begin{array}{c}\text{How much to produce}\\ \text{each time?}\end{array}}$$
  (13-18)

Q_o here is called the *economic production quantity* (EPQ) or optimal production size. The time between successive setups will be

$$\boxed{t_o = \frac{Q_o}{D} \quad \text{When to produce?}}$$
  (13-19)

and the minimum total incremental cost will be

$$\text{TIC}_o = \sqrt{2c_H\left(1 - \frac{D}{p}\right)c_R D} \qquad \text{Minimum incremental inventory cost} \qquad (13\text{-}20)$$

It is worth noting that the only difference in the results between this and the EOQ model is the substitution of c_H by $c_H(1 - D/p)$. As p becomes larger and larger, the two models become identical. The application of the EPQ is illustrated with the following example.

▶ EXAMPLE 13-2

A small company manufactures an electronic device used for aircraft navigation systems. The demand is based on contracted orders for aircraft and is known and uniform at the rate of 6,400 units annually. A voltmeter used for this device can be produced internally at the rate of 128 units/day. There are 250 working days for production each year. The setup cost for each production run is $24, and inventory holding cost is $3 per unit per year. It is desired to develop an inventory policy for this item.

The optimal size of each production run will be

$$Q_o = \sqrt{\frac{2c_R D}{c_H(1 - D/p)}} = \sqrt{\frac{2(24)(6,400)}{3[1 - 6,400/(128)(250)]}} \qquad \text{How much to order?}$$

$$= \sqrt{128,000} = 358 \text{ units/production run}$$

The replenishment cycle time for voltmeters is

$$t_o = \frac{Q_o}{D} = \frac{358}{6,400} \approx 0.056 \text{ yr}$$

When to order?

$$= (.056)(250) \approx 14 \text{ working days}$$

The production time required for each run will be

$$t_p = \frac{Q_o}{p} = \frac{358}{32,000} = .011 \text{ yr} = (.011 \text{ yr})(250 \text{ days/yr}) \approx 2.8 \text{ days}$$

The maximum inventory level will be

$$I_{\max} = (p - D)t_p = (32,000 - 6,400)(.011) \approx 282 \text{ units}$$

The minimum incremental inventory cost will be

$$\text{TIC}_o = \sqrt{2c_H\left(1 - \frac{D}{p}\right)c_R D} = \sqrt{2(3)\left(1 - \frac{6,400}{32,000}\right)(24)(6,400)} \qquad \text{How much will it cost?}$$

$$= \sqrt{737,280} = \$858.65/\text{yr}$$

▶

13-7 INVENTORY MODEL ALLOWING SHORTAGES

A second restrictive assumption in the EOQ model is not allowing for shortages because the unit cost of shortage is considered prohibitive ($c_S = \infty$). For most organizations the shortage cost resulting from being able to satisfy less than the actual demand is usually smaller than the cost of extra inventory required to cover all the demand.

In some extreme cases where the cost of maintaining finished products in stock is very large ($c_H = \infty$), as in the shipping or aerospace industries, the inventory system really operates only with backorders, i.e., with shortages.

In this section we wish to determine the appropriate decision rules for an inventory system that operates with shortages during part of the cycle time.

Inventory-System Specification

The assumptions that describe how an inventory system works when it allows shortages are as follows:

1. *Demand*

$$D = \text{known and constant}$$

2. *Replenishment*

$$p = \infty \text{ (instantaneous addition of order quantity to inventory)}$$

$$L = \text{known and constant}$$

$$b(Q) = b \text{ (no price discounts allowed)}$$

3. *Costs*

$$c_H, c_S, c_R = \text{known and constant unit costs}$$

4. *Decision variables*

$$Q = \text{size of each order or replenishment}$$

$$M = \text{desired maximum, i.e., starting inventory at beginning of cycle time}$$

Inventory-System Relationships

When shortages are allowed during part of the reorder cycle, the operation of the system is shown in Fig. 13-8. We can assume for convenience that the lead time is negligible ($L = 0$); if this is not the case, the only change will be in the timing of an order and not in the decision variables.

At the beginning of the reorder cycle we start out with an amount equal to M, where $M = I_{max}$. As inventory is used up to satisfy demand at a rate D, we reach the zero level after time t_1. However, instead of replenishing our inventory at this point, we continue to accept orders at the same demand rate D. They cannot be met from existing stocks for we have no surplus. Instead a backlog of orders, i.e.,

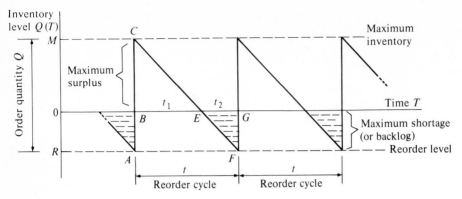

Fig. 13-8   Inventory-level fluctuations for model allowing shortages.

shortages, builds up during time t_2 until we reach the reorder level R. Then an order of size Q is placed. All backorders (equal to an amount R) are taken care of first, and the remainder of the order quantity, an amount $M = Q - R$, is placed in inventory as the surplus from which we shall satisfy part of the demand during the next cycle.

In this system we have the following relationships:

$$\text{Order quantity} \qquad Q = D \cdot t$$

$$\text{Reorder level} \qquad R = M - Q$$

$$\text{Reorder cycle time} \qquad t = t_1 + t_2$$

The determination of the order quantity Q and the starting inventory M completely specifies the values of the reorder level R and the cycle time t.

Next, considering the total inventory cost for the operation of this inventory system, we realize that except for the purchase cost C_B, which will be fixed, all other types will be affected by our decisions concerning Q and M. Thus, in the case of shortages, we seek to minimize the total incremental cost

$$\text{TIC} = C_H + C_S + C_R$$

or

$$\begin{bmatrix} \text{Total incremental} \\ \text{inventory cost} \end{bmatrix} = \begin{bmatrix} \text{holding} \\ \text{cost} \end{bmatrix} + \begin{bmatrix} \text{shortage} \\ \text{cost} \end{bmatrix} + \begin{bmatrix} \text{ordering} \\ \text{cost} \end{bmatrix}$$

The holding cost is

$$C_H = c_H I_H$$

where

$$I_H = \frac{I_{max} + I_{min}}{2} l_1$$

$$\underbrace{\begin{pmatrix} \text{Average} \\ \text{surplus} \end{pmatrix}}_{} \quad \underbrace{\begin{pmatrix} \% \text{ of cycle} \\ \text{surplus exists} \end{pmatrix}}_{}$$

and

$$I_{max} = M, \qquad I_{min} = 0, \qquad I_1 = \frac{t_1}{t}$$

Here $l_1 = t_1/t$ must be expressed in terms of the decision variables Q and M. From the similar triangles BCE and ACF in Fig. 13-8 we have

$$\frac{BE}{AF} = \frac{BC}{AC} \qquad \text{or} \qquad \frac{t_1}{t} = \frac{M}{Q}$$

Therefore,

$$I_H = \left(\frac{M+0}{2}\right)\left(\frac{M}{Q}\right) = \frac{M^2}{2Q}$$

and

$$C_H = c_H \frac{M^2}{2Q}$$

The shortage cost is

$$C_S = c_S I_S$$

where

$$I_S = \frac{I_{\max}^- + I_{\min}^-}{2} l_2$$

$$\left(\begin{array}{c}\text{Average}\\\text{shortage}\end{array}\right) \qquad \left(\begin{array}{c}\text{\% of cycle}\\\text{shortage exists}\end{array}\right)$$

and

$$I_{\max} = R = M - Q, \quad I_{\min} = 0, \qquad l_2 = \frac{t_2}{t}$$

Here $l_2 = t_2/t$ must also be expressed in terms of the decision variables Q and M. Again, from the similar triangles EGF and ACF in Fig. 13-8 we have

$$\frac{EG}{AF} = \frac{GF}{AC} \qquad \text{or} \qquad \frac{t_2}{t} = \frac{R}{Q} = \frac{M-Q}{Q}$$

Therefore

$$I_S = \left(\frac{M-Q+0}{2}\right)\left(\frac{M-Q}{Q}\right) = \frac{(M-Q)^2}{2Q}$$

and

$$C_S = c_S \frac{(M-Q)^2}{2Q}$$

The ordering cost is

$$C_R = c_R I_R = C_R \frac{D}{Q}$$

Combining the above, we have

$$\text{TIC} = c_H \frac{M^2}{2Q} + c_S \frac{(M-Q)^2}{2Q} + c_R \frac{D}{Q} \qquad (13\text{-}21)$$

| Holding | Shortage | Ordering |
| cost | cost | cost |

A graphic representation of the total incremental inventory cost is shown in Fig. 13-9. Since the component costs are second-degree terms in Q and M, TIC corresponds to a parabolic surface which resembles a bowl. Here we are interested in the values of Q and M that yield the minimum point on this surface.

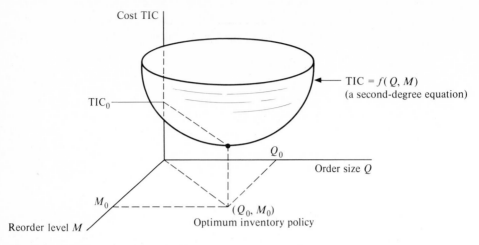

Fig. 13-9   Graphic representation of TIC surface in inventory model allowing shortages.

Optimal Inventory Decision Rules and Minimum Cost

Even though the expression for TIC is rather complex, the determination of the optimal values for Q and M, using calculus, is similar to the previous models (Ref. 11). The desired decision rules are

$$Q_o = \sqrt{\frac{2c_R D}{c_H}} \sqrt{\frac{c_H + c_S}{c_S}} \qquad \text{How much to order each time?} \qquad (13\text{-}22)$$

$$M_o = \sqrt{\frac{2c_R D}{c_H}} \sqrt{\frac{c_S}{c_H + c_S}} \qquad \text{Desired starting inventory} \qquad (13\text{-}23)$$

Substituting the above in TIC, we obtain the minimum value for TIC

$$TIC_o = \sqrt{2c_H c_R D} \sqrt{\frac{c_S}{c_H + c_S}} \qquad \text{Minimum incremental inventory cost} \qquad (13\text{-}24)$$

Once we have computed values for Q_o and M_o, the reorder cycle time and reorder level are determined easily as follows:

$$t_o = \frac{Q_o}{D} \qquad \text{When to order?} \qquad\qquad (13\text{-}25)$$

$$R_o = M_o - Q_o \qquad \text{Reorder level} \qquad\qquad (13\text{-}26)$$

It is important to note that the above results for Q_o and TIC_o are similar to those of the EOQ model except for the second factor, which involves the unit shortage cost. We note that if c_S becomes very large ($c_S \to \infty$), the second term approaches 1 and the decision rules for the model with shortages become identical to those of the EOQ model.

Of greater practical significance is the following conclusion. Suppose that two inventory systems operate with the same demand and the same holding and ordering unit costs and that the first allows for shortages even at a substantial unit shortage cost, then this system can meet the expected demand with lower total incremental cost even though it orders larger lot sizes.

▶ EXAMPLE 13-3

Suppose that the company in Example 13-2 discontinues production of the voltmeters and orders them from an outside supplier at a cost of $20 per unit. The cost of shortage is $40 per unit per year due to the extra work required to disassemble the partially completed devices. The cost of placing an order is $27, and inventory holding cost is estimated at 30 percent of invested capital. Management wishes to know the resulting changes in its inventory replenishment policy for voltmeters.

The optimal initial inventory economic-order quantity and the level are determined as follows:

$$M_o = \sqrt{\frac{2c_R D}{c_H}} \sqrt{\frac{c_S}{c_H + c_S}} = \sqrt{\frac{(2)(27)(6{,}400)}{(.30)(20)}} \sqrt{\frac{40}{6 + 40}}$$

$$= \sqrt{57{,}600}\sqrt{.87} = (240)(.93) = 224 \text{ units}$$

$$Q_o = \sqrt{\frac{2c_R D}{c_H}} \sqrt{\frac{c_H + c_S}{c_S}} = \sqrt{\frac{(2)(27)(6{,}400)}{6}} \sqrt{\frac{6 + 40}{40}} \qquad \text{How much to order?}$$

$$= (240)(1.09) = 257 \text{ units/order}$$

$$R_o = M_o - Q_o = 224 - 257 = -33 \text{ units (maximum shortage)}$$

The reorder cycle time under the new conditions will be

$$t_o = \frac{Q_o}{D} = \frac{257}{6{,}400} = .0402 \text{ yr}$$

$$= (.04)(250) = 10.04 \text{ working days}$$

When to order?

The minimum incremental inventory cost will be

$$TIC_o = \sqrt{2c_H c_R D}\sqrt{\frac{c_S}{c_H + c_S}} = \sqrt{(2)(6)(27)(6{,}400)}\sqrt{\frac{40}{6 + 40}} \qquad \text{How much will}\atop\text{it cost?}$$

$$= (1440)(.7) = \$1{,}252/\text{yr}$$

$$t_1 = \frac{M}{Q_o}t_o = \frac{224}{257}(10.04) = 8.75 \text{ days} \qquad \text{Part of cycle with surplus}$$

▶ $$t_2 = \frac{M_o - Q_o}{Q_o}t_o = \frac{33}{257}(10.04) = 1.29 \text{ days} \qquad {\text{Part of cycle}\atop\text{with shortage}}$$

13-8 INVENTORY MODEL ALLOWING PRICE DISCOUNTS

In the preceding inventory models we focused on situations where the price per unit for the item stocked was fixed regardless of the amount ordered. Some suppliers, however, offer price discounts to encourage large orders from their customers.[1] When this is the case, it is desirable to determine whether the price discounts offered represent any genuine economies in the manner of operating the inventory system.

The key issue here is whether the savings in the purchase cost due to discounts for large orders combined with a reduction in ordering costs are adequate to absorb the additional holding costs that result from increased average inventory.

Inventory-System Specifications

These are the same as for the EOQ model. It is necessary that the unit holding cost be expressed as a percentage f of the unit price $b(Q)$

$$c_H = f[b(Q)]$$

Inventory-System Relationships

1. The same as for the EOQ model except for the total inventory cost.
2. Since the purchase cost C_B is now affected by the order quantity Q, it must be taken into account explicitly. For this case, it is necessary to minimize not the incremental but the total inventory cost TC. Thus, we have

$$TC = C_H + C_R + C_B = f[b(Q)]\frac{Q}{2} + c_R\frac{D}{Q} + b(Q)D \qquad (13\text{-}27)$$

or

$$\begin{bmatrix}\text{Total inventory}\\\text{cost}\end{bmatrix} = \begin{bmatrix}\text{holding}\\\text{cost}\end{bmatrix} + \begin{bmatrix}\text{ordering}\\\text{cost}\end{bmatrix} + \begin{bmatrix}\text{purchase}\\\text{cost}\end{bmatrix}$$

---

[1] This is done by a supplier to achieve economies of scale resulting from larger production runs, hence fewer setups, quantity discounts in his raw materials or parts, etc.

Optimal Inventory Decision Rules and Costs

The procedure for determining how much to order when discounts are allowed Q^* and the minimum total cost TC^* depends on successive evaluation of certain candidate values of Q.

For the sake of illustration, suppose that our supplier proposes the following discounts:

$$b(Q) = \begin{cases} b_1 \text{ dollars/unit} & \text{when } Q < k \text{ units} \\ b_2 \text{ dollars/unit} & \text{when } Q \geq k \text{ units} \end{cases}$$

The expressions for the total inventory cost differ for each price per unit and are given as

$$TC(b_1) = fb_1 \frac{Q}{2} + c_R \frac{D}{Q} + b_1 D \qquad \text{for } Q < k \qquad (13\text{-}28)$$

$$TC(b_2) = fb_2 \frac{Q}{2} + c_R \frac{D}{Q} + b_2 D \qquad \text{for } Q \geq k \qquad (13\text{-}29)$$

The graphs for the TC curves for two different values of k are given in Fig. 13-10. Portions of the curves are shown with dotted lines to indicate that

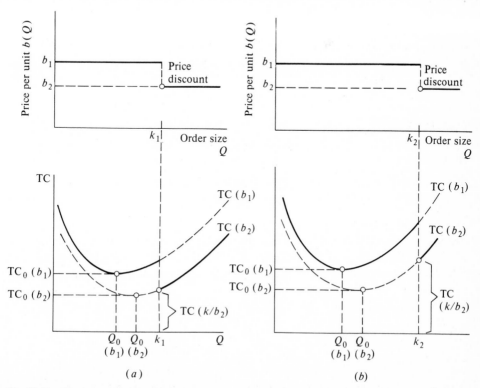

Fig. 13-10 Two cases with one price discount.

different cost curves are not permitted or desirable in different ranges of Q. Since for a given value of Q both holding cost and purchase cost are lower for the discount price while ordering costs are the same, $TC(b_2)$ will be under $TC(b_1)$ for all values of Q.

First, we determine the EOQ $Q_o(b_2)$ at the discounted price, since this yields the lowest possible total cost $TC_o(b_2)$. Here

$$Q_o(b_2) = \sqrt{\frac{2c_R D}{f b_2}}$$

If this value is greater than or equal to the amount k needed to entitle us to the discounted price b_2, this is also the optimal amount to order and the problem is solved.

When $Q_o(b_2)$ is less than k, we cannot order this amount at the reduced price b_2. In this case we compare the costs of ordering in quantities equal to $Q_o(b_1)$, the EOQ at the regular price b_1, and an amount k which is just enough to get us the lower price b_2. Here we have

$$TC_o(b_1) = \sqrt{2 f b_1 c_R D} + b_1 D \qquad \text{when } Q = Q_o(b_1) = \sqrt{\frac{2c_R D}{f b_1}}$$

$$TC(k\,|\,b_2) = f b_2 \frac{k}{2} + c_R \frac{D}{k} + b_2 D \qquad \text{when } Q = k$$

We select the order amount which results in the smallest total cost. Figure 13-10a corresponds to the situation where $TC(k\,|\,b_2)$ is smaller than $TC_o(b_1)$, resulting in $Q^* = k$. Figure 13-10b illustrates the opposite situation, yielding $Q_o(b_1)$. The above procedure can be best specified in a decision flow diagram, as in Fig. 13-11. Such a diagram can be generalized to two or more price breaks.

▶ EXAMPLE 13-4

The supplier of paint to the maintenance department of Example 13-1 has just announced a new pricing policy as follows:

$$b(Q) = \begin{vmatrix} b_1 = \$8 \text{ per gallon} & \text{if } Q < 300 \text{ gal} \\ b_2 = \$6 \text{ per gallon} & \text{if } Q \geq 300 \text{ gal} \end{vmatrix}$$

The data for demand, ordering costs, and holding costs remain the same. It is now desired to determine whether the savings in purchase costs due to the discount and reduction in ordering costs are enough to offset the increase in holding costs due to larger average inventories. Using the logic of the flow diagram for one price break of Fig. 13-10, we proceed as follows.

The EOQ at the lower price will be

$$Q_o(b_2) = \sqrt{\frac{2c_R D}{f b_2}} = \sqrt{\frac{(2)(16)(3,600)}{(.25)(6)}}$$

$$= \sqrt{76,800} = 277.13 \text{ gal/order}$$

This amount is less than the order size of 300 needed to take advantage of the

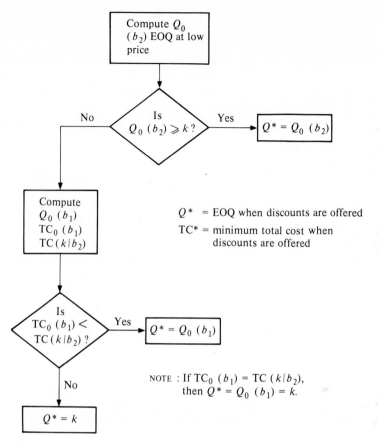

Fig. 13-11   Decision flow diagram for one price break.

discount offered. Therefore, we must calculate the total costs incurred for the EOQ at the regular price and for orders equal to $k = 300$ at the discounted price. When $Q_o = Q(b_1) = 240$ gal, we have

$$TC_o(b_1) = TIC(b_1) + b_1 D$$

$$= 480 + 28{,}800 = \$29{,}280/\text{yr}$$

When $Q = k = 300$ gal, we have

$$TC(Q = k \text{ at } b_2) = f b_2 \frac{k}{2} + c_R \frac{D}{k} + b_2 D$$

$$= (.25)(6)\frac{300}{2} + (16)\frac{3{,}600}{300} + (6)(3{,}600)$$

$$= 225 + 192 + 21{,}600 = \$22{,}017/\text{yr}$$

This situation corresponds to the case of Fig. 13-10*b*.

Thus, to minimize total inventory costs the maintenance department must order in amounts equal to

$$Q^* = 300 \text{ gal}$$

Had the price break been at 250 gal, the optimal order quantity would have been
▶ $Q_o(b_2) = 227$ gal. This would correspond to Fig. 13-10a.

13-9   A SINGLE-STAGE INVENTORY MODEL UNDER CONDITIONS OF RISK

For certain items replenishment of inventory occurs only once during each planning period. They are the reason this type is known as a single-stage inventory problem. Familiar examples in this category include fashion clothes, Christmas trees, special cakes for a holiday, hot dogs for a football game, spare parts for a new complex product or weapons system, and others.

The inventory situations for the above examples have certain common features. To begin with, the demand for such items is uncertain and can be described at best with a statistical distribution if there is some record of past experience. We also know the cost of each unit stocked C and its selling price B. If there is no sufficient demand during the current period, we assume that the leftover units can be sold at a reduced price S. This is generally lower than the cost per unit C. If demand exceeds the number of units stocked, there is a stockout, or shortage, cost per unit equal to the forgone profit $B - C$.

The inventory problem for this case consists of specifying a decision rule that would minimize the expected cost during the period. The solution procedure can be best illustrated with an example.

▶ EXAMPLE 13-5
The Edelweiss Bakery Shop prepares a deluxe cake each weekend for its best customers. The demand for this cake from week to week is uncertain, but the owner of the bakery has kept a record of sales in past weeks, and the statistical distribution for demand is shown in Table 13-2.

TABLE 13-2   **Weekly demand for fresh deluxe cake**

Demand y	0	1	2	3	4	5
Probability $p(y)$	.05	.15	.20	.25	.20	.15

The owner sells the cakes for $8 each and has estimated that they cost $5 to prepare. If any fresh cakes are left over after the weekend, they are put on special sale on Monday of the following week at $3 each. At this price all leftover cakes have always sold. The owner's problem can be formulated as follows:

$$\text{Possible actions on units to stock: } Q = \{0, 1, 2, 3, 4, 5\}$$

$$\text{Possible demand for fresh cakes: } y = \{0, 1, 2, 3, 4, 5\}$$

The consequences are as follows:

1. When demand is less than inventory $(y < Q)$, the bakery, because of leftover cakes, experiences an overestimation or surplus cost per cake c_o equal to the difference between its cost and salvage value. Thus,

$$c_o = C - S = \$5 - \$3 = \$2/\text{cake}$$

2. Similarly, when demand exceeds inventory $(y > Q)$, the bakery, because of shortages, experiences an underestimation, or stockout, cost per cake c_u, equal to the forgone profit. Thus,

$$c_u = B - C = \$8 - \$5 = \$3/\text{cake}$$

The costs associated with surplus or stockout for the bakery are displayed in Table 13-3 for all combinations of Q and y values. The costs shown in Table 13-3 pertain to the particular outcome in a given week, when the bakery stocks Q cakes and actual demand is y. The entries above the diagonal of zeroes apply to stockout costs $(y > Q)$, while those below the diagonal represent surplus costs $(Q > y)$.

TABLE 13-3   Surplus stockout costs for various order quantities

	Actual demand y						
	0	1	2	3	4	5	
Units stocked Q			Prob (y)				Total expected cost TEC(Q)
	.05	.15	.20	.25	.20	.15	
0	0	3	6	9	12	15	$8.55
1	2	0	3	6	9	12	5.80
2	4	2	0	3	6	9	3.80
3	6	4	2	0	3	6	2.80 ← Q_o
4	8	6	4	2	0	3	3.05
5	10	8	6	4	2	0	4.30

Since demand varies at random from period to period, according to the distribution $p(y)$, it is important to know the long-run performance for a given action to stock Q units. This information is provided by the total expected cost of the inventory decision (see Table 13-3).

For a given order quantity Q, the long-run expected cost attributed to surplus, i.e., leftover cakes sold at reduced prices, will be

$$EC(Q) = \sum_{y<Q} c_o(Q - y)p(y) \qquad \begin{array}{l}\text{Expected surplus} \\ \text{cost when } y < Q\end{array} \qquad (13\text{-}30)$$

For $Q = 3$, a surplus will result if demand y is 0, 1, or 2. Thus,

$$EC_o(3) = \sum_{y<3} c_o(3 - y)p(y)$$

$$= (2)(3 - 0)(.05) + (2)(3 - 1)(.15) + (2)(3 - 2)(.20)$$

$$= .30 + .60 + .40 = \$1.30/\text{wk}$$

Similarly, for a given order quantity Q, the long-run expected cost attributed to stockouts, i.e., unsatisfied demand for cakes, will be

$$EC_u(Q) = \sum_{y\geq Q} c_u(y - Q)p(y) \qquad \begin{array}{l}\text{Expected stockout} \\ \text{cost when } y > Q\end{array} \qquad (13\text{-}31)$$

For $Q = 3$, a stockout or shortage will occur if demand y is 4 or 5. Thus,

$$EC_u(3) = \sum_{y\geq 3} c_u(y - 3)p(y)$$

$$= (3)(3 - 3)(.25) + (3)(4 - 3)(.20) + (3)(5 - 3)(.15)$$

$$= 0 + .60 + .90 = \$1.50/\text{wk}$$

The total expected cost TEC associated with stocking Q units is the sum of the expected costs resulting from surplus and stockouts:

$$TEC(Q) = EC_o(Q) + EC_u(Q)$$

or

$$TEC(Q) = \sum_{y<Q} c_o(Q - y)p(y) + \sum_{y\geq Q} c_u(y - Q)p(y) \qquad (13\text{-}32)$$

or

$$\begin{bmatrix}\text{Total expected cost for} \\ \text{an order quantity } Q\end{bmatrix} = \begin{bmatrix}\text{expected cost of} \\ \text{surplus}\end{bmatrix} + \begin{bmatrix}\text{expected cost of} \\ \text{stockout}\end{bmatrix}$$

Continuing with our bakery example, when $Q = 3$,

$$TEC(3) = EC_o(3) + EC_u(3) = 1.30 + 1.50 = \$2.80/\text{wk}$$

Thus, if the bakery stocks three deluxe cakes each weekend, it will experience in the long run an expected cost equal to \$2.80 per week.

The actions to stock 0, 1, 2, ..., 5 deluxe cakes can be evaluated by calculating their total expected cost, as it was done for $Q = 3$. The results are shown in the last ▶ column of Table 13-3.

Solution Using Bayes' Criterion

In order to solve the inventory problem under risk, as typified by our example, we select as the optimal action the one with the minimum total expected cost.

Decision Rule A

For the single-stage inventory problem under conditions of risk, the optimal action on the number of units to stock Q_o is the one yielding the minimum total expected cost, i.e.,

$$TEC(Q_o) = \text{minimum } TEC(Q) \text{ over all } Q \text{ values}$$

Surveying the $TEC(Q)$ column in Table 13-3, we note that the minimum expected cost is obtained when $Q = 3$. Thus, to minimize the long-run losses from the sale of this item the bakery should stock three deluxe cakes each weekend. Considering the customer satisfaction gained from making this deluxe cake available and the maintenance of a reputation as a high-quality bakery, the owner decides to continue making it.

This is just another application of Bayes' decision criterion, discussed in Supplementary Chapter A. Of course, we have assumed that the statistical distribution of demand and the relevant costs remain the same. Any changes in these information inputs must be incorporated in the cost table. $TEC(Q)$ is subsequently recomputed and the optimal action determined on the basis of the revised expected costs.

Solution Using Incremental Analysis

The procedure using Bayes' criterion is simple and computationally manageable as long as the number of alternative actions is fairly small. If in the bakery-shop example actual demand reached a maximum of 100 or more cakes, the calculations required to prepare a table with this many rows and columns would be formidable.

It is apparent that for large single-stage inventory problems under risk we need a more streamlined approach. Such an approach exists and is called *incremental analysis*, based on the cost concepts discussed in Supplementary Chapter B. The basic idea is quite simple. Again, the use of the bakery-shop example can help focus on the key concepts. The problem is represented graphically in Fig. 13-12.

In Fig. 13-12 we observe that when we start with $Q = 0$, the total expected cost $TEC(Q)$ for a given value of Q decreases until it reaches its minimum and then increases. Thus, the increments in total expected cost $\Delta C(Q)$ are negative until we reach the optimal action Q_o. At that point the increment becomes positive and remains so. Under the assumptions stated for this problem it is not possible to have several minimum values for $TEC(Q)$. The increment under discussion is similar to the concept of marginal cost in economics

$$\Delta C(Q) = TEC(Q) - TEC(Q - 1) \qquad \text{Marginal cost for production quantity } Q \qquad (13\text{-}33)$$

Thus, for the example

$$\Delta C(3) = TEC(3) - TEC(2) = \$2.80 - \$5.80 = -\$3.00$$

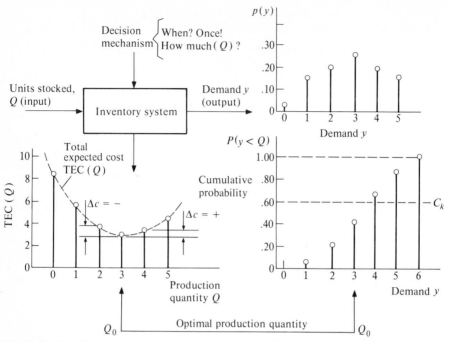

Fig. 13-12   Graphic representation of example for inventory problem under risk.

We can see in Fig. 13-12 that *the optimal action Q_o corresponds to the value of Q at which the increment changes in sign from negative to positive.* This happens because as long as this increment is negative, increasing Q by 1 unit decreases the total expected cost. As soon as it becomes positive, we have just passed the optimal solution. It can be shown[1] that the optimal action corresponds to the value of Q for which the following relationship holds:

$$\text{Prob}(y < Q) \le \frac{C_u}{C_u + C_o} \quad \begin{array}{l}\text{Critical} \\ \text{ratio } C_k\end{array} \qquad (13\text{-}34)$$

In words, the optimal quantity to stock Q_o is the one for which the adjusted cumulative probability of demand being less than Q_o is just less than or equal to the ratio $C_u/(C_u + C_o)$, known as the *critical ratio C_k*.

Decision Rule B

For the single-stage inventory problem under conditions of risk, the optimal action on the number of units to stock Q_o corresponds to the largest value of Q for which

$$P(y < Q) \le \frac{C_u}{C_u + C_o} \qquad \text{Critical-value ratio}$$

---

[1] Rao V. Tummala, *Decision Analysis with Business Applications*, Intext, 1973.

For the bakery-shop example we have

$$P(y < Q) \le \frac{C_u}{C_u + C_o} \quad \text{or} \quad P(y < Q) \le \frac{3}{3 + 2} = .600$$

For a production quantity $Q = 3$

$$P(y < 3) = P(y = 0) + p(y = 1) + P(y = 2)$$
$$= .05 + .15 + .20 = .40$$

while for a production quantity $Q = 4$

$$P(y < 4) = P(y = 0) + P(y = 1) + p(y = 2) + P(y = 3)$$
$$= .05 + .15 + .20 + .25 = .65$$

Therefore, the value of Q for which the cumulative probability is less than or equal to .600 is $Q = 3$. The critical-value ratio is shown in the appropriate graph in Fig. 13-12. This is the same optimal action determined by Bayes' criterion. The obvious advantage of the incremental-analysis method is that it completely by-passes the calculation of the entries in the table for stockout and surplus costs and the expected cost for each action.

13-10 SUMMARY

The objectives of this lengthy chapter were two, to discuss the importance of inventories for a smooth and economic operation and to explain the meaning of such terms as inventory, inventory problem, inventory system, and inventory model.

In operations management, *inventory* refers to idle scarce resources waiting to be used to satisfy demand. Their specific form varies with each organization (materials in process for a factory, cash reserve for a bank, stewardesses for an airline, etc.). The *inventory problem* consists of deciding when and in what amounts to replenish inventory so that demand can continue to be satisfied at minimum cost or maximum profit.

To solve the inventory problem for a specific case we must describe accurately and adequately the *inventory system* that exists for the item(s) handled. This description is really a set of assumptions about certain aspects or components of the inventory system, i.e., the demand and replenishment characteristics, operating constraints, required decisions that define the inventory policy, and the latter's effectiveness as measured by some cost or profit criterion.

An effective approach for solving an inventory problem is with the assistance of an *inventory model*. This is simply a representation, in quantitative form, of the assumptions, the relationships, and the measure of performance of the inventory system. This model is subsequently used to determine an optimal inventory policy and its sensitivity to changes in demand, costs, or other aspects. Our survey included four inventory models with known demand and one model in which demand was described statistically. Simulation is often helpful in handling the uncertainty in demand, lead time, or other aspects.

The scope of this book does not allow space for discussing the truly rich literature of inventory models for a wide variety of operating systems. Of course, the mathematical sophistication required to study many of them is quite demanding. In any event, inventory models have been developed covering one or several items, in one or more installations, under a variety of assumptions concerning the behavior of inventory costs and the demand and lead-time properties. The interested reader can study these advanced topics in the Selected References.

NOTATION

Inventory demand

y = quantity removed from inventory during replenishment cycle
D = demand rate, i.e., amount of inventory used up per unit time

Inventory replenishment

Q = order or production quantity for each replenishment
t = reorder or replenishment cycle
L = replenishment lead time
t_p = replenishment or production period
p = production rate

Inventory level

$Q(T)$ = amount of stock available at time T
I_{max} = maximum surplus inventory during each replenishment cycle
I_{min} = minimum surplus inventory during each replenishment cycle
I_H = average surplus inventory during each replenishment cycle
I_{max}^{-} = maximum shortage (or backlog) during each replenishment cycle
I_{min}^{-} = minimum shortage (or backlog) during each replenishment cycle
I_S = average shortage (or backlog) during each replenishment cycle
I_R = average number of replenishments per unit time

Inventory unit costs

f = percentage of inventory value charged to holding inventory
$b(Q)$ = price per unit when ordering in amounts equal to Q
b = price per unit when no quantity discounts are offered
c_H = cost of holding 1 unit per unit time = $f[b(Q)]$
c_S = cost of being short 1 unit per unit time
c_R = cost per order or production setup

Inventory annual costs

C_H = holding cost per unit time = $c_H I_H$
C_S = shortage cost per unit time = $c_S I_S$
C_R = replenishment cost per unit time = $c_R I_R$
C_B = purchase cost per unit time = $b(Q)D$
TIC = total incremental inventory cost per unit time = $C_H + C_S + C_R$
TC = total inventory cost per unit time = $C_H + C_S + C_R + C_B$

REVIEW QUESTIONS

1. State what is meant by the following:
   (a) Inventory
   (b) Inventory problem
   (c) Inventory system
   (d) Inventory model
2. Discuss the main reasons for maintaining inventories.
3. State the basic decisions required to operate an inventory system.
4. Discuss the components of an inventory system with reference to (a) a hospital supply room, (b) an oil refinery, and (c) a commercial bank's cash reserves.
5. Describe the steps involved in developing an inventory model.
6. Which types of inventory costs are usually relevant in analyzing an inventory system? Which is the most difficult to estimate? Why?
7. What would be the effect of assuming a fixed and known lead time in the EOQ model?
8. When is the cost of purchasing inventories important in the determination of an inventory policy?
9. Which inventory costs increase and which decrease when price discounts are available?
10. Which are the most restrictive assumptions of the classical (or EOQ) inventory model? Why is it important to study it at all?
11. For what reasons is simulation helpful in approaching complex inventory problems?
12. Discuss the interaction of an inventory policy with aggregate planning.

PROBLEMS

1. The administrative services of a government agency require 2,400 rolls of duplicating paper per year for copiers. Holding costs are estimated to be $3.60 per roll per year, and the cost of replenishment for this item is equal to $25 per order.
   (a) Prepare a table showing the average inventory, number of orders, holding cost, ordering cost and total incremental cost for order quantities in multiples of 200 rolls.
   (b) Plot the relevant cost curves for each order-quantity value.
   (c) Identify on the table the minimum-cost order quantity and compare this with the EOQ from the graph of part (b).
2. Refer to Prob. 1.
   (a) Determine optimum order quantity using the EOQ model.
   (b) Compare the optimum Q_o with answers obtained from the tabular and graphical methods.
   (c) Determine the revised Q_o and the error in total incremental cost if we must change the initial estimates as follows:
       (i) Demand rate equals 1,800 rolls (due to budget cuts).
       (ii) Holding costs are $4.90 per roll per year (due to recent price increases in paper).
       (iii) Replenishment costs are $36 per order (due to salary raises).
       (iv) All the above.
3. The demand for a certain item is 48,000 units/yr. Each unit costs $80, and inventory carrying charges have been estimated at 20 percent of inventory value. Management does not allow any shortages and can purchase the item locally in whatever quantity is desired at a cost of $400 per shipment (for ordering, receiving, inspecting, and placing stock on shelves).
   (a) Determine:
       (i) The EOQ

    (ii) The time between orders

    (iii) The number of orders required each year

    (iv) The minimum incremental inventory cost

    (v) What the incremental cost is if by mistake management orders 600 units each time

    (vi) The minimum total inventory cost

(*b*) Plot a graph for inventory-level fluctuations with time and identify quantities (i) and (ii).

(*c*) Plot a graph of the relevant cost curves versus order quantity and identify (i), (iv), (v), and (vi).

4. Suppose that in Prob. 3 management made an error in estimating demand, the true value being 56,000 units/yr.

    (*a*) Determine the revised EOQ and scheduling period.

    (*b*) Calculate the revised minimum incremental inventory cost for the new EOQ.

    (*c*) Determine the percentage error in the incremental inventory cost if the demand error goes undetected and inventory is replenishment with the old decision rules.

5. Refer to Prob. 3. If as a result of inflation the cost per unit increases by 50 percent and the cost per order has gone up 25 percent, determine:

    (*a*) The revised EOQ

    (*b*) The new minimum incremental inventory cost

    (*c*) The percentage error in the inventory cost if the inventory replenishment proceeds with the old decision rules

6. After conducting a feasibility study, the management in Prob. 3 has decided to manufacture the needed item internally. The setup cost for each production run has been estimated at $240 and inventory carrying charges at $15 per unit per year. The production rate is 768 units per day, and there are 250 working days per year.

    (*a*) Determine:

        (i) The optimum production lot (or batch) size

        (ii) The time between production runs

        (iii) The duration of each production run

        (iv) The number of production runs per year

        (v) The minimum incremental inventory cost

    (*b*) Plot the fluctuations in inventory levels versus batch size and identify (i) to (iv).

    (*c*) Plot the relevant cost curves versus batch size and identify (i) and (v).

7. To limit its dependence on imported oil, the Eastern Power Co. has decided to cover a fixed part of the regional demand for electricity using coal. This follows the installation of scrubbers in its electrical plant to reduce pollution in compliance with Environmental Quality Council regulations. The annual demand for the coal input is estimated at 730,000 tons used uniformly throughout the year. The coal can be strip-mined near the power-generating plant at the rate of 5,000 tons/day with a setup cost of $2,000 per mining run. Inventory holding cost is estimated at $3 per ton per day.

    (*a*) Assuming 250 working days per year, determine:

        (i) The economic coal production quantity

        (ii) The duration of each mining run

        (iii) The time between runs

        (iv) The minimum (incremental) inventory cost

    (*b*) Plot a graph showing the coal inventory fluctuations versus time and identify (i) to (iii).

    (*c*) Plot a graph showing the relevant cost curves versus production quantity and identify (i) and (iv).

8. A chemical company supplies hospitals with an antiseptic solution for cleaning surgical equipment. The annual demand is uniform and equal to 180,000 gal/year. The setup cost for preparing each batch is $1,200 at a rate of 2,000 gal/day. The inventory holding cost is estimated at 50 cents per gallon per year
   (a) If no shortages are allowed and the company works 250 days/yr. determine:
      (i) The optimum batch size for the cleaning solution
      (ii) The length of each production period
      (iii) The time between production runs
      (iv) The minimum (incremental) inventory cost
   (b) Plot a graph of the relevant cost curves versus order quantity and identify (i) and (iv).
9. The manufacturer of the Easy-Use office machine has a contract that calls for the delivery of 6,400 machines annually at a uniform rate. Each unit requires three identical small gears produced internally at the rate of 76,800 per day. The holding cost is $3 per gear per year. The plant operates 250 days/yr and the cost per production setup is $60. Determine:
   (a) The economic production quantity (EPQ) for machine gears
   (b) The length of the production period
   (c) The number of necessary setups per year for the EPQ
   (d) The minimum incremental inventory cost
10. The operations manager of Power Lift Inc., a fork-lift truck manufacturer, expects to use 6,400 generators at a cost of $60 per unit. Carrying costs are estimated at $15 per generator per year and the ordering cost is $120 per order. Management allows shortages to occur. However, there is a shortage cost of $20 per generator per week due to production delays from incompletely assembled trucks.
   (a) Assuming 52 wk/yr, and negligible lead times, determine:
      (i) The EOQ
      (ii) The maximum inventory level
      (iii) The maximum allowed backlog for generators
      (iv) The time between orders
      (v) The length of period during which generator shortages exist
   (b) Plot a graph of inventory fluctuations versus time and identify (i) to (v) in part (a),
      (i) The minimum incremental inventory cost
      (ii) The minimum total inventory cost
11. In Prob. 10 the demand for tires is equal to 25,600 per year. The regular supplier, Goodtread Co., charges Power Lift, Inc. $30 per tire for orders less than 2,000 and $25 per tire for larger quantities. The inventory carrying charges are 20 percent of inventory value, and the cost per order is $240.
   (a) *If no shortages are allowed* for this item, determine:
      (i) The total inventory cost equation for each price per tire
      (ii) The EOQ taking into account the price discount
      (iii) The minimum total inventory cost for the EOQ
      (iv) The savings, if any, compared with a no-discount policy
   (b) Sketch the total-cost curves versus order quantity and identify (ii) to (v) above.
12. The demand for an item is 25,000 units/yr. The supplier has offered the following purchasing plan:

$$b(Q) = \begin{cases} \$12 \text{ per unit} & \text{if} & Q < 1{,}000 \\ \$11 \text{ per unit} & \text{if } 1{,}000 \le Q < 5{,}000 \\ \$9 \text{ per unit} & \text{if} & Q \ge 5{,}000 \end{cases}$$

(*a*) If carrying charges have been estimated at 30 percent of inventory value and the cost per order is $60, determine:
  (i) The total-inventory-cost equation for each price
  (ii) The EOQ
  (iii) The minimum total inventory cost possible
  (iv) The savings, if any, made possible due to the available discounts
(*b*) Sketch the total-cost curves versus order quantity and identify (ii) to (iv).

13. Every year Simone Champlain, owner of Boutique Elegante, a downtown fashion shop, buys the latest ready-to-wear creations of the famous French designer Philippe Debussy. From past experience she has accumulated the following data for sales of the most successful design in Europe, which she imports with slight variations in color and cut.

Demand y	0	1	2	3	4	5	6
Probability $p(y)$	.05	.10	.20	.30	.20	.10	.05

After paying customs, etc., each dress costs her $180. The sales tag during the season is $360. However, if her selected customers do not buy the entire shipment, she holds an end-of-the-season sale with a tag of $120 per dress, at which time other customers purchase all the remaining quantity. Determine the optimum order quantity for the above fashion dress for Boutique Elegante and specify the expected value to the owner each season.

14. Rework Prob. 13 if the probability distribution for demand has been revised as follows:

Demand y	0	1	2	3	4	5	6
Probability $p(y)$	.05	.05	.10	.30	.25	.20	.05

15. The manufacturer of Kosteau II, a special vessel for underwater research has experienced a demand for spare parts of a critical component according to a Poisson distribution with $\lambda = 1.0$ per vessel per year. Spare parts are produced once a year. The cost of surplus is $60 per part per year, and the cost of stockout is $150 per part per year. Determine the optimum production quantity of spare parts Q if there is only one research vessel in operation.

16. Refer to Prob. 15. Determine Q if the failure rate of the component is the same but a production run for spare parts is scheduled only every 2 years.

17. Refer to Prob. 15. Determine Q if there are two research vessels in operation and production runs for spare parts are scheduled (*a*) once a year and (*b*) every 2 yr.

18. (This problem requires familiarity with the Supplementary Chapter D.) A camera shop maintains a stock of a special accessory for professional photographers. The probability distributions for weekly demand for this item and the lead time to obtain it are as follows:

Weekly demand, units	Relative frequency	Supply lead time, weeks	Relative frequency
0	0.05	1	0.35
1	0.10	2	0.50
2	0.25	3	0.15
3	0.30		
4	0.20		
5	0.10		

The owner of the camera shop has set a reorder point for this item equal to 10 units and replenishes his stock in lot sizes of 18 units. The inventory carrying cost is equal to $4 per unit per week, the replenishment cost is $30 per order, and the shortage cost is $64 per unit per week. Initial inventory on hand for the upcoming week is equal to 12 units.

(a) Prepare a flowchart for a simulation that will evaluate the average total inventory cost for this item per week.

(b) Perform a 15-wk simulation run and calculate the average total inventory cost per week.

19. Refer to Prob. 18. Perform another 15-wk simulation to evaluate the inventory policy for which the reorder point is (a) 12 and the order size is 15 and (b) 8 and the order size is 21.

SELECTED REFERENCES

1. Bergstrom, G. L., and B. E. Smith: "Multi-Item Production Planning: An Extension of the HMMS Rules," *Management Science*, vol. 16, no. 10, pp. 614–629, June 1970.
2. Brown, R. G.: *Decision Rules for Inventory Management*, Holt, New York, 1967.
3. Buchan, J., and E. Koenigsberg: *Scientific Inventory Control*, Prentice-Hall, Englewood Cliffs, N.J., 1963.
4. Buffa, E. S.: *Operations Management: Problems and Models*, 3d ed., Wiley, New York, 1972.
5. Feltham, G. A.: "Some Quantitative Approaches to Planning for Multi-Product Production Systems," *The Accounting Review*, vol. 25, no. 1, pp. 11–26, January 1970.
6. Love, S. F.: *Inventory Control*, McGraw-Hill, New York, 1979.
7. Magee, J. F., and D. M. Boodman: *Production Planning and Inventory Control*, 2d ed., McGraw-Hill, New York, 1967.
8. Peterson, R., and E. A. Silver: *Decisions Systems for Inventory Management and Production Planning*, Wiley, New York, 1977.
9. Sivaslian, B. D., and L. E. Stanfel: *Analysis of Systems in Operations Research*, Prentice-Hall, Englewood Cliffs, N.J., 1975.
10. Starr, M. K., and D. W. Miller: *Inventory Control: Theory and Practice*, Prentice-Hall, Englewood Cliffs, N.J., 1962.
11. Tersine, Richard J.: *Materials Management and Inventory Systems*, Elsevier, New York, 1976.

Chapter 14

INVENTORY-MANAGEMENT SYSTEMS

14-1 INTRODUCTION

The inventory models discussed previously relate to idealized situations dealing with one item and are most appropriate for an environment with no uncertainty. Real inventory systems, however, have to cope with several factors that increase their complexity and present major difficulties in their design, analysis, and operation. Among the most serious complicating features, we have:

1. The need for handling a large number of items deserving different degrees of control, ordered from several suppliers, and having unique requirements for packaging, storage, and handling
2. The difficulty of estimating with accuracy the relevant costs of holding inventory, ordering or setting up, and stockouts
3. The inherent variability, which is often random, in the demand rate D, the supply lead time L, and the production rate p.

In the following sections, we examine how these complexities are handled in practice and then describe the predominant types of inventory-management systems.

The design of inventory systems has been recently influenced by an important distinction between *dependent* and *independent* demand. Our discussion so far pertains to items with independent demand. In general, these are finished products whose demand is generated externally and is therefore uncertain. For several applications many inventoriable items are materials, parts, and components that are assembled to form a finished product or end item. Once an estimate is available for future demand for the end item, the requirements in parts and components are known exactly from the specifications of the product. Hence, there is no reason to hold safety stocks for such items. The kinds of parts needed, their time phasing for production, and the quantities required can be determined with an approach known as *material requirements planning* (MRP). MRP, which can be viewed as a bridge between inventory management and production scheduling, is discussed later in this chapter and compared with the more traditional inventory systems.

ABC Analysis For Proper Control

An inventory-management system usually handles hundreds or even thousands of different items. It is simply not sound managerial practice to exercise the same degree of control over all such items or all groups of items.

To determine the proper degree of control for the various items held in stock, it is necessary to classify them on the basis of their value or critical nature. The resulting categories are then ranked according to the desired degree of control, which reflects the size of investment in each and the critical nature of an item in securing smooth and economic operation. The more capital management invests in a given category the tighter the required control. The more critical an item is, say a fuse in an electronic device, the closer the surveillance required, even though the dollar value per unit of the item may not be high.

The most effective and widely used approach for establishing the various control categories is a procedure known as *ABC analysis*. In a large number of studies it has been observed that, independently of the field of application, a small percentage, say 15 percent, of the items held in stock represents the greatest part, say 75 percent, of the total value invested in inventories. Next, another 30 percent of the items accounts for 20 percent of the total value, and, finally the major proportion of items, 55 percent, represents only 5 percent of the capital investment in inventory. The specific percentage figures may vary somewhat from one organization to another, but the general form of the distribution of items by value is the same as that shown in Fig. 14-1.[1]

After completion of the ABC analysis, an inventory-management system is set up so that items in class A are placed under tight control, items in class B under intermediate control, and class C items under loose or no control. Control in the present context refers to the degree of attention given to such aspects of inventory as:

1. The time interval between successive reviews of requirements t (see Fig. 14-1)
2. Order frequencies
3. Expected demand rates D
4. Order quantities Q
5. Review of information system operation concerning timing, accuracy, and frequency of reporting relevant data

An ABC analysis can also be used to evaluate which inventory items are profitable, which suppliers or customers are most important, and so on.

Estimation of Inventory Costs

In the models discussed in Chap. 13 inventory unit costs were assumed to be known and constant. In actual applications the estimation of holding, shortage, and ordering costs is usually a very difficult part of the inventory-system analysis.

[1] The ABC analysis diagram is also known as a *Pareto distribution curve*, named after the famous economist. This can be used to describe the distribution of companies in an industry by output value (or volume), the distribution of manufacturers by the extent of energy conservation, water pollution, etc.

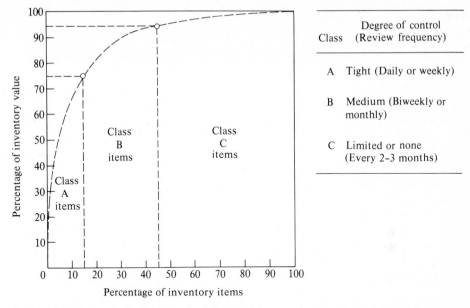

Fig. 14-1 **ABC analysis showing typical relationship between percentage of value invested in various inventory groups and percentage of inventory items.**

Holding costs incurred to maintain surplus inventory are the sum of a variety of costs, i.e., cost of capital tied up, storage or warehouse costs, depreciation, obsolescence, insurance, handling, taxes, etc. The major component is the cost of capital, which depends on the company's rate of return. The latter is a very elusive parameter to estimate and is more frequently assumed than measured. Insurance rates drop as the value of inventory increases; warehouse costs may be determined on square footage or volume, and handling charges may decrease with volume as more efficient equipment is purchased to handle greater traffic. Depreciation and obsolescence are also difficult to assess, and the same may be true for other costs.

Ordering costs are supposed to be incremental in nature and vary linearly with the number of orders. Yet they are primarily related to the salaries of personnel in the purchasing department, where people are not fired if the number of orders for an item drops.

Most elusive of all are the costs related to shortages, especially if the demand is external and stockouts involve loss of customers and goodwill. Nevertheless, these costs are real and cannot be assumed to be infinite, forcing the system to maintain enough inventory to cover all possible demand loads.

Despite the difficulties inherent in the estimation of inventory costs, it is necessary to arrive at specific values. This is done by making realistic assumptions on a case-by-case basis concerning the system's operation. Fortunately for management, *the majority of inventory systems studied display a rather flat total-inventory-cost curve (or dish-shaped surface). This means that the optimal decision rules for when to order and how much to order are rather robust or insensitive to errors in the estimation of unit-cost parameters.*

If there is doubt concerning the robustness of the decision rules, there exist methods for performing sensitivity analyses. The latter help establish the relative impact of errors in the cost estimates on the total inventory cost (Ref. 10).

Safety Stocks for Absorbing Random Variability

The random variability in the demand rate, the supply time, and the production rate represents one of the most difficult yet real problems in inventory management. Let us for a moment consider the effect of random variability only in the demand rate. Unlike the variation attributed to a trend, accounted-for seasonal fluctuations, and business cycles, which can be identified and removed, random variability is unpredictable. In the deterministic models we are concerned with optimal decision rules that apply to a constant and known demand. In a real system this is the average or expected demand.

If for a given period actual demand is less than expected, extra inventory is left, which increases the holding cost. On the other hand, if actual demand exceeds average demand, the stockouts will increase shortage costs. Comparable effects are observed when random variability is displayed by supply lead time or production rate. The problem is manageable when variability occurs in only one of these variables. However, when supply lead time and demand are both variable, the problem is very complex and the only feasible approach is to use simulation (Ref. 9) (see Prob. 13-18).

In order to absorb random variability, especially in demand and lead time, inventory systems rely on safety (or buffer) stocks. By using buffer inventories we seek to reduce the risk of running out of stock. The greater the buffer stock maintained the less the risk of experiencing shortages. However, such an increase in safety stock raises the holding cost. The objective is to reach a balance between the extra holding cost resulting from safety stocks and the expected cost of shortage. An optimum amount of buffer stock would be one that makes the sum of these costs a minimum.

Because of the difficulties involved in obtaining an accurate estimate for the shortage costs, the above method is usually not feasible.[1] Instead, management accepts a reasonable service level and then determines the size of safety stock necessary to keep the risk of stockout within prescribed limits. For example, suppose the desired service level for a given company is 90 percent. This implies a commitment to maintain adequate stock to satisfy actual demand (mainly in terms of orders but sometimes in terms of customers or part of the cycle time) 9 times out of 10.

The determination of the required buffer stock to support a given service level depends on the type of inventory-management system, i.e., whether orders are placed at fixed intervals or in fixed amounts.

---

[1] For the solution method used when shortage costs are available see Refs. 10 and 12.

14-2 DETERMINATION OF SAFETY-STOCK SIZE FOR SPECIFIED SERVICE LEVEL

The following discussion concerns the determination of safety stocks in a fixed-order-quantity inventory system with constant lead time. This is similar in operation to the system assumed in the EOQ model. In that, when the inventory level drops to the reorder point, an order of fixed quantity is placed. With average demand during the lead time the inventory reaches zero, at which time the new order arrives.

In such a system when actual demand during the lead time exceeds expected demand, there will be a stockout. Without safety stocks shortages are likely to occur 50 percent of the time, and so the objective in using safety stocks is to reduce the risk of shortages from 50 percent to a more reasonable level, say 5 or 10 percent. Note that *in a fixed-order-quantity system the lead time is the only time the system is vulnerable to stockouts.*

Let $\bar{D}$ = average demand rate per unit time (usually a year)

D_{max} = maximum reasonable demand rate per unit time

L = supply lead time, days

$\bar{x}$ = average demand during lead time = $D \cdot L$

x_{max} = maximum reasonable demand during lead time for given service level = $D_{max} \cdot L$

B_{FOQ} = safety stock in fixed-order-quantity system

Definition

Safety stock is the amount of extra inventory needed to satisfy maximum reasonable demand for a given service level during the lead time.

Thus,

$$B_{FOQ} = x_{max} - \bar{x}$$

or
$$B_{FOQ} = D_{max} \cdot L - D \cdot L = (D_{max} - D)(L) \tag{14-1}$$

where if x_i occurs with a frequency $p(x_i)$ ($i = 1, 2, \ldots, n$), then

$$\bar{x} = x_1[p(x_1)] + x_2[p(x_2)] + \cdots + x_n[p(x_n)]$$

Safety-Stock Determination for an Empirical Demand Distribution

A camera shop has experienced an uncertain demand for one of its high-priced items and wishes to determine the amount of buffer stock needed for various service levels. The lead time for replenishment is 2 weeks, or 10 working days.

TABLE 14-1   Data on demand during lead time

Demand during L x	Relative frequency $p(x)$	Probability demand exceeds x	Demand during L x	Relative frequency $p(x)$	Probability demand exceeds x
0	.00	1.00	9	.08	.15
1	.02	.98	10	.05	.10
2	.03	.95	11	.03	.07
3	.05	.90	12	.02	.05
4	.08	.82	13	.02	.03
5	.12	.70	14	.01	.02
6	.20	.50	15	.01	.01
7	.15	.35	16	.01	.00
8	.12	.23			

Table 14-1 contains data on lead-time demand for several weeks. The same information could be shown graphically as a bar chart. If the camera shop is to satisfy the average, or normal, demand during a lead time of 10 days ($L = 10$), it must only carry 6 units ($\bar{x} \approx 6$).[1] However, if demand in the future follows the same pattern observed in the past, with 6 units in stock during L the shop will experience shortages 50 percent of the time. On the other hand, with 16 units demand will be met 100 percent of the time.

The manager of the camera shop wants to maintain enough inventory to satisfy demand 90 percent of the time. From Table 14-1 it can be seen that maximum reasonable demand for this service level is 10 units. In other words, actual demand is likely to exceed this amount 10 percent of the time. For this risk level the buffer stock will be

$$B_{FOQ} = x_{max} - \bar{x} = 10 - 6 = 4 \text{ units}$$

If holding cost is 30 percent of the investment in inventory and the purchase cost per unit is \$200, the buffer-stock cost for 90 percent service level is

$$(0.3)(4)\$(200) = \$240$$

Suppose the manager wished to determine how much more it would cost to increase the service level to 95 and 99 percent. Table 14-2 summarizes the results of these calculations.

Note in Table 14-2 that *successive improvements in the service level become increasingly more expensive*. Thus, the improvement from 50 to 90 percent in service level will cost \$240, the next 5 percent improvement costs \$120, and subsequent 4 percent improvement costs \$180. This is true not only for inventory systems but also for the service quality of systems in education, health care, transportation, maintenance, etc.

---

[1] The value for $\bar{x}$ has been rounded down to allow an easier interpretation of the probability data in Table 14-1.

TABLE 14-2 Cost effects for different inventory service levels

	Inventory characteristic			
Service level, %	Maximum reasonable demand x_{max}	Buffer stock B	Extra investment for buffer stock	Extra holding cost
50	6	0	$ 0	$ 0
90	10	4	$ 800	$240
95	12	6	$1,200	$360
99	15	9	$1,800	$540

Safety-Stock Determination for a Theoretical Demand Distribution

If the empirical demand distribution can be approximated satisfactorily by a theoretical statistical distribution, safety-stock calculations can be carried out more easily using the properties of the distribution.

Approximation using the normal distribution   The demand experienced by an inventory system can sometimes be viewed as the sum of demands from many sources each having only a negligible effect. This is often the case with a wholesale distributor receiving orders from many local retailers, each requiring only a limited quantity. Under such conditions, it is reasonable to assume that the total demand can be approximated with the normal distribution.

For example, if total demand during L has a mean value $\bar{x}$ equal to 3,600 units and a standard deviation s_x of 20 units, the maximum reasonable demand during the lead time can easily be determined using the normal-distribution tables. Here

$$x_{max} = \bar{x} + z_\alpha s_x = 3,600 + z_\alpha(20) \qquad (14\text{-}2)$$

where z_α is the number of standard deviations away from the mean that corresponds to a risk level α, that is, a service level equal to $1 - \alpha$. For a 90 percent service level ($\alpha = 10$ percent) inspection of a table for the normal distribution yields $z_\alpha = 1.282$. (Note that this refers only to one tail of the normal distribution on the right side.) Figure 14-2 shows the values of z_α for different risk levels.

Approximation using the Poisson distribution   For certain inventory systems the total quantity demanded is the sum of orders each having a very small probability of materializing. Furthermore, the average demand rate is constant and the amounts ordered in successive time intervals are independent. This situation seems to describe sales at the retail level, where the probability of receiving an order from any one of numerous potential customers is very small. This case can be adequately approximated by the Poisson distribution as long as the mean demand $\bar{x}$ is not

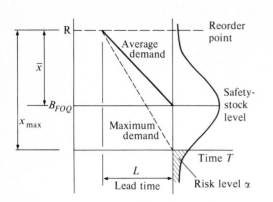

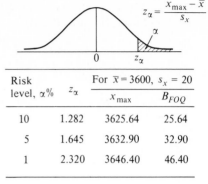

Risk level, α%	z_α	For $\bar{x} = 3600$, $s_x = 20$	
		x_{max}	B_{FOQ}
10	1.282	3625.64	25.64
5	1.645	3632.90	32.90
1	2.320	3646.40	46.40

Fig. 14-2   Calculation of safety stock from normal distribution.

greater than 20. For this situation

$$x_{max} = \bar{x} + z'_\alpha s_x \tag{14-3}$$

$$s_x = \sqrt{\bar{x}} \tag{14-4}$$

where z'_α is the number of standard deviations away from the mean that corresponds to a risk level α, that is, a service level equal to $1 - \alpha$. For a 95 percent service level ($\alpha = 5$ percent) inspection of a table for the Poisson distribution gives $z_\alpha = 1.57$.

Suppose an auto repair shop experiences an average demand for a given part equal to 16 during the lead time. If the demand pattern can be approximated by the Poisson distribution, we can calculate the buffer stock for different service levels, as shown in Fig. 14-3.

From the above discussion, it can be seen that the common business practice of maintaining buffer stock to satisfy a demand of given time period, that is, holding a

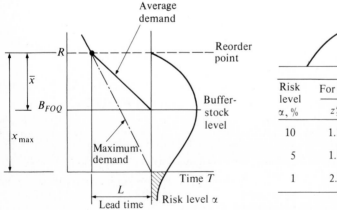

Risk level α, %	z'_α	For $\bar{x} = 16$, $s_x = \sqrt{16} = 4$	
		x_{max}	B_{FOQ}
10	1.12	20	4
5	1.57	22	6
1	2.24	25	9

Fig. 14-3   Calculation of safety stock from Poisson distribution. For other risk levels the value of z' can be obtained from Ref. 4.

3-wk supply, is an expensive and destabilizing approach to inventory management. As shown in the preceding discussion, safety stock, which is defined as

$$B_{FOQ} = x_{max} - \bar{x} = (\bar{x} + z_\alpha s_x) - \bar{x} = z_\alpha s_x \qquad (14\text{-}5)$$

is proportional not to average demand itself but to its standard deviation s_x, which involves the square root of $\bar{x}$.[1] This finding is comparable in significance to the one concerning the economic-order-quantity determination. The change of both is proportional not to the demand but to the square root of demand. These facts suggest that an effective inventory policy must be developed on a rational basis rather than intuitively or with rules of thumb.

14-3 THE FIXED-ORDER-QUANTITY (CONTINUOUS-REVIEW) SYSTEM

Inventory-management systems differ in the way they are triggered to initiate action for replenishment. For each system we are interested in knowing the appropriate decision rule(s), its mode of operation concerning maximum and minimum inventories, required safety stocks, recommended applications, and certain limitations or disadvantages.

Decision Rule A

In a fixed-order-quantity system with lead time shorter than the reorder cycle time $(L < t)$ an order of fixed amount Q is placed when the inventory level drops to a predetermined reorder point R.

The quantity Q can be determined using the appropriate EOQ formula, but in some cases the order quantity is affected by other more dominant considerations or is simply based on judgment or common practice.

Mode of Operation

Under ideal conditions, the operations of the fixed-order-quantity (FOQ) system resembles the system assumed in the EOQ model with the addition of safety stocks, as determined in the preceding section. This is shown in Fig. 14-4. Here each cycle is like any other cycle since demand rate and lead time are constant, assuming their expected values.

Under more realistic conditions, the demand rate will usually vary from its expected value. In this case, the time between successive replenishments will also

---

[1] The only exception is when demand follows a negative exponential distribution for which the standard deviation equals the mean demand, $s_x = \bar{x}$.

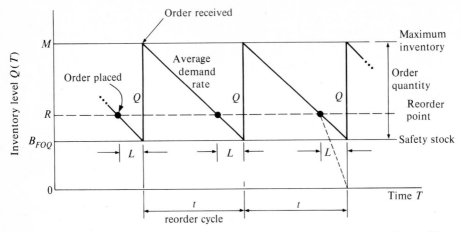

Fig. 14-4 **Inventory-level fluctuations for a fixed-order-quantity system operating under ideal conditions with $L < t$.**

vary, reflecting the demand rate experienced. For a system with a fixed supply time L the inventory-level fluctuations are as shown in Fig. 14-5.

The three cycles shown in Fig. 14-5 differ in that the demand rate D deviates from the average demand rate. As a result the actual lead-time demand x varies from the average demand $\bar{x}$. In the sense that the quantity ordered Q is the same each time, the maximum inventory level fluctuates to reflect the demand experienced in the preceding lead time. The reorder cycle times also vary responding to the demand rate during the previous cycle.

In the above systems it was assumed that the supply lead time was smaller than the reorder cycle time ($L < t$). Whenever the opposite is true, the decision rule must be modified (see Fig. 14-6).

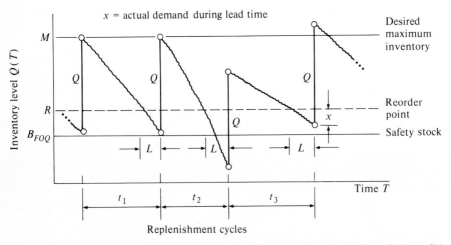

Fig. 14-5 **Inventory fluctuations for a fixed-order-quantity system operating under realistic conditions with $L < t$.**

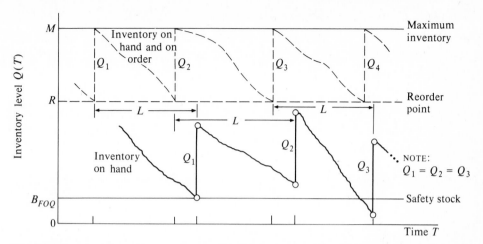

Fig. 14-6 Inventory fluctuations in a fixed-order-quantity system with lead time exceeding the reorder cycle time $L > t$.

Decision Rule B

In a fixed-order-quantity system with lead time longer than the reorder cycle time $(L > t)$ an order of a fixed amount Q is placed when the amount of inventory on hand plus the amount(s) ordered but not yet received reach the reorder point R.

In the FOQ system, where an order is triggered when the inventory level reaches a reorder point, it is essential to maintain a perpetual inventory record.[1] This requirement for high visibility of inventory levels can be handled by maintaining inventory status cards. As the number of items handled may reach several thousand, the need for electronic data processing becomes imperative.

A rather widely used approach for maintaining the equivalent of a perpetual inventory record is the so-called *two-bin system*. Here each item is segregated in a container with two bins. Demand is met from the first bin until its contents are depleted. This corresponds to reaching the reorder point, at which time an order for a fixed amount is placed. Further demand is met from units in the second bin, which contains enough to cover average demand during the lead time plus the safety stock. When the quantity ordered arrives, it is used to bring the amount in the second bin up to the reorder point and the balance is then placed in the first bin. The two-bin system in practice has turned out to be an effective and economical method, especially in organizations where it is not feasible to convert to computerized inventory control.

---

[1] This is the reason this system is sometimes called the *perpetual inventory system* or *continuous-review system*.

Recommended Applications

The FOQ system is widely used in practice, even though it seems to be the most demanding and expensive from the point of view of record keeping. It is primarily recommended for:

1. Items of low value per unit, i.e., class C goods. The rationale here is to allow for inventory to drop to a level that would result in large enough order to make replenishment worthwhile. For items of the "nuts and bolts" variety the comparatively low total value invested in inventory makes it feasible to maintain larger amounts of stock.
2. Items of high visibility for which it is easy and inexpensive to maintain a perpetual inventory record.

Limitations and Disadvantages

One of the major objections to the continuous review system occurs when a large number of items in stock are ordered from the same supplier. The order point here is usually reached at different times for each item. As a result, too many different orders are placed with the same supplier, resulting in higher ordering, packing, and shipping costs than if they were grouped.

A second difficulty is related to the system's orientation. A FOQ system is usually geared to handle the demand placed by the next stage downstream. The time lags present as each stage places orders to the next one upstream have the tendency to produce objectionable oscillations of inventory levels that increase as we proceed upstream. This creates considerable instability that interferes with a smooth and economic operation.

The Need for Proper Maintenance

When the orders placed by a FOQ system are large, they are likely to be infrequent. It is possible under such conditions for significant changes in demand to take place between successive orders. These changes are not reflected in the lot size Q.

If demand has increased, this leads to increased ordering costs since the order point is now reached faster. Holding costs depend on the lot size and will remain the same, but now there is a greater probability of shortages, since the maximum reasonable demand during lead time has also increased. A decrease in demand will have the opposite effect, i.e., reduced ordering and shortage costs, but increased holding costs. This is due to the larger cycle and buffer inventories present for the same risk level as before.

To permit the inventory system to function with the same degree of control in the presence of changing demand, it is necessary to perform periodic reviews of requirements, that is, current demand. The more frequent the reviews the higher the responsiveness of the system. *In practice, it is best to carry out reviews of current requirements with the same frequency of preparing short-term forecasts.* Therefore, tieing the review procedure to a moving average or, preferably, an exponential forecasting system provides an effective control over changes in demand.

The above must be combined with periodic reviews of the cost estimates, so that the order quantity reflects the current operating conditions. Without such maintenance and in the presence of a dynamic environment, the inventory-management system cannot exercise adequate control and is likely to degenerate into a costly and highly erratic operation.

▶ EXAMPLE 14-1

A manufacturing company requires a component at the annual average rate $\bar{D}$ of 1,000 units. Placing an order costs \$48 and has a 5-day lead time. Inventory holding cost is estimated at \$15 per unit per year. The plant operates 250 days/yr. It is assumed that daily demand is normally distributed with an average of $1,000/250 = 4$ units and a standard deviation of 1.2 units. Even though annual demand in this case is probabilistic, it is approximated by its expected or average value.

It has been decided to use a FOQ inventory system for the above item based on a 95 percent service level. For such a system an inventory policy is specified by calculating a reorder point (when to order) and the size of the fixed order (how much to order). In symbols

$$\bar{D} = 1,000 \text{ units/yr} = 4 \text{ units/day}$$

$$s_D = 1.2 \text{ units/day}$$

$$L = 5 \text{ days}$$

$$c_H = \$15/\text{unit per year}$$

$$c_R = \$48/\text{order}$$

$$\alpha = 5\% \ (95\% \text{ service level})$$

Calculation of Reorder Point R

For a FOQ system the reorder point corresponds to the maximum reasonable demand during the lead time at the specified service level. Thus,

$$R = x_{\max} = \bar{x} + z_\alpha s_x$$

where $\bar{x} = \bar{D} \cdot L = (4)(5) = 20$ units = average lead-time demand

$z_\alpha = z_{.05} = 1.645$ = number of standard deviations from mean for 95% service level

s_x = standard deviation of demand during lead time

If we assume that daily demands are independent, the variance of lead-time demand x will be the sum of five daily demand variances

$$s_x^2 = 5s_D^2 = 5(1.2)^2 = 7.2$$

Therefore
$$s_x = \sqrt{7.2} = 2.683 \text{ units}$$

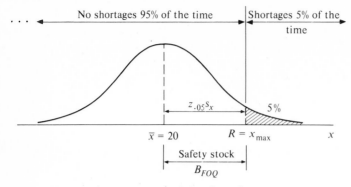

Fig. 14-7   Normal distribution for lead-time demand x.

From the above we conclude that demand during lead time is normally distributed, as shown in Fig. 14-7. Thus,

$$\text{Reorder point } R = x_{\text{max}} = \bar{x} + z_{.05} s_x$$

$$= 20 + (1.645)(2.683) = 20 + 4.41$$

$$\approx 25 \text{ units}$$

From this we have

$$B_{FOQ} = x_{\text{max}} - \bar{x} = 25 - 20 = 5 \text{ units} \qquad \text{Safety stock}$$

In the absence of any safety stock, the system would experience shortages 50 percent of the time.

Calculation of the Fixed Order Quantity Q_o

Using the EOQ model, we obtain the fixed order quantity as follows:

$$Q_o = \sqrt{\frac{2c_R \bar{D}}{c_H}} = \sqrt{\frac{2(48)(1,000)}{15}} = \sqrt{6,400} = 80 \text{ units}$$

This value of Q_o from a model assuming that demand is exactly known is in practice a good approximation because the total inventory cost is not sensitive to deviations of Q around its optimal value; i.e., the TIC curve is quite flat around Q_o. Thus, random fluctuations of annual demand around its mean value $\bar{D} = 1,000$ would not affect inventory costs significantly. The derivation of Q_o by more precise methods is mathematically quite advanced and beyond our scope.

The inventory system will thus operate by placing an order for 80 units when inventory on hand reaches the reorder point of 25 units. At that level there is a buffer of 5 units to protect against stockouts ($x > R$) during the lead time of 5 days. Figure 14-8 shows the fluctuations of the inventory level.

For $Q_o = 80$ there will be an average of $1,000/80 = 12.5$ orders per year (operating cycles). The 95 percent service level would allow shortages to occur 5 percent of the time, or a little more than once every 2 yr $[(12.5)(.05) = .625$ per year, or 1.25

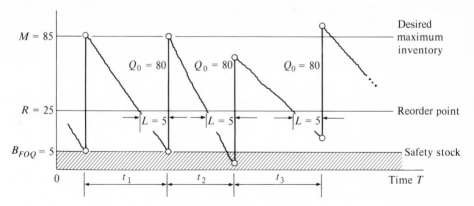

Fig. 14-8   Typical operation of the FOQ system for Example 14-1.

every 2 yr]. Under such conditions, the cost of operating the inventory system will be determined approximately (no stockout costs are included) as follows:

Cost	Cost per year
Holding: $c_H\left(\dfrac{Q_o}{2} + B_{FOQ}\right) = (15)\left(\dfrac{80}{2} + 5\right)$	\$675
Ordering: $c_R\dfrac{D}{Q_o} = (\$48)\dfrac{1,000}{80}$	\$ 600
Total inventory cost	\$1,275

In the absence of uncertainty in demand the holding cost would be equal to $c_H Q_o/2 = (\$15)(80/2) = \$600$, since there would be no need for safety stock. Because in this case demand is probabilistic, there is a cost of uncertainty. This is the extra holding cost for the safety stock, or $(\$15)(5) = \$75$ per year. In setting the service level at 95 percent, management feels that this extra cost more than offsets the expected cost of stockouts avoided with the additional 5 units.

14-4   THE FIXED-ORDER-INTERVAL (PERIODIC-REVIEW) SYSTEM

Instead of ordering a fixed amount at variable time intervals it is possible to operate an inventory system in the opposite way. The system in such a case is known as a fixed-order-interval (FOI) or periodic-review system. In a fixed-interval system orders of variable size are placed at fixed time intervals, i.e., biweekly, monthly, etc. The size of the order depends on the demand rate in the preceding period and is such as to bring the inventory level up to a desired maximum level M.

Decision Rule A

When lead time is less than review time, $L < t$,

$$Q_i = M - Q(T_i)$$

or

$$\begin{bmatrix} \text{Amount ordered} \\ \text{at review time} \end{bmatrix} = \begin{bmatrix} \text{maximum} \\ \text{desired inventory} \end{bmatrix} - \begin{bmatrix} \text{inventory on hand} \\ \text{at review time} \end{bmatrix}$$

The decision variables of interest here are the fixed interval between successive orders t and the maximum inventory level. However, instead of seeking to determine the optimal reorder period (such as $t_o = Q_o/D$) from an EOQ formula, management may specify an ordering interval based on more practical considerations.

Review periods to determine current inventory levels are usually planned for groups of items, e.g., those from the same supplier or having some other common characteristic. This makes ordering possible in such a way that advantage can be taken of lower rates for shipping and easier packaging and handling.

At times practical factors such as convenience of review, supplier's policies, or time required to carry out the process of physical counting may be quite influential in arriving at the ordering interval. Thus, the main decision variable for minimizing inventory costs is the maximum desired inventory M. In general, M must be enough to cover average demand during a planning period equal to $t + L$ and also protect against stockouts at the specified service level.

Mode of Operation

For constant demand rate and lead time the period-review system would be the same as the continuous review. Variability in demand only, however, results in the type of operation shown in Fig. 14-9, which assumes that the constant lead time is shorter than the recorder (or review) cycle time ($L < t$). Let $O(T_i)$ represent inventory ordered but not received at time T_i. Then we have

---

Decision Rule B

For a fixed interval system in which the lead time is longer than the review period ($L > t$),

$$Q_i = M - [Q(T_i) + O(T_i)]$$

or

$$\begin{bmatrix} \text{Amount ordered} \\ \text{at review time} \end{bmatrix} = \begin{bmatrix} \text{maximum desired} \\ \text{inventory} \end{bmatrix} - \left(\begin{bmatrix} \text{inventory on hand} \\ \text{at review time} \end{bmatrix} + \begin{bmatrix} \text{inventory ordered} \\ \text{but not received} \end{bmatrix} \right)$$

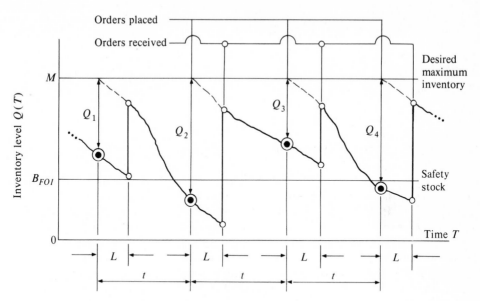

Fig. 14-9 **Inventory-level fluctuations for a fixed-order-interval system $L < t$.**

With regard to buffer stock, the periodic-review system must carry enough extra inventory beyond normal requirements to cover maximum reasonable demand not just during the lead time but during an interval equal to the sum of the lead time and a review period, $t + L$.

Let y = demand during planning period $t + L$
y_{max} = maximum reasonable demand during planning period

Then
$$M = y_{max} = \bar{y} + z_\alpha s_y$$

where $\bar{y} = \bar{D}(t + L)$ = average demand during $t + L$
s_y = standard deviation of demand during $t + L$
z_α = number of standard deviations from mean $\bar{y}$ for $1 - \alpha$ service level.

From this it follows that the FOI-system safety stock will be

$$B_{FOI} = y_{max} - \bar{y} = z_\alpha s_y \qquad (14\text{-}6)$$

These relationships are shown in Fig. 14-10.

Recommended Applications

The FOI system is also widely used in actual applications, especially when:

1. The majority of items held in stock are ordered from one or a few suppliers. In this case orders can be grouped according to supplier in order to take advantage of lower shipping rates and handling costs.

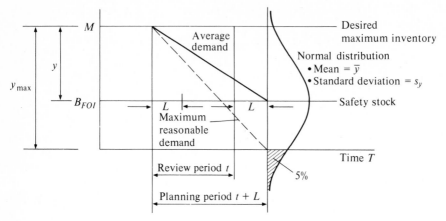

Fig. 14-10   Determination of safety stock in FOI inventory system.

2. The items in stock have a high activity or a high total value. These are class A items, for which it is necessary to maintain tight control. The high responsiveness of the periodic-review system to demand changes makes it very effective for this category.
3. The inventory levels have very low visibility; i.e., it is difficult to keep perpetual inventory records for them. In this case, a convenient review period is determined and the necessary physical count takes place.

The clerical costs in this system are lower than in the FOQ type, except where the switch to computerized data processing is required, in which case this comparative advantage is diminished. With automatic data processing the required periodic reviews are made on the basis of perpetual inventory records. The frequency of such review depends, among other things, on the incremental cost of making the reviews.

Limitations and Disadvantages

An important disadvantage of the FOI system is the higher operating cost due to larger safety stocks and periodic reviews. The requirements for buffer stocks here are greater because the system is vulnerable to extreme fluctuations in demand during an interval equal to the review period and the next lead time $(L + t)$.

A second objection to the periodic-review system is the tendency by those responsible for its operation to outguess changes in the demand rate. Like the continuous-review system, this one also operates to meet the demand of the next stage downstream. As a result of the information time lags and the temptation to interpret random demand fluctuations as genuine trends, the periodic-review system is likely to experience oscillations in the inventory levels that lead to considerable instability. The proper course of action in this case is to leave the system alone and allow such random fluctuations in demand to be absorbed by the safety stocks.

The unwarranted intervention of operations managers with a manual system tends to neutralize the effectiveness of an otherwise well-designed inventory-control system. This is generally avoided with automatic data processing, which tends to treat random as well as genuine changes in demand levels with a rational approach.

The Need for Proper Maintenance

The FOI system also requires periodic reviews of demand rates and unit-cost estimates for holding and ordering inventory as well as shortages. Such reassessments may result in revising the reorder cycle time t and the desired maximum inventory M.

However, by virtue of its mode of operation the FOI system provides more frequent information of shifts in demand rates, since it constantly responds to the direct demand experienced in the preceding period.

▶ EXAMPLE 14-2

Suppose that the company in Example 14-1 recognizes that several components are also ordered from the same supplier and decides to employ a FOI system. Using the data for the company of Example 14-1, it is desired to formulate a periodic-review inventory policy. This involves specifying the review period (when to order) and the desired maximum inventory level, which indirectly determines the order quantity (how much to order).

Repeating for convenience the data of Example 14-1 in symbols, we have

$$\bar{D} = 1,000 \text{ units/yr} = 4 \text{ units/day}$$

$$s_D = 1.2 \text{ units/day}$$

$$L = 5 \text{ days}$$

$$c_H = \$15/\text{unit per year}$$

$$c_R = \$48/\text{order}$$

$$\alpha = 5\% \ (95\% \text{ service level})$$

Calculation of Review Period t

The length of the review period corresponding to the economic order quantity is

$$t_o = \frac{Q_o}{D} \quad \text{where} \quad Q_o = \sqrt{\frac{2c_R \bar{D}}{c_H}}$$

Thus
$$t_o = \sqrt{\frac{2c_R}{c_H \bar{D}}} = \sqrt{\frac{2(48)}{15(1,000)}} = 0.08 \text{ yr}$$

$$= (0.08 \text{ yr})(250 \text{ days/yr}) = 20 \text{ days}$$

This result means that management should review the inventory level every 20 working days. Again, for a probabilistic demand this is just an approximation, useful in practice, which avoids the complex mathematics of accounting for shortage costs explicitly.

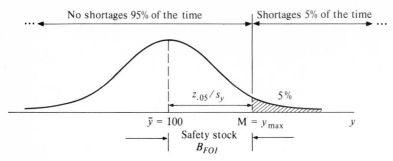

Fig. 14-11   Normal distribution for demand y during the planning period.

In the description of the FOI inventory system it was stated that the desired maximum level M must be enough to cover average demand during a planning period equal to $t + L$ and also protect against stockouts at the specified service level.

For a review period equal to 20 days and a lead time of 5 days the average demand is

$$\bar{y} = \bar{D}(t + L) = (4)(20 + 5) = 100 \text{ units}$$

The standard deviation s_y is calculated with the same method as used in Example 14-1. Thus,

$$s_y^2 = 25s_D^2 = 25(1.2)^2 = 36 \quad \text{and} \quad s_y = \sqrt{36} = 6 \text{ units}$$

Demand during the planning period $t + L$ is normally distributed,[1] as shown in Fig. 14-11.

For a service level of 95 percent the desired maximum inventory will be

$$M = y_{\max} = \bar{y} + z_{.05}s_y$$

$$= 100 + (1.645)(6) = 100 + 9.87$$

$$\approx 110 \text{ units}$$

The safety stock that will provide the desired protection against stockouts will be

$$B_{FOI} = y_{\max} - \bar{y} = 110 - 100 = 10 \text{ units}$$

According to the above specification of the inventory policy, the FOI system will operate as follows. Management will review the inventory level $Q(T_i)$ for the component every 20 days ($t = 20$). The size of the order placed at time T_i ($T_i = 0, t,$ $2t, 3t, \ldots$) will be equal to

$$Q_i = M - Q(T_i) = 110 - Q(T_i) \qquad T_i = 0, 20, 40, \ldots, \text{days}$$

---

[1] Demand during the planning period is the sum of $t + L$ daily demands. Therefore, it is following a normal distribution exactly or approximately, depending on whether daily demand follows the normal or other distribution.

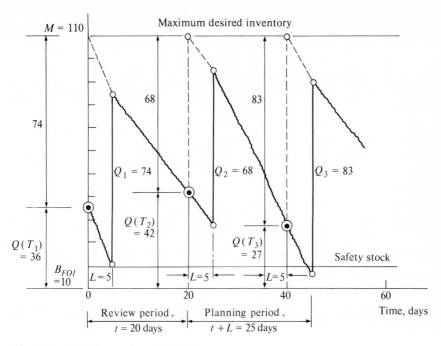

Fig. 14-12 Typical operation of a FOI inventory system.

This amount will be added to stock 5 days later $(T_i + 5)$. In Fig. 14-12, in the first review $(T_1 = 0)$ the inventory level was 36 units. The order quantity Q_1 must be equal to $110 - 36 = 74$ and will be added 5 days later $(T = 5)$. On the second review $(T_2 = 20)$ the inventory level is 42, so the order quantity will be 68 units and will be added 5 days later $(T = 25)$ and so on.

In comparing the FOI and FOQ systems of Examples 14-1 and 14-2 using the same data, we note that the FOI must maintain a larger buffer stock than the FOQ (10 versus 5). The cost of operating this FOI system will be determined approximately (no stockout costs are included) as follows:

	Annual cost
Holding: $c_H \dfrac{M - B_{FOI}}{2} = (\$15)\dfrac{110 - 10}{2}$	\$ 900
Ordering: $c_R \dfrac{D}{Q_o} = (\$48)\dfrac{1,000}{80}$	\$ 600
Total inventory cost	$\overline{\$1,500}$

In this case the cost of uncertainty due to probabilistic demand is equal to

1,500 − 1,200 = 300 per year.[1] The difference in the cost of uncertainty between the FOI and the FOQ system (300 − 75 = 225) is due to the need for a larger buffer stock to protect the system against shortages over a longer period of time (25 versus 5 days).

▶

14-5 THE BASE-STOCK (OPTIONAL-REPLENISHMENT) SYSTEM

We have seen that both the continuous-review and periodic-review systems have distinctive advantages and limitations. It is desirable in practice to combine these advantages with as few of the limitations as possible. This has been accomplished to a considerable extent with a third type known as the base-stock,[2] or optional-replenishment (OR), inventory-management system. In such a system both the order quantity and the time between successive orders may be variable.

Decision Rule A

The inventory on hand is reviewed at fixed time intervals t. If the inventory level is at or below a reorder point R, an order is placed to bring the inventory up to a desired maximum level M. If the inventory is above the reorder point, the replenishment decision is postponed for the next review using the same rules.

---

[1] In the absence of uncertainty the total incremental inventory cost per year is

$$\text{TIC} = c_H \frac{Q}{2} + c_R \frac{D}{Q} = (\$15)\frac{80}{2} + (\$48)\frac{1,000}{80} = 600 + 600 = \$1,200/\text{yr}$$

[2] In the literature it is also referred to as an (S, s) system, where $S = M$ and $s = R$.

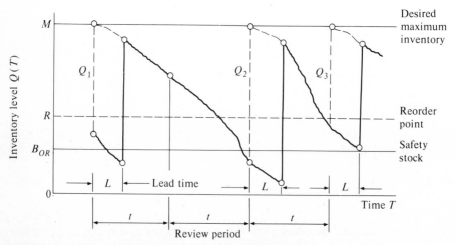

Fig. 14-13   Inventory-level fluctuations for a base-stock (OR) system $1 < t$.

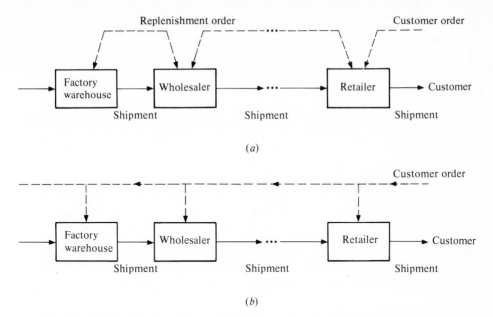

Fig. 14-14   Comparison of information and shipment flows in the (*a*) FOQ and FOI and (*b*) OR systems.

Mode of Operation

The operation of a base-stock system is shown in Fig. 14-13. Here we wish to determine three decision variables, i.e., the maximum M and minimum R inventory desired and the time between reviews t. The comparison of information and shipment flows in the FOQ, FOI, and OR systems is shown in Fig. 14-14.

It has been assumed so far that the lead time is shorter than the review period ($L < t$).

Decision Rule B

If the lead time is longer than the review period, the decision rule is adjusted so that an order is placed at review time when the inventory on hand plus the amount on order is at or below the reorder point R.

The buffer stock desired for this inventory system must provide protection for a time interval equal to $t/2 + L$. Thus,

$$B_{OR} = (D_{max} - \bar{D})\left(\frac{t}{2} + L\right) = z_\alpha s_D \sqrt{\frac{t}{2} + L} \qquad (14\text{-}7)$$

The maximum desired (or base stock) level at each stage of the production-distribution chain is determined on the basis of (1) the maximum demand for the item during the lead time for that stage and (2) the minimum amount that is to be ordered for that item (computed from an EOQ formula). The maximum demand during the lead time is based on customer orders that are reported to all stages, either as they occur or periodically. In the latter case the base stock must be adjusted to cover maximum demand during the lead time plus the time between reporting of customer demands (see Ref. 8).

Recommended Applications

The OR system is appropriate when tight control is necessary, e.g., for class A items. By relying on a reorder point it triggers action for replenishment when the order quantity is at least of the minimum desirable size. Because of the use of a reorder point, the OR system requires less safety stock than the periodic-review system.

Through regular reviews at fixed intervals the base-stock system displays a high degree of responsiveness to changes in the demand rate and inventory levels like the periodic-review system. Furthermore, by operating against customer demand rather than that of the next stage, the OR system avoids the time lags in the flow of information that result in objectionable inventory-level fluctuations and instability.

Limitations and Disadvantages

The use of the OR system in actual applications to date is somewhat limited compared with the other two basic types. One of the difficulties stems from the complex analysis required to determine the values for the decision variables of maximum M and minimum R inventories. Due to the different structure of the information system, the base-stock system is also more demanding in terms of the quantity and frequency of information required.

Need for Proper Maintenance

The importance of periodic evaluation of the system's cost parameters and reviews of any changes in demand rates is as great for the OR system as it is for the others. The additional investment for a more elaborate information system makes the need for proper maintenance imperative.

The operating aspects of all three basic inventory-management systems are summarized for comparison in Table 14-3.

14-6 MATERIAL-REQUIREMENTS PLANNING

General

The preceding inventory-management systems are designed for items with independent demand. These are end items, i.e., finished products, whose demand is estimated by some forecasting technique. Independent demand reflects the market's response to a firm's final output.

TABLE 14-3 Summary of operating characteristics of basic inventory systems ($L < t$)†

Characteristic		System: Fixed order quantity (FOQ)	Fixed order interval (FOI)	Optional replenishment (OR)
Decision rule	When to order?	When inventory on hand reaches reorder point $$Q(T) = R$$	At fixed time intervals equal to review period $$t_o = \frac{\bar{D}}{Q_o}$$	Inspect at fixed intervals and order if inventory on hand is at or below reorder point $$Q(T) \le R \qquad T = 0, t, 2t, \ldots$$
	How much to order?	A fixed quantity to cover normal requirements during average reorder cycle $$Q_o = \bar{D}t = \sqrt{\frac{2c_R \bar{D}}{c_H}}$$	Order enough to bring inventory level to desired maximum $$Q_i = M - Q(T_i)$$ $$T_i = 0, t_o, 2t_o, \ldots$$	Order enough to bring inventory level to desired maximum $$Q_j = M - Q(T_j)$$ $$T_j = \text{integer multiple of } t$$
Maximum inventory		Sum of normal requirements during average reorder cycle plus safety stock $$M = Q_o + B_{FOQ}$$	Sum of normal requirements during planning period $t + L$ plus safety stock $$M = \bar{D}(t + L) + B_{FOI}$$	Sum of normal requirements during $t/2 + L$ plus safety stock $$M = \bar{D}\left(\frac{t}{2} + L\right) + B_{OR}$$
Minimum inventory		Safety stock B_{FOQ}	Safety stock B_{FOI}	Safety stock B_{OR}
Average inventory		$$\frac{Q_o}{2} + B_{FOQ}$$	$$\frac{M - B_{FOI}}{2} + B_{FOI}$$	$$\frac{M - B_{OR}}{2} + B_{OR}$$
Safety stock (for service level $1 - \alpha$)		Maximum reasonable demand minus normal requirements during lead time $x_{max} - \bar{x}$ $$B_{FOQ} = z_\alpha s_x = z_\alpha s_D \sqrt{L}$$	Maximum reasonable demand minus normal requirements during planning period $y_{max} - \bar{y}$ $$B_{FOI} = z_\alpha s_y = z_\alpha s_D \sqrt{t + L}$$	Maximum reasonable demand minus normal requirements during $t/2 + L$ $$B_{OR} = z_\alpha s_D \sqrt{\frac{t}{2} + L}$$

† For systems with $L > t$ substitute "inventory on hand" above by "inventory on hand and on order."

For some organizations a finished product is assembled from several parts and subassemblies. Other products are made by mixing or blending several ingredients. Given a production plan for such an end item, the requirements for parts can be determined exactly. Demand for a finished product is generally uncertain. Its estimation often involves a statistical forecasting approach. The demand for components and parts, however, can be calculated with certainty. Consequently, safety stocks are not required as they would be for the finished product. In short, demand for components needed to produce a finished product is dependent, i.e., derived from the technology used within the organization. This realization has led to an alternative approach for managing inventories for dependent demand items known as *material-requirements planning* (MRP).

Definition

Material-requirements planning (MRP) is a method which, starting with a forecast for the independent demand of a finished product, determines the dependent, or derived, demand for (1) the kinds of components (materials, parts, or ingredients) needed, (2) the exact quantities required, and (3) the time phasing of the above orders to satisfy a production plan.

With MRP the emphasis is more on when-to-order than on the how-much-to-order aspect of the problem. In this sense, MRP might be viewed more as a scheduling than as an inventory-management technique. For items with dependent demand, inventories are held to support production schedules. The paramount problem in their management is not monitoring their inventory levels but ensuring their availability in desired quantities at the proper time and at the right place.

As an illustration consider the case of a TV manufacturing company. Here demand for finished sets is subject to random variations and is independent. Having a period-by-period estimate of demand for such TV sets, the requirements for chassis, cathode-ray tubes, printed circuits, transistors, knobs, etc., can be determined exactly given the product design, supply lead times, scrap losses, and the like. The amounts and time phasing for these components constitute the dependent demand.

MRP Operating System

Stripped of its technical jargon, MRP is quite simple. Early applications can be traced to construction projects as far back as Roman times. However, its use with today's complex products requires large-scale computers to handle the tremendous number of components at various levels of detail. The basic logic of MRP is outlined in Fig. 14-15 in the form it would be used for a computer application.

MRP inputs   MRP processing   MRP outputs

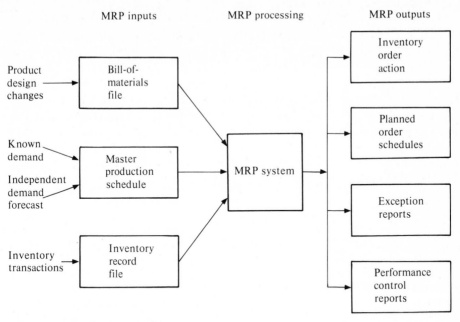

Fig. 14-15 MRP system description.

MRP Inputs

In order to run an MRP program, a company must provide three key inputs:

1. A master production schedule
2. A bill-of-materials file
3. An inventory-records file

The *master production schedule* specifies what end item is to be produced, when, and in what amounts. For each time period in the planning horizon management must specify the total demand for each end item. This usually consists of two parts, an amount determined by orders received from known customers and an estimate of the uncertain demand for the period, obtained by statistical forecasting. It is the latter we refer to as independent demand, subject to random variations, and managed by one of the inventory systems (FOQ, FOI, or OR) described previously.

A proposed master production schedule, like that in Table 14-4, is assumed to be feasible. In other words, before it can be employed by the MRP system, it is assumed to satisfy constraints on productive capacity. Such a schedule is obtained by trial and error, and it may be adjusted before or after it is run if it violates existing capacity restrictions.

TABLE 14-4   A master production schedule for end item A

Week number	1	2	3	4	5	6	7	8
Requirements		60		40	20		80	50

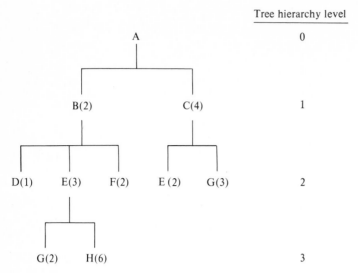

Fig. 14-16   Tree representation of product structure for end item A.

The *bill of materials file* is a "recipe" of how a finished product is made from raw materials, parts, or purchased components. The product structure can be graphically described by a tree like that in Fig. 14-16. Note that product A, the end item (level 0 in the tree hierarchy), is made of two subassemblies B and four subassemblies C (level 1). Each subassembly B consists of one part D, three parts E, and two parts F (level 2). Similarly, each subassembly C consists of two parts E and three parts G (also level 2), and so on. Since the same part may be used for subassemblies at different levels, it is more efficient for a computer to operate with a single-level explosion. Accordingly, each component is listed showing only its parent and the number of units required for each parent unit (see Fig. 14-17). When all identical components are listed at the same level for each end item, the computer can easily scan across each level and total the number of units required for each item.

The *inventory-records file* covers each item separately, indicating its inventory status on a period-by-period basis. It also includes many other details about the item, i.e., supplier, lead time, lot size, etc. Any changes due to stock removal or receipt, canceled orders, scrap losses, etc., are posted in an inventory-transaction file.

MRP Processing

Given a feasible master production schedule for a specific end item, the next step is to translate the period-by-period demand into requirements for subassemblies, parts, and materials needed to make it. This translation is performed with the bill-of-materials file. Once *total requirements* for components and parts are calculated from the master production schedule and the bill-of-materials file, **MRP** proceeds to determine the *net requirements* in conjunction with the inventory-records file.

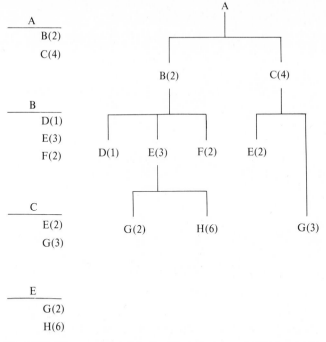

Fig. 14-17 Tree representation of product structure and bill-of-materials list for single-level explosion.

For each period MRP determines the amount needed for each part, exploding requirements level by level. By referring to the inventory file, the total requirement for an item in that period is reduced by the amount on hand to arrive at *net requirements*. Based on production lead times, net requirements for the item are set back in time so that they will be available when needed. The inventory-status file is then updated by posting inventory changes due to stock removals, receipts, cancellations, and scrap losses.

The inventory-record file in MRP generally does not specify safety-stock levels for items with dependent demand. Some practitioners, however, feel that random variations in production lead times, scrap losses, and breakdown rates may call for buffer stocks to absorb them. Often, however, such adjustments are handled with overplanning, i.e., overstating requirements, lead times, or other features.

Relying on economic order quantities or lot sizes in MRP is considered practical only for items at the lower levels of the product structure (raw materials, nuts and bolts, transistors, and the like). As we move to higher levels, i.e., subassemblies, the use of lot sizes exaggerates the demand for the lower-level items.

MRP Outputs

The most important output of the MRP program consists of reports for production and inventory control. These are known as primary reports, in contrast to the secondary types, which are optional and are designed to aid management in planning and performance control.

Primary reports include schedules of planned orders, changes in due dates, cancellations or suspensions of open orders, and inventory-status data. *Secondary reports* consist of planning reports to specify future requirements, performance reports to pinpoint variances between plans and actual performance, and exception reports focusing on problem areas (late orders, excessive scrap, etc.).

Most of the companies that use MRP run their programs to obtain the above outputs once a week or biweekly. Each time the master scheduler (an individual) follows an iterative procedure until the primary reports are feasible with available productive capacity.

The ultimate value of the MRP outputs depends on the accuracy of the three key inputs, the master production schedule, the bill-of-materials file, and the inventory-records file. For example, inaccuracies in the bill of materials may be due to an unaccounted product design change. In the inventory-record file inaccuracies can be traced to unreported stock removals or receipts. Similarly, a master production schedule may fail to report order delays, cancellations, or new orders received. Unless management can control such sources of errors, the usefulness of the MRP output can be no better than the quality of input information.[1]

▶ EXAMPLE 14-3 AN ILLUSTRATION OF MRP

Speedex, Inc., a sports-equipment company, specializes in skateboards of the type shown in Fig. 14-18a. The product-structure tree for a skateboard is given in Fig. 14-18b. For the next 10 weeks management has developed estimates of demand based on firm contract sales and random independent demand, as shown in Table 14-5.

To release a planned order for production of skateboards in a given period, all required parts and subassemblies must be available in that period. Therefore, the planned-order release date for the parent unit becomes the due date for the gross requirements of its components. Using a MRP system in this example would provide a production schedule identifying each kind of component needed, the period in which it is required, and the appropriate quantities for each item. If such a production schedule violated some capacity restriction, there would be a manual

---

[1] For a more detailed treatment of MRP see Refs. 11 and 15.

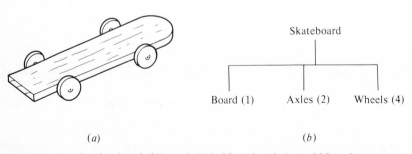

Skateboard

Board (1)   Axles (2)   Wheels (4)

(a)   (b)

Fig. 14-18   Speedex skateboard of Example 14-3: (a) product design and (b) product-structure tree representation.

TABLE 14-5 Anticipated sales of Speedex skateboards

					Week number					
1	2	3	4	5	6	7	8	9	10
Firm contract sales		180			210		130		190
Independent demand		120			120		120		120
Total requirements		300			330		250		310

adjustment until it became feasible. The proper time phasing of established requirements is performed on the basis of the lead time for each component.

For the Speedex skateboard example, the development of the master schedule for parts and components is illustrated with the help of Table 14-6. We assume that the inventory on hand in week 1 is 60 boards, 100 axles, and 200 wheels.

The demand for 300 skateboards in week 3 can be met if in the same period we have available the component requirements, i.e., 300 boards, 600 axles, and 1,200 wheels. Since the inventory on hand for boards in week 3 is 60, carried over from week 1, the net requirement for this part is 240. However, boards are produced in lot sizes of 700. In order to be available in week 3 with a lead time of 1 wk, they must be produced in week 2. Hence, we need a planned-order release in week 2 for 700 boards, 240 of which are required in week 3. The balance of 460 units is carried in stock and in week 6 another 330 are removed to meet the demand for 330 skateboards in the same period. This leaves an inventory on hand of 130 units, which must be replenished with another planned-order release in week 7 to satisfy the demand for end items in week 8.

Using similar analysis, we arrive at the time phasing and quantities for planned orders of axles and wheels. For these items the table also includes additional quantities, indicated by a dagger, required for other products of Speedex, Inc. The production schedules for components to satisfy the given demand for end items are summarized in Table 14-7. To repeat, this schedule is checked for feasibility and adjusted manually as necessary. In our example, the wheel assembly could be further exploded into bearings, lug nuts, pins, etc. The minimization of costs in MRP is not as explicit in the phases indicated but has been calculated in the stage of determining lot sizes.

Comparison of Traditional Inventory Systems and MRP

To appreciate the differences between inventory systems for dependent and independent demand, Table 14-8 has been constructed to show the contrast in the most relevant characteristics. A variety of computer programs is available to handle both dependent and independent demand inventory systems.[1]

---

[1] For a list of commercially available computer packages for inventory systems see N. Paul Loomba, *Management—A Quantitative Perspective*, Macmillan, 1978, p. 387.

TABLE 14-6 MRP schedules for skateboards and components

Master schedule for skateboards

Week number	1	2	3	4	5	6	7	8	9	10
Requirements			300			330		250		310

Component MRP schedule

Boards: L = 1 wk, Lot size = 700 units

Week number	1	2	3	4	5	6	7	8	9	10
Gross requirements			300			330		250		310
On hand	60	60	60	460	460	460	130	130	580	580
Net requirements			240			(−130)		120		(−270)
Scheduled receipts			700					700		
Planned order release		700					700			

Axles: L = 1 wk, Lot size = 800 units

Week number	1	2	3	4	5	6	7	8	9	10
Gross requirements			600		280†	660		500		620
On hand	100	100	100	300	300	20	160	160	460	460
Net requirements			500		20	640		340		160
Scheduled receipts			800			800		800		800
Planned order release		800			800		800		800	

Wheels: L = 2 wk, Lot size = 3,000 units

Week number	1	2	3	4	5	6	7	8	9	10
Gross requirements			1,200		540†	1,320		1,000		1,240
On hand	200	200	200	2,000	2,000	1,460	140	140	2,140	2,140
Net requirements			1,000		1,460	(−140)		860		(−900)
Scheduled receipts			3,000					3,000		
Planned order release	3,000					3,000				

† Refer to requirements for other products.

586

TABLE 14-7 Production schedules for MRP planned orders for Speedex skateboards

	Planned-order release			
Week no.	Skateboards	Boards	Axles	Wheels
1	—	—	—	3,000
2	—	700	800	—
3	300	—	—	—
4	—	—	—	—
5	—	—	800	—
6	330	—	—	3,000
7	—	700	800	—
8	250	—	—	800
9	—	—	800	—
10	310	—	—	—

▶

TABLE 14-8 Inventory systems for independent and dependent demand

Characteristic	Independent demand	Dependent demand
Items handled	Finished product(s)	Materials, parts, components, ingredients
Determination of demand	Statistical forecasting	Bill of materials
Nature of demand	Random	Predetermined (or derived)
Time distribution of demand	Dispersed	Lumpy
Special features or requirements: Inventory	Total inventory costs rather insensitive to small errors in estimation of demand and unit costs	Need for accuracy in master schedule, bill of materials, and inventory files
Safety stocks	Needed to absorb random fluctuations in demand	Indirect buildup and use of safety stocks for randomness in delivery times and scrap losses through overplanning
Lot sizes	To minimize setup and holding costs	Limited use for lower-level items

14-6 SUMMARY

In approaching the design of real inventory-management systems, one must tackle three important questions.

1. We must ask whether a given item the system will deal with has independent or dependent demand. If the item(s) under consideration are end items for the firm, their demand is shaped by the marketplace and is subject to uncertainty. Given a statistical forecast which specifies the demand level for the end item, the requirements for any materials, parts, or components needed to assemble the

final product can be determined exactly. Inventory problems for independent demand, i.e., end items, are handled with any one of the traditional inventory systems, the fixed-order quantity, fixed-interval, or optional-replenishment type. Items with dependent demand, i.e., materials, parts, and subassemblies, are most effectively controlled with material-requirements planning, which can be also viewed as a scheduling technique.

2. Management must determine the appropriate level of control for the hundreds or thousands of end items held in stock. This problem is usually resolved by ABC analysis. The objective here is to vary the degree of control on the basis of the value of a particular item. Such a value is established either by the size of investment required to keep an item in stock or by its criticalness in maintaining a smooth operation. The ABC analysis diagram identifies three classes of items requiring tight (A), intermediate (B), and loose (C) control procedures.

3. It is important to devise means of handling the random variability in certain aspects of the system. The dominant method for handling this problem is the use of safety stocks acting as a buffer against randomness, analogous to the shock absorbers in a car. For independent-demand items the safety-stock size can be determined from the statistical distribution of demand and/or lead time. For items with dependent demand, the random variability is not in the "how much" aspect but in production or delivery lead times and in scrap losses. Any safety stock maintained for such protection is normally determined indirectly, i.e., by overplanning. This means the calculation of requirements by allowing for longer lead times or higher scrap-loss rates.

Whatever the final form of an inventory-management system, it is of paramount importance to keep it updated so that it reflects actual operating conditions accurately. Lack of such maintenance results in a costly control procedure that deprives the system of the stability and effectiveness to meet demand smoothly and economically. Symptoms of instability include extreme fluctuations in inventory levels and production rates, along with considerable delays in meeting schedule deadlines and delivery dates.

NOTATION

D = actual demand rate
$\bar{D}$ = average demand rate
s_D = standard deviation of demand rate
Q = order quantity
t = reorder or review period
L = lead time
M = desired maximum inventory
R = reorder point
α = risk level for stockouts
$1 - \alpha$ = service level
z_α = number of standard deviations from the mean for $1 - \alpha$ service level
x = actual demand during lead time L
$\bar{x}$ = average demand during lead time L

x_{max} = maximum reasonable demand during lead time L
s_x = standard deviation of demand during lead time L
y = actual demand during planning period $t + L$
$\bar{y}$ = average demand during planning period $t + L$
y_{max} = maximum reasonable demand during planning period $t + L$
s_y = standard deviation of demand during planning period $t + L$
B_{FOQ} = safety stock in fixed-order-quantity system
B_{FOI} = safety stock in fixed-order-interval system
B_{OR} = safety stock in optional-replenishment system

REVIEW QUESTIONS

1. What factors complicate the design of a real inventory system?
2. What is the purpose of ABC analysis? How does it work?
3. What aspects of an inventory system are affected by different degrees of control?
4. Discuss some of the difficulties encountered in estimating inventory costs.
5. What aspects of an inventory system are subject to random variability?
6. Describe the procedure for the determination of safety stocks given the desired service level.
7. State the decision rule for the replenishment of a fixed-order-quantity (FOQ) inventory system. How is this rule modified when the lead time is longer than the reorder cycle period?
8. Discuss the cases where FOQ is recommended and indicate the major limitations and disadvantages.
9. State the decision rule for the replenishment of a fixed-order-interval (FOI) system. How is this rule modified when the lead time is longer than the reorder cycle period?
10. Discuss the cases where FOI is recommended and indicate the major limitations and disadvantages.
11. State the decision rule for the replenishment of a base-stock (OR) system. How is this rule modified when the lead time is longer than the review period?
12. Discuss the cases where OR is recommended and indicate the major limitations and disadvantages.
13. Describe the differences between dependent and independent demand.
14. What is the main output of a material-requirements planning system? How often is it usually made available?
15. How can inaccuracies develop in the application of MRP?
16. Discuss how random variability is handled in MRP and contrast it with the inventory systems used for independent demand.

PROBLEMS

1. The management of a small firm has decided to establish a new inventory-control system and has asked for a list showing the annual use and unit cost for each of the 12 items maintained in stock. The information obtained is as follows:

Item	Annual use	Unit cost	Item	Annual use	Unit cost
X-14	1,500	$1.80	Z-22	600	$2.90
X-16	2,800	1.40	Z-24	33,000	1.10
X-18	30,500	1.20	Z-26	1,200	2.05
Y-05	7,200	1.15	W-31	75,000	2.20
Y-07	5,100	1.60	W-35	21,000	1.50
Y-09	82,000	1.40	W-39	2,300	.40

(a) Calculate for each item the annual dollar use and prepare a list showing each item in order of its annual dollar weight.

(b) Starting with a list ranking the items by annual dollar use, determine in adjacent columns (i) the cumulative dollar use and (ii) the cumulative percentage of investment corresponding to (i).

(c) Using ABC analysis, group the items in classes A, B, and C and suggest the appropriate degree of control for each category.

2. The probability distribution for lead-time demand for an item has been estimated as shown:

Lead-time demand	60	61	62	63	64	65	66	67	68
Probability	.05	.15	.20	.20	.18	.12	.05	.04	.01

Determine the reorder point and safety stock for (a) 90 percent level, (b) 95 percent level, and (c) 99 percent level.

3. The lead-time demand distribution for a spare part used by the service department of an imported-car dealer is as follows:

Lead-time demand	20	21	22	23	24	25	26
Probability	.05	.05	.25	.30	.25	.05	.05

Determine the apropriate reorder point and safety stock for a 90 and 95 percent service level.

4. Suppose that each part in Prob. 3 costs $300 per unit and that inventory holding costs are estimated at 20 percent of the investment in stock. Determine the extra holding cost and the extra investment required to provide the 90 and 95 percent service level.

5. Rework Example 14-1 for service levels of 90 and 99 percent.

6. Rework Example 14-1 if lead-time demand is Poisson with same mean.

7. Rework Example 14-2 for service levels of 90 and 99 percent.

8. Rework Example 14-2 if daily demand is Poisson with same mean.

9. In a FOQ inventory system an item has *a lead-time demand* distribution with a mean equal to 18 units. Determine the reorder level and required safety stock for service levels equal to 90, 95, and 99 percent, if the distribution is (a) normal with a standard deviation equal to 2 units and (b) Poisson.

10. The *daily* demand for an item kept in stock is a random variable with a mean equal to 9 units. The price per unit is \$243, and inventory carrying charges amount to 30 percent. The replenishment cost is \$64 per order and the lead time is 6 days. The firm operates 250 days/yr. If daily demand is normally distributed with a standard deviation equal to $s_D = 2$ units, determine:

   (a) An inventory policy for a FOQ system with 95 percent service level
   (b) An inventory policy for a FOI system with 95 percent service level
   (c) The cost of uncertainty for (a) and (b)

11. Rework parts (a), (b), and (c) in Prob. 10, if daily demand follows a Poisson distribution with the same mean, $\bar{D} = 9$.

12. An electronics firm has an annual demand for a part equal to 5,000 units. The replenishment cost is \$60 per order with a lead time of 7 working days, and the holding cost is \$16 per unit per year. The shop operates 250 days/yr.

   (a) Assuming that *daily demand* is normally distributed with a standard deviation of 6 units, determine an inventory policy for (i) an FOQ system based on a 99 percent service level and (ii) a FOI system based on a 99 percent service level.
   (b) Compare the holding cost, replenishment cost, and total cost for the above FOQ and FOI systems and calculate the cost of uncertainty for each.

13. The master production schedule for a toy is shown below:

Week	1	2	3	4	5	6	7	8
Demand		40		70	20	50		60

   The toy is assembled from parts and components as shown in the tree representation of the product structure. Starting inventory on hand is 80 for A, 65 for B, and 90 for C. These components are produced in lot sizes of 200, 150, and 120, respectively. All components have a lead time of 1 wk except for B, E, and G which have a lead time of 2 wk.

   (a) Determine the material-requirements planning schedules for the components in level 1.

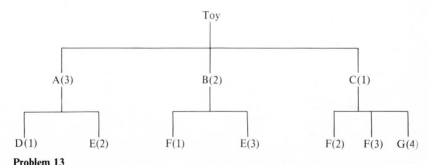

Problem 13

(*b*) Continue with MRP schedules for components at level 2 if lot sizes for all components are 500, initial inventory is 200 for each component, and *L* is 1 wk.

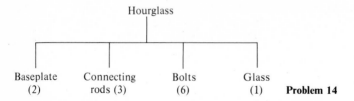

Problem 14

14. A manufacturer of an hourglass requires the components and parts shown in the accompanying product tree. The master production schedule for the next 8 wk calls for 120
units in week 3, 200 in week 5, 150 in week 6, and 400 in week 8. The required lot sizes
for parts, lead times, and initial inventory are as shown below.

Part	Lot size	Lead time, wk	Initial inventory
Baseplate	600	2	300
Connecting rods	1,000	1	1,500
Bolts	2,400	1	2,000
Glass	500	2	400

Determine the material-requirements planning schedule for this end item.

SELECTED REFERENCES

1. Brown, R. G.: *Decision Rules for Inventory Management*, Holt, New York, 1967.
2. Brown, R. G.: *Statistical Forecasting for Inventory Control*, McGraw-Hill, New York, 1959.
3. Buchan, J., and E. Koenigsberg: *Scientific Inventory Management*, Prentice-Hall, Englewood Cliffs,
   N.J., 1963.
4. Buffa, E. S., and W. H. Taubert: *Production-Inventory Systems: Planning and Control*, rev. ed., Irwin,
   Homewood, Ill., 1972.
5. Fetter, R. B., and W. C. Dalleck: *Decision Models for Inventory Management*, Irwin, Homewood, Ill.,
   1961.
6. Love, Stephen F.: *Inventory Control*, McGraw-Hill, New York, 1979.
7. Magee, J. F.: *Industrial Logistics*, McGraw-Hill, New York, 1968.
8. Magee, J. F., and D. M. Boodman: *Production Planning and Inventory Control*, 2d ed., McGraw-Hill,
   New York, 1967.
9. McMillan, C., and R. F. Gonzalez: *Systems Analysis: A Computer Approach to Decision Models*, rev.
   ed., Irwin, Homewood, Ill., 1968.
10. Naddor, E.: *Inventory Systems*, Wiley, New York, 1966.
11. Orlicky, Joseph: *Materials Requirements Planning*, McGraw-Hill, New York, 1975.
12. Starr, N. K., and D. W. Miller: *Inventory Control: Theory and Practice*, Prentice-Hall, Englewood
    Cliffs, N.J., 1962.
13. Tersine, Richard J.: *Materials Management and Inventory Systems*, North-Holland, New York, 1976.
14. Thurston, Phillip H.: "Requirements Planning for Inventory Control," *Harvard Business Review*,
    May–June 1972, pp. 67–71.
15. Wight, Oliver W.: *Production and Inventory Management in the Computer Age*, Cahners, Boston,
    1974.

Chapter 15

OPERATIONS SCHEDULING

15-1   INTRODUCTION

The General Scheduling Problem

For the short run, i.e., for periods ranging from a few days to a month, management has the task of scheduling operations for existing orders and/or imminent forecast demand. Scheduling involves the fine tuning of aggregate production plans. Actual orders, in this phase, are first assigned to specific resources (facilities, employees, and equipment), and then at each processing center they are sequenced to achieve an optimum utilization of existing capacity or other objective.

In aggregate planning forecast demand was assigned to successive production periods without considering specific products. In scheduling, however, demand must be broken down by product and assigned to specific hourly, daily, or weekly periods at given processing centers.

Significance of Scheduling

Scheduling derives its importance from two different considerations: (1) Inefficient scheduling results in poor utilization of available resources. An obvious symptom here is the idleness of facilities, human resources, and equipment waiting for orders to be processed. As a result, production costs increase, and this reduces the competitiveness or effectiveness of the organization. (2) Poor scheduling frequently creates delays in the flow of some orders through the system. This calls for expediting measures that again increase costs, upset previous plans, and delay other orders, whose late delivery results in unhappy customers.

Even though overall capacity may have been designed to minimize the total cost from alternating periods of idle resources and waiting orders, incompetent scheduling can aggravate the problem beyond any reasonable limit in terms of production costs and service levels.

Factors Affecting Scheduling

Even though the general scheduling problem is the same for all organizations, the specific methods used to solve it in a given context depend on the type of production process used. Since scheduling is used to regulate work flow through the system, the key factor that dominates scheduling strategy is the *type of flow* allowed by the process design. Thus, the choice of a scheduling method depends on whether we are dealing with a continuous process, such as an oil refinery, a flow shop (with flexible or rigid mass production), a job shop for custom-ordered items, or a project involving a unique product or service.

In all cases the effectiveness of scheduling decisions requires adequate consideration of the interactions that exist with other decision systems responsible for forecasting, aggregate planning, inventory, maintenance, and quality control. This network of interactions is shown in Fig. 15-1, where schedules are prepared in response to actual orders and short-term demand forecasts. The specific form of a schedule is affected by the short-term capacity provided in the aggregate plan

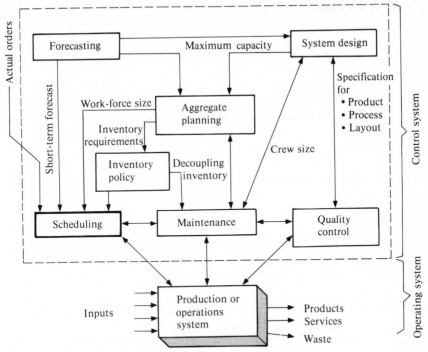

Fig. 15-1   Interaction of scheduling system with other decision areas.

(work-force size, subcontracting, etc.), by available inventories, and by the requirements for maintenance activities to keep the process in good working condition.

15-2   THE SCHEDULING SYSTEM

Having examined the major interactions of scheduling with other functions, we can focus now on the scheduling system itself, in terms of its key elements. The scheduling methods, as they apply to different kinds of production processes, will be examined in subsequent sections.

Activities (or Outputs) of Scheduling System

To ensure a smooth work flow through the various stages, a scheduling system must perform the following activities:

1. *Loading.* This involves matching the capacity requirements of orders received (or expected) to the existing capacity. Loading is accomplished by assigning orders to specific facilities, operators, and equipment.
2. *Sequencing.* This entails the assignment of job priorities so that we can determine the sequence in which orders will be processed.
3. *Dispatching.* This refers to authorizing actual performance of orders scheduled.

4. *Controlling schedule performance by:*
   a. Reviewing the status of orders as they advance through the system.
   b. Rearranging the sequencing, i.e., expediting orders that fall behind or have a top priority.
5. *Updating schedules.* This is done as needed to reflect current operating conditions and/or revised priorities.

   The complexity of these tasks can be handled systematically with graphic displays or computer printouts that assist management in the evaluation and control of schedule performance.

Information Requirements (or Inputs) of Scheduling System

The tasks of allocating capacity to orders, assigning job priorities, and controlling the production schedule require detailed information, representing the input to the scheduling decision system.

At this point we must determine the *capacity requirements* of the orders to be scheduled in terms of the kinds and amounts of resources to be used. For a given product or service this information can be obtained from an *operation sheet* (skills and equipment needed, time standards, etc.) and a *bill of materials* (components, parts, and supplies requirements). The quality of scheduling decisions is seriously affected by the accuracy of these estimates. For this reason, it is important to maintain updated records both on the status of manpower and equipment available and on the capacity-requirement changes effected by alterations in product or process design.

Scheduling-System Constraints

Arriving at a final schedule represents a complex task. Even in small to medium firms the number of possible solutions is staggering. This arises from the enormous number of possible combinations for processing a set of orders with different but equivalent assignments to facilities, equipment, and personnel.

As indicated in Chap. 11, in the short term the major problem is to cope with uncontrollable random occurrences affecting demand, equipment availability, absenteeism, etc. The scheduling system constraints relate to:

1. Process technology (sequencing of activities)
2. Capacity limits (normal capacity and standby equipment)
3. Aggregate plan provisions for:
   a. Inventories
   b. Work-force size
   c. Limits on overtime, etc.
4. Maintenance requirements
5. Availability and size of buffer inventories between stages

Decision Variables for Scheduling System

The variables controlled by management in preparing, controlling, and updating a production schedule include:

1. The exact size of the work force on a daily basis
2. Setting the actual production rate adjusted for overtime or undertime
3. The specific allocation of orders to resources (employees, machines, etc.)
4. The sequencing, i.e., time phasing, of orders through the processing centers

Performance Criteria for Scheduling System

Manipulation of these control variables is aimed at optimizing scheduling performance, although some of the criteria are rather difficult to quantify. Basically, the effectiveness of scheduling depends on (1) the degree of promptness of deliveries as they affect customer satisfaction and (2) the utilization of available capacity.

Customer satisfaction can be measured by the percentage of deliveries made as promised, assuming that quality does not suffer when expediting occurs. In some instances late deliveries, especially for construction projects or government contracts, may result in penalties beyond the loss of goodwill.

The utilization of capacity can be evaluated in terms of the percentage of idle time of various work centers as determined by a work-sampling study (see Chap. 8). The scheduling system and its major components are shown in Fig. 15-2.

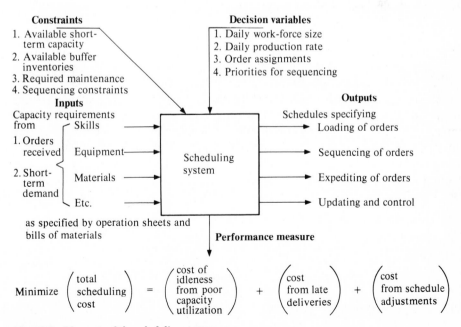

Fig. 15-2   Elements of the scheduling system.

15-3 FLOW-SHOP SCHEDULING

A great deal of the scheduling effort required to operate a flow shop has been contributed in the design phase of the system. Here we have a virtually continuous movement of units through a series of work stations laid out by product. As stated in Chap. 7, a flow-shop arrangement can be justified for products with a stable design and high production volume to justify the investment in special-purpose equipment.

A critical problem for a flow shop is grouping the necessary tasks in work stations so that they satisfy sequencing constraints and are balanced in their output rate. If the output rate varies for each work station, the production line is out of balance. This results in uneven or erratic flow and poor capacity utilization of those stages which must slow down to the speed of the bottleneck station or operate intermittently.

Another serious problem in scheduling flow shops relates to the severe strain this flow arrangement places on workers because of the limited work content of each station and the usual lack of control over the pace of the production line. In order to enhance job satisfaction and productivity management may encourage job rotation, decompose a long production line into shorter segments whose pace can be controlled by a smaller group of workers, and provide rewards for high quality and productivity rates. To overcome the boredom and frustration of employees in narrow jobs, management must attempt to maintain a work atmosphere that satisfies social and psychological needs through the development of activities tying workers into cohesive groups that identify with organizational goals.

Line-Balancing Problem

The grouping of tasks that will result in a balanced production line requires information about the task-performance times, the precedence requirements which govern the feasible sequences, and the desired output rate or cycle time per unit. The main features of the line-balancing problem are shown in Fig. 15-3.

The line-balancing problem is most pervasive in assembly (rather than fabrication) processes. Fabrication of parts usually requires heavy machines with long cycles. When several operations with different equipment are required in series, it becomes very difficult to balance their lengthy machine cycles, resulting in poor

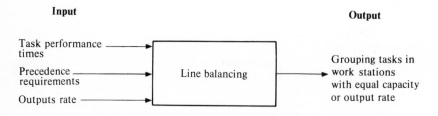

Fig. 15-3 **The major elements of the line-balancing problem.**

capacity utilization. Continuous movement, however, is more likely to be achieved with assembly operations performed manually when such operations can be subdivided into small tasks of very short duration. The greater the flexibility in combining such tasks the higher the degree of balance that can be achieved. This permits a smooth flow with high labor and equipment utilization.

Fabrication processes are usually operated as intermittent-flow, or batch-type, systems. When the production volume is very large and the product specifications stable, a continuous-flow arrangement is possible through automation of the necessary operations so that the entire production line functions like one giant machine.

Line-Balancing Methods

The specific method used to balance a production line depends on the length of processing time and the availability of units at each stage. Here we recognize three possible types.[1]

Mechanically paced production line. In this case the processing time of each work station is constant, and the units are advanced mechanically through the successive stages.

Stochastic production line. When the processing time at each station is variable, specified by a statistical distribution, we have a series of queueing systems. The alternating conditions of congestion and idleness for each station make it difficult to achieve a balanced production line. The allowance of in-process inventories may reduce the unevenness in the overall output rate but does not solve the balance problem completely.

Mixed production line. This is a combination of the two previous types and is quite prevalent in practice when large segments of a production system are considered.

Even though the majority of actual systems are of the stochastic type, waiting-line theory has not been of any significant value in solving the line-balancing problem, except for some insights in conceptualizing its underlying structure. Most methods advanced to date address themselves to the simplified case of a mechanically paced line for which service times are constant and units always available in the form of in-process inventories.

Coupling Scheduling to Aggregate Planning

For a flow shop, translating an aggregate production plan covering several months into a detailed schedule on a daily or weekly basis runs into several serious problems:

1. The period-by-period allocation of capacity (labor-hours, machine-hours, inventories) to all products must now be decomposed into resource allocation for specific products. This is known as the *product-mix problem.*

---

[1] For a detailed discussion of line-balancing methods see Refs. 1, 2, and 3.

2. A flow shop represents only one stage in a multistage production-distribution system involving flows of materials and information along a chain including suppliers, factory, factory warehouse, distributors, retailers, and final consumers of the product(s). Several stages in this chain are beyond management's control, and the presence of information and supply-time lags in the replenishment cycle for each stage tends to amplify any fluctuations in demand at the consumer level as we go upstream. The result is increasing fluctuations in the inventory levels of the stages upstream, which in turn induce undesirably large fluctuations in the actual production rates needed but not visualized in the aggregate-planning phase (see Ref. 2).

3. As we go from general-capacity allocation to the specific assignment of resources to orders, the degree of required detail expands and the complexity of the information needed becomes a great challenge for management both in terms of the volume of data and the frequency of updating them.

Within the limits of effective capacity provided in each period by the aggregate plan, management must solve the economic problem of the more detailed resource allocation to specific products. Different products may require similar resources (machine-hours, labor-hours, etc.), but they may have different profitabilities. Furthermore, the detailed allocation must satisfy a variety of constraints due to the technology of the production process, the maximum capacity for each resource type (regular time, overtime, etc.) as set in the aggregate plan, or both.

The restrictions due to technology increase with the degree of process integration. Thus, for a steelmill, a papermill, or an oil refinery the nature of transformation dictates that as we make more of one type of product, say one grade of steel, paper, or gasoline, we must make less of the other varieties. In less integrated systems, i.e., those used for mass production of automobiles, home appliances, typewriters, etc., most restrictions in the product-mix problem depend on available capacity in each processing center, labor-union agreements, market-saturation levels, and the like.

In theory, then, the product-mix problem in scheduling is a complex mathematical programming problem. For a wide variety of applications (oil refineries, forest products, etc.) this has been successfully solved using linear programming (see Supplementary Chapter C). In practice, however, despite the availability of powerful methods such as linear programming, the product-mix problem is usually solved by simpler methods. Accordingly, management starts with each product's previous percentage sales and then adjusts this figure subjectively in the light of perceived trends or market changes. This approach yields a solution which after a series of adjustments satisfies the border constraints of the aggregate plan.

Once the product-mix problem has been resolved, we can proceed to determine detailed schedules for production, for work-force requirements (through specific amounts of layoffs or hiring), and for materials procurement. The degree of flexibility in setting production rates and work-force schedules for individual products may vary from one organization to another, depending on the process technology.

If the production line cannot be rebalanced for different output rates, the approach taken is to rely on overtime or undertime. If the assembly line is quite rigid and mechanically paced, it may also be possible to adjust the line speed to achieve different output rates. This is common in bottling plants, food-packaging plants, and others.

When rebalancing of the line is feasible, i.e., with appliance assembly plants, it may be a good alternative to meet the need for varying output rates. This is especially true when the changes in output rate are too drastic to be absorbed with varying working hours. *Rebalancing usually entails hiring and layoffs*, and its desirability is taken into account in broader terms when developing an aggregate plan.

The entire procedure of coupling a detailed schedule to an aggregate plan is a series of trial-and-error approximations in which proposed schedules are checked for feasibility against the broader constraints of the aggregate plan. The specific steps are shown in Fig. 15-4.

In summary, scheduling for a continuous system begins by first solving the product-mix problem. This is done within the framework established by the aggregate plan, utilizing information about the profitability of individual items and market characteristics. Next we examine whether the aggregate plan calls for a change in the work-force size for the upcoming period. If so, this usually requires rebalancing the production line and preparing a revised work-force plan incorporating orders for the needed hiring or layoffs.

Large companies may have predetermined work-force requirement schedules for various output rates. Given the desirable output rate and the corresponding work-force plan, they prepare detailed schedules that assign individual orders to specific facilities and subcontractors (if needed) on a daily basis. Such schedules must take into account the maintenance schedule for the equipment used, work rules specified in contracts between the firm and labor unions, and the capacity provided by the aggregate plan.

A proposed detailed schedule is next checked for feasibility against the restrictions on overtime, hiring or layoffs, inventory levels, subcontracting, etc., specified in the aggregate plan. Since the latter represents the optimum utilization of existing capacity, a feasible schedule is interpreted as one that achieves the desired optimum allocation of available resources. If a proposed schedule violates any of the aggregate-plan constraints, it must be adjusted, as many times as necessary, until it becomes feasible. At present, we have no well-developed methods for selecting the best among several feasible schedules. This is an instance in which the tremendous complexity of the scheduling task makes it appropriate to use a *satisficing* rather than an optimizing approach (see Chap. 2).

The development of a feasible schedule for the next period and the adjustment of the current schedule to reflect present conditions (status of orders already started, actual versus projected inventory levels, and revised demand forecasts) are combined to produce detailed schedules for one or two periods ahead, specifying product assignments to facilities, worker and equipment assignments, and desired inventory levels and shipment dates.

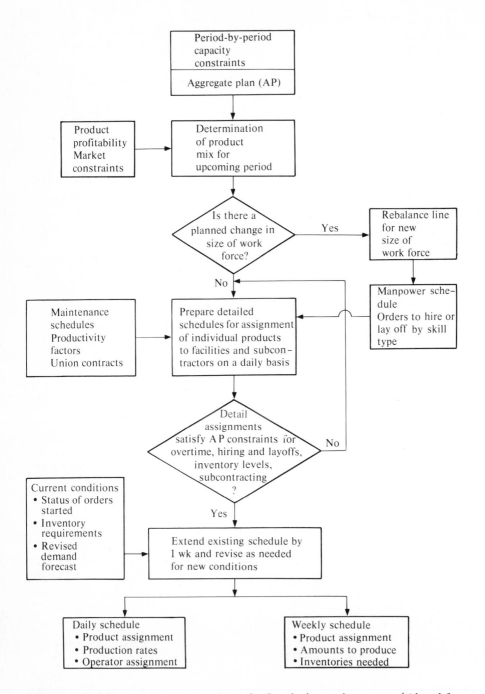

Fig. 15-4 Scheduling procedure for a continuous (or flow-shop) operations system. (*Adapted from E. S. Buffa, Operations Management: The Management of Productive Systems, John Wiley & Sons, Inc., New York, 1975, by permission of the publisher.*)

15-5   JOB-SHOP SCHEDULING

General

Scheduling a job shop is much more complex than scheduling a flow shop for three reasons: (1) job shops handle a large variety of products, with different flow patterns through the work centers; (2) equipment in a job shop is time-shared by the various orders in process, whereas in a flow shop it is used exclusively for one product type; and (3) different jobs may be governed by different priorities. This in turn affects the order in which they are selected for processing once they are assigned to a work center. The uniformity of output produced for stock by a flow shop, however, does not create such a problem. Order priorities for flow shops affect mainly their shipping rather than processing dates.

These factors result in an extremely large number of possible loading and sequencing combinations. The computational task of identifying and evaluating possible schedules is formidable. For this reason, job-shop scheduling has received a great deal of attention in past research. Except for small problems, preparing a job-shop schedule and adjusting and updating it require a considerable investment in computational facilities.

In this section we discuss job-shop scheduling by considering the problems of job loading and job sequencing. In *loading* we must decide which of several work centers a job will be assigned to. In *sequencing* we must determine the order of processing the various jobs assigned to a particular machine or work center. Our discussion will focus on some important considerations in scheduling by examining a variety of simple problems in which each order can be treated as a single job that cannot be split either in loading or sequencing. Since many job shops also handle orders that involve several identical units or batches, we shall conclude with methods for batch scheduling with or without prescribed lot sizes.

Job-shop scheduling has been important in manufacturing. It can play an equally helpful role in the service sector as well. In Chap. 7 we noted that many service organizations are operated as job-shop arrangements. This is true for hospitals, court systems, universities, consulting firms, police or fire departments, and others. As such they can be improved and their increasing costs brought under control by applying, with appropriate modifications, scheduling techniques employed in manufacturing systems. The requirement for employees with high skills and the considerable control they exercise over their work are elements conducive to the development of a well-motivated and productive work force. Here ample opportunities exist to form cohesive groups in which members can satisfy job-related, psychological, and social needs.

Job-Shop Loading

When orders arrive in a job shop, the first scheduling task is to assign them to the various work centers for processing. They may be patients to be assigned to physicians or operating rooms, cases to be assigned to a court or a judge, insurance claims to be assigned to adjusters, fabrication jobs to various machine centers, and so on. In general, there are several processing centers that can handle a given order or job, each one having different performance characteristics.

Definition

Shop loading involves the assignment of jobs to various processing centers in a way that satisfies some stated objective, such as minimizing the total processing time or cost. In other words, shop loading is a resource-allocation process.

The loading problem is simpler when a job cannot be split. Even though this occurs frequently, it is also common practice in industry to split a job and assign different parts to different work centers as a means of improving resource utilization. For small problems, in which we can assume no job splitting, shop loading can be performed easily by using a Gantt chart. If additional assumptions can be made about the nature of the relationships that hold, it may be possible to use special cases of linear programming, such as the assignment or the transportation method.

Loading may be centralized (for all departments to achieve greater coordination) or decentralized. In the latter case, a supervisor can use discretion in assigning jobs to workers to reward and motivate individuals more directly for their performance. Decentralized loading thus becomes an important instrument for achieving greater job satisfaction and productivity through more responsive management of a given situation.

Loading with a Gantt chart   A Gantt chart represents the oldest, simplest, and most widely used method for scheduling various activities. With reference to shop loading, the construction of the chart requires listing the various processing centers as rows and placing the various jobs in each row plotted against a time axis, as shown in Fig. 15-5 for the fabrication of a machine part.

Despite its simplicity and visual appeal, a Gantt chart is very limited in evaluating alternative loading arrangements. Users must rely on trial and error for improvements. As the number of jobs increases, this process becomes quite complicated and unreliable.

Loading with the assignment method   In order to use the assignment method we must formulate a problem so that the following conditions are satisfied:

1. Each job must be assigned to one processing center only and vice versa; i.e., there is no job splitting.
2. For each possible assignment we must have a performance index related to processing time, cost, or other variable. Nonfeasible assignments are indicated

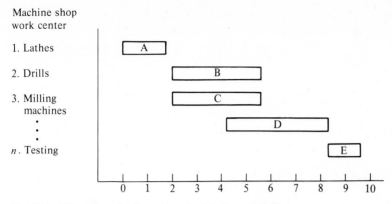

Machine shop
work center

1. Lathes — A

2. Drills — B

3. Milling
   machines — C

   ⋮

   D

n. Testing — E

0 1 2 3 4 5 6 7 8 9 10

Fig. 15-5 Illustration of a Gantt chart for job-shop scheduling.

by a very large penalty. This is shown by a large number M, say $999\ldots$, for the index, making that pairing highly undesirable.

3. The number of jobs n must be equal to the number of processing centers. Otherwise we create one or more fictitious (or dummy) jobs or processing centers. An assignment involving a dummy job or machine has a zero value for the performance index since it is never really done.

The assignment method can be best illustrated with an example. Consider the service department of WMB Auto Imports Co., which operates with four mechanics (Bill, Doug, George, and Jim) all of comparable training. Suppose that one day there are four jobs scheduled for service. For a given job the estimated labor requirements vary with each mechanic, reflecting his experience and skill. Processing times for each possible assignment are shown in Table 15-1.

To determine the optimum, i.e., least total labor-time, assignment with the suggested method, known as the *Hungarian method*, we must go through a series of steps aimed at minimizing the total opportunity cost, i.e., the cost of failing to make the best assignments.

1. In each row, subtract the smallest entry from all row values. This creates at least one zero per row, indicating the most desirable assignment(s).

TABLE 15-1 Labor requirements for service jobs at WMB Auto Imports, Inc.

Job	Time, min			
	Bill	Doug	George	Jim
A	70	50	50	60
B	30	30	90	110
C	30	10	20	60
D	50	20	70	60

2. In each column, subtract the smallest entry from all column values. This may create additional zero values in each column if none were there from step 1.
3. Draw the minimum number of lines needed to cover all the zero values in the table. If this number equals the number of rows (or columns) *n* an optimum assignment can be made as follows:
   a. Make unique assignments for each row, eliminating zero values in the same column.
   b. Repeat the same for each column until each job has been assigned to each operator.
4. If the minimum number of lines is less than the matrix size *n*, additional zero entries can be created as follows. After all zero entries have been covered by lines, identify the smallest uncovered positive entry, subtract it from all uncovered values, and then add it to those values at the intersections of the lines. Then repeat steps 3 and 4 on the revised matrix until a complete assignment is possible.

For the WMB Auto Imports, Inc. example, the above steps are illustrated in Table 15-2.

In the preceding example the objective was the minimization of total labor time (or cost). The Hungarian method identified the opportunity costs of failing to make optimal assignments and sought to minimize them by making assignments in matrix cells with zero values.

Sometimes a loading problem is best formulated so that each assignment is evaluated on the basis of its projected profit rather than cost, e.g., assigning analysts in a consulting firm to different clients. Now the objective is to maximize total profit. To solve this type of problem we proceed as follows:

1. Identify the cell with the largest profit entry in the matrix.
2. Subtract each entry in the original table from the largest profit entry found in step 1. The new table indicates the opportunity cost of not using a particular combination.
3. Apply the previous minimization method on the transformed table.
4. After an optimal assignment is found, obtain the maximum total profit from the corresponding entries in the original table.

In more complex situations the loading problem can be formulated as a transportation problem. For some interesting illustrations see Refs. 11 and 12.

Job-Shop Sequencing

Once several jobs have been assigned, i.e., loaded, to a particular work center, the next step involves determining a sequence for their processing. Processing order is important because it affects the time a job will spend in the system and therefore the date it can be available for delivery. Equally important is the effect of job-processing sequence on the utilization of an organization's resources, especially those in critical supply.

TABLE 15-2 Steps in applying the assignment method

Step 1: Row reduction					Step 3: Covering zero entries				
Job	Bill	Doug	George	Jim	Job	Bill	Doug	George	Jim
A	20	0	0	10	A	~~20~~	0	~~0~~	~~0~~
B	0	0	60	80	B	~~0~~	0	~~60~~	~~70~~
C	20	0	10	50	C	20	0	10†	40
D	30	0	50	40	D	30	0	50	30

Minimum number of lines < 4;
no optimum solution yet

Step 2: Column reduction					Step 4: Creating new zero entry.				
Job	Bill	Doug	George	Jim	Job	Bill	Doug	George	Jim
A	20	0	0	0	A	~~20~~	10	~~0~~	~~0~~
B	0	0	60	70	B	~~0~~	10	~~60~~	~~70~~
C	20	0	10	40	C	~~10~~	0	~~0~~	~~30~~
D	30	0	50	30	D	20	0	40	20

Number of lines = 4, optimum
solution possible

Assignment sequence	Bill	Doug	George	Jim	Optimal assignment	Time, min
Fourth A	20	10	X	0	Job A to Jim	60
First B	0	10	60	70	Job B to Bill	30
Third C	10	X	0	30	Job C to George	20
Second D	20	0	40	20	Job D to Doug	20

Minimum total labor time = 130

† Smallest uncovered positive entry.

Definition

Job sequencing involves the time ordering of jobs through one or more processing centers according to some stated criterion of performance such as optimum resource utilization, prompt delivery, or other.

Job-shop characteristics relevant to sequencing Before we determine a job sequence, it is necessary to specify the following characteristics:

1. The *number of jobs* to be processed n.
2. The *number of machines* in series a job must be processed through m. The word "machine" here may also refer to a work station or a production stage.

3. The *job arrival pattern*, which can be static or dynamic. In the *static* pattern S all jobs to be scheduled on a machine are available at the beginning of a shift, and no others are allowed to be included in the schedule. In the *dynamic* arrival pattern D, in addition to jobs already waiting to be processed others may arrive at random or regularly. Depending on their assigned priority, later arrivals may be incorporated in the present schedule.
4. The *job-flow pattern* specifies the sequence of machines an order will go through before completion. If all jobs go through the same sequence of machines, we have a flow-shop pattern F; otherwise we have a job-shop pattern J.
5. The *job-selection rule* for a given work center specifies the order in which jobs will be processed. Common rules include:
   a. First come, first served (FCFS).
   b. Random order (RO).
   c. Shortest operation time (SOT); this rule sequences jobs assigned to a work center in order of increasing processing time.
   d. Slack time left until due date (STD); this is equal to the number of days left until due date minus the number of remaining processing days.
   e. Slack time per operation remaining (STO); this is equal to the difference between the time remaining to due date and the remaining machine processing time divided by the number of remaining operations.
6. The *schedule-evaluation criterion* specifies the type of performance desired to satisfy stated organization objectives.

Some scheduling criteria emphasize high utilization rates for critical resources of a job shop. In *human-limited* systems people represent the important capacity bottlenecks. They may be physicians in a hospital, professors in a university, mechanics in an auto-repair shop, etc. *Machine-limited* systems are those in which expensive equipment represents the critical resource, i.e., a blood-testing machine in a medical laboratory, a computer facility for a business consulting firm, the number of milling machines in a fabrication shop, and so on.

In certain cases, however, it is more important to concentrate on prompt or rapid deliveries. It is common in some industries to develop a schedule by trying to minimize the percentage of late orders, even though this may result in inefficient resource utilization.

The following are the most commonly used schedule evaluation criteria:

1. *Criteria aimed at improving customer service*
   a. Average processing time[1] (APT)
   b. Average waiting time of jobs (AWT)
   c. Percentage of late jobs (%L)
2. *Criteria aimed at improving resource utilization*
   d. Labor utilization (LU)
   e. Machine utilization (MU)
   f. In-process inventory cost (IP)

---

[1] Processing time = operation time + waiting time at a work center.

Once a criterion is adopted for evaluating alternative schedules, it tends to favor one or very few of the job-selection rules. Several studies have tested various selection rules by different criteria in extensive simulation runs, and have shown that there is no superior selection rule for all the criteria used in practice. For high levels of customer service, the shortest-operation-time (SOT) rule has the lowest average processing time (APT) for all selection rules tested.[1] However, since in practice the importance of a job is usually positively correlated with its processing time, there is a tendency for jobs to be sequenced in order of decreasing operation times. Given that no selection rule is best for all schedule criteria, most job shops attempt to do well on some limited but dominant objective.

One may view a job-shop scheduling problem as a complex queueing problem (see Refs. 1 and 3). The symbols for the key features of a job shop can be combined to represent various scheduling situations. For example, in a situation where we have n jobs to be processed in two machines ($m = 2$), with a static arrival pattern S, a flow-shop pattern F, and a criterion of minimizing average processing time (APT), the abbreviated notation would be ($n/m = 2/S/F/$APT).

Case 1: n jobs, one machine, flow shop with static arrivals ($n/m = 1/S/F$)   Let us consider a production stage with one machine ($m = 1$) and n jobs waiting to be processed in a static arrival pattern. This is a flow-shop arrangement since all units undergo the same transformation.

Let t_i = operation time for job i $i = 1, 2, \ldots, n$
 x_i = waiting time for job i
 T_i = processing time for job i $T_i = x_i + t_i$
 $\bar{T}$ = average processing time $\bar{T}$ = APT

We want to determine the sequence in which the n jobs must be processed through the one machine to minimize the average processing time $\bar{T}$.

To illustrate, suppose a medical laboratory on a given day receives five samples for analysis on a special machine. The operation times for each sample are as follows:

Lab. sample i	A	B	C	D	E
Operation time t_i, h	1.2	0.3	0.8	0.5	0.2

Since the laboratory manager believes that customers, i.e. hospitals, clinics, etc., evaluate performance on the basis of the time until they get back the results on requested tests, she wishes to minimize the average processing time for all jobs handled by the special machine.

The average processing time depends on the particular sequence in which

[1] E. S. Buffa and William F. Taubert, *Production-Inventory Systems: Planning and Control*, rev. ed., Irwin, Homewood, Ill., 1971.

TABLE 15-3   Processing times for different job sequences

Lab. sample	Operation time	Waiting time	Processing time, h
Sequence A-B-C-D-E, which may reflect arrival order			
A	1.2	0	1.2
B	.3	1.2	1.5
C	.8	1.5	2.3
D	.5	2.3	2.8
E	.2	2.8	3.0
Total			10.8

$$\text{Average processing time } \bar{T} = \frac{T_A + T_B + \cdots + T_E}{n} = \frac{10.8}{5} = 2.16 \text{ h}$$

Sequence E-D-C-B-A, the reverse of the previous one			
E	.2	0	.2
D	.5	.2	.7
C	.8	.7	1.5
B	.3	1.5	1.8
A	1.2	1.8	3.0
Total			7.2

$$\text{Average processing time } \bar{T} = \frac{T_E + T_D + \cdots + T_A}{n} = \frac{7.2}{5} = 1.44 \text{ h}$$

For sequence E-B-D-C-A			
E	.2	0	.2
B	.3	.2	.5
D	.5	.5	1.0
C	.8	1.0	1.8
A	1.2	1.8	3.0
Total			6.5

$$\text{Average processing time } \bar{T} = \frac{T_E + T_B + \cdots + T_A}{n} = \frac{6.5}{5} = 1.30 \text{ h (optimum)}$$

samples are analyzed. This can be seen using different sequences and then computing the corresponding average processing time. For three possible sequences the relevant calculations are shown in Table 15-3.

The effect of sequencing on average processing time can be seen more vividly in Fig. 15-6, in which we use a Gantt chart for each sequence. The total waiting time for each sequence is equal to the shaded area under the bars for the operation times. Since this is the only part affected by the particular sequence used, *the average processing time is shortest when the total waiting time is minimized. This occurs when jobs are arranged in order of increasing operation times.*[1] For the medical laboratory this is shown in Fig. 15-7.

Sometimes the various jobs to be processed have different priorities. In our example the laboratory samples may be assigned ratings based on the degree of

---

[1] This is proved in Ref. 4.

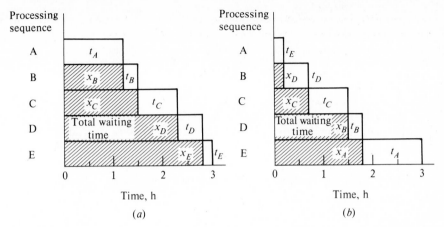

Fig. 15-6 Gantt-chart representation of different processing sequences: (*a*) A-B-C-D-E and (*b*) E-D-C-B-A.

urgency for obtaining the results. The weights of the jobs $w_1, w_2, \ldots, w_n$ on some scale, say 1 to 10, are assigned so that the larger the value of w the more important the job. In such a situation, *we can minimize the average weighted processing time* $\bar{T}_w$ *by sequencing jobs so that the ratios of operation times to weights* (t_i/w_i) *are in increasing order.*

Suppose that the weights for the laboratory samples are as shown below, with the ratios t_i/w_i calculated in the adjacent column:

Job	Operation time t_i	Weight w_i	Ratio t_i/w_i	Job sequence
A	1.2	4	.30	5
B	.3	2	.15	3
C	.8	10	.08	1
D	.5	5	.10	2
E	.2	1	.20	4

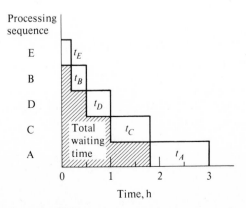

Fig. 15-7 Gantt chart for optimum schedule sequence in the example.

To minimize the average weighted processing time the proper sequence in order of increasing t_i/w_i ratios must be

$$C \rightarrow D \rightarrow B \rightarrow E \rightarrow A$$

corresponding to ratios: $.08 < .10 < .15 < .20 < .30$

Case 2: n jobs, two machines, flow shop with static arrivals $(n/m = 2/F/S)$ The preceding arrangement can be expanded to include processing of n jobs in two work centers in series. For simplicity, we assume that all jobs have arrived at the beginning of a shift; i.e., we have a static arrival pattern. If there is no priority rule for job completion, the optimum sequence of n jobs through two machines can be found by *Johnson's rule,*[1] as follows:

1. List operation times for each job on the two machines.
2. Select the shortest operation time on the list.
3. If the shortest time from step 2 is for machine 1, sequence the corresponding job as early as possible. If it is for machine 2, place the job as late as possible. A tie in shortest operation times can be broken arbitrarily.
4. Cross off both operation times for the job selected in step 3.
5. Repeat steps 2 and 3 on list of remaining jobs until all are included in a complete sequence.

Johnson's rule identifies the sequence with the shortest total elapsed time. This criterion is satisfactory for flow shops in which the cost and volume of in-process inventory is low. Otherwise, the holding inventory costs may be significant for some jobs, and priority rules may be necessary to expedite scheduling delays.

For an illustration, suppose that the seamstress for a large department store receives each morning a set of alteration jobs which require work in two steps, cutting and preparation done by herself and sewing, etc., done by her assistant. On a given day, the jobs requiring alterations and their operation time at each work station are listed below (step 1):

Work station	Job operation time, min					
	1	2	3	4	5	6
Seamstress	30	30	60	20	35	45
Assistant	45	15	40	25	30	70

The shortest operation time, equal to 15 min, is identified with job 2 (step 2). Since this is associated with the second work station, it is placed last in sequence, as

[1] S. M. Johnson, "Optional Two- and Three-Stage Production Schedules with Set-Up Times Included," *Naval Research Logistics Quarterly*, March 1954.

shown below (step 3) and the times for job 2 are crossed off in the initial list (step 4):

Iteration 1:

					↓
					2

Repeating the same procedure on the reduced list for jobs 1, 3, 4, 5, and 6, the shortest time is 20 min for job 4. This is now placed first because the shortest time is on work station 1. The times for job 4 are then deleted from the list.

Iteration 2:

↓					
4					2

In searching for the next shortest time, we find that jobs 1 and 5 have one operation time equal to 30. The tie is broken arbitrarily by selecting job 1. This is placed as early as possible, i.e., after job 2, since it is associated with work station 1. Job 5 is next placed as late as possible, i.e., before job 2.

Iteration 3:

	↓			↓	
4	1			5	2

From the reduced list of jobs 3 and 6 the shortest time is 40 for job 3 in work station 2. Job 3 is placed before job 5, leaving only one position empty to be filled by job 6.

Iteration 4:

			↓		
4	1		3	5	2

Optimum sequence:

		↓			
4	1	6	3	5	2

This yields the sequence with the minimum total elapsed time as shown in the bar chart for the work stations in Fig. 15-8. The percentage utilization of each work station is equal to the ratio of the productive over the total elapsed time.

Case 3: n jobs, m machines, flow shop with static arrivals $(n/m/F/S)$ For sequencing n jobs when the number of machines or stages in series exceeds 2 $(m \geq 3)$ there is no exact method which identifies an optimum solution. Instead, available methods rely on heuristics, which decompose the original problem of n jobs and m machines into a series of subproblems with n jobs and 2 machines.[1] The subproblems are then treated with Johnson's rule and the final heuristic solution corresponds to the best sequence for the subproblems.

[1] For details, see Barry Shore, *Operations Management*, McGraw-Hill, New York, 1973.

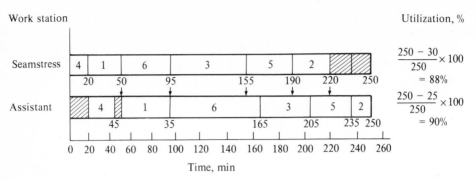

Fig. 15-8 Sequence of six jobs in two work sections using Johnson's rule.

Complex job-shop configurations: queueing and simulation models Several procedures have been devised for determining an optimal sequence of jobs given other types of arrival pattern and flow configuration. An exact graphical method is available for scheduling two jobs on *m* machines in series with static arrivals (see Ref. 13, Chap. 10). Methods for scheduling job shops with dynamic arrival patterns have been analyzed with queueing models, but the most successful approach by far to realistic job-sheet scheduling is simulation. This realization has led to the development in recent years of special computer programs, such as the one used by Hughes Aircraft Co.[1] Relying on a large simulation model, it prepares, monitors, and updates a shop schedule on a weekly basis allowing for dynamic arrivals and priority setting. Another successful program package developed by General Electric Co. is known as GJSCH$ (general shop scheduler).[2] It is intended for shops hand-ling one-of-a-kind jobs with little or no production of items for stock. These are processed in several work stations with special requirements. Using two input files (one on machine centers and one on jobs), GJSCH$ can schedule forward given a starting date or backward from a desired due date. The program, which requires the user to input values for schedule parameters (days per week, capacity per mechanic, etc.), can produce a job-schedule report and a machine-center load report, neither of which guarantees an optimum utilization of facilities.

Job-Shop Batch Scheduling

A job shop may receive an order for several identical units, i.e., a batch. For a "closed" job shop the orders originate within the same organization and are triggered to replenish various stock points in the total production-distribution system. Batch scheduling has the objective of producing to cover demand at fore-cast rates of use. Sometimes the scheduling must also take into account prescribed order batch sizes. In closed job shops such an order size may well be an economic

[1] Michael H. Bulkin, et al., "Load Forecasting Priority and Simulation in a Job Shop Control System," *Management Science*, October 1966, p. B-29.

[2] General Electric Co., *User's Guide to General Shop Scheduler GJSCH$*, 1970.

production quantity, i.e., one that minimizes the setup and inventory holding costs (see the finite-production-rate inventory model in Chap. 13).

Faced with several orders at the beginning of a scheduling period, say a week, a job shop is expected to determine which orders to run and how much to produce of a given item in that period. This problem can be handled by assigning available production capacity on the basis of *runout*, or depletion, times for different items.

Definition

The *runout time* for an item is the time that inventory on hand, if any, plus already scheduled production for that item will cover demand at the current rate of use.

Inventory on hand and scheduled production may be expressed in physical units or some common unit of capacity for the various orders processed, e.g., labor-hours or machine-hours.

For a given item the runout time is computed as follows:

$$\text{Runout time} = \frac{\text{inventory on hand at end of scheduling period}}{\text{forecast demand for scheduling period}}$$

$$= \frac{\begin{bmatrix} \text{inventory on hand} \\ \text{at beginning} \end{bmatrix} + \begin{bmatrix} \text{scheduled} \\ \text{production} \end{bmatrix} - \begin{bmatrix} \text{forecast demand for} \\ \text{scheduling period} \end{bmatrix}}{\text{forecast demand for scheduling period}}$$

Suppose a job shop prepares a schedule at the beginning of each week. If the inventory on hand for an item is 185 units, the scheduled production is 60 units and the weekly demand is 70 units, then for this item we have

$$\text{Runout time} = \frac{185 + 60 - 70}{70} = 2.5 \text{ wk}$$

This means that the amount for that item available at the end of the week will cover demand at the current rate of use for a period equal to $2\frac{1}{2}$ wk.

Decision Rule

In batch scheduling various orders, the items and batch sizes are selected so that the runout times for all items handled will be as nearly equal as possible.

Batch scheduling with prescribed order sizes   To illustrate batch scheduling using runout times, consider a job shop about to prepare a weekly schedule for the items and conditions shown in Table 15-4. The job shop operates two shifts daily, 5 days/wk, and requires 6.5 h for maintenance each week. So the production time, i.e., capacity, available weekly is $(8)(2)(5) - 6.5 = 73.5$ machine-hours. The order size specified for each item can be viewed as an economic production quantity although in practice this may not be the case.

In Table 15-4 the total number of 79.5 machine-hours required to run all items at the prescribed order sizes exceeds the available capacity of 73.5 machine-hours.

TABLE 15-4   Data required for batch scheduling using runout times

			Production		
Item	Forecast weekly demand, units	Beginning inventory on hand, units	Order size, units	Time per unit, h	Time per order, machine-hours
A	50	160	90	.05	4.5
B	35	120	80	.20	16.0
C	45	60	120	.25	30.0
D	30	130	100	.08	8.0
E	40	170	150	.14	21.0
Total					79.5

To decide which of the items to schedule in the week ahead, we must first compute runout, or depletion, times for all items. The schedule is then determined by starting with the item expected to be depleted first and then including additional ones in the order of increasing runout times until available capacity is all used up.

Since for the week ahead there is no intermediate scheduling period, the amount already scheduled for each item is zero and run-out time is computed by dividing beginning inventory by weekly rate of use. The run-out times and processing sequence for each item in the prescribed lot sizes is shown in Table 15-5.

TABLE 15-5   Determination of runout times for batch scheduling with prescribed order sizes

Item	Beginning inventory	Weekly demand	Runout time	Processing sequence
A	160	50	3.20	2
B	120	35	3.43	3
C	60	45	1.33	1
D	130	30	4.33	5
E	170	40	4.25	4

Item C, with the smallest runout time (1.33 wk), must be scheduled first. For a prescribed batch size of 120 units for C, the production time will be 30.0 machine-hours. This reduces available capacity to $73.5 - 30.0 = 43.5$ h. The item to be depleted next will be A with a runout time equal to 3.20 wk. This will reduce capacity by 4.5 machine-hours to 39.0 h for a batch of 90 units. Additional items are added to the weekly schedule until all capacity is used up, as shown in Table 15-6.

TABLE 15-6   Determination of schedule sequence with prescribed order sizes

Schedule sequence	Runout time, wk	Order size (prescribed)	Production time, machine-hours	Remaining capacity, machine-hours
				73.5
C	1.33	120	30.0	43.5
A	3.20	90	4.5	39.0
B	3.43	80	16.0	23.0
E	4.25	150	21.0	2.0
D	4.33	100	8.00	−6.0

Since item D requires 8 machine-hours and the remaining capacity when we get to it is only 2 h, the prescribed order of 100 units for D can only be partially completed in the current period. The balance of the order requiring 6 h must be scheduled first in the following week. Upon completion of this week's schedule the inventory figures are updated for the next period and the procedure repeated in the following week with the remaining capacity of $73.5 - 6 = 67.5$ h. The runout method for batch scheduling can be integrated with the aggregate planning method for the entire organization.

Batch scheduling without order-size restrictions   Sometimes we can remove the constraint that different items be scheduled in prescribed order sizes. It is then possible to prepare a schedule that yields a runout time for each item equal to an aggregate runout time computed as follows:

$$\begin{bmatrix} \text{Aggregate} \\ \text{runout time} \end{bmatrix} = \frac{\begin{bmatrix} \text{total requirements for end of} \\ \text{scheduled period, machine-hours} \end{bmatrix}}{\begin{bmatrix} \text{forecast requirements for scheduled} \\ \text{period, machine-hours} \end{bmatrix}}$$

where

$$\begin{bmatrix} \text{Total requirements for} \\ \text{end of scheduled period} \end{bmatrix}$$

$$= \begin{bmatrix} \text{requirements for aggregate} \\ \text{inventory on hand} \end{bmatrix} + \begin{bmatrix} \text{aggregate scheduled} \\ \text{production} \end{bmatrix} - \begin{bmatrix} \text{forecast requirements} \\ \text{for period} \end{bmatrix}$$

all expressed in machine-hours or units of capacity for any other critical resource.

TABLE 15-7   Determination of machine-hour requirements

Item	Forecast weekly demand, units (1)	Beginning inventory on hand, units (2)	Production time per unit, machine-hours (3)	Machine-hour requirements	
				Weekly demand (1) × (3)	Inventory on hand (2) × (3)
A	50	160	.05	2.50	8.00
B	35	120	.20	7.00	24.00
C	45	60	.25	11.25	15.00
D	30	130	.08	2.40	10.40
E	40	170	.14	5.60	23.80
Total				28.75	81.20

The previous quantities can be determined from Table 15-4 by ignoring order sizes for each item, after converting inventory on hand and rates of use from physical units into machine-hour requirements, as shown in Table 15-7.

The aggregate runout time for all these items is equal to

$$\frac{81.20 + 73.5 - 28.75}{28.75} = 4.38 \text{ wk from end of period being scheduled}$$

To provide enough ending inventory for each item so that all items run out after 4.38 wk, our schedule for the current week is determined as shown in Table 15-8.

The difference between the available and scheduled production capacity (73.50 − 73.51 = −.01 machine-hour) is due to rounding errors in determining the ending inventory for each item, so that they all yield the same aggregate runout time of 4.38 wk. For more details on this method see Ref. 6.

TABLE 15-8   Determination of production schedule for equalizing runout times†

Item	Forecast weekly demand, units (1)	Desired ending inventory for 4.38-wk runout time, units (4)	Total require-ments for 4.38-wk runout time, current period, units (1) + (4)	Beginning inventory on hand, units (2)	Production schedule	
					Units (5) = (1) + (4) − (2)	Machine hours (5) × (3)
A	50	219	269	160	109	5.45
B	35	154	189	120	69	13.80
C	45	197	242	60	182	45.50
D	30	132	162	130	32	2.56
E	40	175	215	170	45	6.30
Total						73.51

† (2) and (3) refer to columns in Table 15-7.

15-6   PROJECT SCHEDULING

General

We have previously noted that a project usually refers to one-of-a-kind undertaking. The uniqueness of a productive activity termed a project is often established by the unusual features of the product or service being created. However, at times the uniqueness is due to the circumstances under which the required activities have to be performed. At the level of a firm, a project may involve the R&D effort for a new product or a new process, construction of a new facility, or planning a new marketing strategy. Large projects may require the coordinated efforts of several government agencies and/or private organizations. Examples of large projects might be the development of a national health-insurance program, the design of a mass-transit system, the construction of a dam for flood control, or the Alaska pipeline.

Elements of a Project

Regardless of size and complexity, a project is described by certain key elements, which include the set of required activities, events, precedence or sequencing restrictions on the activities and critical resources defined as follows:

Activities   These refer to time- and resource-consuming tasks with clearly recognizable beginning and end points, e.g., writing a computer program or a legal contract or testing a computer program or a new piece of equipment.

Events   An event is a condition which signals the start or completion of an activity. It does not consume time or other resources but represents a point when one or more tasks have been performed. Certain events are called *milestones* because they represent the completion of important phases of the project. For example, signing a law or the approval of a new facility construction signal permission to start subsequent activities for implementation; completing the debugging of a computer inventory-control program allows change-over from a manual system.

Precedence restrictions   These specify the order or sequence in which the various activities can be performed. To determine precedence relationships for a given activity we must ask:

1. Which activities must be completed immediately before the activity under consideration can begin? These are called *prerequisite* activities.
2. Which activities must immediately follow this activity? These are called *immediate successors*.
3. Which activities can be performed at the same time with this activity? These are called *concurrent* activities.

For example, writing a computer program for a new inventory system must precede testing it, but analyzing the specific items it will be used for can be done concurrently.

Resources   The performance of project activities depends on the type and amounts of required resources, i.e., special skills, money, equipment, materials, testing facilities, etc. Such resources in critical supply, including time, are taken into account in order to achieve objectives related to their optimum utilization or schedule deadlines.

Objectives in Project Scheduling

Preparing a project schedule, regardless of the method used, is undertaken in order to answer one or more of the following questions:

1. What is the shortest time for completing the entire project?
2. Which activities are bottlenecks that must be monitored closely?
3. How much flexibility or slack is there with nonbottleneck activities?
4. What are the effects of shifting resources from ordinary to bottleneck activities?
5. If the duration of activities is uncertain, what is the probability of meeting specific schedule deadlines?

Management can respond to the above questions by using one of the methods discussed in the following sections. In addition, the graphical network representations of a project employed with these methods can prove extremely valuable as a communication device in the phases of project planning, coordination, and control. The Gantt chart, discussed previously, is simple, versatile, and easy to use for rather small projects, but as the complexity of a project increases, the use of techniques like the critical-path method, explained below, becomes indispensable for coordinating the various activities and the necessary resources.

Project Scheduling with
Critical-Path Method

Critical-path scheduling methods have revolutionized the management of complex projects in numerous fields of application. This is especially true in large construction, in R&D programs for new products, in planning new facilities, in government programs and projects, in conducting market surveys, performing complicated surgical operations, etc.

Procedure for applying critical-path scheduling   Once a decision is made to use critical-path scheduling, management proceeds in a series of steps designed to answer the questions posed previously:

1. *Determine project objectives, required activities, and key events (or milestones) for major project phases.* To do so requires specification of the project elements as follows:
   a. Prepare a list of required activities (A, B, C, ..., X)
   b. Estimate how long each activity will take T_x and required resources
   c. Indicate the precedence relationships for each activity. Thus, if activity A must precede activities B and C, in the row for A we show A < B, C, etc.

2. *Convert the information from step 1 into a network diagram* using the following conventions:

   a. An event indicating the start or completion of an activity is represented by a numbered circle or a network node. We have *merge nodes*, at which several activities converge (3 and 4 in Fig. 15-9*b*); *burst nodes*, from which several activities emanate (1 and 2 in Fig. 15-9*b*), and mixed types.

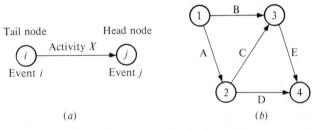

Tail node   Head node

Activity *X*

Event *i*   Event *j*

(*a*)   (*b*)

Fig. 15-9   **Representation of (*a*) events and (*b*) nodes.**

   b. An activity consuming time and resources is represented by an arrow connecting the starting and ending event nodes. The activity is specified by a letter for the arrow or by the two nodes it connects (Fig. 15-9*a*).

   c. A dummy activity, represented by a dashed line, is used to differentiate activities with the same starting and ending nodes (see Fig. 15-10), especially when the analysis is performed by a computer.

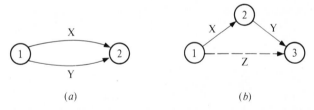

(*a*)   (*b*)

Fig. 15-10   **(*a*) Incorrect and (*b*) correct representation of activities with the same end nodes.**

   d. A dummy activity is also used to show precedence relationships accurately that could not be specified otherwise. For example, suppose we have a project in which activity X precedes Z and W (X < Z, W) and activity Y precedes Z and W (Y < Z, W). This can be shown in the network in Fig. 15-11*a*. If the precedence relationships were modified to read activity X precedes Z and W (X < Z, W) and activity Y precedes W only (Y < W), it would not be possible to construct a network without the use of a dummy activity. This problem is overcome by introducing a dummy, as shown in Fig. 15-11*b*.

3. *Perform critical-path calculations to determine:*

   a. Early and late start and completion times for each activity

   b. Critical activities

   c. Activity slack as measured by total and free float

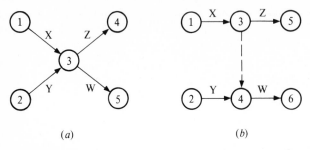

Fig. 15-11 Use of a dummy activity to represent precedence relationships.

4. *Construct project time chart.*
5. *Evaluate resource-leveling alternatives.*

The above steps are illustrated in the example that follows.

▶ EXAMPLE 15-1: ILLUSTRATION OF CRITICAL-PATH SCHEDULING
The firm of Plan-Ahead Consultants, Inc. has prepared a list of activities, their duration, and precedence relationships for a new project to develop a computerized inventory-control system. The relevant information is shown in Table 15-9. This is the first step in the application of critical-path analysis required for all projects whose preliminary budget exceeds $50,000.

TABLE 15-9 Activity list for new inventory-control-system project

Activity	Duration, wk	Required system analysts	Precedence relationships
A	5	6	A < B, C, D
B	7	3	B < E, F, G
C	10	2	C < I
D	6	5	D < G
E	3	3	E < H
F	9	2	F < I
G	7	4	G < I
H	4	7	H < I
I	2	4	

Construction of project network

The information developed as part of step 1 in the example can now be converted into a network showing the activities, their duration, and their sequencing requirements, as shown in Fig. 15-12. This represents step 2 in the analysis.

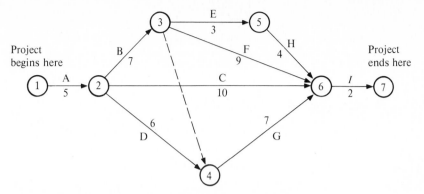

Fig. 15-12   Network representation of activities in Example 15-1.

Critical-Path Scheduling Calculations

In step 3 the analysis proceeds with the calculation of activity start and completion times in order to identify the critical activities in the project. Before doing so, however, it may be helpful to consider the concept of a critical path and its activities intuitively. If we examine the network in Fig. 15-12, we realize that we can reach the last node 7 from the beginning node 1 along any one of the four alternative paths, or connected sequences of activities indicated in Table 15-10.

TABLE 15-10   Network paths and their duration for example

Path	Activities	Sum of durations
I	A-B-E-H-I	$5 + 7 + 3 + 4 + 2 = 21$
II	A-B-F-I	$5 + 7 + 9 + 2 = 23$
III	A-C-I	$5 + 10 + 2 = 17$
IV	A-D-G-I	$5 + 6 + 7 + 2 = 22$

Since the time required to traverse each path depends on the duration of the activities that make it up, we can intuitively conclude that the total time to complete the entire project must be equal to that of the longest path from node 1 to node 7. This is the *critical path*, which *determines the shortest possible project completion time*. All activities included in it are critical, i.e., bottlenecks, since a delay in any one of them will postpone the completion of the entire project. In the example, the critical path in the project network is path II, so activities A, B, F, and I are all critical.

For more realistic projects with hundreds or even thousands of activities the intuitive approach breaks down, because it is difficult to identify all the complete paths in the network. Since the analysis is usually performed by computer, activities must be identified by their nodes and the calculations for early and late start and finish times are based on straightforward relationships.

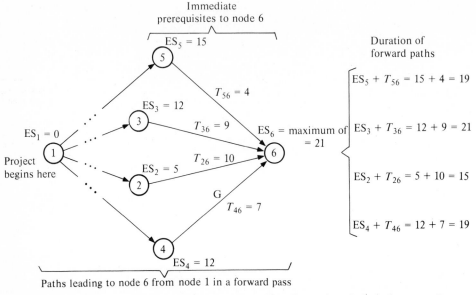

Fig. 15-13   Calculation of earliest start (ES) times from a forward pass through the project network.

Let ES_j be the earliest start time for all activities originating at node j. (For node 1 $ES_1 = 0$, unless it is agreed otherwise.) Intuitively, ES_j is the time needed to reach node j from node 1 on the longest path leading to it. ES_j times are calculated from a forward pass through the project network, as shown in Fig. 15-13.

If the tail nodes for all the immediate prerequisite activities, i.e., those terminating at j are $i - 1, i, \ldots, m$ and their durations are $T_{i-1, j}, T_{i, j}, \ldots, T_{m, j}$, then for node 6 in the example

$$ES_6 = \text{maximum of} \begin{cases} ES_2 + T_{26} = 5 + 10 = 15 \\ ES_3 + T_{36} = 12 + 9 = 21 \\ ES_4 + T_{46} = 12 + 7 = 19 \\ ES_5 + T_{56} = 15 + 4 = 19 \end{cases} = 21 \qquad (15\text{-}1)$$

where $ES_i + T_{i, j}$ is the time needed to reach node j from the starting node 1 on the path through node i. For the example, these calculations for ES times for all nodes are given in Table 15-11.

The ES time for any node can be interpreted as the earliest time an activity originating from that node can begin if all activities on the longest path leading to it are completed as rapidly as possible.

Next, let LS_j be the latest start time for all activities originating at node j to avoid project delays. If we are to avoid any delay in completing a project, then for the last node N in the network the earliest start time ES_N must be equal to the latest start time LS_N. In other words, the earliest time for starting any activity originating at N, say another project, must equal the latest start time for the same

TABLE 15-11   Calculations of earliest start times for example 15-1

Event j	Tail event of prerequisite activities	Earliest start time ES_j	Affected activities
1	0	0	A
2	1	$ES_2 = ES_1 + T_{12}$ $= 0 + 5 = 5$	B, C, D
3	2	$ES_3 = ES_2 + T_{23}$ $= 5 + 7 = 12$	E, F, G
4	2, 3	$ES_4 = $ maximum of $\{ES_2 + T_{24}, ES_3 + T_{34}\}$ $= \{5 + 6, 12 + 0\} = 12$	G
5	3	$ES_5 = ES_3 + T_{35}$ $= 12 + 3 = 15$	H
6	2, 3, 4, 5	$ES_6 = $ maximum of $\{ES_3 + T_{36}, ES_4 + T_{46}, ES_5 + T_{56}\}$ $= \{12 + 9, 11 + 7, 15 + 4\} = 21$	I
7	6	$ES_7 = ES_6 + T_{67}$ $= 21 + 2 = 23$	Next project if any

activities. Thus, for node 7 in the example $LS_7 = ES_7$. In general,

$$LS_N = ES_N \qquad \text{where } N = \text{last node in network} \qquad (15\text{-}2)$$

Intuitively, for node 3 the latest start time LS_3 is equal to the earliest start time for the last node ES_N minus the total time of the longest path leading to 3 from N. LS times are thus calculated from a backward pass through the network, as shown in Fig. 15-14.

The latest time (LS) for any node refers to the latest time an activity originating at that node can start without delaying the shortest completion time possible for the whole project. For node 3 in the example:

$$LS_3 = \text{minimum of} \left\{ \begin{array}{l} LS_4 - T_{34} = 14 - 0 = 14 \\ LS_5 - T_{35} = 17 - 3 = 14 \\ LS_6 - T_{36} = 21 - 9 = 12 \end{array} \right\} = 12 \qquad (15\text{-}3)$$

where $LS_k - T_{jk}$ is the time needed to reach node j from last node N on the path through node k. The calculations of latest start times for the example are given in Table 15-12.

Given the earliest and latest start times for each node in the network, we can determine the earliest and latest finish times EF_{ij} and LF_{ij} for each activity from the following relationships:

$$EF_{ij} = ES_i + T_{ij} \qquad (15\text{-}4)$$

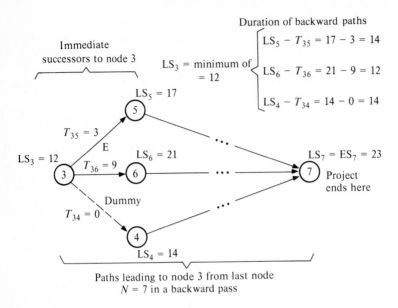

Fig. 15-14   **Calculation of latest start (LS) times from a backward pass through the project network.**

TABLE 15-12   **Calculations of latest start times for example 15-3**

Event j	Head event of activities originating from node j	Latest start time LS_j	Affected activity
$N = 7$	None	$LS_7 = ES_7 = 23$	Next project if any
6	7	$LS_6 = LS_7 - T_{67}$ $= 23 - 2 = 21$	I
5	6	$LS_5 = LS_6 - T_{56}$ $= 21 - 4 = 17$	H
4	6	$LS_4 = LS_6 - T_{46}$ $= 21 - 7 = 14$	G
3	5, 6	$LS_3 = $ min of $\{LS_6 - T_{36}, LS_5 - T_{35}, LS_4 - T_{34}\}$ $= \{21 - 9, 17 - 3, 14 - 0\} = 12$	E, F
2	3, 4, 6	$LS_2 = $ min $\{LS_3 - T_{23}, LS_4 - T_{24}, LS_6 - T_{26}\}$ $= \{12 - 7, 14 - 6, 21 - 10\} = 5$	B, C, D
1	2	$LS_1 = LS_2 - T_{12}$ $= 5 - 5 = 0$	A

or

$$\begin{bmatrix} \text{Earliest finish time} \\ \text{for activity } i, j \end{bmatrix} = \begin{bmatrix} \text{earliest start time} \\ \text{for node } i \end{bmatrix} + \begin{bmatrix} \text{duration of} \\ \text{activity } i, j \end{bmatrix}$$

$$LF_{ij} = LS_i + T_{ij} \tag{15-5}$$

or

$$\begin{bmatrix} \text{Latest finish time} \\ \text{for activity } i, j \end{bmatrix} = \begin{bmatrix} \text{latest start time} \\ \text{for node } i \end{bmatrix} + \begin{bmatrix} \text{duration of} \\ \text{activity } i, j \end{bmatrix}$$

From the above times we can calculate the slack, or total float, time for each activity TF_{ij} as follows:

$$TF_{ij} = LS_i - ES_i = LF_{ij} - EF_{ij} \qquad \text{Total float for activity } (i, j) \tag{15-6}$$

or

$$\begin{bmatrix} \text{Total float} \\ \text{time for } i, j \end{bmatrix} = \begin{bmatrix} \text{latest start} \\ \text{for node } i \end{bmatrix} - \begin{bmatrix} \text{earliest start} \\ \text{for node } i \end{bmatrix}$$

$$= \begin{bmatrix} \text{latest finish} \\ \text{for activity } i, j \end{bmatrix} - \begin{bmatrix} \text{earliest finish} \\ \text{for activity } i, j \end{bmatrix}$$

Start and finish times and total float for all activities in the example are summarized in Table 15-13, where the critical path consists of activities with no slack or total float ($TF = 0$). This can be shown graphically in the project network with a double or heavy line. In managing a project, critical activities must be monitored closely because any delay in them will postpone the completion of the entire project by the same amount. Other activities have more flexibility in their scheduling, so that management can adjust the allocation of limited resources accordingly.

It is helpful at times to distinguish between total float and free float. *Total float* might be shared by all activities in a given sequence, such as E and H in the example, whereas *free float* is exclusively available to a single activity, such as C in the example. The network for the example is repeated in Fig. 15-15, showing early

TABLE 15-13 Summary of activity start times, finish times, and total float

Activity name	i, j	Duration, wk	System required analysts	Start time ES	LS	Finish time EF	LF	Total float TF
A	1, 2	5	6	0	0	5	5	0†
B	2, 3	7	3	5	5	12	12	0†
C	2, 6	10	2	5	11	15	21	6
D	2, 4	6	5	5	8	11	14	3
E	3, 5	3	3	12	14	15	17	2
F	3, 6	9	2	12	12	21	21	0†
G	4, 6	7	4	12	14	19	21	1
H	5, 6	4	7	15	17	19	21	2
I	6, 7	2	4	21	21	23	23	0†

† Critical.

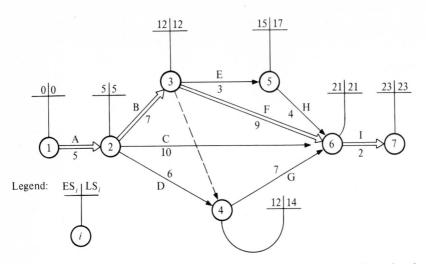

Fig. 15-15 Project network for example, showing earliest and latest start times for each node and critical activities.

and late start times; all critical activities for the project are shown with double lines.

Construction of Project Time Chart and Resource-Requirement Profile

The information in Table 15-13 forms the basis for preparing a time chart and a resource-requirement profile, also known as a load chart. A time chart is in practice the most useful graphical display of the project schedule. It is similar to a Gantt chart in that activities are displayed by solid horizontal bars (or lines) against a time scale for elapsed time. Beyond that, however, a time chart shows the precedence relationships by vertical dotted lines and the total float for noncritical activities by empty bars (or dotted lines). For the example the time chart is shown in Fig. 15-16. This can be accompanied by another chart displaying the requirements for a critical resource, in this case analyst-weeks, to allow management to shift resource allocations as necessary. When critical-path analysis is performed by a computer, time charts and load charts are part of the output that can be updated

▶ and used to monitor the project.

Resource leveling by heuristic methods The presence of fluctuations in the resource-requirement profile implies costly adjustments due to overtime, hiring, firing, or underutilization of available capacity. Thus it is desirable to smooth out such fluctuations by rescheduling noncritical activities. This is done by sliding them back and forth in the range specified by their earliest and latest start times. The time chart and load chart when noncritical activities are rescheduled at their earliest start times are shown in Fig. 15-17.

For simple projects with one or two resources in critical supply the above heuristic method may prove satisfactory, but for large projects with several resource constraints one must resort to more sophisticated methods that rely on some

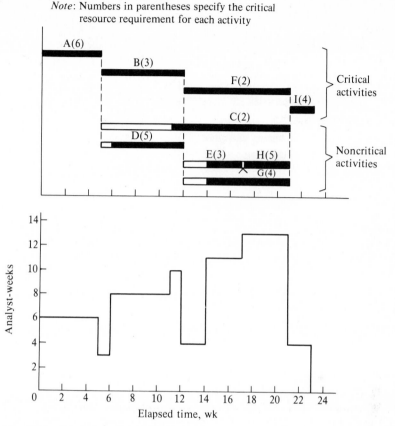

Fig. 15-16 Time chart and critical-resource (analyst-weeks) requirement profile when all activities are scheduled at their latest start times.

optimization technique. One such approach, devised by Wiest and Levy (Ref. 17, p. 124), uses integer programming. When the assumptions of integer programming (integer-valued variables and linear restrictions and objective function) are not met, it is possible to use heuristic computer programs which generate and evaluate a large number of alternative schedules rapidly, using the total float in noncritical activities.

Project rescheduling by changing duration of critical activities Sometimes the objective may be to keep resource requirements below a certain limit (crew size, available machine-hours, budget level, etc.) rather than to smooth them out over the project duration. Alternatively, it may be desired to minimize total project costs rather than meet a particular completion date. Naturally, the first candidates for rescheduling are the noncritical activities. If the resultant adjustments do not achieve the above objectives, however, it may be necessary to change the duration of critical activities or even the types of resources used.

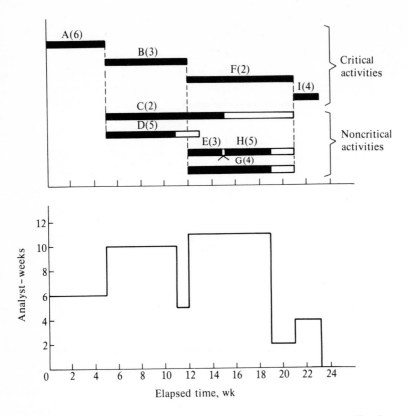

Fig. 15-17 Time chart and critical-resource (analyst-weeks) requirement profile when all noncritical activities are scheduled at their earliest start times.

A change in the duration of critical activities involves two types of cost trade-offs: (1) We must consider the effects on the *direct activity costs*. In general, shorter completion times for an activity require more intensive use of resources (work force, equipment, etc.) which increases direct costs according to some pattern like those indicated in Fig. 15-18*a*. (2) We have to account for the effects of activity duration changes on *indirect project costs*, such as facilities or equipment rentals, supervision, and other costs fixed for the project as a whole. As the project completion time decreases, indirect costs tend to decrease too. This is shown in Fig. 15-18*b*. The net effect of a change in activity duration on relevant costs is shown in Fig. 15-18*c*.

We must keep in mind that as we reduce the duration of one or more critical activities, thus shortening the total time of the critical path, some other path(s) in the network may also become critical. The trade-off analysis must then be expanded to cover a larger number of interactions between costs and activity durations. The "near optimum" schedule, i.e., one that minimizes total cost or meets some other criterion, is usually determined by a computerized heuristic method.

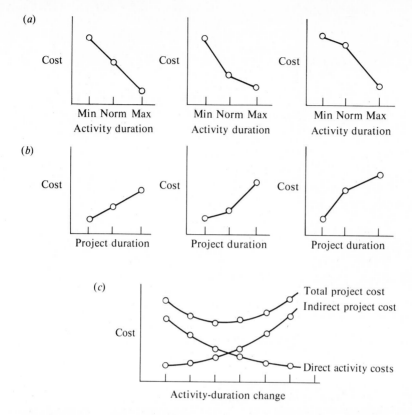

Fig. 15-18 Estimating the cost of trade-offs of changing activity durations: (*a*) direct-activity-cost curves, (*b*) indirect-activity-cost curves, and (*c*) net effect of changes in duration of activity.

Project Scheduling with PERT

So far we have assumed that activity times and resource requirements for the project are known and constant. This is, of course, a highly idealized situation. For projects with activities that have been performed repeatedly in various configurations (maintenance, construction, planning, etc.) the above assumption may approximate reality quite well. The single estimates used represent averages of statistical distributions with variability so small that it can be ignored.

For certain types of work, however, the uncertainty in the duration of activities may be substantial. The project schedule must reflect this fact; otherwise it becomes an unreliable basis for planning and control. Uncertainty is usually significant in R&D for new products and processes, in construction affected by weather, in the execution of programs or plans with limited control over those responsible for implementation, and others.

PERT (program evaluation and review technique) takes account of the uncertainty in activity times explicitly. It does so by providing not a single estimate but three. As a result, we can calculate not only an average duration but also a measure of variability for the time needed to perform an activity.

Since PERT specifies the entire statistical distribution for each activity's duration, we can estimate the probability of completing a particular phase or the entire project by a specific date. In using PERT management follows the same steps as for critical-path scheduling.

Activity-time estimates in PERT When a project with considerable uncertainty is to be managed using PERT, we assume that those responsible for each activity can provide three different estimates concerning its duration, as follows:

An *optimistic estimate a*, which assumes that uncontrollable factors will be exceptionally favorable when the activity is performed

A *most likely estimate m*, which represents a fair share of favorable and unfavorable conditions in the performance of the activity

A *pessimistic estimate b*, which assumes an unusual amount of difficulty from unfavorable conditions while the activity is performed.

In the excavation activity for the foundations of a new structure, *m* would apply to the typical weather prevailing in the month the activity is scheduled, *a* would indicate fewer rainy days than average, and *b* would refer to unusually bad weather in terms of rainfall. Similar comments would apply to the time for performing necessary tests on a new drug or a new automobile antipollution device.

If we can also assume that the above estimates describe a particular statistical distribution for activity duration, known as the *beta distribution* (see Fig. 15-19), we can proceed to determine for each activity (1) its expected or mean duration t_E and (2) its variability as measured by its variance V as follows:

$$t_E = \frac{a + 4m + b}{6} \tag{15-7}$$

and
$$V = [\tfrac{1}{6}(b - a)]^2 \tag{15-8}$$

where t_E = expected time for activity
V = variance for duration of activity

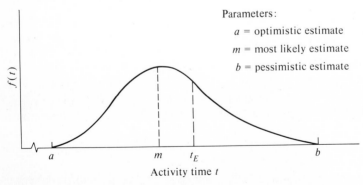

Fig. 15-19 Statistical distribution of activity-time estimates using PERT.

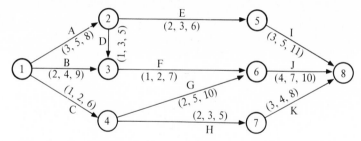

Fig. 15-20   Network and activity times for R&D program of Miracle Drug Co.

▶ EXAMPLE 15-2

Suppose Miracle Drug Co. is about to undertake a research and development program for a new drug treating high blood pressure. The network of activities and their time estimates for this project are shown in Fig. 15-20.

Critical-Path Calculations Using PERT

Before we can identify the critical path in a PERT network, we must calculate the expected time t_E for each activity from the three estimates supplied by management. Following that, we can proceed to determine early and late start and finish times using the expected times as we did the single estimates in critical-path scheduling (see Fig. 15-21). The results from these calculations are shown in Table 15-14. Knowing the variability of each activity as measured by its variance, we can also calculate the variability in the duration of the critical path.[1]

---

[1] For this type of analysis and others that account for projects costs, resource leveling, etc. there are a number of computer programs from the libraries of commercial computer systems. For a representative sample see N. Paul Loomba, *Management—A Quantitative Perspective*, Macmillan, New York, 1978, p. 159.

TABLE 15-14   Critical-path calculations for PERT network of Miracle Drug Co.

Activity	Time estimates, months			Expected time t_E	Standard deviation S	Start time		Finish time		Total float
	a	m	b			ES	LS	EF	LF	
A	3	5	8	5.17	.83	0	0	5.17	5.17	0
B	2	4	9	4.50	1.17	0	3.67	4.50	8.17	3.67
C	1	2	6	2.50	.83	0	3.01	2.50	5.51	3.01
D	1	3	5	3.00	.67	5.17	5.17	8.17	8.17	0
E	2	3	6	3.33	.67	5.17	8.84	8.50	12.17	3.67
F	1	2	7	2.67	1.00	8.17	8.17	10.84	10.84	0
G	2	5	10	5.33	1.33	2.50	5.51	7.83	10.84	3.01
H	2	3	5	3.17	.50	2.50	10.17	5.67	13.34	7.67
I	3	5	11	5.67	1.33	8.50	12.17	14.17	17.6	3.67
J	4	7	10	7.00	1.00	10.84	10.84	17.84	17.84	0
K	3	4	8	4.50	.83	5.67	13.34	10.17	17.84	7.67

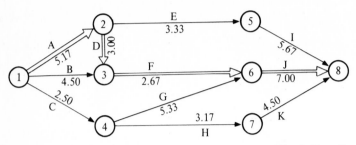

Fig. 15-21   PERT network with expected activity times for Miracle Drug Co.

Property

The variance in the duration of the critical path, hence the total project, is equal to the sum of the variances for all critical activities along that path.

From the total times of the different paths through the network or by using the rules developed to compute early and late start and finish times the critical path for the PERT network of the example consists of activities A, D, F, and J. The sum of the expected times for these activities is as follows, where *cp* stands for critical path:

$$t_{E,\,cp} = t_E(A) + t_E(D) + t_E(F) + t_E(J)$$
$$= 5.17 + 3.00 + 2.67 + 7.00 = 17.84 \text{ months}$$

and the variability for the duration of the critical path is

$$V_{cp} = V_A + V_D + V_F + V_J = S_A^2 + S_D^2 + S_F^2 + S_J^2$$
$$= (.83)^2 + (.67)^2 + (1.00)^2 + (1.00)^2 = (3.14 \text{ months})^2$$
$$S_{cp} = \sqrt{S_A^2 + S_D^2 + S_F^2 + S_J^2} = \sqrt{3.14} = 1.77 \text{ months}$$

From basic statistics we have a fundamental property that the sum of several random variables has a distribution that is approximately normal.[1] Since the project completion time is the sum of the critical activity times, it follows a normal distribution with a mean equal to 17.84 months and a standard deviation equal to 1.77 months (see Fig. 15-22).

The inferred normal distribution for project completion times is based on two assumptions: (1) all activities on the critical path must be independent of each other with respect to duration and (2) their expected times must be unbiased, i.e., estimate the mean activity duration correctly when used repeatedly. If these assumptions can approximate actual project conditions satisfactorily, we can deter-

---

[1] This is known as the *central-limit theorem*. For a more detailed explanation consult any standard text in statistics.

Normal approximation
  mean = t_E = 17.84 months

Standard deviation = S = 1.77 months

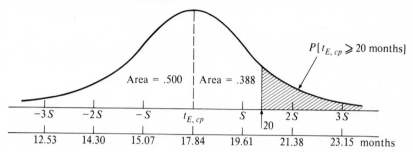

Fig. 15-22 **Statistical distribution for project completion time for Miracle Drug Co.**

mine the probability of meeting a particular project completion date. For example, the probability that the R&D project for Miracle Drug Co. will be completed in less than 20 months will be

$$P(t_{E,\,cp} \le 20) = \text{area under normal curve to right of 20 months}$$

For $t = 20$ we have

$$z = \frac{t - t_{E,\,cp}}{S_{cp}} = \frac{20 - 17.84}{1.77} = 1.22 \qquad \begin{array}{c}\text{Number of standard deviations}\\\text{to right of mean}\end{array}$$

From the table with areas under the normal distribution (see Appendix 2) the value corresponding to $z = 1.22$ is .388 (see Fig. 15-22). Hence

$$P(t_{E,\,cp} \le 20 \text{ months}) = .500 + .388 = .888 = 88.8\%$$

The procedure described must be used very cautiously. If other paths in the network have total durations close to that for the critical path, their activities may exceed their mean duration. When this happens, the almost-critical paths may have longer total times, thus becoming more restrictive than the original critical path. A versatile approach for testing the sensitivity of the original critical path uses simula-
▶ tion with probability distributions of all individual activities.[1]

Some Difficulties in Using Critical-Path Methods

The application of critical-path methods to real projects may be accompanied by difficulties related to both conceptual and implementation problems. Familiarity with the most frequent sources of errors is important so that appropriate allowances can be made in advance.

[1] For an interesting example see Barry Shore, *Operations Management*, McGraw-Hill, New York, 1973, p. 173.

At the conceptual level we must deal with three assumptions about the definition of activities, their duration, and the nature of their interrelationships: (1) Activities as building blocks of a network may not have well-defined starting and endpoints. Instead they may change in content and blend with each other. (2) Activity duration is neither fixed, as assumed in CPS, nor conveniently summarized by a statistical (beta) distribution specified by three estimates (a, m, and b), as in PERT. These are helpful approximations, which in the case of PERT may lead to 10 percent absolute error in the estimation of earliest times and 5 percent error in individual variances. (3) The calculation of the probability of meeting a certain due date assumes the independence of activities along the critical path. In reality this may not be the case.

At the practical level problems may arise in two areas: (1) it is possible that the technical aspects of the method are not well understood by key personnel. Unless such features are adequately explained, implementation of critical-path methods may suffer. (2) Problems may be related to the significance implied for activities on the critical path. If the project is to be performed by one organization, the attention assigned to critical activities is well deserved. When the project employs several subcontractors, political or economic motives may influence their actions to be or not to be on the critical path, depending on the consequences of such visibility.

Despite these difficulties, critical-path methods in the last two decades have become one of management's most versatile planning and control tools employed in simple and sophisticated ways.

15-6 SUMMARY

Scheduling is the last step before managerial plans are converted into productive activities. Its complexity varies with the type of production process and the scale of operation. Our discussion of scheduling methods is structured around the three pure types of a process, flow shop, job shop, and project. Unless scheduling is done efficiently, resources are forced into idleness, delivery times are not met, and previous planning steps become unreliable.

For a flow shop much of the scheduling effort has been invested in the system design phase. This is done when necessary tasks are grouped into successive work stations to achieve a desired output rate. Helpful in this regard is the variety of line-balancing methods. In subsequent phases, given the available capacity per period, management first determines the desirable product mix and then makes the detailed assignments within the constraints of the aggregate production plan. For large systems we rely on *satisficing* rather than optimizing methods. When several primary products use interchangeable parts and components, the linking of the aggregate plan with a production schedule is based on materials-requirement planning, as discussed in Chap. 14.

With a job shop, scheduling consists of two major tasks: (1) The available jobs must be loaded into the various work centers for processing. This is a resource-allocation process performed with a criterion such as minimizing total cost or processing time. (2) For a specific work center assigned jobs must be ordered in time, i.e., sequenced. A sequencing problem can be viewed as a queueing problem in which we treat the queue (or job-selection) principle as a variable and try to satisfy criteria related either to the utilization of limited resources or to customer service times. Here we note that the effectiveness of a job-selection rule for sequencing depends on the criterion employed. Job-shop scheduling is extremely complex, and for real problems it can be handled only with simulation techniques. Two well-integrated systems for this purpose have been developed by Hughes Aircraft Co. and General Electric Co.

In the case of a project, scheduling techniques vary from simple Gantt charts to complex critical-path methods that may rely on a graphical network representation. If some of the key assumptions about activity duration and independence are satisfied, critical-path methods prove very helpful in answering questions related to project completion time, allocation of limited resources, and the like.

Regardless of the type of production process, the complexity of the scheduling task for realistic operations systems requires the use of computer-based information systems to store and process the masses of data needed in the preparation and evaluation of alternative feasible schedules.

NOTATION

Job sequencing

n = number of jobs to be processed
m = number of work centers in series a job must be processed through
S = static arrival pattern, i.e. all jobs to be done available at the beginning
D = dynamic arrival pattern, i.e. some jobs arrive for processing while other work is in progress
F = flow shop arrangement, i.e. work centers placed in series
J = job shop arrangement, i.e. work centers grouped by function
APT = average processing time
AWT = average waiting time
LU = per cent labor utilization
MU = per cent machine utilization
IP = in process inventory cost
t_i = operation time for job i
x_i = waiting time for job i
T_i = processing time for job i $(= t_i + x_i)$
$\bar{T}$ = average processing time
w_i = weight for degree of importance of job i

Critical path scheduling & PERT

T_x = duration of activity x
ES_j = earliest start time for all activities starting at node j
LS_j = latest start time for all activities starting at node j
TF_{ij} = total float for activity defined by nodes i and j
a,m, b = optimistic, most likely and pessimistic duration for an activity with uncertain completion time
t_E = expected duration for an activity
V = variance of duration for an activity
S = standard deviation of duration for an activity

REVIEW QUESTIONS

1. State the major difference between scheduling and aggregate planning.
2. For what reasons is scheduling significant in operations management? How does it affect the image of the firm?
3. Discuss the factors that affect the scheduling function.
4. Describe the general scheduling system in terms of (*a*) activities (or outputs), (*b*) information requirements (or inputs), (*c*) scheduling constraints, (*d*) decision variables, and (*e*) performance criteria.
5. Discuss the use and importance of operation sheets and bills of materials in scheduling production.
6. Describe the information requirements and the objective of the line-balancing problem.
7. What types of production lines are used in a flow shop?
8. Which problems usually arise in going from aggregate planning to scheduling for a flow-shop system?
9. Describe the steps necessary to couple the scheduling and aggregate-planning functions in a flow shop. Is an optimum schedule possible? Why?
10. State the reasons that make scheduling more difficult in job shops than in flow shops.
11. Explain the difference between loading and sequencing in shop scheduling.
12. Explain the use of a Gantt chart for job-shop scheduling. What are its major advantages and limitations?
13. What are the conditions for the use of the assignment method in job-shop scheduling?
14. What is the necessary adjustment in the assignment method (of shop loading) when the performance index is to be maximized?
15. Which characteristics must be specified before analyzing the shop-sequencing problem?
16. What is the meaning of human-limited versus machine-limited systems with regard to scheduling?
17. Why must the schedule-evaluation criterion be specified before selecting the job-selection rule?
18. Which scheduling criteria are aimed at improving (*a*) resource utilization and (*b*) customer service? (*c*) How are some of the above employed for scheduling in (i) industrial applications, (ii) a commercial airline, (iii) a commercial bank, (iv) a hospital operating room, (v) a government agency such as IRS?
19. What is the objective of the runout-time method in job-shop batch scheduling?
20. Describe in your own words the meaning of the following concepts related to critical-path analysis:
    (*a*) Event
    (*b*) Activity
    (*c*) Precedence relationships
    (*d*) Milestone
    (*e*) Critical resource
    (*f*) Critical activity
    (*g*) Critical path
21. With reference to a typical critical-path application specify:
    (*a*) The information input requirements
    (*b*) The usual form of analysis
    (*c*) Possible outputs for use by management
22. Under what circumstances is the use of a probabilistic approach, e.g., PERT, most appropriate?
23. What are some of the conceptual and practical problems encountered in critical-path applications?

PROBLEMS

1. International Consultants, Ltd., has just signed contracts with four clients concerning the preparation of feasibility studies for the construction of power generation plants. Performance of each consultant that will head the study groups is expected to vary in terms of the consultant-days required to prepare the report for each project as shown in the matrix below.

	Project			
Consultant	A	B	C	D
C_1	50	27	32	55
C_2	65	19	38	53
C_3	60	28	35	64
C_4	56	25	56	62

(a) How should the consultants be assigned to the projects to minimize the number of consultant-days used for the feasibility studies?

(b) What is the minimum number of consultant-days required?

2. Suppose that in Prob. 1 the entries in the matrix refer instead to expected profits from each assignment. How should the firm assign its consultants to maximize total expected profit?

3. A computer manufacturer has sold hardware systems to five different customers. Five of the manufacturer's maintenance engineers service the systems periodically. The time each engineer takes on the five installations varies, as shown in the following matrix.

Maintenance engineer	Computer installation				
	1	2	3	4	5
A	8	3	15	2	7
B	10	6	18	2	11
C	4	17	4	2	13
D	11	16	14	2	12
E	9	12	10	2	6

(a) How should the engineers be assigned to minimize the total maintenance time?

(b) What is the minimum maintenance time?

4. Each morning the foreman of a shop gives the milling-machine operator a list of jobs in the order they have arrived with their time estimates. On a given day the list includes the following data:

Job	J_1	J_2	J_3	J_4	J_5	J_6
Time estimate, h	3	7	4	1	2	5

(a) Determine the job sequence that will minimize the average processing time.
(b) What is the percentage improvement over the job sequence according to arrival time?
(c) Draw a Gantt chart for the optimum sequence.
5. Suppose that the jobs in Prob. 4 have priority weights equal to $w_1 = 3$, $w_2 = 5$, $w_3 = 8$, $w_4 = 5$, $w_5 = 10$, $w_6 = 4$. What is the minimum average weighted processing time?
6. Every morning the operator of the duplicating-services department of UpState University is handed a list of job requests in the order they arrive. A time estimate per job is also included on the list based on the number of pages per job. As each order is completed the operator phones the secretary of the requesting department to have the material picked up. In recent weeks there have been several complaints about slow turnaround times. One day the list included the following:

Job request	A	B	C	D	E	F	G
Time, h	1.6	1.3	.7	.5	1.5	1.4	.3

(a) Determine the average turnaround time using the current procedure for first in, first out handling of job requests.
(b) What would be the optimum job sequence on this day to minimize the average turnaround times?
(c) Draw a Gantt chart for the optimum job sequence.
7. In Prob. 6, assume that the list also includes priority weights for the job requests as follows:

$$w_A = 8, \ w_B = 1, \ w_C = 10, \ w_D = 5, \ w_E = 3, \ w_F = 2, \ w_G = 6.$$

How should the jobs be sequenced to minimize the average weighted processing time?
8. Suppose that five jobs await at the beginning of a shift to be processed in two machines. Their operation times in hours have been estimated as follows:

Job	J_1	J_2	J_3	J_4	J_5
Machine A	5	3	6	1	4
Machine B	2	7	5	2	5

(a) What job sequence will minimize the total elapsed time?
(b) What is the percentage idle time for each machine over the total elapsed time?
9. The testing laboratory of Alvon Cosmetics Co. receives requests for sample evaluation before processing large batches at its different processing units. Testing involves sample preparation and sample analysis, which must be done in quick succession by two different chemists. On a given day the list of tests with the estimates for processing times are as follows:

	Time requirement, min	
Job request	Sample preparation	Sample analysis
1	0.7	0.5
2	0.5	0.2
3	0.4	0.1
4	0.3	0.2
5	0.6	0.4
6	0.5	0.3

(a) What is the total elapsed time if the testing lab processes the samples in the order they arrive?

(b) How would you sequence the sample testing to minimize the total elapsed time?

(c) What is the percentage utilization of each chemist?

10. The machine shop of General Home Appliance Co. runs batches of machined parts used for ranges and refrigerators. These parts are carried in stock to satisfy given demand rates. The shop operates one 8-h shift per day, 6 days/week and requires 3 h of weekly maintenance. For the upcoming week the production planning and control department has supplied the following information:

Component	Forecast weekly demand	Beginning inventory on hand	Production time per unit, h	Order size
A	240	570	.03	360
B	180	280	.07	240
C	300	450	.02	400
D	150	330	.05	250

(a) What must the processing sequence for these items be?

(b) What must the amount produced of each item be if no order sizes are prescribed?

11. The maintenance of a large papermill machine requires the activities shown in the accompanying network along with a time estimate in days for each activity.

(a) Prepare an activity time table.

(b) Identify the critical path.

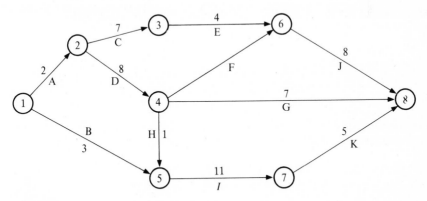

Problem 11

12. Suppose that in Prob. 11 the requirements for maintenance mechanics are specified as follows:

Activity	A	B	C	D	E	F	G	H	I	J	K
Requirements, mechanic-days	8	7	4	3	8	2	4	5	3	2	1

(a) Prepare a manpower requirement profile using LS times for all activities.

(b) How can this profile be leveled to smooth out the utilization of maintenance mechanics?

13. Upon further examination it was realized that in the network of Prob. 12 dummy activities (3, 4) and (4, 7) had been omitted.

(a) Prepare a revised activity timetable.

(b) Identify the critical path in the revised network.

14. Repair work on a flood-control dam will require completion of the activities indicated by the network. Optimistic, most likely, and pessimistic estimates (a, m, b) for activity duration (in weeks) due to weather uncertainty are shown along the activity arrows.

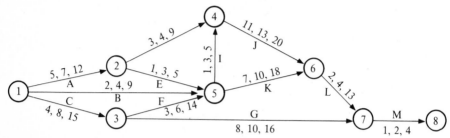

Problem 14

(a) Prepare a table showing for each activity early and late start and finish times and total float.

(b) Determine the critical path for the project.

(c) Calculate the probability that the flood-control dam will be ready no later than 2 wk from its expected completion time.

15. The R&D project for a new scrubber for electrical power plants requires the activities shown in the network along with estimates on activity duration (a, m, b).

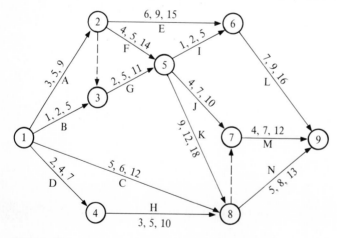

Problem 15

(a) Prepare a table with activity ES, LS, LS, LF times and float.

(b) Identify the critical path for the project.

(c) Calculate the probability that the critical-path duration will be exceeded by (i) more than 3 days and (ii) more than 8 days.

SELECTED REFERENCES

1. Baker, K. R.: *Introduction to Sequencing and Scheduling*, Wiley, New York, 1974.
2. Buffa, E. S.: *Production-Inventory Systems: Planning and Control*, Irwin, Homewood, Ill., 1968.
3. Conway, R. W., William L. Maxwell, and Louis W. Miller: *Theory of Scheduling*, Addison-Wesley, Reading, Mass., 1967.
4. Johnson, L. A., and D. C. Montgomery: *Operations Research in Production Planning, Scheduling, and Inventory Control*, Wiley, New York, 1974.
5. Levin, R. I., and C. A. Kirkpatrick: *Planning and Control with PERT/CPM*, McGraw-Hill, New York, 1966.
6. Magee, J. F., and D. M. Boodman: *Production Planning and Inventory Control*, 2d ed., McGraw-Hill, New York, 1967.
7. Moder, J. J., and C. R. Phillips: *Project Management with CPM and PERT*, 2d ed., Reinhold, New York, 1970.
8. Moodie, C. L., and D. J. Novotny: "Computer Scheduling and Control Systems for Discrete Part Production," *Journal of Industrial Engineering*, vol. 19, no. 7, pp. 648–671, July 1967.
9. Muth, John F., and Gerald L. Thompson: *Industrial Scheduling*, Prentice-Hall, Englewood Cliffs, N.J., 1963.
10. Niland, Powell: *Production Planning, Scheduling and Inventory Control*, Macmillan, New York, 1971.
11. O'Brien, James J.: *Scheduling Handbook*, McGraw-Hill, New York, 1969.
12. Riggs, James L.: *Production Systems*, 2d ed., Wiley/Hamilton, New York, 1976.
13. Starr, Martin K.: *Systems Management of Operations*, Prentice-Hall, Englewood Cliffs, N.J., 1971, chaps. 10 and 11.
14. Wiest, J. D.: "A Heuristic Model for Scheduling Large Projects with Limited Resources," *Management Science*, vol. 13, no. 6, pp. 359–377, February 1967.
15. Wiest, J. D.: "Heuristic Programs for Decision-Making," *Harvard Business Review*, September–October 1966, pp. 129–143.
16. Wiest, J. D.: "Some Properties of Schedules for Large Projects with Limited Resources," *Operations Research*, vol. 12, no. 3, May–June 1964.

Chapter 16

PERFORMANCE CONTROL

16-1 INTRODUCTION

The long-term survival of an organization depends on its continued ability to satisfy consumer or public needs through the products and services offered. The nature of such needs is identified and taken into account in the phase of preparing general and engineering specifications for a product or service with existing technologies.

Quality control as one aspect of performance control is the function within a firm whose purpose is to measure and evaluate quality in the inputs and outputs of a process. *The same concepts and methods developed for quality control can be applied equally well to other important aspects of effectiveness, such as production costs, production or delivery times, and others.* Thus, by providing feedback on various key indicators, performance control informs management on how well its objectives are attained.

The objectives of this chapter are to explain different interpretations of quality, to describe the nature of a quality-control system, and to discuss the most widely employed methods for statistical control of quality, costs, or other measures of performance.

16-2 ASPECTS OF QUALITY

The meaning of quality depends on the observer's point of view. For our purpose, it is helpful to consider quality in three different contexts, i.e., quality inherent in the product design, quality associated with production, and quality related to performance in use.

Quality to the consumer refers to certain tangible and intangible attributes inherent in the design of the product or service and in its performance under normal use. High *design quality* takes the form of better materials, e.g., leather versus vinyl seats for a car, a wider choice on the menu for an airline's first-class passengers, and so on. It also involves superior workmanship for increased precision or better appearance, and for products it is usually expressed by tighter engineering specifications.

Performance quality relates to the product's reliability and the ease of maintenance and repair service when required. Reliability implies satisfactory operation under normal conditions of use for a certain length of time. Performance quality is limited by design quality and may be enhanced through warranties offered to the consumer pertaining to workmanship and parts over a fixed time interval or amount of use.

Design and performance quality of the output represent the targets aimed at by the production process. How well they are achieved in practice is another dimension of quality known as *production or conformance quality*. The latter depends on how well the design of a product or service has been adapted to the capabilities of the process. A good match of a process to a set of output specifications may result in excellent conformance quality even though these specifications apply to an "average" product or service in terms of design quality. Suppose that a machine can produce record-player shafts so that 99.7 percent of its output is in the range of .2560 $\pm$ .0060 in. If the specifications for the shaft were .2560 $\pm$ .0120 in we would say the process is *overmatched* to the output specifications, resulting in higher cost per unit than would be possible with a less precise machine. But if the shaft specifications were .2560 $\pm$ .0015 in, the process would be *undermatched* because a high percentage of its output would fall outside the permissible range and be classified as defective.

The quality-control function attempts to integrate and balance several important decisions in marketing, production, and finance with the purpose of achieving overall objectives for the entire organization. The design-quality and performance-quality decisions must represent the best compromise of what the consumer needs, as interpreted by marketing, and what the organization can deliver, as interpreted by production and engineering. This is a top management decision involving far-reaching implications for the *company's image and competitive ability*. The relationship of the quality-control function to the rest of the organization is shown in Fig. 16-1.

Regardless of how well design decisions are made, the quality of the finished product is in the hands of inspectors and/or operators responsible for conformance quality. Thus, the existence of a successful system for monitoring customer satisfaction, with services received or products in use, is essential for the necessary feedback on performance quality. It is only through a continual readjustment and balance of all three aspects of output quality that the organization can adapt and compete successfully in serving the needs of the consumer as a means of advancing toward its long-term objectives.

16-3 SETTING QUALITY STANDARDS

When considering the multitude of factors that influence quality decisions, we realize that an optimum quality standard is at best a relative concept. High quality in a product or service can be used as a powerful reason to secure a higher price and instill pride in the work force. It also can be incorporated in a strategy to confront competitors and enter new markets. Both these approaches serve to increase revenues, but increasing quality through superior design is subject to the law of diminishing returns as measured by additional revenues. Furthermore, the

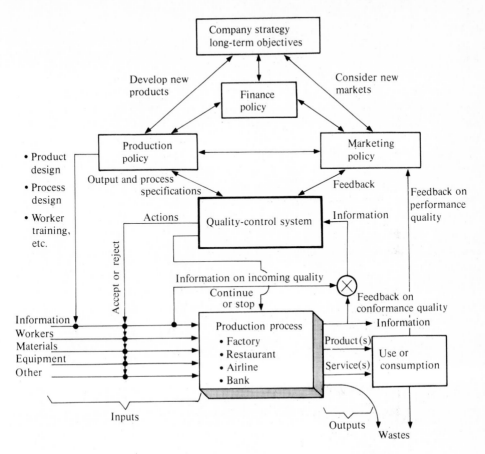

Fig. 16-1   Relationship of the quality-control system to other parts of the organization.

accelerating increases in production and inspection costs required to provide additional improvements act as a brake against further quality refinements. The conflicting pressures in deciding the appropriate quality level are shown in Fig. 16-2. According to the concepts of marginal analysis in economics, the optimum quality level is reached at the point where the marginal, or incremental, revenue from a quality improvement equals the marginal, or incremental, cost to secure it.

16-4   THE QUALITY-CONTROL SYSTEM

Our understanding of the quality control (QC) system and its operation can be strengthened if we view it as one part of the operations-management control function discussed in Chap. 1. Figure 16-3 provides the framework needed for a more detailed discussion, using an input-output description.

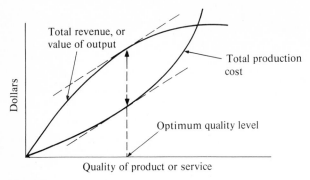

Fig. 16-2   **Factors influencing determination of the optimum quality level.**

The Basic Quality-Control Problem

Given a set of specifications, i.e., a desired quality level as a target, control of quality involves keeping track of the variability from these specifications, observed in actual units of the product or service. Measurement of actual quality may be based on inspection of all or part of the items produced, although 100 percent inspection is rarely an attractive alternative. When possible, it is expensive, not necessarily error-free, and may induce poor performance from employees in the belief that poor work will be detected later. For the output of an ongoing process, 100 percent inspection is not possible. Furthermore, in instances where inspection is destructive or detrimental to the item produced the use of 100 percent inspection would wipe out the entire output of a process. Thus, it is preferable to rely on sampling, which can yield extremely reliable results when it is carried out according to statistical methods.

Quality control can be generally exercised over a process that may or may not be feasible to control directly. The semifinished output from a critical operation or the finished product of a firm's own process is normally under direct control. This, however, is not the case with materials or parts purchased from suppliers. *It is always assumed that a process* (ours or someone else's) *operates satisfactorily unless the evidence in the sample(s) taken indicates otherwise.*[1]

The key issue in quality control is to select a sample of items representative of the process output being evaluated. These may be assembly parts, accounting entries, airline customers served, etc. The evidence of output quality contained in the sample becomes the basis for accepting or rejecting the hypothesis that the process it came from is satisfactory, i.e., under control. If the evidence in the sample leads us to accept the hypothesis, we allow the process to continue if it is under our control or we accept its output, say a shipment from a supplier, if we do not control it. When the sample indicates that the process is not satisfactory, we can stop the process if we can control it and look for possible sources causing poor quality or reject the lot the sample came from.

---

[1] This is the *null hypothesis* tested when we sample the process output.

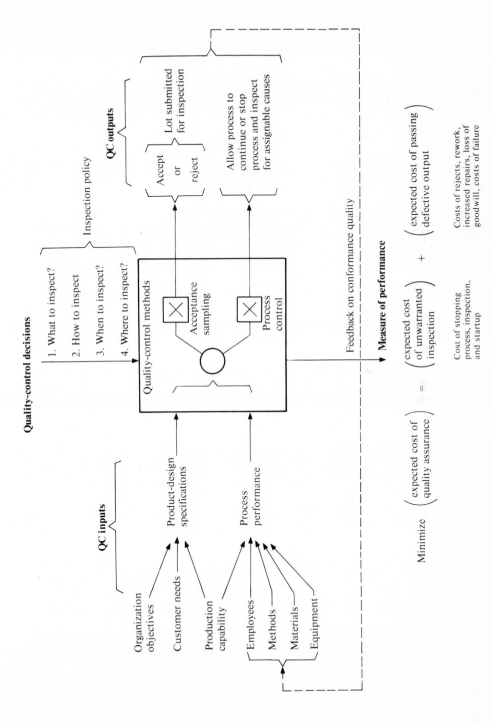

Fig. 16-3 The components of a quality-control system.

This procedure is generally quite effective and reliable, but since the decision concerning what to do with the process is based on a sample, i.e., incomplete information, it is possible to make one of two types of errors.

The sample may indicate that the process is not satisfactory when in fact it is. This is known as *Type I error*, i.e., rejecting a hypothesis when it is true. The consequences here involve the costs generated by stopping the process and inspecting for trouble when there is none. Thus, the consequences of Type I error relate to the costs of stopping the process, inspection, lost production, and startup again.

In the opposite case, the sample may suggest that the process is in control when in fact it is not. This is known as *Type II error*, i.e., accepting a false hypothesis. Associated with this is the cost of passing on defective output to subsequent stages. In a manufacturing situation, occurrence of Type II error results in increased costs for rejects or rework of parts and increased assembly costs. Furthermore, we may incur higher maintenance or repair costs and potential loss of goodwill if the finished product reaches the ultimate consumer. The types of error involved and their possible consequences are shown in Table 16-1.

TABLE 16-1   Types of errors and risks involved in quality control

Quality-control decisions	Actual condition of process (or its output)	
	Under control (satisfactory)	Out of control (unsatisfactory)
Reject output as bad	Type I error, related to producer's risk Costs: Stop process Inspection Start process	OK
Accept output as good	OK	Type II error, related to consumer's risk Costs: Rejects Rework Repairs Loss of goodwill

Objective of QC System

Operations management aims to achieve a level of output quality consistent with desired product specifications and process capabilities. The objective of the QC system is to ensure the desired level of quality while minimizing the total expected cost from sampling errors. In other words, we try to minimize the sum of costs related to passing on defective items (due to Type II error) and costs related to unnecessary process inspections (due to Type I error).

QC-System Decision Variables

In order to provide the desired level of outgoing quality at minimum expected cost the management of the QC system can control the following variables:

1. *What* to inspect
2. *How* to inspect
3. *When* to inspect
4. *Where* to inspect

Specific answers to the above questions define the QC system's inspection policy. Unfortunately, the search for answers requires much more than the knowledge of a few statistical techniques. Sound QC programs are based on a combination of experience, art, and well-developed statistical methods. The following sections summarize key considerations that must be taken into account in answering the what, how, when, and where of an inspection program.

What to Inspect

A particular product or service can be described by a large number of attributes relating to physical, chemical, functional, or aesthetic characteristics. A ready-to-wear suit can be described by the fabric used, its style or cut, its size, cleaning requirements, etc. Similarly, an airline transportation service may be described in terms of ground and in-flight characteristics, such as ease of making reservations, airport checking time, amenities aboard, and so on.

From the point of view of quality control, it is desirable to focus on a few critical characteristics whose values determine whether a product or service is satisfactory. When these vary within certain limits, they represent good quality, and when they go beyond such limits, they are viewed as unacceptable. A critical characteristic may be one that is not necessarily visible to the final user or consumer. Since design quality specifications define a range of expected performance quality, *the main focus of quality control is on conformance quality.* However, the QC system provides important information in preparing output specifications and receives valuable input from users of the process output. Table 16-2 suggests examples of possible critical characteristics susceptible to quality control in the manufacturing or service sectors.

TABLE 16-2 Examples of possible QC aspects in product and service systems

Product or service	Critical characteristic
Ball bearing	Internal and/or external diameter
Automobile	Fuel efficiency, power rating, polluting emissions, reliability of brakes, etc.
Bank customer service	Waiting time and service time per visit; accuracy of bank statements
Restaurant service	Service quality and time, food quality, atmosphere

How to Inspect: Measurement by Variables
or by Attributes

The issue of how to inspect for quality control involves (1) the type of measurement (variables versus attributes) and (2) the method of measurement (choice of an appropriate man-machine system). In certain cases inspection to establish quality in a product or service involves detailed measurement of some critical characteristic along a continuous scale. Thus, we may wish to measure a shaft diameter with a micrometer in hundreds or thousands of an inch, the content of a drug in some critical ingredient in milligrams, or an airplane's flying time on a given route in hours and minutes. When it is worthwhile to have the degree of detail provided by measuring the specific value of a critical characteristic, we have *control by variables*. This yields a great deal of information about the process and its output, albeit at considerable cost.

For many applications, however, all that is necessary to assess quality is an indication of whether a particular attribute is present or not in the product or service being controlled. This is especially appropriate whenever the process output can be easily classified in one of two categories. For example, a light bulb or a transistor is good or defective, an employee is either present or absent, a machine is running or idle, and so on. In all these cases the process or its output can be unambiguously classified with regard to the characteristic of interest. This is known as *measurement by attribute*. It does not provide as much information as measurement by variables, but it is less expensive and is often sufficient for control purposes. So much so that product characteristics amenable to measurement by variables are often converted for measurement by attributes.

An example of such a characteristic is the diameter of a record-player shaft. Instead of using a micrometer to obtain a reading in inches or millimeters it is possible to construct a *go–no-go gauge*, as shown in Fig. 16-4. If the shaft can pass through the hole AA' but not through hole BB', it is classified as good. If it is too

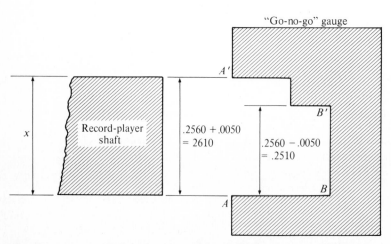

Fig. 16-4   An example of a go–no-go gauge. Critical dimension x, say a shaft diameter for a record player. Product design specification, $x = .2560 \pm .0050$ in.

wide to pass through AA' or too narrow, thus passing through BB', it is classified as defective. This approach reduces the cost of inspection per shaft, even though we sacrifice some information concerning the process variability.

In the service sector, customer service at a given facility, say an airlines reservation desk, may be considered good if waiting time does not exceed a certain limit, say 5 min, and poor if such a limit is exceeded as a matter of routine procedure. Such limits are taken into account in evaluating the quality of service at telephone switchboards, banks, restaurants, etc.

The second part of the question of "how to inspect," i.e., the method of measurement, depends on the type of measurement needed. The greater the need for precision and consistency, the more one relies on inspection methods using sophisticated instruments. The final choice is an economic one, in which the costs of increased precision do not outweigh the costs saved through a less accurate method.

When to Inspect: Acceptance Sampling versus Process Control

The decision when to inspect is important because it determines the QC method to be used. Inspection can occur either while the process is going on or after it has been completed, producing a desired batch of items. The first type of inspection is part of *process control*, while the second is required for *acceptance sampling*. The choice between acceptance sampling and process control depends on both economic and technological considerations.

In general, the *selection of process control is appropriate whenever:*

1. The inspection cost per unit is low.
2. The consequences of passing on defective output are high in terms of costs, customer goodwill, or other.
3. The inspection is not destructive or detrimental to the items.
4. The process can be adjusted, or stopped, inspected, and started up again at a reasonable cost.

If one or more of these conditions do not apply, management usually resorts to *acceptance sampling*, which *is most appropriate whenever:*

1. Inspection (or audit) cost per unit is high.
2. Consequences of passing on defective items are not serious.
3. Inspection is destructive or detrimental to the items produced.
4. Process control is not feasible.

Both methods rely on the selection of a sample representative of the process output, in progress or completed and submitted as a lot. Details of each approach and the tools employed to perform quality control with them are presented in the sections that follow. According to the type of measurement performed and the time of the inspection, we have a variety of QC schemes, as illustrated in Table 16-3.

TABLE 16-3   Inspection methods classified by measurement type and inspection timing

Type of measurement	Time of inspection	
	Acceptance sampling	Process control

By variable	Sampling plan:
	  Single
	  Double
	  Sequential
		$\bar{X}$ chart
		R chart

By attribute	Sampling plan:
	  Single
	  Double
	  Sequential
		p chart
		c chart

Where to Inspect

Converting a set of inputs into desired products and services usually requires a large number of operations. Inspection may take place before, during, or after any of these microconversions.

Production inputs such as raw materials, parts, etc., may be tested at points where the shipments arrive, in special laboratories, or even at the supplier's site. After such inputs enter the production process, the location of inspection stations depends on the process layout and the technical requirements of needed tests.

In a flow-shop layout, with a predetermined sequence of operations, inspection stations are positioned along the production line, but in a job shop, where the sequence may vary with each order, it is necessary to have roving inspectors who test samples as an order is advanced through various processing centers (lathes, drilling machines, etc.). For a fixed-position layout on large projects the inspection equipment and personnel are brought to the location of the unique product or service, whether it is the construction of a tanker, staging a play, or a surgical operation.

With regard to technical testing requirements, inspection may be conducted on site, i.e., where production takes place, or in special laboratories. The latter are preferred when the skills, procedures, and equipment needed are too expensive to maintain internally for the volume of tests handled. Occasionally, a stamp of approval by a prestigious testing laboratory may be sought to enhance a product's image.

Where to inspect may thus vary between the extremes of no inspection at all, which abandons the responsibility of quality control to the consumer, and inspection of all inputs and in-process items after every operation. As one might expect, the optimum number of inspection stations and their location is some alternative between the highly risky approach of no inspection and the prohibitively costly control of every step of the production process.

A satisfactory solution of where to inspect depends on the costs of inspection and the costs of passing defectives to other production stages and the consumer. With respect to location, inspection is desirable before operations that are irreversible or too costly. Thus, it is preferable to inspect before a critical part is welded to

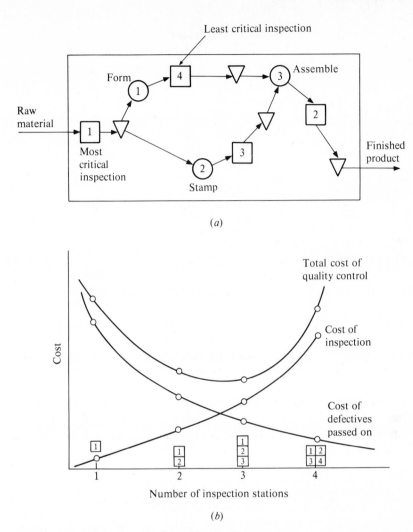

(a)

(b)

Fig. 16-5 Variations in cost of quality control with number of inspection stations: *(a)* **a simplified process and possible inspection stations and** *(b)* **costs associated with different inspection efforts and resulting defectives.**

another, before two chemicals are mixed to produce a drug, before a housing or a container is sealed, and so on.

Here we are confronted with the familiar economic problem of diminishing returns. Beyond a certain point, the marginal cost of another inspection exceeds the marginal cost of passing some defectives. Specific solutions may be developed by trial-and-error methods or more sophisticated heuristic procedures. The relevant aspects of this problem are summarized graphically in Fig. 16-5. The process in Fig. 16-5*a* consists of forming one part and stamping another, both from the same material. The two parts are then assembled and stored. Inspections are possible before and after each operation. The most important inspection is that of the pieces of material used to make the parts, since defects in the material will certainly result in an unsatisfactory product. The next most important inspection is after the parts have been assembled and then the inspections following the stamping and forming operations. The relative importance of these inspections is indicated by the number inside the squares, with 1 being the most critical. The cost of inspection as a function of the number of locations that will be used is shown in Fig. 16-5b.

16-5   ACCEPTANCE SAMPLING

General

Whenever it is not physically possible or economically desirable to exercise direct control of a process, we have the option of acceptance sampling. In a typical case a lot of N items is submitted for quality inspection. This may be an economic order quantity or some other amount representing a shipment of parts from a supplier or a batch of semifinished or finished products of our own process. It is customary to identify the source of the lot as the *producer* and the user of the items as the *consumer*.

In acceptance sampling the key decision is to accept or reject the submitted lot. Since 100 percent inspection may not be possible when inspection is destructive or uneconomical, the decision to accept or reject the lot is usually based on the evidence about quality contained in one or more samples. As a result of possible sampling errors, acceptance sampling may at times reject lots of good quality, a risk assumed by the producer, or accept lots of poor quality, a risk assumed by the consumer.

Definition

Acceptance sampling is a quality-control screening procedure for lots of purchased or internally processed items. Based on the avidence about quality contained in the sample(s) taken, acceptance sampling leads to acceptance or rejection of the submitted lots.

Once a lot is rejected, it may be sent back or submitted to 100 percent inspection, at the producer's expense, followed by substitution of defective units by good ones.

The objective of acceptance sampling is to minimize the total expected cost resulting from sampling errors. This presumes an agreement between producer and consumer as to what constitutes "good" and "bad" quality and acceptable risks of error for each quality level. Rejecting a satisfactory lot (Type I error) penalizes the producer by unwarranted inspection and replacement costs. On the other hand, accepting poor-quality lots (Type II error) forces on the consumer the costs of passing on defective units to subsequent stages. These may involve high reject rates, increased rework and assembly costs for subsequent production stages, or increased repair costs and loss of goodwill if defectives are passed on to the final user or consumer of the product or service.

Types of Acceptance Sampling

In order to achieve the above objective management can control the sample size, the maximum number of samples to be taken before a decision, and the type of measurement used to evaluate quality of incoming shipments. Thus, for given quality levels and risks it is possible to arrive at a decision to accept or reject a lot on the basis of one, two, multiple but fixed, or an undetermined number of samples.

In some cases it is desirable to exercise control on some measurable characteristic, e.g., length or weight, thus using a *sampling plan by variables*. The use of measurements on a continuous scale is naturally expensive but provides detailed information about the source of the items inspected. For most applications, however, all that is needed is the classification of a unit in the sample as good or defective. Here we employ a *sampling plan by attributes*, which is easier to implement, more economical on inspection costs, but less informative about the process and incoming quality. The variety of sampling plans used in practice is shown in Fig. 16-6.

In the following sections we illustrate the key features of a single sampling plan $(k = 1)$ for lot defectives, i.e., by attributes, and discuss the remaining types briefly.

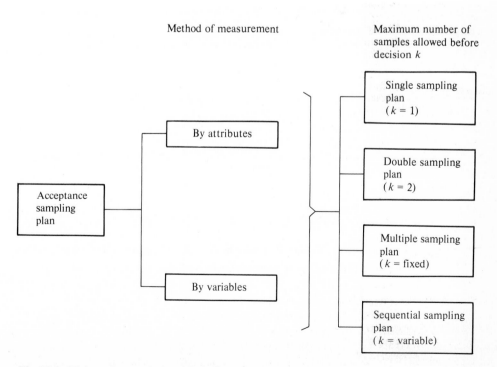

Fig. 16-6   Variety of acceptance-sampling plans.

Acceptance Sampling for Lot Defectives

Suppose that the assembly department of Stereo Products, Inc. periodically receives a lot of 10,000 record-player shafts used to assemble the complete units. The source of this shaft may be an outside supplier or another department of the same company. For both conformance and performance quality of a record player the shaft diameter is a critical characteristic. Instead of measuring shaft diameters with a micrometer it has been decided to use a go–no-go gauge that classifies each shaft as good or defective.

Quality control of this part can be exercised through acceptance sampling as follows. In a plan that relies on one sample, we are given the sample size n, say 100 units, and an acceptance number c, say 5. After a representative sample is taken from the lot and the units are inspected, we count the number of defectives x. If x is less than or equal to $c = 5$, we accept the lot; otherwise we reject it.

The sample size n and acceptance number c are determined so that we have an effective screening procedure, i.e., a sampling plan which is discriminating. Such a plan would have a high probability of accepting a lot of good quality, and a low probability of accepting a lot of poor quality. The discriminating ability of a sampling plan is normally specified by an operating-characteristic (OC) curve. This gives the probability of accepting a lot P_a for different quality levels as measured by the percent defective in the lot p.

Derivation of an OC curve requires that we specify in advance what producer and consumer agree to be good and bad quality and what risks each side will accept as a result of sampling errors. From this information we can determine the sample size n and acceptance number c of a sampling plan that can be applied to incoming lots to discriminate between good and bad lots with the agreed risks. These concepts are given more precise meaning as follows:

Definitions

1. $p_1 = $ *acceptable quality level* (AQL) = good quality; expressed as a decimal for percentage defectives in the incoming lots. AQL is what the consumer considers good quality consistent with his product specifications.
2. $\alpha = $ *producer's risk*; this is the probability of rejecting good lots, i.e., lots whose percentage defective is AQL or less. It is the measure of risk of Type I sampling errors undertaken by the producer.
3. $p_2 = $ *lot-tolerance percent defective* (LTPD) = bad quality; expressed as a decimal for percentage defectives in the incoming lots, LTPD is what is viewed as the most unsatisfactory or bad quality the consumer can tolerate.
4. $\beta = $ *consumer's risk*; or the probability of accepting lots of unsatisfactory quality LTPD. It is a measure of the risk of Type II sampling error undertaken by the consumer.

An ideal OC curve would have a probability equal to 1 of accepting incoming lots with percentage defective equal to AQL or less and zero probability of acceptance for lots with quality above AQL (see Fig. 16-7a). This situation could be achieved only with 100 percent error-free inspection, i.e., when $n = N$. A sampling plan with $n < N$ introduces sampling errors that result in the risks discussed previously. Hence, the OC curve will be as shown in Fig. 16-7b.

When incoming lots have zero defects ($p = .00$), they are always accepted ($P_a = 1.00$). As the quality deteriorates, i.e., with p increasing, the probability of acceptance P_a decreases. When lots arrive with all units defective ($p = 1.00$), they will always be rejected ($P_a = 0$). How the probability of acceptance decreases as the lot percentage defective increases will depend on the selection of the sample size n and the acceptance number c.

We want an OC curve such that the probability of acceptance P_a decreases by an amount equal to the producer's risk α as incoming quality goes from $p = 0$ to $p_1 = $ AQL and then gradually drops to the consumer's risk level β as incoming quality reaches $p_2 = $ LTPD. To obtain such a curve we must solve a set of two equations in two unknowns, n and c. The terms on the left-hand side in the two

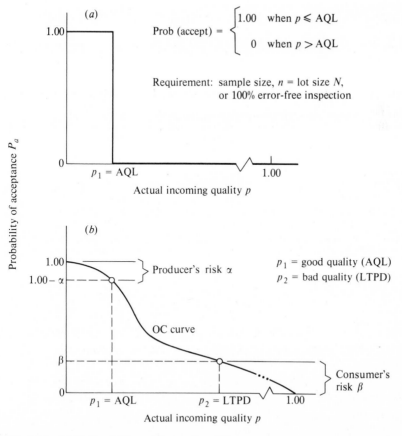

Fig. 16-7 (*a*) **Ideal and** (*b*) **usual forms of an OC curve.**

equations represent probabilities computed by the binomial or Poisson distribution given AQL, LTPD, α, and β. The solution for n and c can be found using trial-and-error methods, available tables or nomograms, or commercial computer programs. The procedure is illustrated below by an example.

▶ EXAMPLE 16-1

Suppose that the assembly department of Stereo Products, Inc., has agreed with its supplier on the following quality levels and risks for the acceptance-sampling control of record-player shafts in shipments of 10,000:

Quality level	Risk
p_1 = AQL = .01	α = .05
p_2 = LTPD = .08	β = .10

This means that the producer of shafts aims at shipping lots with 1 percent defectives, the customer's quality specifications, and agrees to have such lots rejected due to sampling errors 5 percent of the time. The assembly department would like to protect itself against lots with 8 percent or more defectives and will reject them 90 percent of the time. The values chosen for the sample size n and acceptance number c must satisfy the following relationships:

1. For lots with incoming quality $p = p_1 = $ AQL = .01 (good quality)

$$\text{Prob (acceptance of lots with } p_1 \text{ defective)} = 1.00 - \alpha = .95$$

or

$$P(x \le c \mid p_1) = P(x = 0 \mid p_1) + P(x = 1 \mid p_1)$$
$$+ P(x = 2 \mid p_1) + \cdots + P(x = c \mid p_1) = .95 \quad (16\text{-}1)$$

2. For lots with incoming quality $p = p_2 = $ LTPD = .08 (bad quality)

$$\text{Prob (acceptance of lots with } p_2 \text{ defective)} = \beta = .10$$

or

$$P(x \le c \mid p_2) = P(x = 0 \mid p_2) + P(x = 1 \mid p_2)$$
$$+ P(x = 2 \mid p_2) + \cdots + P(x = c \mid p_2) = .10 \quad (16\text{-}2)$$

The probability that in a sample of size n the number of defects x equals a value k, given the lot quality p, can be determined using the binomial distribution. However, when p is small ($p < .10$) and n is large ($n > 20$), we can simplify the calculations by approximating the binomial with a Poisson distribution with a mean equal to np

$$P(x = k \mid p) = \frac{n!}{k!\,(n-k)!} p^k (1 - p)^{n-k} \xrightarrow[\substack{np < 5 \\ n > 20 \\ p < .10}]{\text{when}} \frac{(np)^k e^{-np}}{k!} \quad (16\text{-}3)$$

$$\underset{\text{Binomial}}{} \qquad \underset{\text{Poisson}}{}$$

Solutions of Eqs. (16-1) and (16-2) for different values of AQL, LTPD, α, and β have been extensively tabulated to reduce the burden of trial-and-error calculations.[1] One such table for $\alpha = .05$, $\beta = .10$, and various combinations of AQL and LTPD levels is Table 16-4. For AQL $= .01$ and LTPD $= .08$ in the example, Table 16-4 provides values for $n = 60$ and $c = 2$ specifying an OC curve which comes closest to the sampling-plan specifications of (AQL, α) $= (.01, .05)$ and (LTPD, β) $= (.08, .10)$. Since we require both n and c to be integers, there will always be some deviation from the original specifications. In our example

$$\text{Prob (accept given } p = .01) = P(x \leq 2 \mid p = .01)$$

$$= P(x = 0 \mid p = .01) + P(x = 1 \mid p = .01)$$

$$+ P(x = 2 \mid p = .01)$$

$$= \frac{[(60)(.01)]^0 e^{-(60)(.01)}}{0!} + \frac{[(60)(.01)]^1 e^{-(60)(.01)}}{1!}$$

$$+ \frac{[(60)(.01)]^2 e^{-(60)(.01)}}{2!}$$

$$= .5488 + .3293 + .0988 = .9769$$

$$\text{Prob (accept given } p = .08) = P(x \leq 2 \mid p = .01)$$

$$= P(x = 0 \mid p = .08) + P(x = 1 \mid p = .08)$$

$$+ P(x = 2 \mid p = .08)$$

$$= \frac{[(60)(.08)]^0 e^{-(60)(.08)}}{0!} + \frac{[(60)(.08)]^1 e^{-(60)(.08)}}{1!}$$

$$+ \frac{[(60)(.08)]^2 e^{-(60)(.08)}}{2!}$$

$$= .0082 + .0395 + .0948 = .1425$$

The above calculations indicate that for a sampling plan with $n = 60$ and $c = 2$ the revised risk of having lots with 1 percent defective rejected is now $1.000 - .977 = .023$ or 2.3 percent. Similarly, the revised risk of accepting lots with 5 percent defective is .142, or 14.2 percent. Both risks can be further adjusted by altering the sample size n and/or the acceptance number c.

Effect of Changes in Sample Size n and Acceptance Number c

It is possible to change the discriminating ability of a sampling plan by varying the sample size n, the acceptance number c, or both. If we increase the sample size n while holding the ratio of sample size to acceptance number constant, 100/2, 150/3,

---

[1] For an illustration of the trial-and-error method see E. H. Bowman and R. B. Fetter, *Analysis for Production and Operations Management*, 3d ed., Irwin, Homewood, Ill., 1967.

TABLE 16-4 Suggested *n* and *c* values for single sampling plans where α = .05 and β = .10, given AQL and LTPD

AQL	LTPD						
	4.51–5.60	5.61–7.10	7.11–9.00	9.01–11.2	11.3–14.0	14.1–18.0	18.1–22.4
.451 to .560	80 1	60 1	60 1	50 1	15 0	15 0	10 0
.561 to .710	100 2	80 1	50 1	50 1	40 1	10 0	10 0
.711 to .900	100 2	80 2	50 1	40 1	40 1	30 1	7 0
.901 to 1.12	120 3	80 2	60 2	40 1	30 1	30 1	25 1
1.13 tp 1.40	150 4	100 3	60 2	50 2	30 1	25 1	25 1
1.41 to 1.80	200 6	120 4	80 3	50 2	40 1	25 1	20 1
1.81 to 2.24	300 10	150 6	100 4	60 3	40 2	30 2	20 1
2.25 to 2.80	n c	250 10	120 6	70 4	50 3	30 2	25 2
2.81 to 3.55	n c	n c	200 10	100 6	60 4	40 3	25 2
3.56 to 4.50	n c	n c	n c	150 10	80 6	50 4	30 3
4.51 to 5.60	n c	n c	n c	n c	120 10	60 6	40 4

SOURCE: James L. Riggs, *Production Systems*, John Wiley & Sons, Inc., New York, 1976, p. 577, reprinted by permission of the publisher.

200/4, etc., the OC curve becomes more discriminating; i.e., it provides lower risks of rejecting a good lot or accepting a bad one. This is shown in Fig. 16-8, where we note that as *n* increases, the OC curve becomes steeper and approaches the ideal OC curve ($n = N$). Since a larger sample provides higher accuracy because it is more representative of the entire lot, we must strike a balance between the increased costs of inspection for larger *n* and the costs associated with the sampling errors. In Fig. 16-8 we note that as we increase *n* from 100 to 200 and then 300 while *c* goes from 1 to 2 and 3 (100/1, 200/2, 300/3) the producer's risk α at AQL = .005 goes from .10 to .05 and then to .03. Comparable decreases occur with the consumer's risk at LTPD = .03.

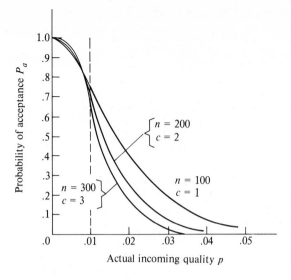

Fig. 16-8 Effect of sample-size changes on discriminating ability of OC curve (fixed proportion of acceptance number to sample size).

If we hold the sample size n constant and decrease the acceptance number c, we make the sampling plan tighter by lowering the OC curve toward the origin. Such a change results in higher rejection probabilities for all quality levels and therefore forces more lots to undergo 100 percent inspection. This is shown in Fig. 16-9, where for a sample size of 100, the probability of rejection[1] of a lot with $p = .02$ is equal to .31 for $c = 3$, .58 for $c = 2$, and .85 for $c = 1$.

Average Outgoing Quality (AOQ)

The effectiveness of the screening effort associated with a specific sampling plan is evaluated by the *average outgoing quality* (AOQ) for the plan. Here we assume that

---

[1] The probability of rejection is equal to one minus the probability of acceptance, i.e., $(1 - P_a)$.

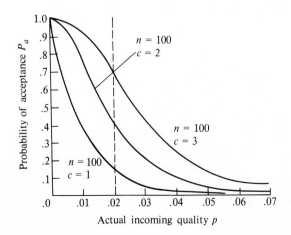

Fig. 16-9 Changes in OC curve with variation in acceptance number c when the sample size n is held constant.

if the lot is accepted $(x \leq c)$, all defectives in the sample are replaced by good units, and if the lot is rejected $(x > c)$, it undergoes 100 percent rectifying inspection, in which all defective units in the lot are replaced by good ones.

Except for the two extreme cases in which a lot is either perfect and goes through or completely bad and is rejected and returned with all units good, in all other cases there will always be some defective units in the lots that are accepted.

In a lot of size N from which we take a sample n and proceed to accept it when $x \leq c$, the percentage defectives p are to be found in the remaining units $(N - n)$. The total number of defectives in the accepted lot will therefore be equal to $p(N - n)$. This number of defectives, $p(N - n)$, divided by the lot size N gives the proportion of defectives remaining in the lot. Since this will be accepted with a probability of P_a, which depends on the incoming quality p, the average outgoing quality for an accepted lot can be stated as follows:

$$AOQ = P_a \frac{p(N - n)}{N}$$

$$\approx P_a p \quad \text{for small } n/N$$

Average outgoing quality assuming all defectives are replaced by good units   (16-4)

If we plot the values of AOQ that correspond to different levels of incoming quality p, we obtain a curve like that in Fig. 16-10. The AOQ curve starts at zero for $p = 0$, increases to a maximum level, known as the average outgoing quality limit (AOQL) for intermediate quality levels, and then decreases, approaching zero again for lots of very poor quality due to rectifying inspection of rejected lots. *The AOQL represents the worst quality likely to pass through the screening provided by a sampling plan.* Its value depends on n, c, and N rather than the actual incoming quality p.

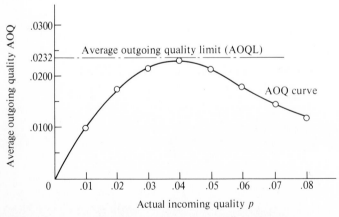

Fig. 16-10   An AOQ curve for $n = 60$, $c = 2$, and $N = 10,000$.

Sometimes it is not feasible after inspection to replace defective units discovered in the sample or the lot by good ones. This in effect reduces the size of submitted lots. The average outgoing quality, using similar reasoning as before, is now computed by the formula

$$AOQ = P_a \frac{p(N - n)}{N - pn - p(1 - P_a)(N - n)} \qquad \text{Average outgoing quality assuming defectives are not replaced} \qquad (16\text{-}5)$$

The denominator in (16-5) represents the average lot size resulting when defectives found in it cannot be replaced with good units.

▶ EXAMPLE 16-2

For the assembly department of Stereo Products, Inc., the AOQ curve, assuming rectifying inspection, for a sampling plan with $n = 60$ and $c = 2$ and $N = 10,000$ can be determined by the values developed in Table 16-5. When the sample size n is small compared with the lot size N, it simplifies calculations considerably to approximate AOQ by $P_a p$. The values of P_a for different quality levels p can be estimated from an OC curve or computed as cumulative probabilities from the Poisson distribution with a mean equal to np.

The AOQ values when plotted yield the AOQ curve shown in Fig. 16-10. It can be seen that for the sampling plan with $n = 60$, $c = 2$, and $N = 10,000$, the worst quality on the average that would be allowed to reach the consumer through the
▶ above inspection scheme would be lots with 2.32 percent defectives.

Alternative Plans for Acceptance Sampling

In the preceding method for acceptance sampling, a decision to accept or reject a lot was based on a single sample and on inspection by attributes. Under certain

TABLE 16-5 Calculations of AOQ values for $n = 60$ and $c = 2$

Quality level p	Sample size n	Poisson mean np	Probability of acceptance P_a	AOQ†
.01	60	.60	.98	.0098
.02	60	1.20	.88	.0176
.03	60	1.80	.72	.0216
.04	60	2.40	.58	.0232 AOQL
.05	60	3.00	.43	.0215
.06	60	3.60	.30	.0180
.07	60	4.20	.21	.0147
.08	60	4.80	.15	.0120

† Assuming all defectives are replaced by good units.

conditions it may be desirable to rely on more detailed measurement of the units inspected or on more than one sample. This creates the need for sampling plans by variables rather than attributes and for plans in which the decision may be to (1) accept the lot, (2) reject the lot, (3) or obtain additional information.

Multiple- and sequential-sampling plans   For psychological and economic reasons, it is sometimes preferable to use more than one sample before a lot is accepted or rejected. The producer may feel that a verdict based on one sample from a lot is too harsh. Additional samples are thus viewed as another chance to evaluate quality more "realistically." From a statistical point of view, a plan based on two or more samples can be as strict or discriminating as a single-sampling plan, but the psychological appeal may be considerable.

From the consumer's point of view a double- or multiple-sampling plan may have economic advantages by reducing the inspection cost. For clearly good- or bad-quality lots, a decision to accept or not can be reached with an initial smaller sample size than would be required for a single-sampling plan. The need for additional samples arises only for lots of average quality.

For the same degree of protection in terms of producer and consumer risks at specified quality levels AQL and LTPD, double- or multiple-sampling plans generally reduce the inspection cost. Variability in the level of quality in the submitted lots, however, results in fluctuating requirements for inspection and presumes considerable flexibility in inspection capability.

For a double-sampling plan assume $n_1 = 40$, $c_1 = 1$ and $n_2 = 60$, $c_2 = 3$. The procedure of evaluating the lot is shown in the flow diagram in Fig. 16-11. The OC curves for this case are shown in Fig. 16-12. Extending the logic of the double-sampling plan to allow for more samples, we have procedures for a multiple- or sequential-sampling plan. After each sample is taken, the cumulative evidence for all defectives observed leads to a decision to (1) accept lot, (2) reject lot, or (3) take another sample. This is shown in Fig. 16-13.

In a *multiple-sampling* plan a decision must be reached within the maximum number of allowed samples as specified in advance. In *sequential sampling*, however, the sampling may continue until the cumulative evidence is conclusive. In either case, a sample may consist of one or several units from the submitted lot.

The construction of such plans follows the same rules as single sampling. The plan's discriminating ability is specified by an OC curve for given quality levels AQL and LTPD and agreed risks α and β (see Ref. 4).

Acceptance sampling by variables   In certain cases the quality of incoming lots cannot be evaluated adequately by classifying an item as good or defective. The need for measuring some critical characteristic(s) of a unit on a continuous scale requires inspection by variables.

An acceptance-sampling plan by variables is also specified by an OC curve for specific quality levels and risks α and β. However, since actual measurements of quality vary in a continuum instead of assuming discrete values, the OC curve is related to a range of tolerance limits, determined by the normal distribution of measurements for the accepted risk levels.

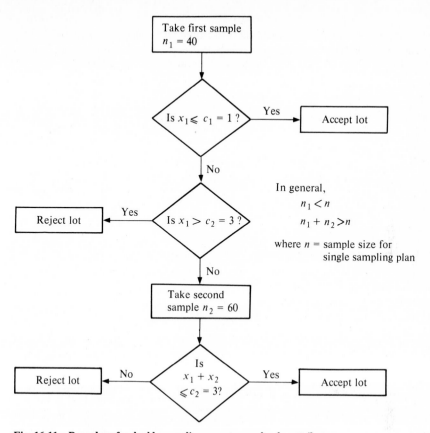

Fig. 16-11 Procedure for double-sampling acceptance plan by attributes.

In general,
$$n_1 < n$$
$$n_1 + n_2 > n$$
where n = sample size for single sampling plan

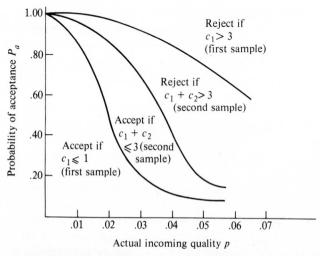

Fig. 16-12 The shape of OC curves for a double-sampling acceptance plan by attributes.

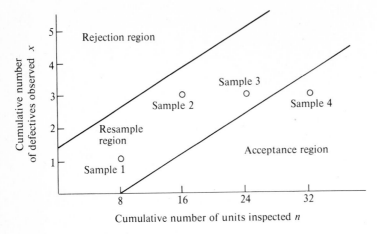

Fig. 16-13 Sequential-sampling plan by attributes.

Since inspection by variables is more elaborate and detailed, it costs more than classification by a go–no-go gauge. However, the increased cost of the inspection per unit is partly offset by the need for smaller samples due to the greater information provided by actual measurements. Furthermore, with sampling by variables it is possible to evaluate not only whether the submitted lot is acceptable or not but also the accuracy and precision of the process used. This is based on the mean and standard deviation of the actual measurements, which allows management to exercise some control over the process as well (see Ref. 4).

16-6   PROCESS CONTROL

As indicated previously, there are cases in which process control is most appropriate because we have access to the process, low inspection costs per unit of output, and serious consequences from defectives that may be passed on.

Process Variability: Random versus Nonrandom Variations

Quality control is exercised by comparing the variation observed in the process output with the variation allowed in the product specifications. Any real process exhibits a natural variation attributed to a stable system of causes. Thus, the weight of a 32-oz box of cereal, the length of tape in a 90-min cassette, the time for an assembly operation or a blood test all exhibit a natural variation from unit to unit. *The stable system of causes that result in random variation consists of the inherent variability in the factors of production*, e.g., the employees, their methods, materials used, equipment, and the conditions that define the working environment (noise level, illumination, heating, etc.). The amount of process variability seems to increase with the extent of human involvement in the desired transformation.

Random variations in the output are attributed to uncontrollable factors, and

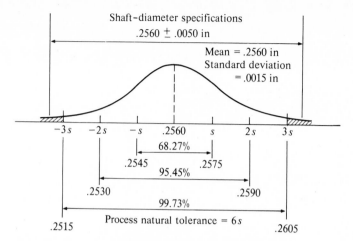

Fig. 16-14   Random variations displayed by shaft diameters.

the only way they can be reduced to improve quality is through a change in the technology used. In short, the normal random variation defines the process capability and can be described by a statistical distribution. For a critical characteristic that can be measured on a continuous scale, such as the shaft diameter in the example of Stereo Products, Inc., the distribution of diameters may appear as in Fig. 16-14.

The value of a particular shaft diameter represents the net result of a multitude of factors none of which plays a more dominant role than the others. It is reasonable, therefore, to assume that the distribution of such values is normal. When the process is centered correctly at the desired value of .2560 in, the technology used generates variation with a standard deviation of $s = .0015$ in. Under such conditions we may expect 68.3 percent of the process output to fall in the range $2560 \pm .0015$ in, 95.5 percent of the output in the range $.2560 \pm (2)(.0015)$ in, and 99.73 percent in the range $.2560 \pm (3)(.0015)$ in. For this application the process capability is well suited to the product specifications since less than 3 out of 1,000 units will fail to meet the product design requirements. The range of six standard deviations is considered a reasonable measure of the process capability and is known as the *natural tolerance of the production process.*

At times, however, an observed value may deviate significantly from the stable pattern of variation. Such an occurrence may be viewed either as an extremely rare event, or it can be attributed to some assignable cause that has upset the stable system generating random variations. In the case of a shaft diameter with a value equal to 0.2640, that is, nearly five deviations from the mean, the probability of such a rare event is less than 27 out of 10,000. Management in this instance would assume that the cause for such a large deviation is more likely related to some assignable cause in the factors of production. Worn-out cutting tools, a poorly trained operator, defective materials, or other unusual conditions in the inputs, the process, or the internal environment have a probability of 99.73 percent of causing the observed significant departure.

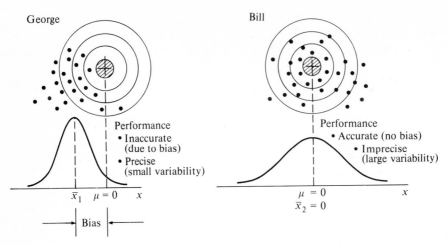

Fig. 16-15   Accuracy versus precision in process control.

Definition

Process control is a procedure designed to identify any significant departure from the natural range of variation of some critical product or process characteristic. The presence of nonrandom variations is attributed to assignable causes and generally prompts management to take corrective action to bring the process under control.

Process Accuracy versus Process Precision

In everyday language the words accuracy and precision are often used as synonyms. In quality control, however, there is an important difference that can be illustrated with an example. Suppose two friends, George and Bill, go to a shooting range for target practice. Their shooting skill can be measured by the distance of their shots from the bull's-eye. Here for convenience we shall consider only the horizontal distance of shots from the bull's-eye. After several rounds we obtain the distribution shown in Fig. 16-15, where for each person the average distance of his shots from the bull's-eye $\bar{x}$ measures his accuracy. In this regard Bill is accurate, while George is inaccurate, as evidenced by the presence of bias in his shots to the left. However, along with the accuracy observed, it is important to keep track of the dispersion, or variability, of the shots as measured by the standard deviation of x or the range. The degree of variability, measured by the standard deviation s, in the shots determines the precision, and in this regard George is more precise than Bill ($s_1 < s_2$).

We can now draw an analogy in which the production process we wish to control is like a person shooting for target practice. The target and the bull's-eye represent the product specifications. The shots fired represent how closely the process comes to meeting them. A process is under control when it is both accurate and precise. The presence of significant bias, i.e., lack of accuracy, and/or excessive variability, i.e., lack of precision, suggests that the process is not meeting the desired product specifications and requires inspection for removing any cause(s) of such deviations that result in poor-quality output.

In process control by variables the accuracy of the process is maintained with the aid of a mean, or $\bar{x}$ chart. The precision is tracked with a range, or R chart. These control devices provide direct feedback for identifying the source of trouble more readily, as opposed to the control charts by attributes (p chart and c chart), which cannot distinguish between process accuracy or precision and simply classify the process as acceptable or not.

Process-Control Charts for Variables

Whenever the evaluation of process performance requires considerable detail, we single out critical output characteristics that can be measured on a continuous scale. This approach can be applied to characteristics such as weight, length, volume, processing time, or other. This type of measurement enables us to evaluate both process accuracy and precision in terms of the average level and the variability in the measurements.

Mean or $\bar{x}$ Chart

The graphical device employed to evaluate the accuracy or average level attained by a process is known as a mean chart or $\bar{x}$ chart.

Definition

An $\bar{x}$ *chart*, or mean chart, is a control chart that monitors the accuracy of a process by observing whether the means from periodic sample measurements fall within predetermined limits.

A mean chart is constructed using sample data from a period considered representative of future operating conditions. For each sample of measurements, taken in the order the items were produced, we compute the sample mean and the range defined by the difference between the maximum and minimum observed values. The control chart is determined by specifying a centerline for the process level and upper and lower control limits (UCL, LCL) usually placed at three standard deviations as follows:

$$\text{Centerline: } \bar{\bar{x}} = \frac{\bar{x}_1 + \bar{x}_2 + \cdots + \bar{x}_n}{N} = \frac{\sum\limits_{j=1}^{N} \bar{x}_j}{N} \qquad (16\text{-}6)$$

where $\bar{x}_j$ = mean for sample j $(j = 1, 2, ..., N)$ based on n observed values
N = number of samples used in base period

Control limits: $\mathrm{UCL}_x = \bar{\bar{x}} + A\bar{R}$ $\mathrm{LCL}_x = \bar{\bar{x}} - A\bar{R}$ (16-7)

where

$$\bar{R} = \frac{R_1 + R_2 + \cdots + R_N}{N} = \frac{\sum\limits_{j=1}^{N} R_j}{N}$$ (16-8)

and A = constant which for small sample sizes n makes $A\bar{R}$ equal to three standard deviations of the mean; that is, $A\bar{R} = 3s_{\bar{x}}$

Values for A are tabulated along with values of similar constants B and C used for the control limits of the R chart in Table 16-6. The presence of one or more sample means outside the control limits implies the lack of process accuracy to meet specifications. To avoid the subsequent occurrence of a large proportion of defective units the process is normally stopped to investigate for assignable causes (poor raw materials, faulty machine settings, or other).

The reader may question the need for using averages rather than individual measurements in constructing the mean chart. The reason lies in what in statistics is a cornerstone property of sample means. According to the *central-limit theorem*, even though individual measurements may not follow a normal distribution, which would not allow us to decide as easily whether the process is in control or not, the sample means for such measurements tend to follow a normal distribution.

According to common practice, control limits are set at three standard deviations from the centerline. This, however, is arbitrary, and the decision should be

TABLE 16-6   Values for constants A, B, and C to set up control limits for $\bar{x}$ and R charts

Sample size n	For $\bar{x}$ chart A	For R chart B	For R chart C
2	1.880	3.268	.000
3	1.023	2.574	.000
4	.729	2.282	.000
5	.577	2.114	.000
6	.483	2.004	.000
7	.419	1.924	.076
8	.373	1.864	.136
9	.337	1.816	.184
10	.308	1.777	.223
12	.266	1.716	.284
14	.235	1.671	.329
16	.212	1.636	.364

made to reflect the costs of Type I and Type II errors more realistically for the particular application under study.[1]

Range, or R, chart

It is entirely possible that the process may be producing an excessive number of defective units even though it displays sufficient accuracy, as evidenced by sample means being within the control limits. This may occur when the *process lacks precision, as indicated by the variability of measurements within a sample.* The latter can be estimated by computing a standard deviation or the range for each sample. Since for small samples the range, which is much easier to compute, can be used to approximate the standard deviation, process precision can be checked through the range, or R, chart.

Definition

An R *chart,* or range chart, is a control chart used to monitor the precision of a process by observing whether the ranges computed from periodic sample measurements fall within predetermined limits.

To construct an R chart we must specify the average range $\bar{R}$, computed previously, and control limits normally placed at three standard deviations, as follows:

$$\text{Centerline:} \qquad \bar{R} = \frac{R_1 + R_2 + \cdots + R_N}{N} \qquad (16\text{-}8)$$

$$\text{Control limits:} \qquad \text{UCL}_R = B\bar{R} \qquad \text{LCL}_R = C\bar{R} \qquad (16\text{-}9)$$

where B, C = constants which for small sample sizes n make $B\bar{R} = 3s_R$ and $C\bar{R} = 3s_R$ or zero if the LCL would otherwise be less than zero.

Lack of process precision would be indicated by a sample range R outside the control limits. Again, management would feel compelled to stop the process and look for assignable causes, such as a worn-out bearing, improper training of personnel, or other.

---

[1] In some applications control charts are constructed with additional *warning limits* at two standard deviations from the centerline, to alert inspectors of potential deviations beyond the regular control limits.

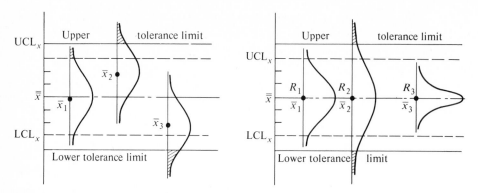

Fig. 16-16   Shifts in process accuracy and variation.

The lack of accuracy and precision in a process is illustrated in Fig. 16-16 and explained with an example. It is important to remember that *lack of accuracy is revealed by excessive variability between samples* and *lack of precision by excessive variability within samples.*

▶ EXAMPLE 16-3
Because of large recent increases in the wholesale price of coffee beans, the owners of a store specializing in imported coffee, tea, and spice varieties want to maintain closer control over the product weight of the most popular coffee blend, the Frescafe, sold in 8-oz bags. The owners want to keep the weight in the range of $8 \pm .15$ oz. The data in Table 16-7 refer to measurements made of actual contents over a 12-day period for random samples of five bags taken each day, in the chronological order the bags were filled. Working conditions for the bag-filling operation during this period were considered normal.

TABLE 16-7   Actual content weight of Frescafe-blend bags

Sample number	Observation					Mean $\bar{x}$	Range R
	1	2	3	4	5		
1	8.02	8.00	8.14	8.15	8.13	8.088	.15
2	8.13	7.91	8.04	7.84	7.95	7.974	.29
3	8.01	8.04	7.81	7.91	7.94	7.942	.23
4	8.17	8.05	7.93	8.08	8.10	8.066	.24
5	7.89	8.07	8.01	7.97	7.93	7.974	.18
6	8.15	7.96	8.07	8.03	7.82	8.006	.33
7	7.99	8.13	7.95	7.92	8.07	8.012	.21
8	8.03	7.99	8.02	8.00	7.83	7.974	.20
9	8.03	8.04	8.04	8.04	8.05	8.040	.02
10	7.88	8.06	8.04	7.96	8.05	7.998	.18
11	8.01	7.99	8.22	7.99	7.91	8.024	.31
12	7.88	7.96	7.90	8.00	7.90	7.928	.12
Total						96.026	2.46

Due to the negligible weight variation in the $\frac{1}{2}$-oz paper bags, observed over a prolonged period of use, the weight variation is attributed to the bag-filling operation factors, e.g., the scale-setting accuracy or the operator. From the measurements taken the average weight of an 8-oz coffee bag is

$$\bar{\bar{x}} = \frac{\bar{x}_1 + \bar{x}_2 + \cdots + \bar{x}_{12}}{12} = \frac{96.026}{12} = 8.002 \text{ oz}$$

The average range for the filling operation is

$$\bar{R} = \frac{R_1 + R_2 + \cdots + R_{12}}{12} = \frac{2.46}{12} = .205 \text{ oz}$$

It is now possible to construct control charts to check on the accuracy and precision of the coffee-bag-filling operation as follows. For the $\bar{x}$ chart:

Centerline: $\bar{\bar{x}} = 8.002$ oz

Upper control limit: $UCL_x = \bar{\bar{x}} + A\bar{R} = 8.002 + (.577)(.205) = 8.120$ oz

Lower control limit: $LCL_x = \bar{\bar{x}} - A\bar{R} = 8.002 - (.577)(.205) = 7.884$ oz

After plotting the values for sample means over the base period, it can be seen that all points are within the control limits. Therefore, the bag-filling operation seems quite accurate (see Fig. 16-17). For the R chart:

Centerline: $\bar{R} = .205$ oz

Upper control limit: $UCL_R = B\bar{R} = (2.114)(.205) = .433$ oz

Lower control limit: $LCL_R = C\bar{R} = (.000)(.205) = .00$ oz

Again plotting the values for observed sample ranges, we can see that the precision of the bag-filling operation is also satisfactory (see Fig. 16-18).

From the above analysis, the owners of the store conclude that the weight of their 8-oz coffee bags is well under control within the specifications they want. Thus, the control charts can be used to monitor the bag-filling operation in the future. The presence of an out-of-control point at a later time would signal the

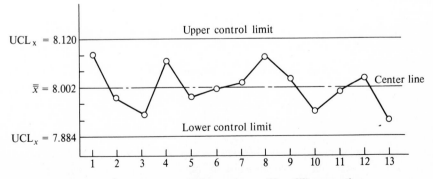

Fig. 16-17   Process-control $\bar{x}$ chart to monitor accuracy of bag-filling operation.

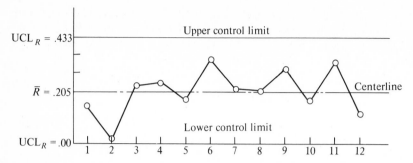

Fig. 16-18   Process-control *R* chart to monitor precision of bag-filling operation.

presence of some assignable cause related possibly to the balance scale, the opera-
▶ tor, or the working environment (lighting, noise, etc.).

Process-Control Charts for Attributes

For many operations all we need to know is whether the quality of an item or some aspect of the process is satisfactory or not. This may not require any detailed measurements, and process control can be assessed by describing the process or its output in terms of some critical attribute.

p Chart, or Chart for Proportion of Defectives

Quite often what we wish to control cannot be measured on a continuous scale. A light fuse or transistor is either good or defective, a machine is working or idle, an employee is present or absent, and so on. Even when continuous measurement is possible, it may be too costly and we may be content to classify some aspect of the process or its output as good or bad using a go–no-go gauge or some other means. For this situation we can use a *p* chart.

Definition

A *p chart*, or proportion-defective chart, is a control chart used to monitor a process by observing the proportion with which some selected attribute appears in samples taken periodically.

A *p* chart is constructed by recording the number of observations x_j in the classification of interest for a sample of size n_j over the number of all samples taken *N*. Since the random outcome of an observation can be classified in only two ways, the results of this sampling procedure can be described using the *binomial distribution*.

Let p = true proportion of the desired classification, i.e., percentage defectives in output, percentage absenteeism for an organization's employees, etc.

$\bar{p}$ = our estimate of p based on the outcome of samples taken, expressed as a decimal

Then, for individual samples

$$p_1 = \frac{x_1}{n_1}, \; p_2 = \frac{x_2}{n_2}, \; \ldots, \; p_N = \frac{x_N}{n_N}$$

and

$$\bar{p} = \frac{\text{total number of observations in category of interest}}{\text{total number of observations for all samples}}$$

In most cases we use a fixed sample size, that is, $n_1 = n_2 = \cdots = n_N$. Thus, for a p chart with control limits at three standard deviations we have

Centerline:
$$\bar{p} = \frac{p_1 + p_2 + \cdots + p_N}{N} = \frac{\sum_{j=1}^{N} p_j}{N} \qquad (16\text{-}10)$$

Control limits:
$$\text{UCL}_p = \bar{p} + 3s_p = \bar{p} + 3\sqrt{\frac{\bar{p}(1-\bar{p})}{n}}$$

$$\text{LCL}_p = \bar{p} - 3s_p = \bar{p} - 3\sqrt{\frac{\bar{p}(1-\bar{p})}{n}} \qquad (16\text{-}11)$$

where s_p is the standard deviation of a binomial distribution given $\bar{p}$ and the sample size n.

When the sample size n is variable, we must either determine an average value $\bar{n}$ if the variations are minor (say up to 5 percent) or we must calculate different control limits to account for the effect of n on s_p. As n increases, s_p decreases and the control limits come closer to the centerline. The converse holds for decreases in n.

Once the values for $p_1, p_2, \ldots, p_N$ have been plotted, the process can be evaluated by noting whether they lie within the control limits or not. Any out-of-control point is investigated and treated in the same way as for the mean chart.

▶ EXAMPLE 16-4

A hospital administrator has been concerned recently with the absenteeism among nurse's aides, as reported by his personnel manager. The problem has been brought up by registered nurses, who feel they often have to perform work normally done by their aides. To get to the facts, the administrator asked the personnel manager to provide him with absenteeism data over the last 2 weeks, which he considers a representative period for future conditions. After taking random samples for each

TABLE 16-8 Absenteeism data on nurse's aides in hospital example

Day	Sample size	Aides absent	Proportion absent
1	64	4	.0625
2	64	3	.0469
3	64	2	.0313
4	64	4	.0625
5	64	2	.0313
6	64	5	.0781
7	64	3	.0469
8	64	4	.0625
9	64	8	.1250
10	64	2	.0313
11	64	3	.0469
12	64	2	.0313
13	64	1	.0156
14	64	3	.0469
15	64	4	.0625
Total	1,080	50	.7815

day and consulting the personnel files, the personnel manager produced the data shown in Table 16-8.

Estimates for average absenteeism $\bar{p}$ and s_p are computed as follows:

$$\bar{p} = \frac{\sum x_j}{\sum n_j} = \frac{50}{1,080} = .0521 \quad \text{or} \quad \bar{p} = \frac{\sum p_j}{N} = \frac{.7815}{15} = .0521$$

and

$$s_p = \sqrt{\frac{\bar{p}(1 - \bar{p})}{n}} = \sqrt{\frac{(.0521)(1.000 - .0521)}{64}} = \sqrt{.0008} = .0277$$

Thus, for a preliminary p chart we have

Centerline: $\bar{p} = .0521$

Control limits:

$$\text{UCL}_p = \bar{p} + 3s_p = .0521 + (3)(.0278) = .1350$$

$$\text{LCL}_p = \bar{p} - 3s_p = .0521 - (3)(.0278) = 0$$

These results mean that expected absenteeism for nurse's aides is about 5 percent and a variation of up to 13.5 percent is considered normal under existing conditions.

After plotting the values for absenteeism during the base period (see Fig. 16-19), we note that all points fall within the control limits. Given a low average value of 5.21 percent and no out-of-control points, it is felt that no further action is warranted other than informing the registered nurses of the study results.

If on day 9, however, there had been 14 aides absent (21.9 percent) instead of 8, the administrator would have to investigate for conditions resulting in this out-of-control point. Assignable causes might be related to poor working conditions, low morale, bad schedules, or other. Such findings would call for revising the prelimin-

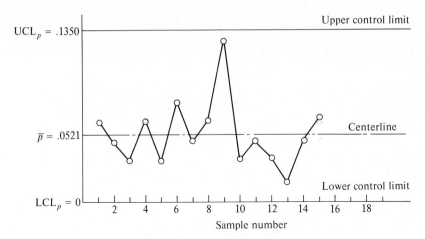

Fig. 16-19 A *p* chart for absenteeism of nurse's aides in hospital example.

ary chart by omitting the data of that sample and recomputing the values for the centerline and control limits. Similar action to investigate would be called for in future periods when observing out-of-control points.

c Chart or Chart for Number of Defects per Unit

The complexity of some products such as automobiles, typewriters, or stereo components makes it unrealistic to classify them as simply good or bad. The same could be said about service rendered by a restaurant, a department store, or a bank. In these examples, it is more relevant to evaluate performance by keeping track of the number of defects per unit or the number of complaints received say per 100 customers served or per $10,000 of sales.

Since the number of opportunities for a defect in a product or a complaint from a customer are numerous but the probability of their occurrence per unit quite small, the outcome of such a sampling process can be described by the Poisson distribution. Performance or quality in such cases can be described by a *c* chart.

Definition

A *c chart* is a control chart used to monitor a process by counting the number of undesirable occurrences *c*, such as defects or complaints, per unit of output samples.

A *c* chart is constructed by calculating the average rate $\bar{c}$ with which such events occur and placing control limits using the standard deviation of the Poisson distribution s_c, which is equal to $\sqrt{c}$.

Thus, we have

$$\text{Centerline:} \qquad \bar{c} = \frac{c_1 + c_2 + \cdots + c_N}{N} = \frac{\sum_{j=1}^{N} c_j}{N} \qquad (16\text{-}12)$$

and

$$\text{Control limits:} \qquad \begin{aligned} \text{UCL}_c &= \bar{c} + 3s_c = \bar{c} + 3\sqrt{\bar{c}} \\ \text{LCL}_c &= \bar{c} - 3s_c = \bar{c} - 3\sqrt{\bar{c}} \end{aligned} \qquad (16\text{-}13)$$

After the values of observed counts per unit sampled $c_1, c_2, \ldots, c_N$ are plotted, we can determine whether the process is in control. With appropriate adjustments, if it is not, we can use it to monitor future performance. The c chart can be used to establish whether a process is under control in a wide variety of applications for which the Poisson distribution is appropriate, e.g., number of fire department calls per so many blocks of a given type of city area, number of crimes per residential district, or number of arrivals at a hospital for emergency treatment.

▶ EXAMPLE 16-5
The chief of the highway patrol in the Carnation City district has been concerned about the traffic accidents resulting in injury on the 15-mi freeway connecting the city with its international airport. His assistant, on request, has prepared Table 16-9, indicating the number of serious accidents reported during each month of last year.

A c chart can be set up by computing an average rate $\bar{c}$ for traffic accidents and determining appropriate control limits assuming a Poisson distribution. Thus we have

$$\text{Centerline:} \qquad \bar{c} = \frac{\sum c_j}{N} = \frac{52}{12} = 4.33$$

TABLE 16-9   Number of reported accidents resulting in injury for the airport freeway

Month	Sample unit	Number of traffic accidents	Month	Sample unit	Number of traffic accidents	Month	Sample unit	Number of traffic accidents
Jan.	1	5	May	5	1	Sept.	9	5
Feb.	2	3	June	6	4	Oct.	10	12
Mar.	3	4	July	7	3	Nov.	11	4
Apr.	4	2	Aug.	8	6	Dec.	12	3

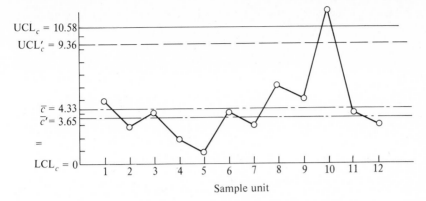

Fig. 16-20 Process-control c chart for injury-causing automobile accidents.

Control limits:
$$\mathrm{UCL}_c = \bar{c} + 3s_c = 4.33 + 3\sqrt{4.33} = 10.58$$
$$\mathrm{LCL}_c = \bar{c} - 3s_c = 4.33 - 3\sqrt{4.33} = 0$$

After plotting the c values from Table 16-9, the chief noted that the number of injury-resulting accidents in October ($c_{10} = 12$) exceeded the upper control limit (see Fig. 16-20).

Upon further investigation, it was found that in October the Weather Bureau had reported thin ice on the freeway that could easily explain the out-of-control point for that month. As a result, the c chart was revised by omitting the data for October and recomputing the centerline and control limits, as shown in Fig. 16-20. The revised c chart would have the centerline at

$$\bar{c}' = \frac{40}{11} = 3.65$$

and control limits

$$\mathrm{UCL}_{c'} = 3.636 + 3\sqrt{3.636} = 9.36$$
$$\mathrm{LCL}_{c'} = 3.636 - 3\sqrt{3.636} = 0$$

It can be seen that all points now fall within the revised control limits. Thus, the chart can be used in the future as a device to monitor traffic conditions for the airport freeway.

The general procedure would have been the same with data about the number ▶ of defects per square yard of fabric or glass and so on.

16-7 PRODUCT LIABILITY

We have previously noted the trend for new legislation to protect the safety of employees (OSHA) and various aspects of the environment (NEPA and others). Another development gaining momentum in recent years relates to laws on product liability intended to protect the consumer. Product-liability laws are of major concern to manufacturing organizations, especially their engineering, production, and quality-control departments. They are also of interest to service organizations that require the use of products and materials in their operations.

Under product-liability laws,[1] a manufacturer may be forced to compensate consumers of his products for any defects in the design or production and for lack of adequate warning or instructions concerning their use and maintenance. Design- and production-related considerations are part of the responsibility of the operation-management function, discussed earlier in this chapter with reference to design and conformance quality. Labeling and advertising considerations are a marketing responsibility, which requires close coordination between production and finance to assess the liability risks of a given policy for the entire organization.

Product-Liability Source 1: Faulty Design

A product's design might be judged to be faulty for one or more of the following reasons:

1. It might include defective or substandard materials, e.g., improper electrical wiring for a generator, or a dangerous ingredient in a drug.
2. A product might have a design feature that makes it dangerous under certain foreseen conditions of use, e.g., dials that are difficult to read or controls that are hard to operate.
3. A manufacturer may be liable for failing to include in the product design any safety features or devices that are appropriate considering the state of the art, e.g., collapsible steering columns in passenger automobiles.

The last item makes the manufacturer responsible for knowing the current state of the art in safety research, so that if certain devices are known to improve safety they will be included at a reasonable cost, whereas unsafe features or materials will be excluded.[2] One criterion for the state of the art in product-design safety is provided by industry standards.

To protect the organization against future product-liability suits it is necessary to adjust and document the selection of the adopted design compared with other alternatives. Furthermore, the product and its components should pass safety tests using current standards of performance with documentation of the results from such tests. The latter should be continued and updated throughout the life of the product. The use of independent testing laboratories for this purpose may add not only prestige but solid proof of adequate consideration given to product-design safety and quality.

---

[1] A major statement on this point includes Sec. 402A of the restatement of torts, issued by the American Law Institute in 1965. This defines *strict liability* of a seller of product to users, consumers, and in some instances to bystanders. This followed the landmark case of *Greenman* versus *Yorba Power Products, Inc.* in 1963.

[2] Recent federal laws that have been passed to promote the safety of various products include those for aircraft (1958), motor vehicles (1966), boats (1971), and, the most comprehensive in coverage, the Consumer Product Safety Act (1972).

Product-Liability Source 2:
Faulty Manufacture

The integrity of a sound product design must be maintained in the production phase through adequate quality control. Otherwise product liability may result from defects during the fabrication, assembly, and packaging stages. This is part of conformance quality and requires that quality-control methods and equipment be employed more thoroughly to ensure that the process performs within the expected product specifications.

The substantial financial expense and loss of goodwill from product-liability suits might force reevaluation of whether acceptance sampling is to be preferred to process control when both are technically feasible. The increased potential cost of passing on defective units might well justify using process control for more stages of a production process than was considered desirable in the past.

Product-Liability Source 3: Inadequate
Instructions or Warnings for Product Use

Whenever the use of a product exposes one to certain dangers, they must be stated clearly in any labels or instructions for the product. This applies to the use and maintenance of products ranging in complexity from toys to home appliances, TV sets, or automobiles. Similar comments apply to the claims made by the manufacturer about quality, performance, and the life of a product. Excessive efforts to play down any dangers associated with a product or to keep claims to quality in the labels, instructions, and advertising vague are likely to increase the risks of liability.

General Conclusions and Recommendations

The increased risks of exposure to liability suits from users or consumers of a product or service have created a new responsibility and additional costs to manufacturers. Adequate protection should proceed in accordance with the adage that an ounce of prevention is worth a pound of cure. This calls for careful evaluation in the product-design selection and testing phase, for increased vigilance in the production and packaging, and for greater responsibility in advertising. The results of efforts to achieve and maintain product quality and safety must be carefully monitored and documented so that they can be used, if the need arises, during the life cycle of the product. A company's image and the attitudes of its employees toward quality can also play an important role in future disputes on product liabilities.

Responsibility for product liability may reside in a quality-control department. However, this will require close coordination with R&D, production, marketing, and the legal department of the organization to ensure a proper balance in the concern for product safety and performance and the economic motive for an adequate return on investment.[1]

---

[1] For more details see Ref. 17.

16-8   SUMMARY

In this chapter quality control has been used to illustrate the basic concepts, the operating system, and the methods employed to monitor quality. The same might apply to other aspects of system performance such as cost, time, safety, or productivity. Quality in the products and services produced is of fundamental importance in both the design and the planning and control of operations. Decisions about quality, however, involve the entire organization at all levels and affect marketing and operations strategies and policies and the day-to-day conduct of business.

Design quality defines the basic character of a business in terms of image and potential markets and sets the requirements in human, material, and other resources. These resources determine the minimum production cost possible, thus setting a limit to the firm's ability to compete. *Conformance quality* reflects how effectively available resources are matched to the level of design quality. *Performance quality* is the true test of the soundness of decisions made for design and conformance quality. The economics of most organizations dictates important trade-offs for all dimensions of quality. Thus, management must settle for less than perfect design quality and must allow for occasional defective output to reach the consumer. Gaps between desired and actual performance are usually bridged through warranties to help maintain the image of a quality producer.

Operations management plays a key role in reaching decisions affecting both design and performance quality. However, its major responsibility is for conformance quality. This is accomplished through a quality-control system that receives information about existing standards and the actual quality of items inspected. It then acts as a filter in what it allows to enter and leave the production system.

The two methods employed to exercise quality control are acceptance sampling and process control. Both aim at minimizing the total expected cost that results from unwarranted inspection and the cost of allowing defectives to pass. Since 100 percent inspection is either impossible or uneconomical, quality control is based on sampling procedures. Therefore, the specific plan used must reflect the consequences of sampling errors, i.e., the risks of rejecting good items and passing defective ones. It is important for quality-control procedures to rely on sound statistical principles, but they must also reflect the technological and economic factors of the situation to which they are applied. Negligence of the quality-control function within an organization simply transfers this responsibility to the ultimate user or consumer, with uncontrollable consequences to the survival and achievement of established objectives.

NOTATION

Acceptance Sampling

N = size of the lot submitted for inspection

n = sample size

k = number of successive samples employed in sampling plan

c = acceptance number, i.e. maximum number of defectives allowed in sample before rejecting the entire lot

p = proportion of defectives generated by process producing lot

p_1 = AQL = acceptable quality level, i.e. proportion of percent defectives considered satisfactory

p_2 = LTPD = lot tolerance percent defective, i.e. proportion of defectives considered unsatisfactory

P_a = probability of accepting a lot given its proportion of defective items

α = producer's risk, i.e. the probability of Type I error, i.e. rejecting a lot of good quality (p_1 = AQL)

β = consumer's risk, i.e. the probability of Type II error, i.e. accepting a lot of bad quality (p_2 = LTPD)

AOQ = average outgoing quality for a sampling plan

AOQL = average outgoing quality limit

Process Control

x = value of a critical dimension for a unit in a sample of n taken for process control

$\bar{x}_j$ = mean or average value for a critical dimension in sample j (j = 1, 2, ..., N)

$\bar{\bar{x}}$ = grand mean for the critical dimension calculated over N samples taken during the base period. This corresponds to the center line of the $\bar{x}$-chart

$s_{\bar{x}}$ = standard error of sample means in base period

R_j = range, i.e. the difference between the maximum and minimum values in sample j

$\bar{R}$ = average range over N samples collected during the base period

UCL_x, LCL_x = upper and lower control limits in $\bar{x}$ chart ($= \pm 3 s_{\bar{x}}$)

A = constant defined so that for small samples n $A\bar{R} = 3 s_{\bar{x}}$

UCL_R, LCL_R = upper and lower control limits for range or $\bar{R}$ chart ($= 3 s_R$)

B, C = constants defined so that for small samples $\text{UCL}_R = B\bar{R}$ and $\text{LCL}_R = C\bar{R}$

p = true proportion of defectives for a production process

p_j = proportion of defectives in sample j

$\bar{p}$ = estimate of p based on outcome of N samples taken during base period

s_p = standard deviation of p given $\bar{p}$ and n (binomial distribution)

$\bar{n}$ = average sample size when n varies from one sample to another

UCL_p, LCL_p = upper and lower control limits in p chart ($= 3 s_p$)

c = "count" of defects found in a sample unit for complex items

$\bar{c}$ = average number of defects for the N samples collected during base period

s_c = standard deviation for number of defects per sample unit (Poisson distribution)

UCL_c, LCL_c = upper and lower control limits in c chart ($= 3 s_c$)

REVIEW QUESTIONS

1. Explain the meaning of:
   (a) Design quality
   (b) Performance quality
   (c) Production, or conformance, quality
2. Discuss the role of marketing, finance, production, and top management in the decision concerning design quality.
3. State the major factors considered in arriving at the *optimum quality level* for a product or service.

4. With reference to the quality-control system, specify:
   (a) The key features of an inspection policy
   (b) The methods by which quality control is exercised
   (c) The outputs provided in the form of recommended action
   (d) The desired information inputs
   (e) The criterion by which the QC system performance is evaluated
5. Explain the reasons that make 100 percent inspection undesirable in most quality-control situations.
6. What is meant by the term *null hypothesis* in quality control?
7. Define (a) Type I error and (b) Type II error.
8. What are the consequences usually associated with Type I and Type II error?
9. Describe the differences between measurement by attributes and measurement by variables.
10. In applying quality-control procedures to the operation of a post office, which aspects can be measured by attributes and which by variables?
11. What are the differences between process control and acceptance sampling?
12. Under what conditions are process control and acceptance sampling most appropriate?
13. Where is it preferable to inspect a process when using process control?
14. Suppose you are applying quality-control procedures in the operation of a commercial bank.
    (a) Select two or three characteristics deserving control.
    (b) What type of measurement (attribute versus variable) would be most appropriate?
    (c) What method would you recommend for each characteristic?
15. What information is conveyed by an OC curve in acceptance sampling? What is its shape under ideal conditions, i.e., 100 percent error-free inspection?
16. Discuss the considerations that enter in the specification of (a) producer's risk and (b) consumer's risk. How are they related to Type I and Type II errors?
17. Discuss the factors considered in arriving at specific values for (a) AQL and (b) LTPD.
18. Define the following characteristics of a single-sampling plan by attributes: (a) AOQ and (b) AOQL.
19. What are some of the reasons for resorting to multiple- or sequential-sampling plans?
20. What is the meaning of (a) *process natural tolerance* and (b) *assignable causes?*
21. What is the meaning of (a) process accuracy and (b) process precision? How are they monitored in process control?
22. Under what conditions are the various control charts most appropriate?
23. Which statistical distribution is associated with each type of process-control chart, and what are the assumptions behind them?

PROBLEMS

1. For a sampling plan by attributes with $n = 30$ and $c = 3$:
   (a) Determine the producer's risk if AQL = 2 percent.
   (b) Determine the consumer's risk if LTPD = 10 percent.
   (c) Calculate acceptance probabilities P for $p = 1, 5, 8$, and 20 percent and plot the OC curve.
2. On the OC curve of Prob. 1 show graphically the effect of (a) increasing n to 60 and (b) decreasing c to 2.
3. Farmeq, Inc., a farm-equipment manufacturer, is negotiating an acceptance-sampling plan with its supplier and producer of ball bearings. Farmeq management suspects that the quality of submitted lots may be in the range above 10 percent defective. The

producer of the ball bearings knows that his output has less than 10 percent defective. After lengthy arguments the choice is to be made from plan A for which $n = 10$ and $c = 2$ and plan B which has $n = 30$ and $c = 4$.

(a) Plot the OC curves for plans A and B by calculating acceptance probabilities P_a for incoming quality levels at $p = 2, 5, 8, 10$, and 20 percent.

(b) Which plan should Farmeq, Inc., prefer and why?

(c) Which plan should the producer of ball bearings prefer and why?

4. A manufacturer of heating and air-conditioning systems receives monthly shipments of 20,000 thermostats from a supplier who claims the defectives of his lots do not exceed 2 percent. This quality level is considered acceptable by the manufacturer, who wishes to reject any lots with more than 10 percent defective.

(a) Assuming that producer and consumer risks have been set at $\alpha = .05$ and $\beta = .10$ initially, determine the sampling-plan values for n and c from Table 16-4 and revise the risks.

(b) Calculate acceptance probabilities for different incoming quality levels if $n = 100$ and $c = 2$ and specify the revised producer and consumer risks at the specified AQL and LTPD values.

(c) Which of the two plans above is preferred by the manufacturer and which by the supplier of thermostats?

5. Determine the AQL and the AOQL for a sampling plan with (a) $n = 60$, $c = 3$ and (b) $n = 100$, $c = 4$.

6. An aluminum-foil manufacturer has recently completed a new plant. After several months of operation the process is believed to be stable. It is assumed that a critical dimension of the product is the length of foil packaged in rolls of 33 ft. During a 10-day base period random daily samples of five rolls produced the following results:

Sample no.	Average length $\bar{x}$	Range R	Sample no.	Average length $\bar{x}$	Range R
1	33.4	1.3	6	31.7	2.2
2	33.2	1.5	7	32.4	2.1
3	32.5	.9	8	34.8	2.0
4	33.1	1.2	9	33.6	1.6
5	34.3	1.7	10	33.3	1.8

Following the base period, three additional samples were taken with

$$\bar{x}_1 = 33.1 \qquad \bar{x}_2 = 36.7 \qquad \bar{x}_3 = 34.3$$

and

$$R_1 = 1.7 \qquad R_2 = 1.5 \qquad R_3 = 2.1$$

(a) Construct the c chart and R chart for the base period.

(b) Is the process under control for the base period?

(c) Are the three samples taken after the base period within the control limits? If not what might be some of the possible assignable causes?

7. The cutting tool of several identical expensive machines is replaced once a week as part of a preventive-maintenance program. Maintenance-crew performance is evaluated by measuring the time taken for each replacement, which follows a predetermined sequence of steps. During a 20-wk base period using samples of 6, the average time required for

the cutting-tool change was estimated at 75.0 min with an average range of 9 min (sample size used included six observations). In the following 4 wk management collected the following data:

Sample week	1	2	3	4
Average replacement time $\bar{x}$	71	82	74	89
Range R	12	8	10	7

(a) Construct a control chart from the base-period data assuming that the process was then under control.

(b) Plot the points corresponding to the samples for the 4 wk after the base period. Is the process out of control? Why?

(c) What might be possible assignable causes for a point outside the upper control limit? Should a point below the lower control limit be investigated and why?

(d) What is the probability of a sample mean exceeding a value of 90 min?

8. The management of a large restaurant has been concerned about mistakes on checks for customers. Waitresses write the amounts for the item served and compute the total. To verify check accuracy an auditor has collected data for a base period covering 20 different days as shown below:

Day	Sample size	Number of inaccurate checks	Day	Sample size	Number of inaccurate checks
1	100	6	11	100	5
2	100	4	12	100	4
3	100	7	13	100	6
4	100	5	14	100	3
5	100	6	15	100	8
6	100	2	16	100	2
7	100	8	17	100	7
8	100	9	18	100	4
9	100	4	19	100	5
10	100	3	20	100	6

(a) Prepare a control chart of the percentage defective, i.e., inaccurate checks written in this restaurant.

(b) Is the check-writing process under control? Why?

(c) If the average percentage of incorrect checks is considered too high, what might be some ways to reduce it?

(d) What might be some objections to using a p chart in this case compared with an $\bar{x}$ chart?

9. Refer to Prob. 8. If the sample size for the last 10 days were 64 instead of 100 with the same number of defectives for each sample, what would the necessary adjustments in the p chart be? Is the process still under control? Why?

10. Inter-American Airlines is striving to meet scheduled departure times for its flights as one quality aspect of its service. Before this can be used as part of its forthcoming new promotional strategy, the operations vice-president has asked for a study on flight delays. A flight is considered delayed if there is more than a 10-min wait in departure time. This excludes delays attributed to weather problems or control-tower instructions. The industry average for the delayed flights on commercial airlines is assumed to be 10 percent. After studying Inter-American flight data on weekly samples considered representative of the overall schedule, the company has obtained the information summarized below:

Week number	Sample size	Delayed flights	Week number	Sample size	Delayed flights
1	64	7	9	64	7
2	64	5	10	64	10
3	64	8	11	64	14
4	64	9	12	64	8
5	64	10	13	64	11
6	64	6	14	64	12
7	64	5	15	64	9
8	64	8	16	64	5

(a) Plot a p chart for the percentage of delayed flights. Is the scheduling process under control?

(b) Based on the results of this study, can Inter-American make a claim for better service in this respect? If not, what can be recommended to improve schedule conformance?

11. The credit department of a multibranch department store has recently reported a large number of delinquent accounts. Management feels that the credit-qualification system may need tightening up. To investigate the problem an auditor has been asked to sample the percentage of delinquent accounts for the last 12 months. The data collected are summarized below:

Month	Sample accounts examined	Delinquent accounts	Month	Sample accounts examined	Delinquent accounts
1	121	4	7	121	6
2	121	5	8	121	3
3	121	3	9	121	5
4	121	6	10	121	7
5	121	2	11	121	4
6	121	5	12	121	18

During months 11 and 12 there was a general strike of the largest local employer.

(a) Set up a control chart and determine whether the process is under control.

(*b*) If the process is not stable, suggest possible assignable causes and modify the chart accordingly if necessary.

(*c*) If the average percentage of delinquent accounts allowed by the present credit system is considered too high, suggest possible changes to improve it.

12. After introducing its new stereo receiver model 2001-X, True Sound, Inc., has allowed the assembly process to settle before setting up any routine quality-control procedures. Data on the number of defects per unit over a base period covering a random sample of 20 units are summarized below:

Sample unit	Number of defects	Sample unit	Number of defects
1	8	11	3
2	5	12	8
3	6	13	6
4	7	14	8
5	7	15	8
6	3	16	4
7	5	17	7
8	9	18	6
9	4	19	10
10	6	20	5

(*a*) Construct the appropriate control chart for the assembly process and state whether it is stable.

(*b*) If in subsequent weeks 3 units sampled at random have 5, 12, and 8 defects, respectively, can we assume that they come from a controlled process? Why?

13. The police of Orange City have received citizen complaints about recent disturbances following home games of its nationally famous university basketball team. Concerned with its public image and the possible loss of financial support, the university administration has asked the police to report the number of complaints on incidents involving property damage or injuries on such occasions. The data collected from a sample of recent games are as follows:

Game	Reported serious incidents	Game	Reported serious incidents
1	3	9	1
2	2	10	1
3	2	11	0
4	3	12	2
5	1	13	3
6	2	14	2
7	0	15†	11
8	2	16‡	12

† Finals.   ‡ Semifinals.

(a) Construct a control chart and determine whether the process is under control.

(b) If the process is not stable, what might be some assignable causes?

(c) How can the number of disturbances be reduced when they are expected to be excessive?

14. The safety manager of a paper-products plant is concerned about the number of major OSHA violations filed with the district OSHA director from recent inspections. For recent months he has collected the following data:

Month	Reported major violation	Month	Reported major violation
1	4	7	3
2	1	8	4
3	3	9	1
4	2	10	2
5	2	11	8
6	5	12	5

(a) Is the plant safety program resulting in a stable process? If not, what might be some assignable causes?

(b) If the average number of violations per month is viewed as excessive, how can it be reduced?

SELECTED REFERENCES

1. Anthony, R. H., J. Deardon, and R. F. Vancil: *Management Control Systems*, Irwin, Homewood, Ill., 1972.
2. Buffa, E. S.: *Operations Management: Problems and Models*, 3d ed., Wiley, New York, 1972.
3. Dodge, H. F., and H. G. Romig: *Sampling Inspection Tables*, 2d ed., Wiley, New York, 1959.
4. Duncan, A. J.: *Quality Control and Industrial Statistics*, 4th ed., Irwin, Homewood, Ill., 1974.
5. Enrick, N. L.: *Quality Control*, 5th ed., Industrial, New York, 1966.
6. Feigenbaum, A. V.: *Total Quality Control*, McGraw-Hill, New York, 1961.
7. Fetter, R. B.: *The Quality Control System*, Irwin, Homewood, Ill., 1967.
8. Gonella, J. A., M. J. Goran, and J. W. Williamson, et al.: "The Evaluation of Patient Care," *Journal of the American Medical Association*, vol. 214, no. 8, pp. 2040–2043, 1970.
9. Grant, E. L., and R. S. Leavenworth: *Statistical Quality Control*, 4th ed., McGraw-Hill, New York, 1972.
10. Hansen, B. L.: *Quality Control*, Prentice-Hall, Englewood Cliffs, N.J., 1963.
11. Harris, D. H., and F. B. Chaney: *Human Factors in Quality Assurance*, Wiley, New York, 1969.
12. Juran, J. M., and F. M. Gryna: *Quality Planning and Analysis: From Productive Development through Usage*, McGraw-Hill, New York, 1970.
13. Kirkpatrick, E. G.: *Quality Control for Managers and Engineers*, Wiley, New York, 1970.
14. Shewhart, W. A.: *Economic Control of Quality of Manufactured Product*, Van Nostrand, New York, 1931.
15. Smith, C. S.: *Quality and Reliability: An Integrated Approach*, Pitman, New York, 1969.
16. Vance, L. L., and J. Neter: *Statistical Sampling for Auditors and Accountants*, Wiley, New York, 1956.
17. Vaughn, R. C.: *Quality Control*, Iowa State University Press, Ames, 1974.
18. Williamson, J. W.: "Evaluating Quality of Patient Care," *Journal of the American Medical Association*, vol. 218, no. 4, pp. 564–569, Oct. 25, 1971.

Chapter 17

MAINTENANCE AND SYSTEM RELIABILITY

17-1   INTRODUCTION

Practically all components of an operations system are subject to deterioration and occasional failure in performing their assigned tasks. How fast deterioration occurs and how frequently breakdowns force idleness on workers, equipment, and perhaps the entire process depends on the design of the process and operating conditions. Poor maintenance can result in defective output, unsafe working conditions, and increased production costs due to repairs and excessive downtime.

Purpose of Maintenance

The purpose of an effective maintenance policy is to keep the production system in optimum operating condition so that it can satisfy expected demands at minimum cost. According to Hardy and Krajewskly (Ref. 8), this requires maintaining the reliability of the production system at a reasonable level and still maximizing profits or minimizing costs using two main types of policies, *reducing* the *frequency of failures* or reducing the *severity of failures*. Specific policies under each category will be discussed in Secs. 17-3 and 17-4.

Alternative Interpretations of Maintenance

In a narrow sense, maintenance is intended to improve the reliability of such physical assets as machines, materials-handling equipment, or computers and the safety of buildings and other facilities. The deterioration and failure patterns for such system components can be observed, recorded, and analyzed quite objectively. Thus, a considerable amount of study in this area has led to the development of both practical and theoretical models that can be used to formulate maintenance policies. The task of collecting data on frequency distributions for breakdowns, estimates of times required for preventive maintenance, probability distribution of repair times, and relevant costs or economic life-spans is difficult and often expensive, but it presents no conceptual problems.

However, except for highly automated processes, most production systems rely heavily on human resources as well as equipment. This is especially true in the service sector. A balanced view of maintenance for a production system must therefore consider in addition the issues involved in the proper maintenance of human resources. A major contribution to the proper maintenance of human resources can be made in the design of jobs, work stations, and the working environment. Successful job design can be an important tool in reducing fatigue and boredom. Combined with a working environment that provides pleasant and sanitary conditions, i.e., low noise levels, clean air, and adequate heating and lighting, job design can accomplish much in reducing the wear on human resources associated with work pressures. Proper training, adequate vacation time, and periodical medical checkups as part of more comprehensive medical insurance plans may also prove valuable means in the form of preventive maintenance for human resources. Finally, the availability of the necessary medical facilities or easy access to them are important for those occasions that workers break down on the job or are involved in serious accidents. The latter are usually the responsibility of other functions within the organization. In any event, the development of maintenance policies for human resources cannot reach the power of models developed for physical facilities because people—unlike equipment—are also members of other systems (families, professional clubs, etc.) and subject to pressures and conditions that management cannot control.

The next logical extension in the scope of a general maintenance program aims to include not only the operating system in terms of its physical and human resources but also the control systems designed to monitor all production and other activities. At the more general level this is the responsibility of top management. However, in the context of operations management the specific control system requiring maintenance is the subfunction of operations control. The deterioration and failures here take the form of large and consistent forecast errors, scheduling delays, poor capacity utilization, congestion in both material and information flows, and customer complaints about late deliveries.

It can be seen that an integrated maintenance program covers not only the hard technology, i.e., equipment and human resources as employed in a process, but the soft technology, i.e., the methods of managing the production system, such as aggregate planning and scheduling. Such an approach requires additional data and skills and a highly developed information system. The result of its successful application, however, is an improvement of the overall reliability of the production system and the organization at large.

Interactions of Maintenance Decisions with Other Operations-Management Functions

The range of available options in selecting a maintenance policy is restricted by decisions in process design and interacts in turn with decisions relating to scheduling, quality control, and inventory. Significant interactions of maintenance with other decision areas are shown in Fig. 17-1, where the interactions of the maintenance function with other decisions made by production management represent potential areas of conflict which are resolved with important trade-offs.

1. *In the short run*
   a. Trade-offs between maintenance and scheduling arise from the conflict of their policies. Maintenance usually tries to keep repair times to a minimum through interruption for preventive maintenance. Scheduling, however, wishes extended operation time to meet optimum completion times, which increases the likelihood of breakdowns.
   b. Trade-offs between maintenance and aggregate planning may result from the former's insistence on decoupling inventories to allow easier and less costly preventive maintenance, while aggregate planning seeks to keep inventories down for a minimum-production-cost plan.
2. *In the long run*
   a. Trade-offs between maintenance and quality control arise due to conflicts in optimum spacing of preventive maintenance and the allowed deterioration in the quality of process output.

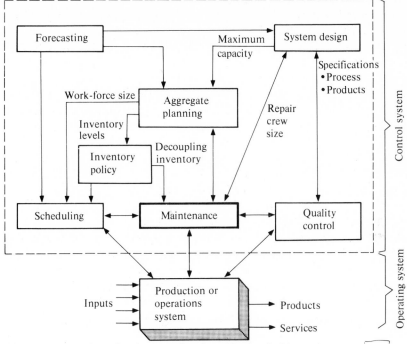

Fig. 17-1 Interactions of maintenance function with other decision areas.

b. Trade-offs between maintenance and system design occur with regard to size of maintenance crew needed. The objective is to balance the expected cost of idle crew time and waiting time of equipment in need of repair. This is further complicated by union contract restrictions on what maintenance personnel may or may not do during idle periods.

As an example, attempting to implement an optimal preventive-maintenance policy for a certain class of equipment, say every 25 working days, may interfere with an optimal schedule in terms of delivery dates for accepted orders. If the effects of deviating from these policies can be measured in added costs, the conflict resolution can be achieved at a higher level with straightforward economic arguments. The issue, however, is often clouded by several intangible factors, such as appeals for equipment safety by maintenance personnel and labor unions or arguments by marketing for customer satisfaction as determined by prompt deliveries. In the absence of clear criteria, the decision is usually a political one, i.e., one that will satisfy all affected parties after considerable pulling and hauling. Other conflicts are also handled in a similar fashion.

17-2 THE MAINTENANCE SYSTEM

The purpose of the maintenance system is to secure reliable performance from the production system. *Reliability is normally measured by the probability of satisfactory operation for a certain length of time under specified conditions.* The mainten-

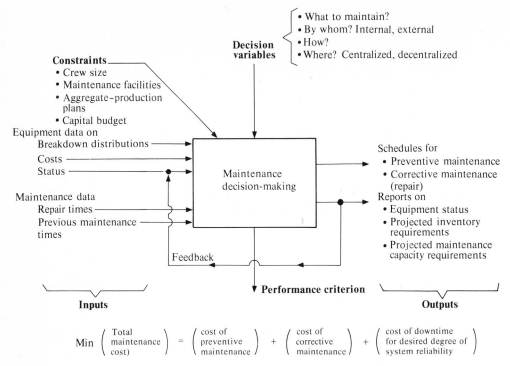

Fig. 17-2 Basic components of an operations management maintenance system.

ance system is called upon either in a predictable manner for preventive maintenance or at random times when failure is signaled by significant deviations from accepted standards in the quality of output or the cost and/or time to produce it.

Our description of the maintenance system and its operation follows the usual format in terms of decision variables, outputs and inputs, constraints, and measures of performance, which are indicated in Fig. 17-2 and covered in more detail in the sections that follow.

Maintenance-System Decision Variables

The alternatives available for the maintenance of a production system differ considerably in the lead time for their implementation. Some may have to be considered in the phase of system design (products, processes, layout, capacity, etc.). Others, however, can be implemented in the short run, given the technology for existing products and processes.

A maintenance policy must address itself to the following questions:

1. *What* is to be maintained?
2. *How* is maintenance going to be performed?
3. *Who* performs the maintenance?

4. *Where* is maintenance to be performed?

The specific answers define a maintenance policy which is as critical to the success of the organization as the other previously discussed functions performed by operations management.

What is to be maintained?   A production system usually consists of many components in the form of facilities, processes, and man-machine systems. Since they are likely to differ in their pattern of deterioration and failure, the maintenance policy selected for one or a group of similar components must take this into account if it is to contribute effectively to achieving desired levels of overall reliability.

The problem of selecting what components to maintain is similar to that of deciding the degree of control needed for an inventory system. In Chap. 12 we saw that this is determined using an ABC analysis, which groups inventory items according to their total value, their critical nature, or some other criterion. For maintenance purposes, production-system components can be grouped, again using an ABC analysis, based on their contribution to overall reliability and its effect on total operating costs. The general relationship is shown in Fig. 17-3.

Class A, or critical components are the parts of an operations system whose failure brings production to a standstill and results in a high cost due to breakdown repair and lost production from downtime. Critical components require tight control and intensive maintenance efforts.

Class B, or major, components are important parts of the system which provide smooth performance but when they fail do not disrupt operations seriously,

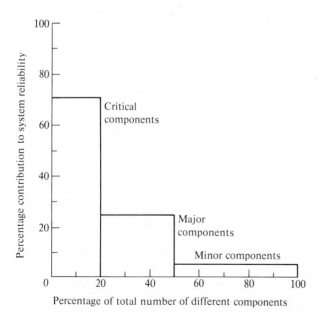

Fig. 17-3   ABC classification of system components based on their contribution to overall reliability.

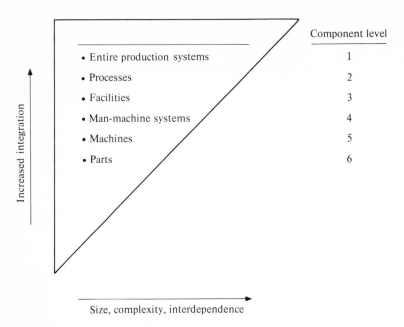

Fig. 17-4 Levels of size, complexity, and interdependence of maintenance activities.

forcing production to stop. They require moderate control and maintenance effort.

Class C, or minor, components are the supportive elements whose failure may contribute to suboptical performance but do not disrupt operations in any obvious way. They require very limited or no formal maintenance policies.

As indicated previously, the degree of seriousness can be measured by the total cost associated with repairs and downtime combined with the cost of late deliveries. An ABC analysis for reliability can be used at various levels in the organization to encompass components of different size, complexity, and interdependence, as shown in Fig. 17-4. The higher the level of the component and the degree of integration with other parts the more difficult it becomes to shut the system down for maintenance without significant costs due to disruptions and lost production. In this sense, a continuous process, such as a steelmill or a chemical plant, offers fewer options for maintenance than a flow shop, such as a bottling line or a typewriter-assembly plant. Similarly, a flow shop offers fewer options than a job shop, which provides multiple processing paths due to the interchangeability of its general-purpose equipment. An ABC analysis yields a priority list so that when several components wait for repairs, the maintenance crew can establish the order in which they should be serviced.

How is maintenance to be performed?   Once a component is selected for maintenance, it is necessary to determine how it will be performed. Our interest here is not on the engineering requirements of the maintenance activity (tools, supplies, etc.) or with normal maintenance requirements specified by the equipment manufacturer.

Instead, we wish to consider alternatives available to management to maintain equipment in satisfactory working condition at minimum cost. They include several categories.

Inspection   This is intended to determine the operating status of a component and may be visual or require some tests for measurement with special equipment. If the outcome of the inspection is satisfactory, the component is allowed to continue in operation until the next inspection unless it breaks down earlier. Sometimes a component is allowed to operate for a fixed period and then is overhauled or replaced.

If the inspection reveals defective performance, the component may be repaired or replaced. This alternative is widely employed for maintenance at all levels, e.g., for moving parts in equipment, an entire assembly line, various facilities such as elevators in buildings, accounting systems through internal audits, or pollution-control devices in cars, airplanes, or factories.

The availability of inspection depends on whether the wear and tear is observable or not. Such items as cutting tools, bearings, cars, appliances, buildings, and others lend themselves to measurement of the degree of deterioration that has occurred. This in turn allows management to decide what to do next. Some items, however, operate satisfactorily until they fail completely, e.g., some electronic equipment or light bulbs. For such items inspection as an alternative to maintenance is not useful in anticipating future breakdowns.

Corrective maintenance or repair   This is the alternative used after a component breaks down and replacement is not advisable. It is also known as *emergency maintenance*. The timing of repair work depends on how critical the component is, as indicated by its priority rating, and whether or not there is a standby component that takes over to avoid production stoppage.

Preventive maintenance   This more comprehensive approach relies on both inspection and repair, according to a predetermined plan of action. For certain items whose deterioration and failure pattern can be described with a probability distribution, inspection may reveal an imminent breakdown. If the effect of a failure is very costly or disruptive and the probability of this event is high, it is advisable to act as soon as the results of the inspection are known. Possible action may range from minor or major repairs to replacing parts or even the entire component and may be scheduled to be performed immediately or at a later time, all at once or sequentially.

An important condition for using preventive maintenance is that the distribution of the component's failure-free run time has a small variance. The key problem, when this is true, is to determine the best timing of inspections, i.e., an optimal inspection schedule.

Which alternative will be best for a given case depends on operating conditions and adequate data about (1) equipment and facilities failure patterns and (2) costs for preventive maintenance, repair, and lost production time. Data requirements are discussed in the section on maintenance-system inputs, but a few words are in order here about the effect of operating conditions.

Some production systems, e.g., steelmills, oil refineries, chemical plants, and nuclear power plants, operate continuously, while others run for one or two shifts a day and may close on weekends. For the first category, maintenance requires that production be stopped, and this can be very costly both in terms of lost production and startup requirements. This considerably limits the attractiveness of preventive-maintenance alternatives. On the other hand, maintenance becomes much easier when normal and planned interruptions in productive activity allow the selection of any one of the three alternatives on the basis of cost. The only way the above restriction is removed is when maintenance can be performed while production goes on, either with the same facilities or standby equipment.

Who performs the maintenance?   Depending on the process technology used and the demand for maintenance services, the maintenance function may be internal or external to the organization. The choice is often an economic one. For a production system with a simple technology, like a machine shop or a typewriter-assembly plant, the skills needed for maintenance often justify the operation of an *internal* maintenance function. However, the maintenance of an electronic computer, a multipurpose blood-testing machine, a chemical reactor, or an airline computer reservation system generally requires maintenance skills available most economically from the manufacturer because of the complex technology of such items and the limited demand for their maintenance within one organization.

When the demand for maintenance is quite intensive or needed on very short notice, it may be necessary to provide this function internally, despite the complex technology of the process. Airlines and nuclear power plants are examples in this category.

Where is maintenance performed?   Assuming that it is best to have an internal maintenance function, we must decide whether it will be centralized or decentralized. The answer depends on the level of demand for maintenance services, the desired specialization of maintenance personnel, the degree of urgency in responding to breakdowns, the travel time to a central shop, the skills of equipment operators, and the like. Physical centralization of maintenance facilities usually results in higher utilization rates of maintenance personnel and equipment but slower response times and increased production downtime. The opposite is true of decentralized facilities. The issue is resolved by an economic analysis supported by some guessing or a simulation model.

Of all variables defining a maintenance policy, the *what*, *who*, and *where* aspects must be considered early in the design of the production system. Afterwards they are reviewed periodically with changes in the production volume and process technology. The *how* part can be reviewed and modified more easily with corresponding adjustments in the function of aggregate planning and scheduling.

Maintenance-System Outputs

The usual output of a maintenance system includes the following:

1. *Schedules for the execution of selected policies*
   a. For inspection to assess the status of equipment and facilities
   b. For repair when breakdowns occur, specifying priorities and expected requirements in skills, parts, etc.
   c. For preventive maintenance when appropriate
2. *Reports prepared covering*
   a. The status of equipment after inspection, repair, or preventive maintenance
   b. The projected requirements for spare parts and decoupling inventories for planned maintenance jobs
   c. The projected requirements for maintenance capacity in terms of skills and worker-hours needed

How many of these outputs are actually made available depends on the quality of the existing information system. For all but the simplest cases, the development of good maintenance policies requires the use of a computer-assisted information system that provides the information covered in the following section.

Maintenance-System Information Inputs

Raw data are scarcely adequate for making managerial decisions. The same applies to data relating to the maintenance of a production system. While it may be possible to generate masses of data pertaining to the performance of various parts, equipment, and facilities, quite often management must rely on approximations and assumptions concerning the behavior of these items.

Available data can be organized to specify both physical and economic characteristics needed to describe the production-system components and the maintenance system itself. The information needed to determine the most appropriate maintenance policies represents the input to the maintenance decision-making system. This is in contrast to the inputs of work force, spare parts, and special equipment for testing and repair that are needed to perform maintenance activities in the same manner as any other productive system.

Information inputs may pertain to the history of components in terms of operating time and repairs performed, to the costs for parts and labor, and to the effects of downtime on lost production and/or delays. Table 17-1 summarizes the most frequently used information inputs.

Constraints on Maintenance System

The number of alternatives considered for developing a maintenance policy is restricted by several constraints. Alternatives requiring long lead times for their implementation (what, who, where) are constrained by the design of the production system, which specifies process technology and layout as well as the capacity, i.e.,

TABLE 17-1   Information inputs for maintenance system

	Characteristic	
System	Physical performance	Economic performance

Production:
  Parts
  Equipment
  Facilities
	Function(s) performed
	Design features
	Age
	Operating condition
	Previous breakdowns
	  and required service
	Deterioration pattern
	Statistical distribution:
	  Breakdowns
	  Useful life
		Purchase price
		Installation cost
		Costs of downtime
		  (opportunity cost per
		  hour of lost production)

Maintenance:	Statistical distribution:
	  Inspection time
	  Repair time
	  Preventive-maintenance
	    time
	Inspection and testing
	  procedures to deter-
	  mine location and
	  nature of failures
		Costs of:
		  Planned inspections
		  Breakdown repair
		    Labor
		    Parts
		    Other
		Cost of idleness of
		  maintenance facilities

crew size, assigned to the maintenance system. These factors also constrain the *how* aspects in terms of technologically feasible alternatives.

Aggregate-planning and capital-budgeting decisions also set limits on the *how* aspects of maintenance in terms of allowances for decoupling inventories affecting the degree of dependence between successive stages and fluctuations in the size of maintenance crews.

Performance Criterion for Maintenance Systems

A maintenance system, like an inventory system, is a supporting function aiming at economic and smooth operation of the production system. Thus, the various policies are evaluated on the basis of the maintenance costs incurred for a desired level of reliability.

Assuming that long-term constraints have determined what is to be maintained, by whom, and where, the selection of an optimal policy in the short run is to be made from the alternatives of breakdown repair and preventive maintenance. The cost relationships for these alternatives are shown in Fig. 17-5. Note that for low or no preventive-maintenance effort the total cost of maintenance is mainly attributed to the cost of breakdown repairs. As we increase the level of preventive mainten- ance, breakdown costs decrease faster than preventive-maintenance costs increase, thus pulling the total cost down. This continues up to the point of optimal

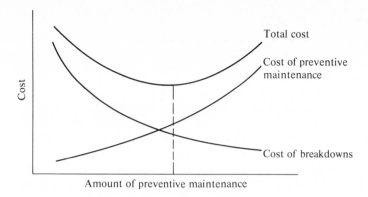

Fig. 17-5   Cost relationship of maintenance alternatives.

preventive-maintenance effort. Beyond that, the reductions in the cost of break-down repairs are not enough to offset the steady increases in the cost of preventive maintenance, causing total cost to rise.

17-3   SHORT-TERM MAINTENANCE POLICIES

For an existing firm with an internal maintenance function many of the critical factors that determine the inherent reliability of the operations system have been decided in the design phase. It is still possible, however, to take a number of steps in the short run that can keep the process in good working condition. They may include the following:

1. Training machine operators
2. Training maintenance-crew workers
3. Making use of decoupling, i.e., work in process and finished-goods inventories, to allow limited operation during maintenance
4. Providing adequate inventory of spare parts to reduce repair time
5. Using overtime to make up for lost production due to repairs
6. Using preventive maintenance to reduce the frequency of breakdowns
7. Using group rather than individual replacement for low-valued items

These alternatives can be used in different combinations to formulate satisfactory short-term maintenance policies. In this section we shall consider only the last two alternatives. The training of operators and maintenance workers can be incorporated in more general plans, while the use of inventories in various forms and overtime may be part of an aggregate-production plan, as discussed in Chap. 12. The evaluation of preventive-maintenance and group-replacement policies requires information about the pattern of deterioration or breakdown, the time required for preventive maintenance and repairs, and the costs incurred for repairs, maintenance, and downtime.

Breakdown-Time Frequency Distributions

The physical performance of a moving part, a machine, or an entire assembly line can be described by a frequency distribution of the failure-free run time between breakdowns T. As with any statistical distribution, we must specify a mean value T_b for the average time until a breakdown occurs and the variability s_T of T.

The shape of the frequency distribution $f(T)$ reflects the complexity of a component and its design quality. For two items with comparable complexity we would expect the variability in T to be about the same. However, the component with higher design quality would be expected to have a larger value for the average time between breakdowns T_b. Variability in failure-free run time increases with the complexity of a component as measured by the number of interacting parts. Figure 17-6 shows the frequency distribution for four different types of components.

Data for failure-free run times are first summarized in the form of a histogram. It is often possible to approximate this by a smooth curve corresponding to a theoretical statistical distribution (normal, negative exponential, etc.) with well-known properties.

In Fig. 17-6 we note that if a component is relatively simple, it tends to break down after a run time close to the average value T_b (case 1). When a component is complex, however, a breakdown may be attributed to failure of any one of its many interacting parts. Therefore, the breakdown time is more unpredictable, as measured by a larger value for its variability (case 2). At times we have to work with components which may run for a long time if adjusted properly when inspected or repaired but which tend to break down very quickly if the adjustment is not correct. This type displays the largest variability of the three examples (case 3). Case 4 exemplifies a component with a dish-shaped frequency distribution. The probability of failure is high in the early period of operation (infant mortality) and near the end of the equipment's life (old-age mortality) due to wear and tear. If the component survives the early-infancy phase, it is likely to operate reliably for an extended period of time until it reaches old age and requires overhaul or replacement.

Selection of Repair versus Preventive-Maintenance Policy

To focus on the key aspects of the procedure for selecting a short-term maintenance policy, we shall assume that we have only one machine, say a milling machine, in a job shop and a maintenance crew of a fixed size. A milling machine is used to create a smooth surface on metal parts and has a number of critical components that wear out or go out of adjustment, causing defects in the parts. A machine breakdown occurs when failure in any one of its critical components causes the machine to stop or to produce an excessive number of defective units.

Management may choose to allow the machine to operate until it breaks down after a run time T. The maintenance crew then proceeds to fix the machine, taking an average repair time equal to T_r, the mean value of a repair-time distribution $g(T)$. After repair the machine runs until the next breakdown, and so on. This policy is shown in Fig. 17-7a.

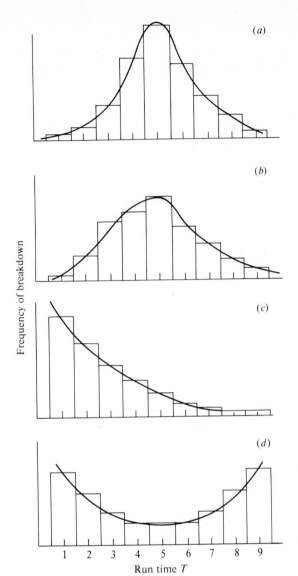

Fig. 17-6 Representative types of frequency of breakdown distributions for various types of production components: (*a*) *case 1*, simple component (few interacting parts) with tendency to break down at almost fixed intervals; (*b*) *case 2*, complex components (many interacting parts) with large variability in breakdown times due to multiple causes of failure; (*c*) *case 3*, component requiring delicate initial adjustment; and (*d*) *case 4*, complex component with high probability of breakdown in early and late stages.

An alternative approach is to operate the milling machine for a certain period T_p and then inspect it to assess its operating status and replace if necessary any critical components for which a breakdown is imminent. The average time for performing this preventive maintenance is T_m, a mean value of a preventive-maintenance time distribution $h(T)$. The fixed time T_p between successive inspections is called the *preventive-maintenance period*. The sum of T_m and T_p is the complete preventive-maintenance cycle. Occasionally, the machine may break down between regular inspections, in which case the maintenance crew will repair it

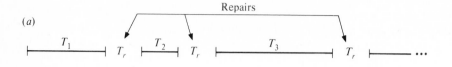

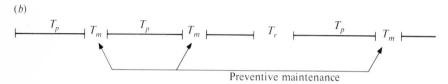

Fig. 17-7 **Alternative short-term maintenance policies: (a) operating a machine with a repair policy and (b) operating a machine with a preventive-maintenance policy.** $T_1, T_2, T_3, \ldots$ = **failure-free run times;** T_p = **run time between preventive-maintenance inspections;** T_m = **average time to perform preventive maintenance;** T_r = **average time for machine repair (using a fixed crew size).**

with the same average repair time T_r. This maintenance policy is shown in Fig. 17-7b.

There are two questions management must consider at this point: (1) Is the expected decrease in repair costs due to fewer breakdowns offset by the cost of preventive maintenance? (2) If preventive maintenance is advisable, what is the optimum time T_p between inspections? The answers depend on the variability of the frequency distribution for breakdowns $f(T)$, on the length of times for preventive maintenance T_m and repair T_r, and on the impact of breakdowns due to downtime.

In general, we can use the following guidelines:

1. Assuming that downtime costs are not significant, preventive maintenance is desirable if the time to perform it is less than the time to perform repairs ($T_m < T_r$). Otherwise, it is just as well to allow the machine to operate until it fails, since this way we are likely to have a larger percentage of run time.
2. Assuming that downtime costs are not significant and that T_m is shorter than T_r, preventive maintenance is advisable if during inspection we have a high probability of identifying imminent breakdowns. This is possible only when the variability of run time is small, because for this case most failure-free run times will be close to the average T_b. Accordingly, a component with a frequency distribution like that in case 1 of Fig. 17-6 would be a better candidate for preventive maintenance than the others. When this condition is satisfied, the preventive-maintenance period T_p can be set equal to some fraction of the average run time T_b. The specific value is selected so that the savings in repair costs will exceed the cost of preventive maintenance and value of remaining life of the component.
3. In the event downtime costs are significant, when a component is idle due to repairs or preventive maintenance, guidelines 1 and 2 may no longer hold. For a production system with a high degree of integration (a steelmill, a chemical

plant, or a mass-production assembly line) preventive maintenance may be preferable to repair during planned periods of equipment idleness (lunch hours, second or third shifts, vacation, etc.), since only repairs would now affect the proportion of failure-free run time.

The frequency of preventive maintenance would be selected to minimize the combined cost of repairs, preventive maintenance, and downtime. The higher the downtime costs from breakdowns the greater the pressure for shorter preventive-maintenance periods T_p and reduced repair time T_r using a larger maintenance capacity (larger crew size, multiple crews, etc.).

▶ EXAMPLE 17-1

Precision Parts Co., specializing in hospital equipment, is in the process of evaluating alternative maintenance policies. In the stamping department there are 60 identical machines ($N = 60$) with the breakdown distribution shown in Fig. 17-8.

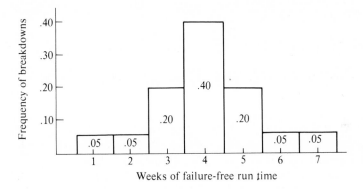

Fig. 17-8   Frequency distribution of breakdowns for a stamping machine.

Downtime costs in the stamping department are negligible ($C_d = 0$) because when a breakdown occurs, the foreman assigns the machine operator to other tasks. Personnel on the maintenance crew are paid an average wage of $10 per hour. A machine breakdown requires an average repair time equal to 8 h ($T_r = 8$ h) by a crew of two workers. For the same crew size the preventive-maintenance time per machine is 3 h ($T_m = 2$ h). Supplies and parts amount to $140 per single repair and $60 per machine for preventive maintenance. Thus

$$\text{Unit cost of repair} = C_r = (8 \text{ h})(2 \text{ workers})(\$10/\text{h}) + \$140$$
$$= \$300/\text{breakdown (for labor and parts)}$$

$$\text{Unit cost of preventive maintenance} = C_m = (2 \text{ h})(2 \text{ workers})(\$10/\text{h}) + \$60$$
$$= \$100/\text{machine (for labor and parts)}$$

The management of Precision Parts Co. must evaluate repair and preventive-maintenance policies and select the one for which the total maintenance cost per week (TMC) is minimum.

Expected Cost of Repair Policy

When each machine is allowed to run until it breaks down and is then repaired, the only cost incurred will be for repairs, since downtime costs are negligible; i.e.,

$$\text{TMC(repair policy)} = \text{TC}_r = \text{expected cost of repairs}$$

Before we can determine TC_r, we must calculate the average run time of each machine T_b and from this the average number of breakdowns per week B. Here

$$\text{TC}_r = B \cdot C_r \tag{17-1}$$

or

$$\begin{bmatrix} \text{Expected cost of} \\ \text{repair policy per week} \end{bmatrix} = \begin{bmatrix} \text{average number of break-} \\ \text{downs/week for } N \text{ machines} \end{bmatrix} \begin{bmatrix} \text{unit cost} \\ \text{of repair} \end{bmatrix}$$

For the stamping department, with $N = 60$ machines, the average number of breakdowns per week is

$$B = \frac{N}{T_b} = \frac{\text{number of machines}}{\text{average run time per machine before failure}} \tag{17-2}$$

From the frequency distribution of breakdowns we have

$$T_b = p_1 T_1 + p_2 T_2 + \cdots + p_7 T_7 = \sum_{i=1}^{7} p_i T_i$$

$$= (.05)(1) + (.05)(2) + (.20)(3) + (.40)(4) + (.20)(5) + (.05)(6) + (.05)(7)$$

$$= 4.0 \text{ wk}$$

This result could be intuitively guessed from the symmetry of the distribution. Returning to the calculation of the cost for a repair policy, we have

$$\text{TC}_r = B \cdot C_r = \frac{N}{T_b} C_r = \frac{60}{4.0} 300 = \$4,500/\text{wk}$$

Expected Cost of Preventive-Maintenance Policy

The expected cost per week of a preventive-maintenance policy will depend on the time between inspections T_p. Since despite the preventive-maintenance effort there will also be some breakdowns between inspections, for negligible downtime costs the cost of a preventive-maintenance policy with inspections every n weeks will be

$$\boxed{\text{TMC}(n) = \text{TC}_r(n) + \text{TC}_m(n)} \tag{17-3}$$

where $n =$ number of weeks between preventive maintenance
$\text{TMC}(n) =$ total maintenance cost per week
$\text{TC}_r(n) =$ repair cost per week
$\text{TC}_m(n) =$ preventive-maintenance cost per week

In theory, there are as many policies to be evaluated as there are feasible values for a machine's failure-free run time. In our example, $n = 1, 2, \ldots, 7$ wk. When the variability of the breakdown frequency distribution is small, the number of policies to be evaluated is reduced to values of n less than or equal to the average run time T_b.

Method

To calculate the total maintenance cost per week for each feasible value of n the method consists of the following steps:

1. Calculate the cumulative expected number of breakdowns B_n for all machines during the preventive-maintenance period $T_p = n$ weeks
2. Determine the average number of breakdowns per week B as the ratio of B_n/n
3. Determine the expected cost of repairs per week, given the preventive-maintenance period

$$TC_r(n) = \left(\frac{B_n}{n}\right) C_r$$

4. Calculate the cost of preventive maintenance per week

$$TC_m(n) = \frac{N \cdot C_m}{n}$$

5. Determine the total maintenance cost $TMC(n)$ by adding 3 and 4

The above procedure can be illustrated with the data of our example.

Preventive-Maintenance Policy for $n = 1$ wk

If preventive maintenance is performed at the end of each week, we have:

1. $B_1 = N p_1 = (60)(.05) = 3$ machines in 1 wk; i.e., the cumulative expected number of breakdowns when $n = 1$ is the number of machines ($N = 60$) multiplied by the percentage of those which will fail after 1 wk of operation.
2. The average number of breakdowns per week will be

$$B = \frac{B_n}{n} = \frac{B_1}{1} = \frac{3}{1} = 3 \text{ machines/wk}$$

i.e., the cumulative number of breakdowns divided by the number of weeks in the preventive-maintenance period.
3. The expected cost of repairs per week will be

$$TC_r(1) = B \cdot C_r = (3 \text{ machines/wk})(\$300/\text{machine}) = \$900/\text{wk}$$

4. The cost of preventive maintenance per week will be

$$TC_m(1) = \frac{N \cdot C_m}{n} = \frac{(60 \text{ machines})(\$100/\text{machine})}{1 \text{ wk}} = \$6,000/\text{wk}$$

5. The total maintenance policy per week will be

$$TMC(1) = TC_r(1) + TC_m(1) = \$900 + \$6,000 = \$6,900/\text{wk}$$

Preventive-Maintenance Policy for n = 2 wk

When preventive maintenance is performed every 2 wk, we have:

1. $B_2 = Np_1 + Np_2 + B_1 p_1 = N(p_1 + p_2) + B_1 p_1$
   $= 60(.05 + .05) + (3)(.05) = 6 + .15 = 6.15$ machines/2-wk period

   i.e., the cumulative number of expected breakdowns in a 2-wk period will be the number of machines ($N = 60$) multiplied by the percentage of those which fail after 1 or 2 wk ($p_1 + p_2$), plus the portion of machines that failed and were repaired in the first week B_1 but may break down again in the second week, i.e., after operating for 1 wk only.

2. The average number of breakdowns per week will be

$$B = \frac{B_2}{2} = \frac{6.15}{2} = 3.075 \text{ machines/wk}$$

3. The expected cost of repairs per week will be

$$TC_r(2) = B \cdot C_r = (3.075)(\$300) = \$922.50/\text{wk}$$

4. The prorated cost of preventive maintenance per week will be

$$TC_m(2) = \frac{N \cdot C_m}{n} = \frac{(60)(100)}{2} = \$3,000/\text{wk}$$

5. The total maintenance-policy cost per week will be

$$TMC(2) = TC_r(2) + TC_m(2) = \$922.50 + \$3,000 = \$3,922.50/\text{wk}$$

It can be seen that all the above calculations are quite straightforward, except perhaps for the cumulative number of expected breakdowns during the preventive-maintenance period. In examining the remaining policies we shall focus on the calculation of B_n, and the other results will be summarized in Table 17-2.

Preventive-Maintenance Policy for n wk

When calculating the value for B_n, we first identify the population sources for breakdowns and then the appropriate probabilities for first-time or repeated failures. For $n = 3$ we have:

1. First-time failures from a population of $N = 60$ machines in the first, second, and third week with probabilities p_1, p_2, p_3, respectively,

$$N(p_1 + p_2 + p_3) = (60)(.05 + .05 + .20) = 18 \text{ machines}$$

TABLE 17-2   Evaluation of preventive-maintenance policies

Preventive-maintenance period n	Cumulative number of expected breakdowns B_n	Average number of breakdowns per week B	Expected repair cost per week $TC_r(n)$	Preventive-maintenance cost per week $TC_m(n)$	Total cost of preventive-maintenance policy $TMC(n)$
1	3.000	3	$900.00	$6,000	$6,900.00
2	6.150	3.075	922.50	3,000	3,922.50
3	18.457	6.1523	1845.70	2,000	3,845.70
4	43.831	10.958	3287.33	1,500	4,787.32
5	59.544	11.909	3572.64	1,200	4,772.64
6	68.920	11.487	3446.00	1,000	4,446.00
7	83.952	11.993	3597.96	857.14	4,455.00

2. Machines repaired in the first and second week B_2 that may fail after 1 wk with a probability equal to p_1

$$B_2 p_1 = (6.150)(.05) = .3075 \text{ machine}$$

3. Machines repaired in the first week that may fail after 2 wk with a probability equal to p_2

$$B_1 p_2 = (3)(.05) = .1500$$

The value of B_3 is found by summing expected breakdowns from all the above sources:

$$B_3 = N(p_1 + p_2 + p_3) + B_2 p_1 + B_1 p_2$$
$$= 18 + .3075 + .1500 = 18.457$$

For $n = 4$ we have

$$B_4 = N(p_1 + p_2 + p_3 + p_4) + B_3 p_1 + B_2 p_2 + B_1 p_3$$
$$= (60)(.05 + .05 + .20 + .40) + (18.457)(.05) + (6.15)(.05) + (3)(.20)$$
$$= 42 + .923 + .307 + .600 = 43.831$$

Figure 17-9 may help visualize the process of generating breakdowns for $n = 4$. The reader can verify the values for B_5, B_6, and B_7 in Table 17-2.

In the example, since 70 percent of all breakdowns occur within 4 weeks ($n = 4$), there would be no reason to evaluate preventive-maintenance policies for n larger than 4. Table 17-2 covers all possible policies, as one must do for distributions with large variability. It can be seen that the optimal policy corresponds to $n = 3$ weeks, a preventive-maintenance period which minimizes the combined cost due to repairs and preventive maintenance. This is also shown graphically in Fig. 17-10, where the costs for various preventive-maintenance policies can be ▶ compared with the cost of a simple repair policy, shown as a horizontal line.

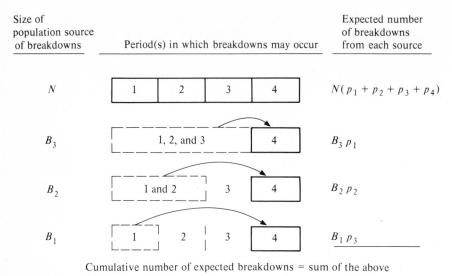

Size of population source of breakdowns	Period(s) in which breakdowns may occur	Expected number of breakdowns from each source

Cumulative number of expected breakdowns = sum of the above

Fig. 17-9   Calculating cumulative number of breakdowns for $n = 4$.

Individuals versus Group-Replacement Policy for Low-Valued Items

A production system may use a large number of identical low-valued components whose probability of breakdown increases with age. Failure of these items may not result in major disruptions, but they still require replacement if the system is to perform satisfactorily. Examples of such items include telephone poles, street lights,

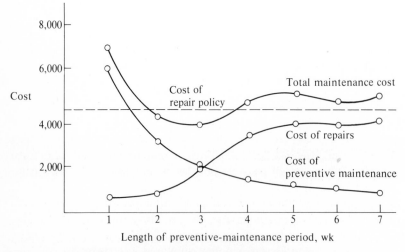

Length of preventive-maintenance period, wk

Fig. 17-10   Comparison of costs for repair and preventive-maintenance policies.

park sprinklers, etc. Even though the unit replacement cost for such items is low, it requires sending a maintenance crew to do the necessary work. With only a limited extra effort we can replace a whole group instead of 1 unit of similar components. This is a situation with a high setup cost and a low variable (replacement) cost per unit.

The main issue in this case is to decide whether there is an economic advantage in replacing a whole group of similar components regardless of age at predetermined intervals rather than replacing units individually as they fail. If we have accurate data on the breakdown frequency distribution for such components and estimates of costs for individual and group replacement, we can analyze the problem in a way similar to that used for evaluating repair versus preventive-maintenance policies in the previous section.

▶ EXAMPLE 17-2

On its production line the Ambrosia Food Co. uses a battery of 100 small sprinklers for cleaning fresh vegetables, fruit, etc., before they are prepared for canning. Failure of a sprinkler, which costs $2 per unit, does not disrupt production flow but may create quality-control problems from insufficient cleaning. Such failures are reported by the line foremen to the maintenance department, which must disassemble the arc-shaped battery frame from the production line before replacing a sprinkler at the end of the shift or on weekends. Due to the high setup cost for this task, management is considering a policy of group replacement. The frequency distribution for sprinkler breakdowns is given in Table 17-3.

TABLE 17-3 Data for sprinkler performance and replacement costs

Run time T_n	1	2	3	4	5	6
Probability of failure p_n	.05	.05	.10	.10	.30	.40

	Replacement cost		
	Purchase	Installation	Per unit
Individually	$2	$7	$9
Group	2	1	3

Our approach will be to compute the expected cost per week for the policy of individual replacements and compare this with the cost per week for group replacements. The interval between successive group replacements will vary with each policy.

Expected Cost of Individual Replacement Policy

When a sprinkler is replaced individually at the end of the shift in which it fails, the expected cost of this policy is equal to the cost of expected individual replacements

$$\text{TRC(individual replacement policy)} = \text{TRC}_i$$

$$= \text{expected cost of individual replacement}$$

To determine TRC_i we must first calculate the average operating time before failure T_b. This can then be used to determine the average number of expected individual replacements R per week:

$$\text{TRC}_i = R \cdot C_i \tag{17-4}$$

or

$$\begin{bmatrix} \text{Expected cost of individual} \\ \text{replacement policy/week} \end{bmatrix} = \begin{bmatrix} \text{average number of individual} \\ \text{replacements/week} \end{bmatrix} \begin{bmatrix} \text{unit cost of indi-} \\ \text{vidual replacements} \end{bmatrix}$$

For the sprinklers in the Ambrosia production line the average number of individual replacements per week is

$$R = \frac{N}{T_b} = \frac{\text{number of sprinklers}}{\text{average operating time before failure}} \tag{17-5}$$

The average operating time T_b for the distribution given is

$$T_b = p_1 T_1 + p_2 T_2 + \cdots + p_6 T_6 = \sum_{i=1}^{6} p_i T_i$$

$$= (.05)(1) + (.05)(2) + (.10)(3) + (.10)(4) + (.30)(5) + (.40)(6)$$

$$= 4.75 \text{ wk}$$

The expected cost per week of a policy for individual replacements is

$$\text{TRC}_i = \frac{N}{T_b} C_i = \left(\frac{100}{4.75}\right)(\$9) = \$189.47/\text{wk}$$

Expected Cost of Group-Replacement Policies

When sprinklers are replaced as a group every n wk, we experience two types of costs: (1) the cost of the group replacements at the lower cost of $C_i = \$3$ per unit and (2) an expected cost due to individual replacements during the n-wk period at the higher cost of $C_g = \$9$ per unit. Both types must be converted to a weekly basis and added to yield a group-replacement-policy cost per week as follows:

$$\boxed{\text{TRC}(n) = \text{TRC}_i(n) + \text{TRC}_g(n)} \tag{17-6}$$

where n = number of weeks between group replacements
$\text{TRC}(n)$ = total replacement cost per week
$\text{TRC}_i(n)$ = expected cost of individual replacements per week
$\text{TRC}_g(n)$ = cost of group replacements per week

Method

For evaluating alternative group replacement policies the method is very similar to the one used for preventive maintenance policies. The steps are:

1. Calculate the cumulative expected number of individual replacements R_n during a period of n wk between group replacements
2. Determine the average number of individual replacements per week

$$R = \frac{R_n}{n}$$

3. Determine the expected cost per week of individual replacements given the group-replacement period

$$TRC_i(n) = \frac{R_n}{n} C_i$$

4. Calculate the cost of group replacement per week

$$TRC_g(n) = \frac{N_g \cdot C_g}{n}$$

5. Determine the total maintenance cost $TRC(n)$ by adding results 3 and 4.

Group Replacement Policy for $n = 1$ wk

When all the sprinklers in the production line are replaced at the end of each week, we have:

1. Expected number of individual replacements in 1 wk

$$R_1 = Np_1 = 100(.05) = 5 \text{ sprinklers}$$

2.
$$R = \frac{R_1}{1} = \frac{5}{1} = 5 \text{ sprinklers/wk}$$

3. Expected cost of individual replacements

$$TRC_i(1) = R \cdot C_i = (5)(\$9) = \$45/\text{wk}$$

4. Cost of group replacement per week

$$TRC_g(1) = \frac{N \cdot C_g}{n} = \frac{(100)(\$3)}{1} = \$300/\text{wk}$$

5. Cost of a policy with group replacement every week

$$TRC(1) = TRC_i(1) + TRC_g(1) = \$45 + \$300 = \$345/\text{wk}$$

Group Replacement Policy for n = 2 wk

If management allows the sprinklers to operate for 2 wk before group replacement, we have the following situation:

1. The cumulative expected number of individual replacements in 2 wk will be

$$R_2 = N(p_1 + p_2) + R_1 p_1 = 100(.05 + .05) + 5(.05)$$
$$= 10 + .25 = 10.25 \text{ sprinklers}$$

That is, R_2 is equal to the expected number of breakdowns of good sprinklers after 1 or 2 wk plus the portion of sprinklers replaced after 1 wk that may fail again in the second.

2. The average number of individual replacements per week is

$$R = \frac{R_2}{2} = \frac{10.25}{2} = 5.125 \text{ sprinklers}$$

3. The expected cost of individual replacements per week is

$$\text{TRC}_i(2) = R \cdot C_i = (5.125)(\$9) = \$46.125/\text{wk}$$

4. The cost of group replacement prorated weekly is

$$\text{TRC}_g(2) = \frac{N \cdot C_g}{n} = \frac{(100)(\$3)}{2} = \$150/\text{wk}$$

5. The cost of a policy with group replacement every 2 wk is

$$\text{TRC}(2) = \text{TRC}_i(2) + \text{TRC}_g(2) = \$46.125 + \$150 = \$196.125/\text{wk}$$

Group-Replacement Policy for a Period of n wk

As with preventive-maintenance policies in the previous section, the main problem in evaluating group-replacement policies is the determination of the expected number of individual replacements R_n in the interval between group replacements. The reasoning here is exactly the same as in calculating the expected number of machine breakdowns B_n. Thus, for $n = 3$

$$R_3 = N(p_1 + p_2 + p_3) + R_2 p_1 + R_1 p_2$$
$$= (100)(.05 + .05 + .10) + (10.25)(.05) + (5)(.05) = 20.763 \text{ sprinklers}$$

and for $n = 4$

$$R_4 = N(p_1 + p_2 + p_3 + p_4) + R_3 p_1 + R_2 p_2 + R_1 p_3$$
$$= (100)(.05 + .05 + .10 + .10) + (20.763)(.05)$$
$$+ (10.25)(.05) + (5)(.10) = 32.051$$

The values for R_5 and R_6 are given in Table 17-3, and the reader is asked to verify them. The remaining calculations for R, $\text{TRC}_i(n)$, $\text{TRC}_g(n)$, and $\text{TRC}(n)$ are performed in the manner illustrated for $n = 1$ and $n = 2$ and tabulated with the previous results in Table 17-3. The optimum group-replacement policy corresponds

TABLE 17-3   Evaluation of group-replacement policies

Group-replace-ment period n	Cumulative no. of expected individual replacements R_n	Average no. of individual replace-ments/wk R	Expected cost of individual replace-ments/wk $TRC_i(n)$	Cost of group replace-ment/wk $TRC_g(n)$	Total cost of group replacement policy $TRC(n)$
1	5	5	$ 45.00	$300	$345.00
2	10.250	5.125	46.125	150	196.12
3	20.763	6.921	62.20	100	162.29
4	32.051	8.013	72.11	75	147.11
5	64.166	12.833	115.50	60	175.50
6	102.412	18.235	164.12	50	214.12

to $n = 4$, or replacing all sprinklers every 4 wk regardless of age and replacing those which fail during this period at the end of the shift in which the breakdowns occur.

The results in Table 17-3 are shown graphically in Fig. 17-11, where we can compare the costs of various group-replacement policies with the policy of replac-
▶ ing sprinklers individually as they fail.

17-4   LONG-TERM MAINTENANCE POLICIES

General

The opportunity to develop sound long-term maintenance policies arises mainly in the design and redesign phases of an operations system. On these occasions deci-

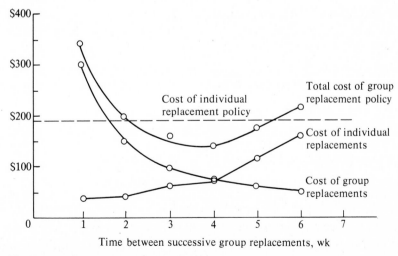

Fig. 17-11   Comparison of costs for individual- and group-replacement policies of low-valued items. All costs are on a weekly basis.

sions about process and equipment selection, job design, and plant layout set the general framework for the types of policies considered in the preceding section.

The focus of long-term maintenance policies may be on one or a combination of the following:

1. Designing reliability into production components or their configuration to achieve overall levels of reliability
2. Selecting processes and equipment that allow:
   a. Easy maintenance
   b. Alternative uses for increased versatility of operation
3. Determining desirable excess capacity in the form of standby equipment for critical operations in the system
4. Determining optimum maintenance-crew size

In the following sections we shall consider in some detail the issues involved in improving system reliability, in providing standby production capacity, and in determining an optimum maintenance-crew size for a given configuration. Designing components with high built-in reliability through greater precision and allowing for easy maintenance and flexible utilization are engineering problems beyond our scope.

Improving Reliability

As stated previously, reliability is a measure of a system's ability to perform the necessary transformations at minimum cost. In Chap. 16 we noted that performance is normally evaluated in terms of standards for quality, production rate, and the time and cost required per unit of output. When actual performance deviates significantly from these standards, the system requires maintenance to restore its reliability to a satisfactory level.

System reliability is mainly a design or redesign problem. It can be increased by improving the reliability of individual components, by rearranging the configuration of components to allow for alternative paths, or both. As the system becomes more complex with increases in the number of interacting parts, management must use the above alternatives to maintain a satisfactory level of overall reliability. The problem becomes more difficult with increasing degrees of human involvement in a given operation. Thus, reliability becomes more difficult to measure and maintain as we move from highly integrated systems (automated oil refineries, chemical plants, etc.) to assembly lines, job shops, and projects, especially those in the service sector. The following discussion treats reliability as applied mainly to manufacturing systems.

To appreciate how complexity affects reliability, let us assume that a production line is made up of three stages with operations performed in sequence by machines A, B, and C, as shown in Fig. 17-12. If the reliability of each machine is 95 percent, i.e., the probability of a machine breakdown is 5 percent, the reliability of the production line is

$$\text{Prob(A and B and C working)} = p_A p_B p_C$$

$$= (.95)(.95)(.95) = .86$$

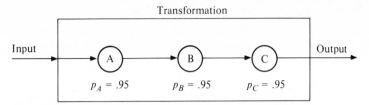

Fig. 17-12 A three-stage production line with specified component reliabilities.

This means that the probability the production line will break down is 14 percent. If the movement of materials between stations is performed by two conveyors that have a reliability of 90 percent, the revised system reliability will be

$$\text{Prob(all machines and conveyors working)} = p_A p_B p_C (p_{MH})^2$$
$$= (.95)^3 (.90)^2 = (.86)(.81) = .69$$

In other words, the probability of this simple production line's stopping due to a breakdown is 31 percent!

As we keep adding more components in series to a production line, the overall reliability drops rapidly, even though the reliability of each component may be high, as in our simple example. In Fig. 17-13 the overall system reliability is shown for specified levels of complexity (as measured by the number of components in series and their individual reliability). For example, a system with 200 components in series, each having a reliability of 99 percent, will have an overall reliability of only 15 percent.

Considering the complexity of modern equipment such as home appliances, cars, or production machines with hundreds or thousands of components, it is a technological miracle that things run as well as they seem to do. For a given system

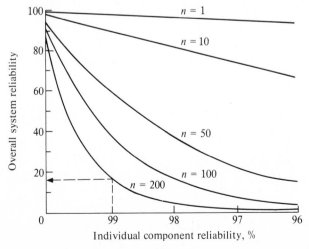

Fig. 17-13 Variation of overall system reliability with system complexity *n* and individual-component reliability for connection in series.

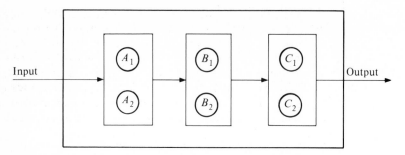

Fig. 17-14   A three-stage production line with two identical machines per stage.

this is accomplished by using parallel components that provide alternative paths for performing the same operation. Figure 17-14 shows the same production line with three stages, one stage for each operation, but this time we allow two machines per stage to perform the same function. We assume that if one machine breaks down in any stage, the other will immediately take over in performing the same function.

Assuming the same reliability for each machine, that is, 95 percent, the reliability for each stage is increased, since if one machine breaks down, the second one will maintain a continuous production flow. The improved reliability per stage can be computed as follows:

$$\text{Prob(stage A breakdown)} = \text{Prob}(A_1 \text{ or } A_2 \text{ breakdown}) = P(A_1)P(A_2)$$

$$= (.05)(.05) = .0025$$

Therefore,

$$\text{Prob(stage A operating)} = 1.00 - \text{Prob(stage A breakdown)}$$

$$= 1.0000 - .0025 = .9975$$

Similar reliability improvements also hold for stages B and C. Thus, the overall system reliability for two parallel machines per stage, assuming no conveyors are needed, has now improved as follows:

$$\text{Prob(system operating)} = \text{Prob(all stages operating)} = P(A)P(B)P(C)$$

$$= (.9975)(.9975)(.9975) = .9925$$

For this arrangement the probability of production stoppage has been reduced from 14 percent to less than 1 percent.

Such an impressive gain in overall reliability has been achieved at the cost necessary to purchase, install, maintain, and operate the extra three machines as needed in this new configuration. *In actual applications we must carefully weigh the trade-off between increased reliability for the entire system and the increase in investment and operating expense necessary to use identical components in parallel.*

In practice, redundancy to improve reliability is quite expensive. For cases where cost is not a limiting factor, redundancy of components may be restricted by weight, space, or other considerations. Thus, redundancy can be justified for components with limited reliability or for components with high reliability but of a very critical nature, like those needed in space missions. The following section examines the desirability of redundancy.

The comments about the effect of complexity on reliability in capital-intensive systems, i.e., systems with heavy investment in equipment, apply with greater force to organizations that are labor-intensive, whether of the flow shop, job shop, or project variety. This is especially true of large service organizations, such as insurance companies, banks, hospitals, the military, and others. For these, complexity can be managed only by using standard operating procedures for handling similar problems. Man-dominated man-machine systems tend to display much greater variability in performance than the other types. This is attributed to the basic need of people for maintaining a variable work pace and the differences between people in their natural pace and their attention span.[1] Under such conditions the concept of overall system reliability is difficult to measure and even more difficult to maintain. Reliable performance in large organizations, especially service-oriented ones, is accomplished at the expense of flexibility. However, this becomes critical if one is to avoid serious risks in applying procedures for landing a jumbo jet, for performing a heart operation, or approving a multimillion-dollar loan.

Determining Requirements in Standby Equipment

For some systems a breakdown in one stage is likely to have serious consequences due to disruptions, downtime costs, or resulting unsafe conditions. In such cases, it is possible to reduce the impact of a breakdown by using standby equipment. In discussing system reliability, we concluded that redundancy through standby machines in a given stage improves the reliability of that stage and the system as a whole but at a certain price. *Standby equipment can be compared to buffer inventories. Both exist to maintain a smooth production flow in the event of undesirable random departures from normal conditions.* Such protection against the risks of random disruptions is secured at a price. Whereas for buffer inventories the price took the form of extra holding costs, for standby equipment it involves the added investment needed and the extra cost of maintaining such equipment in good working condition.

Deciding whether standby machines are desirable and how many there should be requires information about the frequency distribution of breakdowns, the costs associated with downtime, i.e., lost production, and the costs of having standby equipment. As with buffer inventories, the more standby equipment we keep the greater the protection against breakdowns, i.e., the smaller the costs from downtime, but the higher the cost for this normally unused extra capacity. The cost relationships are shown in Fig. 17-15. Our analysis of this problem is best illustrated with an example and is comparable to that used for buffer inventories and for group replacement.

---

[1] Peter Drucker, *Management Tasks, Objectives, Responsibilities*, Harper & Row, New York, 1974.

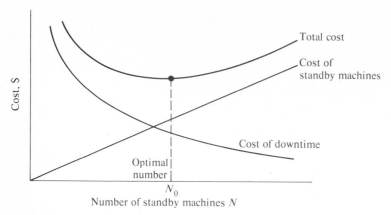

Fig. 17-15 Cost relationships for determination of optimum amount of standby equipment.

▶ EXAMPLE 17-3   DETERMINATION OF OPTIMUM NUMBER OF STANDBY MACHINES
Athena Fashions, Inc., a ready-to-wear company, operates a knitting department with 20 identical knitting machines. Data from previous years about breakdowns of each machine suggest that their frequency distribution can be approximated by a Poisson distribution with an average of three failures per day. The cost of lost production from a breakdown is estimated at $200 per day, but this can be reduced by keeping standby knitting machines at a cost of $30 a day per machine. Management wishes to determine how many standby machines to have available in order to minimize the combined cost from lost production and standby capacity. Since a machine requires an average of 1 day for repairs, it cannot break down more than once in any day.

This problem can be solved by determining for each number of extra machines N

1. The expected cost of downtime, i.e., lost production, $TC_d(N)$
2. The cost of the given number of standby machines $TC_s(N)$
3. The total cost of operating with N standby machines $TSC(N)$, that is, item 1 plus item 2

The expected cost of downtime, given the number of available standby machines, is found by determining the expected capacity shortage per day due to breakdowns and multiplying this by the daily cost of lost production per machine. As an illustration, assume that we have three standby knitting machines. A capacity shortage occurs when the number of breakdowns is greater than 3.

Let x = number of actual breakdowns in given day
   λ = average number of breakdowns per day = 3
   e = 2.7183

Then the probability of x is given by the Poisson formula[1]

$$P(x) = \frac{e^{-\lambda}\lambda^x}{x!} \qquad x = 0, 1, 2, \ldots$$

To determine the expected cost for downtime given the number of standby machines we must first compute the expected capacity shortage using probabilities from the above distribution. The data for such calculations are summarized in Table 17-4. Determining the entries in Table 17-4 is quite straightforward. Assuming that we have three standby machines ($N = 3$), actual capacity shortages occur when the number of breakdowns exceeds 3 and are shown in the row for $N = 3$. The expected capacity shortage ECS(3) given $N = 3$ is computed by multiplying the values of possible actual shortages by the probability that they will occur and summing. Thus

$$ECS(N) = \sum_{x=N+1}^{9} (x - N)P(x)$$

for

$$ECS(3) = (4 - 3)P(4) + (5 - 3)P(5) + \cdots + (9 - 3)P(9)$$

or

$$ECS(3) = (1)(.168) + (2)(.101) + (3)(.050) + (4)(.022) + (5)(.003) + (6)(.001)$$
$$= .168 + .202 + .150 + .088 + .015 + .006 = .629$$

[1] Poisson probabilities for different values of λ and x are given in Appendix 3.

TABLE 17-4   Calculations for actual and expected capacity shortage given N

Number of standby machines N	Number of failures x										Expected capacity shortage ECS(N)
	0	1	2	3	4	5	6	7	8	9	
	.050	.150	.224	.224	.168	.101	.050	.022	.003	.001	
	Actual capacity shortages $x - N$										
0		1	2	3	4	5	6	7	8	9	2.934
1			1	2	3	4	5	6	7	8	1.991
2				1	2	3	4	5	6	7	1.198
3					1	2	3	4	5	6	.629
4						1	2	3	4	5	.284
5							1	2	3	4	.107
6								1	2	3	.031
7									1	2	.005
8										1	.001

The remaining entries are determined in the same manner. The maximum number of standby machines considered is decided by the values of the probability of x breakdowns. After $x = 4$ these decrease rapidly and become negligible for $x > 9$. Probability values for x given the mean ($\lambda = 3$) can be calculated by the Poisson formula or obtained from statistical tables (see Appendix 3).

The expected cost of downtime for N standby machines $TC_d(N)$ is determined by multiplying the expected capacity shortage by the unit cost of downtown $C_d = \$200$ per machine. Thus, on a daily basis we have

$$\begin{bmatrix} \text{Expected cost} \\ \text{of downtime} \end{bmatrix} = \begin{bmatrix} \text{expected capacity} \\ \text{shortage} \end{bmatrix}\begin{bmatrix} \text{cost of downtime} \\ \text{machine} \end{bmatrix}$$

For $N = 3$

$$TC_d(3) = ECS(3)C_d = (.629 \text{ machine})(\$200/\text{machine}) = \$125.80/\text{day}$$

The cost of the standby capacity $TC_s(N)$ is given by

$$\begin{bmatrix} \text{Cost of standby} \\ \text{machines} \end{bmatrix} = \begin{bmatrix} \text{number of standby} \\ \text{machines} \end{bmatrix}\begin{bmatrix} \text{cost/standby} \\ \text{machine} \end{bmatrix}$$

For $N = 3$

$$TC_s(N) = N \cdot C_s = (3 \text{ machines})(\$50/\text{machine}) = \$150/\text{day}$$

Adding the above, we have the total cost $TCS(N)$ of using N standby machines,

$$\begin{bmatrix} \text{Total cost with } N \\ \text{standby machines} \end{bmatrix} = \begin{bmatrix} \text{expected cost} \\ \text{of downtime} \end{bmatrix} + \begin{bmatrix} \text{cost of } N \text{ standby} \\ \text{machines} \end{bmatrix}$$

For $N = 3$

$$TSC(N) = TC_d(N) + TC_s(N)$$

$$TSC(3) = \$125.80 + 150.00 = \$275.80/\text{day}$$

Repeating the above set of calculations for each value of N, we obtain the cost data shown in Table 17-5. The optimum number of standby knitting machines is 4,

TABLE 17-5   Data for downtime, standby capacity, and total cost

Number of standby machines N	Expected capacity shortage $ECS(N)$	Expected cost of downtime $TC_d(N)$	Cost of standby machines $TC_s(N)$	Total cost with standbys $TSC(N)$
0	2.934	$586.80	$ 0	$586.80
1	1.991	398.20	50	448.00
2	1.198	239.60	100	339.60
3	.629	125.80	150	275.80
4	.284	56.80	200	256.80
5	.107	21.40	250	271.40
6	.031	6.20	300	306.20
7	.005	1.00	350	356.00
8	.001	.20	400	400.20
9	0	0	450	450.00

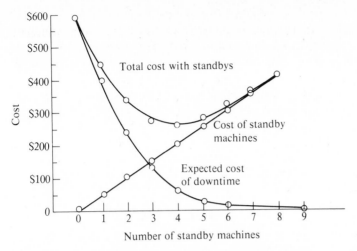

Fig. 17-16 Cost relationships for downtime and standby machines for the Athena Fashions, Inc., example.

since with that much extra capacity in the knitwear department the management of Athena Fashions, Inc., would minimize the combined cost resulting from downtime due to machine breakdowns and that of having the standby machines. A plot of the values for the cost of downtime and the cost of standby machines would reveal the type of relationship shown in Fig. 17-16.

Optimum Size for Maintenance Crew

For a fixed number of machines in a production system, the determination of the optimum size of the maintenance crew is a waiting-line problem with a finite calling population. For simplicity, we shall assume that maintenance relies only on repairs. In this case, the arrivals are machines that break down at random, usually according to a Poisson distribution, and wait to be repaired by a maintenance facility with a crew of s workers. The problem is similar to the waiting-line problems discussed in Chap. 6 on capacity determination for service systems.

The optimum crew size is that for which the combined cost of machines waiting for repair and the cost of maintaining a given crew size is a minimum. This problem can be solved by known mathematical formulas if we can justify certain assumptions about the frequency distributions of breakdowns and repair times and the order in which waiting machines are to be serviced. Otherwise, we must resort to simulation.

17-5 ENVIRONMENTAL IMPACTS OF MAINTENANCE POLICIES

The application of sound long- and short-term policies for the maintenance of an operations system can have important beneficial impacts on environmental problems. Through effective maintenance, management can prolong the life of its facilities and equipment, thus reducing the need for repairs and frequent replacements. This approach conserves resources that would be required if the system components were allowed to deteriorate at a faster pace. The fuel savings for autos, heating systems, and other equipment are just a few instances of impressive energy conservation as a result of proper maintenance. Another beneficial effect is the improvement in quality control. Equipment in good working condition results in less defective output and requires less effort and cost for inspection. This reduction in scrap losses also decreases the amount of solid waste.

Although defective output may be traced to reasons other than improperly working equipment, the reduction of this source of variation in critical product characteristics increases the probability of reliable performance of the final product.

Thus, in addition to the direct economic benefits they bring in the form of lower production costs, good maintenance policies also help reduce the important environmental costs related to resource depletion and pollution.

17-6 SUMMARY

Effective maintenance policies for human and material resources contribute in many ways towards the achievement of short- and long-term objectives. Their importance derives from the direct benefits they provide to the individual firm by reducing production costs, assuring a smooth and reliable operation, and enhancing the safety of facilities and equipment. In addition, maintenance policies contribute toward energy conservation, a reduction in solid waste created by defective output, and improved resource utilization by avoiding unnecessary replacements.

By far the most crucial maintenance considerations enter the decision-making process in the system-design phase. The design of the production process, the selection of equipment, and the layout of the facilities can all contribute toward improving the reliability of the entire system. Long-term maintenance policies relate to the size of maintenance crews, the amount of standby equipment for critical operations, and the methods and hardware employed to perform maintenance tasks.

In the short run, management can develop sound policies within the constraints imposed by the design of the system. At this level, depending on the breakdown characteristics of a component, management may choose preventive versus corrective maintenance and individual versus group replacement for low-valued items. The appropriate levels of decoupling inventories determine the desired degree of independence between successive stages of production, allowing time for preventive maintenance or repairs without serious disruptions. The objective for short-term policies of an internal maintenance system is to minimize the total cost from preventive maintenance, repairs, and forced idleness of a facility, i.e., downtime.

NOTATION

Physical performance characteristics

N = total number of components or machines to be maintained

$T_1, T_2, \ldots, T_j$ = failure-free run times for a component, i.e. time between successive breakdowns

T_b = average run time till breakdown
$f(T)$ = frequency distribution of run time till breakdown
T_m = average time to perform preventive maintenance
T_p = run time between preventive maintenance inspections or replacements
T_r = average time for machine or component repair
n = number of operating periods between inspections or group replacements
P_n = probability of failure after n periods
B_n = cumulative expected number of breakdowns in n periods
B = average number of breakdowns per period

Maintenance costs for preventive-maintenance policy

C_m = unit cost of preventive maintenance in component
C_r = unit cost of repair per component
$TC_m(n)$ = cost of preventive maintenance per period when $T_p = n$
$TC_r(n)$ = expected cost of repairs per period when $T_p = n$
$TMC(n)$ = total maintenance cost per period when $T_p = n$

Maintenance costs for replacement policy

C_i = unit cost of replacing a component individually
C_g = unit cost of replacing a component as one of a group
$TRC_i(n)$ = expected cost of individual replacements per period when $T_p = n$
$TRC_g(n)$ = cost of group replacement per period when $T_p = n$
$TRC(n)$ = total replacement cost per period when $T_p = n$

Costs for standby equipment requirements policy

C_d = unit cost of downtime in \$ per machine
C_s = unit cost of standby equipment in \$ per machine
$ECS(N)$ = expected capacity shortage per period when operating with N standby machines
$TC_d(N)$ = expected cost of downtime per period with N standby machines
$TC_s(N)$ = cost of N standby machines per period
$TSC(N)$ = total cost with N standby machines per period

REVIEW QUESTIONS

1. State the purpose of the maintenance function within an organization.
2. Describe the narrow and broad interpretation of maintenance.
3. Discuss the interactions of maintenance decisions with:
   (*a*) Scheduling
   (*b*) Quality control
   (*c*) Inventory control
   (*d*) Product design
   (*e*) Process design
   (*f*) Plant layout
4. Why are some maintenance decisions usually resolved by political rather than rational approaches?
5. Describe the key features of a maintenance system with regard to:
   (*a*) Inputs
   (*b*) Constraints

(c) Outputs
(d) Decision variables
(e) Performance criterion
6. How can ABC analysis, first examined in inventory control, be used in organizing the maintenance function?
7. Discuss the major aspects of a maintenance policy and some feasible alternatives in each case.
8. What are some of the problems addressed in the formulation of short-term policies?
9. What are some of the problems examined in the development of long-term policies?
10. What do we mean by a breakdown-time frequency distribution, and how is it specified?
11. How does the breakdown distribution influence the choice between preventive- and repair-maintenance policies?
12. Name the types of component costs taken into account in selecting policies related to:
    (a) Preventive versus repair maintenance
    (b) Individual versus group replacement for low-valued items
    (c) Determination of the number of standby machines
13. What approaches are available for improving process or product reliability (a) in the short run and (b) in the long run?
14. Discuss some of the direct and indirect impacts of maintenance policies on the natural environment with respect to (a) energy conservation and (b) reduction of solid waste and other types of pollution.

PROBLEMS

1. A manufacturer of plastic products operates 40 molding machines which break down at random according to the distribution specified below:

	Failure-free time, wk			
	1	2	3	4
Frequency of breakdowns	.10	.30	.40	.20

The repair of a machine breakdown requires a maintenance crew of two men working a full 8-h day whose wage is $12.50 per worker-hour. With the same crew size preventive maintenance takes only 2 h per machine. The cost of supplies and parts is $160 per repair and $40 for preventive maintenance per machine. Downtime costs are assumed negligible due to multiple assignments for machine operators.
    (a) Determine the cost of a maintenance policy based on repairs only for the molding machines.
    (b) Evaluate the cost of alternative preventive-maintenance policies.
    (c) Select the minimum-cost policy from (a) and (b).
2. In Prob. 1, assuming that the cost of preventive maintenance per machine remains the same, how much can the repair cost per machine change before it is desirable to switch policy?

3. Determine the optimum maintenance policy for the problem of Example 17-1 if the failure distribution for the stamping machines is:

Failure-free time, wk	1	2	3	4	5	6	7
Frequency of breakdowns	.40	.20	.15	.10	.05	.05	.05

4. A large aerospace firm uses 120 computer terminals whose breakdown frequency distribution is as follows:

Failure-free time, months	1	2	3	4	5	6	7	8
Frequency of breakdowns	.30	.10	.05	.05	.05	.05	.10	.30

The average cost per terminal repair is $80, while preventive maintenance amounts only to $20 per machine. There is no cost normally associated with terminal downtime in this case.

(a) Determine the cost of maintenance policy based only on repairs.

(b) Calculate the cost of alternative preventive-maintenance policies.

(c) Select the minimum-cost policy from (a) and (b).

5. The Milton International Hotel in the French Riviera operates a large open parking space for its customers. To keep vandalism and car thefts to a minimum management has installed at key points 180 special bright lamps to provide ample lighting at night for easier security inspections and deterrence. These lamps cost $10 per unit and have a failure distribution shown below. Replacement of these lamps requires rental of a special truck. The replacement cost is $30 per lamp if done individually ($10 purchase + $20 installation) but drops to $12 per lamp when all are replaced as a group.

Burning time, months	1	2	3	4	5
Probability of failure	.10	.25	.30	.25	.10

Determine whether management should adopt an individual- or group-replacement policy.

6. Select the minimum-cost replacement policy in Prob. 4 if the breakdown frequency distribution for lamps is:

Burning time, months	1	2	3	4	5
Probability of failure	.40	.30	.20	.05	.05

7. (a) Determine the optimum policy in Prob. 4 if recent equipment rental increases make the cost of a single individual replacement $50 and group replacement $20 per lamp.

(b) Determine the optimum replacement policy for the problem in Example 17-2 if the breakdown frequency distribution is as follows:

Run time	1	2	3	4	5	6
Probability of failure	.30	.10	.10	.10	.10	.30

8. Southeastern Distillers, Inc., employ a fleet of 15 identical fork-lift trucks in their major bottling plant and central warehouse. The breakdown distribution for a truck follows a Poisson distribution with an average of two failures per day. Each breakdown results in added handling costs of $300 per day, mainly from overtime charges to clean congested areas. This cost can be reduced by maintaining standby fork-lift trucks at an added daily cost of $50 per truck. Since the average repair time per truck is 1 day, there can be no more than one breakdown per day for the same truck. What number of standby fork-lift trucks will minimize the total cost?

9. Rework Prob. 8 assuming that the average breakdown rate is four per day and the breakdown costs have increased to $450 per truck per day, while the daily cost per standby truck has gone up to $100.

10. Determine the optimum number of standby machines in Example 17-3 if:
    (a) Breakdowns follow a Poisson distribution with a mean of two failures per day
    (b) $C_s = \$150$
    $\quad C_d = \$200$

11. A chemical processing plant has four stages with individual reliabilities equal to .90, .96, .98 and .95, respectively.
    (a) What is the reliability of the entire system?
    (b) If technological improvements allow the integration of the first two stages into one with an overall reliability of .98, what will the effect on the system reliability be?

12. An assembly line has three stages with machines A, B, and C in series having individual reliabilities equal to .95, .90, and .99, respectively.
    (a) Calculate the reliability of the entire assembly line.
    (b) What is the improvement in reliability if in the second stage we place two machines of type B in parallel?
    (c) What will be the effect of two parallel machines in all production stages?
    (d) What will be the effect of three parallel machines in all production stages?
    (e) If design improvements of machine B in the original layout lead to an individual reliability of .98, what will be the effect on overall reliability?

13. Refer to Fig. 17-15. Calculate:
    (a) The reliability for each stage and the overall system (i) with three components per stage and (ii) four components per stage
    (b) The overall cost for the system for each configuration if each component costs $1,000; plot the graph

SELECTED REFERENCES

1. Barlow, R., and L. Hunter: "Optimum Preventive Maintenance Policies," *Operations Research*, vol. 8, no. 1, pp. 90–100, 1960.
2. Bovaird, R. L.: "Characteristics of Optimal Maintenance Policies," *Management Science*, vol. 7, no. 3, pp. 238–254, April 1961.
3. Buffa, E. S.: *Operations Management: Problems and Models*, 3d ed., Wiley, New York, 1972.

4. Cunningham, C. E., and W. Cox: *Applied Maintainability Engineering*, Wiley, New York, 1972.
5. Gilbert, J. O. W.: *A Manager's Guide to Quality and Reliability*, Wiley, New York, 1968.
6. Goldman, A. S., and T. B. Slattery: *Maintainability: A Major Element of System Effectiveness*, Wiley, New York, 1964.
7. Gradon, F.: *Maintenance Engineering: Organization and Management*, Wiley New York, 1973.
8. Hardy, T. S., and L. J. Krajewski: "A Simulation of Interactive Maintenance Decision," *Decision Sciences*, January 1975, pp. 92–105.
9. Jardine, A. K. S.: *Maintenance, Replacement and Reliability*, Wiley, New York, 1973.
10. Morse, P. M.: *Queues, Inventories, and Maintenance*, Wiley, New York, 1958.
11. Peck, L. G., and R. N. Hazelwood: *Finite Queuing Tables*, Wiley, New York, 1958.
12. Riggs, J. L.: *Production Systems*, 2d ed., Wiley, New York, 1975.
13. Turban, E.: "The Use of Mathematical Models in Plant Maintenance," *Management Science*, vol. 13, no. 6, pp. 342–358, February 1967.
14. Weiss, G. H.: "A Problem in Equipment Maintenance," *Management Science*, vol. 8, no. 3, pp. 266–278, April 1962.

Chapter 18

A REVIEW
AND A LOOK
AHEAD

18-1   GENERAL

We have come to the end of a rather lengthy presentation of key concepts, problems, and decision-making techniques in operations management. It will be helpful to pause for a brief review, a few comments on some critical issues, and an extrapolation from observed trends to likely future developments.

18-2   LOOKING BACK: REVIEW AND SYNTHESIS

There are several ways one can discuss the content of operations management. Our approach has focused on a framework based on major problem areas. Another might have been with reference to the input-process-output formulation or with the types of resources employed (materials, human resources, capital, etc.).

Some define a field, say physics, as what its practitioners do, but operations management encompasses much more than what operations managers do. Decisions concerning a process and its inputs or outputs are of great concern to all levels of management and often involve different parts of an organization. To assist with a review and synthesis we repeat Fig. 1-5 as Fig. 18-1 and present summaries of the most important decision types.

In Table 18-1 we have grouped decisions with significant long-term effects. These define a system's basic character and relate mainly to its design. Long-term decisions are concerned with the design of new outputs (products or services) or processes and with desired capacity as specified by levels of critical resources or the maximum output rate. Included here are also decisions specifying the roles of human resources (work study), desired material flow patterns (facilities layout), and preferred locations of needed facilities. All these belong in the system-design block in Fig. 18-1.

The long-term decisions summarized in Table 18-1 are also called strategic decisions because they affect several parts of an organization and commit large amounts of scarce resources (capital funds, facilities, energy, personnel, etc.). As such, they determine an organization's distinctive competence and set limits on its *effectiveness* in achieving long-term objectives. Strategic decisions for new products, new technologies, or new facilities are made infrequently; they are complex and costly to change. Even though a few analytical methods are available for such problems, their successful resolution requires an understanding of environmental forces that impose constraints and shape new opportunities. In the end they are handled mainly by the organizational and/or political decision-making approaches discussed in Chap. 2.

Table 18-2 covers planning and control decisions required to make the most of available capacity and existing products, technology, and facilities. These decisions are made repeatedly to reflect actual or anticipated changes in demand and are restricted by the framework established by previously made strategic decisions and plans.

Short- and medium-term decisions are usually structured well enough to allow the use of versatile quantitative methods from management science, statistics, and microeconomics. Here we can employ models developed to forecast demand, to allocate limited productive resources (aggregate planning), set inventory levels, prepare production schedules, control quality, and ensure reliable system performance through proper maintenance policies. Such decisions determine how *efficiently* short-term targets are accomplished and provide feedback for the periodic evaluation of both operating standards and long-term objectives.

As stated in Chap. 1, the contribution of operations management to the attainment of organizational objectives is often directed at the reduction of costs. This often assumes specified levels of quality for products and services and reliability in performance. For this reason, the criteria employed for evaluating short-term decisions usually involve the minimization of appropriate cost functions especially formulated for each decision type (see Table 18-2). The effectiveness of decision rules that minimize such costs depends on the availability of a management information system (MIS) capable of providing adequate, accurate, and timely data about operating conditions. In the absence of such information, most decision rules used by management tend to deprive a system of the desired stability and efficiency in satisfying demand for its output.

The decreasing cost of computer processing with recent technological break-

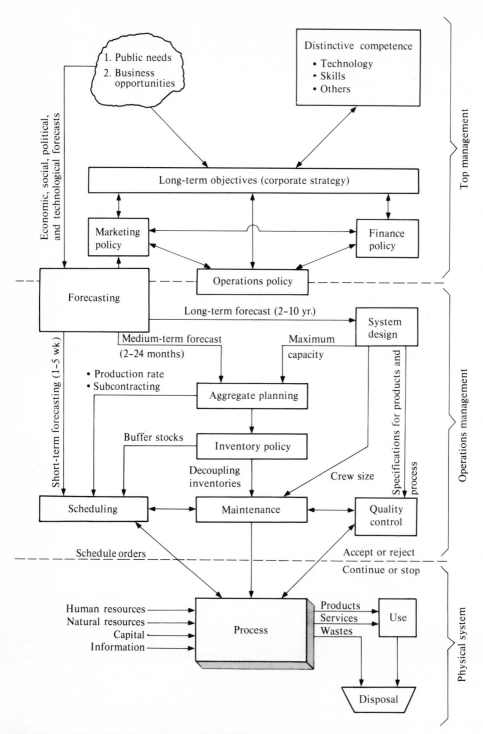

Fig. 18-1 Specific functions of operations management.

throughs has brought the development of a sound MIS within reach for many organizations, public or private. For cases where the alternative of an internal MIS installation is not feasible, the widespread use of computer terminals with access to computer facilities with rental programs and services provides almost unlimited opportunities at reasonable cost.

18-3 LOOKING AHEAD: TRENDS AND FUTURE OUTLOOK

From its emergence as a recognizable field to the present operations management has been subject to dynamic change. The last few decades have seen it evolve, expand, mature, and become increasingly sophisticated. Although the effects from technological, social, and economic change and their impact on our value system cannot be precisely assessed, they are certain to affect operations management. Such changes are likely to affect its focus, its methodology, and its primary concerns or priorities.

A Shift in Focus: Private and Public Service Sector versus Manufacturing

In the initial phases of its development, the focus of operations management (better known then as manufacturing or production management) was the factory. Much of the research in those days had to do with work methods, time standards, workstation design, and plant layout. Recent years have witnessed a strong interest in the service sector, i.e., hospitals, banks, commercial airlines, and others. Furthermore, as the role of government increases, we shall also see a greater concern with government systems at the federal, state, and local level.

An important reason for our interest nowadays in the service sector has been the soaring costs of medical, postal, insurance, and many other services. Medical care, in particular, has become an important issue because of its social significance and the alarming increases in the size of the health-care bill for the United States (13 to 15 percent annual increases in recent years for a total cost of \$206 billion in 1979, or 9.2 percent of the country's GNP). Low productivity combined with salaries higher than the average for United States industry has resulted in similar problems with the postal service. Following intensive studies of the latter and recent efforts for reorganization, many of the problems still persist.

Strong pressures have been also building up for higher productivity in government services. Despite considerable increases in personal income, the loss or stagnation in purchasing power due to inflation and rising taxes has brought about waves of taxpayer protests for more effective use of government funds. Such funds affect the operation of schools, libraries, police and fire departments, and the government agencies themselves. The Gann-Jarvis Proposition 13 in California for reducing the taxpayer's burden and its overwhelming 2 : 1 voter support in 1978 have led the way for similar strong movements across the country. The "heat is on" to use tax money more effectively through increased productivity in government bureaucracy at all levels.

TABLE 18-1 Summary of information inputs and outputs, control variables, and performance criteria for decisions in operations systems design

Decision type	Input information	Output information	Control variables	Performance criteria	Usual approaches
Product or service design	Consumer-revealed needs Public needs Projected derived needs resulting from new projects	General specifications Technical specifications	Mix of source inputs (materials, etc.) Quality levels (tolerances and allowances) Modular components	Maximize product or service effectiveness or utility subject to restrictions on: Operating costs Maintenance costs Safety, reliability, etc.	Economic analysis Market surveys combined with internal information generate general specifications leading through trial and error to technical specifications
Process design and capacity planning	Product technical specifications Available technologies Available skills Costs of production inputs Demand level	Selection of technology and equipment to provide: Desired capacity Ability to meet output specifications	Selection of: Process flow type: Flow shop Job shop Project Equipment types	Minimize production cost per unit subject to constraints on: Input factors Budget Production specifications Environmental factors	Feasibility studies involving technical, economic, and other aspects

TABLE 18-1 (*continued*)

Decision type	Input information	Output information	Control variables	Performance criteria	Usual approaches
Work study	Production volume Process type Layout type Organizational climate	Determination for each work station or work group of: Work content Work method Time standards	Assignment of: Tasks Responsibility	Maximize: Productivity Employee job satisfaction subject to sociotechnical constraints	Trial-and-error methods taking into account the type of industry, socioeconomic factors, and organizational climate
Facilities layout	Production volume Type of process Stability in product design and demand	Selection of overall layout configuration made up of basic types of: Product layout Process layout Fixed-position layout	Spatial allocation of process components and supporting activities	Minimize total cost of materials handling subject to sociotechnical and safety constraints	Trial and error Systematic layout Computer heuristic models (CRAFT, etc.)
Facilities location	Process type Input requirements Desired capacity	Selection of specific site	Centralized vs. decentralized facilities	Minimize total distribution cost for given capacity subject to process and environmental constraints	Location economic analysis Linear and nonlinear programming Miscellaneous techniques

TABLE 18-2 Summary of information inputs and outputs, control variables, and performance criteria for decision operations planning and control

Decision system	Input information	Output information	Control variables	Performance criteria	Usual solution methods
Demand forecasting	External environment: Economic Social Internal environment: Executive surveys History of demand	Estimates for: Level of demand Forecast error by length of planning period and by user	Data used Forecasting method Length of planning period	Benefit-to-cost ratio for effects of forecast: Accuracy Stability vs. responsiveness Objectivity Timeliness	Subjective estimates Causal models Time-series models
Aggregate-production planning	Maximum capacity Medium-term forecast Feasible production options and unit costs Starting conditions	Production plan, specifying by period: Production rate Work-force size Inventory levels Subcontracting	Amount of demand covered by: Regular-time production Overtime production Hiring and firing Inventory and backordering	Minimize total production cost for planning period	Trial and error Linear programming Nonlinear programming Heuristic methods Search methods
Inventory control	Period demand rate Unit cost for inventory: Holding Ordering Replenishment Operating assumptions	Policy on inventory replenishment: When to order How much to order Inventory assets	When to order How much to order	Minimize total inventory cost for planning period	Trial and error Classical optimization Dynamic programming Simulation

TABLE 18-2 (*continued*)

Decision system	Input information	Output information	Control variables	Performance criteria	Usual solution methods
Scheduling	Capacity requirements per unit of output in: Skills (worker-hours) Equipment (machine-hours)	Loading orders Sequencing orders Dispatching, expediting, and control	Assignment of orders to work centers Priorities for sequencing Expediting	Minimize total scheduling cost for planning period	Gantt charts Assignment method Branch-and-bound method Line balancing Batch scheduling PERT, CPM, etc.
Performance control	Product or service specifications Natural process tolerance from process specifications	Accept or reject submitted lot Continue or stop production process	Control method: Acceptance sampling Process control Sample size	Minimize total quality cost for planning period	Acceptance-sampling plans: Single Double Multiple Process-control charts: $\bar{x}$ chart R chart p chart c chart
Maintenance and reliability	Equipment data on: Failure pattern Costs Status Maintenance data on: Repair times Preventive-maintenance times	Schedule for: Preventive maintenance Corrective maintenance Reports on: Equipment status Inventory or capacity requirements	What to maintain By whom How Where	Minimize total maintenance cost for planning period	Trial and error Classical optimization Dynamic programming Simulation

As a result of these economic and social forces at work, we shall see operations-management specialists address themselves with the full spectrum of productive activities placing special emphasis on services in both the private and public sector.

A Shift in Methodology: Better
Implementation versus Better Models

Following a modest beginning with empirical studies of limited scope in the factory, operations-management theoreticians and many practitioners have had lasting love affairs first with the behavioral school of thought and then with the management-science approach and its emphasis on systems, modeling, and computers.[1]

Since the late sixties, however, the increased sophistication in modeling problems has outpaced the ability of managers to put quantitative models to good use. Consequently, we have been experiencing a widening gap between theory and practice. If the adage "nothing is more practical than a good theory" has any truth in it, then either the "theory" of operations management in the form of models is not satisfactory or the means by which it is communicated to practitioners and applied leaves much to be desired. For this reason, a significant shift in methodology is now toward improving model implementation rather than model refinements.

Back in Chap. 2 we examined the rational, organizational, and political approaches to decision making. The majority of models developed for an operations manager fall in the domain of the rational approach. As such they often ignore or bypass certain organizational and political realities. The latter, which are not adequately articulated for modeling purposes, often become extremely critical in the implementation phase. To many managers sophisticated models, e.g., the resource-allocation types, seem like bulldozers threatening to knock down well-respected procedures, traditions, existing communication channels, and power networks. Coupled with the mystique of strange symbols and mathematical techniques, such models tend to reinforce rather than diminish the fear of losing control if the model is accepted for use. Managers in general feel that they understand and can handle with some measure of success several aspects of a problem situation. For this reason, they are inclined to rely on a more practical approach instead of taking the risks they associate with the more mathematical models.

Resolving implementation problems for quantitative or computer models built to assist managers will be a great challenge in the future. It will require some painful adjustments on the part of many model builders fascinated with a search for the "optimum" solution. Easier implementation will involve sacrificing the purity of such creations for something simpler that people can understand, accept, and use.

This adjustment may not be so hard to take if we recognize at the outset that the idea of trade-offs is fundamental even within the quantitative models themselves. To achieve minimum costs we have trade-offs when an inventory system experiences some stockouts, when a service facility has less than 100 percent utiliza-

---

[1] See C. W. Churchman, *The Systems Approach*, Dell, New York, 1968.

tion, when a maintenance system allows for some breakdowns, or when a schedule allows for some slippage. Beyond the model, trade-offs represent compromises between model builders (management scientists) and model users (the managers). Such compromises may take the form of (1) reduction in model complexity to allow easier understanding and communication, (2) aggregation or conversion of some variables to drive the model with available data, or (3) decision rules formulated for ease of application rather than for mathematical elegance.

Another shift in methodology is likely to be the need to view operations problems in increasingly wider contexts. This will force more detailed studies of the interfaces of operations problems with other parts of the organization (marketing, finance, or personnel) and with various aspects of the external environment (national economy, environmental legislation, etc.). An improvement in quality control may do much more than reduce production costs. Inside the firm, it may offer the marketing people ammunition for a more vigorous advertising campaign, it may help those in finance by allowing a better allocation of funds, and it can boost employee morale by generating pride in a superior product. Outside the organization, an improvement in quality can help reduce solid waste from scrap losses, improve the image of the company in the community, and attract more qualified candidates for employment.

Shift in Primary Concerns

As we look back at the development of operations management as a function within a firm, we realize that its history has been one of increasing constraints on its degrees of freedom. If we view its major objective as the improvement of productivity in purposeful and organized human activity, we note the following stages of evolution.

First, we had the objective of productivity improvement restricted only by the resources available to the firm and existing technology. This outlook during the industrial revolution led to increased efficiency in physical transformations, but it often reduced the human role in the system to that of a machine.

In the second stage, the objective for productivity improvement remained, but now in addition to restrictions from available processes and resources new ones were added relating to the well-being and safety of human resources. The latter were brought about mainly by government and labor unions in the 1930s in response to protests about the poor and unsafe conditions of the workplace.

In the third stage, to the above objective and restrictions new constraints have been added to protect consumers, the public, and our natural environment. Environmental considerations have been discussed in detail at different points in the text, as they related to various decision types. In addition to pressure for resource conservation and pollution control, operations management will also be influenced by increased emphasis on providing greater job satisfaction to employees, safer and more reliable products and services at competitive prices (consumerism), and increased liability for meeting advertising claims on performance (product liability).

We now seem to be in a new stage where the economic strength and security of the country are threatened by inflation and undesirable dependence on foreign oil imports. Both these problems are interrelated and their resolution will require some rather painful long-term adjustments in the private and public sectors. Operations management with the central objective of improving productivity can contribute to the solution of both.

If past success in raising our material standard of living is to be enjoyed by future generations without the threats posed by economic, social, and environmental disruptions, comparable achievements are needed in reorganizing some of our values and priorities. Operations management, which has helped harness technology to bring about material progress, can also play a significant role again by raising productivity, using natural resources more wisely, keeping the environment clean, and raising the level of human dignity by making work more satisfying. This is admittedly a great challenge but one we can hardly afford to ignore.

SELECTED REFERENCES

1. Daly, H. È. (ed.): *Toward a Steady State Economy*, Freeman, San Francisco, 1973.
2. Davis, L. E., and A. B. Cherns (eds.): *Quality of Working Life: Problems, Prospects, and State of the Art*, vols. I and II, Free Press, Glencoe, Ill., 1975.
3. Dorf, R. C.: *Technology, Society, and Man*, Boyd & Fraser, San Francisco, 1974.
4. Radford, K. J.: *Complex Decision Problems: An Integrated Strategy for Resolution*, Reston, 1977.

Appendixes

APPENDIX-1 RANDOM NUMBERS

10097	85017	84532	13618	23157	86952	02438	76520	91499	38631	79430	62421	97959	67422	69992	68479
37542	16719	82789	69041	05545	44109	05403	64894	80336	49172	16332	44670	35089	17691	89246	26940
08422	65842	27672	82186	14871	22115	86529	19645	44104	89232	57327	34679	62235	79655	81336	85157
99019	76875	20684	39187	38976	94324	43204	09376	12550	02844	15026	32439	58537	48274	81330	11100
12807	93640	39160	41453	97312	41548	93137	80157	63606	40387	65406	37920	08709	60623	2237	16505
66065	99478	70086	71265	11742	18226	29004	34072	61196	80240	44177	51171	08723	39323	05798	26457
31060	65119	26486	47353	43361	99436	42753	45571	15474	44910	99321	72173	56239	04595	10836	95270
85269	70322	21592	48233	93806	32584	21828	02051	94557	33663	86347	00926	44915	34823	51770	67897
63573	58133	41278	11697	49540	61777	67954	05325	42481	86430	19102	37420	41976	76559	24358	97344
73796	44655	81255	31133	36768	60452	38537	03529	23523	31379	68588	81675	15694	43438	36879	73208
98520	02295	13487	98662	07092	44673	61303	14905	04493	98086	32533	17767	14523	52494	24826	75246
11805	85035	54881	35587	43310	48897	48493	39808	00549	33185	04805	05431	94598	97654	16232	64051
83452	01197	86935	28021	61570	23350	65710	06288	35963	80951	68953	99634	81949	15307	00406	26898
88685	97907	19078	40646	31352	48625	44369	86507	59808	79752	02529	40200	73742	08391	49140	45427
99594	63268	96905	28797	57048	46359	74294	87517	46058	18633	99970	67348	49329	95236	32537	01390
65481	52841	59684	67411	09243	56092	84369	17468	32179	74029	74717	17674	90446	00597	45240	87379
80124	53722	71399	10916	07959	21225	13018	17727	69234	54178	10805	35635	45266	61406	41941	20117
74350	11434	51908	62171	93732	26958	02400	77402	19565	11664	77602	99817	28573	41430	96382	01758
69916	62375	99292	21177	72721	66995	07289	66252	45155	48324	32135	26803	16213	14938	71961	19476
09893	28337	20923	87929	61020	62841	31374	14225	94864	69074	45753	20505	78317	31994	98145	36168

SOURCE: Leonard J. Kazmier, *Business Statistics*, Schaum's Outline Series, McGraw-Hill Book Company, New York, 1976.

APPENDIX-2 PROBABILITIES OF AREA
FOR THE STANDARD NORMAL DISTRIBUTION

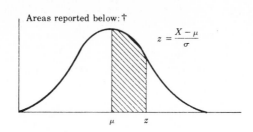

Areas reported below: †

$$z = \frac{X - \mu}{\sigma}$$

z	.00	.01	.02	.03	.04	.05	.06	.07	.08	.09
0.0	.0000	.0040	.0080	.0120	.0160	.0199	.0239	.0279	.0319	.0359
0.1	.0398	.0438	.0478	.0517	.0557	.0596	.0636	.0675	.0714	.0753
0.2	.0793	.0832	.0871	.0910	.0948	.0987	.1026	.1064	.1103	.1141
0.3	.1179	.1217	.1255	.1293	.1331	.1368	.1406	.1443	.1480	.1517
0.4	.1554	.1591	.1628	.1664	.1700	.1736	.1772	.1808	.1844	.1879
0.5	.1915	.1950	.1985	.2019	.2054	.2088	.2123	.2157	.2190	.2224
0.6	.2257	.2291	.2324	.2357	.2389	.2422	.2454	.2486	.2518	.2549
0.7	.2580	2.612	.2642	.2673	.2704	.2734	.2764	.2794	.2823	.2852
0.8	.2881	.2910	.2939	.2967	.2995	.3023	.3051	.3078	.3106	.3133
0.9	.3159	.3186	.3212	.3238	.3264	.3289	.3315	.3340	.3365	.3389
1.0	.3413	.3438	.3461	.3485	.3508	.3531	.3554	.3577	.3599	.3621
1.1	.3643	.3665	.3686	.3708	.3729	.3749	.3770	.3790	.3810	.3830
1.2	.3849	.3869	.3888	.3907	.3925	.3944	.3962	.3980	.3997	.4014
1.3	.4032	.4049	.4066	.4082	.4099	.4115	.4131	.4147	.4162	.4177
1.4	.4192	.4207	.4222	.4236	.4251	.4265	.4279	.4292	.4306	.4319
1.5	.4332	.4345	.4357	.4370	.4382	.4394	.4406	.4418	.4429	.4441
1.6	.4452	.4463	.4474	.4484	.4495	.4505	.4515	.4525	.4535	.4545
1.7	.4554	.4564	.4573	.4582	.4591	.4599	.4608	.4616	.4625	.4633
1.8	.4641	.4649	.4656	.4664	.4671	.4678	.4686	.4693	.4699	.4706
1.9	.4713	.4719	.4726	.4732	.4738	.4744	.4750	.4756	.4761	.4767
2.0	.4772	.4778	.4783	.4788	.4793	.4798	.4803	.4808	.4812	.4817
2.1	.4821	.4826	.4830	.4834	.4838	.4842	.4846	.4850	.4854	.4857
2.2	.4861	.4864	.4868	.4871	.4875	.4878	.4881	.4884	.4887	.4890
2.3	.4893	.4896	.4898	.4901	.4904	.4906	.4909	.4911	.4913	.4916
2.4	.4918	.4920	.4922	.4925	.4927	.4929	.4931	.4932	.4934	.4936
2.5	.4938	.4940	.4941	.4943	.4945	.4946	.4948	.4949	.4951	.4952
2.6	.4953	.4955	.4956	.4957	.4959	.4960	.4961	.4962	.4963	.4964
2.7	.4965	.4966	.4967	.4968	.4969	.4970	.4971	.4972	.4973	.4974
2.8	.4974	.4975	.4976	.4977	.4977	.4978	.4979	.4979	.4980	.4981
2.9	.4981	.4982	.4983	.4983	.4984	.4984	.4985	.4985	.4986	.4986
3.0	.4987									
3.5	.4997									
4.0	.4999									

†Example: For $z = 1.96$, shaded area is 0.4750 out of the total area of 1.0000.

SOURCE: Leonard J. Kazmier, *Business Statistics*, Schaum's Outline Series, McGraw-Hill Book Company, New York, 1976.

APPENDIX-3 POISSON PROBABILITIES†

X	0.1	0.2	0.3	0.4	λ 0.5	0.6	0.7	0.8	0.9	1.0
0	.9048	.8187	.7408	.6703	.6065	.5488	.4966	.4493	.4066	.3679
1	.0905	.1637	.2222	.2681	.3033	.3293	.3476	.3595	.3659	.3679
2	.0045	.0164	.0333	.0536	.0758	.0988	.1217	.1438	.1647	.1839
3	.0002	.0011	.0033	.0072	.0126	.0198	.0284	.0383	.0494	.0613
4	.0000	.0001	.0002	.0007	.0016	.0030	.0050	.0077	.0111	.0153
5	.0000	.0000	.0000	.0001	.0002	.0004	.0007	.0012	.0020	.0031
6	.0000	.0000	.0000	.0000	.0000	.0000	.0001	.0002	.0003	.0005
7	.0000	.0000	.0000	.0000	.0000	.0000	.0000	.0000	.0000	.0001

X	1.1	1.2	1.3	1.4	λ 1.5	1.6	1.7	1.8	1.9	2.0
0	.3329	.3012	.2725	.2466	.2231	.2019	.1827	.1653	.1496	.1353
1	.3662	.3614	.3543	.3452	.3347	.3230	.3106	.2975	.2842	.2707
2	.2014	.2169	.2303	.2417	.2510	.2584	.2640	.2678	.2700	.2707
3	.0738	.0867	.0998	.1128	.1255	.1378	.1496	.1607	.1710	.1804
4	.0203	.0260	.0324	.0395	.0471	.0551	.0636	.0723	.0812	.0902
5	.0045	.0062	.0084	.0111	.0141	.0176	.0216	.0260	.0309	.0361
6	.0008	.0012	.0018	.0026	.0035	.0047	.0061	.0078	.0098	.0120
7	.0001	.0002	.0003	.0005	.0008	.0011	.0015	.0020	.0027	.0034
8	.0000	.0000	.0001	.0001	.0001	.0002	.0003	.0005	.0006	.0009
9	.0000	.0000	.0000	.0000	.0000	.0000	.0001	.0001	.0001	.0002

X	2.1	2.2	2.3	2.4	λ 2.5	2.6	2.7	2.8	2.9	3.0
0	.1225	.1108	.1003	.0907	.0821	.0743	.0672	.0608	.0550	.0498
1	.2572	.2438	.2306	.2177	.2052	.1931	.1815	.1703	.1396	.1494
2	.2700	.2681	.2652	.2613	.2565	.2510	.2450	.2384	.2314	.2240
3	.1890	.1966	.2033	.2090	.2138	.2176	.2205	.2225	.2237	.2240
4	.0992	.1082	.1169	.1254	.1336	.1414	.1488	.1557	.1622	.1680
5	.0417	.0476	.0538	.0602	.0668	.0735	.0804	.0872	.0940	.1008
6	.0146	.0174	.0206	.0241	.0278	.0319	.0362	.0407	.0455	.0504
7	.0044	.0055	.0068	.0083	.0099	.0118	.0139	.0163	.0188	.0216
8	.0011	.0015	.0019	.0025	.0031	.0038	.0047	.0057	.0068	.0081
9	.0003	.0004	.0005	.0007	.0009	.0011	.0014	.0018	.0022	.0027
10	.0001	.0001	.0001	.0002	.0002	.0003	.0004	.0005	.0006	.0008
11	.0000	.0000	.0000	.0000	.0000	.0001	.0001	.0001	.0002	.0002
12	.0000	.0000	.0000	.0000	.0000	.0000	.0000	.0000	.0000	.0001

X	3.1	3.2	3.3	3.4	λ 3.5	3.6	3.7	3.8	3.9	4.0
0	.0450	.0408	.0369	.0334	.0302	.0273	.0247	.0224	.0202	.0183
1	.1397	.1304	.1217	.1135	.1057	.0984	.0915	.0850	.0789	.0733
2	.2165	.2087	.2008	.1929	.1850	.1771	.1692	.1615	.1539	.1465
3	.2237	.2226	.2209	.2186	.2158	.2125	.2087	.2046	.2001	.1954
4	.1734	.1781	.1823	.1858	.1888	.1912	.1931	.1944	.1951	.1954
5	.1075	.1140	.1203	.1264	.1322	.1377	.1429	.1477	.1522	.1563
6	.0555	.0608	.0662	.0716	.0771	.0826	.0881	.0936	.0989	.1042
7	.0246	.0278	.0312	.0348	.0385	.0425	.0466	.0508	.0551	.0595
8	.0095	.0111	.0129	.0148	.0169	.0191	.0215	.0241	.0269	.0298
9	.0033	.0040	.0047	.0056	.0066	.0076	.0089	.0102	.0116	.0132

† Example: $P(x = 5 | \lambda = 2.5) = 0.0668$

SOURCE: Leonard J. Kazmier, *Business Statistics*, Schaum's Outline Series, McGraw-Hill Book Company, New York, 1976.

APPENDIX-3   *(Continued)*

X	3.1	3.2	3.3	3.4	λ 3.5	3.6	3.7	3.8	3.9	4.0
10	.0010	.0013	.0016	.0019	.0023	.0028	.0033	.0039	.0045	.0053
11	.0003	.0004	.0005	.0006	.0007	.0009	.0011	.0013	.0016	.0019
12	.0001	.0001	.0001	.0002	.0002	.0003	.0003	.0004	.0005	.0006
13	.0000	.0000	.0000	.0000	.0001	.0001	.0001	.0001	.0002	.0002
14	.0000	.0000	.0000	.0000	.0000	.0000	.0000	.0000	.0000	.0001

X	4.1	4.2	4.3	4.4	λ 4.5	4.6	4.7	4.8	4.9	5.0
0	.0166	.0150	.0136	.0123	.0111	.0101	.0091	.0082	.0074	.0067
1	.0679	.0630	.0583	.0540	.0500	.0462	.0427	.0395	.0365	.0337
2	.1393	.1323	.1254	.1188	.1125	.1063	.1005	.0948	.0894	.0842
3	.1904	.1852	.1798	.1743	.1687	.1631	.1574	.1517	.1460	.1404
4	.1951	.1944	.1933	.1917	.1898	.1875	.1849	.1820	.1789	.1755
5	.1600	.1633	.1662	.1687	.1708	.1725	.1738	.1747	.1753	.1755
6	.1093	.1143	.1191	.1237	.1281	.1323	.1362	.1398	.1432	.1462
7	.0640	.0686	.0732	.0778	.0824	.0869	.0914	.0959	.1002	.1044
8	.0328	.0360	.0393	.0428	.0463	.0500	.0537	.0575	.0614	.0653
9	.0150	.0168	.0188	.0209	.0232	.0255	.0280	.0307	.0334	.0363
10	.0061	.0071	.0081	.0092	.0104	.0118	.0132	.0147	.0164	.0181
11	.0023	.0027	.0032	.0037	.0043	.0049	.0056	.0064	.0073	.0082
12	.0008	.0009	.0011	.0014	.0016	.0019	.0022	.0026	.0030	.0034
13	.0002	.0003	.0004	.0005	.0006	.0007	.0008	.0009	.0011	.0013
14	.0001	.0001	.0001	.0001	.0002	.0002	.0003	.0003	.0004	.0005
15	.0000	.0000	.0000	.0000	.0001	.0001	.0001	.0001	.0001	.0002

X	5.1	5.2	5.3	5.4	λ 5.5	5.6	5.7	5.8	5.9	6.0
0	.0061	.0055	.0050	.0045	.0041	.0037	.0033	.0030	.0027	.0025
1	.0311	.0287	.0265	.0244	.0225	.0207	.0191	.0176	.0162	.0149
2	.0793	.0746	.0701	.0659	.0618	.0580	.0544	.0509	.0477	.0446
3	.1348	.1293	.1239	.1185	.1133	.1082	.1033	.0985	.0938	.0892
4	.1719	.1681	.1641	.1600	.1558	.1515	.1472	.1428	.1383	.1339
5	.1753	.1748	.1740	.1728	.1714	.1697	.1678	.1656	.1632	.1606
6	.1490	.1515	.1537	.1555	.1571	.1584	.1594	.1601	.1605	.1606
7	.1086	.1125	.1163	.1200	.1234	.1267	.1298	.1326	.1353	.1377
8	.0692	.0731	.0771	.0810	.0849	.0887	.0925	.0962	.0998	.1033
9	.0392	.0423	.0454	.0486	.0519	.0552	.0586	.0620	.0654	.0688
10	.0200	.0220	.0241	.0262	.0285	.0309	.0334	.0359	.0386	.0413
11	.0093	.0104	.0116	.0129	.0143	.0157	.0173	.0190	.0207	.0225
12	.0039	.0045	.0051	.0058	.0065	.0073	.0082	.0092	.0102	.0113
13	.0015	.0018	.0021	.0024	.0028	.0032	.0036	.0041	.0046	.0052
14	.0006	.0007	.0008	.0009	.0011	.0013	.0015	.0017	.0019	.0022
15	.0002	.0002	.0003	.0003	.0004	.0005	.0006	.0007	.0008	.0009
16	.0001	.0001	.0001	.0001	.0001	.0002	.0002	.0002	.0003	.0003
17	.0000	.0000	.0000	.0000	.0000	.0001	.0001	.0001	.0001	.0001

X	6.1	6.2	6.3	6.4	λ 6.5	6.6	6.7	6.8	6.9	7.0
0	.0022	.0020	.0018	.0017	.0015	.0014	.0012	.0011	.0010	.0009
1	.0137	.0126	.0116	.0106	.0098	.0090	.0082	.0076	.0070	.0064
2	.0417	.0390	.0364	.0340	.0318	.0296	.0276	.0258	.0240	.0223

APPENDIX-3   *(Continued)*

X	6.1	6.2	6.3	6.4	λ 6.5	6.6	6.7	6.8	6.9	7.0
3	.0848	.0806	.0765	.0726	.0688	.0652	.0617	.0584	.0552	.0521
4	.1294	.1249	.1205	.1162	.1118	.1076	.1034	.0992	.0952	.0912
5	.1579	.1549	.1519	.1487	.1454	.1420	.1385	.1349	.1314	.1277
6	.1605	.1601	.1595	.1586	.1575	.1562	.1546	.1529	.1511	.1490
7	.1399	.1418	.1435	.1450	.1462	.1472	.1480	.1486	.1489	.1490
8	.1066	.1099	.1130	.1160	.1188	.1215	.1240	.1263	.1284	.1304
9	.0723	.0757	.0791	.0825	.0858	.0891	.0923	.0954	.0985	.1014
10	.0441	.0469	.0498	.0528	.0558	.0558	.0618	.0649	.0679	.0710
11	.0245	.0265	.0285	.0307	.0330	.0353	.0377	.0401	.0426	.0452
12	.0124	.0137	.0150	.0164	.0179	.0194	.0210	.0227	.0245	.0264
13	.0058	.0065	.0073	.0081	.0089	.0098	.0108	.0119	.0130	.0142
14	.0025	.0029	.0033	.0037	.0041	.0046	.0052	.0058	.0064	.0071
15	.0010	.0012	.0014	.0016	.0018	.0020	.0023	.0026	.0029	.0033
16	.0004	.0005	.0005	.0006	.0007	.0008	.0010	.0011	.0013	.0014
17	.0001	.0002	.0002	.0002	.0003	.0003	.0004	.0004	.0005	.0006
18	.0000	.0001	.0001	.0001	.0001	.0001	.0001	.0002	.0002	.0002
19	.0000	.0000	.0000	.0000	.0000	.0000	.0000	.0001	.0001	.0001

X	7.1	7.2	7.3	7.4	λ 7.5	7.6	7.7	7.8	7.9	8.0
0	.0008	.0007	.0007	.0006	.0006	.0005	.0005	.0004	.0004	.0003
1	.0059	.0054	.0049	.0045	.0041	.0038	.0035	.0032	.0029	.0027
2	.0208	.0194	.0180	.0167	.0156	.0145	.0134	.0125	.0116	.0107
3	.0492	.0464	.0438	.0413	.0389	.0366	.0345	.0324	.0305	.0286
4	.0874	.0836	.0799	.0764	.0729	.0696	.0663	.0632	.0602	.0573
5	.1241	.1204	.1167	.1130	.1094	.1057	.1021	.0986	.0951	.0916
6	.1468	.1445	.1420	.1394	.1367	.1339	.1311	.1282	.1252	.1221
7	.1489	.1486	.1481	.1474	.1465	.1454	.1442	.1428	.1413	.1396
8	.1321	.1337	.1351	.1363	.1373	.1382	.1388	.1392	.1395	.1396
9	.1042	.1070	.1096	.1121	.1144	.1167	.1187	.1207	.1224	.1241
10	.0740	.0770	.0800	.0829	.0858	.0887	.0914	.0941	.0967	.0993
11	.0478	.0504	.0531	.0558	.0585	.0613	.0640	.0667	.0695	.0722
12	.0283	.0303	.0323	.0344	.0366	.0388	.0411	.0434	.0457	.0481
13	.0154	.0168	.0181	.0196	.0211	.0227	.0243	.0260	.0278	.0296
14	.0078	.0086	.0095	.0104	.0113	.0123	.0134	.0145	.0157	.0169
15	.0037	.0041	.0046	.0051	.0057	.0062	.0069	.0075	.0083	.0090
16	.0016	.0019	.0021	.0024	.0026	.0030	.0033	.0037	.0041	.0045
17	.0007	.0008	.0009	.0010	.0012	.0013	.0015	.0017	.0019	.0021
18	.0003	.0003	.0004	.0004	.0005	.0006	.0006	.0007	.0008	.0009
19	.0001	.0001	.0001	.0002	.0002	.0002	.0003	.0003	.0003	.0004
20	.0000	.0000	.0001	.0001	.0001	.0001	.0001	.0001	.0001	.0002
21	.0000	.0000	.0000	.0000	.0000	.0000	.0000	.0000	.0001	.0001

X	8.1	8.2	8.3	8.4	λ 8.5	8.6	8.7	8.8	8.9	9.0
0	.0003	.0003	.0002	.0002	.0002	.0002	.0002	.0002	.0001	.0001
1	.0025	.0023	.0021	.0019	.0017	.0016	.0014	.0013	.0012	.0011
2	.0100	.0092	.0086	.0079	.0074	.0068	.0063	.0058	.0054	.0050
3	.0269	.0252	.0237	.0222	.0208	.0195	.0183	.0171	.0160	.0150
4	.0544	.0517	.0491	.0466	.0443	.0420	.0398	.0377	.0357	.0337

APPENDIX-3 *(Continued)*

X	8.1	8.2	8.3	8.4	λ 8.5	8.6	8.7	8.8	8.9	9.0
5	.0882	.0849	.0816	.0784	.0752	.0722	.0692	.0663	.0635	.0607
6	.1191	.1160	.1128	.1097	.1066	.1034	.1003	.0972	.0941	.0911
7	.1378	.1358	.1338	.1317	.1294	.1271	.1247	.1222	.1197	.1171
8	.1395	.1392	.1388	.1382	.1375	.1366	.1356	.1344	.1332	.1318
9	.1256	.1269	.1280	.1290	.1299	.1306	.1311	.1315	.1317	.1318
10	.1017	.1040	.1063	.1084	.1104	.1123	.1140	.1157	.1172	.1186
11	.0749	.0776	.0802	.0828	.0853	.0878	.0902	.0925	.0948	.0970
12	.0505	.0530	.0555	.0579	.0604	.0629	.0654	.0679	.0703	.0728
13	.0315	.0334	.0354	.0374	.0395	.04;6	.0438	.0459	.0481	.0504
14	.0182	.0196	.0210	.0225	.0240	.0256	.0272	.0289	.0306	.0324
15	.0098	.0107	.0116	.0126	.0136	.0147	.0158	.0169	.0182	.0194
16	.0050	.0055	.0060	.0066	.0072	.0079	.0086	.0093	.0101	.0109
17	.0024	.0026	.0029	.0033	.0036	.0040	.0044	.0048	.0053	.0058
18	.0011	.0012	.0014	.0015	.0017	.0019	.0021	.0024	.0026	.0029
19	.0005	.0005	.0006	.0007	.0008	.0009	.0010	.0011	.0012	.0014
20	.0002	.0002	.0002	.0003	.0003	.0004	.0004	.0005	.0005	.0006
21	.0001	.0001	.0001	.0001	.0001	.0002	.0002	.0002	.0002	.0003
22	.0000	.0000	.0000	.0000	.0001	.0001	.0001	.0001	.0001	.0001

X	9.1	9.2	9.3	9.4	λ 9.5	9.6	9.7	9.8	9.9	10.0
0	.0001	.0001	.0001	.0001	.0001	.0001	.0001	.0001	.0001	.0000
1	.0010	.0009	.0009	.0008	.0007	.0007	.0006	.0005	.0005	.0005
2	.0046	.0043	.0040	.0037	.0034	.0031	.0029	.0027	.0025	.0023
3	.0140	.0131	.0123	.0115	.0107	.0100	.0093	.0087	.0081	.0076
4	.0319	.0302	.0285	.0269	.0254	.0240	.0226	.0213	.0201	.0189
5	.0581	.0555	.0530	.0506	.0483	.0460	.0439	.0418	.0398	.0378
6	.0881	.0851	.0822	.0793	.0764	.0736	.0709	.0682	.0656	.0631
7	.1145	.1118	.1091	.1064	.1037	.1010	.0982	.0955	.0928	.0901
8	.1302	.1286	.1269	.1251	.1232	.1212	.1191	.1170	.1148	.1126
9	.1317	.1315	.1311	.1306	.1300	.1293	.1284	.1274	.1263	.1251
10	.1198	.1210	.1219	.1228	.1235	.1241	.1245	.1249	.1250	.1251
11	.0991	.1012	.1031	.1049	.1067	.1083	.1098	.1112	.1125	.1137
12	.0752	.0776	.0779	.0822	.0844	.0866	.0888	.0908	.0928	.0948
13	.0526	.0549	.0572	.0594	.0617	.0640	.0662	.0685	.0707	.0729
14	.0342	.0361	.0380	.0399	.0419	.0439	.0459	.0479	.0500	.0521
15	.0208	.0221	.0235	.0250	.0265	.0281	.0297	.0313	.0330	.0347
16	.0118	.0127	.0137	.0147	.0157	.0168	.0180	.0192	.0204	.0217
17	.0063	.0069	.0075	.0081	.0088	.0095	.0103	.0111	.0119	.0128
18	.0032	.0035	.0039	.0042	.0046	.0051	.0055	.0060	.0065	.0071
19	.0015	.0017	.0019	.0021	.0023	.0026	.0028	.0031	.0034	.0037
20	.0007	.0008	.0009	.0010	.0011	.0012	.0014	.0015	.0017	.0019
21	.0003	.0003	.0004	.0004	.0005	.0006	.0006	.0007	.0008	.0009
22	.0001	.0001	.0002	.0002	.0002	.0002	.0003	.0003	.0004	.0004
23	.0000	.0001	.0001	.0001	.0001	.0001	.0001	.0001	.0002	.0002
24	.0000	.0000	.0000	.0000	.0000	.0000	.0000	.0001	.0001	.0001

APPENDIX-4   VALUES OF $e^{-\lambda}$

λ	$e^{-\lambda}$	λ	$e^{-\lambda}$
0.0	1.00000	2.5	.08208
0.1	.90484	2.6	.07427
0.2	.81873	2.7	.06721
0.3	.74082	2.8	.06081
0.4	.67032	2.9	.05502
0.5	.60653	3.0	.04979
0.6	.54881	3.2	.04076
0.7	.49659	3.4	.03337
0.8	.44933	3.6	.02732
0.9	.40657	3.8	.02237
1.0	.36788	4.0	.01832
1.1	.33287	4.2	.01500
1.2	.30119	4.4	.01228
1.3	.27253	4.6	.01005
1.4	.24660	4.8	.00823
1.5	.22313	5.0	.00674
1.6	.20190	5.5	.00409
1.7	.18268	6.0	.00248
1.8	.16530	6.5	.00150
1.9	.14957	7.0	.00091
2.0	.13534	7.5	.00055
2.1	.12246	8.0	.00034
2.2	.00180	8.5	.00020
2.3	.10026	9.0	.00012
2.4	.09072	10.0	.00005

SOURCE: Leonard J. Kazmier, *Business Statistics*, Schaum's Outline Series, McGraw-Hill Book Company, New York, 1976.

APPENDIX-5   LEARNING CURVES: UNIT VALUES†

Unit	Improvement ratios							
	60%	65%	70%	75%	80%	85%	90%	95%
1	1.0000	1.0000	1.0000	1.0000	1.0000	1.0000	1.0000	1.0000
2	.6000	.6500	.7000	.7500	.8000	.8500	.9000	.9500
3	.4450	.5052	.5682	.6338	.7021	.7729	.8462	.9219
4	.3600	.4225	.4900	.5625	.6400	.7225	.8100	.9025
5	.3054	.3678	.4368	.5127	.5956	.6857	.7830	.8877
6	.2670	.3284	.3977	.4754	.5617	.6570	.7616	.8758
7	.2383	.2984	.3674	.4459	.5345	.6337	.7439	.8659
8	.2160	.2746	.3430	.4219	.5120	.6141	.7290	.8574
9	.1980	.2552	.3228	.4017	.4930	.5974	.7161	.8499
10	.1832	.2391	.3058	.3846	.4765	.5828	.7047	.8433
12	.1602	.2135	.2784	.3565	.4493	.5584	.6854	.8320
14	.1430	.1940	.2572	.3344	.4276	.5386	.6696	.8226
16	.1296	.1785	.2401	.3164	.4096	.5220	.6561	.8145
18	.1188	.1659	.2260	.3013	.3944	.5078	.6445	.8074
20	.1099	.1554	.2141	.2884	.3812	.4954	.6342	.8012
22	.1025	.1465	.2038	.2772	.3697	.4844	.6251	.7955
24	.0961	.1387	.1949	.2674	.3595	.4747	.6169	.7904
25	.0933	.1353	.1908	.2629	.3548	.4701	.6131	.7880
30	.0815	.1208	.1737	.2437	.3346	.4505	.5963	.7775
35	.0728	.1097	.1605	.2286	.3184	.4345	.5825	.7687
40	.0660	.1010	.1498	.2163	.3050	.4211	.5708	.7611
45	.0605	.0939	.1410	.2060	.2936	.4096	.5607	.7545
50	.0560	.0879	.1336	.1972	.2838	.3996	.5518	.7486
60	.0489	.0785	.1216	.1828	.2676	.3829	.5367	.7386
70	.0437	.0713	.1123	.1715	.2547	.3693	.5243	.7302
80	.0396	.0657	.1049	.1622	.2440	.3579	.5137	.7231
90	.0363	.0610	.0987	.1545	.2349	.3482	.5046	.7168
100	.0336	.0572	.0935	.1479	.2271	.3397	.4966	.7112
120	.0294	.0510	.0851	.1371	.2141	.3255	.4830	.7017
140	.0262	.0464	.0786	.1287	.2038	.3139	.4718	.6937
160	.0237	.0427	.0734	.1217	.1952	.3042	.4623	.6869
180	.0218	.0397	.0691	.1159	.1879	.2959	.4541	.6809
200	.0201	.0371	.0655	.1109	.1816	.2887	.4469	.6757
250	.0171	.0323	.0584	.1011	.1691	.2740	.4320	.6646
300	.0149	.0289	.0531	.0937	.1594	.2625	.4202	.6557
350	.0133	.0262	.0491	.0879	.1517	.2532	.4105	.6482
400	.0121	.0241	.0458	.0832	.1453	.2454	.4022	.6419
450	.0111	.0224	.0431	.0792	.1399	.2387	.3951	.6363
500	.0103	.0210	.0408	.0758	.1352	.2329	.3888	.6314
600	.0090	.0188	.0372	.0703	.1275	.2232	.3782	.6229
700	.0080	.0171	.0344	.0659	.1214	.2152	.3694	.6158
800	.0073	.0157	.0321	.0624	.1163	.2086	.3620	.6098
900	.0067	.0146	.0302	.0594	.1119	.2029	.3556	.6045
1,000	.0062	.0137	.0286	.0569	.1082	.1980	.3499	.5998
1,200	.0054	.0122	.0260	.0527	.1020	.1897	.3404	.5918
1,400	.0048	.0111	.0240	.0495	.0971	.1830	.3325	.5850
1,600	.0044	.0102	.0225	.0468	.0930	.1773	.3258	.5793
1,800	.0040	.0095	.0211	.0446	.0895	.1725	.3200	.5743
2,000	.0037	.0089	.0200	.0427	.0866	.1683	.3149	.5698
2,500	.0031	.0077	.0178	.0389	.0806	.1597	.3044	.5605
3,000	.0027	.0069	.0162	.0360	.0760	.1530	.2961	.5530

† Example: $T(n = 25) = (.0933)T(n = 1)$.

SOURCE: A. N. Schreiber, R. A. Johnson, R. C. Meier, W. T. Newell, and H. C. Fischer, *Cases in Manufacturing Management*, McGraw-Hill Book Company, New York, 1965.

APPENDIX-6   INTEREST FACTORS

8% Interest Factors for Discrete Compounding Periods

| | SINGLE PAYMENT | | UNIFORM SERIES | | | | | |
| | Compound Amount Factor | Present Worth Factor | Capital Recovery Factor | Present Worth Factor | Sinking Fund Factor | Compound Amount Factor | Gradient Factor | |
N	(F/P, 8, N)	(P/F, 8, N)	(A/P, 8, N)	(P/A, 8, N)	(A/F, 8, N)	(F/A, 8, N)	(A/G, 8, N)	N
1	1.0800	.92593	1.0800	.9259	1.0000	1.0000	.0000	1
2	1.1664	.85734	.56077	1.7832	.48077	2.0799	.4807	2
3	1.2597	.79383	.38803	2.5770	.30804	3.2463	.9487	3
4	1.3604	.73503	.30192	3.3121	.22192	4.5060	1.4038	4
5	1.4693	.68059	.25046	3.9926	.17046	5.8665	1.8463	5
6	1.5868	.63017	.21632	4.6228	.13632	7.3358	2.2762	6
7	1.7138	.58349	.19207	5.2063	.11207	8.9227	2.6935	7
8	1.8509	.54027	.17402	5.7466	.09402	10.636	3.0984	8
9	1.9989	.50025	.16008	6.2468	.08008	12.487	3.4909	9
10	2.1589	.46320	.14903	6.7100	.06903	14.486	3.8712	10
11	2.3316	.42889	.14008	7.1389	.06008	16.645	4.2394	11
12	2.5181	.39712	.13270	7.5360	.05270	18.976	4.5956	12
13	2.7196	.36770	.12642	7.9037	.04652	21.495	4.9401	13
14	2.9371	.34046	.12130	8.2442	.04130	24.214	5.2729	14
15	3.1721	.31524	.11683	8.5594	.03683	27.151	5.5943	15
16	3.4259	.29189	.11298	8.8513	.03298	30.323	5.9045	16
17	3.6999	.27027	.10963	9.1216	.02963	33.749	6.2036	17
18	3.9959	.25025	.10670	9.3718	.02670	37.449	6.4919	18
19	4.3156	.23171	.10413	9.6035	.02413	41.445	6.7696	19
20	4.6609	.21455	.10185	9.8181	.02185	45.761	7.0368	20
21	5.0337	.19866	.09983	10.016	.01983	50.422	7.2939	21
22	5.4364	.18394	.09803	10.200	.01803	55.455	7.5411	22
23	5.8713	.17032	.09642	10.371	.01642	60.892	7.7785	23
24	6.3410	.15770	.09498	10.528	.01498	66.763	8.0065	24
25	6.8483	.14602	.09368	10.674	.01368	73.104	8.2253	25
26	7.3962	.13520	.09251	10.809	.01251	79.953	8.4351	26
27	7.9879	.12519	.09145	10.935	.01145	87.349	8.6362	27
28	8.6269	.11592	.09049	11.051	.01049	95.337	8.8288	28
29	9.3171	.10733	.08962	11.158	.00962	103.96	9.0132	29
30	10.062	.09938	.08883	11.257	.00883	113.28	9.1896	30
31	10.867	.09202	.08811	11.349	.00811	123.34	9.3583	31
32	11.736	.08520	.08745	11.434	.00745	134.21	9.5196	32
33	12.675	.07889	.08685	11.513	.00685	145.94	9.6736	33
34	13.689	.07305	.08630	11.586	.00630	158.62	9.8207	34
35	14.785	.06764	.08580	11.654	.00580	172.31	9.9610	35
40	21.724	.04603	.08386	11.924	.00386	259.05	10.569	40
45	31.919	.03133	.08259	12.108	.00259	386.49	11.044	45
50	46.900	.02132	.08174	12.233	.00174	573.75	11.410	50
55	68.911	.01451	.08118	12.318	.00118	848.89	11.690	55
60	101.25	.00988	.08080	12.376	.00080	1253.1	11.901	60
65	148.77	.00672	.08054	12.416	.00054	1847.1	12.060	65
70	218.59	.00457	.08037	12.442	.00037	2719.9	12.178	70
75	321.19	.00311	.08025	12.461	.00025	4002.3	12.265	75
80	471.93	.00212	.08017	12.473	.00017	5886.6	12.330	80
85	693.42	.00144	.08012	12.481	.00012	8655.2	12.377	85
90	1018.8	.00098	.08008	12.487	.00008	12723.9	12.411	90
95	1497.0	.00067	.08005	12.491	.00005	18701.5	12.436	95
100	2199.6	.00045	.08004	12.494	.00004	27484.5	12.454	100

SOURCE: James L. Riggs, *Engineering Economics*, McGraw-Hill Book Company, New York, 1977.

APPENDIX-6   *(Continued)*

9% Interest Factors for Discrete Compounding Periods

| | SINGLE PAYMENT | | UNIFORM SERIES | | | | | |
| | Compound Amount Factor | Present Worth Factor | Capital Recovery Factor | Present Worth Factor | Sinking Fund Factor | Compound Amount Factor | Gradient Factor | |
N	$(F/P, 9, N)$	$(P/F, 9, N)$	$(A/P, 9, N)$	$(P/A, 9, N)$	$(A/F, 9, N)$	$(F/A, 9, N)$	$(A/G, 9, N)$	N
1	1.0900	.91743	1.0900	.9174	1.0000	1.0000	.0000	1
2	1.1881	.84168	.56847	1.7591	.47847	2.0899	.4784	2
3	1.2950	.77219	.39506	2.5312	.30506	3.2780	.9425	3
4	1.4115	.70843	.30867	3.2396	.21867	4.5730	1.3923	4
5	1.5386	.64993	.25709	3.8896	.16709	5.9846	1.8280	5
6	1.6770	.59627	.22292	4.4858	.13292	7.5232	2.2496	6
7	1.8280	.54704	.19869	5.0329	.10869	9.2002	2.6572	7
8	1.9925	.50187	.18068	5.5347	.09068	11.028	3.0510	8
9	2.1718	.46043	.16680	5.9952	.07680	13.020	3.4311	9
10	2.3673	.42241	.15582	6.4176	.06582	15.192	3.7976	10
11	2.5804	.38754	.14695	6.8051	.05695	17.559	4.1508	11
12	2.8126	.35554	.13965	7.1606	.04965	20.140	4.4909	12
13	3.0657	.32618	.13357	7.4868	.04357	22.952	4.8180	13
14	3.3416	.29925	.12843	7.7861	.03843	26.018	5.1325	14
15	3.6424	.27454	.12406	8.0606	.03406	29.360	5.4345	15
16	3.9702	.25187	.12030	8.3125	.03030	33.002	5.7243	16
17	4.3275	.23108	.11705	8.5435	.02705	36.972	6.0022	17
18	4.7170	.21200	.11421	8.7555	.02421	41.300	6.2685	18
19	5.1415	.19449	.11173	8.9500	.02173	46.017	6.5234	19
20	5.6043	.17843	.10955	9.1285	.01955	51.158	6.7673	20
21	6.1086	.16370	.10762	9.2922	.01762	56.763	7.0004	21
22	6.6584	.15018	.10591	9.4423	.01591	62.871	7.2231	22
23	7.2577	.13778	.10438	9.5801	.01438	69.530	7.4356	23
24	7.9109	.12641	.10302	9.7065	.01302	76.787	7.6383	24
25	8.6228	.11597	.10181	9.8225	.01181	84.698	7.8315	25
26	9.3989	.10640	.10072	9.9289	.01072	93.321	8.0154	26
27	10.244	.09761	.09974	10.026	.00974	102.72	8.1905	27
28	11.166	.08955	.09885	10.116	.00885	112.96	8.3570	28
29	12.171	.08216	.09806	10.198	.00806	124.13	8.5153	29
30	13.267	.07537	.09734	10.273	.00734	136.30	8.6655	30
31	14.461	.06915	.09669	10.342	.00669	149.57	8.8082	31
32	15.762	.06344	.09610	10.406	.00610	164.03	8.9435	32
33	17.181	.05820	.09556	10.464	.00556	179.79	9.0717	33
34	18.727	.05340	.09508	10.517	.00508	196.97	9.1932	34
35	20.413	.04899	.09464	10.566	.00464	215.70	9.3082	35
40	31.408	.03184	.09296	10.757	.00296	337.86	9.7956	40
45	48.325	.02069	.09190	10.881	.00190	525.83	10.160	45
50	74.353	.01345	.09123	10.961	.00123	815.04	10.429	50
55	114.40	.00874	.09079	11.014	.00079	1260.0	10.626	55
60	176.02	.00568	.09051	11.047	.00051	1944.6	10.768	60
65	270.82	.00369	.09033	11.070	.00033	2998.0	10.870	65
70	416.70	.00240	.09022	11.084	.00022	4618.9	10.942	70
75	641.14	.00156	.09014	11.093	.00014	7112.7	10.993	75
80	986.47	.00101	.09009	11.099	.00009	10950.6	11.029	80
85	1517.8	.00066	.09006	11.103	.00006	16854.8	11.055	85
90	2335.3	.00043	.09004	11.106	.00004	25939.2	11.072	90
95	3593.1	.00028	.09002	11.108	.00003	39916.6	11.084	95
100	5528.4	.00018	.09002	11.109	.00002	61422.7	11.093	100

APPENDIX-6   *(Continued)*

10% Interest Factors for Discrete Compounding Periods

	SINGLE PAYMENT		UNIFORM SERIES					
	Compound Amount Factor	Present Worth Factor	Capital Recovery Factor	Present Worth Factor	Sinking Fund Factor	Compound Amount Factor	Gradient Factor	
N	(F/P, 10, N)	(P/F, 10, N)	(A/P, 10, N)	(P/A, 10, N)	(A/F, 10, N)	(F/A, 10, N)	(A/G, 10, N)	*N*
1	1.1000	.90909	1.1000	.9091	1.0000	1.000	.0000	1
2	1.2100	.82645	.57619	1.7355	.47619	2.0999	.4761	2
3	1.3310	.75132	.40212	2.4868	.30212	3.3099	.9365	3
4	1.4641	.68302	.31547	3.1698	.21547	4.6409	1.3810	4
5	1.6105	.62092	.26380	3.7907	.16380	6.1050	1.8100	5
6	1.7715	.56448	.22961	4.3552	.12961	7.7155	2.2234	6
7	1.9487	.51316	.20541	4.8683	.10541	9.4870	2.6215	7
8	2.1435	.46651	.18745	5.3349	.08745	11.435	3.0043	8
9	2.3579	.42410	.17364	5.7589	.07364	13.579	3.3722	9
10	2.5937	.38555	.16275	6.1445	.06275	15.937	3.7253	10
11	2.8530	.35050	.15396	6.4950	.05396	18.530	4.0639	11
12	3.1384	.31863	.14676	6.8136	.04676	21.383	4.3883	12
13	3.4522	.28967	.14078	7.1033	.04078	24.522	4.6987	13
14	3.7974	.26333	.13575	7.3666	.03575	27.974	4.9954	14
15	4.1771	.23940	.13147	7.6060	.03147	31.771	5.2788	15
16	4.5949	.21763	.12782	7.8236	.02782	35.949	5.5492	16
17	5.0544	.19785	.12466	8.0215	.02466	40.543	5.8070	17
18	5.5598	.17986	.12193	8.2013	.02193	45.598	6.0524	18
19	6.1158	.16351	.11955	8.3649	.01955	51.158	6.2860	19
20	6.7273	.14865	.11746	8.5135	.01746	57.273	6.5080	20
21	7.4001	.13513	.11562	8.6486	.01562	64.001	6.7188	21
22	8.1401	.12285	.11401	8.7715	.01401	71.401	6.9188	22
23	8.9541	.11168	.11257	8.8832	.01257	79.541	7.1084	23
24	9.8495	.10153	.11130	8.9847	.01130	88.495	7.2879	24
25	10.834	.09230	.11017	9.0770	.01017	98.344	7.4579	25
26	11.917	.08391	.10916	9.1609	.00916	109.17	7.6185	26
27	13.109	.07628	.10826	9.2372	.00826	121.09	7.7703	27
28	14.420	.06935	.10745	9.3065	.00745	134.20	7.9136	28
29	15.862	.06304	.10673	9.3696	.00673	148.62	8.0488	29
30	17.448	.05731	.10608	9.4269	.00608	164.48	8.1761	30
31	19.193	.05210	.10550	9.4790	.00550	181.93	8.2961	31
32	21.113	.04736	.10497	9.5263	.00497	201.13	8.4090	32
33	23.224	.04306	.10450	9.5694	.00450	222.24	8.5151	33
34	25.546	.03914	.10407	9.6085	.00407	245.46	8.6149	34
35	28.101	.03559	.10369	9.6441	.00369	271.01	8.7085	35
40	45.257	.02210	.10226	9.7790	.00226	442.57	9.0962	40
45	72.887	.01372	.10139	9.8628	.00139	718.87	9.3740	45
50	117.38	.00852	.10086	9.9148	.00086	1163.8	9.5704	50
55	189.04	.00529	.10053	9.9471	.00053	1880.4	9.7075	55
60	304.46	.00328	.10033	9.9671	.00033	3034.6	9.8022	60
65	490.34	.00204	.10020	9.9796	.00020	4893.4	9.8671	65
70	789.69	.00127	.10013	9.9873	.00013	7886.9	9.9112	70
75	1271.8	.00079	.10008	9.9921	.00008	12709.0	9.9409	75
80	2048.2	.00049	.10005	9.9951	.00005	20474.0	9.9609	80
85	3298.7	.00030	.10003	9.9969	.00003	32979.7	9.9742	85
90	5312.5	.00019	.10002	9.9981	.00002	53120.2	9.9830	90
95	8555.9	.00012	.10001	9.9988	.00001	85556.8	9.9889	95
100	13780.6	.00007	.10001	9.9992	.00001	137796.1	9.9927	100

APPENDIX-6 *(Continued)*

11% Interest Factors for Discrete Compounding Periods

	SINGLE PAYMENT		UNIFORM SERIES					
	Compound Amount Factor	Present Worth Factor	Capital Recovery Factor	Present Worth Factor	Sinking Fund Factor	Compound Amount Factor	Gradient Factor	
N	$(F/P, 11, N)$	$(P/F, 11, N)$	$(A/P, 11, N)$	$(P/A, 11, N)$	$(A/F, 11, N)$	$(F/A, 11, N)$	$(A/G, 11, N)$	N
1	1.1100	.90090	1.1100	.9009	1.0000	1.000	.0000	1
2	1.2321	.81162	.58394	1.7125	.47394	2.1099	.4739	2
3	1.3676	.73119	.40922	2.4437	.29922	3.3420	.9305	3
4	1.5180	.65873	.32233	3.1024	.21233	4.7097	1.3698	4
5	1.6850	.59345	.27057	3.6958	.16057	6.2277	1.7922	5
6	1.8704	.53464	.23638	4.2305	.12638	7.9128	2.1975	6
7	2.0761	.48166	.21222	4.7121	.10222	9.7831	2.5862	7
8	2.3045	.43393	.19432	5.1461	.08432	11.859	2.9584	8
9	2.5580	.39093	.18060	5.5370	.07060	14.163	3.3143	9
10	2.8394	.35219	.16980	5.8892	.05980	16.721	3.6543	10
11	3.1517	.31729	.16112	6.2065	.05112	19.561	3.9787	11
12	3.4984	.28584	.15403	6.4923	.04403	22.712	4.2878	12
13	3.8832	.25752	.14815	6.7498	.03815	26.211	4.5821	13
14	4.3104	.23200	.14323	6.9818	.03323	30.094	4.8618	14
15	4.7845	.20901	.13907	7.1908	.02907	34.404	5.1274	15
16	5.3108	.18829	.13552	7.3791	.02552	39.189	5.3793	16
17	5.8950	.16963	.13247	7.5487	.02247	44.500	5.6180	17
18	6.5434	.15282	.12984	7.7016	.01984	50.395	5.8438	18
19	7.2632	.13768	.12756	7.8392	.01756	56.938	6.0573	19
20	8.0622	.12404	.12558	7.9633	.01558	64.201	6.2589	20
21	8.9490	.11174	.12384	8.0750	.01384	72.264	6.4490	21
22	9.9334	.10067	.12231	8.1757	.01231	81.213	6.6282	22
23	11.026	.09069	.12097	8.2664	.01097	91.146	6.7969	23
24	12.238	.08171	.11979	8.3481	.00979	102.17	6.9554	24
25	13.585	.07361	.11874	8.4217	.00874	114.41	7.1044	25
26	15.079	.06631	.11781	8.4880	.00781	127.99	7.2442	26
27	16.738	.05974	.11699	8.5478	.00699	143.07	7.3753	27
28	18.579	.05382	.11626	8.6016	.00626	159.81	7.4981	28
29	20.623	.04849	.11561	8.6501	.00561	178.39	7.6130	29
30	22.891	.04368	.11502	8.6937	.00502	199.01	7.7205	30
31	25.409	.03935	.11451	8.7331	.00451	221.90	7.8209	31
32	28.204	.03545	.11404	8.7686	.00404	247.31	7.9146	32
33	31.307	.03194	.11363	8.8005	.00363	275.52	8.0020	33
34	34.751	.02878	.11326	8.8293	.00326	306.83	8.0835	34
35	38.573	.02592	.11293	8.8552	.00293	341.58	8.1594	35
40	64.999	.01538	.11172	8.9510	.00172	581.81	8.4659	40
45	109.52	.00913	.11101	9.0079	.00101	986.60	8.6762	45
50	184.55	.00542	.11060	9.0416	.00060	1668.7	8.8185	50

APPENDIX-6   *(Continued)*

12% Interest Factors for Discrete Compounding Periods

| | SINGLE PAYMENT | | UNIFORM SERIES | | | | | |
| | Compound Amount Factor | Present Worth Factor | Capital Recovery Factor | Present Worth Factor | Sinking Fund Factor | Compound Amount Factor | Gradient Factor | |
N	$(F/P, 12, N)$	$(P/F, 12, N)$	$(A/P, 12, N)$	$(P/A, 12, N)$	$(A/F, 12, N)$	$(F/A, 12, N)$	$(A/G, 12, N)$	N
1	1.1200	.89286	1.1200	.8929	1.0000	1.0000	.0000	1
2	1.2544	.79719	.59170	1.6900	.47170	2.1200	.4717	2
3	1.4049	.71178	.41635	2.4018	.29635	3.3743	.9246	3
4	1.5735	.63552	.32924	3.0373	.20924	4.7793	1.3588	4
5	1.7623	.56743	.27741	3.6047	.15741	6.3528	1.7745	5
6	1.9738	.50663	.24323	4.1114	.12323	8.115	2.1720	6
7	2.2106	.45235	.21912	4.5637	.09912	10.088	2.5514	7
8	2.4759	.40388	.20130	4.9676	.08130	12.299	2.9131	8
9	2.7730	.36061	.18768	5.3282	.06768	14.775	3.2573	9
10	3.1058	.32197	.17698	5.6502	.05698	17.548	3.5846	10
11	3.4785	.28748	.16842	5.9376	.04842	20.654	3.8952	11
12	3.8959	.25668	.16144	6.1943	.04144	24.132	4.1896	12
13	4.3634	.22918	.15568	6.4235	.03568	28.028	4.4682	13
14	4.8870	.20462	.15087	6.6281	.03087	32.392	4.7316	14
15	5.4735	.18270	.14682	6.8108	.02682	37.279	4.9802	15
16	6.1303	.16312	.14339	6.9739	.02339	42.752	5.2146	16
17	6.8659	.14565	.14046	7.1196	.02046	48.883	5.4352	17
18	7.6899	.13004	.13794	7.2496	.01794	55.749	5.6427	18
19	8.6126	.11611	.13576	7.3657	.01576	63.439	5.8375	19
20	9.6462	.10367	.13388	7.4694	.01388	72.051	6.0201	20
21	10.803	.09256	.13224	7.5620	.01224	81.698	6.1913	21
22	12.100	.08264	.13081	7.6446	.01081	92.501	6.3513	22
23	13.552	.07379	.12956	7.7184	.00956	104.60	6.5009	23
24	15.178	.06588	.12846	7.7843	.00846	118.15	6.6406	24
25	16.999	.05882	.12750	7.8431	.00750	133.33	6.7708	25
26	19.039	.05252	.12665	7.8956	.00665	150.33	6.8920	26
27	21.324	.04689	.12590	7.9425	.00590	169.37	7.0049	27
28	23.883	.04187	.12524	7.9844	.00524	190.69	7.1097	28
29	26.749	.03738	.12466	8.0218	.00466	214.58	7.2071	29
30	29.959	.03338	.12414	8.0551	.00414	241.32	7.2974	30
31	33.554	.02980	.12369	8.0849	.00369	271.28	7.3810	31
32	37.581	.02661	.12328	8.1116	.00328	304.84	7.4585	32
33	42.090	.02376	.12292	8.1353	.00292	342.42	7.5302	33
34	47.141	.02121	.12260	8.1565	.00260	384.51	7.5964	34
35	52.798	.01894	.12232	8.1755	.00232	431.65	7.6576	35
40	93.049	.01075	.12130	8.2437	.00130	767.07	7.8987	40
45	163.98	.00610	.12074	8.2825	.00074	1358.2	8.0572	45
50	288.99	.00346	.12042	8.3045	.00042	2399.9	8.1597	50

APPENDIX-6   (*Continued*)

15% Interest Factors for Discrete Compounding Periods

N	SINGLE PAYMENT		UNIFORM SERIES					N
	Compound Amount Factor	Present Worth Factor	Capital Recovery Factor	Present Worth Factor	Sinking Fund Factor	Compound Amount Factor	Gradient Factor	
N	(F/P, 15, N)	(P/F, 15, N)	(A/P, 15, N)	(P/A, 15, N)	(A/F, 15, N)	(F/A, 15, N)	(A/G, 15, N)	N
1	1.1500	.86957	1.1500	.8696	1.0000	1.000	.0000	1
2	1.3225	.75614	.61512	1.6257	.46512	2.1499	.4651	2
3	1.5208	.65752	.43798	2.2832	.28798	3.4724	.9071	3
4	1.7490	.57175	.35027	2.8549	.20027	4.9933	1.3262	4
5	2.0113	.49718	.29832	3.3521	.14832	6.7423	1.7227	5
6	2.3130	.43233	.26424	3.7844	.11424	8.7536	2.0971	6
7	2.6600	.37594	.24036	4.1604	.09036	11.066	2.4498	7
8	3.0590	.32690	.22285	4.4873	.07285	13.726	2.7813	8
9	3.5178	.28426	.20957	4.7715	.05957	16.785	3.0922	9
10	4.0455	.24719	.19925	5.0187	.04925	20.303	3.3831	10
11	4.6523	.21494	.19107	5.2337	.04107	24.349	3.6549	11
12	5.3502	.18691	.18448	5.4206	.03448	29.001	3.9081	12
13	6.1527	.16253	.17911	5.5831	.02911	34.351	4.1437	13
14	7.0756	.14133	.17469	5.7244	.02469	40.504	4.3623	14
15	8.1369	.12290	.17102	5.8473	.02102	47.579	4.5649	15
16	9.3575	.10687	.16795	5.9542	.01795	55.716	4.7522	16
17	10.761	.09293	.16537	6.0471	.01537	65.074	4.9250	17
18	12.375	.08081	.16319	6.1279	.01319	75.835	5.0842	18
19	14.231	.07027	.16134	6.1982	.01134	88.210	5.2307	19
20	16.366	.06110	.15976	6.2593	.00976	102.44	5.3651	20
21	18.821	.05313	.15842	6.3124	.00842	118.80	5.4883	21
22	21.644	.04620	.15727	6.3586	.00727	137.62	5.6010	22
23	24.891	.04018	.15628	6.3988	.00628	159.27	5.7039	23
24	28.624	.03493	.15543	6.4337	.00543	184.16	5.7978	24
25	32.918	.03038	.15470	6.4641	.00470	212.78	5.8834	25
26	37.856	.02642	.15407	6.4905	.00407	245.70	5.9612	26
27	43.534	.02297	.15353	6.5135	.00353	283.56	6.0318	27
28	50.064	.01997	.15306	6.5335	.00306	327.09	6.0959	28
29	57.574	.01737	.15265	6.5508	.00265	377.16	6.1540	29
30	66.210	.01510	.15230	6.5659	.00230	434.73	6.2066	30
31	76.141	.01313	.15200	6.5791	.00200	500.94	6.2541	31
32	87.563	.01142	.15173	6.5905	.00173	577.08	6.2970	32
33	100.69	.00993	.15150	6.6004	.00150	664.65	6.3356	33
34	115.80	.00864	.15131	6.6091	.00131	765.34	6.3705	34
35	133.17	.00751	.15113	6.6166	.00113	881.14	6.4018	35
40	267.85	.00373	.15056	6.6417	.00056	1779.0	6.5167	40
45	538.75	.00186	.15028	6.6543	.00028	3585.0	6.5829	45
50	1083.6	.00092	.15014	6.6605	.00014	7217.4	6.8204	50

APPENDIX-6 *(Continued)*

20% Interest Factors for Discrete Compounding Periods

	SINGLE PAYMENT		UNIFORM SERIES					
	Compound Amount Factor	Present Worth Factor	Capital Recovery Factor	Present Worth Factor	Sinking Fund Factor	Compound Amount Factor	Gradient Factor	
N	(F/P, 20, N)	(P/F, 20, N)	(A/P, 20, N)	(P/A, 20, N)	(A/F, 20, N)	(F/A, 20, N)	(A/G, 20, N)	N
1	1.2000	.83333	1.2000	.8333	1.0000	1.0000	.0000	1
2	1.4400	.69445	.65455	1.5277	.45455	2.1999	.4545	2
3	1.7280	.57870	.47473	2.1064	.27473	3.6399	.8791	3
4	2.0736	.48225	.38629	2.5887	.18629	5.3679	1.2742	4
5	2.4883	.40188	.33438	2.9906	.13438	7.4415	1.6405	5
6	2.9859	.33490	.30071	3.3255	.10071	9.9298	1.9788	6
7	3.5831	.27908	.27742	3.6045	.07742	12.915	2.2901	7
8	4.2998	.23257	.26061	3.8371	.06061	16.498	2.5756	8
9	5.1597	.19381	.24808	4.0309	.04808	20.798	2.8364	9
10	6.1917	.16151	.23852	4.1924	.03852	25.958	3.0738	10
11	7.4300	.13459	.23110	4.3270	.03110	32.150	3.2892	11
12	8.9160	.11216	.22527	4.4392	.02527	39.580	3.4840	12
13	10.699	.09346	.22062	4.5326	.02062	48.496	3.6596	13
14	12.839	.07789	.21689	4.6105	.01689	59.195	3.8174	14
15	15.406	.06491	.21388	4.6754	.01388	72.034	3.9588	15
16	18.488	.05409	.21144	4.7295	.01144	87.441	4.0851	16
17	22.185	.04507	.20944	4.7746	.00944	105.92	4.1975	17
18	26.623	.03756	.20781	4.8121	.00781	128.11	4.2975	18
19	31.947	.03130	.20646	4.8435	.00646	154.73	4.3860	19
20	38.337	.02608	.20536	4.8695	.00536	186.68	4.4643	20
21	46.004	.02174	.20444	4.8913	.00444	225.02	4.5333	21
22	55.205	.01811	.20369	4.9094	.00369	271.02	4.5941	22
23	66.246	.01510	.20307	4.9245	.00307	326.23	4.6474	23
24	79.495	.01258	.20255	4.9371	.00255	392.47	4.6942	24
25	95.394	.01048	.20212	4.9475	.00212	471.97	4.7351	25
26	114.47	.00874	.20176	4.9563	.00176	567.36	4.7708	26
27	137.36	.00728	.20147	4.9636	.00147	681.84	4.8020	27
28	164.84	.00607	.20122	4.9696	.00122	819.21	4.8291	28
29	197.81	.00506	.20102	4.9747	.00102	984.05	4.8526	29
30	237.37	.00421	.20085	4.9789	.00085	1181.8	4.8730	30
31	284.84	.00351	.20070	4.9824	.00070	1419.2	4.8907	31
32	341.81	.00293	.20059	4.9853	.00059	1704.0	4.9061	32
33	410.17	.00244	.20049	4.9878	.00049	2045.8	4.9193	33
34	492.21	.00203	.20041	4.9898	.00041	2456.0	4.9307	34
35	590.65	.00169	.20034	4.9915	.00034	2948.2	4.9406	35
40	1469.7	.00068	.20014	4.9966	.00014	7343.6	4.9727	40
45	3657.1	.00027	.20005	4.9986	.00005	18281.3	4.9876	45
50	9100.1	.00011	.20002	4.9994	.00002	45497.2	4.9945	50

Index